Iran

Andrew Burke, Mark Elliott, Kamin Mohammadi

Contents

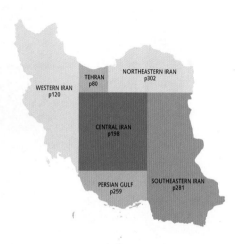

Lonely Planet books provide independent advice. Lonely Planet does not accept advertising in guidebooks, nor do we accept payment in exchange for listing or endorsing any place or business. Lonely Planet writers do not accept discounts or payments in exchange for positive coverage of any sort.

کتاب های لانلی پلنت توصیه های مستقلی فراهم می کنند. انتشارات لانلی پلنت آگهی کردن در کتاب راهنماها را قبول نمی کند همچنین ما هیچ پولی در مقابل ذکر نام محل یاتجارت خاص نمی پذیریم. نویسنده های لانلی پلنت هیچ گونه تخفیف یاپرداختی رادر مقابل گزارش مثبت از جایی قبول نمی کنند.

Destination Iran

Travellers have been raving about Persia since long before Marco Polo meandered through more than 700 years ago. It's Iran these days, but the praise for one of the great cultural, social and historical destinations on earth hasn't stopped. If you want simply to walk in the footsteps of some of history's most outstanding figures, you can hardly be disappointed by the kaleidoscope of architectural wonders they left behind: the awesome beauty of Persepolis; the sublime harmony of Esfahan; or the immensity of the ancient ziggurat at Choqa Zanbil.

While the monuments to glories past are indeed worthy of a trip (or several trips), it is the ancient and complex Iranian culture that many visitors find most memorable – few countries have embraced so many civilisations. Myriad cultural elements have been adapted into a national identity with strong links to Cyrus the Great and beyond. The result is neither East nor West, modern nor ancient, and will repeatedly seduce you with its irresistibly warm welcome. It's a country where, if you dare, you will find yourself in Iranian homes and treated as an honoured guest not once, but over and over again – chances are that by the time you leave Iran you'll have a whole new definition for hospitality.

Not that a daring nature is needed. You will inevitably face the 'Iran? Is it safe?' line of questioning from friends and family not yet familiar with Iran. And while Iran is neither a paragon of democracy nor a legitimate member of any evil axis, you'll probably feel safer than in your home town – except when in Tehran's diabolical traffic. So pack your bags and soak up the history, the subtle cultural shifts and the hospitality. You won't regret it.

CLINT LUCAS

MASULEH (p156)
Lush, green and the most visitor-friendly of Iran's memorable stepped villages

TEHRAN (p80)
Iran's fast-beating heart is a mad mix of good museums and restaurants; heavy traffic and make-up

TAKHT-E SOLEIMAN (p170)
Windswept 3rd-century ruins amid volcanic peaks and timeless mountain villages

KASHAN (p203)
A fine bazaar, exquisitely restored Qajar-era mansions and a wonderfully relaxed atmosphere

YAZD (p230)
An ancient forest of windtowers and brown, twisting lanes full of romantic hotels and restaurants

ESFAHAN (p210)
Shah Abbas's majestic capital, with its grand mosques, enchanting bridges and incomparable Imam Square

CHOQA ZANBIL (p192)
Lonely 3000-year-old stepped pyramid in semidesert between the biblical cities of Shush and Shushtar

SHIRAZ (p241)
The heartland of Persian culture, sophisticated Shiraz gave us poetry, roses, nightingales and wine

PERSEPOLIS (p252)
All the power and grace of the Achaemenids summed up in one of the world's greatest ancient sites

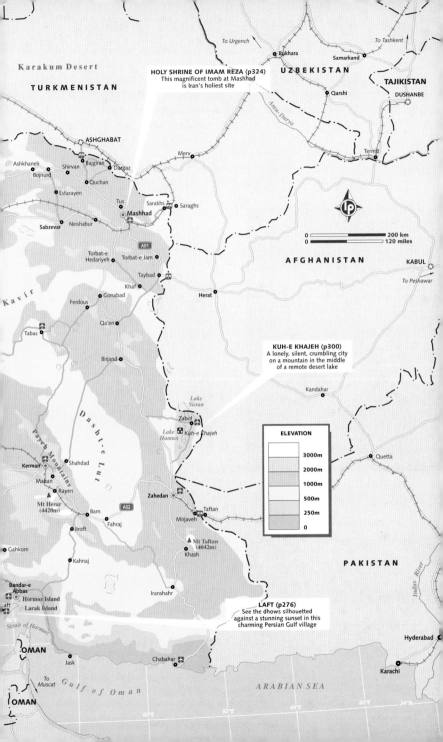

HOLY SHRINE OF IMAM REZA (p324)
This magnificent tomb at Mashhad is Iran's holiest site

KUH-E KHAJEH (p300)
A lonely, silent, crumbling city on a mountain in the middle of a remote desert lake

LAFT (p276)
See the dhows silhouetted against a stunning sunset in this charming Persian Gulf village

ELEVATION

	3000m
	2000m
	1000m
	500m
	250m
	0

0 ————— 200 km
0 ————— 120 miles

Karakum Desert

TURKMENISTAN

UZBEKISTAN

TAJIKISTAN

To Urgench
To Tashkent

Bukhara
Samarkand

ASHGHABAT
Qarshi
DUSHANBE

Ashkhaneh
Shirvan
Bajgiran
Dargaz
Merv
Amu Darya
Termz
Bojnurd
Quchan
Esfarayen
Tus
Sarakhs
Saraghs

Sabzevar
Neishabur
Mashhad

Kavir

Torbat-e Hedariyeh
Torbat-e Jam
A01
Taybad
Khaf
Herat

AFGHANISTAN

KABUL

To Peshawar

Ferdous
Gonabad
Qa'en

Tabas

Birjand

Kandahar

Lake Sistan

Dasht-e Lut

Lake Hamun
Zabol
Kuh-e Khajeh

Pāveh Mountains

Shahdad
Quetta

Kerman
Mahan
Rayen
Zahedan
Taftan

Mt Hezar
(4420m)
Bam
Fahraj
Mirjaveh

A02

Jiroft

Gahkom
Kahnaj
Mt Taftan
(4042m)
Khash

PAKISTAN

Indus River

Bandar-e Abbas
Hormoz Island
Larak Island
aft
Iranshahr

Hyderabad

Strait of Hormoz

OMAN
Jask
Chabahar
Karachi

To Muscat
Gulf of Oman

ARABIAN SEA

OMAN

60°E
62°E
64°E
66°E
24°N

Some claim that Iran's greatest contribution to world culture has been its architecture. The awesome **Imam Mosque** (p216) and **Chehel Sotun Palace** (p219) in Esfahan and the **Holy Shrine of Imam Reza** (p324) in Mashhad impress with their scale, elegance and deceptively simple lines. But Iran has its architectural curios as well – the stepped villages at **Masuleh** (p156), the 55m-tall, millennium-old tomb tower at **Gonbad-e Kavus** (p313) and the fairy chimneys of **Kandovan** (p140).

View the four *badgirs* (wind towers) of Yazd (p233)

MARTIN MOOS

WAYNE WALTON

Marvel at the grandeur of Esfahan's Imam Mosque (p216)

Soak up the splendour of Esfahan's Imam Sq (p216)

PHIL M WEYMC

SIMON RICHMOND

Wander around the fascinating Amir Chakhmaq Complex, Yazd (p234)

CLINT LUCAS

Shake the famous minarets at
Esfahan's Manar Jomban (p221)

Delight in the sumptuous decoration
of the Imam Mosque, Esfahan (p216)

COREY WISE

The greatest unsung highlight of Iran is its people. Many are the tales that travellers recount of unexpected kindnesses, of hands extended in friendship, of the gregarious, hospitable and generous Iranians. Come prepared for a spontaneous and warm welcome.

PHIL M WEYMOUTH

Visit a Shiraz teahouse (p250)

PATRICK BEN LUK

Shop for souvenirs in one of the bazaars in the pleasant desert city of Kerman (p284)

Experience the friendly openness of Iranians in Tehran (p80)

JOHN BORTHWICK

Boasting three millennia of recorded history, Iran is bestowed with a great legacy of ruins and hallowed stonework. Here is your chance to ramble around the relics of bygone empires at the Elamite ziggurat at **Choqa Zanbil** (p192) and the ruined fire-temple complex of **Takht-e Soleiman** (p170). Or follow in the footsteps of the Greats – Darius and Alexander – at **Persepolis** (p252).

Discover Zoroastrianism at
Takht-e Soleiman (p170)

PHIL M WEYMOUTH

ANTHONY HAM

Gasp at the mysteries, and the splendid isolation, of Choqa Zanbil's magnificent ziggurat (p192)

Soak up the atmosphere at Persepolis (p252), one of the wonders of the world

PHIL M WEYMOUTH

The harshness of Iran's terrain and the tumultuousness of its history have fostered the vibrancy of Iranian arts. Iranians have sought to brighten their lives and sustain their culture through the richness of their artistic traditions. Here is a nation where poetry is still venerated, where the countless knots of the nomad's *gabbeh* (rug) and the delicacy of the miniaturist's brushstrokes tell the story of the land and its people.

PHIL M WEYMOUTH

Watch craftsmen pock marking a large copper pot in Esfahan (p210)

Admire the art of the miniaturist (p60)

PHIL M WEYMOUTH

Gaze at intricate frescoes in the Chehel Sotun Palace, Esfahan (p219)

PHIL M WEY

CLINT LUCAS

Learn new skills as you watch an enamelled copperware artist at work in Esfahan (p210)

PHIL M WEYMOUTH

Discover limitless outlets for artistry in Esfahan's Bazar-e Bozorg (p215)

Appreciate the age-old skills involved in firing mosaic tiles (p57)

PHIL M WEYMOUTH

PHIL M WEYMOUTH

Be inspired by the colours of Esfahan's carpets and the creativity of their makers (p226)

The great majority of Iranians live in cities – they're sprawling, bustling and sometimes smoggy, but always pulsing with life. Get delightfully lost in the bazaar in **Shiraz** (p241), **Kerman** (p284) and **Kashan** (p201), take tea in the courtyard of a traditional *chaykhuneh* (teahouse) or join the crowds for an evening stroll in **Tabriz** (p133) and you'll come to appreciate the atmosphere that makes Iran so distinctive.

PHIL M WEYMOUTH

Stroll Shiraz's Bazar-e Vakil (p245)

Join the modern throngs for a Friday night amble in Shiraz's city streets (p241)

PHIL M WEYMOUTH

Chat with the welcoming locals at one of Esfahan's marvellous teahouses (p225)

MARK

Getting Started

WHEN TO GO

Extremes of temperature are the main factors in determining when to visit Iran. Temperatures can vary wildly: when it's -5°C in Tabriz it might be 35°C in Bandar-e Abbas. Spring and autumn are easily the best times to come, and if you come in spring you avoid having countless Iranians tell you: 'Oh, but you must come back in the spring, it's beautiful.' The most agreeable time to visit the south coast is during winter, while the northwest and northeast are at their best between mid-April and early June, and late September and early November.

High summer is unpleasantly hot in most of the country, but most especially so along the Persian Gulf coast and when the smog hangs heavy over Tehran. Nights during winter can be bitter but the days (often clear and about 15°C in much of the country) are far more pleasant than the summer heat.

Unless you're on the Persian Gulf coast, hotel prices tend to be higher during summer, usually by about 20% but, as in the case of the Caspian Sea resorts, sometimes up to 400%. Prices are at their highest and rooms hardest to find during No Ruz (Iranian New Year, about 21 March), when the country virtually shuts down for 10 days. Hotels across the country are booked solid from about 10 March until 5 April.

There is no one date that high season prices and summer opening hours begin. However, many hotels, airlines, monuments and museums up their prices and keep their doors open longer from mid-March to early October. For the sake of clarity, in this book when you see 'summer' opening hours it will usually refer to these dates. Hotel prices throughout are summer prices.

Many people prefer not to visit Iran during Ramazan, the Muslim month of fasting, when most restaurants close between dawn and dusk and tempers can be strained (p350–1). However, cafés in hotels and bus stations still operate and while buses may be less frequent, Ramazan is the least crowded time to travel on trains and planes.

See Climate Charts (p343) for more information.

The price of petrol, kept so ridiculously low by subsidies of about US$4 billion a year, is set to rise in coming years – initially from about IR600 to IR800 a litre. Costs of everything, from transport to food, are likely to rise with it.

DON'T LEAVE HOME WITHOUT...

There is not much you can't buy in Tehran or the big cities, though the selection is often limited. Things you should consider bringing include sunscreen and a hat; a teaspoon; a short-wave radio (p336); a universal plug; and pictures of your family, which are a great way to break the language barrier with your new Iranian friends. A couple of decent books should soak up your free hours at night and on transport (but make sure they don't have pictures of scantily clad women on the cover). Earplugs are useful for when you've finished reading and want to sleep. Women should bring tampons since these are almost impossible to find; and if you can't do without a specific brand of shampoo or cosmetic, stock up.

The question of clothing vexes many a visitor, but the rules are simple enough and you don't need to start scouring the Muslim neighbourhoods of your home town looking for chadors – unless you really want to. Just pack (in your hand luggage) a scarf and a loose-fitting jacket that reaches at least to mid thigh. For full details on dress, see p364).

Remember that US-passport holders almost always need to be booked on some form of guided tour before they will be issued a visa; and Israelis and anyone with an Israeli stamp in their passport will be denied entry.

COSTS & MONEY

While prices have risen steadily in Iran in recent years, it is still dirt cheap and great value by Western standards.

Backpackers can get by on as little as IR125,000 a day, even less if all luxuries are foregone; however, you would need to stay in a basic hotel, known as a mosaferkhuneh (from about IR30,000/US$3.70), eat the simplest food in local restaurants and limit the number of historical sites you visit.

Not a complete ascetic? You'll be looking at about IR180,000 to IR200,000 (US$22 to US$24) a day. This will usually be enough for budget or simple mid-range accommodation (with a bathroom), one good cooked meal a day, transport by the better Volvo buses or savari, chartered taxis around town (and sometimes in the countryside) and visits to all the important tourist attractions.

For IR300,000 (US$36) a day you could take a couple of internal flights, eat at restaurants serving 'exotic' Western fare to break up the kebabs, and lodge in mid-range hotels with Western toilets and satellite TV. If you want to stay in top-end hotels you'll be looking at more than IR632,000 (US$76) a day. Discounts on single rooms are minimal, so couples will pay less than the amounts quoted here.

Getting around Iran is wonderfully cheap; comfortable buses work out at about US$1 (IR8310) per 100km, while a bed on an overnight train can be cheaper than US$10 (IR79,000).

Domestic flights are no longer as ridiculously cheap as they were, but you can still fly from Tehran to Esfahan, for example, for only IR144,000 (US$17).

One of your biggest costs will be the entrance fees to museums and historical sites – the authorities seem to like the number 30,000 and that is how much it costs to see most of them. A busy day in Esfahan could easily cost you IR150,000 (US$18) in admission fees alone.

Remember that travellers cheques and credit cards don't work in Iran, so bring all the money you'll need in cash (see p354).

TRAVEL LITERATURE

The past few years have seen a rush of new travel literature about Iran. Most have a decidedly political bent, if not necessarily an agenda, and are generally quite readable.

Interestingly, several of the following are by female authors. It's worth noting that most of these books are not available in Iran. However, you shouldn't have any trouble bringing them, or almost any other books, through Iranian customs – but you can forget *Not Without My Daughter* or anything by Salman Rushdie. For more on customs restrictions, see p344.

Persian Pilgrimages by Afshin Molavi sees the US-educated Iranian journalist explore his homeland through a series of 'pilgrimages' to historical sites, poets' tombs and martyrs' cemeteries. This is a really great read, full of illuminating insight into Iranian culture and fairly balanced politically.

Searching for Hassan by Terence Ward recounts the author's return to Iran with his family in search of Hassan, the family's 1960s housekeeper. However, Hassan is really a subplot to a revealing look at the history and culture of Iran. Some have criticised Ward's soft approach to the Islamic government.

The Road to Oxiana by Robert Byron is a classic. A vividly observed travel diary of the author's 1930's passage from England to Afghanistan

HOW MUCH?

Meal in a cheap restaurant
IR20,000

One hour online
IR10,000

Short taxi ride
IR5000

Average museum ticket
IR30,000

Two-pack of toilet paper
IR700

LONELY PLANET INDEX

Litre of petrol
IR600

1.5L bottle of water
IR2000

Pot of tea in a teahouse
IR4000-6000

Souvenir qalyan
(water pipe)
IR60,000

Street snack – *sausis*
(sausage) sandwich
IR3500

TOP TENS
GREAT READS

Iran's complex culture and long history have seen plenty of words written about them, with most authors finding the truth far more interesting than fiction – there aren't many novels. For more information, see p64.

- *All the Shah's Men* by Stephen Kinzer
- *Answering Only to God* by Geneive Abdo and Jonathon Lyons
- *In Search of Zarathustra* by Paul Kriwaczek
- *Journeys in Persia & Kurdistan* by Isabella Bird
- *My Uncle Napoleon* by Iraj Pezeshkzad

- *Persepolis: The Story of a Childhood* by Marjane Satrapi
- *Persian Mirrors* by Elaine Sciolino
- *Persian Pilgrimages* by Afshin Molavi
- *Reading Lolita in Tehran* by Azar Nafisi
- *Shah of Shahs* by Ryszard Kapuscinski

MUST-SEE MOVIES

There have been few decent films about Iran made by foreigners, but that has been more than made up for by local film-makers. For more on films, see p66.

- *A Moment of Innocence*
- *The Apple*
- *Blackboards*
- *Children of Heaven*
- *The Desert of the Tartars*

- *Gabbeh*
- *The Little Stranger*
- *Paper Airplanes*
- *Taste of Cherry*
- *The White Balloon*

TEMPTING TEAHOUSES

With no bars, teahouses are among the most social places in Iran. These 10 make it as much for their atmosphere as anything else.

- Aramgah-e Hafez, Shiraz (p250)
- Chaykhaneh-ye Vakil, Kerman (p289)
- Chaykhuneh Baharestan, Hamadan (p184)
- Chubi Bridge, Esfahan (p225)
- Ghavam Restaurant, Bushehr (p264)

- Haji Dadashi, Zanjan (p170)
- Hamum-e Khan, Yazd (p238)
- Qeysarieh Tea Shop, Esfahan (p226)
- Sofre Khane Sonnati Sangalag, Tehran (p105)
- Towhid Teahouse, Shiraz (p250)

via Iran. Famous for its descriptive prose and often biting sketches of local people, its tone can verge uncomfortably close to racism by today's standards.

Honeymoon in Purdah by Alison Wearing seems to be either loved or hated by readers. Some decry Wearing's ignorance when embarking on her 'honeymoon' in Iran – with a friend posing as her husband – while others find much in common with her and enjoy the witty episodes she recounts.

Neither East Nor West by Christiane Bird is another new travelogue with more background but less humour than Wearing's book. Both do a decent job of getting behind the veil.

Black on Black: Iran Revisited by AM Briongos recounts this Spanish woman's return to visit friends in the country where she had studied before the Islamic Revolution.

INTERNET RESOURCES

Iran Chamber Society (www.iranchamber.com) Easily the best site around for historical, cultural and background information, with plenty of practical detail as well.

Lonely Planet (www.lonelyplanet.com) The latest news from travellers on the road in the Postcards section and the Thorn Tree bulletin board.

Net Iran (www.netiran.com) Dry but informative Iranian Government site lists embassy contact details, customs rules etc.

Pars Times (www.parstimes.com/ltravel.html) A virtual encylopaedia of good links to sites on Iran, this branch linking you to just about everything you need to know before you go.

Salam Iran (www.salamiran.org) A site created by the Iranian embassy in Ottawa. Useful for visa information, links to other embassy websites and downloadable application forms.

Tehran Times (www.tehrantimes.com) An online edition of the daily English-language *Tehran Times*, together with an archive.

Itineraries

CLASSIC ROUTES

THE FOOTSTEPS OF EMPIRE
Two Weeks / Tehran to Tehran

Two weeks is long enough to get a taste of the jewels of Iran's rich history. Fly into **Tehran** (p80) and spend two days seeing the **Golestan Palace** (p92) and **Tehran Bazaar** (p89). Fly to **Ahvaz** (p195), from where you can spend a day seeing **Shush** (p191) and **Choqa Zanbil** (p192). Take a bus (10 hours) to **Shiraz** (p241), where in three days you can see the mosques and gardens of the Zand dynasty and magnificent **Persepolis** (p252).

Take a bus and stop in **Abarqu** (p240) on the way to **Yazd** (p230), and wander the old town, gaping at the **Jameh Mosque** (p233) and the Zoroastrian **Towers of Silence** (p236). On your second day, tour **Meybod** (p240), the Zoroastrian pilgrimage site at **Chak Chak** (p240) and the mud village of **Kharanaq** (p239).

Catch a bus to **Esfahan** (p210), Iran's most architecturally stunning city, and explore Shah Abbas's **Imam Sq** (p216), the **Bazar-e Bozorg** (p215), the sublime **bridges** (p220) across the Zayandeh River and the Armenian community at **Jolfa** (p220). An easy bus trip brings you to **Kashan** (p203), where you can scramble over the roofs of both the bazaar and the incredible Qajar-period **traditional houses** (p205), and take a day trip to **Abyaneh** (p209).

By plane, bus and taxi and on a tight timetable you'll be able to hot-foot it around most of Iran's highlights. This 2850km ramble offers you a taste of Iran's pre-Islamic legacy, it's bustling modern megalopolises and its stately former capitals. Add in some rural retreats and regional bazaars and this two-week loop will give you an emphatically Iranian experience.

EAST BY SOUTHEAST

One Month / Turkey to Pakistan

Travellers with an adventurous bent have been following this classic overland route from Europe to subcontinental Asia for centuries. A month is the minimum time needed to do it justice. **Maku** (p123) makes a pleasant introduction on the way to **Tabriz** (p133), from where you can spend three days checking out **Jolfa** (p141) and **Kandovan** (p140), before heading for **Zanjan** (p168) for a look at **Soltaniyeh** (p167).

Stop for a day in historic **Qazvin** (p162) then head into the Alamut, to walk among the ruined **Castles of the Assassins** (p166). **Masuleh** (p156) is a charming place to chill out. Consider splicing in the 'Canyons, Forests & Paddyfields…In Iran?!' itinerary here.

Spend three days in **Tehran** (p80) seeing the museums and taking in the hustle and bustle, and then head south for two days in **Kashan** (p203) and **Abyaneh** (p209). Bus it to **Esfahan** (p210) where you'll need at least three days to see the sights, and then head off to **Shiraz** (p241), where one of your three days will be spent gaping at the ruins of magnificent **Persepolis** (p252). You could spend a night in **Abarqu** (p240) en route to **Yazd** (p230), where three days should include a trip to the historic towns of **Meybod** (p240) and **Kharanaq** (p239), plus the spectacular Zoroastrian pilgrimage site at **Chak Chak** (p240).

Splurge on a night in the restored **Caravanserai Zein-o-din** (p240) on the way to **Kerman** (p284), where three days will be enough to see **Mahan** (p290) and the 'New Arg' at **Rayen** (p293), before stopping for a night in **Bam** (p293) to see what remains of the Arg. **Zahedan** (p296) will detain you only as long as you need to prepare for the long trip to Quetta (Pakistan).

Follow in the footsteps of the hippies of old, crossing the Iranian plateau from the fringes of Europe to the edge of the subcontinent. En route you'll absorb and appreciate Iran's diversity, this 4420km traverse passing through rocky mountain gorges, green hillsides, the grand cities of central Iran and the great expanse of the arid southeast.

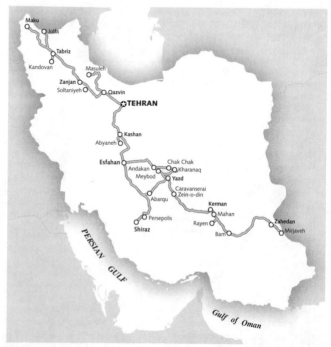

ROADS LESS TRAVELLED

CANYONS, FORESTS & PADDYFIELDS...IN IRAN?!

10 Days / Tabriz to Masuleh

Challenge Iran's desert image in the lush and rarely visited mountains of northwestern Iran. In the remotest sections you'll need to charter taxis, but with rides at US$3 per hour they're an affordable luxury.

Start in **Tabriz** (p133), where you can explore the **bazaar** (p136) and the **Valiasr District** (p139). Allow a day or two for an excursion to quaint **Kandovan** (p140). Take the train to **Jolfa** (p141) and spend the afternoon at the ancient **Church of St Stephanos** (p142) and in nearby **canyons** (p142). In Jolfa arrange a taxi for next morning's early start: reaching Kaleybar along the fascinating **Aras River Valley** (p142) will take a long day. Be aware you're driving alongside international borders; permit requirements might be imposed should political developments in the Caucasus make the region sensitive. Unwind in **Kaleybar** (p144) after hiking up the soaring crag of nearby **Babak Castle** (p144).

Take a savari from nearby **Ahar** (p143) via **Meshgin Shahr** (p145) to Ardabil for impressive views of Mt Sabalan. While in **Ardabil** (p145) visit the **Sheikh Safi od-Din mausoleum** (p147), one of western Iran's finest monuments. Descend to the Caspian Sea coast either via **Astara** (p149), or through nomad country via **Kivi** and **Khal Khal** (both p149). Stop in **Bandar-e Anzali** (p155) or **Rasht** (p151) to enjoy the garlic-stoked food, then escape through paddyfields and thick forests to the mountain village of **Masuleh** (p156).

This intriguing 10-day meander through alternative Iran is ideal for those who've already seen the main desert city sites and who are confident in navigating through areas unaccustomed to foreign visitors. The basic route is 865km (plus 175km in side excursions), of which a sizable chunk (265km) is covered during one long day on the splendid taxi ride between Jolfa and Kaleybar.

DESERT DETOUR

10 Days / Esfahan to Kerman

After a few days in bustling cities, the wide open spaces, ancient mud-and-straw towns and tiny oasis villages in and around the Dasht-e Kavir desert are a tonic for the soul. Start this detour in **Esfahan** (p210) and take a short bus trip to **Na'in** (p229), where if you arrive too late the caretaker at the **Imamzadeh Soltan Said Ali** (p229) will happily offer you pilgrim status and a basic room.

From Na'in hitch or take the 5pm bus east to Khur, and any transport you can find to take you the last 38km to **Garmeh** (p229). The silence in this oasis village is profound, and the hospitality at **Ateshoni** (p229) heartfelt; you could easily be here longer than planned.

Take a bus to **Yazd** (p230) and check into one of the great-value hotels in the old town. Visit the Zoroastrian **Towers of Silence** (p236) and a **qanat** (p234), the veins that have supplied water for centuries.

Take a day trip to **Meybod** (p240), **Chak Chak** (p240) and the mud-brick ghost town of **Kharanaq** (p239), before lashing out on a night of Safavid-era luxury in the restored **Caravanserai Zein-o-din** (p240) as you continue south.

Hardier souls could try the **Kermanshah caravanserai** (p240), 30km further south, where you can sleep soundly next to local shepherds and their flocks.

Move to **Kerman** (p284), where you can arrange camel or 4WD tours, including to the beautiful sand castles at **Kaluts** (p292).

Do not even think of doing this trip during summer. October to April is the best time to travel.

Find yourself on this 1330km odyssey through the seared expanses of emptiness. Here you can enjoy the silence and the solitude as you venture on through the heat haze towards the next town, shimmering like a gem on the horizon.

TAILORED TRIPS

THE CRADLE OF PRE-ISLAMIC RELIGIONS
Two weeks / Off the beaten track in Western Iran

Fire your imagination with millennia of religious history and myth. Start in ancient **Shush** (p191), visiting the tomb of the Jewish hero Daniel as well as the nearby **Choqa Zanbil** (p192), a magnificent 3000-year-old Elamite ziggurat (stepped pyramid). Climb into the mountains along the Babylonian 'Royal Road' via **Kermanshah** (p176) and **Tyuserkan** (p186) to **Hamadan** (ancient Ecbatana; p180) to see the tomb of biblical Jewish Queen Esther. Alternatively, from Kermanshah (via Paveh) roller-coaster the bumpy hairpins of the **Howraman** valley (p174), where the spectacularly set **Howraman-at-Takht** (p175) holds the last extant Mithraic midwinter festival. Further north, amid idyllic rural villages, explore the lonely ruins of **Takht-e Soleiman** (p170), once the world's greatest Zoroastrian fire-temple complex.

David Rohl's book *Legend* claims that the area around bustling **Tabriz** (p133) is the historical Garden of Eden, and that Mt Sahand, above lovely **Kandovan** (p140) village, is the Old Testament's Mountain of God. Northwest of Tabriz is **Bazargan** (p123), from where Mt Ararat (Noah's Ark crash landing spot) is clearly visible. Nearby **Jolfa** (p141), in the beautiful valley of the **Aras River** (the Bible's Gihon; p142), charming Church of St Stephanos was originally founded just a generation after Christ. To the east of Tabriz, around **Ardabil** (p145), is Genesis's Land of Nod guarded by the magnificent volcanic peak of **Mt Sabalan** (p145), the metaphorical fire-sword of the Cherubim.

THE TRANSIT-VISA DASH
Five Days / Turkey to Pakistan

The days of extendable transit visas are over. But if a transit visa's all you can get, overnight buses mean that you can still get a taste of Iran's two gem-cities while crossing the country for barely US$20 all in. On day one leave Van (Turkey) in the early morning, cross the border at **Sero** (p122) to arrive in **Orumiyeh** (p127) by early afternoon. At 4pm take the overnight bus to glorious **Esfahan** (p210), avoiding relatively uninteresting Tehran. Spend two days in Esfahan then on the third evening take a night bus (six hours) to wonderful **Yazd** (p230). Book the next night's ticket to Zahedan before spending the day exploring Yazd. With luck you're not too tired to enjoy its splendid alleys and windtowers. From **Zahedan** (p296) it's only an hour to the Pakistani border.

22

The Authors

ANDREW BURKE
Coordinating Author, Tehran, Central Iran, Persian Gulf, Southeastern Iran, Eastern Northeastern Iran

Andrew's first exposure to Iran came through news reports of the 1979 revolution. He was fascinated, and when his career in journalism took him to London it provided the opportunity to spend months exploring the Middle East. During research for this book Andrew was one of the first journalists in Bam following the earthquake, reporting on it and the political crisis for newspapers in Australia and Hong Kong. Fortunately his arrest by militiamen on charges of being a spy was soon resolved: 'But I'm Australian! Why would I want to spy for the British?' When he's not wandering the world Andrew lives in Phnom Penh, Cambodia.

My Favourite Trip

I've always enjoyed the desert and in Iran I found that the harsher was the environment the warmer the hospitality. The route I enjoyed most started in Na'in (p229) and went through Khur on the way to Garmeh (p229), probably the only place in Iran where you can live rural life in an oasis village. Skirting the desert, I moved on to Yazd (p230), Caravanserai Zein-o-din (p240) and Kerman (p284), where the bazaar reveals the first real taste of the subcontinent. I continued through Rayen (p293), Bam (p293) and Zahedan (p296) to get to the classic 'wild east' frontier town, Zabol (p299). The last leg was to Kuh-e Khajeh (p300), an ancient city on the side of a mountain in the middle of a lake. Totally worth it.

MARK ELLIOTT
Western Iran, Western Northeastern Iran

Travel writer Mark Elliott has been captivated by Iran's hospitality since his first visit in 1984. On one early trip he found himself caught up in the middle of a vast 'Down with America' demonstration celebrating the anniversary of the storming of the US embassy. Far from being a threatening experience, demonstrators merrily welcomed him along, took him for tea and reminded him that lacking discos, this was the nearest Tehran came to entertainment. Mark is best known as a travel writer and tourism consultant and he specialises in Iran's neighbour, Azerbaijan, about which he has written three books.

My Favourite Trip

While I adore the gem cities of Yazd (p230) and Esfahan (p210), my greatest delights are random adventures in the beautiful, utterly untouristed mountain areas of Kordestan, Lorestan and Azarbayjan provinces. Especially thrilling is the newly possible route along the Aras River from Jolfa (p141) to Khudaferin (p145), with spectacular canyons, ancient churches, mud-walled fortresses and quaint villages added to the geopolitical frisson of glimpses into Armenia, Azerbaijan and occupied Karabagh. Cap off the trip by cutting inland on a lovely mountain road up to the magnificent, emotionally powerful crag-top ruins of Babak Castle (p144), near Kaleybar.

CONTRIBUTING AUTHORS

Kamin Mohammadi Although based in London, where she grew up, Kamin travels back to Iran frequently. When in Iran she becomes the consummate contortionist, shifting between the twin allures of family duty and travelling the land. Kamin has written and broadcast on all aspects of Iran and she is working on her first novel.

Dr Caroline Evans Having studied medicine at the University of London, Caroline completed general practice training in Cambridge. She is the medical adviser to Nomad Travel Clinic, a private travel-health clinic in London, and is also a GP specialising in travel medicine. Caroline has acted as expedition doctor for Raleigh International and Coral Cay expeditions. She wrote the Health chapter in this edition.

Martha Brekhus Shams Martha has studied Middle Eastern culture for 25 years at the University of Maryland and University of Tehran and has lived in Iran for the last 15 years. She has worked with the Iranian Cultural Heritage Organization for 10 years as a consultant. She has also worked in the Iranian film industry on their annual Dah-e Fajr film festival and on the *Iranian Economic Review*. Martha has dual American–Iranian citizenship and describes herself as living in an 'exotic and interesting place in interesting times'.

Snapshot

Twenty-five years after Ayatollah Ruhollah Khomeini flew into Tehran to take charge of the world's first Islamic republic (p35), Iran finds itself at a crossroads. The revolution has, according to most Iranians, run its course. It's time to move on, they say, both politically and economically. But just how Iran will move forward is far from clear. With President Mohammad Khatami and his reform movement stripped of power through a sustained campaign of interference by the country's conservative forces, the obvious path to change has been blocked (p38).

So, where to now? Iranians want greater democracy, transparency, accountability of elected officials, civil rights and freedoms, but as long as the mullahs maintain their grip on power through the Supreme Leader, Ayatollah Ali Khamenei, and the Guardian Council (p38), it is hard to see how change will be achieved. What everyone from taxi drivers to young soldiers will tell you – every Iranian has an opinion on politics – is that there is no going back to the strictures of pre-Khatami Iran.

Not that there is much suggestion of that. The conservative government believes the best way forward is to put political differences aside and improve the economy. The theory is that if people are able to work and feed their families they won't be so concerned about their lack of democracy. But fixing the economy won't be easy. Foreign earnings are based almost exclusively on the sale of oil, an industry that in Iran has grown extraordinarily inefficient. Widespread corruption, a US trade embargo and unemployment, which is steadily rising as the 30 million children born during the '80s enter the job market, don't help. And Iran's isolation from international banking systems means significant foreign investment is still a long way off; and travellers can leave their credit cards at home (p353).

Chronic air pollution is among the most noticeable problems, from a visitor's point of view (p72), and can be loosely tied to that other old chestnut, the Bushehr nuclear power plant. The plant was near to completion in 2004 and is officially there to provide clean energy and help wean Iran off its dependence on oil. But any nuclear power at all depends on Israel stepping back from its promise to bomb the reactor before it comes online.

On the streets of Iran, what you wear is often as much a political statement as a reflection of fashion. While the chador (all-enveloping robe) is still widely worn, it is not unusual to see young women in Tehran wearing open-toed shoes, jeans, figure-hugging manteaus (overcoats), masses of make-up and scarves that seem to be constantly on the verge of falling off. This growing fashion liberalism is reluctantly accepted by the mullahs, who see it as cultural poison from the West, but it has made visiting Iran as a woman a little easier (p362). For men, before you decide to grow a beard for your Iran trip, note that goatees are in but full beards are not – they suggest an uncool affinity with the Islamic regime.

FAST FACTS

Population: 70 million

Population growth rate: 1.1% per year

Part of population under 15: 29%

Surface area: 1,648,000 sq km

Highest point: Mt Damavand 5671m

Lowest point: Caspian Sea -28m

Rate of inflation: 16%

Per capita GDP: US$6800

Number of Paykans on Iran's roads: 1.72 million

University places taken by women: 63%

Women as a percentage of paid workforce: about 11%

History

Historians are still debating when the first inhabitants settled in what is now Iran, but archaeologists suggest that during Neolithic times small numbers of hunters probably lived in caves in the Zagros and Alborz Mountains and in the southeast of the country.

THE ELAMITES & MEDES

Iran's first organised settlements were established in Elam, the lowland region in what is now Khuzestan province, as far back as the middle of the 3rd millennium BC. Elam was close enough to Mesopotamia and the great Sumerian civilisation to feel its influence and what few records there are suggest the two were regular opponents on the battlefield. The Elamites established their capital at Shush (p191) and derived their strength through a remarkably enlightened federal system of government which allowed the various states to interchange the natural resources unique to each region. The Elamites system of inheritance and power distribution was also quite sophisticated for the time, ensuring power was shared by and passed through various family lines.

For the most complete history of Iran on the web, including a full translation of Herodotus's writings and detailed articles on each dynasty, see www.iranchamber.com.

By the 12th century BC the Elamites are thought to have controlled all of western Persia, the Tigris Valley and the coast of the Persian Gulf. They even managed to defeat the Assyrians, carrying off in triumph the famous stone inscribed with the Code of Hammurabi, a battered copy of which is in the National Museum of Iran (p93), the original having been carried off to the Louvre in Paris.

About this time Indo-European Aryan tribes began to encroach on northern Persia. The Persians eventually settled in what is now Fars province, while the Medes took up residence in western Persia, establishing a capital at Ecbatana, now buried under modern Hamadan (p180). The Medes first crop up in Assyrian records in 836 BC, but little more is heard of them until Greek historian Herodotus writes of how Cyaxares of Media expelled the Scythians, who had invaded from the Caucasus, in about 625 BC. According to Herodotus, the Scythians were defeated when their kings attended a party and became so drunk they were easily disposed of.

Under Cyaxares the Medes became a most formidable military force, repeatedly attacking the neighbouring Assyrians. In 612, having formed an alliance with the Babylonians, the Medes sacked the Assyrian capital of Nineveh and chased the remnants of this once mighty empire into history. Exactly how the conquering powers divided the spoils of this heady success is uncertain, but it is believed the Medes assumed control of the highland territories. This meant that at his death in 575 BC Cyaxares is thought to have controlled an area that stretched from Asia Minor in the west as far as present-day Kerman in the east. However, little did the Medes know that within a few years one of their satrapies (subject states) in the south would make the Median conquests seem almost trivial.

Dawn of the Greatest Persian: The Childhood of Cyrus the Great is a recent historical novel by CJ Kirwin, which weaves fact with fiction in reconstructing Cyrus's coming of age in the last days of the Median Empire.

TIMELINE **c 2500–1200 BC**
Elamites establish themselves in present-day Khuzestan province

c 12th century BC
Elamites defeat neighbouring Assyrians and loot the Code of Hammurabi

THE ACHAEMENIDS & THE FIRST PERSIAN EMPIRE

In the 7th century BC the king of one of the Persian tribes, Achemenes, created a unified state in southern Iran, giving his name to what would become the First Persian Empire, that of the Achaemenids. By the time his great-grandson Cyrus II ascended the throne in 559 BC aged just 21, Persia was clearly a state on the up. In less than 20 years it would become the greatest empire the world had known.

Having rapidly built up a mighty military force, Cyrus the Great (as he came to be known) ended the Median Empire in 550 BC when he defeated the hated Mede king Astyages – who was also Cyrus's grandfather – in battle at Pasargardae. Within 11 years, Cyrus had campaigned his way across much of what is now Turkey; east into modern Pakistan; and finally defeated the Babylonians. It was in the aftermath of this victory in 539 BC that Cyrus marked himself out as something of a sensitive, new age despot. Rather than putting the Babylonians to the sword, he released the Jews who had been held there and, according to Herodotus in *The Persian Wars*, declared, among other things, that he would 'respect the traditions, customs and religions of the nations of my empire and never let any of my governors and subordinates look down on or insult them... I will impose my monarchy on no nation. Each is free to accept it, and if any one of them rejects it, I never resolve on war to reign.'

Cyrus the Great by Jacob Abbott tells the story of the fair-minded empire builder through the writings of Greek historian Herodotus and general Xenophenon, with extensive commentary from Abbott.

> When Tomyris heard what had befallen her son and her army, she sent a herald to Cyrus, who thus addressed the conqueror: 'Thou bloodthirsty Cyrus, pride not thyself on this poor success: it was the grape-juice...it was this poison wherewith thou didst ensnare my child, and so overcamest him, not in fair open fight. Now hearken what I advise, and be sure I advise thee for thy good. Restore my son to me and get thee from the land unharmed... Refuse, and I swear by the sun, the sovereign lord of the Massagetae, bloodthirsty as thou art, I will give thee thy fill of blood'.

Cyrus colonised the old Median capital at Ecbatana, redeveloped Shush and built for himself a new home at Pasargadae (p256), establishing the pattern whereby Persian rulers circulated between three different capitals. Unfortunately for him, the Massagetaes from the northeast of the empire decided he was indeed imposing his monarchy on them and they didn't like it. Herodotus writes that Cyrus incurred the wrath of the Massagetae queen Tomyris after he captured her son and slaughtered many of her soldiers in a battle made especially one-sided because the Massagetae army were all drunk. Even worse, they had over-imbibed on Achaemenid wine, found after they had overrun a camp at the rear of the enemy lines. Herodotus writes:

Cyrus paid no heed to Tomyris, who gathered all the forces of her kingdom for what Herodotus described as the fiercest battle the Achaemenids had fought. Cyrus and most of his army were slain. When his body was recovered she ordered a skin filled with human blood and, making good on her threat, dunked Cyrus's head in it. Cyrus's body was eventually buried in the mausoleum that still stands at Pasargadae (p256).

Cyrus's son, Cambyses II, headed west to capture most of Egypt and coastal regions well into modern Libya. Before he embarked on his Egyptian foray in 525 BC, Cambyses had quietly arranged the assassination of

c 750–550 BC	550–330 BC
Median Empire created in north and western Persia, with capital at Ecbatana	Achaemenid's create the First Persian Empire, with capitals at Shush, Persepolis and Ecbatana; Zoroastrianism established as state religion

his brother, Smerdis. However, while he was distracted in Egypt, a minor official called Magus Gaumata, who had an uncanny resemblance to Smerdis, seized the throne. Cambyses died mysteriously in 522 BC while still in Egypt, and Darius I (Darius the Great), a distant relative, moved quickly to be rid of Gaumata, whom history knows as the False Smerdis. This act was glorified in the giant relief at Bisotun (p179), near Hamadan, where you can see Darius's foot on Gaumata's head.

Darius had won an empire in disarray and had to fight hard to re-establish it, dividing his sprawling inheritance into 23 satrapies to make it easier to govern. The magnificent complex at Persepolis (p252) was created to serve as the religious hub of an empire whose primary faith was Zoroastrianism (p235), while the Median capital at Shush became the administrative centre. Persepolis was liberally decorated with images reflecting the scope of the empire; the Apadana Staircase (p253) shows 23 subject nations paying tribute to the Achaemenid king. Darius eventually expanded the empire to India and pushed as far north as the Danube River in Europe.

At the height of their power the Achaemenids ruled over one of the greatest of early civilisations. Paved roads stretched from one end of their empire to the other, with caravanserais at regular intervals to provide food and shelter to travellers. The Achaemenids introduced the world's first postal service, and it was said the network of relay horses could deliver mail to the furthest corner of the empire within 15 days.

After the Greek colonies of Asia Minor rebelled against their Persian overlord, Darius decided to invade mainland Greece in the hope of suppressing the city-states that supplied them. In 490 BC Darius's armies were defeated at Marathon near Athens while he was busy putting down an uprising in Egypt. He died in 486 BC.

The subsequent defeat of Darius's son Xerxes at Salamis in Greece in 480 BC marked the beginning of a long, slow decline for the First Persian Empire. Artaxerxes made one last attempt to pull the splintering satrapies back together but could not resist the rising power of Macedonia to the west.

ALEXANDER THE GREAT & THE END OF PERSEPOLIS

The end of the First Persian Empire finally came at the hands of Alexander the Great, king of Macedonia. Having defeated the Greeks and Egyptians, and Persian armies at Issus in Turkey (333 BC) and Guagamela in present-day Iraq (331 BC), Alexander arrived in Persia and routed Darius III, who fled east to Bactria, only to be murdered by his cousin. Alexander spent several months at Persepolis, which was later burned down – the jury is still out on whether this was the accidental result of a drunken party or deliberate retaliation for the destruction of Athens by Xerxes.

In 311 BC the Macedonian ruler Cassander had Alexander the Great's Persian widow, Roxana, and their son, Alexander IV, put to death to stave off any threat to his rule.

Alexander's empire soon reached across Afghanistan, Pakistan and India, but after his death in 323 BC it was divided between three squabbling dynasties, with Persia controlled by the Macedonian Seleucids. Gradually the Greek language replaced Aramaic as the lingua franca, new towns were set up all over the region and Greek culture stamped itself on the older Persian one. But the Seleucids were soon in trouble with the ambitious satraps and the numerous feisty ethnic minorities nominally under their control, in particular with the nomadic Parthians.

512 BC	330 BC
Darius the Great wins his way as far as the Danube River in Europe	Alexander the Great invades Persia and sacks Persepolis

THE PARTHIAN TAKEOVER

The Parthians had settled the area of Persia between the Caspian and Aral Seas many centuries before. Under their great king Mithridates (171–138 BC), they swallowed most of Persia and then everywhere between the Euphrates in the west and Afghanistan in the east, more or less re-creating the old Achaemenid Empire. They had two capitals, one at what is now Rey (p116), the other at Ctesiphon, in present-day Iraq.

Those Roman soldiers fortunate enough to survive the carnage at Carrhae reported that the Parthians fought under dazzlingly bright flags. It was Europe's first glimpse of silk.

Expert horsemen and archers, the Parthians spent much energy fighting with Rome for control of Syria, Mesopotamia and Armenia – territories the Romans felt were rightly theirs. This ended, however, after the Roman general Crassus wrongly concluded his armies had the measure of their Parthian counterparts. In 53 BC Crassus saw, until he lost his head, his armies routed at Carrhae. Peace followed, but within a century the two were again fighting. Not nearly as despotic as later dynasties, the Parthians were responsible for the first flowering of Persian architecture.

THE SASSANIANS & THE SECOND PERSIAN EMPIRE

Like the Achaemenids before them, the Sassanian rise from small-time dynasty to empire builders was nothing short of staggering. Beginning in their home province of Fars in AD 224, Ardeshir I (r 224–41) led a push for power that would not only see the Sassanians replace the ailing Parthians in Persia, but within 40 years become a threat to the very existence of the Roman Empire.

Between 241 and 272 Ardeshir's son, Shapur I, added Bactria to the empire and fought repeatedly with the Romans. In one of the most celebrated of all Persian victories, Shapur's armies defeated the Romans at Edessa in 260 and took the Roman emperor Valerian prisoner. You can still see the city of Shapur (p257), where Valerian was kept until he died, and bas-reliefs depicting the victory at Naqsh-e Rostam (p256).

The Sassanians re-formulated Zoroastrianism into a state religion incorporating elements of Greek, Mithraic and ancient animist beliefs. They then indulged in sporadic bursts of repression against other religions, including newly emerging Christianity. They had their own language, Pahlavi, from which modern Farsi slowly developed. A few fire temples built during this period remain, as do the ruins of Firuz Abad (p257); but perhaps the most impressive sight is the giant Statue of Shapur I (p258) hidden in a cave near Shapur. The Sassanian capital was at Ctesiphon in modern Iraq.

In the late 5th century a socialist called Mazdak won a huge following by preaching that nobles should share their wealth and their women with the oppressed masses.

The Sassanians developed small industries, promoted urban development and encouraged trade across the Persian Gulf but eventually they, too, were weakened by seemingly never-ending conflict with Byzantium. Ironically it was in its last years that the empire was at its largest. Khusro II (590–628) managed to recapture parts of Egypt, Syria, Palestine and Turkey. However, after Khusro was murdered by his son in 628, 11 rulers, including Persia's first two women monarchs, came and went in the following five years. Persia was in no state to resist when the Arabs attacked in 633.

THE ARABS & ISLAM

A crucial chapter in Persian history started when the Arabs defeated the Sassanians at Qadisirya in AD 637, following up with a victory at Nehavand near Hamadan that effectively ended Sassanian rule.

312–162BC	247 BC-AD 224
Seleucids attempt to 'Hellenise' Persia, but face constant small-scale resistance	The Parthian Empire is formed and Persian architecture blossoms

By the time of Mohammed's death in 632 the Arabs were firm adherents of Islam. The Persians found plenty to like in Islamic culture and religion, and happily forsook Zoroaster for the teachings of Mohammed without much need of persuasion from their conquerors. Only Yazd and Kerman (both of which clung to Zoroastrianism for a few centuries more) and a few isolated tribes in the mountains near the Caspian Sea held fast to their old religions.

At first the Umayyad caliphs held sway over Persia from their capital in Damascus, but in 750 a Shiite rebellion led to the elevation of the Abbasid dynasty, which set up its capital near Baghdad. The Abbasid caliphs presided over a period of intellectual exuberance in which Persian culture played a major role. Persians also held many high offices at court, but the Arabic language and script became the norm for day-to-day business.

During the 9th century AD, Abbasid power started to crumble, and regional governors snatched the chance to set up their own local power bases. In eastern Iran these new Iranian dynasties included the Safavids (868–903), the Tahirids (820–72) and the Samanids (874–1042), who set up their capital at Bukhara and revived the Persian language.

THE COMING OF THE SELJUKS
Inevitably, these local dynasties could not hold onto their power. The Samanids became fatally dependent on Turkish soldiers, one of whom soon elbowed them aside to found his own Qaznavid dynasty (998–1045); his son went on to grab what is now Sistan va Baluchestan province.

In turn they were ousted by the Seljuk Turks who pushed on through Persia, capturing Esfahan in 1051 and turning it into their capital. By the mid-11th century they had added eastern Turkey to their empire and, despite numerous rebellions, managed to maintain control with a large and well-paid army.

The Seljuk dynasty heralded a new era in Persian art, literature and science, distinguished by geniuses such as the mathematician and poet Omar Khayyam (p65). Theological schools were also set up throughout Seljuk territories to propagate their own Sunni branch of Islam.

The death of Malik Shah in 1092 marked the end of real Seljuk supremacy, and once again a powerful empire splintered into weaker fragments.

In 1079 mathematician and poet Omar Khayyam calculated the length of the year as 365.242198 days. This preceded the Gregorian calendar by almost 500 years.

GENGHIS KHAN & AFTER
In the early 13th century, the Seljuk Empire came to a final and bloody end when the rampaging Mongols swept across the Iranian plateau on their horses, leaving a trail of cold-blooded devastation and thousands of dismembered heads in their wake.

Under the leadership first of Genghis Khan, and then of his grandson, Hulagu, the Mongol rulers managed to seize all of Persia, as well as an empire stretching from Beijing (China) to İstanbul (Turkey). Eventually they established a capital at Tabriz (too close, as they later found out, to the Turks). It was Hulagu Khan who put an end to the stealthy power of the Assassins, destroying their castles around Alamut (p116). After a flirtation with Christianity and Buddhism, Hulagu was forced by social pressures in Persia to adopt Islam. He called himself *il khan* (provincial khan or ruler), a name later given to the entire Ilkhanid dynasty (1259–1335).

AD 224-642

Sassanian Empire, Second Persian Empire; Zoroastrianism the state religion

637–876

Arabs invade Persia, from 649 part of the Umayyad Caliphate; imposition of Islam becomes stricter from 755 under the Abbasids

THE SILK ROAD

Silk first began moving westward from China more than 2000 years ago when, records suggest, the Parthians became quite enamoured with the soft, fine fabric. By about 100 BC, the Parthians and the Chinese had exchanged embassies and inaugurated official bilateral trade. Within a few centuries silk would become more valuable than gold to the Romans, who even engaged in some early industrial espionage when the Emperor Justinian sent teams of spies to steal silk worm eggs in the 6th century.

It took many months to traverse the 8000km route, though geographically the Silk Road was a complex and shifting proposition. It was no single road, but rather a web of caravan tracks threading through some of the highest mountains and bleakest deserts on earth. The network had its main eastern terminus at the Chinese capital Ch'ang-an (now Xian). Caravans entered Iran anywhere between Merv (now in Turkmenistan) and Herat (now in Afghanistan), and passed through Mashhad, Neishabur, Damghan, Semnan, Rey, Qazvin, Tabriz and Maku, before finishing at Constantinople (now İstanbul). In the winter, the trail often diverted in a more westerly direction from Rey, passing through Hamadan to Baghdad. Caravanserais every 30km or so acted as hotels for traders, and many can still be visited today; Rubat Sharaf (p333) is an especially good example.

Unlike the Silk Road's most famous journeyman, Marco Polo, no traders traversed the entire route. Caravanners were mostly short and medium-distance hauliers who marketed and took on freight along a given beat. Goods heading east included gold, silver, ivory, jade and other precious stones, wool, Mediterranean coloured glass, grapes, wine, spices and – early Parthian crazes – acrobats and ostriches. Going west were silk, porcelain, spices, gems and perfumes. In the middle lay Central Asia and Iran, great clearing houses that provided the horses and Bactrian camels that kept the goods flowing in both directions.

The Silk Road gave rise to unprecedented trade, but its true glory lay in the interchange of ideas. Religion alone presents an astounding picture of diversity and tolerance that would be the envy of any modern democratic state: Manichaeism, Zoroastrianism, Buddhism, Nestorian Christianity, Judaism, Confucianism, Taoism and shamanism coexisted until the coming of Islam.

Eventually the Silk Road was abandoned when the new European powers discovered alternative sea routes in the 15th century.

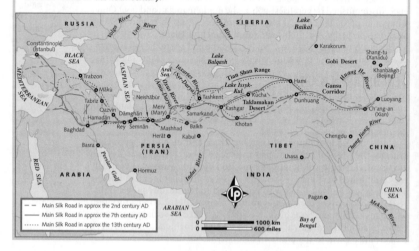

AD 1010

Poet Ferdosi finishes his epic *Shahnamah*, the Book of Kings, with its 50,000 to 60,000 couplets

AD 1051

Seljuk Turks capture Esfahan and rule from there until 1220; Persian literature thrives

Tragically, the Mongols destroyed many of the Persian cities they conquered, obliterating much of Persia's documented history. Perhaps feeling guilty about all the violence, they became great arts patrons leaving many fine monuments, including the wonderful Oljeitu Mausoleum (p167), near Zanjan. It was during the ascendancy of the Mongols that Marco Polo followed the Silk Road across Persia (see the boxed text 'Silk Road', opposite), and that Farsi replaced Arabic as the lingua franca. In 1335 the Mongol Empire came to an end when the death of Sultan Abu Said left it with no successor.

Marco Polo crossed Iran en route from Italy to China in the 13th century. On his way he passed through Tabriz, Kashan, Yazd, Kerman, Hormoz, Bam, Tabas and Neishabur.

The fragmented remnants of the Mongol Empire soon succumbed to invading forces from the east led by Tamerlane (Lame Timur) who swept on to defeat the Ottoman Turks in 1402. Tamerlane came from a Turkified Mongol clan in what is now Uzbekistan. During his short reign, he managed to stop the constant warring and moved the capital from Tabriz to Qazvin (p162). Tamerlane was yet another of the great contradictions who ruled Persia over the years: he was both an enthusiastic patron of the arts and one of history's greatest killers; after one rebellion 70,000 people are said to have been executed in Esfahan alone.

When he died in 1405, Tamerlane's empire immediately started to struggle. Despite their waning powers, the Timurids in eastern Iran maintained their support of Persian art, encouraging in particular the miniaturists of Shiraz. Gohar Shad, the wife of one of the Timurid rulers, was responsible for the beautiful mosque at the heart of Mashhad's Holy Shrine to Imam Reza (p322).

While the Mongols and Timurids were slogging it out in eastern Iran, assorted Turkman tribes were vying for power in the west. Eventually the Kara Koyunlu (Black Sheep) tribe, managed to set itself up in Tabriz and grab power in eastern Turkey. Having held strong for almost two centuries (1275–1468), they, in turn, gave way to the Ak Koyunlu (White Sheep) tribe who continued in power until 1514.

THE SAFAVIDS & THE THIRD PERSIAN EMPIRE

A Sufi called Sheikh Safi od-Din (d 1334) was the inspiration for and progenitor of the Safavi, a powerful sect of Shiite followers from Ardabil (p145). Ismail Savafi, a distant descendent of Safi od-Din, was eventually to conquer all the old Persian imperial heartlands, from Baghdad to Herat. He ruled as Persian Shah (r 1502–24) and although forced out of western Iran by the Ottoman sultan, Selim the Grim, at the disastrous battle of Chaldoran, his Safavid dynasty ushered in a great Iranian revival.

Under Ismail's son Tahmasp (r 1524–76), the capital was moved from Tabriz to Qazvin, and Western monarchs started to take an interest in Persia. The Safavids reached their peak under the brilliant Shah Abbas I (Abbas the Great; r 1587–1629), who, with military advice from English adventurer Robert Shirley, finally crushed all the assorted Turkmen and Turkish factions to create what is considered the Third Persian Empire.

For millennia Iran was called Persia. However, Reza Shah hated the name, and in 1934 changed it to Iran – derived directly from Aryan (meaning 'of noble origin').

The Safavid era saw a great flowering of Persian art and architecture. The capital was moved once again, this time to Esfahan, which Abbas rebuilt around what is today Imam Square (p216). The splendour of the Safavid court can still be seen in the fantastic frescoes of the Chehel Sotun Palace (p219). It was also under the Safavids that Shiism was enshrined

AD 1220–1335	AD 1380
The Mongols hack their way through Persia before turning into patrons of the arts, governing from Tabriz	Tamerlane exercises his sword arm in establishing the Timurid dynasty; they govern from Qazvin until 1502

as Persia's state religion, bringing it into direct conflict with the Sunni Ottoman Empire.

During this time European powers looked to Persia as a market. English companies were given business concessions, although the Portuguese, who controlled Hormoz Island in the Persian Gulf, were eventually expelled (p278).

The death of Abbas was the signal for a renewed period of bickering and fighting, which left the door wide open for the Afghans, who invaded in 1722. The Afghans besieged Esfahan and eventually took control of the city, slaughtering thousands but sparing the architectural wonders. The first Afghan ruler, Mahmud, eventually went mad and was murdered by a member of his own army.

NADER SHAH & KARIM KHAN ZAND

The Safavids were briefly rescued from oblivion by a soldier of fortune, Nader Shah, who in 1729 scattered the Afghans, along with the Russian and Turkish forces that were encroaching in the north. Nader Shah ruled Persia in all but name until 1736, when he decided he could do a better job as shah himself, thus ending once and for all the Safavid dynasty. To describe Nader Shah as a brilliant but war-loving mercenary is something of an understatement. He was a megalomaniac who, in a show of supreme self-confidence, invaded India in 1738 and returned with loot that included the Kuh-e Nur and Darya-e Nur diamonds, the latter of which you can marvel at in the National Jewels Museum (p94). His constant warring rapidly wore out the country. It was a relief to all, both inside and outside Persia, when he was assassinated in 1747.

After Nader Shah's murder, a Lor from western Iran, Karim Khan Zand (r 1750–76), grabbed power. Almost uniquely, he had little interest in warfare. Instead he is remembered for moving the capital to Shiraz, where he built the impressive Arg-e Karim Khani (p243) and the Regent's Mosque (Masjed-e Vakil; p245). Karim Khan ruled with far more compassion and humility than most of his predecessors and refused to take the title of shah, insisting instead on being called *vakil* (regent).

THE QAJARS & THE CONSTITUTIONAL REVOLUTION

The Qajar dynasty was a disaster for Iran, transforming 2500 years of empire and influence into an international laughing stock in just a few decades. Following Karim Khan Zand's death in 1779, the bitter and twisted eunuch Aga Mohammed Khan united the Azari Qajars and created a new capital in the village of Tehran. By 1795 he had wrested control of Persia from Lotf Ali Khan, but just a year later Aga Mohammed Khan was murdered by his own servants.

What Went Wrong? by Bernard Lewis sees the famed Islamic scholar argue why the Islamic Persian and Ottoman civilisations went from world leaders to 'Third World' so quickly. Thought-provoking stuff.

The Russians, as well as the British, had their eyes on Iran. The Russians were determined to gain access to the Persian Gulf and India, while the British were equally determined to deny them. During the undistinguished reign of big-bearded Fath Ali Shah (r 1797–1834) Russia captured Georgia, Shirvan (today's Azerbaijan), eastern Armenia and Daghestan, all semi-independent entities that previously had fallen within Persia's sphere of influence.

While responsible for a broad campaign of modernisation, Nasser al-Din Shah (r 1848–96) was generally more interested in collecting art,

AD 1502–1722

Safavid dynasty governs Third Persian Empire from Tabriz, Qazvin then Esfahan; Shiite Islam becomes state religion

AD 1514

Battle of Chaldoran; Iran loses the western empire to the Ottomans and the scorched-earth policy that follows decimates Kurdish civil society

building museums and servicing his numerous wives. He sired hundreds of princes, all of whom took from the national treasury at will. Inevitably, the Russians asserted control over northern Iran while the British ran things in the south.

The Qajar shahs spent so much money on luxuries such as the Golestan Palace (p92) in Tehran that the treasury constantly needed topping up through hasty sales of state assets. Foreign buyers were more than happy to pick up the bargains. In one particularly notorious incident, Nasser al-Din tried to sell exclusive rights to exploit all Iran's economic resources (including all the banks, mines and railways) for a one-off sum of UK£40,000 to be followed by payments of UK£10,000 for the next 25 years. He was forced to cancel the deal once news of its absurdity leaked out.

Eventually, popular resistance to the sell-off of Persian resources boiled over into revolt and the third-last Qajar shah, Muzaffar al-Din (r 1896-1907), was forced to introduce an embryo parliament, the first Majlis, in 1906, and a constitution to ensure new laws would be in line with Shiite doctrine. It became known as the Constitutional Revolution.

Worried that such a helpful shah was being weakened, the Russians persuaded him to backtrack on his promises. In 1908 martial law and dictatorship were introduced by his ruthless son Shah Mohammed Ali, leading to an uprising in Tabriz in 1909. Shah Mohammed Ali was forced to abdicate in favour of his son, who was still a child. The furore soon died down and in 1911 Shah Ahmad quietly abolished the second Majlis.

During WWI both Britain and Russia occupied parts of Iran while the Turks ravaged the partly Christian northwest. Inspired by the new regime in Russia, Gilan (the west-Caspian area) broke away in 1920 to form a Soviet republic under Kuchuk Khan. The weak Qajar shah seemed unable to respond, so Britain backed charismatic army officer Reza Khan, who swiftly retook Gilan before ousting Shah Ahmad.

THE PAHLAVIS

From the moment in 1921 that Reza Khan staged a coup d'etat to end Qajar rule, the poorly educated but wily soldier was king of Persia in all but name. Initially he had installed a puppet prime minister, but by 1923 Reza Khan felt confident enough to take that role himself. By 1925 he had declared himself the first shah of the Pahlavi line and crowned himself in a Napoleonlike coronation at the Golestan Palace.

Reza Shah, as he became known, set himself an enormous task; to drag Iran into the 20th century in the same way his neighbour Mustafa Kemal Ätaturk was modernising Turkey. Literacy, transport infrastructure, the health system, industry and agriculture had all been neglected and were pathetically underdeveloped. Like Ätaturk, Reza Khan aimed to improve the status of women and to that end he made the wearing of the chador (black cloak) illegal. Like Ätaturk, too, he insisted on the wearing of Western dress and moved to crush the power of the religious establishment.

Despite being nominally neutral during WWII, Reza's outspoken support of the Nazis proved too much for Britain and Russia, who maintained powerful spheres of influence in much of the country. In 1941 Reza was forced into exile in South Africa. The British arranged that he be succeeded

All The Shah's Men by Stephen Kinzer is the incredible true story of the CIA's coup to overthrow Mohammad Mossadegh. It reads like a thriller and draws a line between the coup and the rise of Islamic terrorism. Highly recommended.

AD 1722–29	AD 1736
Brief period of Afghan rule	Nader Shah battles his way to power, plunders Delhi and is finally assassinated in 1747

MOHAMMAD MOSSADEGH & THE CIA'S FIRST COUP

Before Lumumba in Congo, Sukarno in Indonesia and Allende in Chile, Mohammad Mossadegh was the first democratically elected leader toppled by a CIA coup. Mossadegh, a highly educated lawyer, paid the price for seeking a better deal for Iran from the hugely profitable oilfields run by the Anglo-Iranian Oil Company. When the British refused to offer a fairer share to Iran, he nationalised the company and expelled British diplomats whom he rightly suspected of plotting to overthrow him. The significance of this act went far beyond the borders of Iran, and Mossadegh was named *Time* magazine's Man of the Year in 1951 for his influence in encouraging developing nations to shake off the colonial yoke.

The British were desperate to get 'their' oil back. They encouraged a worldwide boycott of Iranian oil and worked hard to muddy Mossadegh's name both at home and abroad. After arch-colonialist Winston Churchill was re-elected in 1952, he managed to persuade the new Eisenhower administration in the USA that Mossadegh had to go. The CIA's Operation Ajax was the result, and it soon won the shah's support. Kermit Roosevelt, grandson of Theodore Roosevelt and one of the agency's top operatives, established a team in the basement of the US Embassy in Tehran and soon won the shah's support. As much as US$2 million was spent buying support from senior clerics, military officers, newspaper editors and thugs.

However, the CIA was new at the coup game and at first it seemed the operation had failed when Mossadegh loyalists arrested the coup leaders on 16 August. The shah fled to Rome, but three days later there was a second, ultimately successful, attempt and Mossadegh was toppled. The shah returned and the oil industry was denationalised, but the British monopoly was broken and the USA now held a 40% stake.

The 96-page CIA history of the coup can be viewed at www.payk.net/politics/cia-docs.

by his 22-year-old son, Mohammed Reza. In 1943 at the Tehran Conference, Britain, Russia and the USA signed the Tehran Declaration, accepting the independence of Iran. The young Mohammed Reza regained absolute power, but was being heavily influenced by the British.

By now the Anglo-Iranian Oil Company (later British Petroleum) was churning out petro-dollars by the million and there were calls for it to be nationalised. When prime minister Ali Razmara was assassinated in 1951, 70-year-old nationalist Dr Mohammad Mossadegh leader of the National Front Movement, swept into office on the back of promises to repatriate that money. Mossadegh succeeded in getting Anglo-Iranian nationalised as the National Iranian Oil Company (a fact still celebrated with an annual public holiday), but in 1953 he was removed in a coup organised by the USA and Britain (see boxed text above).

With Mossadegh gone, the US government encouraged the shah to press right ahead with a program of social and economic modernisation, dubbed the White Revolution because it was intended to take place without bloodshed. But although some headway was made with reducing illiteracy and emancipating women, it was all too fast for a conservative, and mainly rural, Muslim population. The religious establishment, the *ulema*, also took exception to land reforms that deprived them of some of their rights as well as to electoral reforms which gave votes to non-Muslims.

By 1962 Ayatollah Khomeini, then living in Qom, had started to emerge as a figurehead for opposition to the shah. In 1964 the shah approved a bill that gave US soldiers in Iran complete immunity from arrest. Khomeini

In 1971 the Arabic Islamic calendar was replaced by a new 'Persian' calendar (p342).

AD 1747

Karim Khan Zand grabs power and rules relatively peacefully from a new capital at Shiraz

AD 1779–1925

Qajar dynasty sees Iranian assets, including oil rights, sold to foreigners; the capital is moved to Tehran

responded by claiming that he had 'reduced the Iranian people to a level lower than that of an American dog' since if anyone ran over a dog in America they would be prosecuted for doing so, while now if an American ran over an Iranian he could do so with impunity. The shah reacted by banishing Khomeini, who fled first to Turkey and then to Iraq.

In 1971 the shah organised lavish celebrations for the 2500th anniversary of the founding of the Persian Empire, hoping to make himself more popular by fanning the flames of nationalism. It didn't work, and the remains of a vast tent city built to accommodate the mostly foreign guests still stand at Persepolis (p252).

The 1974 oil price revolution turned out to be the shah's undoing. In just one year the income from oil shot from US$4 billion to US$20 billion, but the shah allowed US arms merchants to persuade him to squander much of this vast new wealth on weapons that then stood rotting in the desert. As the world slipped into recession oil sales slumped and several planned social reforms were cut. The public was not happy.

THE ISLAMIC REVOLUTION

Since the beginning of the Pahlavi dynasty there had been smouldering resistance that occasionally flared into violence. Students wanted faster reform, devout Muslims wanted reforms rolled back, and everyone attacked the Pahlavis' conspicuous consumption. As the economy went from bad to worse under the shah's post oil-boom mismanagement, the growing opposition made its presence felt with sabotage and massive street demonstrations. The shah responded with all the force available to the absolute ruler. His security force, Savak, earned a horrific reputation for torture and killing.

In the late 1970s the shah's efforts to save his tottering regime became increasingly desperate and brutal, and US support began to falter. In November 1978, he imposed martial law and hundreds of demonstrators

Shah of Shahs by journalist Ryszard Kapuscinski is a fast-paced yet perceptive account of Iran in the decade leading to the revolution, written in a style that draws attention to the absurdities of a deadly serious situation.

AYATOLLAH KHOMEINI

An earnest, belligerent and intensely committed man, Ayatollah Ruhollah Khomeini was reviled and little understood in the West but revered as a saint by many Iranians. Khomeini was a family man of modest means whose wife hennaed her hair orange until his death; a religious leader who reduced the age at which 'women' could marry to nine; a war leader who sent wave upon wave of young men to their deaths on the Iraqi front by persuading them they would go straight to paradise as martyrs; the man who proclaimed the infamous fatwa against Salman Rushdie.

Born in the village of Khomein in central Iran, Seyed Ruhollah Musavi Khomeini followed in the family tradition by studying theology, philosophy and law in the holy city of Qom. In the 1920s he earned the title of ayatollah (the highest rank of a Shiite cleric) and settled down to teach and write.

He first came to public attention in 1962 when he opposed the shah's plans to reduce the clergy's property rights and emancipate women. In 1964 he was exiled to Turkey, before moving on to Iraq where he remained until 1978. Eventually he wound up in Paris where, with his friend Abol Hasan Bani-Sadr, he plotted the overthrow of the shah . After the shah fled in 1979, Khomeini returned to take control of Iran with ruthless efficiency. When he died in 1989, 10 million mourners turned out for his funeral (p115).

AD 1906	AD 1921
Constitutional Revolution; first parliament is established	Soldier Reza Khan stages a coup that will, by 1925, make him the first Pahlavi shah

were killed in street battles in Tehran, Qom and Tabriz. In December the shah made one last attempt to save the situation by appointing Shapur Bakhtiari as prime minister. However, Mohammed Reza Pahlavi and his third wife, Farah Diba, finally fled the country on 16 January 1979 (now a national holiday). He died in Egypt in 1980.

Although in exile in Paris, Ayatollah Khomeini, the leading Shiite cleric, was acknowledged as the leader of the opposition, a ragbag group including everyone from fundamentalist Muslims to Soviet-backed leftists. Many saw him as a figurehead, who, once the shah was ousted, would retire to a position akin to that of a constitutional monarch. They were wrong.

Khomeini's fiery nationalism and Islamic fundamentalism had been at the forefront of the revolt, but few Westerners had realised how deep-rooted was his support. When Khomeini returned to Iran on 1 February 1979 he told the exultant masses of his vision for a new Iran, free of foreign influence and true to Islam: 'From now on it is I who will name the government,' he proclaimed.

THE AFTERMATH OF THE REVOLUTION

Once in control, Ayatollah Khomeini set about proving the adage that 'after the revolution comes the revolution'. His intention was to set up a clergy-dominated Islamic Republic, and he achieved this with brutal efficiency.

Much of the credit for undermining the shah's regime lay with groups such as the People's Feda'iyin and the Islamic People's Mojahedin, as well as the communists. But once the shah was safely out of the way they were swept aside. People disappeared from the streets, executions took place after brief and meaningless trials, and minor officials took the law into their own hands. The facts, that the revolution had in fact been an effort by a range of groups with the same objective (to see the end of the shah), were quickly revised and the idea of the Islamic Revolution was born.

Following a referendum in March 1979, in which an alleged 98.2% of the population voted in favour, the formation of the world's first Islamic Republic was announced on 1 April 1979. Ayatollah Khomeini became the Supreme Leader.

At the urging of the new Islamic government, Iranian women had, on average, six children each during the 1980s; the population doubled in a decade.

Almost immediately, the Islamic Republic found itself up against the rest of the world, accused of adopting confrontational policies designed to promote other Islamic revolutions. In November 1979, 400 Revolutionary Guards burst into the US embassy and took 52 staff hostage; an action quickly blessed by Khomeini. For the next 444 days the siege of the US embassy dogged US President Jimmy Carter. Worse still, a *Boy's Own*-style attempt to rescue the hostages ran aground quite literally when the helicopters supposed to carry them to safety collided in the desert outside Tabas. In the middle of this crisis the first presidential elections were held in Iran and Abol Hasan Bani-Sadr, Khomeini's friend since the days of his Paris exile, was selected, with Mohammed Ali Rajai as his prime minister.

THE IRAN-IRAQ WAR

All this pales into insignificance, however, compared with the Iran-Iraq War, which raged from 1980 to 1988 and is officially estimated to have

AD 1941	AD 1953
The British and Russians force Reza Shah to abdicate in favour of his son Mohammed Reza Pahlavi	Prime Minister Mohammad Mossadegh is ousted in a coup d'etat organised by the CIA

killed 500,000 on each side. In 1980, hoping to take advantage of Iran's domestic chaos, Iraq's President Saddam Hussein made an opportunistic land grab on oil-rich Khuzestan province, claiming that it was a historic part of Iraq. It was a catastrophic miscalculation.

Saddam presented the shaky Islamic Revolution with an obvious enemy to rally against and an opportunity to spread the revolution by force of arms. Although much smaller, Iraq was better equipped; however, Iran could draw on a larger population and a fanaticism fanned by its mullahs. Believing the Iraqi government to be the lesser of two evils, the Western powers and the USSR took Iraq's side, and weapons were only sold to Iran at vastly inflated black-market prices.

Fighting was fierce, with poison gas and trench warfare being seen for the first time since WWI. A group of Islamic volunteers called Basijis, many as young as 13, chose to clear minefields by walking through them, confident they would go to heaven as martyrs. By July 1982 Iran had forced the Iraqis back to the border, but rather than accept peace Iran adopted a new agenda that included occupying Najaf and Karbala, two Iraqi towns of particular importance to Shiite Muslims. The war dragged on for another six years.

During the war Iraq bombed nearly 3000 villages and 87 Iranian cities, virtually obliterating Abadan and Khorramshahr. About five million Iranians lost their homes and jobs, and some 1.2 million were forced to flee the area, many migrating to far-away Mashhad. A cease-fire was finally negotiated in mid-1988 but war only ended officially in August 1990, just before Iraq became embroiled in the Gulf War. Prisoners were still being exchanged shortly before the Iraq War in 2003.

For a thorough description of the eight-year Iran-Iraq War, see www.iranchamber.com /history/iran_iraq_war.

Iranians refer to the war as the 'Iraq-imposed war' and it remains a huge influence on the country. Pictures of martyrs can be seen in every city; barely a day passes without television broadcasting interviews with veterans.

While the war was raging, different factions within Iran continued to jostle for supremacy. In June 1981 a bomb blast at the headquarters of the Islamic Republican Party killed its founder Ayatollah Beheshti and 71 others, including four cabinet ministers. A second bomb in August killed President Rajai and the new prime minister. The Islamic People's Mojahedin, once co-revolutionaries but now bitter enemies of the clerics, were blamed. However, suspicion also fell on ex-president Bani-Sadr, who fled to France. By the end of 1982 all effective resistance to Khomeini's ideas had been defeated.

AFTER KHOMEINI

When Ayatollah Khomeini died on 4 June 1989 he left an uncertain legacy. Khomeini's position as Supreme Leader passed to the former president, Ayatollah Ali Khamenei. The presidency, which had previously been a largely ceremonial post, was transformed with the election of Hojjat-ol-Eslam Rafsanjani, who began a series of much-needed economic reforms. Rafsanjani was re-elected in 1993 and Iran's domestic policy took on a far more pragmatic tone.

Bashu, the Little Stranger, Behram Beiza'i's 1986 film, tells the story of a little boy finding a new mother in southern Iran. It was the first antiwar film, made at the height of the Iran-Iraq War.

On the international front, however, Iran continued to be unpopular. In 1995 the USA slapped a trade embargo on Iran on the grounds that it was a state sponsor of terrorism. The embargo was still in effect in mid-2004.

AD 1979	AD 1980–88
The Islamic Revolution brings Ayatollah Khomeini to power; the world's first Islamic Republic is created in 1980	The futile Iran-Iraq War claims 500,000 Iranian lives

However, Iranian politics started getting interesting around the presidential elections of mid-1997. Much to the surprise of everyone, especially the mullahs, the moderate, reform-minded Ayatollah Hojjat-ol-Eslam Seyed Mohammad Khatami won in a landslide. Khatami was a liberal by Iranian standards, but he was also an insider. He had studied theology in Qom and served as Minister of Culture and Islamic Guidance for 10 years until he was forced to resign in 1992 – for being too liberal. During the Iran-Iraq War his roles included a stint as head of the Armed Forces Joint Command and chairman of the War Propaganda Headquarters.

He had been the only reform-minded candidate allowed to run for the presidency among seven conservatives, and his victory sent an overwhelming message of discontent to the Islamic conservatives running the country. In 2000 the reformers won a large majority in the Majlis, or parliament, and when Khatami was re-elected with 78% of the vote in 2001 hopes were high that much of the promised social and economic liberalisation would be carried out.

IRAN TODAY

Sadly, the Majlis has proved unable to live up to its reform promises, though it's not been for a lack of trying. Of the 295 pieces of legislation the Majlis had passed up until early 2004, 111 of the most daring changes were blocked by the conservative Guardian Council. The council is made up of 12 members: six Muslim clerics, who are appointed by Supreme Leader Ayatollah Ali Khamenei, and six Islamic jurists, who are appointed by the head of the judiciary, who is himself appointed by the supreme leader. The Guardian Council can veto any bill passed by the Majlis.

Modern Iran: Roots and Results of Revolution by Nikki R Keddie is a thorough analysis of the causes and effects of the revolution, focusing on the economic more than religious factors.

The conservative backlash against reform went further than a simple veto. Reformist intellectuals were assassinated; students beaten for protesting; dozens of reform-minded newspapers were closed and editors arrested. In essence, the credibility of the reformers was so badly damaged by their failure to deliver change that the public lost faith that change could come from 'within'.

'Within' refers to President Khatami's reform agenda, which was based on a policy of avoiding confrontation with the clerics and engineering change from within the theocratic system. Significant gains have been made and almost every Iranian you meet will agree life is better today than it was in 1997. They will also tell you that change has not come quickly enough, and ultimately the reform movement has failed. Such was the backdrop to the Majlis elections in February 2004, which coincided with the 25th anniversary of the Islamic Revolution. More than 2000 mostly reformist candidates, including 82 sitting members, were barred from running by the Guardian Council. Many elected not to vote and the conservatives were swept back into power, leaving Khatami as a lame-duck president for the final year of his term. For more on the Iranian political situation, see Snapshot (p24).

A few weeks before those elections Bam was devastated by an earthquake that killed more than 26,000 people and destroyed the ancient Arg-e Bam; see p293 for a full description.

AD 1989	AD 1997
Ayatollah Khomeini dies and Ayatollah Ali Khamenei takes his place	President Khatami is elected and reformists win a majority in the Majlis, but can't force change

The Culture Kamin Mohammadi

THE NATIONAL PSYCHE

Iranians are the most surprising people. Where you might expect them to be austere, they are charming; rather than dour, they are warm, and instead of being hostile to foreigners, they are welcoming and endlessly curious.

The truth lies in the gap between reality and Western perception. Before the revolution, the West's experience of Iranians was drawn from the country's elite that travelled and came abroad for their education. The revolution turned that image on its head. Suddenly Iranians were scary, hysterical people chanting 'Death to America', covering their women in black chadors, and supporting a fundamentalist regime that apparently took their society back to the Middle Ages.

Let's dispel these images. Despite the Islamic government and the Sharia laws that rule the country, Iranians are not frightening people. They are generally warm and welcoming to a degree that can be embarrassing to Westerners. Any rhetoric that comes from the regime regarding countries such as the USA rarely extends to individuals from those countries.

Iranians take their role as hosts very seriously; there are well-developed rules governing social conduct and interaction. This comes from a genuine desire to put others' needs first and please where possible. *Ta'arof*, the Iranian system of courtesy, can be a minefield if unknown (see the boxed text 'Ta'arof', p40), but it makes Iran a haven for travellers – you will be treated with unfailing politeness wherever you go.

The Iranian spirit is tolerant and eternally buoyant. The Iranian plateau can be a harsh land, hence the necessary creativity of the Iranian soul. The traditional Persian garden, walled in from the desert and divided by water channels, occupies a profoundly primal place in the Iranian heart, inspiring the designs of rugs, informing the brilliance of miniatures and lending its colours to the tiled domes of mosques. The play of light and colour preoccupies all aspects of Iranian art and even Shiism can be seen as an expression of this, based as it is on the 'Light of Mohammad', a spiritual thread passed on through the imams.

A glance at Iran's history will give another insight into the Iranian character. Despite several devastating invasions, Iranians have always managed to keep their own unique culture alive and somehow subvert the invading culture and assimilate it with their own. Thus the Iranian way is to bend to the prevailing wind only to spring back in time with regained poise. Ever-changing fortunes have taught Iranians to be indirect people, unwilling to ever answer with a bald negative and unable to countenance rudeness or public displays of anger.

Iran's attitudes to the West are contradictory. Whereas most Iranians can talk at length about the faults of Western governments, holding first the British and then the Americans responsible for much of Iran's 20th-century history (with some justification), they can nonetheless admire Western attitudes. They will alternately boast of Iran's superiority in terms of culture, home life and morality and then apologise for Iran's inferiority. Most Iranians have a sense of pride in their ancient culture as well as an acute sense of their own society's shortcomings.

Remember that Iranians are proud of their Aryan roots, which distinguish them from the people of south Asia or the Middle East. Iranians intensely dislike being classed as Arabs, who remain unforgiven for their

Kamin Mohammadi is based in London, where she grew up, but she travels back to Iran frequently. She has written and broadcast on all aspects of Iran and she is working on her first novel.

The area of land that is Iran has been continuously inhabited by a single nation for longer than any other land.

invasion of Iran in the 7th century. Iranian racism is reserved for Afghan refugees and the Arabs of neighbouring countries, who are regarded as having no culture aside from what their invasion of Iran gave them. But such is the power of Iranian courtesy and hospitality that you will never see such attitudes displayed openly and especially not extended to travellers.

Ancient Persia by Josef Wiesehöfer is a study of the country's origins and why it collapsed so dramatically after the Arab invasions of the 7th century.

The young people of Iran are particularly curious about foreigners and are much more aware of Western popular culture than you might expect. They love practising their English and will want to bombard you with questions about everything from AIDS to J.Lo, so be prepared to be overwhelmed!

In essence the Iranian soul is a deeply sensual one – perhaps the biggest surprise for Westerners expecting religious fanaticism and austerity. What is universal in the Iranian character is the enjoyment of the cadences of poetry read aloud, their wonderful food and their admiration of natural beauty. They are tied absolutely to the land, although most now live urban lives.

Somewhere in every modern Iranian the desires expressed by Omar Khayyam in his 12th-century poem *Rubaiyat* still resound:

> A book of verses underneath the bough
> A jug of wine, a loaf of bread and thou
> Beside me singing in the wilderness
> And wilderness is paradise enow.

LIFESTYLE

The majority of Iran's urban dwellers live in flats, and more and more houses in Tehran and the major cities are being razed, with apartment blocks taking their place. Land in Tehran is very expensive and the cost of living increasingly prohibitive, particularly for young couples who can rarely afford their own place. Many newly married couples will live with in-laws for years before they can move into a place of their own. With the monthly rent for a two-bedroom property in Tehran coming in at around US$420, and the salary of a mid-ranking civil servant US$120 a month, the struggle to make ends meet dominates many people's lives. Hence,

---

TA'AROF

This system of formalised politeness may seem very confusing to outsiders, but is a mode of social interaction in which everyone knows their place. It may seem that *ta'arof* just means that a person says something merely out of politeness, but in reality it is all about sensitivity to another's position. *Ta'arof* gives everyone the chance to be on equal terms: this ritual display of vulnerability is never abused. So for example, an offer of food will be turned down several times first, giving the person making the offer the chance to save face if in reality they don't have the ability to provide a meal. A good rule is to always refuse any offer three times but, if they continue to insist, do accept. When a taxi driver or shopkeeper routinely refuses payment when asked for a bill, do remember that this is just *ta'arof* – don't leave without paying!

Ta'arof also involves showing consideration of others in your physical actions, so try not to sit with your back to people, especially your elders, and be prepared for a delay at every doorway as Iranians insist that whoever they're with goes through the door first with repeated *'befarmayid'*, 'please'. Be prepared for lots of small talk at the beginning of any exchange, as the health of every member of your family is inquired after. Try to return this courtesy as it will be well appreciated. Also be prepared to be asked questions that are considered quite personal in the West, such as your salary, marital status, why you don't have children and so on. This is quite normal. Steer away from politics or religion unless your Iranian host broaches the subject first.

many ordinary Iranians hold down more than one job and in the case of the middle classes, both men and women work.

The gap between rich and poor is huge, with the middle class shrinking. Teachers, earning around US$180 a month, are the sort of state employee hardest hit by inflation rates running at around 16% per annum (the unofficial figure is 25%). On the other hand, a fortunate minority, some of whom have made a fortune from land and property speculation, continue to build lavish villas with swimming pools behind high walls in Tehran's breezy northern suburbs. Or they live lavishly in one of the glistening new skyscrapers punctuating the hilly north of Tehran, in marble-and-glass apartments filled with cappuccino machines, Le Corbusier chairs and home gyms. The women of such families tend not to work but instead lead lives revolving around their children, visiting parents and friends and working out with personal trainers.

Dara and Sara are dolls developed by a government agency to promote traditional values and rival Barbie (though so far Barbie is winning hands down!).

In contrast a middle-class couple may leave their modest apartment together in the morning after the typical Persian breakfast of bread, cheese, jam and tea. Their children, if small, will mostly be looked after by grandparents while the couple go to work. One or the other may make it back for lunch unless living in Tehran where distances are greater and traffic hideous. In the evening the family meal will be taken together, often with the wider family and friends. Iranians are social creatures and many visits take place after dinner.

In poorer or more traditional families it is likely that the woman will stay at home, in which case her whole day revolves around providing meals for her family and shopping (in ultraconservative families the men may do the shopping), as well as looking after the home and preparing meals.

Iranian meals can take time to prepare and though supermarkets exist and some pre-packaged ingredients are available, mostly there is no convenience food and just buying, cleaning and chopping the requisite bunch of herbs served with every meal can take the best part of an afternoon. Working women generally see to these tasks in the evenings, when they may prepare the next day's lunch. Perhaps in more enlightened families men help with the cooking and housework, but mostly it is safe to say that men's role in the home is largely confined to appreciating the quality of the cooking. Which they do well, Iranians being true gourmands.

Jafar Panahi directs a Kiarostami script in Crimson Gold. This Cannes award-winning film is a dark tale of the ruin of a young pizza delivery boy and the madness of modern life in Tehran.

Family life is still of supreme importance although there is much talk of the erosion of family values since the Iran-Iraq War. Children tend to live with their parents until – and sometimes after – they are married and often families include grandparents and other elderly relatives. As a result Iranian society is more multigenerational than Western society. It is extremely unusual to live alone and children only leave home to attend university in another town or for work. Although the young people of Iran long for independence and their own space, just like their Western counterparts, there is not much cultural precedence for this. Those who do live alone – men as a rule – are pitied and women living alone are regarded with extreme suspicion, the presumption being that they are of dubious moral character. Being married and having a family is regarded as the happiest – not to mention the most natural – state of being.

Education is highly regarded; literacy is well above average for the region at around 80%. Many middle-class teenagers spend up to two years cramming for university entrance exams, though the sheer number of entrants, ideological screening and places reserved for war veterans and their offspring make it very hard to get in. And once out of university, there is no guarantee of work. With the sexes still segregated at school and boys and girls not encouraged to socialise together, it is safe to say that

It has been estimated that there are more than one million drug addicts in the Islamic Republic. Drug dealing and even drug use can be punishable by death, so avoid drugs at all costs.

trying to get to know members of the opposite sex is a huge preoccupation for Iranian teenagers. They hang around shopping malls, in parks, parade up and down main boulevards and spend lots of time driving around in cars. This is very noticeable in Tehran, where you see youngsters on dates in cafés while nonchalantly playing with mobile phones.

Drugs are available and increasingly a problem, from the army of war-veteran addicts to middle-class kids with nothing better to do. Social taboos make it hard for parents to seek help for addicted children. The phenomena of teenage runaways, especially girls, is another social problem that gives weight to those decrying the breakdown of traditional family structures.

For the most part, though, the average Iranian family is a robust unit and, despite economic and social differences, most operate in broadly the same way. They provide an essential support unit in a country with no state benefit system. On public holidays and weekends, you will see many examples of the typical, multigenerational Iranian family out together, walking, laughing and picnicking in the countryside and parks.

POPULATION

When Iranians meet they inevitably ask: 'Where are you from?' This is because Iran has a multiplicity of distinct ethnic identities who are all, nevertheless, Iranian. It is important to understand that though the indigenous ethnicities are very much part of life, there is a unifying Iranian identity that keeps all these separate peoples part of a bigger whole. The name Iran – from the Middle Persian Eran – comes from the term for Aryan, 'the land of the nobles'. It was first used in the 1st millennium BC.

The population of Tehran is 14 million – almost one-fifth of Iran's population. That's comparable to 50 million people living in New York City.

Iran's population has more than doubled since the revolution, as contraception was outlawed and large families encouraged. This policy was hastily reversed when the economic implications became clear and since 1998 the annual population increase has halved. The population now skims 70 million, with almost 70% of the population under 30. Unemployment is high, with about 28% of 15- to 29-year-olds out of work. About one-third of Iran's population is under 15.

The rapid urbanisation of Iranian society started well before 1979, but was intensified by the Iran-Iraq War. Now an estimated 60% of the population live in the cities. About one sixth live in Tehran – just under 14 million – so traditional life in the countryside is fast becoming a thing of the past.

Persians

Persians are the descendents of the original Elamite and Aryan races who populated the plateau from around the 3rd millennium BC. The Persians, or Farsis, were originally the tribes that came to establish the Achaemenid Empire and now make up about 50% of the population. Farsi is the main Iranian language.

Azaris

Commonly called 'Turks' in Iran, the Azaris make up about 25% of the population. They speak Azari Turkish, a dialect mixing Turkish with Farsi. They are concentrated in northwest Iran, in the Azarbayjan province. Although many have relations in the Republic of Azerbaijan over the border, the years of border control between the Iranians and USSR have weakened ties. Unlike the neighbouring Turks in Turkey, the Azaris are Shiite, which keeps them well integrated with the general population, and there is little tension. A small group of Azaris in Azerbaijan are Baha'i.

Azaris are famously active in commerce, and in bazaars all over Iran their voluble voices can be heard. Older Azari men wear the traditional goat's wool hat and their music and dances have become part of the mainstream culture. Azaris are well integrated and many Azari Iranians are prominent in Farsi literature, politics and the clerical world.

Kurds

Iran has 6.8 million Kurds, 10% of the population. The Kurds can lay claim to being the oldest Iranian people in the region, descended from the Medes. Kurds also live in neighbouring Syria, Iraq and Turkey. They speak their own language descended from the same root as modern Farsi. The Kurds are subdivided into several tribes and each tribe has its own distinct version of the traditional dress and dialect.

In Iran, the Kurds live in the mountainous west, particularly Kordestan, though there are settlements in Khorasan province in the east and outside Esfahan in and around Shahr-e Kord. Unlike the Azaris, they have not traditionally migrated to Tehran and so their way of life is little known to other Iranians.

Kurds are mostly Sunni Muslims and have had several run-ins with the government. The worst was a bloody confrontation with Khomeini's troops after the revolution, although by and large, Iranian Kurds just want a degree of cultural and political autonomy rather than independence. Institutional discrimination keeps their province poor, with the second lowest social indicators in Iran.

Kurdish men wear the traditional dress of a short jacket and baggy trousers with a winding cummerbund. The women wear colourful and often sparkly long dresses over baggy trousers, rarely covered with a chador. At celebrations the real finery comes out and caps covered in gold coins over cascading stitched tulle scarves are usual, although each Kurdish tribe has its own variation of the traditional dress.

Kurdish music and dance is very distinctive and the light-footed Kurds love nothing more than to form a circle and perform their lively group dances.

Arabs

Arabs make up about 3% of the Iranian population and are settled mostly in Khuzestan, along the Persian Gulf coast, in the Persian Gulf islands and so are often called *bandari* (*bandar* means port). They rarely settle in Tehran or the provincial towns and so are considered exotic. Arabs in Khuzestan are mostly Shiite while those along the Persian Gulf are mainly Sunni.

Arabs speak a dialect of Arabic and are darker skinned than other Iranians. *Bandari* women tend to wear distinctive clothes, often with jangling ankle bracelets over flip-flops, and have tattoos on their faces and hands. They wear a unique chador with sleeves and may have their faces covered. Several fine cloths in black, one folded over to hang down from the head with another fastened above the ears, means their eyes can be uncovered, or a flick of the cloth can have them disappear completely behind this black curtain. Some women wear an owl-like mask. The men wear the *abba*, a long sleeveless tunic, usually in white, with sandals and perhaps an Arabic turban. Elsewhere you will see the men in *dishdasha*, the traditional floor-length shirt-dress, with the long headscarf known as *gutra*.

They have their own music which is characterised by the *ney ammbooni* (a sort of bagpipe) and a strong beat, and is accompanied by a shimmying dance much like belly dancing.

Lors

These proud people constitute 2% of Iran's population and are commonly thought to be descendants of the first peoples in the region, the Kassites

Chess *(shatranj)* originally came from India, but it was refined into the version that is played today in ancient Persia.

Bahman Ghobadi's film *A Time for Drunken Horses* shared Cannes' 2000 Caméra d'Or prize with Hassan Yektapanah's *Djom'eh*. Another masterful film using children and nonprofessional actors to follow the story of Kurdish orphans living in a border village.

and the Medes, and they speak a mixture of Arabic and Farsi. About half the Lori population is still nomadic and those settled live in the western province of Lorestan. They were almost independent under their own viceroys until Reza Shah brought them under the control of the central government and deported some to Khorasan and Zanjan provinces, where pockets of Lors still exist.

They speak Lori, which is their own language, or Avesta, a dialect of Old Persian. They are renowned for their horsemanship, sheep farming, metalwork and carpet weaving. They make a sort of *gabbeh*, which has tufts on both sides and is used as a blanket. As with the Kurds and the Bakhtiyari, Lor women have traditionally had more freedom than other Iranian women. Also like the Kurds, their refusal to integrate fully has kept their province of Lorestan poor and underdeveloped.

Farhad Mehranfar's 1997 feature debut *Paper Airplanes* is charming. A travelling projectionist assigned to show movies to villagers in remote areas takes his son with him to the northern region of Iran.

Turkmen

Making up 2% of the population, Iranian Turkmen are descended from the nomadic Turkic tribes that once ruled Iran. They live in the northeast of the country. They speak their own Turkic language and have very distinctive looks, being tall with slightly Mongolian features. The Turkmen women wear heavy, full-length dresses in bright colours over trousers and shawls with floral designs while some men still sport large sheepskin hats called *telpek*, knee-length cotton jackets and baggy trousers tucked into boots.

They tend to stay on their own plains and excel in horsemanship, being famous for breeding and racing horses, as well as sheep farming. They are Sunni Muslims and have a liking for Sufism.

Baluchis

The population of the dry, barren province of Sistan va Baluchestan is by and large Baluchi, making up around 2% of the country's population. These Baluchis are part of a greater whole that is spread across Pakistan and Afghanistan and about half are nomadic. They have distinctive facial features and dark skin, and speak Baluchi, a language related to Pashtu. They wear the *shalwar kameez*, a long loose shirt worn over baggy trousers, as in Pakistan, and their handiwork and embroidery is similar to that found in Pakistan and India, often incorporating mirrorwork. Baluchis are Sunni Muslims and are famous for camel races.

Nomads

During the last century authorities insistently tried to settle Iran's many nomadic tribes, but there are still about a million nomads left in Iran. They are mostly the Turkic Qashqa'i and the Bakhtiyari, but there are also nomadic Kurds, Lors and Baluchis.

Gabbeh, directed by Mohsen Makhmalbaf, is a beautiful film centring on a *gabbeh*, a type of Persian carpet made by Qashqa'i nomads, and on the love story of a nomad girl with the same name.

The Bakhtiyari are concentrated in an area extending southward from Lorestan province to Khuzestan province and westward from Esfahan to near the Iraqi border, moving their tribes and herds of sheep and goats between summer and winter pastures. They speak a dialect of Lori.

The Qashqa'i are based in central Iran where they move between summer and winter pastures in the province of Fars. Their migration routes are among the longest and most difficult of all of Iran's pastoral tribes. They have become famous for their production of simple rugs, the *gabbeh*, which have proved very popular with Westerners (Iranians are rather snobbish about *gabbeh*). You can usually spot Qashqa'i women in the Shiraz bazaar.

Nomadic women wear amazingly colourful long layered dresses with much jewellery and no chadors. The men sometimes wear tall hats with a rounded crown.

SPORT

Football (soccer) is the country's most popular sport and something of a national obsession. Please note that women can only attend women's sports (likewise men are restricted to men-only sports), apart from some football matches that feature segregated areas for women. For more information, see below.

Second only in popularity to football is wrestling, a sport at which Iranians excel. Iran has competed internationally and won medals at the Olympic Games.

An ancient sport peculiar to Iran is the *zurkhaneh* (literally, 'the house of strength'); for details, see the boxed text 'Zurkhaneh' (below).

Cricket is played mainly in the south of Iran. In northern Tehran, there are tennis clubs and an 18-hole golf course. Both run separate women's sessions.

Polo is believed to have originated in Iran and was certainly played during the reign of Darius the Great. A couple of millennia later, the huge main square of Esfahan was used for polo matches which would be watched by the Safavid Shah Abbas I from the balcony of the Ali Qapu Palace. Although the game didn't survive the revolution, horse riding is still popular in Iran.

Other popular sports in which Iran competes at international levels are weight lifting, volleyball, shooting, fencing, track and martial arts. More adventurous sports include scuba diving from Kish Island in the Persian Gulf, hang-gliding outside Tehran near Larijan (towards Amol) and sailing and water-skiing off the Caspian coast. Karaj Dam, about 42km west of Tehran, was, until recently, a popular place for water sports, though this has been temporarily stopped for environmental reasons.

Recently Iran has developed an enthusiasm for yoga and you can find single-sex classes in Tehran, Shiraz and Esfahan.

Also popular are skiing (Iran has sent both cross-country and downhill skiers to the Winter Olympics), mountaineering and hiking. Iranians are great walkers and like nothing better than to hike in the mountains or take a leisurely walk (accompanied by elaborate picnics) in the city parks on holidays. For more information, see p338.

Football Iranian Style, Maziar Bahari's 1998 documentary, was filmed in Tehran during the World Cup. By showing the country's passion for football, Bahari's affectionate film draws a portrait of Iranian society that challenges Western views of the Islamic Republic.

Football

The world noticed Iranian football when, in the 1998 World Cup, the Iranian team did surprisingly well and played a historic game against

---

ZURKHANEH

Unique to Iran, the *zurkhaneh* (literally, the 'house of strength') dates back thousands of years. As it was refined through the ages, the *zurkhaneh* picked up different components of moral, ethical, philosophical and mystical values of Iranian civilisation, making it unique. Incorporating the spiritual richness of Sufism, traditional rituals of Mithraism and the heroism of Iranian nationalism, its appeal lies somewhere between sport, theatre and a religious experience. A group of 10 to 15 men, standing around the perimeter of a lowered pit, perform a series of ritualised feats of strength, all to the accompaniment of a leader pounding out a frenetic drumbeat. The leader sings epic songs such as the *Shahnameh* and recites poetry by Hafez, while the performers whirl dervishlike in the centre of the floor. The performance, which takes place in a small, traditional gymnasium decorated like a shrine, is open to the public and usually free (a small donation is sometimes expected). You won't see too many local women in attendance – Western women are welcomed as honorary men.

For more information about *zurkhaneh*, see the website www.pahlavani.com.

the USA. In Iran the progress of the football team through the championship was greeted by cheering crowds the likes of which had not been seen on Iranian streets since the revolution. In addition, hundreds of women forced their way into the Azadi Sports Complex in Tehran to welcome home the victorious national team, to which the authorities turned a blind eye. That same year a women's football league was formed. All-women football matches are held indoors and no males are allowed to watch.

The national team is a source of pride, especially since the football international body FIFA placed Iran 17th in the world in April 2004 – the highest position ever reached by Iran. Several Iranian players play for top teams in Europe. Games are played most Thursdays and Fridays during the season (October to June).

IMMIGRATION & EMIGRATION

Iran hosts more refugees than any other country in the world, with little international assistance. It is estimated there are some 2.5 million Afghans in Iran and half a million Iraqi Shiites. During Saddam Hussein's reign of terror in the 1990s, up to 1.5 million Iraqi Kurds took refuge in Iran, though many were later repatriated. During the Iran-Iraq War, the Iraqi government expelled over 200,000 ethnic Iranians into Iran. Many of these people were descended from Iranians who had settled in Iraq centuries before. Along with Iraqi Shiites who fled Saddam's Iraq, Iran resettled them all, despite the war-torn economy.

My Name Is Rocky, Bahman Moshar's 2001 documentary, paints a heartbreaking picture of the growing population of runaway girls in Tehran. It's an unflinching account of a hopeless generation of young Iranians trying to survive.

Afghan refugees started arriving in Iran in 1980 and soon spread out from the camps provided on the eastern border into the bigger towns such as Mashhad and Tehran, where they became street vendors or worked on construction sites. Afghanis still work mostly in menial jobs and are routinely blamed for most of Iran's crimes.

Khatami's reformist government took some serious measures to reduce the number of immigrants on its hands. Citing high unemployment, the government has set several deadlines in recent years for refugees to leave the country. It also began implementing a new policy of fining and imprisoning employers who provided jobs to foreigners without work permits.

Since the revolution of 1979, there has been a small but steady emigration of educated Iranians abroad. Estimates of the number vary from 750,000 to 1.5 million. Most of these emigrants have preferred to settle in Western Europe or the USA, although there are also sizable communities of Iranians in Turkey. These early Iranian emigrants tended to be highly educated. Some were members of the prerevolutionary political elite who succeeded in transferring much of their wealth out of Iran.

In the Eye of the Storm: Women in Post-Revolutionary Iran, edited by Mahnaz Afkhami and Erica Friedl, explores issues such as temporary marriage, education and the strategies used by women to gain control.

Other émigrés included members of religious minorities, especially Baha'is and Jews; intellectuals who had opposed the old regime, which they accused of suppressing free thought and who had the same attitude towards the Islamic Republic; political opponents of the government in Tehran; and young men who deserted from the military or sought to avoid conscription.

Iran currently suffers from the worst 'brain drain' in the world. The country's lack of world-class educational facilities, high unemployment and restrictions on personal freedom mean that many of its educated young people feel forced to leave. Economists reckon Iran needs to create more than a million jobs a year just to keep pace with its growing population. In reality, though, only about 300,000 new jobs are added each year. The unemployment rate is around 20% and much higher for young people. Hidden in the statistics is massive underemployment, with many graduates forced to take jobs below their qualifications.

So every year more than 150,000 educated young people leave Iran for countries such as the USA and Canada where Iranians are the most educated group of immigrants. Some four million Iranians now live abroad. Few of these will ever return. Estimates put the economic loss to Iran at some US$50 billion a year. The rate of emigration has not slowed under Khatami as his government has failed to deliver any meaningful change for many people. And although there has been talk of trying to attract educated elites back home, any evidence of expats returning is purely anecdotal.

MEDIA

In recent years the struggle for influence and power has been played out in the country's media. The relative freedom of the press, an achievement of President Khatami's government, has been a target for conservatives. Many pro-reform publications have sprung up and been subsequently closed and reformist writers and editors jailed. Iran still leads the region in having the highest number of journalists in jail. Officially, the constitution provides

---

AN AMERICAN WOMAN IN TEHRAN *Martha Brekhus Shams*

The first time I flew into Tehran, I was mesmerised by the mountains surrounding the city. After growing up in the densely forested Blue Ridge Mountains, the jutting snowcapped peaks of the Alborz Mountains (in mid-July) were something else entirely! When I saw a soldier running across the tarmac with a machine gun ready, I thought, 'I've arrived!'.

I was travelling with my Iranian husband and eight-year-old son – it was the first time back for Mr M in 14 years. We had decided to check out the country after the end of the Iran-Iraq War and if it passed the test, we would move to Iran.

We exited the airport to find about 20 people waiting for us, all with huge smiles and flowers – from the mother-in-law to sisters, brothers, aunts, uncles, and a few other miscellaneous acquaintances, they all made a horrific ruckus greeting their new foreign 'bride'. I found out later that they had waited 12 hours at the airport, just for us.

My first impression of the city was of a lack of colour. The buildings were all the same sooty dun-beige or grey, punctuated by painted signs above the stores – incomprehensible pot-hooks and dots which I knew meant something to everyone else in the city but me. My six-month Farsi course had not prepared me for the high-speed crazy drive across the city, and by the time I read half a word, we were past it.

The first month of our visit was a whirlwind of visitors, dinners, and superb Iranian hospitality. I learned that I didn't need to pull that headscarf down to my eyebrows and observed that many women on the street wore more make-up than I would for a night on the town in the USA.

That little piece of silk is such a small thing, but it's also a very important thing in Iranian culture. It can be uncomfortable in the summertime, and I'm grateful for it in the winter…in fact, I've grown so used to wearing a scarf that I must wear something on my head in cold weather even when I'm out of the country. But I made a decision: that little less than 250g of silk wasn't going to keep me from doing what I wanted to do.

Now, 14 years later, I'm still in Iran and I feel like a local. I can read those signs and speak Farsi fluently (even with a Southern accent). I've learned to make and appreciate Persian food, and will never use a teabag again.

I'll never forget the old man in the pastry store who pulled my husband aside and said, 'Be good to her and be kind – she's a stranger here'. Or the man at the airport who telephoned my house an hour later to make sure I arrived safely. Or the old woman in Esfandabad, my husband's village in the middle of the Fars Desert. She is an Ashayer, descended from the nomads who roam the region. A huge, strong woman in colourful skirts, she made *noon tiree* (paper-thin bread made over an open fire on a steel disc) just for me because I mentioned that I liked it.

This is indicative of Iranian culture – supremely gracious, hospitable, fun-loving people who have become my second family. It's a wonderful, exotic, interesting place to be in interesting times.

for freedom of the press as long as published material accords with Islamic principles. The publisher is required by law to have a valid publishing licence and those perceived as being anti-Islamic are not granted a licence. In practice, the criteria for being anti-Islamic have been broadly interpreted to encompass all materials that include anti-regime sentiment.

In the broadcast media, the biggest recent change has been the appearance of satellite television. Although still officially banned, it is tolerated to some extent. Around a dozen opposition television stations beam Persian-language broadcasts into Iran, mostly from the USA. Arab and Turkish stations are also picked up as are some news channels such as CNN. As with the liberal newspapers, clamp-downs come in waves, generally after political unrest or student uprisings.

The five state-run Islamic Republic of Iran Broadcasting (IRIB) national networks are supplemented by a dozen provincial channels. More than 80% of the population watches TV (as likely to be Turkish MTV as IRIB programming).

IRIB's main radio channel broadcasts around the clock. IRIB also operates a parliamentary network and Radio Koran. Many foreign broadcasters target listeners in Iran. The BBC World Service's Persian service is universally popular and easily picked up throughout the country.

The Internet has also been used as a way of circumventing the barriers of censorship. It is estimated that one in 10 Iranians have access to the Internet. Internet service providers are prevented from allowing access to sites deemed to be pornographic or anti-Islamic, but the Internet remains the main forum for dissident voices. Internet access is easy to arrange and affordable for middle-class households.

RELIGION

The Islamic Republic of Iran is the only Shiite Muslim regime in the world, distinguishing it from its Sunni neighbours. Ninety-nine percent of the population are Muslim, made up of around 89% Shiites and 10% Sunnis. There are other religions followed in Iran, with Zoroastrians, Jews, Christians and Baha'is making up the numbers. Although freedom of worship is guaranteed in the constitution (apart from the open practice of the Baha'i religion, which is outlawed), it is safe to assume that the minorities number more than the official statistics allow. Iranians will happily accept that visitors are Christians, but it may be best not to admit to being Jewish. Atheists and agnostics may be met with incomprehension.

Muslims believe that Jesus was a prophet second only to Mohammad. The concept that he is the son of God is considered heretical.

Islam

Muslims accept that there is no God but Allah and that Mohammad was his final prophet. These two precepts form the first pillar of Islam, the *shahada*. The other four pillars, which a Muslim must try to follow, are *salat* (*namaz*; praying five times a day, though Shiites only pray three times), *zakat* (alms-giving), *sawm* (*ruzeh*; fasting during Ramazan) and *haj* (the pilgrimage to Mecca that those able should perform at a given time).

Shiites were historically persecuted by the Sunni majority and so developed a doctrine whereby it is fine to conceal one's faith in order to escape persecution.

SHIISM

When the Prophet Mohammad died in AD 632, there was disagreement over his successor. The majority backed Abu Bakr, the Prophet's father-in-law and friend. He became Caliph. However, there were those who backed the claim of the Prophet's son-in-law and cousin, Ali bin Abi Taleb, one of the first converts. However, Ali was passed over in the succession two more times and eventually became the fourth Caliph in 656, but he was assassinated five years later and his son Hussein abdicated his succession.

THE 12 IMAMS

For Shiites, the rightful spiritual leadership passed from Ali into the hands of successive descendants of the Prophet, none of whom were recognised by the Caliphate. There are 12 imams ('leaders') in total with the first, Ali, the third, Hossein, and the eighth, Reza, the most important. The 12th Imam, known as the Mahdi, is the Hidden Imam, said to have disappeared into a cave under a mosque at Smarra in Iraq in 878, waiting to return at a later date when, with the prophet Jesus by his side, he will guide the world to peace and righteousness. Only the imams can interpret the Quran and the clergy act as their representatives until the Hidden Imam returns. Ayatollah Khomeini was given the honorary title imam after his death.

The Muslim community was by now divided into two factions, the Sunnis who followed the Umayyad Caliphate and the Shiite (from 'Shiat Ali', meaning 'Partisans of Ali'). Hussein's martyrdom at the Battle of Karbala in 680 at the hands of the Caliph's troops made the division permanent.

Shiism reached its greatest influence in Iran. Iranian converts to Islam were attracted by the idea of the imam as a divinely appointed leader possibly because the Iranians possessed a long heritage of government by a divinely appointed monarch.

Iran is the only officially Shiite state. Shiism's bloody history and its mourning rites and rituals are unique in Islam.

A popular part of Shiism is the representation of its imams. You will see pictures of Imam Ali everywhere.

SUNNISM

Sunni comes from the word *sonnat*, which means tradition and refers to the fact that the Sunnis follow the traditional line of succession after the Prophet Mohammad. Sunnism has developed into the orthodox branch of Islam and most of the world's Muslims are Sunni, except in Iran. All Muslims, regardless of whether Sunni or Shiite, are forbidden to drink alcohol or eat anything containing pork, blood or any meat that died in any way other than being slaughtered in the prescribed manner (halal).

SUFISM

A mystical aspect of Islam that is particularly close to Iranian hearts, *tassawof* (mysticism), is a discovery made by Iranians within Islam, derived from the Quranic verses. According to Sufis, God must be felt as a light that shines in the believer's heart and the heart must be pure enough to receive the light. The two are the same, but separated: man's soul is in exile from the Creator and longs to return 'home' to lose himself again in Him. Sufism has various orders and throughout Iran you can find *khaneqas* (prayer and meditation houses) where people go to worship. Sufism in no way conflicts with Shiism or Sunnism.

Some of Iran's greatest thinkers, poets and scholars have had Sufi mystic tendencies and the greatest of them are Sohrevardi, Ghazali, Attar, Rumi, Hafez and Sa'di (p65).

Ayatollah Khomeini was a published Sufi poet.

Aryana Farshad's lovely documentary, *Mystic Iran: The Unseen World,* claims to journey to the heart of spiritual Iran, but is most remarkable for its unique footage of the sacred trance dances of dervishes in Kordestan.

Other Religions

Throughout history Iranians have shown tolerance towards other people's religious beliefs (with the exception of Baha'is), and since the adoption of Islam they have been particularly tolerant of Christians and Jews, who are 'People of the Book'. Christians, Jews and Zoroastrians are all officially recognised and exempt from military service, and have representatives in the Majlis (parliament). Minorities are free to convert to Islam, though conversion from Islam to another faith is punishable by death.

ZOROASTRIANISM

Religious Minorities in Iran by Eliz Sanasarian is drawn from a large number of interviews. This useful book explores the relationship between Iran's religious minorities and the state from the beginning of the Islamic Republic to the present day.

Zoroastrians, the followers of Iran's pre-Islamic religion, are based mainly around Yazd with its fire temple (where the fire is said to have been burning for 4000 years) and the Zoroastrian pilgrimage site in its desert (p230). Sizable communities can also be found in Tehran. Estimates as to the number of Zoroastrians in Iran vary, anywhere from 30,000 to 100,000. Zoroastrianism is the world's first monotheistic religion and has influenced those that have followed such as Judaism, Christianity and Islam. Zoroastrian symbolism is evident everywhere as it has gained importance as a nationalistic symbol. The Iranian New Year, No Ruz, Iran's main festival celebrated on the spring equinox, is descended directly from a Zoroastrian festival, as is Chaharshanbe Soori which takes place on the Wednesday before New Year and involves people jumping over a series of small bonfires. Shab-e yalda, celebrated on the winter solstice, is another Zoroastrian festival still observed by all Iranians.

CHRISTIANITY

The Christian community in Iran consists mainly of Armenians who settled, historically, at Jolfa, in the north of Iran, and were then moved to New Jolfa in Esfahan in Safavid times. Christians were present in Iran before the arrival of Islam and some of their saints were martyred here.

Today, Iran's 250,000 Christians also include Roman Catholics, Adventists, Protestants and Chaldeans as well as about 20,000 Assyrians. There are churches in most large towns and the Anglican Episcopal Church of Iran has churches in Tehran, Esfahan, Shiraz and Kerman. Christians are allowed to consume alcohol in private and hold mixed-sex parties with dancing. They also have a nonsegregated sports centre in Tehran. Christmas trees can be seen outside florists in Tehran every December.

JUDAISM

Esther's Children: A Portrait of Iranian Jews by Houman Sarshar is a comprehensive history of Iran's Jews from the Achaemenid Empire to the community that remains following the revolution of 1979.

Since Cyrus the Great freed the Jews of Babylon, there has been a strong Jewish presence in Iran. Since the revolution, however, their number has fallen sharply, to around 25,000. Traditionally active in the bazaars and jewellery trade, Iranian Jews tend to live in the big cities such as Tehran, Esfahan and Shiraz. About 30 synagogues remain in Iran, but they are not easy to find. Anti-Zionist sentiment can make life tricky for anyone suspected of Zionist sympathies.

BAHA'ISM

www.bahai.org is a comprehensive site for and about the Baha'i religion and community.

The most persecuted religious minority in Iran, Baha'is suffered greatly after the revolution. Today, it remains illegal to practise the religion in public and Baha'is are routinely discriminated against when it comes to jobs and education. Of the world's five million Baha'is, around 300,000 remain in Iran – they form the country's largest religious minority. Most Baha'is are urban, but there are some Baha'i villages, especially in Fars and Mazandaran provinces. Baha'ism originated in Iran during the 1840s as a reformist movement within Shiite Islam. The political and religious authorities joined to suppress the movement and hostility to Baha'ism has remained intense ever since. Baha'i doctrines are strictly egalitarian, teaching the complete equality of men and women and the unity of all humanity. The headquarters of the Baha'i are in Haifa, Israel.

MANDAEISM

An ancient gnostic religion, the exact origin of Mandaeism is unknown. Because they speak a form of Aramaic, some credence is given to the

Mandaeans' claim that they are descended from followers of John the Baptist; others believe they may be descended from the Essene sect. They practise weekly baptisms as a sacrament, and claim to follow the teachings of John the Baptist. They are considered by Muslims to be 'People of the Book' and identified as the Sabeans of Quranic legend. The small community of around 10,000 are centred on the Shatt al Arab in Khuzestan. Another 15,000 live in southern Iraq.

www.mandaeanworld.com is a good site for those interested in finding out more about Mandaeism.

WOMEN IN IRAN

When Samira Makhmalbaf's first film, *The Apple*, made waves in the West, people were confused. How could Iran – the land of female oppression and Sharia law – produce an 18-year-old female film-maker of such vision? Samira Makhmalbaf's answer was simple: 'Iran is a country where these two contrasts coexist.'

For news and issues concerning the rights of Iranian women, check out www.bahai.org run from Iran.

Nowhere are the contradictions in Iranian society more apparent than in the position of women. Historically, women in Iran have lived in a progressive society and enjoyed more equality and freedom than their neighbours. In Iran women are able to sit in parliament, to drive, to vote, to buy property and to work.

There is a long precedence for this. In pre-Islamic Iran, archaeological evidence suggests that ordinary women were able to work, own, sell and lease property and that they paid taxes. Women managers were mentioned at work sites and women were also known to have held high level military positions. By the Sassanian period, though, women's rights were not formally enshrined.

The Prophet Mohammad was the first to specifically address women's rights, recognising men and women as having different (rather than unequal) rights and responsibilities. Men are expected to provide financially, therefore women are not seen as needing legal rights as men are there to protect and maintain them.

www.badjens.com is an Iranian feminist online magazine mainly addressing readers outside Iran.

In reality, for Iranian women, the arrival of Islam after the Arab conquest saw a decline in their position at every level. Most of their rights evaporated, the Islamic dress code was imposed, polygamy was practised and family laws were exclusively to the advantage of the male.

Reza Shah started legislating for women when in 1931 the Majlis approved a bill that gave women the right to seek divorce. The marriage age was raised to 15 for girls. In 1936, a system of education was formed for boys and girls equally and in the same year, legislation was passed to abolish the veil. Reza Shah also encouraged women to work outside the home.

The last shah gave women the vote in 1962 and six years later the Family Protection Law was ratified, the most progressive family law in the Middle East. Divorce laws became stringent, and polygamy was discouraged. The marriage age was raised to 18.

Many Iranian women were active in the revolution that overthrew the shah, but it's safe to say that few women foresaw how the adoption of Sharia law and the Islamic Republic would affect their rights. Within a couple of years of the revolution women were back in the hejab (veil) – and this time it was compulsory. The legal age of marriage for girls had plummeted to nine (15 for boys), and society was strictly segregated. Women were not allowed to appear in public with a man who was not a husband or a direct relation, and they could be flogged for displaying 'incorrect' hejab or showing strands of hair or scraps of make-up. Travel was not possible without a husband or father's permission and a woman could be stoned to death for adultery, which, incidentally, included being raped. Family law again fell under the jurisdiction of the religious courts

Daughter of Persia by Sattareh Farman Farmaian is an engaging memoir by the daughter of a Qajar prince who introduced social work to Iran. It covers much of Iran's modern history and illustrates the changing roles of women.

and it became almost impossible for a woman to divorce her husband without his agreement, and in any case of divorce she was almost certain to lose custody of her children. Women holding high positions – such as Shirin Ebadi who became a judge in 1979 and won the Nobel Peace Prize in 2003 – lost their jobs and many gave up promising careers.

However, women did not disappear behind a curtain this time. Iranian women had been emancipated, and they resisted a total return to the home. There were many rights that women did not lose – such as the right to vote and the right to hold property and financial independence on marriage. In fact, the rates of education and literacy for women have shot up since the revolution for the simple reason that many traditional families finally felt safe sending their daughters to school once Iran had adopted the veil. Women made up 63% of university entrants in 2002–03 – though their subsequent employment rate was only 11%. Although women's importance in the workforce is acknowledged – maternity leave, for example, is given for three months at 67% of salary – there is still widespread discrimination.

In 1997 reformist president Khatami was voted in by mostly women and young people, promising change. By 2000, there were 11 women in the Majlis and many members are speaking out for women's rights. One of Iran's most prolific Islamic feminists is Faezeh Rafsanjani, the daughter of the ex-president, who herself was a member of parliament, a magazine proprietor, an academic, a mother and an Olympic horse rider.

Nine Parts of Desire by Geraldine Brooks is an insightful look into Muslim women's lives. The author interviews women throughout the Middle East, including, in Iran, Faeze Rafsanjani and Khomeini's widow.

In recent years there has been a series of hard-fought minor victories. The reformists managed to win the right for single women to study abroad, to raise the legal age for marriage from 9 to 13 for girls (though they had proposed 15), to defeat an attempt to limit the percentage of female students entering university and to improve custody provisions for divorced mothers. However, a woman's testimony is still only worth half that of a man in court and in the case of the blood money that a murderer's family is obliged to pay to the family of the victim, females are estimated at half the value of a males. *Sigheh* (the Islamic practice of temporary marriage) is seen by many as a sort of legalised prostitution.

On the street you will see that superficially the dress code has eased and the sea of black chadors is offset by shorter, tighter, brightly coloured coats and headscarves worn far back on elaborate hairstyles. Young girls have lost the fear of being seen outside the home with unrelated men, and many defy the regular clampdowns. Activists such as Shirin Ebadi, who works as a lawyer and champions human rights, are insistent that within Islam are enshrined all human rights and that all that is needed is more intelligent interpretation.

Through the portrayal of Behnaz Jafari, an ambitious young Tehran actress, Pirooz Kalantari's 1999 film *Alone in Tehran* shows the difficulty of being an independent woman in Iran.

Any visit to an Iranian home will leave you in no doubt as to who is really in charge in the home – and family life is the most important institution in Iran. Iranian women are feisty and powerful and they continue to educate themselves. Most women in Iran will tell you that the hejab is the least of their worries; what is more important is to change the institutional discrimination inherent in Iranian society and the law. As ex-reformist MP Elaheh Koulaie says: 'We have to change the perceptions that Iranians have of themselves, the perception of the role of men and women.'

In 2004, conservatives once more took control of the Majlis after banning many reformist members from standing for elections. Voter turnout was very low but it remains to be seen what path Iran will now follow. What is certain, however, is that Iranian women will continue to assert their rights and slowly chip away at the repressive system, be it with a defiant splash of red lipstick, making visionary movies or becoming expert at interpreting the law and winning the Nobel Peace Prize.

Arts Kamin Mohammadi

Most Iranian art forms predate the Arab conquest, but since nearly all of them reached their peak within the Islamic era, religious influences are rarely completely absent. What distinguishes Iran from other Islamic countries, however, is that the Persian culture that predates the Islamic conquest was already over 1000 years old when the Arabs arrived.

In Iran Islamic art favours the nonrepresentational, the derivative and the stylised over the figurative and the true-to-life. Geometrical shapes and complex floral patterns are especially popular in Iranian art. Traditionally, Islam has forbidden the representation of living beings, but if you're more used to travelling in countries that follow Sunni Islam, where such images rarely appear, it may come as a surprise to see examples of portraiture and images of animals in Iran.

CARPETS

The best-known Iranian cultural export, the Persian carpet, is far more than just a floor covering to an Iranian. A Persian carpet is a display of wealth, an investment, an integral part of religious and cultural festivals, and is used in everyday life.

History

The earliest known Persian carpet, which probably dates back to the 5th century BC, was discovered in a remote part of Siberia, suggesting that carpets were made in Persia more than 2500 years ago.

Historians know that by the 7th century AD, Persian carpets made of wool or silk had become famous in court circles throughout the region. Their quality and subtlety of design were renowned, and carpets were exported to places as far away as China.

The early patterns were usually symmetrical, with geometric and floral motifs designed to evoke the beauty of the classical Persian garden. Towards the end of the pre-Islamic period, stylised animal and human figures (especially royalty) became more popular.

After the Arab conquest, Quranic verses were incorporated into some carpet designs, and prayer mats began to be produced on a grand scale; secular carpets also became a major industry and were highly prized in European courts. Very few examples dating from before the 16th century remain, however.

During the 16th and 17th centuries, carpet making was patronised by the shahs and a favoured designer or weaver could expect great privileges. Sheep were bred specifically to produce the finest possible wool for weaving, and vegetable plantations were tended with scientific precision to provide permanent dyes of just the right shade. Carpet designs were inspired by book illumination which had, by this period, reached a degree of unsurpassed sophistication and elegance. The reign of Shah Abbas I (Abbas the Great; r 1587–1629) marks the peak of Persian carpet production, when the quality of the raw materials and all aspects of the design and weaving were raised to a level never seen before or since.

Towards the end of the 17th century, as demand for Persian carpets grew, standards of production began to fall and designs became less inspired. Although a long period of relative stagnation followed, this has to be seen in perspective, for the finest Persian carpets of the 18th century and later still led the world in quality and design.

Although nominally *Reading Lolita in Tehran* by Azar Nafisi is a work of literary criticism, in reality Nafisi writes a beautiful and powerfully moving memoir of her life in Iran after the revolution.

Shortly after the 1989 publication in Iran of *Women Without Men*, the author, Shahrnush Parsipur, was arrested and jailed. Banned in Iran, the novel is an allegory of women's lives, following five women who come to live around a garden.

Today, Persian carpets are a huge export earner for Iran but there are problems: the hand weaving, which made Persian carpets so special, is being supplanted by modern factories; young Iranians are not interested in learning traditional weaving methods; and cheaper, often blatantly copied, versions of 'Persian' carpets are being produced in India and Pakistan (where child labour is sometimes used).

Iran relies on the prestige evoked by the term 'Persian carpet' and recently recaptured a large slice of the world's trade in carpets and rugs. While some authorities hope that the export of Persian carpets will top US$17 billion a year by 2020, pragmatists concede that the cost of making genuine handmade carpets and rugs will increase until consumers are happier admiring them in museums than buying them.

Types of Carpets & Rugs

Oriental Rugs in Colour by Preben Liebetrau is probably the most useful carpet guide to carry around. This pocket-sized book includes an explanation of the carpets and rugs of Iran and Turkey.

Persian carpets come in three main sizes: the *mian farsh* carpet is up to 3m long and up to 2.5m wide; the *kellegi* carpet is about 3.5m long and nearly 2m wide; and the *kenareh* carpet is up to 3m long and 1m wide. The best are made from wool (from sheep and goats, and occasionally camels), although the quality varies from region to region.

Modern designs are symbolic or religious (eg a lamp indicating the sacred lamp in Mecca), or reflect the everyday life of the weaver. They may also be inspired by whatever surrounds the weaver, eg trees, animals and flowers, particularly the lotus, rose and chrysanthemum. Common designs include *miri-bota*, the leaf pattern that is probably a forerunner to the paisley patterns of the West.

One different type of rug you may come across is the kilim, a double-sided flat-woven mat without knots. These rugs are thinner than knotted carpets.

WEAVING

Most handmade carpets are woven from wool. The wool is spun, usually by hand, and then rinsed, washed and dried. It is then dyed to ensure an even colour throughout the rug. In the past, dyes were extracted from natural sources such as herbs, skins of fruit and vegetables, and plants (eg indigo for blue, madder for red and reseda for yellow). These days, however, chemical dyes are used, mainly aniline (which sometimes fades) and chrome. Later the rug is washed again to enhance the natural colours. Chemicals are sometimes used in this washing process.

Traditionally, nomad carpet-weavers (usually women) used horizontal looms, which are lightweight and transportable. Their carpets and rugs were less detailed and refined because their equipment was not sophisticated, but the quality of wool was often high. Designs were either conjured up from memory, or made up as the weaver worked. These carpets and rugs were woven for domestic use or occasional trade, and were small because they had to be portable.

In the villages, small workshops have simple upright looms, where men and women can create better designs and more variety. Designs are usually standard or copied from existing carpets or designs. Recently, city factories and village workshops mass producing carpets of monotonous design and variable quality have more or less pushed nomad weavers out of the picture.

KNOTS

You may come across the terms 'Persian (or *senneh*) knot' (known in Farsi as a *farsi-baf*) and 'Turkish (or *ghiordes*) knot' *(turki-baf)*. Despite the names, both are used in Iran: the Turkish knot is common in the Azarbayjan provinces and in western Iran.

As a rough guide, an everyday carpet or rug will have up to 30 knots per sq cm, a medium-grade piece 30 to 50 knots per sq cm, and a fine one 50 knots or more per sq cm. A prize piece might have 500 or more knots per sq cm, but nowadays museums are the only places where you will find these. The higher the number of knots per sq cm, the better the quality. A nomad weaver can tie around 8000 knots a day; a weaver in a factory, about 12,000 knots a day.

Finding the Best

Experts argue over their favourite regions. Some claim that the carpets from Kerman province are the most colourful and soft; that those from Tabriz offer the greatest variety; that those from Na'in boast the highest number of knots; that those from Qom are often the most traditional; and that those from Kashan are stronger and more dependable. The widest range – but not the cheapest prices – can be found in the bazaars in Tehran, Esfahan and Shiraz. Usually the name of a carpet indicates where it was made or where the design originated.

Persian Kilims by A Hull & N Barnard is a lavishly illustrated volume covers most of what you'll need to know about Persian carpets and rugs.

You could try and hunt out something special in the following places:

Azarbayjan province The carpets found near the Azerbaijan border have bold designs, often featuring hunting scenes and tales from Ferdosi's poem *Shahnamah* on a mud-coloured background with bizarre fringes. Weavers invariably use Turkish knots.

Kerman province This province is renowned for its soft and often very large carpets. They are very colourful and usually made from locally grown cotton. Designs feature flowers, nuts and fruit, as well as portraits.

Khorasan province Carpets from this area are influenced by the nomadic Turkmen and the Arabs. They are often made from cotton and feature designs in red.

Kordestan province The two main centres for production are Sanandaj and Bijar, where particularly hard-wearing rugs are made. *Sajadeh* (Kurdish kilims) are worth buying here.

Lorestan province Lori carpets are normally made from local wool; the dyes are made from the skin of fruit such as pomegranates, and from herbs that are now hard to find. Designs may contain sporting and hunting scenes, local monuments or mosques.

Qom In Qom, you are more likely to find *gul-i-bulbul* carpets, made from goat's wool and featuring designs with birds and flowers. The best are gorgeous, but these days many carpets sold in Qom are mass-produced for pilgrims.

Buying Carpets & Rugs

Iranians have had more than 2000 years to perfect the art of carpet-making – and just as long to master the art of carpet-selling. If you don't know your warp from your weft, it might be worth reading up before visiting Iran, or taking an Iranian friend with you when you go shopping (bearing in mind that professional 'friends' who make a living from commission are a fact of life in Iran).

If you know what you're doing, you might be able to pick up a bargain, but it's worth remembering that dealers in Western countries often sell Persian carpets for little more than you'd pay in Iran (plus postage) – and carpet sellers in your home country know the market, bargain better, buy in bulk and save on costs. Unless you're an expert, don't buy a carpet or rug as an investment – buy it because you like it, and even then only if you have some idea what sort of price you'd pay for a similar piece back home.

Before buying, lie the carpet flat on the floor and check for bumps or other imperfections. Small bumps will usually flatten out with wear but big ones are probably there to stay; if you're still sold on the carpet, look disappointed and expect a price cut. To check if a carpet is handmade, turn it over; on most handmade pieces the pattern will be distinct on the underside (the more distinct, the better the quality), although this is not an absolute rule. The most common pile material is wool, which is tough and practical, and the best wool used is Iranian. Silk carpets are magnificent but they're largely decorative. Wool and silk mixtures are a little more practical and very beautiful, with the fine use of silk giving an interesting texture.

Taking Them Home

Clearing a carpet through customs and getting it to your doorstep usually takes one month (but allow two) and adds roughly one-third to the cost. Some of the larger, older and more valuable carpets cannot be exported without special permission, so always check that yours doesn't fall into this category before paying for it. Also make absolutely sure whether you'll have to pay transport costs or duties on delivery, and get everything down on paper. If in doubt, it's better to arrange to pay on delivery so you don't risk being charged twice. The service is generally reliable, but it's up to you to work out a fail-safe agreement with the agent.

'Regulations for exporting carpets can be confusing, so check the current situation with a reputable dealer.'

Regulations for exporting carpets can be confusing, so check the current situation with a reputable dealer. Currently, each foreigner can take out of Iran one Persian carpet, or two small Persian rugs, totalling 12 sq metres in size. If you want to buy anything larger, or buy more than two rugs, and take them out of Iran, the authorities might regard you as a carpet trader.

More Information

For more information about Persian carpets and rugs visit the annual Persian Carpet Grand Exhibition in Tehran, held in August, or visit the exquisite collection in Tehran's Carpet Museum (p96). You could also contact the **Export Promotion Center of Iran** (☎ 021-212 896; fax 204 2858; PO Box 1148, Tajrish, Tehran), which organises the carpet fair. The Iran Carpet map, produced by Ramezani Oriental Carpets and available at the Gita Shenasi map shop in Tehran (p84), indicates the location of carpet-weaving centres.

Some of the oldest and finest Persian carpets and rugs are housed in museums outside Iran: for example, in the national museums in Munich and Berlin, the royal palaces in Denmark, and the Victoria & Albert Museum in London, which houses the Ardabil Carpet (p147), one of the best known of all Persian carpets.

ARCHITECTURE

Persian architecture has a long and complex history, and is often regarded as the field in which Persia made its greatest contribution to world culture. Although Persian styles differ sharply from those of other Islamic architectural traditions, they have strongly influenced building throughout much of the Islamic world, especially in Central Asia, Afghanistan, Pakistan and India.

The two important religious influences on Persian architecture have been Zoroastrianism (dominant before the Arab conquest of AD 637) and Islam. Most of the greatest buildings were built for a religious purpose, and even in secular buildings religious influences are rarely entirely absent – even Persian churches often incorporate Islamic features.

What Makes Persian Architecture Unique?

The defining aspects of Persian architecture are its monumental simplicity and its lavish use of surface ornamentation and colour. The ground plans of ordinary Persian buildings are usually very simple, mixing only a few standard elements: a courtyard and arcades, lofty entrance porticoes and four *iwan* (barrel-vaulted halls opening onto the courtyard).

The typical Persian mosque design consists of a dome above an entrance *iwan* which leads into a large courtyard surrounded by arched cloisters. Behind these are four inner *iwans*, one of them featuring a decorated niche indicating the direction of Mecca. In the Islamic world in general this is usually called a mihrab although in Iran this term is also used to refer to the cut-out space in the ground in front of it. According to many commentators, the four-*iwan* design can be traced back to old Zoroastrian ideas about the four elements and the circulation of life.

These basic features are often so densely covered with decoration that observers are led to imagine that the architecture is far more complex than it actually is. The decorations are normally geometric, floral or calligraphic. A wall's decoration sometimes consists of nothing but mosaics forming the names of Allah, Mohammed and Ali, repeated countless times in highly stylised script.

TILES

The tiled domes of Iranian mosques, reminiscent of Fabergé eggs in the vividness of their colouring, are likely to remain one of your abiding memories of Iran.

The art of Persian tile production dates back to the Elamite period. However, the glorious period of tile-making came during the Safavid era (1502–1722). Tiles from that period come in two main forms. The very best are really mosaics *(moarraq kashi)* – patterns are picked out in tiny pieces of tile rather than created in one piece. Less fine are the *haft rangi* (seven-coloured) tiles, which are square with a painted surface. *Haft rangi* tiles normally appear only on the inside of buildings.

By the time of the Qajars, Persian tile making had passed its prime. But Qajar buildings often make up in quantity of tiles for what they lack in quality. Examples are the courtyard walls of the Golestan Palace (p92) in Tehran and the walls of the wonderful Takieh Mo'aven ol-Molk (p176) in Kermanshah.

Persepolis: The Story of a Childhood was produced as a comic book, but Marjane Satrapi's snappy cartoons and witty text make this memoir of growing up through the revolution and the formation of the Islamic Republic compelling, funny and, ultimately, heart-rendingly sad.

QUIRKS OF PERSIAN ARCHITECTURE

All along the great trade routes from east to west caravanserais (hostels with stabling for animals) were set up to facilitate trade. Although the earliest caravanserais date to Seljuk times, many of those surviving date from the reign of Shah Abbas I who was credited with establishing a network of 999 such structures. In cities they were often built right beside the bazaar to facilitate the transfer of goods from beast to shelf and back again. It's easy to see this arrangement in Esfahan (p210).

In the hot southern deserts you will see the remains of mud-brick ice houses which were built to store ice through the summer. Most have a long wall against which water was thrown. As soon as it froze it was scraped off and stored in an adjoining building, often a stepped dome. The one at Abarqu (p240) near Yazd resembles a circular ziggurat (tiered temple) with the wall peeling off to one side.

In the countryside near Esfahan you may see curious circular towers standing alongside village houses. These were pigeon houses where pigeons were reared for meat and manure.

For details about windtowers, see the boxed text 'The Badgirs of Yazd' (p233).

Pre-Islamic Architecture

The only substantial remains left from before the 7th century BC are those of the remarkable Elamite ziggurat at Choqa Zanbil (p192). The ancient inhabitants of Persia imbued their mountains with great religious symbolism and built the characteristic pyramidal ziggurats to imitate them. The earliest builders used sun-dried mud bricks; baked brick was already being used for outer surfaces by the 12th century BC.

The surviving sites from the Achaemenid era (550–330 BC) include the magnificent ceremonial palace complexes and royal tombs at Pasargadae (p255), Naqsh-e Rostam (p255), Persepolis (p252) and Shush (p191). These are decorated with bas-reliefs of kings, soldiers, supplicants, animals and the winged figure of the Zoroastrian deity Ahura Mazda.

Remains from the Achaemenid era show links with the old ziggurats, both in their shape and decoration. The Achaemenid style also incorporated features taken from Egyptian and Greek architecture. They built colossal halls supported by stone and wooden columns with typically Persian bull's-head capitals. The most usual building materials were sun-dried brick and stone.

Alexander the Great's arrival in 331 BC effectively ended the Achaemenid style of architecture in Persia. Instead the influence of Greece and Macedonia grew even stronger. No great examples remain today, although the Anahita Temple Ruins at Kangavar (p180) was built with Greek capitals to honour a Greek goddess. Under the Parthians (247 BC–AD 224), a few characteristically Persian features, including the *iwan*, began to appear.

In the Sassanian period (AD 224–642), buildings became larger, heavier and more complex. The four-*iwan* plan with domed, square chambers became increasingly common, with the distinctive Persian dome seen for the first time. Decoration became more adventurous and more use was made of colour. The Sassanians built fire temples throughout their empire, and the simple plan of the earliest examples was retained throughout the pre-Islamic era, even in the design of churches.

The Arab Conquest & Early Persian Islamic Style

The Arab conquest didn't supplant the well-developed Sassanian style but it did introduce the Islamic element that was to have such a pervasive impact on the Persian arts. Not only did the Arab period (AD 637–1050) shape the nature and basic architectural plan of religious buildings, but it also defined the type of decoration – no human representation was to be permitted, and ceremonial tombs or monuments also fell from favour. In place of palace complexes built as symbols of royal majesty came mosques designed as centres of daily life for ordinary people.

As Sassanian and Arab ingredients merged, a distinctly Persian style of Islamic architecture evolved. From the mid-9th century, under the patronage of a succession of enlightened rulers, there was a resurgence of Persian nationalism and values. Architectural innovations included the high, pointed arch, stalactites (elaborate stepped mouldings used to decorate recesses) and an emphasis on balance and scale. Calligraphy became the principal form of architectural decoration. A good example is the Jameh Mosque (p229) in Na'in.

The period also marks the emergence of a series of remarkable tower tombs, more secular than religious in purpose. Built of brick and usually round, they show a development of ornamentation starting with little more than a single garter of calligraphy and graduating to elaborate basket-weave brickwork designed to deflect the harsh sunlight.

The Steppe Peoples: the Seljuks, the Mongols & the Timurids

Many of the Seljuk rulers (1051–1220) took a great personal interest in patronage of the arts. Architectural developments included the double

The word Persian doesn't exist in Farsi. It is the ancient Greek word for Iranians.

dome, a widening of vaults, improvement of the squinch and refinement of glazed tilework. A unity of structure and decoration was attempted for the first time, based on rigorous mathematical principles. Stucco, incorporating arabesques and Persian styles of calligraphy, was increasingly used to enhance brick surfaces.

Although often seen as a dark age in Iranian history, the Mongol period (1220–1335) saw new developments in Persian architecture. The conquest by Genghis Khan and rampaging hordes was initially purely destructive, and many architects fled the country, but later the Mongols, too, became patrons of the arts. The Mongol style, designed to overawe the viewer, was marked by towering entrance portals, colossal domes, and vaults reaching up into the skies. It also saw a refinement of tiling, and calligraphy, often in the formal angular Kufic script imported from Arabia. Increasing attention was paid to the interior decoration of domes.

The White Balloon, written by Abbas Kiarostami and directed by Jafar Panahi, tells the story of a young girl who loses her money while on the way to buy a goldfish. It won several international awards.

The Timurids (1380–1502) went on to refine the Seljuk and Mongol styles. Their architecture featured exuberant colour and great harmony of structure and decoration. Even in buildings of colossal scale, they avoided the monotony of large empty surfaces by using translucent tiling. Arcaded cloisters around inner courtyards, open galleries, and arches within arches were notable developments.

The Safavids

Under a succession of enlightened and cultivated rulers, most notably Shah Abbas I, came the final refinement of styles that marked the culmination of the Persian Islamic style of architecture. Its greatest expression was Shah Abbas I's royal capital of Esfahan (p210), a supreme example of town planning, with one of the most magnificent collections of buildings from one period anywhere in the world. At its centre is the vast Imam Sq, one of the world's largest squares, with the superb Imam Mosque as its focal point. Other fine examples of Safavid architecture are at Qazvin (p162), while the Holy Shrine of Imam Reza (p322) at Mashhad gained much of its present magnificence in Safavid times.

Farsi (Persian) has changed less since the 10th century than English since Shakespeare's day.

The death of Shah Abbas I in 1629 marked the beginning of the end for the golden age of Persian architecture. The Madraseh-ye Chahar Bagh

THE BEST OF PERSIAN ARCHITECTURE

- **Choqa Zanbil** Perhaps the most impressive structure from before the 7th century BC (p192).
- **Esfahan** This magnificent city (p216) contains many Safavid masterpieces.
- **Golestan Palace and Takieh Mo'aven ol-Molk** Two of the finest examples of overblown Qajar style in Tehran (p92) and Kermanshah (p176), respectively.
- **Great Mosque of Gohar Shad and Blue (Kabud) Mosque** The best-surviving examples of Timurid architecture inside Iran, in Mashhad (p324) and Tabriz (p136) respectively.
- **Jameh Mosque** The finest building remaining from the Seljuk period, in Esfahan (p214).
- **Mil-e Gonbad** The most extraordinary structure from the 11th century (p313).
- **Oljeitu Mausoleum** This mausoleum (p167), in Soltaniyeh near Zanjan, is the most magnificent surviving Mongol structure in Iran, probably the world.
- **Persepolis** The most important surviving site from the Achaemenid period (p252).
- **Taq-e Bostan** These rock carvings (p176), northeast of Kermanshah, are the best-preserved examples of Sassanian sculpture.

(p219) in Esfahan is an outstanding architectural work for its period, but it and other buildings of the late Safavid period are really little more than a swan song.

The Qajars

The Qajar period marks the rather unhappy transition between the golden age of Persian Safavid architecture and the creeping introduction of Western-inspired uniformity from the mid-19th century. Now widely regarded as tasteless, flimsy and uninspired, the Qajar style did produce some fine buildings, including the Kakh-e Eram (p247) in Shiraz and the Golestan Palace (p92) in Tehran.

PAINTING

The earliest known distinctively Persian style of painting dates back to the Seljuk period (1051–1220) and is often referred to as the Baghdad School. Early painting was mainly used to decorate manuscripts and Qurans, though some fine 13th-century pottery found near Tehran also reveals a unique early Persian style of art. During the Mongol period (1220–1335), paintings were used to decorate all sorts of books, especially poetry books.

In the 16th century an important school of Persian art developed in Tabriz, under the guidance of Sultan Mohammed. Designs and patterns produced by this school also influenced the design of contemporary carpets. Persian art later flourished under the auspices of the great Shah Abbas I, who turned Esfahan into a flourishing centre for the arts. By the 18th century artists fell under the influence of India and Europe.

Since early Persian artists rarely signed their names to their work, not much is known about most of these artists.

During the Qajar period (1775–1925) a European style of painting became popular as the shahs created a royal iconography with life-sized portraits, rarely seen in the Middle East. For more information, read *Royal Persian Paintings: The Qajar Epoch* edited by Layla Diba.

CALLIGRAPHY

With the arrival of Islam several distinctly Persian calligraphic styles emerged, some of them so elaborate that they are almost illegible, eg *nashki*, which later developed into another renowned style known as *thulth*. Not only was the Quran faithfully reproduced as a whole in calligraphic form, but verses from it, and the holy names of Allah and Mohammed, were used as decorations on religious buildings and elsewhere, as they are to this day.

By about the 16th century, Shiraz and Esfahan were producing some of the finest calligraphy in the Islamic world. Some of the very best examples of ancient and modern calligraphy can be seen at the Reza Abbasi Museum (p101) in Tehran. Reza Abbasi was himself a renowned 16th-century calligrapher. The art continues to flourish in modern Iran.

MINIATURES

The Persian miniature-painting tradition arose in the 15th century, and had a second flowering in Qazvin during the Safavid period. Later, artists from eastern Iran, who had studied under the great Mohammadi in Herat (now in Afghanistan), also started to influence this art form.

Persian miniature paintings are now deservedly famous throughout the world. The best examples show great intricacy and attention to detail. Favourite subjects include courting couples in traditional dress, polo matches and hunting scenes. Some of the best modern miniatures come from Esfahan. Although a few fine examples can be seen in Iranian museums, most of the early works are housed in museums and private collections in the West.

ILLUSTRATED MANUSCRIPTS

Neatly combining Persia's two traditions of fine penmanship and miniature painting are the illustrated manuscripts you can see on display at the Reza Abbasi Museum (p101) in Tehran. Most of the manuscripts are books of poetry with the themes beautifully illustrated alongside the text. However, some manuscripts are decorated Qurans that, while still non-figurative, go beyond just beautiful handwriting.

Bihzad, Master of Persian Painting by Ebadollah Bahari is the lavishly illustrated life of Kamal al-Din Bihzad, the great 15th-century Persian artist and manuscript illustrator.

MODERN ART

One of the best-known and loved modern Iranian artists and sculptors is Sayyed Ali Akhbar Sanati, whose work is on display in the Kerman Contemporary Arts Museum and the 13 Aban Museum (p94) in Tehran. The contemporary art scene is currently the most vibrant it has been since the revolution, with artists producing work in a variety of media. Despite the limited resources available to Iranian artists – there are very few professional galleries and institutions capable of launching an artist's career – the restrictions themselves seem to inform their aesthetic. The Tehran Museum of Contemporary Art (p96) sometimes showcases modern Iranian artists while, increasingly, exhibitions outside the country include artists from inside Iran as well as the diaspora. Established modern artists include Aidin Aghdashlou, Habibollah Sadeqi and Gholamhossein Nami while Khosrow Hassanzadeh (a student of Aghdashlou) leads the new generation of artists.

Photojournalist Kaveh Golestan's documentary, *Recording the Truth*, made for British television, led to his two-year house arrest. He joined the BBC in 1999 and was killed in 2003 in Iraq.

GLASSWARE

Small, translucent glass vessels dating back to the 2nd millennium BC have been found at Choqa Zanbil (p192). During the Sassanian era, there was major trade in Persian glassware with objects appearing as far afield as Japan. By early Islamic times, two principle techniques were used: mould-blown to produce thicker items, and free-blown for more delicate articles. Glassware was usually green, lapis lazuli, light blue or clear with a tinge of yellow, and decorations were cut into the glass. The art reached its peak during the Seljuk era when the manufacture of enamelled and gilded glassware flourished. With the Mongol invasion, Iranian masters moved west to Syria and Egypt and under Safavid rule Shiraz became the most important centre. Rose-water sprinklers, long-necked wine bottles, flower vases and bowls were popular. By the reign of Karim Khan Zand, the famous wine from Shiraz was exported in locally crafted jugs and bottles. Typical decorations now include gilded or enamelled floral patterns, sun and lion emblems, or glass strings wound around a tall necked vessel.

The world's first ever 'pane' glass was produced at Choqa Zanbil. It was used to cover the panels of doors and windows of the ziggurat.

LACQUER WORK

Some consider this the most interesting of Iran's decorative arts. It can be traced back to early Islamic times as an independent art form, decorating smaller private objects. Wooden or papier-mâché objects are painted then a transparent sandarac-based varnish is applied in successive layers, from three to more than 20 coats. The result gives an impression of depth and provides great durability. Common designs are the popular Persian motif of the nightingale and the rose, flowers, hunting scenes, battles or classic love stories. Pen boxes are the most common form of lacquer work.

MARQUETRY

One of the most intricate styles of woodwork is a form of marquetry *(moarraq)* called *khatam*. A Persian style of marquetry slowly developed

A pair of doors from 1590, now in the Islamic Museum of Berlin, is one of the earliest existing examples of Persian *khatam*.

through the centuries and by the 17th-century *khatam* was so prestigious that several Safavid princes learned the technique.

Several different woods, including betel, walnut, cypress and pine are used, with the inlaid pieces made from animal bones, shells, ivory, bronze, silver and gold. The final product is coated with varnish. Genuine Persian *khatam* contains no paint; the colours come from the inlaid pieces. *Khatam* can be used for furniture but visitors usually buy it in the form of ornamental boxes or picture frames.

METAL WORK

Persian metalworking can be traced back at least to Achaemenid times when silverware was common at court. As well as working with copper, bronze, silver and gold, Iranian metalworkers were unique in producing a wide variety of steel objects, as well as arms and armour. The shapes and decorative motifs used then still survive in the bazaars, where there are alleyways of copperworkers, tinsmiths and engravers producing trays and table tops with scenes depicting hunts or calligraphy.

Enamelling *(minakari)* is another way of working with metal, the earliest-known example being an enamelled copper mihrab dating from 1556. The metal surface is painted with fine patterns usually in turquoise, white and black (the main colour might also be brown, dark blue or green) and then varnished. It is delicate work, easily chipped and needs to be handled with care. The best examples come from Esfahan and are usually bought as small vases or decorative plates.

POTTERY

Pottery is one of the oldest Persian art forms and examples have been unearthed from burial mounds dating from the 5th millennium BC. Early pieces were probably ornamental rather than for domestic use, with elaborately detailed animals dominating the design. Persian pottery was initially unglazed, but glazed pottery dating back to the Elamite period has been unearthed from Choqa Zanbil (p192). In the 1st millennium AD, pottery was painted with the simple geometric, floral and animal motifs that developed into the characteristic Persian style. The lotus flower (called a *niloofar* in Farsi) has always been recognised as a symbol of life and of women; it features on much Persian pottery, and its importance predates the Arab conquest.

From the 9th century onwards, Persia's detailed and colourful (mainly blue and green) glazed pottery became world famous. The nomads of the Khorasan province had by then created their own style of glazing, adding early Islamic lettering styles such as Kufic to the design. Persian pottery reached its zenith in the 13th century, when a new type of clay was used to make the pottery more durable and several dazzling new colours were introduced. Chinese influences became very strong during the Mongol period, when figurative designs became quite commonplace.

The earliest evidence of textiles comes from Seh Gabi in Kordestan province where 5th millennium BC pottery vessels have imprints of fabric wrapped around them as textile fragments.

TEXTILES

You will see hand-printed cloth everywhere you go, mostly made in Esfahan, and used as bedspreads or tablecloths. Wooden blocks are used to apply patterns in black, red, blue, yellow and green to what are basically beige cloths. These are then washed in the river to fasten the colours. It is thought that textile printing has been practised since Sassanian times. Other parts of Iran have their own textile traditions: for example in Yazd you can buy intricately woven textiles known as *termeh*, with paisley patterns worked in cotton.

MUSIC

Most Iranians are familiar with the big names of Western pop, thanks to satellite TV and the Internet. Almost every taxi driver, especially in Tehran, seems to keep a cache of Turkish pop classics stashed under the dashboard. Increasingly, shops selling cassettes and CDs are taking their place on main streets, with most of the musicians featured being Iranian.

There are occasional music festivals, such as the annual 10 Days of Dawn (1-11 February). It can be hard to track down exact details, but if you're particularly interested in attending a festival ask a tour company for up-to-date information (p381). Women performers were banned for many years but now women-only concerts are commonplace.

Sima Bina was born in Khorasan province and first performed publicly at the age of nine. She continues to record the folk music of Khorasan, holds women-only concerts in Iran and tours worldwide.

Classical

Traditional Persian music is poetry set to a musical accompaniment – for Iranians there is no distinction between poetry and lyrics. Like epic poems, some 'epic songs' are very long and masters can spend most of their lives memorising the words. The instruments used as backing include the *tar,* a stringed instrument rather like the Indian sitar; the *dahol* and *zarb,* large and small drums respectively; the *nay* and *sorna,* a flute and oboe; the *kamanceh* a kind of viola played like a cello; and the *daf* and *daryereh,* different sizes of outsized tambourine. Most of these instruments can be seen in the Ethnographical Museum in the Golestan Palace (p92) in Tehran.

Two singers particularly worth listening out for are Shajarian and Shahram Nazeri, both reviving Persian music with their honey-voiced renditions of the classics.

Folk

The most appealing and melodious forms of traditional music are heard among the ethnic minorities, such as the Turkmen in the remote regions of Khorasan province. The Azaris favour a unique style of music, often based around a love song, whereas the Kurds have a distinctively rhythmic music based mainly around the lute and their own versions of epic songs, called *bards.*

The Lors often use an oboe-like instrument, while along the Persian Gulf a type of bagpipe called the *demam* is popular. The music of Sistan va Baluchestan is understandably similar to that of Pakistan and played on instruments such as the *tamboorak* (similar to the Pakistani *tambura,* a type of harmonium).

Perhaps not surprisingly, the lyrics of most traditional music revolve around Islam although some songs are based on love and others celebrate victories over invading armies centuries before.

The Kamkars, a Kurdish family ensemble, started as a semiprofessional group in 1967. Since then, they have been celebrated for their concerts featuring traditional Iranian music, and rousing Kurdish folk songs. They tour both in Iran and worldwide.

Pop

Iranian pop music is slowly starting to re-emerge under the watchful eye of the Iranian authorities, while there is an increasingly prolific underground rock scene. Many of the best Iranian musicians (including the much-admired 'Ebi') fled Iran after the Islamic Revolution. They still perform abroad (the female singer Googosh's comeback concert in Toronto attracted an audience of 12,000) and tapes of their concerts circulate illicitly within Iran.

Shadmehr Aghili is a modern pop star with a huge teenage following. Holding his own against younger newcomers is Mohammed Noori, who was popular before the revolution and still sings songs about nationalism. Clarinet-playing Farhad has performed with the likes of Eric Clapton.

Rock

Two Iranian rock albums
of 1382 (2003) include
A'rabi's album *Penhan*
combined the poetry of
Rumi with heavy metal
tunes, and Barad released
an eponymous album
mixing rock and folk
music. Both albums sold
well in Iran.

Groups such as O-Hum have been shaking the foundation of popular Iranian music, blending lyrics from Hafez with what can only be described as retro '90s grunge rock. Iran's rock scene is still underground, but there are regular unofficial gigs and an ever-changing alliance of bands and musicians trying to find a Persian way to rock.

LITERATURE

Overwhelmingly the most important form of writing in Iran is poetry, and it could be said that Iran is a nation of poets. The population's familiarity with the famous poets and their works is universal: ask the man on the street and he will quote you lines from Hafez or Rumi. The big-name writers are all primarily poets – eg Omar Khayyam, Sa'di and, above all, Ferdosi (see the boxed text 'The Great Iranian Poets', p65). Many Iranians write poetry themselves and the Sufi form, poems addressed to the divine beloved, are still popular.

Poetry

*Modern Persian Poetry (An
Anthology in English)*, edited by Mahmud Kianush,
is a thorough anthology
that includes 129 poems
by 43 poets of the 20th
century. Featured poets
include all the modern
innovators such as Nima
Yushij, Fereydun Tavalloli
and Forough Farrokhzad.

While no-one knows the exact date of origin of the *Avesta*, the first-known example of Persian literature, it is known that Persian poetry first blossomed in the 9th century AD. Various forms of Persian poetry developed. Typical were the *masnavi*, with its unique rhyming couplets, and the *ruba'i*, similar to the quatrain (a poem of four lines). Both were unknown forms in Arabic, as was epic poetry. Poems of more than 100 nonrhyming couplets, known as *qasideh*, were first popularised by Rudaki who flourished under the Samanid ruler Nasr II (913–43).

These styles later developed into the long and detailed 'epic poems', the first of which was Ferdosi's *Shahnamah*, (see the boxed text 'The Great Iranian Poets', p65). Many epic poems celebrated the glories of the old Persia before whichever foreigners had most recently invaded and occupied the country. The last truly great 'epic poem', *Zafarnamah*, covered the history of Islam from the birth of Mohammed to the early 14th century.

Moral and religious poetry became enormously popular following the success of Sa'di's most famous poems, the *Bustan* and *Golestan*. By the 14th century, smaller *qazal* poems, which ran to about 10 nonrhyming couplets, were still being used for love stories. Qazal poetry, which developed around the same time as *qasideh*, was made famous by Hafez and is still practised today.

The Blind Owl by Sadeq
Hedayat, published in
1941, a seminal and
influential book, is a dark
and powerful portrayal
of the decadence of a
society failing to achieve
its own modernity.

Early in the last century modernist Persian poetry changed the poetic landscape. This style is exemplified by the work of Nima Yushij. Poets such as Forough Farrokhzad and Sohrab Sepehri were influential from the 1950s onwards. Ahmad Shamloo's *Fresh Air*, a book of poems published in 1957, marked the introduction of a lyrical style that was also political and metaphoric. Parvin E'tesami is a noted female poet, renowned for her religious poems, *Mecca of the Heart* and *Eye and Heart*. She died in 1941 at 35.

Novels

More and more Iranian novels are now available in English. The 20th-century writer Sadeq Hedayat is the best-known Iranian novelist outside Iran, and one whose influence has been most pervasive in shaping modern Persian fiction. The most popular of Iran's female writers is probably Simin Daneshvar, whose novel *A Persian Requiem* (*Shavushun* in Farsi) deals with life in Iran between the two world wars. Her husband was the

THE GREAT IRANIAN POETS

Iranians venerate their great poets, often because they protected the Persian language and culture during times of occupation. Many poets have large mausoleums, and streets and squares named after them: Ferdosi and Omar Khayyam are buried in huge (separate) gardens near Mashhad; and Sa'di and Hafez have mausoleum complexes devoted to them in Shiraz.

For further information about Hafez and Sa'di, contact the **Hafez & Sa'di Study Centre** (☎ /fax 0711 21071; PO Box 71455-414, Shiraz).

Ferdosi

Hakim Abulqasim Ferdosi, first and foremost of all Iranian poets, was born in about AD 940 near Tus. He was famous for developing the *ruba'i* (or quatrain) style of 'epic' historic poems. His most famous work is undoubtedly the *Shahnamah* (Book of Kings), which he started when he was 40, and finished some 30 years later. When completed, this truly epic poem included 50,00 to 60,000 couplets. However, the Turkish king to whom he presented it was incensed that it contained no references to Turks and so rejected it. Ferdosi died old, poor and grief-stricken.

These days Ferdosi is seen as the saviour of Farsi, which he chose to use at a time when the language was under threat from Arabic. Without his writings many details of Persian history and culture might also have been lost. All in all, Ferdosi is credited with having done much to help shape the Iranian self-image.

Hafez

Khajeh Shams-ed-Din Mohammed, or Hafez (meaning 'One Who Can Recite the Quran from Memory') as he became known, was born in Shiraz in about 1324. His father died while he was still young, so the boy was educated by some of the city's leading scholars. Apart from memorising the Quran at an early age, he also became very interested in literature and wrote many verses that are still used in everyday speech. His collection of poems, known as the *Divan-e Hafez*, has a strong mystical and virtually untranslatable quality; much of it was also about wine, nightingales and courtship. Although he lived in turbulent times, Hafez refused many generous invitations to some of the great courts of the day, both inside and outside Iran, because of his love for his birthplace. He died in 1389.

Omar Khayyam

Omar Khayyam (Omar the Tentmaker) was born in Neishabur in about 1047. He is probably the best-known Iranian poet in the West because many of his poems, including the famous *Rubaiyat*, were translated into English by Edward Fitzgerald; in Iran he is more famous as a mathematician, historian and astronomer, in particular for his studies of the Gregorian calendar and algebra. Although there is some speculation about what he actually wrote, Omar Khayyam is famous for his *ruba'i* (quatrain) poems. He died in 1123.

Rumi

Born Jalal ad-Din Mohammad Balkhi – known as Rumi – in 1207 in Balkh (in present-day Afghanistan). His family fled west before the Mongol invasions and eventually settled in Konya in present-day Turkey, where first his father and then he retreated into meditation and study of the divine. His first great work was the *Masnevi*. He was inspired by a great dervish, Shams-e Tabrizi, and many of his poems of divine love are addressed to him. He is credited with founding the Maulavi Sufi order – the whirling dervishes. He is also known as Maulana ('the Master' in Arabic).

Sa'di

The other great Shirazi poet, Sheikh Mohammed Shams-ed-Din (known by his pen name of Sa'di), lived from about 1207 to 1291. Like Hafez, he lost his father at an early age. His education was entrusted to some of the leading teachers of Shiraz and many of his elegantly phrased verses are still commonly used in conversation. His most famous works, the *Golestan* (Rose Garden) and *Bustan* (Garden of Trees), have been translated into many languages and his tomb has become something of a pilgrimage site.

prominent social commentator Jalal Al-e Ahmad whose novels – *The School Principal* and *The Pen* – have also been translated into English.

Iranians themselves tend to prefer short stories to novels. A selection of these are included in Minou Southgate's compendium *Modern Persian Short Stories*.

My Uncle Napoleon by Iraj Pezeshkzad, published in the early 1970s, was an instant bestseller. In 1976 it became a television series and its story – of three families living under the tyranny of a paranoid patriarch – became a cultural reference point.

Story-Telling

In a preliterate society, formal story-telling was often an extremely popular art form and Iran was no exception, with story-tellers taking their seat in teahouses every evening to entertain the assembled men. Unfortunately, the coming of television has more or less seen off the story-tellers, so tracking down a genuine teahouse with traditional story-tellers is extremely difficult. The Sofre Khane Sonnati Sangalag teahouse (p105) in Tehran's Shahr Park occasionally stages 'tourist' versions, which can be fun.

CINEMA

Close Up: Iranian Cinema: Past, Present and Future by Hamid Dabashi is an academic history book of Iranian cinema that is nevertheless extremely readable. Dabashi sets the great directors in their national context as the descendants of the modern poets.

Iran's love affair with cinema started at the dawn of the last century. The first Iranian to look through a camera, Mirza Ebrahim Khan Akkas-Bashi, recorded a royal visit to Belgium in 1900. In the same year, the first public cinema opened in Iran, in Tabriz. By 1904 the first commercial movie house was opened in Tehran; since then cinema in Iran has been the most popular form of entertainment. Avanes Oganian's *Abi & Rabi* (1930) was the first silent Iranian movie, and *The Lor Girl* (1933), directed by Arde-shir Irani in India, the first talkie. Producer Abdolhossein Sepanta's love for Iranian history and literature helped him to craft films that appealed to Iranian tastes. Esmail Kushan's 1948 *The Tempest of Life* was the first film to be made in Iran and since then, the home-grown industry has not looked back.

It was not until the 1960s, however, that the first signs of a very distinctive Iranian cinematic language emerged. Poet Forough Far-rokhzad's 1962 film of life in a leper colony, *The House is Black*, antici-pated much of what was to come. Darius Mehrjui's 1969 film, based on a story by modern playwright Gholamhossien Sa'edi, was the period's most important landmark film. Sohrab Shahid Sales's early 1970s films such as *Still Life* introduced a new way of looking at reality; the influ-ence of his still camera and simple stories is seen in Kiarostami and Makhmalbaf's work.

Friendly Persuasion: Iranian Cinema After the Revolution is a feature-length documentary by Jamsheed Akrami which examines the phenomenon of Iranian post-revolutionary cinema. Those inter-viewed represent three generations of Iranian filmmakers.

The first 'new wave' of Iranian cinema is marked by the work of those who first captured the attention of arthouse movie fans around the world: Abbas Kiarostami, Dariush Mehrjui and Bahram Beiza'i, Khosrow Hari-tash and Bahram Farmanara. The post-revolutionary directors, such as Mohsen Makhmalbaf, Rakhshan Bani Etemad and Jafar Panahi, have helped develop a reputation for Iranian cinema as arthouse, neorealist and poetic – the second 'new wave'. Arguably, film-makers such as Kiarostami are continuing the great tradition of Persian poetry, albeit in a visual me-dium. The strict censorship of the post-revolutionary state has encouraged use of children, nonprofessional actors and stories that are fixated on the nitty-gritty of life. This has all proved hugely popular overseas.

While Iranians have finally learned to love their own cinema (though it took a revolutionary ban on Hollywood movies first) and flock to it in droves, many of these 'arthouse' films never get a mainstream release in Iran, and rely on the bootleg market. Recently there has been a feeling that the masters are making movies specifically for foreign markets and film festivals.

A lot of Iranian films are churned out every year for the domestic market, most of them action flicks. There are, however, signs of improvement here too, with social issues increasingly taking centre stage.

If you happen to be in Tehran during the annual Fajr Film Festival (usually in early February; p349), try to see a couple of new Iranian masterpieces, bearing in mind that they will be in Farsi, without English subtitles. The latest festival included screenings of *The Lizard* (Marmulak) by Kamal Tabrizi. This comic story of a convict who impersonates a mullah while trying to arrange his escape from the country had people queuing around the block. Another noteworthy film is *Duel*, directed by Ahmadreza Darvish. The most expensive film in the history of Iranian cinema, it is remarkable because, for the first time since the revolution, a war movie makes no ostentatious show of martyrdom and sacrifice.

Children of Heaven, Majid Majidi's film, was nominated for the Best Foreign Language Film Oscar in 1998. It is a delicate tale centring on two poor children losing a pair of shoes. Humorous and tender.

THEATRE

Most forms of Iranian theatre have their roots in Islam. The most important is the *ta'ziyeh*, or passion play, which means 'mourning for the dead', and actually predates the introduction of Islam into Iran. These plays are staged in every Iranian city, town and village during the anniversary of Karbala, the battle in AD 680 in which Imam Hossein, the grandson of the Prophet, was murdered (p350).

During the two days of mourning, boys and men dressed in black walk through city streets, hitting their chests and backs with a chain called a *shallagh*. Others play drums and brass instruments, lead the chanting, and carry flags and weapons symbolising the struggle against the infidels. The highlight for the participants and the hundreds of spectators comes when mounted warriors dressed in traditional fighting outfits re-enact the martyrdom of Hossein.

The groups then move to a public place where a temporary platform or stage has been erected. Here actors carrying dangerous-looking weapons continue to re-enact the martyrdom. The followers of Hossein are usually

Taste of Cherry, directed by Abbas Kiarostami, was co-winner of the prestigious Palme d'Or at the 1997 Cannes Film Festival, despite being very controversial inside Iran because it deals with suicide, a taboo subject in Islam.

THE MAKHMALBAF FAMILY – A CINEMA DYNASTY

Born in 1957 in Tehran, Mohsen Makhmalbaf first gained infamy when he was imprisoned for five years after fighting with a policeman. He was released during the Islamic Revolution in 1979 and started to write books before turning to film-making in 1982. Since then he has produced more than a dozen films, including *Boycott*, *Time for Love*, *Gabbeh* and, more provocatively, *Salaam Cinema*. Many of his films are based on taboo subjects: *Time for Love* was filmed in Turkey because it broached the topic of adultery; and *Marriage of the Blessed* was a brutal film about the casualties of the Iran-Iraq War.

Although Makhmalbaf refuses to follow the strict Islamic guidelines for local film-making, he enjoys comparative artistic freedom because he is so well known. In 1997 Makhmalbaf's daughter Samira produced her first film, *The Apple*, to critical acclaim. In 2000 her second film, *Blackboards*, was a smash hit at the Cannes Film Festival; she was the youngest director ever to have shown a film there. Her latest film *At Five in the Afternoon* is set in Afghanistan.

The Makhmalbaf movie factory continues to churn out winners. Samira's younger brother made a 'making-of' documentary about *Blackboards*; then younger sister Hana directed a feature about the shooting of *At Five in the Afternoon*. On the strength of that film, *Joy of Madness*, Hana beat Samira to a 'youngest-ever' record by being invited to the Venice Film Festival at the age of 14. Even Mohsen Makhmalbaf's second wife (the sister of his first wife who died tragically), Marzieh Meshkini, has directed an acclaimed film, *The Day I Became A Woman*, a film featuring three linked short stories that examine what it is to be a woman in Iran. 'These women have to sever their emotional ties to gain independence,' says Meshini.

dressed in green, while the followers of his enemy Yezid are dressed in red. One actor has to play Shemr, the man believed to have killed Hossein. It's a dangerous role since in the past some audiences have become so caught up in the play that they have actually killed 'Shemr'. Traditional poems are recited and dramatic songs sung to an accompaniment of Iranian flutes and drums. Many spectators openly weep while others pray. Note that this is a time when passions can run particularly high. It may not be especially wise to attend a passion play unless accompanied by Iranians.

Environment

THE LAND

If you're lucky enough to fly into Iran, be sure to ask for a window seat – you might be surprised by what you see. Rather than the featureless wasteland many perceive, Iran is a diverse land where starkly beautiful mountains border vast deserts, mountain villages contrast with tiny oases, and the southern fringes of the Central Asian steppes give way to the waters of the Persian Gulf and Oman Sea.

Half the country is covered by mountains, of which four ranges are most prominent. The smaller, volcanic Sabalan and Talesh Mountains in the northwestern Azeri provinces provide fertile pastures for nomads. Nearby, the majestic Alborz Mountains skirt the Caspian Sea from the border of Azerbaijan as far as Turkmenistan, and are home to forests, ski fields and the permanently snowcapped Damavand (5671m; p117), Iran's tallest mountain. Sitting on what is believed to be a lucrative bed of oil and natural gas, the immense Zagros Mountains stretches from Kordestan province to Bandar-e Abbas like the ridged and gnarled back of a great crocodile – if you're flying from Dubai this is really something to see from the sky.

Only about 11% of Iran is arable land; 8% is forest; 47% is natural (ie nonarable) pastures; and the remaining 34% is infertile land, including desert.

All these mountains exist because Iran sits at the junction of three major tectonic plates – the Arabian, Eurasian and Indian – making the country highly susceptible to earthquakes (see the boxed text 'Shaking Iran's Confidence', p69, and Bam p293). East of the Zagros Mountains is the central plain and its two vast deserts, the Dasht-e Kavir (more than 200,000 sq km) in the north and the Dasht-e Lut (more than 166,000 sq km) in the southeast. The deserts are punctuated with occasional salt lakes and, in total, account for almost 25% of the country. This area is roughly 1000m above sea level.

Unlike many ancient civilisations (eg those in Egypt and Mesopotamia), Persian settlements did not develop around major rivers. The

SHAKING IRAN'S CONFIDENCE

To say that Iranians are anxious about earthquakes is quite the understatement. The country sits on dozens of seismic fault lines, and every year scores of tremors of varying size rattle homes and gnaw away at nerves. When a major quake strikes, as it did in Bam in 2003 at a cost of more than 26,000 lives (p294), Iranians everywhere start speculating about who will be next.

Iran has had more than 20 major earthquakes (above 6 on the Richter scale) in the past century, and seismologists believe a sizable population centre will be hit by one of these every eight years or so. While the vast majority of seismic activity occurs along the Zagros Mountains, where the Eurasian and Arabian tectonic plates meet, it is in central Iran that the biggest movements are felt. Ferdows (1968, 7.3 on the Richter scale, up to 20,000 dead), Tabas (1978, 7.8, more than 1500 dead), and Bam (6.6) are all in this area.

However, the mountainous regions in the north are also susceptible, and Tehran reportedly has two major faults running directly beneath it. In the wake of the Bam disaster there was much speculation in Tehran about what kind of hell would be unleashed if – or as many people feel, when – a large quake rocks the capital. The citizenry are right to worry. Building standards in Iran are poor, and corruption among inspectors ensures even those standards are seldom met. A government report in March 2004 stated that of the 15 million homes in Iran, 7.2 million are vulnerable to a major earthquake.

As a visitor, there's not really much you can do. If you're unlucky enough to be in the wrong place at the wrong time, just pray your room has space under the bed or in the cupboard.

With an area of 1,648,000 sq km, Iran is more than three times as large as France; nearly one-fifth the size of the entire USA; and nearly as big as Queensland, Australia.

longest and sole navigable river is the Karun (890km) in the southwest, and it's no Nile. Instead, settled areas are almost entirely confined to the foothills of mountains, where natural springs and melting snow can usually provide sufficient water.

Considering it shares borders with seven countries, Iran has a surprisingly long coastline. In the north, the Caspian Sea (Darya-ye Khazar) at 370,000 sq km is the world's largest lake (or is it? see p159). To the southeast, the Persian Gulf coast is 965km long and becomes the Gulf of Oman east of the strategic Strait of Hormoz. The Gulf contains dozens of tiny islands, most of them uninhabited. Those that are, notably Qeshm (p276) and Kish (p265), are being developed, attracting investors and tourists from the Gulf States. Other islands are used as bases for oil prospecting.

Iran boasts an abundance of hot- and cold-water mineral springs. The most developed is Sara'eyn (p148) near Ardabil, which is now a full-blown spa resort. Even in the desert, however, you can find springs – swimming in the spring at the Garmeh oasis (p229) is a treat.

WILDLIFE

Iran is not blessed with an enormous amount of wildlife and that which is especially notable is often on the endangered list. As such, few visitors come to Iran solely to look at flora and fauna, partly because facilities are almost nonexistent (p71).

Animals

Drug smugglers have been known to load heroin into the humps of camels near the Afghan and Pakistani borders, release them, then retrieve the drugs when the camels arrive, unguided, at points beyond Kerman.

Of the 160 or so species of mammals found in Iran, about one-fifth are endemic. Most of the larger species (wolves, jackals, wild boars, hyenas, black bears and lynx) are more common in the unexplored forests of Mazandaran province, but not common enough that you'll see many. In the deserts and mountains, you're more likely to come across mongooses, galloping Persian gazelles, porcupines and badgers, the endemic Iranian wild ass, and the red, Jabir and Mesopotamian deer. Camels still roam the deserts of the eastern provinces of Kerman, Sistan va Baluchestan and Khorasan, and while they might look wild they almost certainly belong to nomadic or seminomadic communities.

BIRDS

More than 500 species of birds have been sighted in Iran, both indigenous and migrants moving between Europe and Africa via the Middle East. The most common species include black-and-white magpies, blue rollers, brown-and-green bee-eaters, and black-and-grey hooded crows. Among the less common birds are the golden eagle, found in the Caspian provinces; the tiny jiroft, found in Kerman province and along the Persian Gulf; the red-wattled lapwing; the yellow partridge; the delijeh and balaban falcon, found mainly in Hamadan province; and the black vulture and black kite, which live in the central plateau and deserts. Some migratory water birds include the greater flamingo, found in the thousands on Lake Orumiyeh in spring, as well as the glossy ibis and the Smyrna kingfisher.

Birds of the Middle East by RF Porter, S Christensen and P Schiermacker-Hansen is the best book to buy if you're serious about birding in Iran.

If you're staying in Tehran you may also spot green parrots swooping from tree to tree in the grounds of the Sa'd Abad Museum Complex (p97) or flitting between the trees around the British embassy and the Hotel Naderi.

MARINE LIFE

The Persian Gulf is home to a wide range of tropical fish, as well as swordfish, porpoises and an alarmingly large number of sharks. The Caspian

Sea is home to salmon and other fish, as well as to the Caspian seal, whose origins so far from the open seas remain a mystery to science. It also has large shoals of sturgeon, which produce the world-famous caviar, although stocks are threatened by pollution and overfishing. Some of the more common fish found in the streams around the Alborz Mountains include trout, chub and catfish.

ENDANGERED SPECIES

Iran's most exciting endangered animal is the Asiatic cheetah, families of which are mainly found in and around the Dasht-e Kavir. These are believed to be the world's last wild Asiatic cheetahs, and with the support of the United Nations the government has taken a refreshingly proactive approach to saving them by designating several parks and reserves and upping the punishments for poaching. Unfortunately, however, a lack of education about the importance of the cheetah combined with the one million hunting licenses (each with 300 free bullets from the state) issued each year tends to cancel out much of the good work. Families of Asiatic cheetahs are known to live in several national parks and reserves around the Dasht-e Kavir.

Other endangered mammals include the huge ibexlike Alborz red sheep, with its black beard and curvy horns, found in the Alborz Mountains; the wild boar; and the Oreal ram, with a white beard and enormous spiralling horns, found near the border with Turkmenistan.

In the mountains of northwestern Iran, the bearded vulture (also known as the lammergeier) has been shot and poisoned to the brink of extinction due to a misconception among farmers that they attack sheep. Instead, this fascinating bird usually eats only what other vultures have left behind, and often breaks bones by dropping them onto rocks from a great height. They apply the same method to the unfortunate Greek spur-thighed tortoises in the area.

Plants

Despite extensive deserts and unrestrained urban development, Iran still harbours more than 8200 species of flora, about 2500 of them endemic. The northern slopes of the Alborz Mountains (up to about 2500m) are densely covered with broad-leaved deciduous forest, which forms the largest area of vegetation in Iran. Here you will find the same types of trees as in many European forests (oak, maple, pine and elm) as well as the less-common Caucasian wing nut *(Pterocarya fraxini-folia)*. Extracts from some of these trees are used to produce glue, and various resins and dyes. The loveliest pockets of forest are around Masuleh, in the Golestan National Park east of Minudasht and, more accessibly, at Nahar Khoran (p311), just south of Gorgan.

There are smaller, less dense forests of oak and juniper on the higher slopes of the central and northwest Zagros Mountains, and in some southern parts of the province. In contrast, southern and eastern Iran are almost bare, except for some scattered juniper trees. Palm trees grow on the southern coastal lowland, especially near the Strait of Hormoz, and around the luxuriant oases dotted about the bone-dry nothingness. Most will be date palms of which there are a bewildering 60-plus varieties.

NATIONAL PARKS & RESERVES

National parks, and the wildlife they are designed to protect, are luxuries that most Iranians don't really have the time or money to be concerned with. As a result, most national parks are terribly underfunded and understaffed

Check all the latest news on Iran's population of Asiatic cheetahs at the comprehensive www.asiaticcheetah.org. It even has regularly updated photos of the cheetahs taken by remote cameras.

Ancient Greek playwright Aechylus was killed when a tortoise landed on his bald head. This story was thought to be a myth until a bearded vulture was seen dropping a tortoise onto rocks to crack it open. It now seems a bearded vulture confused poor Aechylus's head for a stone.

while the most accessible zones tend to be carelessly rubbish-strewn picnic sites. Unauthorised hunting is an ongoing problem, as is illegal cultivation of protected areas. Attitudes are slowly changing in cities such as Tehran and Shiraz, but it could be decades before Iran's nature reserves have anything like the status of their Western counterparts.

So what does this mean for the visitor? Basically, almost all of Iran's 16 officially mandated national parks and 137 other protected areas have no fences, few if any rangers, no maps, no guides and no facilities. Even finding certain parks can be difficult, as they don't appear on maps, there is no public transport and few if any signs. Other parks such as Sisingan on the Caspian suffer an opposite problem: small, overused and all too quickly overrun by weekenders.

Hardy souls might choose to strike out on their own, but unless time is no problem and you have at least basic Farsi, it will probably be a pretty frustrating experience. Your best bet is to employ a travel agency near to the park you want to visit; at least they should know how to get you there. Alternatively, some agencies offer ecotours (p380).

A selection of Iran's better and more accessible national parks and protected areas are listed below. Due to the limited facilities, there is no extra detail in the destination chapters. But if you're keen, these are a start.

Arjan Protected Area Lake and wetland area near Shiraz; home to masked tits, waterfowl and, seasonally, migratory birds.

Bakhtegan National Park Incorporating Lakes Bakhtegan and Tashk, about 80km east of Shiraz; flamingos and other migratory birds loiter here during winter.

Bijar Protected Area About 15km north of Bijar town in Kordestan; home to Alborz red sheep, hyenas and jackals; best visited in spring and autumn.

Golestan National Park Forested mountains between Gorgan and the Caspian Sea; home to wild boars, Oreal rams, brown bears, wolves, leopards, goitred gazelles and assorted bird life; best visited in spring. Permits are required.

Lake Orumiyeh National Park An important wetland reserve, it sees a multitude of birds migrating between Europe and Africa; it's relatively accessible (p131).

Tandoureh National Park Rocky, mountainous terrain favoured by Oreal rams, ibex and even the odd leopard, near Daragaz on the border with Turkmenistan.

ENVIRONMENTAL ISSUES

Air pollution is the biggest of the litany of environmental problems facing Iran. And like the others it is that much worse for having been ignored until it has reached crisis point. To get an idea of the scale of the problem, which affects all Iranian cities to varying degrees, consider that in Tehran alone 1.5 million tonnes of pollutants are pumped into the air every year.

Tehran has one of the highest automobile fatality rates in the world.

Perhaps the greatest tragedy is that much of the pollution is eminently preventable. More than 70% of it comes from vehicles, a majority of which are frighteningly inefficient. The ubiquitous Paykan (p379), modelled on the 1960s Hillman Hunter, guzzles about 15L of leaded petrol for every 100km – more in city traffic. Worse, few cars are fitted with catalytic converters, which remove many of the worst pollutants from car exhaust before it heads out the pipe.

There are other problems. The Persian Gulf has been repeatedly contaminated by leaks from oil rigs and tankers, untreated sewage, and overly rapid development on the islands of Kish (p265) and Qeshm (p276). Pollution in the Caspian Sea is also a growing problem, one that now threatens the internationally recognised wetlands of the Anzali Lagoon (p159) at Bandar-e Anzali.

Unrestrained urban and industrial development have also caused irreparable damage. The most depressing example of unplanned urban sprawl can be seen along the main road skirting the Caspian Sea. What could be described in guidebooks of only 25 years ago as a collection of quaint villages is quaint no more; concrete homes and apartment-resorts stretch almost the entire way from Rasht to Sari.

Deforestation, erosion and overgrazing are also evident, especially on the southern slopes of the Alborz Mountains. At the time of writing, a scheme to replant millions of trees was getting plenty of television time. Earnest-looking chador-clad women and schoolchildren were planting eucalypts in the name of the Revolution.

As grim as this sounds, it's not all bad news. Public awareness of the environment has risen to the point that a political party, Iran-e Sabz (Green Party of Iran) has been formed to agitate for change. This change includes long-overdue plans to close the Paykan factory in 2004, although few are holding their breath on this one – it was also supposed to cease production in 2002. Taxes on more efficient foreign cars were cut in March 2004, and the agonisingly slow conversion to unleaded fuel continues.

However, you don't need to be Einstein to see that the environment is suffering because fuels are virtually free. The government subsidises petrol and diesel to the tune of at least US$4 billion a year, in order to supply petrol at IR600 per litre and diesel at a ridiculous IR160 per litre in 2003 – that's US2c a litre. As a result there is no value in pursuing efficiency. The same applies to natural gas, which Iran possesses in vast quantities. It is not uncommon to find a kettle on the gas all day long, while heating and cooling systems are routinely left running whether people are around or not.

The government has realised that the only way to change this culture is to make people actualy feel the impact of wasting energy in their back pocket. Petrol prices are rising (the government says it is happy to sell at cost, and will raise prices slowly until it is). The country's stop-start nuclear program is also going (p24), with officials citing clean energy as the main reason.

Elsewhere, dozens of dams have been built in an effort to avert the crisis caused in the late '90s when a three-year drought caused chronic water shortages. Some of these will also serve as electricity generators, but many believe their benefit is limited by the huge impact on the environment.

More than 1000 wetland sites around the world are protected under the framework of an agreement signed in Ramsar, on the Caspian Sea coast, in 1971. It is known as the Ramsar Convention, and birds and their wetland habitats are the greatest beneficiaries.

Food & Drink

Far more than simply the fuel of empires, the food of Iran forms part of a rich cultural experience that has been evolving since Achaemenid times. The tradition of food incorporates medicinal and philosophical perspectives that are as valid today as they were 2000 years ago.

Food is used to honour guests, see in new years and celebrate various social milestones. The ideas of ancient physicians and philosophers aim to combine food and drink in a manner that is integral in maintaining strength in both body and mind. Long before Weight Watchers, these wise Persians concluded that a good diet did not involve an excess of fats, red meats, starch or alcohol – these transformed men into wicked, selfish brutes. However, fruit, vegetables, chicken and fish were encouraged as the food of gentler, more respectable people.

The Persian philosophy of food also dictates that to maintain a balanced diet, 'hot' and 'cold' foods be eaten together. For example, if you order *dugh* (a drink made from churned sour milk or yogurt and mixed with water) with your fish meal the waiter is likely to look at you as if you have two heads. These are both cold foods and constitute a risky proposition. The hot and cold philosophy dates from the Achaemenid era but is still widely adhered to. Yogurt, cheese, radishes and fresh green herbs are all 'cold' and are as common on Iranian tables as salt and pepper is in the West. They act as a balance to the ever-present meats and any sweet desserts, which are both 'hot'.

Even so, as a visitor, you might find it difficult to keep a balance. Outside Tehran the eating options are largely limited to fast food and Iranian restaurants that serve little other than kebabs. To enjoy more variety and the best of Iranian cooking you really need to be invited into Iranian homes. If you get the chance, take it: as a guest you will be a 'gift of God' and the fabulous food and humbling hospitality will make for a memorable meal.

The ancient Persians believed eating walnuts in place of red meat made a person gentler, and that memory could be improved by eating dried red grapes before breakfast.

Yogurt has been regarded as both food and medicine in Iran since ancient times, with early records suggesting it was the only food to be eaten by people suffering dysentery or diarrhoea. It's still good advice.

STAPLES & SPECIALITIES

Almost every meal in Iran is accompanied by *nun* (bread) and/or *berenj* (rice). *Nun* is dirt cheap and usually fresh. There are four main varieties: *lavash* is common for breakfast and is flat and thin (it's mouthwatering when fresh but quickly turns cardboard-like when left to cool); *barbari* is crisp and salty and more like Turkish bread (and is often covered with sesame seeds); *sangak* is the elite of Iranian breads, long and thick and baked on a bed of stones to give it its characteristic dimpled appearance (always check carefully for gravel that may remain!); and *taftun* is crisp with a ribbed surface.

Chelo (boiled or steamed rice) forms the base of many an Iranian meal, and especially at lunch is served in vast helpings. Rice cooked with other ingredients, such as nuts, spices or barberries, is called *polo* and is worth asking for specifically. Saffron is frequently used to add flavour and colour (see the boxed text 'Worth Its Weight', p327). If rice is served with a knob of butter on top, blend this in as the Iranians do. If you get the chance, be sure to try *ta-dig*, the crunchy, savoury crust at the bottom of the pan – it's great.

Iranian Meals
STARTERS

A standard Iranian meal starts with a basic, prefabricated green salad, radioactive-pink dressing and a *sup* (soup) usually featuring lentils or pearl barley. Some places include these in a total set-meal price but often they're charged separately.

TRAVEL YOUR TASTEBUDS

Some dishes just shouldn't be missed...others aren't quite so appealing.

dizi – also called *abgusht;* a delicious soup-stew combination that involves an age-old eating process (see the boxed text 'Getting Dizi', p130). It's considered by Iranians to be poor man's food.
dolme bademjun – eggplant stuffed with meat, raisins, rice and eggplant and steamed. This is a truly delectable dish!
fesenjun – a sauce of pomegranate juice, walnuts, eggplant and cardamom served over roast chicken and rice. It's a Persian classic and it's quite an honour to be served *fesenjun* in an Iranian home; if you are lucky, you might find a few restaurants that also have it.

We dare you to try **kalleh pache** – a breakfast delicacy that can contain one or all of the following: *cheshm* (eye), *maghz* (brain), *zaban* (tongue) and *pache* (foot). They're boiled together and garnished with a thick sauce made from fat from the boiling process.

MAINS

Even in a restaurant with a long menu, 90% of the main-dish options are likely to be kebabs. These are served either on bread (preferably hot from the *tandir* clay oven) or as *chelo kabab* on a mound of rice with a pair of grilled tomatoes. Contrasting with greasy doner kebabs so often inhaled at the end of a rough night in the West, Iranian kebabs are tasty, healthy and cooked shish-style over hot charcoals. The cheapest, standard version is *kubide* (literally, 'ground') kebab, made out of pressed, minced meat. *Makhsus* (special) kebabs use better-quality lamb, *kabab-e barg* (literally, 'leaf kebab') is thinner and more variable in quality, and *fille kabab* uses lamb fillet, while *juje kabab* are chunks of marinated chicken. They are usually sprinkled with acidic *somaq* (sumach) and accompanied by raw onion and *mast* (yogurt).

After a couple of weeks, many travellers start suffering from what could be called 'kebab shock'. However, it's not too hard to find treatment. Even when not on the menu it's worth asking for the common stand-by *zereshk polo ba morq* (chicken on rice made tangy with barberries), *ghorme sabzi* (stewed beans, greens and mince) or *bademjun* (eggplant served in various styles).

New Food of Life: Ancient Persian and Modern Iranian Cooking and Ceremonies by Najmieh Khalili Batmanglij is so good it's on the gift table at almost every Iranian wedding in the US. Clear, concise and accurate.

DESSERT & SWEETS

Dessert is usually a bowl of fruit, which can be quite a relief after so much rice. Iranian fruit is generally excellent. Particularly recommended are pomegranates, peaches, watermelons, rosy-fleshed grapefruits, and sweet oranges and mandarins.

Everywhere you go in Iran you'll find cake shops selling a wide range of sweet titbits (the macaroons are especially delicious). Cakes are sold by weight so it's easy to try plenty of different types. Iranian confectionary is delicious; don't miss the refreshing *paludeh* (a sorbet made of rice flour, grated fresh fruit and rose water from Shiraz) or chewy *gaz* (nougat-like and very sweet) from Esfahan.

DRINKS
Nonalcoholic Drinks

Drinking in Iran almost inevitably involves *chay* (tea). Whether you're in a *chaykhuneh* (teahouse), a carpet shop, someone's home, an office or even a tent, chances are there will be a boiling kettle nearby. According to the rules of Iranian hospitality, a host is honour-bound to offer a guest at least one cup of tea before considering any sort of business, and the guest is expected to drink it.

STOP (SMOKING) PRESS

Puffing on a qalyan over tea and dates might have been legislated into history by the time you visit Iran. In mid-2004 the Majlis passed a law banning smoking in public places, and promised the qalyan would not be spared.

The tea tray is always set with a bowl of *ghand* (sugar cubes), often crudely hacked from huge rocks of sugar. It is customary to dip the sugar into the glass of tea to 'clean' it, then to place the cube between the front teeth (or on the tongue) before sucking the brew through it. In the mouth of a novice the *ghand* lasts just seconds; an Iranian can keep it going for a whole cup or more.

Good coffee can be hard to find, though this situation is changing as more dedicated cafés open. Iranian *qhaveh* (coffee) is the same as Turkish coffee – it's served strong, black and sweet. In most instances, however, the only option will be Nescafé.

> Iranians have been eating pistachios for more than 5000 years. Today Iran produces 53% of the world's pistachios, many varieties of which are available in markets across the country.

You'll never be too far away from delicious fresh fruit *abs* (juices) and fruit *shirs* (milkshakes). Both are about IR3500. Depending on the season, you'll find pomegranate (the dark-red *ab anar*), honeydew melon (*ab talebi*), watermelon (*ab hendune*), orange (*ab porteghal*), apple (*ab sib*) and carrot (*ab havij*). Popular shakes include banana (*shir moz*), pistachio (*shir peste*) and strawberry (*shir tut farangi*). The shakes are often loaded with sugar.

Tap water is drinkable almost everywhere and bottled water is widely available in cities. Despite the US embargo, Coca-Cola is still bottled under licence at a Mashhad plant, though you're far more likely to be served Zam Zam (cola), Parsi Cola or some other black or orange soft drink. Canned drinks can cost five times more than bottled soft drinks.

Alcoholic Drinks

> Shiraz (aka Syrah) was first produced in Shiraz more than 1000 years ago, and is believed to have been taken to the Rhone Valley in France by the Crusaders. Sadly, the wine is almost impossible to find in Shiraz today.

Think of your trip to Iran as a cleansing experience, where your body can recover from all that overindulgence in evil alcohol. This way, at least, you'll feel better about not being able to get a drink. While alcohol is quietly tolerated in Christian communities, such as in the Armenian areas of Tehran and Esfahan, it is strictly forbidden to Iranian Muslims. There is, of course, a black market and you'll occasionally hear a man whisper 'whiskey' as you go by. But, believe us, the sickly sweet clear spirit you'll likely be sold is merely rocket fuel.

If you're desperate for a beer, there's always *ma'-osh-sha'ir* (Islamic beer). Locally produced Delster, which comes in several 'flavours', is the most widely available and popular, mainly because it doesn't pretend to taste like beer. It's more like cider. A bottle of Delster will cost you about IR3000.

WHERE TO EAT & DRINK

'If anyone asks you to their home for dinner, accept the invitation!' This piece of advice, delivered by a long-term expat in Tehran, should not be ignored. Eating in an Iranian home is where you're most likely to experience the real joys of Persian cuisine.

However, even in Iran you'll need more charm than Hugh Grant to be invited home for every meal. At other times, your options will be fast-food/pizza joints, kababis, traditional restaurants and teahouses, hotel restaurants and the occasional place serving foreign cuisine.

Many traditional restaurants are buried below street level and can be hard to find. Even if there is an English sign there's no guarantee there will be a menu in English. Fast-food joints and kababis, on the other hand, tend to be at street level near the main squares and along main roads.

Iranian infatuation with 'pizza' seems to be out of control. In Shiraz, for example, 60 new pizza places opened in the three years to 2004. Beware that Iranian pizza is rarely to Western tastes with a flabby base, tasteless cheese and mounds of anaemic (porkless) sausage. Tomato paste isn't part of the recipe, though locals slosh on ketchup to taste.

Fancy trying some food in an Iranian restaurant before leaving home (or upon your return)? Check the growing list at www.farsieats.com.

Quick Eats

Iran's many fast-food joints serve reheated felafel, sausage or hamburger meat ('*sausis*' and 'hamburger' are usually understood) loaded into a fresh roll and topped with tomatoes and pickles. These are Iranian-style hamburgers and they cost about IR5000 with a soft drink. Simple kababis (kebab shops) selling doner kebabs and cold drinks are everywhere; just follow your nose. These places are usually fairly clean, but remember that the popularity of the eatery is inversely proportional to your chances of spending the next 24 hours on the porcelain throne, so eat where the locals eat.

Tipping is not expected; a 10% service charge is often added to the bill.

Some no-frills places serve *ash e sabzi* (thick, green vegetable soup) all day. It makes a great, cheap breakfast or lunch; just look for the huge metal dish and mountains of bread. Little food is sold on the street itself.

VEGETARIANS & VEGANS

Vegetarianism is foreign to most Iranians. Sure, there are a lot of good vegetarian dishes in Iranian cuisine, but most restaurants don't make them. Even if there is an ostensibly meat-free dish on the menu, such as *ash e sabzi*, it will often come with surprise extras, usually small pieces of mutton.

Solace can be found, however, in the felafels, samosas and potatoes sold in street stalls. *Mirza ghasemi* (mashed eggplant, squash, garlic and egg; see the boxed text 'Cut the Caviar', p154) should be eaten wherever it's found, and the various *kuku* (thick omelette dishes) – *kuku ye sabzi* (omelette with mixed herbs), *kuku e bademjun* (with eggplant) or *kuku e gol e kalam* (with cauliflower) – make great snacks, served hot or cold.

In Tehran there is a range of restaurants serving foreign cuisine. Elsewhere better restaurants may provide steaks, schnitzels and occasionally spaghetti bolognaise. They're usually relatively expensive (at least IR30,000).

Vegans will have a hard time finding anything completely free from animal products; even rice is usually cooked with butter. Fortunately, fresh

IRAN'S TOP FIVE TRADITIONAL RESTAURANTS

- **Malek-o Tojjar, Yazd** (p237) In a restored mansion in the middle of the bazaar, this place is romance on a stick, and the food's pretty good, too.
- **Khayyam Traditional Restaurant, Tehran** (p105) Beautifully restored, this 300-year-old building is both a historical and culinary treasure. It's pricey, but the selection of Persian classics is hard to beat.
- **Karavansara Sangi, Zanjan** (p168) The carpeted platforms and vaulted ceilings of this 400-year-old caravanserai are perfectly complemented by great *bademjun* (eggplant paste with tahini and lemon) and traditional music.
- **Yord Restaurant, Shiraz** (p249) A nomad restaurant in a giant tent. The traditional food is served on dozens of carpets and kilims with traditional music in the background. Atmosphere plus!
- **Bastani Restaurant, Esfahan** (p224) Hidden in the corner of Imam Sq, you can sit down to fantastic *fesenjun* (see p75) in the shadow of the magnificent Imam Mosque.

and dried fruit, myriad varieties of nuts, and vegetables are widely available and very good. Cheaper hotels will usually let you use the kitchen.

WHINING & DINING

The Art of Persian Cooking by Forough Hekmat is the most affordable and readily available cookbook you'll see in Iran. There are plenty of good recipes and descriptions of the ceremonial role of food.

Eating with the family is the norm in Iran, and taking your kids into a restaurant will not only be welcome but often bring you more-attentive service. While few menus include special children's meals, staff are usually happy to tailor the size of the meal to the size of the child. As most food is low on spice it shouldn't be too hard to persuade your child to give it a try.

HABITS & CUSTOMS

At dinner in an Iranian home the host or hostess will never sit at the head of the table. Rather, they stay in the background to make sure the guests have everything they need. No host sits while a guest is standing.

Lunch is the main meal of the day for Iranians and is generally eaten with copious amounts of rice between noon and 2pm. Dinner is from about 8pm onwards. Most restaurants, except those in hotels, close by 7pm on Friday. On religious holidays, almost everywhere selling food will shut, markets and bazaars included. During Ramazan (p380) the majority of eateries will be closed from dawn until dusk. Many won't open at all during the month and many of those that open after dusk are full with prebooked parties and close early. However, because travellers don't have to fast, most hotel and bus station restaurants stay open throughout Ramazan, albeit hidden discreetly behind heavy blinds (and may thus look shut). Eating, drinking or smoking in public is bad form during Ramazan, even if locals push you to do so.

Eating on the floor is normal here. Remember to always remove your shoes before sitting around the plastic sheet that acts as a 'table'. Cutlery normally consists of fork and spoon. If you need to eat with your hands, avoid putting your left hand into a communal dish; the left hand is used for something else altogether. Once the meal has arrived, conversation often dies as diners work through their meal in silence. Tea and conversation flow freely after dinner.

EAT YOUR WORDS

Here are a few hints to help you order successfully. For pronunciation guidelines, see p390.

Useful Phrases
I'm a vegetarian. — *man sabzi khar am*
Does this dish have meat? — *in ghaza gusht dare?*
I can't eat dairy products. — *man nemintunam labaniyyat bekhoram*
What do you recommend? — *shoma chi pishnahad mikonin?*
I'll try what s/he's having. — *man az ghazayi ke un mikhore mikham*

Menu Decoder
One of the most complete lists of Persian recipes (110 of them!) on the web can be found at www.ee.surrey.ac.uk /Personal/F.Mokhtarian /recipes.

SOUPS & STARTERS
ash – a type of soup often made from yogurt and barley
ash e jo – barley soup with cream, butter, parsley and pepper
ash e reshte – noodle soup with beans and vegetables; a very common dish
kashk-e bademjun – slices of eggplant fried and covered with tomato, thick whey and mint

MAIN COURSES
abgusht – see *dizi*
chelo kabab – chopped lamb or beef barbecued and served with rice
chelo morgh – chicken and rice
dizi – lamb stew made with lentils, potatoes and tomato paste, served with bread. For how to eat it, see the boxed text 'Getting Dizi', p130. Also known as *abgusht*.

khoresht – any kind of thick, meaty stew made with vegetables and chopped nuts and served with rice
khoresht e bademjun – stew of chicken or meat, eggplant and tomato paste, served with rice or bread
kubide kabab – mince and onion ground together and barbecued
zereshk polo ba morgh – roast chicken served with rice and barberries (small, red berries)

English–Farsi Glossary

apple – sib
banana – moz
beans – lubiya
beef – gusht e gav
bread – nun
butter – kare
cheese – panir
chicken – morgh
eggplant – bademjun
eggs – tokhm e morgh
fruit – mive
kebab eatery – kababi
mandarin – narengi
meat – gusht

milk – shir
orange – porteghal
pomegranate – anar
potato – sib zamini
prawns – meygu
rice – berenj or ruz
rice (boiled or steamed) – chelo
salt – namak
sugar – shekar
tea – chay
teahouse – chaykhuneh
tongue – zaban
vegetables – sabzijat
water – ab
yogurt – mast

Tehran تهران

With its relatively short history, ugly masks of concrete and smog, and manic streets flowing hot with machines, many travellers and no small number of Tehranis will tell you there's no reason to hang around in the capital. But to take their advice is to miss out. For while Esfahan or Persepolis could mount a convincing case for being the soul of Iran, Tehran is indisputably its big, loud, chaotic, vibrant and ugly beating heart.

This city of about 14 million is where change happens first. Politically and socially it's Iran's cutting edge, and from the relatively bold fashion statements of its youth to the range of restaurants, as a visitor you can't help but notice. Most of the spark comes from the north, and a wander through southern Tehran is a telling contrast – not everyone wants political change.

As fascinating as Tehran is, however, there's no getting around the fact that uncontrolled urban sprawl has turned it into an incredibly unattractive city. Blocks of unsightly concrete units march all the way to the foothills of the Alborz Mountains. Sadly, the mountains are often almost indistinguishable through clouds of smog.

Most of that smog is pumped out of the two million-plus cars that choke Tehran's streets, and it's this often-frightening traffic that will likely leave the deepest of first impressions. Some will undoubtedly find Tehran true to its name – it literally means 'end of the road', as it was once the last settlement on the road from the then capital, Rey. But persist with Tehran – or better, make short repeat visits – and you'll find it opening up to you in ever-more rewarding ways.

Tehran's less-subtle saving graces include a decent choice of hotels and restaurants a class above what you'll find elsewhere in Iran. There are enough museums to keep you interested, and compared with residents of many capitals, Tehranis are surprisingly welcoming.

HIGHLIGHTS

- Take in the over-the-top opulence of the **Golestan Palace** (p92), monument to Qajar excess
- Gaze in wonder at the 51,366-gem Globe of Jewels in the **National Jewels Museum** (p94)
- Escape the chaos of southern Tehran for the serenely beautiful **Khayyam Traditional Restaurant** (p105) and its fabulous food
- Ski the slopes of **Dizin** (p118) and **Shemshak** (p118) for a fraction of what you'd pay at home
- Climb the rocky slopes of **Park-e Jamshidiyeh** (p100) for stunning views and excellent ethnic food
- Gird your loins and climb aboard a **motorcycle taxi** (p113) for a trip across peak-hour Tehran – a white-knuckle ride you're unlikely to forget

★
Dizin;
Golestan Palace;
Khayyam Traditional Restaurant;
Motorcycle Taxi;
National Jewels Museum;
Park-e Jamshidiyeh;
Shemshak

■ TELEPHONE CODE: 021 | ■ POPULATION: ABOUT 14 MILLION

TEHRAN

HISTORY
Archaeologists believe people have lived in this area since Neolithic times, but apart from some 11th-century AD records suggesting the village produced high-quality pomegranates, little was written about Tehran until the 13th century. In his book *Mo'jamol Boldan,* writer Yaqoot Hamavi described Tehran as a village of Rey, then the major urban centre in the region, where 're-bellious inhabitants' lived in underground dwellings. He went on: 'They not only disregard their governors, but are in constant clashes among themselves, to the extent that the inhabitants of its 12 quarters cannot visit each other'.

In 1220 the Mongols sacked Rey as they swept across Persia, executing thousands in the process. Most of those who escaped wound up in Tehran and the village developed into a small, moderately prosperous trading centre.

In the mid-16th century Tehran's natural setting, many trees, clear rivers and good hunting brought it to the attention of the early Safavid king, Tahmasb I. Under his patronage, gardens were laid out, brick houses and caravanserais built and a wall with 114 towers was erected to protect the town and its merchants. As it continued to grow under the later Safavid kings, European visitors wrote of its many enchanting vineyards and gardens.

Threatened by the encroaching Qajars, Karim Khan Zand transferred his army here from his capital at Shiraz in 1758, intending to move in on his enemy. At the same time he refortified Tehran and began the construction of a royal residence. Perhaps he had intended to move his capital here eventually, but when his army killed the Qajar chieftain Mohammed Hasan Khan and took his young son Agha Mohammed Khan hostage, Karim Khan abandoned the unfinished palace and returned to Shiraz.

In 1795, the victorious Agha Mohammed Khan declared this dusty town of around 15,000 souls his capital, and as the centre of Qajar Persia it grew steadily into the 20th century.

Since around 1900 Tehran has grown from a modest city of about 250,000 people into the megalopolis you see today. With this growth has come an influence far greater than most realise. The capital has fomented and hosted two revolutions, two coups d'etat and much intrigue. As the setting for the CIA's first coup in 1953 (see the boxed text 'Mohammad Mossadegh & the CIA's First Coup', p34) it had a profound impact on post-World War II world politics; and as pronouncements from Tehran have been the driving force behind the growth of radical Islam since 1979, that influence has not waned.

Today it is fascinating to walk in the footsteps of that modern history; you can see the White Palace, where the last shah hosted the CIA's Kermit Roosevelt as they plotted the overthrow of Prime Minister Mohammad Mossadegh; gaze up at the Azadi Monument, where hundreds of thousands of people gathered to mark the 1979 revolution; or visit the haunting Behesht-e Zahra cemetery (p116), where the faces of soldiers who died in the Iran-Iraq War stare out from endless fields of glass boxes.

ORIENTATION
Tehran is so vast and so congested that getting lost here is inevitable. Thankfully, most of the streets you're likely to visit have signs in English, though there are still some areas without signs in any language.

As you move through the city the huge social and economic gaps between northern and southern Tehran are plain to see. The south is cheaper, more congested and generally less appealing. However, it has plenty of budget hotels, especially around Imam Khomeini Sq, which also hosts a local bus terminal and the main station on the growing Tehran Metro. The north is more inviting and more expensive and has marginally less chaotic traffic, cleaner air and a range of better hotels and more exotic restaurants.

Valiasr Ave runs from Rah-Ahan Sq in the south all the way to the foothills of the Alborz Mountains in the north – a distance of more than 20km. It's a great street to find when you're lost. One of the main east–west thoroughfares is Azadi Ave, which starts at the Azadi Monument, near the airports, and becomes Enqelab Ave east of Enqelab Sq.

It's handy to remember that the Alborz Mountains are known locally as the North Star of Tehran for a reason – yes, they're in the north. The huge telecoms building at Imam Khomeini Sq dominates inner southern Tehran.

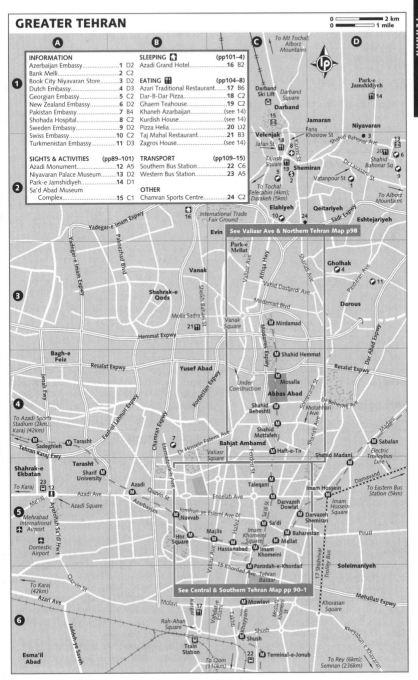

GREATER TEHRAN

0 —————— 2 km
0 —————— 1 mile

INFORMATION	
Azerbaijan Embassy	1 D2
Bank Melli	2 C2
Book City Niyavaran Store	3 D2
Dutch Embassy	4 D3
Georgian Embassy	5 C2
New Zealand Embassy	6 D2
Pakistan Embassy	7 B4
Shohada Hospital	8 C2
Sweden Embassy	9 D2
Swiss Embassy	10 C2
Turkmenistan Embassy	11 D3

SIGHTS & ACTIVITIES	(pp89–101)
Azadi Monument	12 A5
Niyavaran Palace Museum	13 D2
Park-e Jamshidiyeh	14 D1
Sa'd Abad Museum Complex	15 C1

SLEEPING	(pp101–4)
Azadi Grand Hotel	16 B2

EATING	(pp104–8)
Azari Traditional Restaurant	17 B6
Dar-B-Dar Pizza	18 C2
Ghaem Teahouse	19 C2
Khaneh Azarbaijan	(see 14)
Kurdish House	(see 14)
Pizza Helia	20 D2
Taj Mahal Restaurant	21 B3
Zagros House	(see 14)

TRANSPORT	(pp109–15)
Southern Bus Station	22 C6
Western Bus Station	23 A5

OTHER	
Chamran Sports Centre	24 C2

See Valiasr Ave & Northern Tehran Map p98

See Central & Southern Tehran Map pp 90–1

TEHRAN

A REVOLUTION IN STREET NAMES

Across Iran you'll find streets named after the same few revolutionaries, historical figures and revolutionary buzzwords. In many places the government has conveniently painted a huge mural or erected a mosaic likeness of the person beside the street that bears his (it's almost always a man) name. So who are these dead men?

Ayatollah Beheshti founded the Islamic Republic Party (IRP) in 1979. He took part in the negotiations over the US embassy hostages but was killed a year later by a bomb planted in IRP headquarters by the Mojahedin Khalq Organisation (MKO).

Ayatollah Taleqani was a much-admired cleric who was repeatedly exiled and later tortured by the last shah. He led the first Friday prayers after the revolution but died soon afterwards.

Amir Kabir was the nickname of Mirza Taghi Khan, a reformist prime minister (1848–1851) and who was executed at the command of Nasser al-Din Shah in the Bagh-e Tarikhi-ye Fin near Kashan.

Dr Ali Shariati returned to Iran from France in 1964 with a doctorate in sociology from the Sorbonne. He combined radical political thought with socially conscious traditionalism and became an inspiration to many women. Barred from teaching, he went to England in 1977 but was found dead in his apartment three weeks later – apparently a victim of the shah's secret police.

Ayatollah Morteza Motahhari was a close confidant of Ayatollah Khomeini who railed against communism and the effect it would have on Islam. He became president of the Constitutional Council after the revolution, but was assassinated by a rival Islamic group in May 1979.

Streets are also named after buzzwords of the revolution and key Islamic phrases. These include Vali-asr, which means 'Prince of This Time' and is a nickname for Mehdi, the 12th imam who will one day return as the messiah; Azadi, which translates to 'freedom'; Jomhuri-ye Eslami, which means 'Islamic Republic'; and Enqelab, which means 'revolution'. Check out www.iranchamber.com/personalities.

If you plan to use public transport, it helps to learn the names and locations of the main squares as soon as you can.

Arriving in Tehran

If you're flying in, see p112. Travellers arriving by bus will be dropped at one of four bus stations: most will come to the western bus station or the southern bus station, near the train station; fewer to the central (Arzhan-tin) station in the city centre or the eastern bus station. At the time of writing only the southern bus station connected to the Tehran Metro; elsewhere you're best taking a taxi. For details see Getting Around (p112).

Maps

If you're only stopping in Tehran for a few days and seeing the major sights, the maps in this chapter should be adequate. You'll need a more detailed map if you want to walk a lot, visit remote suburbs, or – if you have an uncontrollable yearning for danger – drive. The best one is the Tourist Map of Tehran by Ketab-e-Avval (IR90,000), which is actually a street directory with most hotels and other sights marked. You'll find it in

bookstores at large hotels, museums and palaces. For a more traditional map head straight for the **Gita Shenasi Map shop** (Map pp90–1; ☎ 670 9335; www.gitashenasi.com; 15 Valiasr Crossroads, Razi St, 15 Ostad Shahrivar St) and take a look at its various offerings.

INFORMATION
Bookshops

Books in English (or any European language) can be frustratingly hard to find. The Book City chain has a few stores around town, or else you could try the dozens of mainly Farsi bookshops on Enqelab Ave opposite Tehran University – one of the longest stretches of bookshops on earth. Most top-end hotels have small stores with good ranges of books about Iran, as do some museums and palaces.

Book City Hafez Store (Map p98; ☎ 880 5733; www.ourbooksite.com; 743 Nth Hafez St) The biggest store of the best chain of bookshops in Tehran. A decent but not huge range of fiction and nonfiction in English, but fewer books on Iran than you'd expect.

Book City Niyavaran Store (Map p83; ☎ 228 5969; Shahid Bahoner St) Some people like this store even more than the Hafez store.

Gulestan Bookshop (Map pp90–1; ☎ 311 5416; Manucheri St) Classic chaotic bookshop, with a good range of coffee-table books on Iran.

Evin Bookshop (Map pp90–1; ☎ 896 5021; Laleh International Hotel; 50 Taleqani St) Tiny, with an excellent range of books, including the *Cambridge History of Iran* and Sylvia Matheson's hard-to-find *Persia: An Archaeological Guide*.

Jahanelm Institute (Map pp90–1; ☎ 695 0324; Enqelab Ave) Huge range of foreign magazines – everything from *The Economist* to *Vogue*. It's on the floor just below ground level in a large arcade. Buy your mag and head downstairs to the student restaurant to read it.

National Museum of Iran (Map pp90–1; ☎ 670 2061; Si Tir St) Good range of postcards and English-language books at tourist prices.

Sa'd Abad Museum Complex (Map p83) One of the best ranges of tourist-oriented books in English about Iran – if it's open.

Emergency

If you find yourself in an emergency situation that is not life threatening, it's best to contact your embassy or your hotel's front desk – they should be able to send you to the most appropriate hospital or police station and perhaps help with translation. If that is impossible call one of these numbers:

Ambulance (☎ 115)
Fire Brigade (☎ 125)
Iran Emdad (☎ 643 6662) A private ambulance service.
Police (☎ 110)

Internet Access

Internet cafés, or coffeenets as they're called here, seem to open and close at a remarkable rate in Tehran – and that's even before the government gets involved. In the months leading up to the February 2004 Majlis elections more than 200 of the capital's coffeenets were closed. But there are still plenty around. If these cafés have disappeared into cyberspace by the time you arrive, ask at your hotel, as there's a fair chance they'll be online themselves.

Ferdosi Coffeenet (Map pp90–1; Ferdosi Sq, Enqelab Ave; per hr IR9000) On the 1st floor, on the southeastern corner of the square, this denlike place is often crowded.

Pars Internet (Map pp90–1; ☎ 392 4173; 369 Ferdosi St; per hr IR9000; 9am-11pm) Adjacent to the British embassy, Ali and the friendly guys here have relatively fast machines running XP so you can plug your digital camera in; they also have webcams, sell phonecards and offer the cheapest international calls at IR1000 a minute.

Rahyabnet Cafenet (Map pp90–1; ☎ 880 1316; 40 Keshavarz Blvd, 4th fl; per hr IR12,000; 8am-8.30pm Sat-Thu) Located near the Iranian Traditional Restaurant.

Sepanta Internet (Map pp90–1; ☎ 670 1725; Si Tir St; per hr IR10,000; 10am-10pm Sat-Thu) Small place with just four machines.

Internet Resources

There are few English-language websites devoted to Tehran. For sites that might have Tehran links, see Internet Resources (p15).

Farsinet (www.farsinet.com/Tehran) Useful links to other Tehran sites, though some of the information here is long out of date.

Old Tehran (www.ghandchi.com/iranscope/Fun/OldTehran/ot) Great pictures of Tehran from a bygone era.

TEHRAN IN...

Two Days

Start early in the **Tehran Bazaar** watching the hustling, bustling and haggling of the country's biggest market. Stop in the **Imam Khomeini Mosque** at prayer-time for a taste of Islam in action, then head over to **Park-e Shahr** for some headspace and lunch at the **Sofre Khane Sonnati Sangalag**. Spend the afternoon looking at the ancient wonders of the **National Museum of Iran**, then wander past the peak-hour traffic on Khayyam St (or take the Metro) down to the **Khayyam Traditional Restaurant** for some well-earned *chay* and a truly special meal. On day two check out the **Golestan Palace**, then after a coffee with the paper at **Cafe Naderi**, head down for the 2pm viewing of the **National Jewels Museum**. Round the day out with some alternative cuisine (eg Indian, Chinese) in northern Tehran.

Four Days

Follow the two-day plan, then head north to check out the **S'ad Abad Palace Complex** and take a hike around the trails of **Darband**. Duck across to **Park-e Jamshidieh** for an ethnic dinner and spectacular views of Tehran by night. Use your last day to take in the relaxed **Tehran Museum of Contemporary Art** before chilling out in the cafés of **Gandhi Ave**, and feasting at **Monsoon**.

You'll cry when you see what Imam Khomeini Sq used to look like, and Valiasr Ave without a single car.

Tehran 24 (www.tehran24.com) Well-presented pictures of Tehran updated daily.

Tehran Avenue (www.tehranavenue.com) Undoubtedly the pick of Tehran-focused sites. Well-written café and restaurant reviews share space with razor-sharp evaluations of those films you've seen advertised all over town. What's on in the world of galleries, theatre and music is also assessed. Unfortunately, though, there is often no address for the places reviewed.

Tehran Metro (www.tehranmetro.com) Excellent site with information and maps about the underground and more. Comprehensive list of bus routes and numbers.

Tehran Times (www.tehrantimes.com) Not much cultural news here, but at least you'll get a (fairly conservative) idea of the latest political action.

Laundry

Tehran is not overrun with laundries and dry-cleaning services, although your hotel should be able to arrange something.

Left Luggage

Your hotel is the best option for leaving luggage. There is a left-luggage office at Mehrabad International Airport charging IR12,500 per 24 hours for a large bag and IR17,000 a day for a carpet.

Medical Services

DENTISTS

Dentists regularly advertise in the *Tehran Times*, although you might want to check with your embassy for a recommendation first.

Dr Fereidoun Badal (☎ 884 0193; 18 Kamkar St, Mirzaye Shirazi, 1st fl; ⏱ 4.30-7.30pm Sat-Wed) Highly recommended English-speaking dentist.

HOSPITALS

Tehran has by far the largest concentration of doctors and hospitals in Iran, and the quality of medical care is reasonably high by international standards. Many of the doctors in Tehran received training in the West, and you should have few problems finding one who speaks English (or French or German).

It's best to ask your embassy to recommend a doctor or hospital but if you have no luck getting their advice, the following hospitals are accessible, clean and reputable:

Arad Hospital (Map p83; ☎ 760 1001; Somayyeh St, btwn Shariati Ave & Bahar Sts)

Day Hospital (Map p98; ☎ 801 7111; cnr Valiasr Ave & Tavanir St)

Mehrad Hospital (Map p98; ☎ 874 7401; Motahhari Ave, Mir Embad St)

Shohada Hospital (Map p83; ☎ 271 8009; Tajrish Sq)

Tehran Clinic (Map p98; ☎ 872 8113; Farahani St)

PHARMACIES

Tehran is reasonably well stocked with pharmacies although whether they will have a full range of medications is another matter. If you need to find a 24-hour pharmacy you're best off asking your hotel receptionist for assistance; if they don't know of somewhere, ask them to phone the **pharmacy line** (☎ 191) to find out where the nearest one is.

Money

Tehran has perhaps the greatest concentration of bank branches of any city on earth; along or just off a 1.5km stretch of Enqelab Ave there are more than 20 branches! Only a few of these will change your money, and none deal with credit cards or travellers cheques (see Money, p353).

Below are branches that definitely will deal with foreign currencies. You might find others – look for 'exchange' signs in the windows. Most banks open from 7.30am to 1.30pm but don't change before 9am; the process can be tedious and don't forget your passport.

Many hotels also change money, though the rates aren't good. Then there are the official moneychanging shops, on Ferdosi St just south of Jomhuri-ye Eslami Ave; and the thousands of moneychangers: you'll find them conveniently located outside the banks on Ferdosi St; on the southern side of Ferdosi Sq; and along Jomhuri-ye Eslami Ave west of Ferdosi St, among many other places (see p355 for advice on moneychanging).

If you arrive by air, you will probably have to change some money at the airport in order to get into town. If you're plain out of cash, see the boxed text 'Show Me the Money' (p355).

Bank Melli (Central Branch; Map pp90-1; Ferdosi St) Easily the best place to change money. Relatively fast, friendly service from Mr Abdollahi at counter 14.

Bank Melli (Map p83; Shariati St, Elahiyeh)

Bank Tejarat (Map pp90-1; Nejatollahi St) Handy to Iran Air and all the travel agencies on this street.

Bank Sepah (Map pp90-1; Ferdosi Sq) At the southwestern corner of the square, with plenty of moneychangers outside.

Newsstands

Pavement newsstands can be found all over Tehran, selling a large and ever-changing selection of Farsi newspapers (they're only one critical story away from being closed down) and magazines, and the four English-language dailies. Those mentioned below also stock a random selection of pre-revolution second-hand books.

Enqelab Newsstand (Map pp90-1; Enqelab Ave)

Ferdosi Newsstand (Map pp90-1; Ferdosi St) Just north of Manucheri St.

Post

DHL (Map p98; ☎ 871 5906-9; 353 Dr Beheshti Ave; ☺ 5.30am-9pm Sat-Thu & 9am-2pm Fri)

Main Post Office (Map pp90-1; Sa'di St; ☺ 8am-7pm) About 200m north of Amir Kabir St, this is where you come to send packages, though smaller items can often be posted from any post office. You won't see too many postboxes other than those outside the numerous post offices.

Telephone

Telephone cards for local calls can be bought at most newsstands; cards for international calls are less common but can often be found in Internet cafés. Public telephones are plentiful, conveniently dotted along the main streets where traffic noise is loudest. Coin phones are also common but are less reliable; they are slowly being phased out. The huge telephone office on Imam Khomeini Sq has gone out of the telephone-call business, and has not been replaced. Instead you will need to use one of the small offices scattered around town, or an Internet café with the appropriate hardware.

Pars Internet (Map p90-1; ☎ 392 4173; 369 Ferdosi St; ☺ 9am-11pm) is probably the cheapest option, charging IR1000 a minute for international Internet calls.

Telephone office (Map pp90-1; Ekbatan St; per min IR1590; ☺ 7.30am-10pm) is also worth a go.

Toilets

AYou will find that almost all the museums, palaces and other buildings open to the public have clean toilets, as do all but the smallest restaurants. In an emergency duck into the grounds of the nearest mosque or into a park, where the state of cleanliness or otherwise will depend upon the local caretaker. And remember that old maxim of Iranian travel: 'The wise traveller carries his own paper; the unwise can use this page'.

Tourist Information

Incredibly, there is no tourist office in this city of 14 million. There will probably be an information office at the new airport, but if it's anything like the one at Mehrabad, it's unlikely to have anything as sophisticated as a map.

Travel Agencies

Travel agencies abound in Tehran but for choice and quality the best place to look is along Nejatollahi St in central Tehran. Most sell tickets for domestic and international flights and seats on trains, and those listed here have had good reports. For a list of reliable agencies that also run local tours, see p380.

Asia2000 Travel Agency (Map pp90-1; ☎ 889 6947-58; asia2000@sanapardaz.com; Nejatollahi St) Located next to Iran Air, this professionally run place has friendly English-speaking staff.

Mohajeri Travel Agency (Map pp90-1; ☎ 880 8302; fax 880 7113; Nejatollahi St)

Taban Travel & Tourism (Map pp90-1; ☎ 395 6560-1; taban@sanapardaz.com; Sarcheshmeh Cross, Amir Kabir St) At the end of Amir Kabir St this is handy to the budget accommodation.

Universities

Tehran University (Map pp90-1; Enqelab Ave) At the centre of political change in Iran, this is a fascinating place to wander around. There is, however, a ban on foreign nonstudents entering but its enforcement is haphazard. If you're worried, just hang around the front gate for a few minutes and you're sure to be 'adopted' by someone keen to practise their English.

Visa Extensions

Do anything you can to avoid the **Disciplinary Force for Islamic Republic of Iran Department for Aliens Affairs building** (Map p98; ☎ 880 0000; Valiasr Ave; ☺ 7.45am-1.30pm Sat-Wed & 7.45am-noon Thu). If you think the name sounds bad, wait until you get inside. It is peopled by perhaps the most bureaucratic bunch of contrarians in all Iran. The normal procedure of extending tourist visas by a month on two occasions does not apply here – you'll be lucky to get 10 days. No debate is tolerated. No discussion entered into.

If you are forced to use this office, give yourself several days (it took us eight) and no matter what is said remain courteous and deferential. The nominated **Bank Melli** branch (Map p98) is about 300m down

TEHRAN

Valiasr Ave on the opposite side of the road. In summary, do everything in your power to be in Esfahan, Shiraz or Yazd – anywhere else – when your 30 days is up. For full details on the (normal) process, see the boxed text 'More Time, Please' (p362).

DANGERS & ANNOYANCES
Traffic
Even for the experienced Asia hand, the traffic in Tehran is likely to come as quite a shock. Almost anything goes on these roads, and often does. It's not unusual to see motorcycles weaving between pedestrians on the footpath in an attempt to escape the gridlock; Paykans reversing at speed along an expressway – in the wrong direction, of course; and all manner of cars and buses hurtling towards each other in a high-stakes game of chicken.

The sheer volume of traffic can be overwhelming and makes crossing the street seem like a game of Russian roulette, only in this game there are fewer empty chambers. Indeed, it is hard to overestimate the risk of an accident in this nightmarish traffic, whether you're in a vehicle or on foot.

However, after the initial shock subsides visitors are often surprised there are not more accidents. You might feel as if you've had three near-death experiences in the course of a single cab ride, but in reality drivers are adept at getting you near to

death without actually killing you (see the boxed text 'Bad Driving? It's All in Your Head', below). As a pedestrian, the best way to ensure a safe negotiation of the mean streets is to do what the locals do. Safety in numbers is the usual tactic – wait for one or two other road-crossers to appear and step boldly out into the flow. Be aware of the ubiquitous contra-flow bus lanes, which turn relatively harmless one-way streets into a far more dangerous street-crossing challenge, and don't expect traffic lights to work for more than a couple of hours a day.

But perhaps the most reassuring thing of all is to remember that no matter how 'crazy' a driver appears to be, he will do everything he can to avoid running you over simply because doing so is just too much hassle. For more on Iran's roads, see p376.

Pollution
Tehran is one of the most polluted cities on earth. And it's that dangerous and annoying traffic that produces most of it. According to the government, 71% of the smog that covers Tehran for about 200 days a year comes straight out of the exhaust pipes of the city's two million cars, trucks and motorbikes. Many of those cars are Paykans, the engines of which are staggering in their inefficiency (see the boxed text 'The Perennial Paykan', p379). When pollution levels reach crisis point – usually during summer –

BAD DRIVING? IT'S ALL IN YOUR HEAD

The physical danger notwithstanding, the main problem you face as a visitor on Tehran's streets is mental: how to deal with this manic mass of metal. After much testing, we believe the following attitudinal adjustments will not only free you of some of the traffic-induced anxiety, but make your Tehran experience all the more memorable.

Try not to think of Tehrani drivers as 'hopeless', 'crazy' or 'stupid', it will just make you more scared.

Instead, look at all the tiny gaps your taxi driver is negotiating without recourse to the brakes, the countless sticky situations from which he extricates himself, and you start to realise these guys are actually GOOD drivers.

Watch your driver closely: he almost never uses his mirrors (if he has any); he drapes his seatbelt across his chest only when driving onto an expressway, where he can be fined; he rarely indicates; and he happily makes U-turns in the middle of major roads – all without raising his heartbeat.

Then think of how well you'd have to drive to get through this nightmarish traffic without being involved in some kind of accident. That's right, don't fight it, you know these guys are actually REALLY GOOD!

Finally, embrace the chaos! Head to the corner of Jomhuri-ye Eslami Ave and Ferdosi St and engage a motorbike taxi for a trip across town. Tell him you're in a hurry, and hold on. At Disneyland you'd pay good money for this kind of white-knuckle ride, in Tehran it's just part of life. Enjoy it!

schools are closed and radio warns the old and unwell to stay indoors. Still, reports say about 4500 people die every year as a result of the atrocious air quality.

However, there is some light filtering through from the end of this foggy tunnel. After years of doing nothing, in 2003 the government launched a 10-year plan to try and curb pollution. The plan includes closing the Paykan assembly line and making catalytic converters – which clean many pollutants from exhaust before it leaves the vehicle – mandatory on all new cars, as they have been for years in many other countries. But the most effective means of cleaning the air will be the completion of the Tehran Metro, and that is still many years away.

If the pollution really starts to hurt your throat, or you have asthma, head for the hills and relative purity of Darband or Park-e Jamshidiyeh.

Scams

There are many more dangerous places in the world than Tehran, where crime against foreigners (especially violent crime) is very rare. There is, however, the odd scam to watch out for. The most popular of these is the bogus police scam – for a full description of the scam and how to deal with it, see p346.

SIGHTS

It's not that long ago that southern Tehran was the centre of the city. Today, the area south of Jomhuri-ye Eslami Ave is the oldest and poorest part of town and is home to many of Tehran's best museums, including the National Museum of Iran and the glittering National Jewels Museum, as well as the Golestan Palace complex and the Tehran Bazaar. A little north of here is the area loosely referred to as central Tehran, on the edge of which is Park-e Laleh – home to the Carpet Museum and the Museum of Contemporary Art.

Most locals refer to anywhere north of Valiasr Sq as northern Tehran, and much of this area was semirural until about 35 years ago. The frenetic expansion of the city has spread apartment buildings all the way to the foothills of the Alborz Mountains, engulfing the last shah's opulent Sa'd-Abad and Niyavaran Palaces in the process.

In this guide we have included South & Central Tehran on one map (pp90–1); the

area either side of Valiasr Ave heading north of Valiasr Sq on the Valiasr Ave & Northern Tehran map (p98); while places that don't fall in these two areas can be found on the Greater Tehran map (p83). Places are listed starting at the Tehran Bazaar in the south and heading north from there.

Central & Southern Tehran   Map pp90–1
TEHRAN BAZAAR

The maze of bustling alleys and the *bazaris* that fill them make the **Tehran Bazaar** a fascinating, if somewhat daunting, place to explore (see the boxed text 'The Bazaris', p92). This bazaar has traditionally been the Wall St of Tehran and hence Iran, where the prices of staple commodities were fixed. However, as a growing number of merchants have moved their businesses to more salubrious surroundings the bazaar has gradually declined in both size and importance. Visiting the bazaar is primarily a people-watching and shopping experience – it's no architectural jewel.

There are several entrances to the bazaar, which includes more than 10km of covered stores. The main entrance is along 15 Khordad Ave. The bazaar is a city within a city, encompassing more than a dozen mosques, several guesthouses, a handful of banks (not for changing money), one church and even a fire station. Each corridor specialises in a particular commodity: copper, paper, gold, spices and carpets, among others. In the carpet area expect to be pounced on and whisked off on a tour that inevitably ends with a highly professional demonstration of the hard sell.

You'll also find tobacconists, shoemakers, tailors, broadcloth sellers, bookbinders, flag sellers, haberdashers, saddlers, tinsmiths, knife makers and carpenters. Among the more interesting 'streets' is the one with more than a dozen stores selling fake designer labels – everything from Nike to Yves Saint-Laurent.

The best way to explore the bazaar is simply to wander its labyrinth of streets and alleys. Don't, whatever you do, attempt anything but the vaguest navigation – you will almost certainly get lost and it's more fun to just go with it. Try and visit in the morning, when business is brisk but not yet frantic, as it becomes at lunchtime and between about 5pm and 7pm. During these

CENTRAL & SOUTHERN TEHRAN

To Carpet Museum (800m)

Park-e Laleh

To Laleh International Hotel; Evin Bookshop (700m)

Keshavarz Blvd

Felestin Square

Taleqani Ave

Tehran University

Enqelab Square

Enqelab Ave

Daneshgu Park

Ostad Shahriar St

Dr Labafinezhad St

Nofl Loshato St (France Ave)

Amirkabeir University

Jomhuri-ye Eslami Ave

Talegani Ave

15 Khordad Ave

Bazar-e Bozorg

Bazar-e Ketablorushha

Sirus Crossroads

Masjed-e Jameh Alley

Seyyed Mohmad Sayyed Sarraf Alley

Mirza Amin Alley

Bazar-e Chehel Tan

Esma'il Alley

Tehran Bazaar

Bazar-e Najjarha

Sayyed Esma'il Square

Armenian Church of St Thaddeus

Shahid Musavi Alley

Mostafa Khomeini St

Bazar-e Hazrati

Majlis

Imam Khomeini St

Hassanabad

Fayyazbakhsh St

Park-e Shahr

15 Khordad Ave

Sabt St

Imamzadeh Seyyed Nasreddin Mosque

Vahdat-e Islami St

Maghfoul St

0   300 m
0   0.2 miles

INFORMATION		SIGHTS & ACTIVITIES	(pp89–101)
Arad Hospital.....................................1 F1		13 Aban Museum...........................31 E4	
Armenian Embassy...........................2 C2		Bagh-e Melli..................................32 E4	
Asia 2000 Travel Agency...................3 D2		Glass & Ceramics Museum..............33 D3	
Bank Melli Central Branch................4 E4		Golestan Palace Ticket Office..........34 E5	
Bank Sepah.....................................5 E2		Haft-e-Tir Sports Stadium...............35 D5	
Bank Tejarat....................................6 D2		Iranian Photographers' Centre.........36 D1	
British Embassy...............................7 E3		Madraseh va Masjed-e Sepahsalar...37 G4	
Enqelab Newsstand..........................8 B2		Malek National Museum & Library...38 E4	
Fair & Shop for Products of		Mountaineering Federation of Iran...39 F1	
Self-Sufficiency of Imam		National Jewels Museum..............(see 4)	
Khomeini's Relief Committee........9 E2		National Museum of Iran................40 D4	
Ferdosi Coffeenet...........................10 E2		National Museum of the	
Ferdosi Newsstand..........................11 E3		Islamic Period.........................(see 40)	
French Embassy..............................12 D3		Shahid Shirudi Sports Centre..........41 F1	
German Embassy.............................13 E3		Shohada Museum..........................42 E1	
Gita Shenasi Map Shop...................14 C2		Skiing Federation...........................43 F1	
Gulestan Bookshop.........................15 E3		Tehran Museum of	
Iran Peyma Booking Office..............16 E2		Contemporary Art......................44 A1	
Iran Touring & Tourism Organisation			
(ITTO)..17 B1			
Italian Embassy..............................18 C3			
Jahanlei Institute............................19 B2			
Kassa Mountaineering & Tourism....20 G1			
Main Post Office.............................21 E4			
Mohajeri Travel Agency..................22 D2			
National Museum of Iran			
Bookshop................................(see 40)			
Pars Internet..................................23 E3			

Persepolis Tour & Travel Agency.....24 D2	
Rahyabnet Cafenet.....................(see 72)	
Sepanta Internet............................25 D3	
Taban Travel & Tourism..................26 F4	
Tavakoli International	
Travel & Tour............................27 E2	
Tehran University...........................28 B2	
Telephone Office...........................29 F4	
Turkish Embassy............................30 E3	

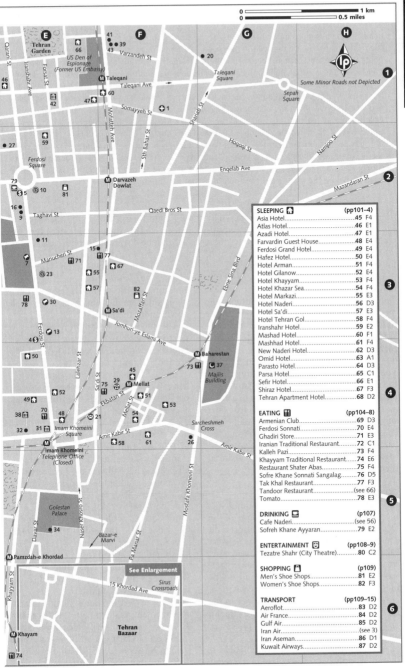

SLEEPING	(pp101–4)
Asia Hotel	45 F4
Atlas Hotel	46 E1
Azadi Hotel	47 E1
Farvardin Guest House	48 E4
Ferdosi Grand Hotel	49 E4
Hafez Hotel	50 E4
Hotel Arman	51 F4
Hotel Gilanow	52 F4
Hotel Khayyam	53 F4
Hotel Khazar Sea	54 F4
Hotel Markazi	55 E3
Hotel Naderi	56 D3
Hotel Sa'di	57 E3
Hotel Tehran Gol	58 F4
Iranshahr Hotel	59 E2
Mashad Hotel	60 F1
Mashhad Hotel	61 F4
New Naderi Hotel	62 D3
Omid Hotel	63 A1
Parasto Hotel	64 D3
Parsa Hotel	65 C1
Sefir Hotel	66 E1
Shiraz Hotel	67 F3
Tehran Apartment Hotel	68 D2

EATING	(pp104–8)
Armenian Club	69 D3
Ferdosi Sonnati	70 E4
Ghadiri Store	71 E3
Iranian Traditional Restaurant	72 C1
Kalleh Pazi	73 F4
Khayyam Traditional Restaurant	74 E6
Restaurant Shater Abas	75 F4
Sofre Khane Sonnati Sangalag	76 D5
Tak Khal Restaurant	77 F3
Tandoor Restaurant	(see 66)
Tomato	78 E3

DRINKING	(p107)
Cafe Naderi	(see 56)
Sofreh Khane Ayyaran	79 E2

ENTERTAINMENT	(pp108–9)
Tezatre Shahr (City Theatre)	80 C2

SHOPPING	(p109)
Men's Shoe Shops	81 E2
Women's Shoe Shops	82 F3

TRANSPORT	(pp109–15)
Aeroflot	83 D2
Air France	84 D2
Gulf Air	85 D2
Iran Air	(see 3)
Iran Aseman	86 D1
Kuwait Airways	87 D2

THE BAZARIS

In Iran a bazaar is much more than just a place to stock up on a few essential shopping items. The *bazari*, the men who run the stalls in the bazaar, are frequently very wealthy and wield enormous political power, most of them being politically and religiously conservative. In an attempt to weaken their power the last shah bulldozed new roads through parts of the bazaar, gave subsidised credit to competing supermarkets, and set up state purchasing bodies to handle sugar, meat and wheat. Not surprisingly, the Tehran *bazaris* hit back during the Islamic Revolution by closing the bazaar and wreaking havoc on the economy. They were equally influential in the 1906 Constitutional Revolution and the coup that ousted Prime Minister Mohammad Mossadegh in 1953 (see the boxed text 'Mohammad Mossadegh & the CIA's First Coup', p34, for more detail).

It has been estimated that the Tehran Bazaar controls a third of Iran's entire retail and trade sector. The carpet dealers and other merchants have access to foreign currency and are able to supply loans as readily as the banks. Inevitably they tend to put their short-term commercial interests before the long-term investment needs of the country.

times, the chances of being mowed down by some piece of fast-moving haulage equipment are significant. From late afternoon on Thursday through to Saturday morning the bazaar resembles a ghost town.

IMAM KHOMEINI MOSQUE

Tehran has surprisingly few interesting mosques and mausoleums but one that's well-worth visiting is the **Imam Khomeini Mosque** (Shah Mosque), right inside the bazaar. This is very much a working mosque, one of the largest and busiest in Tehran. The building itself, though dating from the early 18th century, is not the attraction; rather, you come here to see Islam in action. Since the courtyard is not cut off from the surrounding area and hundreds of people crisscross it on their way to and from the bazaar, it's no problem for non-Muslims to stand and watch the faithful performing their ablutions and praying.

GOLESTAN PALACE

In what was once the heart of Tehran is this monument to the glories and excesses of the Qajar rulers. Set around a square, a short walk south from Imam Khomeini Sq, the **Golestan Palace complex** (☎ 311 3335-8; www.golestanpalace.org; Ark Sq; several tickets required; 9am-3.30pm Fri, Sat & Mon-Wed) is made up of several grand buildings set around a lovely garden; seven of these are open to the public. Annoyingly, tickets for each building must be bought individually and only at the front gate. These prices are outlined in each section.

Although there was a Safavid citadel on this site, it only became a palace in the reign

of Karim Khan Zand. It was the Qajar ruler Nasser al-Din Shah (r 1848–96), impressed by what he'd seen of European palaces, who built it up into the fine complex you see today. Originally it would have been much bigger, with inner and outer sections to encompass offices, ministries and private living quarters, but much of it was pulled down under the Pahlavis.

The following description assumes you start your visit at the Ivan-e Takht-e Marmar then continue in a clockwise direction around the courtyard.

Immediately opposite the entrance is the **Ivan-e Takht-e Marmar** (Marble Throne Veranda; admission IR10,000), a mirrored, open-fronted audience hall dominated by a magnificent throne supported by human figures and constructed from 65 pieces of alabaster. It was made in 1801 for Fath Ali Shah, a monarch who managed a staggering 200-odd wives and 170 offspring. This hall was used on ceremonial occasions, including the Napoleon-style coronation of Reza Shah in 1925.

A narrow corridor leads off to a side room covered with murals of the fictional kings described in Ferdosi's *Shahnamah* – look for Zahhak, the king with a snake on his shoulder that had to be fed with human brains. Don't miss the painting of Fath Ali Shah – he's the one with the beard so thick you'd swear it was a falsie!

If you leave the Ivan-e Takht-e Marmar and turn left you'll come to the **Negar Khane** (Art Gallery; admission IR15,000), which displays a fine collection of Qajar-era art. It was the brainchild of Nasser al-Din Shah, who'd been particularly captivated by European museums.

Especially interesting are the portraits of the shahs wearing the jewels and crowns you can see in the National Jewels Museum, and pictures of everyday life in 19th-century Iran by Kamal ol-Molk and Mehdi. Women were certainly wearing chadors back then, too. The difference is that the men were also swaddled in three layers of clothing.

Continue in a clockwise direction around the courtyard and you'll come to the **Haze Khane** (Pool Room; admission IR10,000), used to house a collection of mediocre works of art given to the shahs by European monarchs. It's a pretty room with the eponymous pool in the middle but if you're pushed for time this would be one of the more missable parts of the complex.

The next museum you come to is the **Shams-Al Emarat** (Edifice of the Sun; admission IR20,000), the tallest palace of its day and designed to mix European and Persian architectural traditions. Born of Nasser al-Din Shah's desire to have a palace that afforded him a panoramic view of the city, it was designed by master architect Moayer al-Mamalek and built between 1865 and 1867. A sequence of mirrored and tiled rooms display a collection of photographs, together with furniture and vases given to the shahs by European monarchs, especially the French.

The four soaring structures nearby that look like minarets are, in fact, **windtowers**, first erected in the reign of Fath Ali Shah. They're not open to the public, but you might be able to climb up onto the podium level through a door in the back of the building.

Next up is a basement room containing a fountain and the **Historic Photograph Gallery** (admission IR10,000), with pictures of Nasser al-Din's wives in curious tutu-like skirts. Most interesting of all is a photograph showing the inside of one of the Zoroastrian Towers of Silence, with bodies in varying states of decay, some still sitting upright.

The tiny **Talar-e Almas** (Diamond Hall; admission IR15,000) displays 19th-century decorative arts in a room with red walls and tiled floor. Unless you're especially interested in 18th- and 19th-century French ceramics, save your money.

Finally you come to the **Ethnographical Museum** (☎ 311 0653; admission IR20,000), which contains some fascinating tableaux, including one of a Qajar wedding and another of a traditional teahouse complete with story-

teller. Particularly interesting is the model of a dervish, his clothes completely covered with Quranic texts, carrying a *kashkool* (a sort of handbag on a chain) and an axe.

There's a pricey but pretty **teahouse** and a decent **book-cum-souvenir shop** in the grounds.

PARK-E SHAHR

If you're staying in southern Tehran and need a break from the traffic, head straight for **Park-e Shahr** where you can go ice skating (when it's cold enough), take a boat trip on the tiny lake (in summer) and enjoy tea or a qalyan (water pipe) at the laid-back **Sofre Khane Sonnati Sangalag** (p105) year-round. It's also a great place to just sit and watch Tehranis – with a much-reduced likelihood of becoming a traffic statistic.

NATIONAL MUSEUM OF IRAN

The modest **National Museum of Iran** (Iran Bastan Museum; ☎ 670 2061; www.nationalmuseumofiran.com; Si Tir St; adult/student IR60,000/30,000 incl admission to Museum of the Islamic Period; 9am-5pm Tue-Sun, until 6pm summer) is no Louvre, but it is chock-full of Iran's rich history and should be on every visitor's list of things to see in Tehran. The contents will probably mean more to you if you come here after you've seen the main archaeological sites – particularly Persepolis – so you might want to wait until the end of your trip.

The museum's grand recessed entrance, designed by the French architect André Godard, is modelled on a Sassanian palace. Inside you'll find a marvellous collection, including ceramics, pottery, stone figures and carvings, mostly taken from excavations at Persepolis, Ismail Abad (near Qazvin), Shush, Rey and Turang Tappeh. Unfortunately, the presentation of these treasures is less than inspired, and several readers have been disappointed by the lack of thorough explanations. There is some English labelling and free guides are promised, though you'll probably have to wait around to get one.

Among the finds from **Shush**, there's a stone capital of a winged lion, some delightful pitchers and vessels in animal shapes, and colourful glazed bricks decorated with double-winged mythical creatures. A copy of the stone detailing the Code of Hammurabi found at Shush is also displayed – to see the original you'll have to go to Paris.

Among the finds from **Persepolis**, you can see a magnificent human-headed capital; a cuneiform inscription from the Talar-e Bar proclaiming the might and godly affinity of Xerxes; and a striking frieze of glazed tiles from the central hall of the Apadana Palace. Also on display are a famous trilingual inscription from the time of Darius I; a bull-headed capital and carved staircase; a statue of a sitting dog that looks as if it was carved just weeks ago; and four foundation tablets inscribed in cuneiform.

One of the more startling exhibits is the **Salt Man** from Zanjan, thought to have been a miner who died in the 3rd or 4th century, whose head with white hair and beard, leg in a leather boot and tools were also preserved by the salt in which he was buried. Rather more comical is a **bronze statue of a prince**, a huge moustache bristling on a head obviously made separately from the body and better suited to a smaller monument. Look out also for a selection of **Lorestan bronzes** dating back to the 8th century BC (p188).

Entry is from Si Tir St – it's behind the small park on the corner of Imam Khomeini Ave.

MUSEUM OF THE ISLAMIC PERIOD

Next to the National Mseum, this **museum** (☎ 670 2061; Si Tir St; adult/student IR60,000/30,000 – the same ticket as for National Museum; 🕑 9am-5pmTue-Sun, until 6pm summer) contains two floors of exhibits from a selection of Islamic arts, including calligraphy, carpets, ceramics, woodcarving, stone carving, miniatures, brickwork and textiles. Look out for the silks and stuccowork from Rey, portraits from the Mongol period, a collection of Sassanian coins and gorgeous 14th-century wooden doors and windows. Look also for the beautiful **Paradise Door**, a 14th-century lustre-painted *mihrab* (niche in a mosque indicating the direction of Mecca) from Qom, and a 19th-century inlaid door from Esfahan.

Captions are in English, and English-speaking guides are – in theory – available at the reception. There's also a plastic-coated page of explanations you can use while in the museum – ask at the ground-floor counter. The **bookshop** on the 1st floor is excellent, with many titles in English. Postcards, videos, maps and dictionaries are also on sale.

To see both museums you should probably allow two to three hours. There's no food in either place.

MALEK NATIONAL MUSEUM & LIBRARY

Heading back from the National Museum of Iran towards Imam Khomeini Sq you'll see on your left the impressive **Bagh-e Melli** (National Garden Arch), a huge tiled arch with a pedestrian street beyond it. About 100m along this street on your left is the **Malek National Museum and Library** (☎ 672 6653; Imam Khomeini Sq, Bagh-e Melli Portico; admission IR10,000; 🕑 9am-1pm Sat-Wed), which contains a small but varied collection of 19th-century furnishings, decorative arts, miniatures, and paintings by Kamal ol-Molk. One vast painting shows Nasser al-Din Shah reviewing the troops with his son and Commander-in-Chief Mirza Mohammed Khan – they're huge and the troops tiny, to reflect their relative importance. For lovers of coins, there's an excellent, well-labelled collection dating back to the 6th century BC.

The basement contains a collection of stamps and several fine carpets, some of them made to order for the museum's benefactor Haji Hossein Agha Malek.

13 ABAN MUSEUM

Through a nondescript, recessed door right on the northwestern corner of Imam Khomeini Sq is a small building that was once used as a stable by the shah. Now the **13 Aban Museum** (Sizdah-e Aban; ☎ 670 1915; admission IR1000; 🕑 8am-noon & 2-7pm), it's crammed solid with life-sized bronze statues by the famous modern Iranian sculptor Seyed Ali Akbar-e San'ati. Most striking is a group sculpture representing the political prisoners taken by the Pahlavis. Unsurprising statues include those of the poets Ferdosi and Sa'di, and Shah Abbas I and Nader Shah. What the crucified Christ and Victor Hugo are doing here is more of a mystery. It's worth a look if only because it's good value.

NATIONAL JEWELS MUSEUM

Through a large iron gate at the northern end of Bank Melli, past a couple of well-armed guards, you'll find the cavernous vault that is the **National Jewels Museum** (☎ 311 2369; Ferdosi St; adult IR30,000, child under 12 not permitted; 🕑 2-4.30pm Sat-Tue). Owned by the Central Bank but actually housed underneath the central branch of the Bank Melli, this museum is probably *the* biggest tourist drawcard in Tehran. If you've already visited the art gallery at the Golestan Palace you will have seen the incredible jewellery with which the Safavid monarchs adorned themselves. Come here to gawp at the real things.

Believe it or not, at least one war has been fought over these jewels. Most of the collection dates back to Safavid times when the shahs scoured Europe, India and the lands of the Ottoman Empire for booty with which to decorate the then capital, Esfahan. However, when Mahmud Afghan invaded Iran in 1722, he plundered the treasury and sent its contents to India. On ascending the throne in 1736, Nader Shah Afshar despatched courtiers to ask for the return of the jewels. When their powers of persuasion proved unequal to the task, he sent an army to prove that he was serious. To get the soldiers off his back Mohammed Shah of India was forced to hand over the Darya-ye Nur and Kuh-e Nur diamonds, a Peacock Throne (though not the one you'll see here) and other assorted treasures. After Nader Shah's murder in 1747, Ahmed Beg plundered the treasury and dispersed the jewels. The Kuh-e Nur diamond found its way into the sticky fingers of the colonial British and has been locked up in the Tower of London since.

You can pick up a guidebook at the shop as you enter for IR6000, or take one of the regular and professional tours in English, French, German, Arabic or Turkish – it's included in the ticket price. Make sure you don't miss the **Darya-ye Nur** (Sea of Light), a pink diamond weighing 182 carats and said to be the largest uncut diamond in the world; the **Peacock (or Naderi) Throne** outside the vault door (see the boxed text 'The Peacock Throne', p95); the tall **Kiani Crown** made for Fath Ali Shah in 1797; the crowns worn by the last shah and his wife, Farah; and the incredible 34kg **Globe of Jewels**, made in 1869 using 51,366 precious stones – the seas are made from emeralds, the land from rubies (Iran, England and France are set in diamonds).

Not surprisingly, cameras and bags must be left at reception, and unless you can hide it under your manteau (overcoat) you'll be forced to leave this book outside too. Be careful not to touch *anything* or you'll set off ear-piercing alarms.

GLASS & CERAMICS MUSEUM

North of the National Museum of Iran is the impressive **Glass & Ceramics Museum** (☎ 670 8153; Si Tir St; adult IR30,000; ☺ 9am-5pm Tue-Sun, until 6pm summer), housed in a beautiful building dating back to Qajar times. Built as a private residence for a prominent Persian family, it later housed the Egyptian embassy and was converted into a museum in 1976.

The building marks a move away from purely Persian traditions, successfully blending features of both Eastern and Western styles. The graceful wooden staircase and the classical stucco mouldings on the walls and ceilings are particularly delightful, and there are many delicate carvings and other decorations.

The museum itself is probably the best-designed in Iran. It has hundreds of exhibits, mainly from Neishabur, Kashan, Rey and Gorgan, dating from the 2nd millennium BC. They're organised chronologically into galleries, with each piece labelled in English and lovingly displayed as if individual thought had been given to it; there are even explanations in English about, for example, the Persian glass-blowing tradition. The ground-floor shop sells an English guidebook to the museum.

THE PEACOCK THRONE

In 1798 Fath Ali Shah ordered a new throne encrusted with 26,733 gems to be made for himself. Set into its top was a carved sun, studded with precious stones, so the throne became known as the Sun Throne. Later Fath Ali married Tavous Tajodoleh, nicknamed Tavous Khanoum or Lady Peacock, and the throne became known as the Peacock Throne in her honour. This throne now sits at the entrance to the National Jewels Museum.

Fath Ali certainly had a taste for gems, but one of his predecessors, Nader Shah, liked the finer things too. So much, in fact, that he invaded India in order to recover the Kuh-e Nur diamond. During the expedition he also bagged the Moghuls' famous Peacock Throne. But during the haul back to Iran this piece of booty fell into the hands of rebellious soldiers, who hacked it up to spread the wealth among themselves. Subsequently, the stories of the Peacock Thrones have become muddled and later commentators believed the throne had been brought to Iran from India.

MADRASEH VA MASJED-E SEPAHSALAR

The **Madraseh va Masjed-e Sepahsalar** (Masjed-e Motahari; Baharestan Sq, Mostafa Khomeini St), at the eastern end of Jomhuri-ye Eslami Ave, is one of the most noteworthy examples of Persian architecture of its period, as well as one of the largest. Built between 1878 and 1890, the multiple minarets and poetry inscribed in several ancient scripts in the tiling are famous. It still operates as an Islamic college and is usually open to the public, though some readers have reported being turned away. Be careful taking photos in this area as the Majlis building is not far away.

IRANIAN PHOTOGRAPHERS' CENTRE

The **Iranian Photographers' Centre** (☎ 880 7062/3; Somayyeh St; admission free; 🕒 9am-7pm Sat-Thu & 3-7pm Fri) has rolling exhibits of the work of local and, occasionally, international photographers. The shop next door sells and processes slides.

US DEN OF ESPIONAGE

More than any other single building in Iran, events emanating from the former US embassy in Tehran have had a dramatic and profound influence on the recent history of this country and, indeed, the whole Middle East. From a bunker beneath the embassy building at the junction of Taleqani and Mofatteh Sts, CIA operatives in 1953 orchestrated a coup d'etat that brought down the government of Mohammad Mossadegh (see the boxed text 'Mohammad Mossadegh & the CIA's First Coup', p34).

For the next 25 years US support for and influence over Mohammed Reza was implemented largely from this building. When the shah was finally pushed out, students fearing a repeat of the 1953 coup stormed the embassy and held 53 diplomats hostage for 444 days (p36). The rest – the birth of the Islamic Republic and the rise of fundamentalism throughout the region – is history.

Today, the former embassy is known as the **US Den of Espionage** (Taleqani Ave) and is used by the Sepah militia, a hardline group dedicated to defending the revolution. It is not open to the public. On the walls outside you'll see the predictable 'Down with the USA' sign, and at the entrance gates you'll be able to see the old embassy insignia, its details methodically hacked out but still distinguishable.

All along the wall overlooking Taleqani Ave are striking **murals** affirming the evil of the 'Great Satan' (the USA) and Israel, including one in which the face of the Statue of Liberty is rendered as a skull. There's no sign saying you can't take pictures of these highly photogenic murals but be warned that more than one traveller has had their film confiscated by gun-toting soldiers. Then again, some readers have reported snapping away with no such problems.

Diagonally opposite the US Den of Espionage is the **Shohada Museum** (Martyrs' Museum; cnr Taleqani Ave & Forsat St; 🕒 8.30am-3.30pm Sat-Thu), which has rolling exhibitions of photographs, usually from the Iran-Iraq War or the 1979 revolution.

PARK-E LALEH

Near the centre of Tehran, **Park-e Laleh** (Keshavarz Blvd) is one of those places that is more than the sum of its parts. Certainly, it is a well-designed space, but due to its location amid so much traffic the park is a veritable oasis. As you wander through, perhaps on your way to the Carpet Museum or Tehran Museum of Contemporary Art located at its fringes, you'll notice plenty of young Tehranis refining their flirting techniques. This is a great place for people-watching.

TEHRAN MUSEUM OF CONTEMPORARY ART

On the western side of Park-e-Laleh, the **Tehran Museum of Contemporary Art** (☎ 896 5411; Kargar Ave; admission IR3000; 🕒 9am-6pm Sat-Thu & 2-6pm Fri, until 7pm summer) is housed in a striking building vaguely reminiscent of the Guggenheim Museum in New York. It contains an interesting collection of paintings by modern Iranian artists, as well as regular temporary exhibitions featuring Iranian and foreign photographers, designers and calligraphers. The museum is popular with locals, not least because of the cheap admission fee and the wonderfully comfortable seats around the corridors. It's a great place to meet young, educated, English-speaking Tehranis.

CARPET MUSEUM

Just north of the Museum of Contemporary Art, the two floors of the **Carpet Museum** (☎ 896 7707; cnr Fatemi St & Kargar Ave; admission IR30,000; 🕒 9am-5pm Tue-Sun, until 6pm summer) house more than 100 pieces from all over Iran, dating from the 16th century to the present day; the older pieces are mostly upstairs. This is a spectacular place to visit and you should certainly come here if you have even the slightest interest in Persian carpets – although seeing the quality of these pieces will make it much harder to settle for buying something more affordable.

Inside, a shop sells postcards and books and there's a pleasant café selling drinks and snacks. Cameras must be left at the door.

Valiasr Ave & Northern Tehran   Map p98
Almost everything along Valiasr Ave and the surrounding parts of northern Tehran has been built in the last 50 years, so there aren't many actual 'sights' here. Instead, this is modern Tehran, home to hip coffee shops, fancy restaurants and embassies.

To get there, shared taxis head north from Valiasr Sq so it's probably simplest to just jump in and out as you need. If you're heading somewhere near to or north of Mirdamad Blvd, however, consider taking the Metro to Mirdamad station and a shared taxi the short hop across to Valiasr – just say 'Valiasr' to the drivers waiting outside and you'll be pointed in the right direction.

SARKIS CATHEDRAL
In case you assume that Islam has a monopoly on Iranian life, visit the surprisingly large **Sarkis Cathedral** (☎ 889 7980; cnr Nejatollahi & Karim Khan-e Zand Sts; ☒ 8am-noon & 1-5pm Mon-Sat). Built between 1964 and 1970, it's wondrous not so much for any great age or beauty but because of what it is and where it is. It's by far the most visible and important non-Islamic religious building in Tehran. The area immediately to the south is the Armenian quarter of Tehran, the centre of a still-thriving community.

Although most of the Christians in Iran are Armenians, there's also a sprinkling of Protestants, Assyrians, Catholics and Orthodox Christians, all of whom have churches in Tehran, most behind large walls in the same district as the Sarkis Cathedral.

PARK-E MELLAT
Many Tehranis say **Park-e Mellat** (Mellat Park; Valiasr Ave) is their favourite in-town getaway, and if you're here around dusk on any spring or summer afternoon you'll find plenty of people enjoying the shaded areas around a small lake. A visit to the park could ideally be combined with a meal at the **Jaam-e**

Jam Food Court (Map p98; p106), from where many of the flirting young couples in the park have probably just come.

Greater Tehran   Map p83
This section covers the palaces and walking trails of the far north of Tehran; the Reza Abbasi Museum; and the Azadi Monument in the west.

For all the sights in the far north head first to Tajrish Sq in the suburb of Shemiran, from where shared taxis leave almost continuously for the Sa'd Abad and Niyavaran Palaces; the popular walking trails at Darband and Darakeh; the cable car to Tochal at Velenjak; and the ethnic restaurants scattered through Park-e Jamshidiyeh.

SA'D ABAD MUSEUM COMPLEX
Scattered among the tall, imposing trees standing on a slope of the Alborz Mountains, the dozen or so buildings that constitute the **Sa'd Abad Museum Complex** (☎ 228 2031; www.saadabadpalace.org; Valiasr Ave, Taheri St; several tickets required; ☒ 8.30am-4pm, until 5pm summer) were once the summer home of the all-powerful shah. While the setting in 104 hectares of parkland is spectacular, many of the buildings themselves are not – or they raise serious doubts about the ruler's taste in design. Still, it is fascinating to walk in the footsteps of history in the White Palace where, for example, a young and paranoid Mohammed Reza held his midnight meetings with CIA agent Kermit Roosevelt to plan the 1953 coup (see the boxed text 'Mohammad Mossadegh & the CIA's First Coup', p34).

Today, most of the buildings house museums. Some of these are more interesting than others, but the ridiculous pricing policy and the fact you can only buy tickets at the main entrance mean you will need to decide first what you want to see. Walking up to the Green Palace can be hard work, so it might be worth using the free minibus that trundles round the grounds at regular intervals.

What is now called the **White Palace** (Palace of the Nation; admission IR30,000) was once the last shah's summer residence, with 54 rooms. The two bronze boots outside are all that remains of a giant statue of Reza Shah Pahlavi – he got the chop after the revolution. The palace is no Versailles – it's a modern building filled

VALIASR AVE & NORTHERN TEHRAN

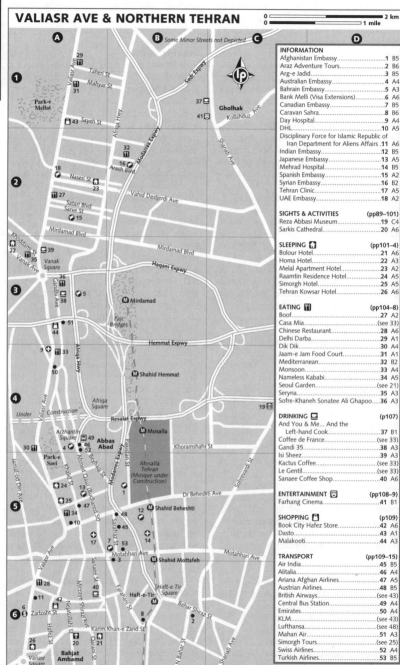

0 _____ 2 km
0 _____ 1 mile

Some Minor Streets not Depicted

INFORMATION
Afghanistan Embassy...............................**1** B5
Araz Adventure Tours..............................**2** B6
Arg-e Jadid..**3** B5
Australian Embassy..................................**4** A4
Bahrain Embassy......................................**5** A3
Bank Melli (Visa Extensions)...................**6** A6
Canadian Embassy....................................**7** B5
Caravan Sahra..**8** B6
Day Hospital..**9** A4
DHL..**10** A5
Disciplinary Force for Islamic Republic of
    Iran Department for Aliens Affairs .**11** A6
Indian Embassy......................................**12** B5
Japanese Embassy...................................**13** A5
Mehrad Hospital.....................................**14** B5
Spanish Embassy....................................**15** A2
Syrian Embassy.......................................**16** B2
Tehran Clinic..**17** A5
UAE Embassy..**18** A2

SIGHTS & ACTIVITIES   (pp89–101)
Reza Abbasi Museum..............................**19** C4
Sarkis Cathedral.....................................**20** A6

SLEEPING 🛏   (pp101–4)
Bolour Hotel...**21** A6
Homa Hotel..**22** A3
Melal Apartment Hotel..........................**23** A2
Raamtin Residence Hotel.......................**24** A5
Simorgh Hotel..**25** A5
Tehran Kowsar Hotel..............................**26** A6

EATING 🍴   (pp104–8)
Boof...**27** A2
Casa Mia...(see 33)
Chinese Restaurant................................**28** A6
Delhi Darba..**29** A1
Dik Dik...**30** A4
Jaam-e Jam Food Court..........................**31** A1
Mediterranean.......................................**32** B2
Monsoon..**33** A4
Nameless Kababi....................................**34** A5
Seoul Garden....................................(see 21)
Seryna..**35** A3
Sofre-Khaneh Sonatee Ali Ghapoo.....**36** A3

DRINKING 🍷   (p107)
And You & Me... And the
    Left-hand Cook.................................**37** B1
Coffee de France...............................(see 33)
Gandi 35..**38** A3
Isi Sheez..**39** A3
Kactus Coffee...................................(see 33)
Le Gentil...(see 33)
Sanaee Coffee Shop...............................**40** A6

ENTERTAINMENT 🎭   (pp108–9)
Farhang Cinema......................................**41** B1

SHOPPING 🛍   (p109)
Book City Hafez Store............................**42** A6
Dasto...**43** A1
Malakooti...**44** A3

TRANSPORT   (pp109–15)
Air India...**45** B5
Alitalia...**46** A4
Ariana Afghan Airlines...........................**47** A5
Austrian Airlines....................................**48** B5
British Airways..................................(see 43)
Central Bus Station................................**49** A4
Emirates...**50** A4
KLM..(see 43)
Lufthansa...(see 48)
Mahan Air..**51** A3
Simorgh Tours..................................(see 25)
Swiss Airlines...**52** A4
Turkish Airlines......................................**53** B5

TEHRAN

with a hodge-podge of extravagant furnishings and paintings, some of them European, some of them Iranian. The tiger pelt in his office, among other things, reveals the shah as a man of dubious taste.

Whatever you think of the furnishings, the White Palace was the height of luxury and opulence in its day. Look for the discreet air-conditioning units that fold away into the walls; or the shah's 20 cues in the billiards room – little has changed since the shah fled in 1979. In the upstairs Ceremony Hall is a 143-sq-metre carpet, woven with an incredible 130 to 150 knots per square inch, which is said to be one of the largest ever made in Iran. The nearby Dining Hall contains a similar carpet, and it is here that the shah, convinced the palace was bugged, dragged a table into the middle of the room and insisted both he and the American general he was entertaining climb on top of it before they spoke.

Don't miss the trippy stainless steel staircases at the back of the ground floor, which spiral down to the **Nation's Art Museum** (admission IR20,000) in the basement. Most will want to save their money here, but it's worth taking the stairs for a look.

Uphill from the White Palace, the more classical-looking **Green Palace** (Shahvand Palace; admission IR30,000) was used by the shah as a private reception hall for special guests. Its three rooms are covered in wall-to-wall mirror tiles and contain a collection of carpets, furniture and other oddments. This is another place where if money's tight you can look in from the outside and get a pretty good idea.

Other small, specialist museums in the complex include the **Abkar Miniature Museum** (admission IR25,000), displaying miniatures by the artist Clara Abkar; the **Bihzad Museum** (admission IR25,000) containing paintings by the artist Bihzad; the **Museum of Ethnological Research** (admission IR30,000) with a few waxworks and ethnological artefacts; and the **Mir Emad Calligraphy Museum** (admission IR25,000), with samples of Iranian calligraphy from different periods.

The **Museum of Fine Arts** (admission IR30,000) houses some charming Persian oil paintings dating back to the 18th century and some beautiful inlaid furniture. The **Military Museum** (admission IR30,000) is housed inside and around another palace that belonged

to the shah's nephew Shahram; just look for the helicopter.

The grounds are quite extensive, so allow plenty of time for wandering around. It's not a bad idea to combine a visit with lunch in nearby Darband.

If pushed for time and/or money, the White and Green Palaces are the most highly recommended. The bookshop at the entrance boasts a pretty good range of tourist-oriented and English-language books about Iran – if it's open.

Getting There & Away

To get to the museum complex, either walk or take a shared (or private) taxi the 1.5km from Tajrish Sq along Ja'fari St.

NIYAVARAN PALACE MUSEUM

About 6km east of the Sa'd Abad Museum complex is what used to be the last shah's second palace. It has been converted into the **Niyavaran Palace Museum** (☎ 228 2050; www .niavaranpalace.org; Shahid Bahonar Sq, Niyavaran Ave; individual tickets required; ☺ 9am-5pm, Sahebqerameh closed Sat), set in five hectares of landscaped gardens and with four separate museums to visit.

The first place you'll come across after entering is the **Ahmad Shahi Pavilion** (admission IR25,000), an attractive two-storey kiosk used to house assorted but not especially interesting gifts to the shah. Save your money, it's best viewed from the outside.

Straight on is the actual **Niyavaran Palace** (admission IR30,000), which is an austere, functional building built between 1958 and 1968 and stuffed full of elaborate furniture and carpets. The jarring styles, try-hard opulence and plethora of royal junk are almost a caricature of the classic royal palace. It gives the place an unreal quality, one that leaves you wondering whether the shah felt his position brought with it a need to be surrounded by the trappings of European palaces, or whether he just had poor taste. Whatever you decide, don't miss the magnificent Kerman carpet in the main hall, which shows all the Iranian kings right back to the Achaemenids, as well as some European sovereigns, including Napoleon Bonaparte.

Across the park and through a gate in the wall is the **Sahebqerameh** (King's Special Office; admission IR30,000), which is probably the pick of the bunch. It contains a very fine collection of paintings, but it is the insight into the shah's daily life that makes it fascinating. Some of the very attractive rooms include a private basement teahouse, private dental surgery and a bar resembling an overdone British pub. Keep an eye out for the shah's golden phone and gold-coloured pistols, and for photos displayed in the Ambassador's Waiting Room; the mixed bunch sees Mao Zedong share space with Pope Paul VI, while Hitler, Queen Elizabeth II, Richard Nixon and Kemal Ataturk stare out from the past nearby. The custodians will make you join a guided tour which might include some English.

Through another wall beside the Sahebqerameh is the **Jahan-Nama Museum & Gallery** (Queen's Private Museum; admission IR25,000). Two main rooms and a few offshoots are filled with the shah's eclectic collection of art, including Iranian archaeological artefacts alongside finds from sites in Mexico and Egypt and icons alongside contemporary Iranian paintings. They're beautifully displayed but it won't take you long to look around.

As at Sa'd Abad you buy tickets for all the museums at the main gate. If you can only manage one museum, the Sahebqerameh is the most interesting.

Getting There & Away

Take a shared taxi east of Tajrish Sq (IR1000), and ask to be dropped off at Shahid Bahonar Sq, about 100m downhill from the entrance to the museum.

DARAKEH & DARBAND

On a sunny day few things could be nicer than fleeing the traffic fumes of the town centre for the foothills of the Alborz Mountains and the **walking trails** of Darakeh and Darband.

Both the trails strike north, bypassing waterfalls and crossing streams. At Darband you need to walk for 45 minutes to get past the development, at Darakeh for 30 minutes. The trails are very crowded on Thursday afternoon and Friday.

Both trails are lined with cafés, kababis and drink stalls, some of which close midweek and in winter. A dish of *dizi* (soupy meat stew, see p130) a kebab or two, a cold drink or a huff and a puff on a qalyan at a café by the stream will soon help you forget the Tehran traffic. Among other tasty treats to sample on the way up are dates, apricots,

pickled walnuts, *lavashak* (sheets of pressed dried fruit), fresh mulberries and steamed lima beans.

Darband also has a **ski lift** (6am-5pm Sat-Thu, until 7.30pm summer), with tickets IR4000/8000 one way/return to the only station.

Getting There & Away

The starting point for getting to either trail is the northern side of Tajrish Sq. For Darband, either walk uphill north along Fana Khosrow St from Tajrish Sq (or take a shared taxi), or leave the grounds of Sa'd Abad from the rear, cross Meydan-e Darband and continue uphill to where you see the ski lift on the left. The walking trail veers off to the right. A visit to Darband can easily be combined with a visit to Sa'd Abad.

To get to Darakeh take a shared taxi from Tajrish Sq (IR2500). At the end of Darakeh St you'll be dropped in a square; the trail leads off from the northeastern corner. A private taxi costs about IR10,000.

PARK-E JAMSHIDIYEH

Meaning Stone Garden, **Park-e Jamshidiyeh** (7am-midnight) climbs steeply up the lower reaches of the Alborz Mountains and offers a clean and relatively quiet atmosphere in which to enjoy some wonderful ethnic food. It's the sort of place you could happily while away an entire afternoon sipping tea and watching the lights of this huge city slowly come to life. For details of the restaurants, see p105.

TOCHAL TELECABIN

Tehran's popular **Tochal Telecabin** (Velenjak Telecabin; ☎ 240 4001-5; www.tochalcomplex.com; Velenjak Ave; IR50,000 for full journey; 7-11am going up, coming back until 4pm, closed Sat & Sun) runs 7.5km up Mt Tochal (3957m), stopping at two stations along the way.

You can walk some or all of the way up the mountain (plenty of masochistic locals walk it on Friday), and use the telecabin when your legs have given up. From the top station there's still a good two-hour walk to the summit. Teahouses at the stations will help to ease your recovery, and there's a restaurant a short walk from the last stop. The views of Tehran are superb, though the mountains are astoundingly barren.

The telecabin is frightfully busy on Friday but can be virtually empty other days. It's possible to ski at the top, and you can rent skis at stations 7 and 8. You can buy one-way/return tickets to whichever station you want. The first stop is **Station 2** (IR10,000/20,000, seven minutes one way), then **Station 5** (IR20,000/28,000, 22 minutes) and it finishes at **Station 7** (IR30,000/50,000, 38 minutes). While the telecabin runs fairly limited hours, you can walk along the trails up the mountain any time you like.

Getting There & Away

From the northern side of Tajrish Sq, ask for a shared taxi (IR2000) to Tochal Telecabin. From where the taxi drops you, a short walk leads through a car park to a stop from where you can walk or catch a bus (IR1000) to the telecabin ticket office.

REZA ABBASI MUSEUM

Named after one of the great artists of the Safavid period, the **Reza Abbasi Museum** (☎ 863 001; www.rezaabbasimuseum.ir; 972 Shariati Ave; admission IR25,000; ☯ 9am-5pm Tue-Sat, until 6pm summer) is one of the best and most professionally run in Tehran. The museum is organised chronologically starting with the top-floor Pre-Islamic Gallery, where you'll find a stunning collection of **Achaemenid gold** bowls, drinking vessels, armlets and decorative pieces, often decorated with exquisite carvings of bulls and rams. Here, too, you'll find fine examples of **Lorestan bronzes** (see the boxed text 'The Lorestan Bronzes', p188).

The middle-floor Islamic Gallery exhibits a collection of ceramics, fabrics, and brassware, while the ground-floor Painting Gallery shows samples of fine calligraphy from ancient Qurans and illustrated manuscripts, particularly copies of Ferdosi's *Shahnamah* and Sa'di's *Golestan*.

To reach the museum you could try taking a shared taxi from the junction of Shariati and Enqelab Aves, but not all of them continue as far north as this so you might be better going by private taxi. Alternatively, take the Metro to Mosalla and then a shared taxi down the Resalat Expressway and ask to get out at Shariati Ave.

AZADI MONUMENT

Way out west at the end of Azadi Ave is the inverted Y-shaped **Azadi Monument** (Freedom Monument; Azadi Sq), built in 1971 to commemorate the 2500th anniversary of the Persian Empire. If you arrive at either of the airports or at the western bus station you can hardly help but notice it. The park surrounding the 45m-high monument was the scene of much protest during the 1979 revolution. The museum at the top has been due to reopen for several years – don't hold your breath. To get here, take a bus or shared taxi west along Enqelab Ave.

SLEEPING

While Tehran has a decent range of accommodation, like the city itself the vast majority of these buildings are pretty uninspired both on the inside and out. Still, apart from the 10 days either side of No Ruz, the Iranian New Year (about 21 March), you shouldn't have too much trouble finding something that will keep you happy.

If you haven't booked a room beforehand, try telephoning your chosen hotel when you arrive, take a taxi to check it out and have a couple of back-ups in mind in case it doesn't meet your approval. Facilities in Tehran hotels are fairly reliable; air-conditioners, fans, heaters and bathrooms usually work. But when looking at a room you also need to be aware of how much street noise there is. Tehran's traffic can be deafening, so if you're a light sleeper look for something away from a main road, or at least at the back of the building.

Fortunately, most hotels tend to be concentrated in a couple of areas, making comparisons relatively easy if you're in a taxi. See the specific sections for more details on locations.

Unless stated otherwise, all places listed here have their names in English near the door.

Budget

Almost all cheap places – and all of those reviewed here – are in the southern part of the city, within about a 1km radius of Imam Khomeini Sq and its Metro station. Most of them are nothing to write home about. The cheapest and most basic places are on or near Amir Kabir St. Unfortunately, this is a noisy, grubby area full of car workshops and spare-parts shops. There aren't many decent restaurants nearby and not a lot of women around – though it's not unsafe. Other concentrations of cheap hotels are in the Tehran Bazaar area, which is more atmospheric but just as noisy, and on or near Jomhuri-ye Eslami Ave.

Hotel Khayyam (Map pp90-1; ☎ 311 3757; www .hotelkhayyam.com; 3 Navidy Alley; s/tw US$18/25; 🅿 🛏 🖳) One of the best in this range and as quiet as it gets in the Amir Kabir area, the Khayyam has well-furnished rooms with bathroom and TV. The English-speaking management is happy to discount and will pick up guests at the airport if you book by email. Look for the yellow sign at the end of the alley.

Mashhad Hotel (Map pp90-1; ☎ 311 3062; www .mashhadhotel.homestead.com; 416 Amir Kabir St; dm/s/tw IR25,000/30,000/50,000; 🖳) The rooms and shared bathrooms here are as tiny as any, but the savvy management (and their excellent guest book) mean it's the place you're most likely to see other backpackers, especially Japanese. However, a couple of women readers have written to say that one of the staff was more tactile than necessary. Don't confuse this Mashhad with the more expensive Mashad Hotel, near the former US embassy.

Hotel Khazar Sea (Map pp90-1; ☎ 311 3860; Amir Kabir St, Ohadi Ln; s/tw IR25,000/40,000) Several readers have written favourably about this place, where the shared bathrooms are relatively clean and the manager speaks English. Look for the small sign in English at the second lane on the left as you head east of the intersection of Amir Kabir and Mellat Sts.

Hotel Sa'di (Map pp90-1; ☎ 322 7653; Lalehzar St; s/d IR60,000/100,000) The friendly, family-run Sa'di has also proved a hit with readers. The clean rooms have showers but toilets are shared, and there's a restaurant serving good Iranian food from 7am to 9pm.

Hotel Arman (Map pp90-1; ☎ 311 2323; fax 392 0600; Sa'di St, Ekbatan St; s/tw with breakfast US$15/25) Seemingly always busy, the clean rooms are big and have a bathroom and TV. It's fairly quiet and the management are happy to help. Look for it a few metres down a lane off the southern side of Ekbatan St. Nearby is the **Asia Hotel** (Map pp90-1; ☎ 311 8320; Mellat St; s/tw with breakfast US$15/25).

Hotel Tehran Gol (Map pp90-1; ☎ 311 3477; Amir Kabir St; s/tw IR40,000/60,000) A simple but more spacious place than some of its neighbours, but still noisy. Bathrooms are shared and there's a restaurant and a pleasant lounge.

Hafez Hotel (Map pp90-1; ☎ 670 9063; fax 670 1367; Ferdosi St, Bank Melli Alley; s/d US$14/22) In a lane beside the Bank Melli, the modern rooms here

THE AUTHOR'S CHOICE
Hotel Naderi (Map pp90-1; ☎ 670 1872; Jomhuri-ye Eslami Ave; s/d US$10/20; 🛏) The Naderi is probably the most atmospheric hotel in Tehran, partly because it's right on top of the bohemian Cafe Naderi (p107), but also because it's like stepping back about 50 years. Everything from the switchboard to the radio in the downstairs 'salon' is a modern antique. The wide staircase leads to two floors of huge old high-ceilinged rooms, complete with fridge, prehistoric bakelite phones, large bathrooms and 'period' '50s furnishings. Those at the back (room numbers 107–112 or 207–212) overlook a garden and are definitely worth asking for if you're a light sleeper. Rooms 104 and 204 have balconies, but like all the front rooms are frightfully noisy. The Armenian management is helpful, without being effusive, and Mohammad at reception is both friendly and an expert on the area.

are quiet, clean and have TV, fridge, fan and pokey bathroom. The hotel has a small restaurant, too. Fair value.

Hotel Markazi (Guest House Central; Map pp90-1; ☎ /fax 391 4798; Lalehzar St; per person IR35,000) is friendly enough and the rooms with internal bathrooms are very reasonably priced.

Hotel Shams (Map pp90-1; ☎ 390 0446; Bazar-e Marvi; s/tw IR30,000/40,000) Right in the bazaar, this is about as cheap and basic as it gets. Staff are friendly and will direct you to the hammam, deeper into the bazaar, for a wash; there are no showers at the Shams.

Misaq Hotel (Map pp90-1; ☎ 392 8164; tw IR40,000) This cheap, friendly and rudimentary hotel is also in the bazaar area.

On Ferdosi St north of Imam Khomeini Sq there are two more cheapies: the male-dominated **Farvardin Guest House** (Map pp90-1; ☎ 391 2777; 654 Imam Khomeini Sq, First Ferdosi St; s/tw IR55,000/70,000), with shared bathrooms and the grubbiest rugs in Iran; and **Hotel Gilanow** (Map pp90-1; ☎ 311 8264; Ferdosi St; s/tw IR35,000/45,000), opposite Bank Saderat, where the rooms have bathrooms.

Mid-Range

Most of the mid-range hotels are in central and northern Tehran, meaning you'll find them on the top half of the Central &

Southern Tehran map (pp90–1), and on the Valiasr Ave & Northern Tehran map (p98). It also means you'll have to walk further or take a taxi to most of the museums in the south, but will be closer to decent restaurants, parks and cafés when you get back afterwards. Prices in this range start at about US$25 for a twin or double room. All rooms have bathrooms, though some will have squat toilets, and most will have a fridge, TV and air-con. There is usually someone who speaks English at reception and a restaurant that opens for lunch and dinner.

Atlas Hotel (Map pp90–1; ☎ 890 6058; www.atlas -hotel.com; 206 Taleqani St; s/d US$35/52; 🗙) The Atlas is something of a sanctuary in the heart of Tehran, especially if you choose to stay in the more modern building at the back. The rooms are quiet, tastefully decorated, have huge bathrooms and some overlook a colourful courtyard that is home to plenty of frolicking felines. Service is friendly and efficient (they're happy to negotiate) and the Indian/Pakistani restaurant is good value. Recommended.

Omid Hotel (Map pp90–1; ☎ 641 4564; www.omid -hotel.com; 20 East Nosrat St; s/d with breakfast US$38/58; 🗙) We've had several emails praising the Omid's excellent service and large, modern rooms, which come with a basic kitchen, fridge, TV and video. It's not far from lovely Park-e Laleh; booking ahead is advisable.

Ferdosi Grand Hotel (Map pp90–1; ☎ 671 9991; info@ferdosigrand.com; Ferdosi St, 24 Sabt St; s/d US$60/ 75; 🗙) Just a short stroll to the museums and Golestan Palace, the comfortable rooms here have fridge and TV but it's the location that is the main draw. The restaurant here is not bad.

New Naderi Hotel (Map pp90–1; ☎ 670 9530; new_naderihotel@hotmail.com; Jomhuri-ye Eslami Ave, 53 Gohar Shad Alley; s/d US$20/30; P 🗙) Far enough off Jomhuri-ye Eslami to be away from the noise, the rooms in this cavernous place are good value, as is the restaurant.

Parasto Hotel (Map pp90–1; ☎ 670 2442; fax 672 0839; Jomhuri-ye Eslami Ave, Mohammad Buyk Alley; s/d with breakfast US$18/25; P 🗙) At the bottom end of the mid-priced range, this hotel's clean and comfortable rooms with TV and fridge are reasonable value. The restaurant downstairs isn't bad and is open during Ramazan.

Iranshahr Hotel (Map pp90–1; ☎ 883 4976; www .hotel_iranshahr.com; Iranshahr Ave; s/d with breakfast US$35/52; P 🗙) Crystal-clean, comfortable

rooms and really welcoming service make this a good option. Suites with kitchens are also available for US$52/64. There's a handy shop in the lobby.

Raamtin Residence Hotel (Map p98; ☎ 872 2786; raamtinhotel@yahoo.com; 1081 Valiasr Ave; d/studio/apt US$55/65/80 plus 19% tax; 🗙 💻) Like the second-cheapest bottle on the wine menu, this place is solid, won't disappoint anyone but won't really inspire rave reviews. The rooms and apartments are big, management are eager and there is a gym and sauna, so it's not bad value. The new Bistango Restaurant is excellent, but pricey.

Bolour Hotel (Map p98; ☎ 882 3080; www .bolourhotel .com; 191 Qarani St; s/d US$30/42; 🗙) Near Sarkis Cathedral, the small, mirrored foyer leads to big rooms with huge bathrooms, but it's best to ask for one away from the main road.

Tehran Apartment Hotel (Map pp90–1; ☎ 880 4180; info@tehranapartmenthotel.com; 513 Hafez St; 1-/2-bedroom apt US$92/142; 🗙 💻) South of Enqelab Ave, the hotel's teahouse under the foyer is quite atmospheric (and does garlic bread!), but the uninspired self-catering apartments aren't worth the asking price. They did, however, come down to a more reasonable US$60-a-single pretty quickly.

There are many more mid-range options. Some worth considering include the good-value **Sefir Hotel** (Map pp90–1; ☎ 830 0873; www.hotelsafir.com; Mofatteh Ave, 10 Ardalan St; s/tw with breakfast US$35/45; 🗙), behind the old US embassy; **Azadi Hotel** (Map pp90–1; ☎ 831 6670-2; www.azadihotel.net; Somayyeh St; r US$45), where rooms at the back are best; **Parsa Hotel** (Map pp90–1; ☎ 646 9211-7; fax 646 5482; Taleqani Ave; s/d with breakfast US$50/60; 🗙), near the junction with Valiasr Ave; **Tehran Kowsar Hotel** (Map p98; ☎ 890 8121; fax 889 1615; Valiasr Sq, 8 Malaee Alley; s/d US$59/76; P 🗙 💻), with its Chinese restaurant and stuffed lioness on the porch; **Shiraz Hotel** (Map pp90–1; ☎ 392 5342; shiraz-hotel@kovash.net; Sa'di St; s/d with breakfast US$30/45; 🗙); and **Mashad Hotel** (Map pp90–1; ☎ 882 5145; mashad_hotel@hotmail.com; Taleqani Ave, 190 Mofatteh St; s/d US$40/60; 🗙), right opposite the old US embassy, where the quality of the plumbing (or lack thereof) has been mentioned in dispatches. Don't confuse this with the Mashhad Hotel in Amir Kabir St.

Top End

Tehran has a few five-star hotels, most of them built in the '70s by big chains and renamed after the revolution. There's a certain retro-cool to those older hotels, while a couple of new places are more like what you'd find in the West. Following is a selection of places that are comparatively central and reasonable value.

Simorgh Hotel (Map p98; ☎ 871 9911; 1069 Valiasr Ave; s/d with breakfast US$99/109; ☒ 🖵 ☎) The newest and probably the savviest pure hotel in Tehran, where rates for the stylish rooms include use of the gym, Jacuzzi and pool (on a sex-based rotation). In-room Internet connection costs US$15 a day. The adjoining travel agency, **Simorgh Tours** (www.simorghtours.com), offers well-organised but pricey two-day ski tours.

Laleh International Hotel (Map pp90-1; ☎ 896 5021; www.lalehhotel.com; Dr Hossein Fatemi Ave; s/d/ste US$110/130/220 plus 16.2% tax; 🅿 ☒ 🖵) At the northeastern corner of Bagh-e Laleh, this place was once the InterContinental and still has some of Tehran's best rooms, everything you'd expect in a five-star establishment, plus a great location and amazing views of the city. The ground floor boasts a good bookshop and several restaurants, but the pool, like the bar, is a dry argument.

Melal Apartment Hotel (Map p98; ☎ 879 0543; www.melal.com; 68 Naseri St, Valiasr Ave; apt for 2 people US$240 plus 17% tax; 🅿 ☒ 🖵 ☎) Undoubtedly the best accommodation in Tehran, these apartments just breathe luxury. For your bundles of cash (just imagine the rials!) you get beautiful rooms, a terrace swimming pool, Jacuzzi, gym, sauna, a café, two classy restaurants and a chauffer to bring you to and from the airport.

Two other old stand-bys are the **Homa Hotel** (Map p98; ☎ 877 3021; www.homahotel.com; 51 Khoddami St; d/ste US$120/160; 🅿 ☒ 🖵), nee Sheraton, which is almost worth it for the *Saturday Night Fever* flashbacks; and the **Azadi Grand Hotel** (Map p83; ☎ 207 3021; www.azadigrandhotel.com; Evin Crossing, Chamran Expressway; s/d US$110/132 plus 17% tax), which was the Hyatt in a previous incarnation and is a looooong way from anywhere except the International Trade Fair Ground.

EATING

It's not Paris or Sydney, but Tehran has a fast-growing selection of restaurants and an impressive variety of cuisines that puts it several leagues ahead of the rest of Iran. The variety makes a welcome change, but there

are also plenty of atmospheric traditional establishments where you'll be able to try all that Iranian cuisine has to offer (see the Food & Drink chapter, p74). Tehrani eateries are expensive by Iranian standards, but even something as exotic as a Malay yellow curry (see Monsoon, p106) will probably cost you less than you'd pay for a couple of beers back home. For non-Iranian food you'll almost certainly have to go to northern Tehran.

Restaurants are open for lunch and dinner daily unless otherwise stated. Kababis are usually open all day. Note that most of the restaurants listed as Iranian & Regional are also excellent places to stop for tea, qalyan and sweets.

Fast Food & Kababis

The kababi might be under pressure from such foreign influences as the burger joint and pizzeria, but you still won't have to look too hard to find one in Tehran. The area around Imam Khomeini Sq is particularly well stocked. This area and the Tehran Bazaar boast plenty of felafel joints, and wherever you go you'll find cheap sandwich places.

Ferdosi Sonnati (Map pp90-1; ☎ 670 0595; Ferdosi St; meals IR23,000) A popular place just north of Imam Khomeini Sq, the full chicken kebab meal, including salad, rice, drinks and bread is probably the favourite. Great lunch spot.

Tak Khal (Map pp90-1; Sa'di St; meals IR15,000) No frills here, but the *khoresht* (a meaty stew with vegetables and rice; IR8000) is good and the fresh-from-the-oven bread superb. Good value.

Dar-B-Dar Pizza (Map p83; ☎ 270 8185; Tajrish Sq, 21 Ja'fari St; large pizzas IR75,000) Heading north from Tajrish Sq towards Darband you'll find a branch of this stylish chain-pizzeria which does easily the best (although probably the priciest) pizzas in Iran, and will deliver.

Boof (Map p98; ☎ 225 3262; Valiasr Ave; meals IR20,000) This is the closest Iran comes to a McDonald's-like chain restaurant. The burgers are huge and there are a few Iranian alternatives.

Tomato (Map pp90-1; ☎ 671 1579; Jomhuri-ye Eslami Ave; pizzas IR20,000; ⏰ 9am-11pm) A trendy, café-like place that serves probably the best pizzas in southern Tehran, good sandwiches and decent coffee.

Other small places worth looking for include the **nameless kababi** (Map p98; Valiasr Ave;

THE AUTHOR'S CHOICE

Khayyam Traditional Restaurant (Map pp90–1; ☎ 580 0760; Khayyam St; meals IR60,000; 🕑 lunch & dinner) About 200m south of the Khayyam Metro station and opposite the Imamzadeh Seyyed Nasreddin Mosque (look for the dome), this beautifully decorated restaurant is an oasis amid the chaos of the bazaar and southern Tehran. Originally part of the mosque, the 300-year-old building was separated when Khayyam St intervened. It was restored in 2002. The food is not cheap (the special *dizi* is IR25,000), but it is worth every rial. The chef's special kebab (IR50,000) will appeal to carnivores, while the various *bademjun* (eggplant) dishes should keep vegetarians happy. In fact, you can try just about any Persian dish you fancy here, or just kick back with tea, qalyan and sweets (IR25,000) and listen to the music men in the evening.

dizi IR8000), which does excellent *dizi* for a mostly male bunch of regulars; **Dik Dik** (Map p98; ☎ 877 7811; Valiasr Ave; 🕑 lunch & dinner), serving good barbecued chicken; and **Pizza Helia** (Map p83; ☎ 229 9060; Bahonar Ave), which is handy to the Niyavaran Palace.

For breakfast, you'll notice some low-key looking places selling *kalleh pache* (sheep innards). One such **kalleh pazi** (Map pp90–1; Mostafa Khomeini St) worth checking out is conveniently near to Amir Kabir St at Baharestan Sq, opposite the old Majlis building.

Restaurants

Many Iranian restaurants are hidden away underground, so be on the lookout for anonymous-looking stairwells.

IRANIAN & REGIONAL RESTAURANTS

Iranian Traditional Restaurant (Agha Bozorg; Map pp90–1; ☎ 890 0522; 28 Keshavarz Blvd; meals IR30,000; 🕑 noon–midnight) This is Iranian social interaction in microcosm. Full of young Iranians flirting, smoking and eating (in that order) under the vaulted and tiled ceilings, it successfully combines tradition with modern Tehran – the nightly music programme consists of pop and jazz as often as traditional Iranian music, and there's a very untraditional mixed bathroom. The *dizi* (IR15,000) here is as good as you'll find in

Tehran. There is no sign in English but it's tucked away down an ornate staircase, just east of the Canon/Konica shop.

Azari Traditional Restaurant (Azari Coffeehouse; Map p83; ☎ 537 3665; Rah-Ahan Sq, Valiasr Ave; meals IR50,000) About 250m north of Rah-Ahan Sq, this restored 'coffeehouse' is as 'old Tehran' as it gets. Set up in the traditional *andarouni* (private part of a home) and *birouni* (outer part) style, it actually serves as something of a local community centre so is always busy. Flamboyant waiting staff serve endless *chay* and date biscuits while traditional or folk music is played each evening; the food, too, is topnotch. If you're lucky and have someone to translate, the tiny white-bearded dervish man might tell your fortune. It's probably best with a group of people; if you do get one together, call ahead.

Sofre Khane Sonnati Sangalag (Map pp90–1; ☎ 671 8342; Park-e Shahr; meals IR45,000; 🕑 11am–9pm) If you're visiting the museums or Golestan Palace this is a good place to stop for lunch (or a cup of tea). *Dizi* is the favourite fare here and while the food is perhaps a little overpriced, the attractive, airy surrounds and lack of cars are worth the extra. Musicians sometimes play between noon and 3pm.

Sofre-Khaneh Sonatee Ali Ghapoo (Map p98; ☎ 877 7803; Gandhi Ave; meals IR65,000) Complete with waiters in traditional dress, this big, noisy underground place is popular with Tehranis and tour groups alike. The food is pretty good but prices get even higher after the traditional band starts playing at 9pm.

Restaurant Shater Abas (Map pp90–1; ☎ 311 5077; Sa'di St; meals IR30,000; 🕑 lunch & dinner Sat–Thu) At the northern end of the Sa'di St flyover, this no-frills place is handy to the cheap accommodation on Amir Kabir St and is deservedly popular for its good kebabs, *bademjun* (eggplant served in various styles) and a couple of fish dishes.

Armenian Club (Map pp90–1; ☎ 670 0521-2; 68 Khark St, cnr France Ave; meals IR50,000; 🕑 noon–3pm & 8pm–midnight Sat–Thu, noon–3pm Fri) The Armenian Club is almost a one-off in Tehran. Because it's a Christian establishment, women can legally eat or just hang out *sans* hejab! The most elegantly furnished old dining room has a certain grandmotherly feel to it, but you'd be lucky if your Nan could serve up barbecued sturgeon (IR36,000) or the better-than-average chicken schnitzel (IR33,000).

The club doesn't advertise its existence – look for a yellow awning and a tiny buzzer – but welcomes guests. Note that Muslims (at the government's direction) cannot enter.

Literally on the side of a mountain, **Park-e Jamshidiyeh** (Stone Park; Map p83; Feizieh Ave, Niyavaran St, Tajrish; ☼ all restaurants about 9am–midnight) is home to four restaurants serving the food of some of Iran's ethnic minorities. It's a charming setting, with the landscaped garden shaded by tall trees giving way to the rocky and barren slopes of the Alborz Mountains and spectacular views of the city, which make it worth a visit even though the food is relatively expensive. Starting from the bottom of the hill, the first restaurant is **Khaneh Azarbaijan** (☎ 229 7540; meals IR40,000). Climbing further you'll come to **Kurdish House** (☎ 280 1309; meals IR50,000), which does a good Kurdish *chelo khoresht* (IR35,000), plus a few European dishes. Take the stairs to the left for **Turkmen Restaurant** (☎ 281 0106; meals IR35,000), which has the best and cheapest food; the garlic-and-eggplant *mirza ghasemi* (IR15,000) is special, as is the *broke* (minced meat with potatoes and vegetables; IR20,000) – the friendly management will happily explain the dishes to you. If you have thighs of steel, **Zagros House** (☎ 281 0107; meals IR50,000) is that one right up there; you'll feel like you're climbing the Zagros Mountains themselves! But the views from the balcony are 'totally awesome, man', as one expat Iranian told us, even if the tea is better than the food.

On balmy evenings in summer Tehranis head for **Darband** and **Darakeh** (both Map p83), where the walking trails are lined with cafés and restaurants serving everything from full kebab meals to generous helpings of *dizi, ash* (yogurt and barley soup) or just snacks.

OTHER CUISINES

It's quite possible that by the time you get to Tehran you'll be desperate for something a little more exotic than kebab – even a little spicy! Fortunately, this is the town to get it. You'll have to pay for the privilege, of course, but you'd probably pay much more for far less at home.

Monsoon (Map p98; ☎ 879 1982; Gandhi Shopping Centre, Gandhi Ave; meals IR80,000; ☼ closed Fri) With influences from across Asia – from sushi to a divine yellow curry (IR50,000) – classy service and an intimate setting, this is one of Tehran's best restaurants. The menu changes regularly. In the same complex, the **Casa Mia** (Map p98; ☎ 879 1959; meals IR45,000-70,000) does pretty good Italian fare.

Delhi Darba (Map p98; ☎ 204 0874; Valiasr Ave; meals IR45,000) A good Indian option with a big menu, though pandering just a little too much to the Iranian dislike of spice.

Seryna (Map p98; ☎ 877 3735; Vanak Sq, 30 Khoddami St [Bijan St]; meals IR75,000; ☼ 6.30-11pm Sat-Thu) The teppanyaki and sushi are considered the best Japanese cuisine in Tehran, and the grill and surrounding tatami seating afford a fairly authentic atmosphere.

Mediterranean (Map p98; ☎ 204 1434; Afriqa Hwy, 29 Saba Blvd; meals IR60,000) Excellent Lebanese food served in classy surroundings, with cheaper lunches available.

Chinese Restaurant (Map p98; ☎ 890 0714; Valiasr Ave, 3 Abdo St; meals IR55,000) Offers Western-style Chinese dishes and a few surprises done reasonably well.

Jaam-e Jam Food Court (Map p98; Jaam-e Jam Shopping Centre, cnr Valiasr Ave & Taheri St) It doesn't sound that exciting, but this, Iran's first food court, was the hottest place in town when we were there. This is as close to a Western-style pick-up bar as you'll find in Tehran, and you'll see plenty of make-up and designer clothing on the young rich here. As for the food, it's not bad and the choice is unbeatable. Among others, you'll find Western-style Chinese food at **Orient Express**; gyro (IR25,000) and Greek salad at **Mediterranean**; try **Paris** for veal filet in a crepe (IR25,000); **Lester** pays homage to British food with the immensely popular binder steak (IR42,000), a plate of meat somehow infused with cheese; **BBQ** is more steak or grilled fish; and **Giro Italy** has pastas (IR40,000) or jambalaya. There's also an expensive coffee shop in the food court.

HOTEL RESTAURANTS

Two of Tehran's better Indian restaurants are located in hotels.

Taj Mahal (Map p83; ☎ 803 5444; Vanak Sq, Mollasadra Ave, 29 Sheikh Bahaei St; meals IR55,000) In the hotel of the same name, this is widely regarded as the best Indian food in Iran. The curries here are mouth-watering and there is a good range of vegetarian options. Pity about the location.

Tandoor Restaurant (Map pp90-1; ☎ 830 0873; meals IR60,000) Located under the Sefir Hotel, the service here is not so good but the curries, especially the chicken Patiala (IR27,000), aren't bad. There are a few vegetarian dishes for about IR25,000 each.

Seoul Garden (Map p98; ☎ 882 3080; meals IR30,000) On the 1st floor of the Bolour Hotel, the extensive menu is as much Chinese as Korean but is still good value.

Also good is the Iranian restaurant in the **Omid Hotel** (Map pp90-1; ☎ 641 4564; meals IR35,000).

Drinking

Many of the best places to drink tea are also good places to eat; these are reviewed under Iranian & Regional Restaurants (p105). Similarly, the teahouses listed in this section also serve food. On a sunny day the walking trails at Darband and Darakeh are popular tea-drinking locales. Tehran's café and coffee-shop scene is also on the up, with many places opening in the northern suburbs in recent times.

Ghaem Teahouse (Map p83; ☎ 0912 320 0113; Tajrish Sq; ☽ noon-midnight) Behind a curtain and up an unmarked stairwell on the southeastern corner of Tajrish Sq, this is a great place from which to people-watch over tea, qalyan and dates (IR15,000).

Sofreh Khane Ayyaran (Map pp90-1; ☎ 676 0376; ☽ noon-midnight) A traditional-style *chaykhuneh* (teahouse), this subterranean place is perfect for escaping the fumes of Ferdosi Sq.

Cafe Naderi (Map pp90-1; ☎ 670 1872) Underneath the Hotel Naderi, this café has long been a favourite of intellectuals and artists. One traveller described the Naderi as managing to perfectly create a bustling yet disinterested atmosphere, well suited to reading alone, people-watching and lingering over coffee. The décor is circa 1940s Paris. Apart from Turkish, instant, mocca or iced coffee, you can enjoy pastries. Don't expect the grumpy-grandad waiters to offer you any change.

And You & Me...And the Left-hand Cook (Map p98; Chapdast; ☎ 261 6830; Shariati Ave, 38 Khaghani St; coffee & pie IR13,000; ☽ 10am-midnight) This a tiny café under a large yellow sign in Farsi, and the coffee is excellent. It's run by right-handed former potter Parham Nadimi, whose signature Parham Coffee mixes three kinds of espresso with milk and is great with the Ardeshir Apple Pie. Great after a movie at the Farhang Cinema around the corner.

Gandhi Ave is turning into something of a trendy strip, especially for coffee shops. The **Ghandi Shopping Centre** (Map p98; cnr Gandhi Ave & 4th St) is home to several cool little cafés that are about as close to the atmosphere of a small pub as you'll find. Peopled largely by young and fairly liberal Tehranis, they're a good place to hang out for an evening. Look for **Kactus Coffee**, **Coffee de France** and **Le Gentil**. 'French' (black) coffee will cost about IR10,000 and a cappuccino about IR12,000. Up the road, **Gandi 35** (Map p98; ☽ 11am-11pm Sat-Thu, 5-11pm Fri) is also pretty trendy, and does toasted sandwiches and lasagne (IR20,000).

Other places to find good coffee include **Isi Sheez** (Map p98; ☎ 877 5180; Valiasr Ave; ☽ 10am-11.30pm) in a lane not far north of Vanak Sq; and the tiny **Sanaee Coffee Shop** (Map p98; Sanaee St, St 13) around the corner from Ikea, which makes and sells all manner of imported bean, and some of the richest and best chocolate milkshakes on earth (yes, big call; you be the judge).

Self-Catering

No matter where you are, fresh fruit and vegetables and various types of flat bread won't be far away (see p74 for the different types of bread). Similarly, small grocery stores stocking food such as tinned fish, Iranian fetta cheese, flavoured and unflavoured yogurt, fruit juices, cold meat, pasta, rice and a few other staples are common in most parts of the city, though less so around Amir Kabir St.

For a good range of local and imported foods at reasonable prices, head for Manucheri St and the nearby stretch of Jomhuri-ye Eslami Ave, just east of Ferdosi St. On Manucheri St, the **Ghadiri Store** (Map pp90-1; ☎ 311 5949; ☽ 9.30am-9pm Sat-Thu) is one of a few shops catering for the ever-expanding Iranian palate, with stacks of imported goods. It will appeal to those wanting a bit more fire in their bellies, with sauces including such exotic pleasures as soy, chilli, HP and, believe it or not, Nando's lime and coriander. Other delights include sesame and olive oils, coconut milk, Lavazza coffee, Nutella, cereals including Kellogg's Corn Flakes and Fruit'n'Fibre, even diabetic jams. Down on Jomhuri-ye Eslami are several shops selling fresh fish plus a few high-turnover butcheries and greengrocers.

In northern Tehran you'll find more extravagant options; the store full of luxury foods underneath the **Jaam-e Jam Food Court** (Map p98; Valiasr Ave) is guaranteed to get the mouth watering. Coffee lovers should go to the tiny **Sanaee Coffee Shop** (Map p98; Sanaee St, St 13) for an unbelievable range of imported coffee.

ENTERTAINMENT

Although Iran has loosened up considerably since 1997, no-one's singing 'Tehran, Tehran ...a city that never sleeps' just yet. There's not a whole lot to do at night. All those nightclubs and discos lovingly described in guidebooks published before the revolution have long-since gone, and are unlikely to reappear anytime soon.

The one time when there is quite a lot of organised entertainment is over the 10 Days of Dawn (1 to 11 February), when you will be able to attend plays, films and concerts of traditional Iranian music as well as music from around the world (p349).

Otherwise, there is a growing number of billiards halls opening around town. They're usually underground and signed in copious neon, and you'll seldom see women playing (or even in the premises).

Cinemas

If you want to see an action flick, Iranian-style, head for one of the cinemas along southern Lalehzar St or eastern Jomhuri-ye Eslami Ave, in southern Tehran. Every day, films are shown about every two hours between 10am and 8pm. A ticket costs about IR5000, and the films are in Farsi. Given the recent international success of Iranian films you might get lucky and catch one of them showing, though don't count on it. For more on films, see p66.

If you fancy a bit of Hollywood, the **Farhang Cinema** (Map p98; ☎ 200 2088; www.fcf-ir.com; Shariati Ave, Gholhak; tickets IR10,000) shows a few carefully chosen foreign films, some in English. Find out what's on where at the first-rate cultural website www.tehranavenue.com.

Music

Trying to find organised public performances of Iranian music – or any music – is difficult in Tehran. There is still much debate in Iran about the religious eligibility of such performances, so anyone trying to promote one is treading a particularly fine line. As a result, most concerts are traditional: a solo male performer plucking at a *tar* (a traditional stringed instrument), with or without singing, for example.

Your best chance of seeing music will be in a traditional restaurant or teahouse (see p105 for possibilities). Otherwise, wander on to the trusty www.tehranavenue.com to see what's on where.

Nightclubs

Dream on.

Theatre

Foreign-language students at the universities occasionally perform plays by writers such as Shakespeare in the original script and in period dress. If you're interested you will have to ask one of the English-language students who are bound to approach you if you spend much time in Tehran, particularly around **Tehran University** (Map pp90-1; Enqelab Ave).

Other theatre productions (in Farsi) are staged at the huge, circular **Tezatre Shahr** (City Theatre; Map pp90-1; ☎ 646 0595; cnr Valiasr & Enqelab Aves). The easiest way to find out what's on is simply to visit and ask, otherwise www.tehranavenue.com should have details and maybe even a review. Performances are normally nightly at 7pm.

Sports

Iran's favourite sport is football (soccer), which is played at 10 major stadiums around the city. The most important games fill the 100,000-capacity Azadi Sports Stadium Complex, way out in the western suburbs. However, finding out when they're on is no easy feat; matches are usually played on Thursdays and Fridays but your best bet is to ask one of the men who work in your hotel. If Esteqlal (blue shirts) or Persepolis (red shirts) are playing, tickets will be in short supply.

At the **Azadi Sports Stadium Complex** (Map p83; ☎ 9161; Karaj Hwy) you might be able to see some wrestling, or motor racing with six categories of cars – all of them Paykans with different-sized engines. Or you could save your time and money and just sit in the middle of any main square in Tehran.

You can watch a variety of sports at the **Haft-e-Tir Sports Stadium** (Map pp90-1; ☎ 673 365;

Young women, Tehran (p80)

Qajar-era tiles, Golestan Palace, Tehran (p92)

Azadi Monument, Tehran (p101)

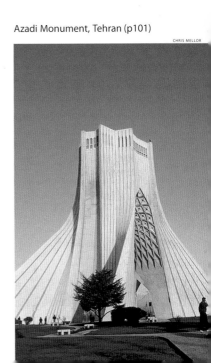

Traditional restaurant, Tehran (p104)

SIMON RICH

Qareh Kalisa (p125)

PATRICK BEN LUKE SYDER

Zagros Mountains (p229)

Allah-Allah tower, Ardabil
(p147)

PA

CHRIS MELLOR

Elgoli (Shahgoli) Park, Tabriz (p137)

Fayyazbakhsh St) on the northern side of Park-e Shahr; the **Chamran Sports Centre** (Map p83; ☎ 221 3034-5; Shariati Ave); and the **Shahid Shirudi Sports Centre** (Map pp90-1; ☎ 882 2113-5; Mofatteh St), where many sports clubs have their headquarters.

SHOPPING

Souvenir shopping is easier and more fun in Esfahan or Shiraz. But if you're out of time or options, you'll definitely be able to find what you're looking for in Tehran. The best approach is to give yourself at least half a day and head straight for the bazaar (p89), where if you can't find what you're looking for, then a carpet salesman will almost certainly find it for you – after you've stopped for tea, of course.

Otherwise, there are a few souvenir shops around town that offer a good choice. Ferdosi St around Ferdosi Sq is a good place to start looking for carpets, miniatures, qalyans, lacquerware etc; check out the place with the snappy title of the **Fair & Shop for Products of Self-Sufficiency Plan of Imam Khomeini's Relief Committee** (Map pp90-1; Ferdosi St), just south of the square. Prices at **Dasto** (Map p98; cnr Valiasr Ave & Sayeh St) will be higher, but the range is huge and quality high. Also worth a trawl are Taleqani St (especially opposite the US Den of Espionage) and Nejatollahi St, or perhaps the shops in the southwestern corner of Park-e Laleh. Prices are generally fixed but tend to fall fast if you show any bargaining form.

Locals claim that Valiasr Ave is the world's longest thoroughfare and it's one of Tehran's major shopping districts. Ladies, this is also a good place to start looking for a manteau. Stores around Valiasr Sq and Vanak Sq both sell a decent selection, both in the long, conservative style and more trendy, shorter modes. You can expect to pay about IR80,000 for a standard manteau, up to IR1,000,000 for something 'sexier' in the boutiques of Afriqa Hwy, near Vanak Sq. If you really want to lash out, try **Malakooti** (Map p98; Gandhi Ave) for the latest styles. Further south, both sides of Dr Labafinezhad St, just west of Valiasr Ave, are lined with women's clothing stores.

While you probably don't think of Iran as a shopping destination for trendy gear, if you're prepared to buy unusual brands you could kit yourself out in the latest European trends for a pittance. Shoes, in particular, are stylish and dirt cheap. Women should head for the boutiques along Mozaffari St (Map pp90-1) in southern Tehran, while men can see the head-spinning choice on Enqelab Ave (Map pp90-1), east of Ferdosi Sq.

GETTING THERE & AWAY

Tehran is the hub of almost all bus, train and air services. Every town and city of any size is directly linked to Tehran; always by bus, usually by air and sometimes by train. Getting a ticket out of Tehran can be difficult; so as soon as you know when you're leaving, book your ticket.

Air

Every day there are flights between Tehran and every major city you are likely to want to visit on one of the two main domestic airlines – Iran Air and Iran Aseman. Less often there are flights to and from Tehran on the smaller airlines, which include Mahan Air, Saha Air, Caspian Air and Kish Airlines.

At the time of writing there was much talk about the long-awaited Imam Khomeini International Airport (IKIA) finally opening for business (see the boxed text 'Imam Khomeini International Airport', p112). However, as IKIA remained no more than speculation, what you read here refers to the old airport at Mehrabad.

For more information, ask a travel agent (many of those in Tehran speak English). Alternatively, you could try contacting the airline offices listed here, or ringing the airport information number (☎ 199).

AIRLINE OFFICES

Many airline offices are along, or near, Nejatollahi St. Staff usually speak good English. Airline offices are generally open from about 9am to 4pm, Saturday to Thursday.

The following international airlines are represented in Tehran:
Aeroflot (Map pp90-1; ☎ 880 8480; 23 Nejatollahi St)
Air France (Map pp90-1; ☎ 670 4111; 882 Enqelab Ave) Near Ferdosi Sq.
Air India (Map p98; ☎ 873 9762; Sarafraz St)
Alitalia (Map p98; ☎ 871 1512; Arzhantin Sq)
Ariana Afghan Airlines (Map p98; ☎ 855 0156-60; 29 Khalid St)
Austrian Airlines (Map p98; ☎ 875 8984; Dr Beheshti Ave, 2 Sarafraz St)
British Airways (Map p98; ☎ 204 4552; Valiasr Ave, Sayeh St, Sayeh Tower, 10th fl)

Emirates (Map p98; ☎ 879 6786; 1211 Valiasr Ave)
Gulf Air (Map pp90-1; ☎ 225 3284-7; Nejatollahi St)
Iran Air (Map pp90-1; ☎ 880 8472; Nejatollahi St) Sells only international tickets; use a travel agent for domestic flights.
KLM (Map p98; ☎ 204 4757; www.klm.com; Valiasr Ave, Sayeh St, Sayeh Tower, 12th fl)
Kuwait Airways (Map pp90-1; ☎ 225 3284; 86 Nejatol-lahi St)
Lufthansa (Map p98; ☎ 873 8701; Dr Beheshti Ave, 2 Sarafraz St)
Swiss Airlines (Map p98; ☎ 874 8332; Arzhantin Sq, 69 Buchharest St)
Turkish Airlines (Map p98; ☎ 874 8450; 239 Motahhari Ave)

It's almost always easier to buy a ticket at a reputable travel agency (p87); especially a ticket on one of the smaller internal airlines (ie Kish, Saha, Mahan and Caspian). In fact, the Iran Air office in Nejatollahi St will send you to a travel agency to buy a domestic seat. If you must contact the domestic airlines, these two have offices in Tehran as follows: **Iran Aseman** (Map pp90-1; ☎ 889 5567; www.iaa.com; Nejatollahi St) and **Mahan Air** (Map p98; ☎ 877 0593/4; www.mahanairlines.com; Vanak Sq, Gandhi Ave)

INTERNATIONAL ARRIVALS
Though the crowds and noise may be in-timidating to anyone who has not travelled in this part of the world before, customs and immigration procedures at Mehrabad Inter-national Airport are slow but generally has-sle-free. Immigration is painless (don't lose the yellow piece of paper they give you) and these days tourists are usually waved through customs. Provided it's open, the tourist infor-mation counter is staffed by a bunch of very helpful ladies who can book hotels for you, though you'll be lucky if they have a map.

Despite the sign in English at the Bank Melli office immediately after immigration, you do not have to fill out a currency dec-laration form unless you're importing huge sums of money. Officially, it's US$1000, but the bank is not interested unless you have quite a bit more. The small bank in the baggage collection area can change cash at competitive rates.

INTERNATIONAL DEPARTURES
The hardest part about leaving Tehran is getting to the airport on time. Unless your flight is very early or very late, give yourself well over an hour to get through the traffic from central Tehran, then at least two hours once you get to the airport to get through customs and immigration. Make sure you go to the correct airport; the international and domestic airports are about 1km apart. If you have changed money legally at a bank, and have a receipt to prove it, you can convert unused rials into US dollars cash at the busy bank near where you check in. There are a couple of pricey souvenir shops in the international departure lounge where you can offload any remaining rials.

Bus
Masses of buses leave from Tehran every few minutes to just about every city, town and village throughout the country, but as the city has four bus stations you will need to know which one your bus leaves from. To add to the confusion, some buses leave from two or more stations.

There is only one specific bus ticket office in the city: the **Iran Peyma booking office** (Map pp90-1; Taavoni No 1; ☎ 670 9964; Ferdosi Sq, Ferdosi St; ☒ 8.30am-4.30pm Sat-Wed, 8.30am-noon Thu). Generally speaking you will need to go to the stations to check times and prices. A good place to check bus schedules and buy advance tickets for any of the major bus companies is the office marked in English 'The Union of Countries Travelling Companies' at the central (Arzhantin) bus station at Arzhantin Sq. You will be lucky to find any English-speaking staff at the bus ticket offices.

The following tables show services to all major destinations on direct buses from Tehran. Where two prices are given, the higher will be for travel on a Volvo or similar bus.

For details of international bus services to/from Tehran, see p110.

CENTRAL BUS STATION
The **central bus station** (Arzhantin, Sayro Safar or Beyhaqi terminal; Map p98; ☎ 873 2535; Arzhantin Sq) is accessible by shared taxis and local buses from most places in the south. Buses leav-ing this station are almost always the sexier (and exier) Volvos. This list represents the minimum number of services – it's possible more buses run these routes. Prices quoted here are for Volvo buses.

TEHRAN

Destination	Price (IR)	Duration (hr)	Departures
Bushehr	70,000	19	1.30pm
Esfahan	30,000	7	hourly
Kerman	60,000	15	3-8pm
Mashhad	58,000	14	4.30pm
Shiraz	40,000	13	2.45-4.45pm
Tabriz	40,000	10	9am, 8.30pm
Yazd	40,000	10	9pm

EASTERN BUS STATION

The **eastern bus station** (terminal-e shargh; Map p83; ☎ 786 8080) has buses to Khorasan province and the Caspian region. It's a small, compact station and quite easy to use. Take a shared taxi to Imam Hossein Sq, and then another shared taxi, or try the trolleybus directly to the station. A private taxi will cost about IR20,000 from central Tehran. Taavonis Nos 1 (Iran Peyma) and 14 have the most services running from this station. Prices here are for Mercedes/Volvo buses.

Destination	Price (IR)	Duration (hr)	Departures
Gonbad-e Kavus	19,500/32,000	9	frequent 5am-noon; 5pm, 9pm & 11pm
Gorgan	17,500/30,000	7	3 per day
Mashhad	35,000/55,000	15	hourly 7am-noon; 2pm & 6pm
Sari	13,000/20,000	5	5.30am, frequent after noon

SOUTHERN BUS STATION

The **southern bus station** (terminal-e jonub; Map p83; ☎ 559 163) has buses to the south and southeast of Tehran. It's an extremely huge circular building with a restaurant and information booth. To get here take the Metro to Terminal-e Jonub station or grab a shared taxi heading south from Imam Khomeini Sq. Try to avoid the very expensive taxi agency that operates from this station. Departure times are the minimum you can expect, and where only one price is quoted it is for a Volvo or quality bus. Otherwise, prices are for Mercedes/Volvo buses.

Destination	Price (IR)	Duration (hr)	Departures
Ahvaz	35,000/50,000	15	3pm, 4pm, 9pm
Bandar-e Abbas	52,500/95,000	20	every 2 hr 7.30am-6pm
Bushehr	75,000	19	10.30am, 2pm (No 14)
Esfahan	17,500/30,000	7	hourly 6am-10pm
Kashan	9500/15,000	4	hourly
Kerman	38,000/60,000	15	3pm, 4pm, 6pm, 9pm
Qom	5000/8000	1½	hourly
Shiraz	35,000/54,000	13-16	hourly 3-9pm
Yazd	27,000/44,000	10	5.30pm, 7.30pm
Zahedan	60,000/96,000	20	every 2 hr 8am-6pm

WESTERN BUS STATION

The **western bus station** (terminal-e gharb; Map p83; ☎ 606 2854) is Tehran's busiest, catering for the Caspian region and places to the west of Tehran, as well as for a few other destinations, including Ankara and İstanbul (Turkey), Baku (Azerbaijan) and Damascus (Syria). The station is well set up with dozens of bus company offices, and a restaurant, post office, police station and information booth.

To get to the bus station, take a shared taxi heading west from Imam Khomeini Sq, or catch anything going to Azadi Sq, and walk northwest to the huge station.

Prices here are for Mercedes/Volvo buses.

Destination	Price (IR)	Duration (hr)	Departures
Ardabil	29,000/45,000	10	hourly 6am-10pm
Astara	18,500/35,000	9	every 1-2 hr
Chalus	14,500/26,000	6	every 15 min
Hamadan	15,000/28,000	6	every 15 min
Kermanshah	25,000/40,000	9	every 30 min
Orumiyeh	38,000/50,000	2	hourly
Qazvin	7500/10,000	2	every 15 min
Ramsar	18,000/30,000	6	hourly
Rasht	12,500/28,000	6	hourly
Tabriz	25,000/40,000	10	hourly

Minibus

A few towns in central Iran and nearby parts of the Caspian provinces are linked to Tehran by minibus. Minibuses are generally a little more expensive than buses, but leave more regularly. They leave from specially designated sections within the eastern, southern and western bus stations, depending on the destination.

Savari

Most towns within about three hours' drive of Tehran are linked by savari (long-distance shared taxi), eg Amol, Sari, Kashan, Qom, Zanjan and Rasht, and anywhere along the way. Prices are two to three times the price of the cheapest bus tickets, but are often worth paying to enjoy some comfort and speed, making them an excellent option for day trips from Tehran. Savaris leave from specially designated sections inside, or just outside, the appropriate bus stations, depending on the destination. Just say your destination and 'savari' and you'll soon be pointed in the right direction.

Train

All train services around the country start and finish at the impressive **train station** (Map p83; Rah-Ahan Sq) in southern Tehran. The destinations and the arrival and departure times are listed in English on a board at the entrance. The staff at **tourist information** (☎ 565 1415) speak English and are walking timetables. For planning, use the excellent www.rajatrains.com website, which has up-to-date schedules and prices. If you're on a budget note that it's normal to have huge differences in price between 1st-class express trains and slower-than-a-wet-week 2nd-class trains.

The train station is easy to reach in any shared taxi heading south from the southwestern corner of Imam Khomeini Sq – ask to be dropped at Rah-Ahan Sq.

BUYING TICKETS

You can buy tickets a week or more in advance at a travel agency – there are several situated along Nejatollahi St that will be able to sort you out. At the station you can only buy tickets for travel on the same day; you will find the **ticket office** (☺ 8am-9pm) is up the stairs on the right as you enter the building.

SCHEDULES

The prices and days of departure in the timetable listed here are liable to change; in particular, what are daily services in

summer may well become much less frequent in winter.

Qazvin is served by train services to Tabriz and Zanjan.

Note that trains to Mashhad vary quite considerably in speed, comfort and price. Prices shown are for 1st/2nd class,

Destination	Price (IR)	Duration (hr)	No of trains daily
Ahvaz	103,400/16,700	15/17	2
Bandar-e Abbas	80,600*	20	1
Esfahan	30,300*	7	1
Gorgan	36,150/15,600	10½	1
Kerman	57,400/36,150	13	1
Mashhad	112,800/24,850	12/16	11-15
Qom	3850**	2½	3
Sari	16,150/6000	7	1
Tabriz	52,550/25,000	13	2
Yazd	32,700*	8	1
Zanjan	21,900/15,800	4	2

*1st class only **2nd class only

GETTING AROUND
To/From the Airport

Before you read further, first read the boxed text 'Imam Khomeini International Airport' (p113).

BUS

If you're confident, and don't have much luggage, public buses (IR300) leave every 15 to 20 minutes from immediately outside the domestic airport for Enqelab and Vanak Sqs.

TAXI

Unless you're travelling light and know Tehran, it's wise to bite the bullet and pay for a private taxi to your hotel. Most of the drivers who frequent Mehrabad International Airport are pretty straight. A few might try to take you to a hotel of their choice; but insist on your own preference.

Whether you're coming from the international or domestic terminals, which are about 1km apart, the fares are fixed. A taxi to southern Tehran or the city centre will cost IR30,000, and up to IR50,000 to northern Tehran. If it's peak hour, drivers will probably ask you for an extra IR10,000, which is pretty fair considering the trip will

TEHRAN

IMAM KHOMEINI INTERNATIONAL AIRPORT

Tehran's Mehrabad International Airport is on borrowed time. And if you believe the pronouncements of the government, that time is short. However, Tehranis have been waiting more than 30 years for the Imam Khomeini International Airport (IKIA) and as one deadline after the other has come and gone, so too has any faith in those deadlines. In early 2004 Tehranis were told the airport 'will open in three weeks for domestic services, and for all flights by April'. It was an announcement made to coincide with the 25th anniversary of Khomeini's return to Iran and was treated with the scepticism it deserved; Mehrabad was still struggling along in May.

It is possible, however, that by the time you fly into Tehran the new airport will be open. If so, you'll find taxis much more expensive (it's about 35km to central Tehran), but the Metro will, *in sh'Allah*, be running all the way from IKIA into town for only a couple of thousand rial.

---

probably take twice as long. If you find you're being quoted something significantly greater than this, check with the taxi dispatcher who is located in a booth outside the terminal – he's pretty straight up.

If you want a shared taxi (about IR7000 from the airport to the city centre), ask around or tell a taxi driver you want to share, and he will look for other passengers going the same way.

Car & Motorcycle

If you're driving in Tehran try to put out of your mind everything you've ever learned about road rules – none of it applies here. Out of a basic instinct for survival you'll soon enough assimilate the lawless aggression of the locals and be driving with 100% attention at all times.

One adrenalin-inducing way to get across town in a hurry is on a motorcycle taxi. You'll see them loitering on corners all over town, though the corner of Jomhuri-ye Eslami Ave and Ferdosi St is a good place to look for one going north. They cost as much as taxis but take half the time. Good luck!

CAR RENTAL

It's not only difficult to find a car without a driver, but usually unnecessary too. There is little incentive when you can get a car and English-speaking driver for less than a car alone. Any of the travel agencies listed under Tours (p381) will be able to lease you a car with driver. The cost depends on many variables, not least whether you want an English-speaking driver who can double as a guide, but reckon on paying between US$40 and US$65 a day.

One driver-cum-translator who is highly recommended is **Ali Taheri** (☎ 443 1105; 0912

134 9345; r_alitaheri@yahoo.com). Ali speaks excellent English and knows Tehran (and much of its history) like the back of his hand. He and his air-con Peugeot will cost you US$50 a day.

To charter one of the airport shuttle taxis for the day would probably cost about US$30; to charter a Paykan in worse condition about US$20.

Public Transport

BUS

Buses cover virtually all of Tehran, but as they're often crowded and slow, most travellers end up using taxis. Buses run from roughly 6am until 10pm or 11pm, finishing earlier on Friday and public holidays. Tickets cost slightly more than nothing – IR200. You buy them from ticket booths near bus stops or at bus stations, and then give them to the driver when you board the bus.

Buses normally travel from one local bus station to another, so you may need to take more than one. Major bus departure points you might use include Imam Khomeini Sq, for the south of the city; the station on the opposite side of Imam Khomeini Ave from the National Museum of Iran, for the west; Arzhantin, Vanak and Valiasr Sqs, for the north; Azadi Sq, for further west; and Rah-Ahan Sq, for the far south.

The buses often have Roman numerals, but never show the destinations in English. Some handy numbers going north–south include the 18 from Arzhantin Sq to Tajrish Sq; the I-22 between Imam Khomeini Sq and Arzhantin Sq; the I-24 from Imam Khomeini Sq to Tajrish Sq; and the I-33 from Valiasr Sq to Tajrish Sq. Bus numbers apply to services in both directions.

TEHRAN

METRO

The **Tehran Metro** (www.tehranmetro.com) underground rail network is this city's great hope of salvation from both the chronic pollution problems and seemingly endless traffic jams. In the planning since before the revolution, it will eventually have nine lines, but that is a very long way off. At the time of research, sections of Line 1 (or the red line), Line 2 (navy blue) and all of Line 5 (green) were operating and an estimated US$800 million a year was being spent on new tunnels and stations.

The red line is by far the most useful for travellers. It runs from Mirdamad in the north to Haram-e Motahar in the south, making it the cheapest and easiest way to get to the Behesht-e Zahra cemetery and the Tomb of Imam Khomeini. Heading south it stops at Terminal-e Jonub station for the southern bus terminal. Construction is continuing and when completed this line will reach Tajrish in the north – that will indeed be a happy day – and the new Imam Khomeini International Airport in the south.

At the time of writing, Line 2 ran from Dardasht in the east of the city to Tehran (Sadeghieh) in the west, from where it is easy to get a share taxi to the western bus station. It will eventually extend to the eastern bus station, providing a fast link from Imam Khomeini Sq.

The completed green line is largely above ground and is, in effect, an extension of the navy blue line. It runs from Tehran (Sadeghieh) out past Karaj to Golshahr. From Karaj you can find onward transport to Chalus on the Caspian by a most picturesque route.

Tickets cost IR650 per trip (you need two if you're going to change, or a IR1000 ticket on Line 5) and the whole process is pretty low-tech; you buy as many as you think you'll need from a window near the entrance of the station, then hand one on immediately to a man sitting a few metres away near a partition. Trains start at about 6am and stop around 10pm, running every 10 or 15 minutes.

This lack of frequency is a real problem and during peak hours just getting on to the Metro is a test of strength. Inside is a frotteur's paradise, so while women are free to ride in any carriage they like, making use of the one female-only car (usually) at the front of the train might be worthwhile at these times.

Station announcements are in Farsi only, so keep an eye on the English maps inside the trains.

MINIBUS

Crowded public minibuses are found in the suburbs and most travellers are unlikely to need them. If you do, finding the right minibus is not easy, so ask, ask and ask again. The place you're most likely to need one is going north of Tajrish Sq; for an idea of prices, the trip from Tajrish costs IR600 to Darakeh or Tochal.

TROLLEYBUS

One excellent but, unfortunately, unique innovation is the electric trolleybus. Currently, the one line runs between the eastern bus station and Khorasan Sq.

Taxi

Tehran taxis come in a variety of colours that, in theory, govern what services they can offer. In practice, however, it's anything goes. The vast majority of taxis are Paykans, many of them shitboxes of the first order. Then there is every other car on Tehran's roads, almost all of which have the potential to be a taxi if the driver needs a few quick rial.

PRIVATE TAXI

In practice, chartering a private taxi on the street is not as easy as you might expect because most taxis are looking for shared fares; you may have to stop several before you hit the jackpot.

The alternative is to get your hotel to call a taxi or call one yourself (☎ 133), although this costs more than flagging a taxi on the street.

Once you've found a taxi prepared to take you, agree on a price before setting out. Most drivers demand IR10,000 even before they know where you want to go. Sometimes this will turn out to be an extortionate sum for a short trip; at other times they'll be grumbling and complaining when they realise what a bargain you've landed.

To get from Imam Khomeini Sq to Vali-asr Sq should cost about IR15,000; from Imam Khomeini Sq to Tajrish Sq will cost about IR30,000. To hire a taxi for an hour or so to visit several sites shouldn't cost much more than IR25,000. To get from southern Tehran to the north even in a private taxi takes a minimum of half an hour, much longer in peak hour. You can expect prices to rise during peak hour.

SHARED TAXI

Taxi fares in Tehran are higher than in the rest of Iran and the minimum fare of IR500 won't get you very far. For most trips expect to pay between IR1000 and IR2000. Always watch what other passengers are paying: you'll soon get an idea of the going rate.

Using shared taxis is hard in Tehran partly because of the sheer volume of people but also because the one-way streets make it difficult for an outsider to be sure where they will be going. It's easy to use the shared taxis plying the main roads between the following squares: Imam Khomeini, Vanak, Valiasr, Tajrish, Arzhantin, Azadi, Ferdosi, Enqelab, Haft-e Tir, Rah-Ahan and Imam Hossein. However, even these squares may have several ministations for shared taxis heading in different directions, so you usually have to ask around. You might be lucky and get a shared taxi all the way from, say, Imam Khomeini Sq to Tajrish Sq (IR3000), but often you will have to change in Valiasr or Vanak Sq.

When trying to hail a shared taxi don't bother with anything in any language along the lines of 'Iran Hotel, on the corner of': the driver will have lost interest after the word 'hotel', picked up someone else and be halfway there before you know it's. Use a major landmark or a town square as a destination, even if you are getting off before then. Shout it quickly and loudly: 'FeDOSe!' will do for Ferdosi St or square; similarly, 'eHESHTe!' for Beheshti St or Sq; and so on. The driver will either ignore you, or give you a quick beep on the horn and pull over for half a second while you leap in. It's best to practise outside Tehran and build up to the big city.

AROUND TEHRAN

Away from the hyperactive streets of the capital, Tehran province offers barren hills to scramble around, lush valleys to explore and even a majestic mountain to climb. Most visitors to Tehran will want to visit the Holy Shrine of Imam Khomeini and the adjacent military cemetery, Behesht-e Zahra, to the southwest of the city. Mountaineers might want to head for the slopes of Iran's highest mountain, Mt Damavand (5671m), while skiers can head for one of the resorts in the Alborz Mountains.

HOLY SHRINE OF IMAM KHOMEINI
حرم قم

When future generations look back on the historical periods of Iran, the early years of the Islamic Republic will be remembered as a time of great endeavour on the building front. This, the resting place of His Holiness Imam Khomeini, is the grandest of those endeavours. But while the scale of the **Holy Shrine of Imam Khomeini** (Map p116; ☾ 24hr) is quite enormous, for the time being it looks more like a shoddily built and empty aircraft hangar than one of Iran's holiest sites.

The mausoleum is flanked by four towers, each 91m high – Khomeini was 91 when he died. The huge gold dome is adorned with 72 tulips, symbolising the 72 people who fought and died with Imam Hossein in Karbala.

It's fine for non-Muslims to enter the shrine provided they've removed their shoes, but cameras are not allowed. Inside you'll find the actual shrine tucked into a corner of what looks a bit like an ice-skating rink minus the ice. This vast empty space is often full of families having picnics, kids rolling coins

---

THE FUNERAL OF AYATOLLAH KHOMEINI

In 1989, the Islamic Republic's final send-off for its founder and inspiration, Ayatollah Khomeini, culminated in the largest funeral ever held in the world – a crush of 10 million inconsolable mourners. As the hearse tried in vain to move through the crowd towards the cemetery, it was twice stopped and the crowd eventually took the coffin from the hearse and started passing it over their heads. It was pandemonium, and as a helicopter was hastily pressed into service even the armed Komiteh guards couldn't stop the unedifying scene of the crowd pushing forward and ripping pieces off the shroud as holy relics.

Unless you thrive on chaos, you're advised not to come here on or around 4 June, the anniversary of the ayatollah's death, when hundreds of thousands of mourners visit the shrine.

AROUND TEHRAN

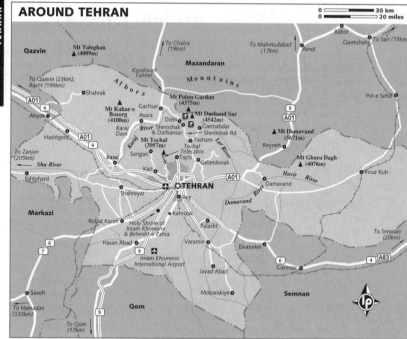

along the floor and homeless men sleeping. Apparently the ayatollah wanted his shrine to be a public place where people could enjoy themselves, rather than a mosque where they must behave with reverence.

The complex has a few simple **food shops**, places flogging tacky souvenirs and a post office.

Appropriately enough, the shrine is on the road between Tehran, the town that launched the 1979 revolution, and Qom, where the great man underwent his theological training. It's right in front of Behesht-e Zahra, so you can see both on one trip.

Getting There & Away
The Tehran Metro Line 1 runs all the way to the Haram-e Motahar station and at just IR650 it is both the easiest and cheapest way to get here. Shared taxis and buses do make the trip, but why would you bother?

BEHESHT-E ZAHRA   بهشت زهرا
As well as being a normal cemetery, **Behesht-e Zahra** is the main resting place for those who died in the Iran-Iraq War (1980–88). And

it is the sheer scale of the death represented in the roughly 200,000 glass boxes here that is most moving. To many visitors it will be familiar from the TV and newspaper images taken during the war itself: hysterical mourners surrounded by countless pictures of the dead, most of them portraits of the dead, most of them housed in small glass boxes on stilts and holding a watch, a knife, a letter that belonged to the lost father, son, husband. The pine trees have grown since then, but the faces of the dead remain.

Right at the heart of the cemetery there's a shrine to Iranian pilgrims killed during the annual haj (pilgrimage to Mecca), when Saudi Arabian soldiers opened fire on a crowd during the mid-1980s.

A visit here can easily be combined with a trip to the Holy Shrine of Imam Khomeini. Behesht-e Zahra is packed on mourning days but is eerily empty on other days.

REY   ری
One of the most historically important places in Tehran province is Rey, although these days it has been swallowed up by the

urban sprawl of the capital. In the 11th and 12th centuries, Rey was the regional capital and much larger than Tehran, but it was destroyed by the rampaging Mongols, who left very few buildings standing.

The main reason to visit Rey is to see the really lovely **Imamzadeh Shah-e Abdal-Azim**, built for a descendant of Imam Hossein. This mausoleum has elaborate tilework, a golden dome, a pool in the courtyard and a 14th-century sarcophagus with intricate carvings, constructed from betel wood. In the same complex is a shrine to Imam Hamzeh (brother of Imam Reza). Women need to wear a chador here.

Other attractions include the remains of the Sassanian **Ghal'-e Tabarak**, a fortress on a nearby hill; the 12th-century **Gonbad-e Toghoral**, the 20m-high tomb tower of a Seljuk king in the town centre; and the **Cheshmeh Ali** mineral springs with some Qajar-period **carvings** nearby.

Finding these sites without a guide and a vehicle is likely to prove frustrating, and although you could hire a taxi in Rey for a negotiable IR20,000 per hour it will be hard to find a guide who can speak English.

Getting There & Away
It's simple, just take Metro Line 1 south to Shahr-e Rey station. Alternatively you can take a tour organised by a Tehran travel agency (p381). Costs start at about US$30 depending on the number of people you can get together.

KARAJ   کرج
Karaj, 42km west of Tehran, is primarily a dormitory town for people working in the capital. It's also the starting point for a pleasant drive along a spectacular road forced north through the Alborz Mountains to Chalus on the Caspian Sea by Shah Reza Khan. The drive takes you past the Karaj Dam where you can either walk and enjoy the scenery or take part in a variety of water sports.

Karaj is easily accessible on Metro Line 5 from Tehran (IR1000). To get to the dam you will need to find a shared taxi, which will be easiest on Fridays.

MT DAMAVAND   کوه دماوند
Shaped like Mt Fuji, **Mt Damavand** (5671m) is the highest mountain in Iran and easily accessible from Tehran, although it is actually in Mazandaran province. Damavand is a volcano and still belches out sulphuric fumes strong enough to kill unfortunate stray sheep.

Most people approach the peak from Reyneh, where there is a mountaineering club at the junction where the main road enters the village. Tragically, the manager of the club, an expert local mountaineer, and his sons died a few years ago while trying to climb the mountain, giving you some idea of the potential dangers.

You can see Mt Damavand on the IR10,000 note, on bottles of Damarvand spring water and from the air as you fly into Tehran, smog permitting. Don't confuse the mountain of Damavand with the village of Damavand to its south.

Reyneh   رینه
One possible starting point for exploring the mountain and the nearby countryside is the pretty village of Reyneh. From Reyneh, there are fine views of other picturesque villages on the far side of the valley. Even if you don't want to climb the mountain, there are plenty of other local walking trails to enjoy.

There is no hotel, but if you ask around, especially if you want to climb the mountain, someone will put you up in their home for about IR40,000 per person and they'll probably put you in touch with someone who could act as a guide. There are a couple of kababis and other shops in the village.

Climbing the Mountain
From a technical point-of-view, Damavand is basically a walk-up. And the fact that you climb so far so quickly is the most dangerous aspect of this climb. As you ascend be sure to watch out for the signs of altitude sickness – dizziness, headaches, nausea and swollen fingers – which kills people here every year. Most first-timers use a guide.

Starting at Reyneh, it's possible to take an ordinary vehicle as far as Gusfand Sara (3200m), where you can sleep in the mosque. However, if you want to acclimatise before climbing the mountain it may be better to walk up, taking perhaps four or five hours to get there. In summer local families will be able to provide simple food for small groups of people but for most of the year you must bring your own food.

From Gusfand Sara, you can walk, or ride a donkey, for about four hours to Barghah-e-Sevvom (4150m), where you can stay overnight in a mountaineers' hut and clean water is available. There's no water en route so you should bring some up with you. The hut may be full, so bringing a tent (and leaving it there during the final ascent) is a good idea. You will also need to bring a sleeping bag, warm clothes and perhaps a gas camping stove for making hot drinks – even in July it can be freezing here at night and -10°C at the summit. A reader has pointed out that you should fill your water bottle in the evening since the water will be frozen when you get up before dawn.

Next morning you should get up at about 3am to make the tough seven-hour climb to the summit in time to enjoy the views before clouds cover the peak and the sulphur fumes become overpowering. In August you should be able to get up without special equipment. It's another four to five hours back to the hut from the peak.

Bear in mind that the weather can change suddenly and that snowfalls are a possibility, even in high summer. What's more, many of the rocks are treacherously loose and at places the path is not as obvious as you'd expect.

Hot Springs

After expending all that energy climbing Mt Damavand you'll be pleased to know that just 4km east of Reyneh, at **Ab Karm**, several hotels have been built around hot springs. You can rent a room for the night for around US$10, including breakfast, tea and a dip in one of the baths.

Getting There & Away

Reyneh is not particularly easy to reach. Take a savari or minibus from Tehran's eastern bus station towards Amol and get off at the junction to Reyneh, which is not signed in any language but is not far after the 'Amol 75' sign. (You will have to pay the full Tehran–Amol fare.) At the junction, where there is a decent restaurant, a shared taxi should be waiting for passengers going to Reyneh. Either wait for it to fill up, or charter the taxi up the hill to the village. You may want to walk back from Reyneh to the highway, but the road up is very steep.

Getting back to Tehran from the highway, especially on a public holiday, might take some time.

Alternatively, you can charter a taxi between Tehran and Reyneh for about IR120,000. This allows you to stop along the way for a picnic, or for lunch at one of the many restaurants along the road; take photos of the majestic mountains; explore streams and caves along the way; and to drive further up the mountain beyond Reyneh.

ALBORZ SKI RESORTS

Skiing in the Alborz Mountains above Tehran can be one of the most unexpected pleasures of a trip to Iran. There are four resorts within day-trip distance of Tehran, all of which have good facilities, equipment for hire and which cost virtually nothing for a day on the slopes. **Darbansar** (Map p116; day pass IR40,000; ☒ 8.30am-3.30pm Jan-Mar), near the village of Shemshak, has three easy slopes and is best for beginners; while the slopes and resort at **Tochal** (Map p116; ☎ 242 1502; www.tochalcomplex.com; day pass IR40,000; s/d US$20/60; ☒ 8.30am-3.30pm Jan-Mar) are most-easily accessible via the Tochal Telecabin (p100) in northern Tehran. The pick of the bunch, however, are Shmshak and Dizin.

Shemshak   شمشک

Just down the road from Darbansar, **Shemshak Resort** (Map p116; ☎ 0221-355 2912; day pass IR40,000; ☒ 8.30am-3.30pm Jan-Mar) has the slopes that will get hardcore skiers most excited. There are six lifts, the longest being about 1450m long with a vertical descent of about 500m (some of it at an adrenalin-inducing 45-degree angle) and plenty of moguls. Snowboards are welcome. There is something of an après-ski scene here, as well, with one young Tehrani describing Shemshak by night as 'out-of-control and mind-boggling'. If you don't actually know someone (or meet someone on the slopes) who is having a party in one of the chalets, however, you'll struggle to find much of a nightlife. Night-skiing is sometimes possible.

Dizin   دیزین

The largest field in Iran and home to Iranian skiing, **Dizin Resort** (Map p116; ☎ 0262-254 2449; day pass IR50,000; ☒ 8.30am-3.30pm Nov-Apr) is *the* place to be seen. The slopes aren't as difficult as those at Shemshak, but with a vertical drop of about 900m it will still appeal to anyone feeling the need for speed. With base camp being at about 2700m and the upper slopes about 3500m, Dizin is one of the world's 40 highest ski resorts, so there is usually a good cover of snow here for almost six months of the year. From the base, you take an antique-looking gondola to the mid-station, and another to the top. A third gondola ferries you to some of the eastern slopes.

Pistes are sometimes groomed and there is plenty of scope for off-piste if you manage to get a fresh snowfall. Apart from Friday, waiting for lifts is almost unheard of. Hiring skis can be a hit-and-miss affair, and you might find that the cost of hiring a guide will be significantly defrayed by the savings you make when hiring skis. As a rough guide, a day's ski-hire starts at about IR75,000 but can climb as high as IR250,000 – shop around and you should be able to get a decent pair of carve skis, boots and poles for about IR140,000.

Dizin boasts summer activities such as grass-skiing, hiking, horse riding and tennis, and a children's playground.

Sleeping & Eating

All the resorts have up-market hotels, with prices starting at about US$35/50 per single/twin. There are dozens of chalets at Dizin, but they can be pricey. Rooms at **Dizin Hotel** (☎ 0262-254 2449; tw US$50; **P**) are adequate in an ageing sort of way – those in the main building have better views. In the basement there is a very (retro) cool pizza place.

A few restaurants serve Western and Iranian food at reasonable prices.

Getting There & Away

Undoubtedly the easiest option is to arrange your whole package through a travel agency. Most local travel agencies sell one- and two-day trips that include transport, accommodation and lift passes for reasonable prices (those sold by foreign agencies tend to be ludicrously expensive considering the costs). Look for trips advertised in the English-language newspapers, or ask at the up-market hotels.

With access to a vehicle, you can pick and choose between any of the resorts along the main road that runs north of Karaj to Chalus, and stay wherever you want (or just take a day trip from Tehran). For example, Dizin is 123km and roughly 2½ hours from Tehran; you'll need chains on your wheels or a 4WD for the last 10km or so. The Shemshak and Darbansar resorts are 55km north of Tehran on the Shemshak Rd, and you can use this road to get to Dizin more quickly than the Chalus Rd (it's about 12km further than Shemshak).

If you are relying on public transport (ie shared taxis or minibuses from the eastern bus station in Tehran), you will be limited to the three major resorts mentioned earlier. You will also need to do a bit of hitching to get from the main road to the slopes.

Western Iran
ایران غربی

Probably the historical site of the Garden of Eden, western Iran has been at the centre of many of civilisation's earliest empires. Standing at the frontiers with Mesopotamia and Turkey, the region's fortunes have oscillated between trading glories and military decimation. The border areas have suffered during Persian–Ottoman conflicts and, most recently, during the Iran-Iraq War of the 1980s. Mostly mountainous, and in places densely forested, you can expect blizzards in the higher mountain passes from November. This deeply hospitable region is a rare first choice for Westerners, which makes it all the more fascinating.

Western Iran is a linguistic and cultural patchwork: Kurds predominate in Kordestan and Kermanshah provinces; Lors in Ilam and Lorestan; Arabs inhabit southern Khuzestan; Talesh and Gilaki are the traditional languages of Gilan (the southwest Caspian hinterland); and Azaris whose language is more Turkish than Persian, predominate in the rest of the northwest. In the most remote regions, and more generally in Kurdish towns, tribal dress is still worn.

This chapter starts from the Turkish border as a loop around Lake Orumiyeh to Tabriz, continuing through the Azari heartlands to Ardabil and down the Caspian coast via Rasht to Chalus. Then it returns via Qazvin and Soltaniyeh to Zanjan. Next we consider the central mountains, the former 'Royal Road' through Kordestan and the historical cities of Kermanshah and Hamadan before descending towards the ancient sites of Shush, Shushtar and Choqa Zanbil. From Ahvaz one can easily continue along the Gulf coast to Bushehr and on to Shiraz.

HIGHLIGHTS

- Hike into flower-filled valleys amid the ruined 12th-century **Castles of the Assassins** (p166)
- Challenge Iran's desert image in the paddy fields and forests of Gilan that lead to the delightful stepped village of **Masuleh** (p156)
- From Jolfa explore ancient churches, mud-walled castles and grand canyons along the biblical **Aras River Valley** (p142)
- Stagger up to **Babak Castle** (p144), the dramatic emotional heart of Azarbayjan
- Venture into **Howraman** (p174), a magical, rarely visited valley of traditional Kurdish villages
- Be awed by lonely **Choqa Zanbil's** (p192) massive, brick ziggurat which somehow managed to get 'lost' for 2500 years
- Relax in an atmospheric teahouse beside the world's highest brick dome at **Soltaniyeh** (p167)
- Cross sparsely populated mountainscapes from Zanjan to reach **Takht-e Soleiman** (p170), history's foremost fire temple
- Potter about between the fairy-chimney homes of **Kandovan** (p140), Iran's mini-Cappadocia

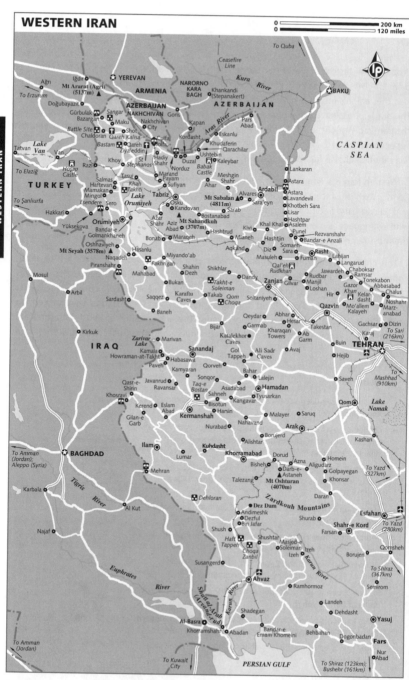

WESTERN IRAN

0 ——— 200 km
0 ——— 120 miles

To Quba

Ceasefire Line

Kura River

YEREVAN

Agrı
Iğdır
Mt Ararat (Agri) (5137m)
To Erzurum
Doğubayazıt
Gürbulak
Bazargan
Sangar
Maku
Shot
Battle Site
Chaldoran
Bastam
Qareh Kalisa
Qareh
Ziya'eddin

ARMENIA
NARORNO KARA BAGH
Khankandi (Stepanakert)

AZERBAIJAN
NAKHCHIVAN
Nakhchivan City
Goris
Kapan

AZERBAIJAN

BAKU

Pars Abad

Aras River
Eskanlu
Kordasht
Khudaferin
Qarachilar

CASPIAN SEA

Tatvan
Lake Van
Van
Hoşap Castle
Razi
To Elazig
Khoy
St Stephanos
Hadiy Shahr
Jolfa
Duzal
Ushtebin
Kaleybar
Babak Castle
Norduz
Marand
Payam
Sufiyan
Ahar
Meshgin Shahr

Lankaran
Astara
Astara
Lavandevil
Khotbeh Sara
Lisar
Asalem

TURKEY
To Şanlıurfa
Hakkari
Salmas
Haftevan
Mamakan
Mingol
Esendere
Sero
Khan Takhti
Tasuj
Tabriz
Osku
Kandovan
Alvares
Mt Sabalan (4811m)
Sara'eyn
Sarab
Ardabil

Hashtpar
Punel
Rezvanshahr
Bandar-e Anzali

Yüksekova
Orumiyeh
Bandar-e Golmankhaneh
Oshnaviyeh
Mt Seyah (3578m)
Naqadeh
Piranshahr
Hasanlu
Azar Shahr
Aziz Abad
Mt Sahandkuh (3707m)
Bonab
Maragheh
Hashtrud
Hashtjin
Kivi
Khal Khal
Somaeh Sara
Rasht
Fuman
Lahijan
Langarud
Chaboksar
Ramsar
Tonekabon
Abbasabad
Chalus
Noshahr
Marz-anabad

Mosul
Fakhrigah
Miyando'ab
Shahin Dezh
Bostanabad
Bukan
Shikhlar
Dandy
Diz
Masuleh
Qal'eh Rudkhan
Gilvar
Rudbar
Jawardeh
Manjil
Loshan
Hir
Gazor
Kelardasht
Khan
Mo'allem Kalayeh

Arbil
Mahabad
Karaftu Caves
Saqqez
Takht-e Soleiman
Takab
Qom Choqa
Soltaniyeh
Zanjan
Abhar
Qazvin

IRAQ
Sardasht
Baneh
Bijar
Qeydar
Garmab
Hesar
Kharaqan Towers
Takestan
Buin
Gachsar
Dizin
To Sari (216km)

Kirkuk
Zarivar Lake
Marivan
Kamala
Howraman-at-Takht
Habasawa
Paveh
Katalekhor Caves
Gol Tappeh
Ali Sadr Caves
Avaj
Ab Garm
Hejib
Karaj
Mashhad (910km)

Sanandaj
Kamyaran
Qorveh
Bahar
Lalejin
Saveh
Qom
Lake Namak

Qasr-e Shirin
Javanrud
Ransavar
Sonqor
Taq-e Bostan
Asadabad
Sahneh
Kangavar
Hamadan
Tyusarkan

Khosravi
Kerend
Eslam Abad
Bisotun
Harsin
Kermanshah
Nurabad
Malayer
Nahavand
Saruq

Gilan-e Garb
Boroujerd
Arak
Kashan

Ilam
Kuhdasht
Alishtar
Khorramabad
Dorud
Azna
Aligudarz
Homein
Golpayegan
Khonsar
To Yazd (327km)

To Amman (Jordan); Aleppo (Syria)
BAGHDAD
Lumar
Mehran
Bisheh
Darb-e Astaneh
Mt Oshturan (4070m)

Karbala
Talezang
Zardkouh Mountains
Daran
Esfahan
To Yazd (280km)

Dehloran
Dez Dam
Andimeshk
Dezful
Bin Jafar
Shurab
Shahr-e Kord
Farsan

Najaf
Shush
Haft Tappeh
Choqa Zanbil
Shushtar
Masjed-e Soleiman
Izeh
Karun River
Borujen
Qomsheh
To Shiraz (367km)
Semirom

Susangerd
Ahvaz
Ramhormoz
Landeh
Dehdasht

Euphrates River
Shadegan
Yasuj
Fars

Al-Basra
Khorramshahr
Abadan
Bandar-e Emam Khomeini
Behbahan
Dogonbadan
Nur Abad

To Amman (Jordan)
Tigris River
Al Kut

To Kuwait City
PERSIAN GULF
To Shiraz (123km); Bushehr (161km)

BAZARGAN   بازرگان
☎ 0462

Bazargan is a gun-barrel straight strip of shops, car repair yards and cheap hotels pointed towards the silhouette of Mt Ararat's twin peaks. The village ends abruptly at the outer border gate, from which a gated road winds 2.5km up a hill to the immigration post. While westbound travellers arriving late will save money by sleeping in Bazargan, eastbound it's recommended to continue to Maku. Ten kilometres along the Maku road, a muddy 2km track leads to **Farhad Dameh**, a mildly interesting cave-dwelling with churchlike niches. It's thought to be part of the Urartian citadel of **Sangar**. There are fine views of Ararat, and more modest views of Sangar village across the unbridged river.

Sleeping & Eating
There are nine cheap hotels, all on the northern side of the main drag, Imam St.

Hotel Hamid (☎ 337 2435; Imam St; tw IR50,000) Some 300m from the outer border gate, Hamid has the only rooms in town with (squat) toilet. It's simple but spacious and clean. There's a fairly pleasant ground-floor restaurant.

Hotel Jafapoor (☎ 337 2058; Imam St; dm/tw IR15,000/30,000) Right beside the outer border gate the friendly Jafapoor is basic and rather shabby. Some rooms have showers, but un-exciting, shared toilets.

Qods Lokantasi (☎ 337 2928; Imam St; meals IR9000-20,000; 24hr incl Ramazan) Downstairs beside the Jafapoor this basement dive's speciality is *ät*, hunks of boiled-on-the-bone beef. Many other roadhouse restaurants serve similar Azari food.

Getting There & Away
There is no need to take the expensive taxis whose drivers tout outside the immigration post. Instead take the IR500 shuttle bus down to Bazargan village (or walk for 30 minutes). Just beyond the outer border gate, Bazargan's main taxi stand is in front of the Hotel Jafapoor. From here to Maku you should pay IR2000 to IR3000 per person, IR10,000 per car direct or IR20,000 with an excursion to Sangar. A savari to Tabriz costs IR20,000 per person, or charter a savari for US$20, including a side trip to Qareh Kalisa. There are no longer any minibuses.

MAKU   ماکو
☎ 0462 / pop 38,000 / elevation 1630m

Boxed into a soaring rocky canyon, little Maku is a particularly appealing introduction to Iran. Long a key fortress and citadel

---

CROSSING THE TURKISH BORDER AT BAZARGAN

The customs/immigration post sits on a hilltop 2.5km from Bazargan village. On the Turkish side it's called Gürbulak but there's no village whatever, the nearest accommodation being 40km away in Doğubayazıt. The border is busy and can be somewhat chaotic, especially westbound on the Turkish side: most foreigners need a Turkish visa sticker to enter Turkey; these are available from a separate office and it's frustratingly pointless to join the melee of locals fighting for an entry stamp till you've got one. This office might close in the evenings even though the border itself theoretically works all night (with go-slows at meal times). International buses cross the border but you might wait anywhere between three and 16 hours to clear customs.

A vehicle crossing can take as little as 1½ hours, assuming you have the correct carnet (now virtually impossible to get on arrival). Drivers' insurance purchased at the border costs US$45; it can be more cheaply arranged in Tabriz with the help of the tourist information office.

Eastbound you're strongly recommended to change money at a little bank office on the Iran side. It's right within the immigration building behind the (normally closed) tourist information office and gives excellent rates for US dollars cash (but won't change anything else). For Turkish lira you'll have to deal with moneychanging rogues on either side who are expert at a dozen varieties of note-counting scams. Moharram, the gregarious owner of the Hotel Jafapoor in Bazargan village, is more reliable. Note that Turkish lira are virtually worthless in Iran beyond Bazargan.

Dolmuşlar (minibuses) costing US$1.40 in lira take 25 minutes between Gürbulak and Doğubayazıt, where they depart from the junction of Ağrı and Sehiltik Sts, 300m beyond the Ağrı *dolmuş* stand, or five minutes' walk from the little bus station. The last Gürbulak *dolmuş* leaves around 5pm, after which a taxi will cost around US$20. On foot it takes about an hour.

guarding the Ottoman–Persian frontier, Maku was one of the many Azerbaijani khanates which gained semi-independence in the chaotic period following the death of Nadir Shah in 1749. Although rejoining Iran in 1829, the khanate was only finally abolished a century later. Today there are enough curiosities to keep you interested for half a day, and Maku makes a sensible base for visits to the old Armenian church of Qareh Kalisa.

Orientation & Information

Small but very long, Maku starts with a lobe of new town, 14km south of Bazargan. The single main street, dual carriageway Resalat Blvd, funnels into narrower Imam Khomeini Ave, reaching the centre (little Chahara Sq) after 7km and the bus station 3km beyond. Super-keen freelance guide **Islam Suleymani** (☎ 324 2428) is likely to find you before you look for him. He claims he can show you the best areas for hiking, ice climbing and mountain ecology. **Kafenet Misaq** (☎ 322 6518; per hr IR10,000; ☺ 7.30am-midnight) is the handiest Internet café, hidden in a passage of new shops just west of Bank Melli, 300m west of Chahara Sq.

Sights

Just off Chahara Sq, Taleqani St passes an old **fire station** facing a **former hospital**. Beside the latter, a side street leads swiftly to **Karkh**, a celebrated century-old house with filigree wrought-iron balconies. Nearby pathways lead steeply up through a largely derelict **citadel** between remnant brick fortifications culminating in a vertical cliff above the **Abu Fazl Mosque**, which some claim was originally an Armenian church. It's worth the sweaty hike (40 minutes up, 15 minutes down) to poke about the vestiges of a 17th-century fortress, including the ruined **Zindan Shah Abbas** (royal prison). At the top, amid the wax of votive candles, are great views from a pool of holy water that bleeds from the cliffside.

The attractive **Baqcheh Juq Palace Museum** (☎ 324 3719; admission IR20,000; ☺ 9am-1pm & 3-5pm Tue-Sun) was originally built for the *sardar* (military governor) of Muzaffar al-Din, Qajar shah (1896–1907). Eclectically furnished rooms with colourful, quaintly tacky fruit murals are set around a wonderfully over-the-top mirror-tiled atrium. It's set in an appealing orchard at the far west end of town, 2km off the main Bazargan road via a big roundabout 7km west of Chahara Sq: IR5000 by taxi. Behind is a traditional village of hay-topped mud houses rising steeply into a tree-dotted chasm.

Sleeping & Eating

All accommodation is close to Chahara Sq along Imam Khomeini Ave.

Makoo Tourist Inn (Mehmunsara Jahangardi; ☎ 322 3212; fax 322 3184; tw/ste US$15/23; ℗) Appealing and quiet, the Tourist Inn is a green three-storey block set well back off Imam Khomeini Ave, signed in English 400m west of Chahara Sq. Despite a little peeling paint and lack of toilet paper, the rooms are relatively up-market with shower and squat toilet, towels, soap, shampoo and fridge. Prices are negotiable.

Hotel Alvand (☎ 322 3491; s/tw IR35,000/45,000) Just west of the square, the friendly Alvand has fans, shared squat toilets on both floors, a hot shower downstairs and glimpsed views of the citadel from some quieter back rooms.

Hotel Laleh (☎ 322 3441; s/tw IR40,000/60,000) Directly opposite the Alvand, the Laleh has showers in the rooms, but shared squat loos.

Delgosha (☎ 322 3623; s/tw/tr IR21,400/26,100/31,500; ℗) Of three very basic mosaferkhunehs (lodging houses), the most bearable is this one, with shared squat toilets and washbasins, but no showers.

There are bakeries, nut shops and simple kababis around Chahara Sq, but smarter places such as **Pasha Baba** (☎ 324 4419; Resalat Blvd; meals IR13,000-18,000; ☺ 8am-10pm) are over 2km further west. The Makoo Tourist Inn's **restaurant** (meals IR15,000-25,000), the town centre's smartest option, has excellent soup, but Fawlty Towers service and very little food in stock.

Getting There & Away

From the bus station at the eastern (Tabriz) end of town there are buses to Tehran (IR45,000, three daily), Tabriz (IR12,000, four hours, six daily), departing at 6.30am, 7.15am, 8.30am, 9am, 12.30pm and 1.30pm, and Orumiyeh (IR10,000 to IR13,000, 4½ hours, five daily), departing at 7am, 7.30am, 8am, 2.30pm and 3.30pm, via Khoy (IR5000). Alternatively use savaris via Khoy or Marand.

AROUND MAKU

An interesting one-day taxi charter would take you from Maku via Qareh Kalisa to Chaldoran and on via Bastam to Qareh Ziya'-eddin, whence there are frequent savari connections to Khoy.

Qareh Kalisa   قره كليسا

The road between Shot and Chaldoran rolls through arid hills that spring turns into bright green flower-filled meadows. Some 8km off this road beyond a photogenically low-rise Kurdish village is the splendid **Qareh Kalisa** (Black Church; admission IR20,000; ☺ 8am-1pm & 2-7pm), the best maintained of all Iran's medieval churches. It is more accurately known as Kalisa-ye Tadi (Church of St Thaddaeus) because St Thaddaeus (aka Tatavoos) supposedly founded a church here in AD 43. Some say he came with apostle St Bartholomew, others that he was St Bartholomew. Whatever the case, Thaddaeus' preaching proved a little too successful and the jealous Armenian king reacted by killing him and massacring his 3000 converts in AD 66. In a curious twist, Armenia later became the world's first Christian nation (AD 301) and Thaddaeus' memory was revived with a chapel built here at his supposed grave (AD 371).

Mostly rebuilt after an earthquake, the smaller black-and-white striped chapel dates from 1319–29. It was much restored and enlarged in 1810 when the main beige-white stone section was added. This is richly carved with saints, angels, kings and crosses, best observed from the chunky fortress-style walls which surround the church site. The interior is mostly whitewashed and was full of scaffolding at the time of research. The only Christian services are held during a brilliant three-day summer pilgrimage; dates vary and are announced shortly beforehand. Contact the Armenian diocesan office in Tabriz for details. Bring a tent.

There is no public transport. Taxis don't like to take the narrow, painfully potholed road from Bazargan via Kalisa Kandi and Chaldoran, which crosses rolling, mostly empty moorland. Access is quicker and easier from Maku (IR70,000 return) via Shot on a newly upgraded road.

Chaldoran   چالدوران

The scraggy little market town marked as Siyah Cheshmeh on most maps has recently reverted to the medieval name of Chaldoran (Chaldiran, Chaldran), known to all Iranians for its historically pivotal battle. In 1514, 6km from the present town, the Ottoman forces of Selim-the-Grim devastatingly defeated Safavid shah Ismail's formerly invincible Persian–Azari army. Of 27,000 Iranian soldiers a phenomenal 26,000 died, cut down by Selim's newfangled secret weapon, the cannon. The battle was followed by a scorched-earth policy that devastated agricultural settlements across much of west Azarbayjan and Kordestan, leaving the emptied land to grazing nomads for centuries to come.

The lonely battlefield, **Chaldoran Changi**, is newly commemorated by an impressively large, bulbous, brick-domed tomb tower and a statue of Seyid Sadraddin, the Persian army's hapless commander.

There are three buses per week to Tehran and two daily to Qareh Ziya'-eddin (1pm and 2pm, returning 11am and noon). Savaris are infrequent so combining Chaldoran with a taxi charter to Qareh Kalisa makes sense. The battlefield is a IR5000 taxi ride from Chaldoran market, beyond the quaint village of Jala Ashaqi.

Bastam   بسطام
& Qareh Ziya'-eddin   قره ضياء الدين

Of Iran's many Urartian sites, Bastam (aka Rusai-Urutur) is probably the most impressive. That's not saying much. It's simply a steep unfenced rocky hill, but if sheer age excites you, reflect that the occasionally visible, eroded steps were probably carved into the rock around 685–645 BC. Along with slithering sheep-paths, these teeter up the edge of a precipice forming a veritable stairway to heaven. After a 30-minute scramble the summit reveals what looks like a Bronze-Age helipad. There are lovely views into the valley beyond. The site is 6km down a dead-end road that starts at the far-western edge of Qareh Ziya'-eddin, signed south off the Chaldoran road. Park where the asphalt stops and the archaeology department incredibly appears to be rebuilding the massive lower ramparts, which till now have appeared only as partly defined rock-terraces. Taxis from Qareh Ziya'-eddin want IR25,000 return, including the necessary 90-minute wait.

From unexciting low-rise Qareh Ziya'-eddin (population 23,000) to Khoy there are frequent buses (IR2600) and savaris (IR6000, 50 minutes). Head 3km northeast of the centre to the main Bazargan road to pick up passing transport for Maku or Tabriz.

KHOY خوی
☎ 0461 / pop 170,000

Occupied since Median times, Khoy (Salt) was named for the salt mines that made it an important spur of the silk route. While not worth a lengthy detour, Khoy is more appealing than much bigger Orumiyeh, with which it shares a long history as an important Christian centre.

Orientation & Information

The town centre is Imam Khomeini Sq where Enqelab (east), Imam (west), Shari'ati (north) and Taleqani (south) Sts all intersect.

With several name changes, initially attractive Imam St passes **Khoy Kafenet** (Internet per hr IR8000; ◷ 8am-7pm Sat-Thu), Basij Sq, the telephone office, Gumsal Sq (aka Kesarvaz Sq), Kochari Sq, a flashy Imamzade and Imam Hossein Sq, where many shared taxis turn around or swing right along 22 Bahman St. Taleqani St leads south to Valiasr Sq and eventually to the Salmas bus station 2km beyond. From Valiasr Sq, diagonally eastbound Chamran St converges with Enqelab St, continuing well past the post office and Motahhari St to the Tabriz bus terminal 2km east. **Bank Melli** (Enqelab St) changes money.

Sights

The roofless **Motalleb Khan Mosque** (Taleqani St; admission by request) is a huge 13th-century Ilkhanid edifice of unadorned brickwork, which claims to have the world's largest mihrab. Ask nicely and you might be shown up onto the roof through passages in the super-thick walls. It's just off Imam Khomeini Sq, through a triple-arched gateway. A short block east, the long, one-street **vaulted bazaar** paralleling Taleqani St links two more modest historic mosques and emerges into Perastori Park at the **Darvazeh Sangi** (stone gate). This black-and-white stone arch with two carved lions is the last remnant of the former city wall.

The squat, stone cube of **St Sarkis Church** (Kalisa Sorop Serkis; Imam St), just beyond Gumsal Sq, looks ancient, though how much of it really dates from the 4th century is questionable. It was mostly rebuilt in the 1730s.

SHAMS TABRIZI

If you find Khomeini-style Islam a little stony faced, don't be put off. Iran has produced other inspirational Muslim thinkers. One such was Sufi philosopher Shams Tabrizi. Bravely and often with humour he was keen to point out that religion is not an end in itself, merely the first step in a personal journey of spiritual discovery. His *Khatesevom* is generally translated as *The Third Line*. But *The Third Path* might be more accurate, echoing the middle way of the Buddha.

The **Shams Tabrizi Minaret** is a unique 300-year-old tower encrusted with protruding animal horns, many now hanging like old party balloons. It's named for the 13th-century dervish who inspired the more famous poet Rumi (see the boxed text 'Shams Tabrizi', above). The tower is hidden away in unpromising back alleys off 22 Bahman St, north of Imam Hossein Sq.

Pol-e-Khatoon is an attractive 18th-century bridge, 2km south of the Salmas terminal. Views are spoilt by the busy Salmas road, which thunders beside it.

Sleeping & Eating

The best central cheapies are both within a block of Imam Khomeini Sq.

Khoy Tourist Inn (Mehmunsara Jahangardi; ☎ 244 0351; fax 244 0352; Enqelab St; tw US$20) Modern yet cosy, and with English-speaking staff, this super-clean place has rooms with Western toilets and excellent showers. It has a pleasant enough kebab **restaurant** (meals IR15,000-20,000; ◷ 7am-9.30pm).

Hotel Saadat (☎ 222 3560; Shari'ati St; tw IR30,000) Meaning 'happiness' this place is an unusually clean mosaferkhuneh with fresh new sheets.

Sepid (☎ 222 4234; Taleqani St; tw IR30,000) Slightly mustier than the Saadat, the Sepid's shared hot shower is hidden away through the central kitchen.

There are several cheaper kababis and snack bars along Taleqani St, food barrows appear in the evening on nearby Imam Khomeini Sq and there's a small, sweet if fairly standard teahouse **Eram** (tea IR500) with qalyans (water pipes) and plenty of questions as to why you ventured in.

Getting There & Away

From the Salmas terminal buses leave at least hourly to Orumiyeh from 5.15am to 4.30pm (IR650) along with minibuses when full to Salmas. For Tabriz, Maku, Marand and Qareh Ziya'eddin use the easy-to-miss Tabriz terminal at the corner of Motharikh Hagihosinlus St behind a tatty grocery shop.

SALMAS   سلماس
☎ 0461 / pop 75,000

Archaeologists suggest that Gül Tappeh (Ash Hill) once housed one of the world's first settled civilisations (7th millennium BC). Today the site is a mere muddy mound in a field 5km from Salmas accessed by a 600m-long orchard track off the lane to Keleshan village. Salmas itself was known to the Medes as Zarvand, and was founded under Assyrian king Salmansar III (3rd millennium BC) as a bulwark against Babylonian incursions. The Sassanid Persians staked a claim with the royal inscription **Khan Takhti** carved into a cliff 14km south of the city. That's now highlighted with white-and-green painted 'frame' at the Sero turning of the Salmas–Orumiyeh road.

Influenced by Armenia and Caucasian Albania, Salmas later became a major Christian centre. Although ravaged by the Turkish invasion of 1915 it remains a Chaldean Catholic bishopric, though the original Chaldean spiritual centre was **Haftevan**, 4km to the south. Haftevan village retains its 17th-century cubic stone **church** with wobbly polygonal tower, albeit locked in a fenced garden.

Known as Shahpur under the Pahlavis, Salmas lost most other visible remnants of its history to a massive 1930 earthquake and today it's an unremarkable apple- and pumpkin-processing town.

The Orumiyeh–Khoy road bypasses Salmas on a new ring road, but it's easy to visit on frequent minibuses from either town. To reach Sero via Mamakan you'll need to charter a taxi (IR100,000, 1¾ hours). It's easy to visit Khan Takhti and Haftevan en route, but add at least an hour extra if you want to reach and explore Gül Tappeh too. Savaris to Tabriz (IR20,000, 2½ hours) go via **Tasuj**, which has an historic Jameh Mosque.

SERO   سرو
Four kilometres west of the minuscule village of Sero is a secondary border-crossing point between Iran and Turkey, and it is much quieter, and therefore quicker, than at Bazargan (p123).

At the layby before the immigration post, bolshy waiting taxis want IR50,000 per car (45 minutes) to Orumiyeh, and threaten to beat up passing drivers who offer to charge less. So to hitch it's best to walk as far as possible away from the border. Walk 6km downhill to the first police post (Mingöl road junction) for the nearest minibus.

The direct route to Salmas by taxi (IR100,000, 1¾ hours) is quieter and more scenic than the Orumiyeh road, especially in the first section through the upper Gonbadchay Valley. Although there is a 25-minute unpaved section between Mingöl and Mamakan, the road is easy enough for a Paykan, no matter what taxi drivers might claim.

ORUMIYEH   ورميه
☎ 0441 / pop 500,000

Unexpectedly huge, Orumiyeh (Urmia, Urumiyeh) was known as Rezaiyeh during the Pahlavi era. It's culturally Azari and deeply historic, but offers little of visual tourist interest. However it has good transport connections and a wide choice of mid-range accommodation. It is an inevitable connection point if you're circling Lake Orumiyeh.

CROSSING THE TURKISH BORDER AT SERO

Called Esendere on the Turkish side, this border post is just a few lonely buildings below a mountain pass. Immigration supposedly works 8am to 10.30pm (9.30am to midnight Turkish time); there is no accommodation so try to cross in daylight in case it closes early. Even in winter a gaggle of moneychangers (Iran side) shiver outside the compound.

Turkish-side transport is by dolmuş to/from Yüksekova 40km away, a town served by Van- and Hakkari-bound buses (roughly every two hours). The route to/from Van (three hours) passes the magnificent ruins of Hoşap Castle halfway.

If you're on a short Iranian transit visa, use the Sero border: if you leave Van early in the morning you'll reach Orumiyeh in time for the night bus to Esfahan.

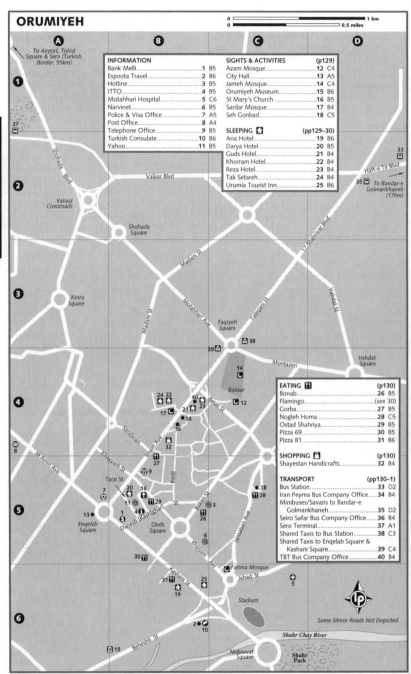

ORUMIYEH

0 _____ 1 km
0 _____ 0.5 miles

To Airport, Tohid Square & Sero (Turkish Border; 55km)

INFORMATION	
Bank Melli.................................1	B5
Espoota Travel...........................2	B6
Hotline.....................................3	B5
ITTO..4	B5
Motahhari Hospital.....................5	C6
Narvinet...................................6	B5
Police & Visa Office....................7	A5
Post Office................................8	A4
Telephone Office........................9	B5
Turkish Consulate.....................10	B6
Yahoo....................................11	B5

SIGHTS & ACTIVITIES	(p129)
Azam Mosque..........................12	C4
City Hall..................................13	A5
Jameh Mosque.........................14	C4
Orumiyeh Museum.....................15	B6
St Mary's Church........................16	B5
Sardar Mosque..........................17	B4
Seh Gonbad.............................18	C5

SLEEPING	(pp129–30)
Ana Hotel................................19	B6
Darya Hotel.............................20	B5
Guds Hotel..............................21	B4
Khorram Hotel..........................22	B4
Reza Hotel...............................23	B4
Tak Setareh.............................24	B4
Urumia Tourist Inn.....................25	B6

EATING	(p130)
Bonab....................................26	B5
Flamingo............................(see 30)	
Gorba....................................27	B5
Nogleh Homa...........................28	C5
Ostad Shahriya.........................29	B5
Pizza 69..................................30	B5
Pizza 81..................................31	B6

SHOPPING	(p130)
Shayestan Handicrafts.................32	B4

TRANSPORT	(pp130–1)
Bus Station..............................33	D2
Iran Peyma Bus Company Office.....34	B4
Minibuses/Savaris to Bandar-e	
Golmankhaneh.......................35	D2
Seiro Safar Bus Company Office......36	B4
Sero Terminal...........................37	A1
Shared Taxis to Bus Station...........38	C3
Shared Taxis to Enqelab Square &	
Kashani Square.......................39	C4
TBT Bus Company Office...............40	B4

Haft-e Tir Blvd

To Bandar-e Golmankhaneh (17km)

Shohada Blvd

Valiasr Blvd

Valiasr Crossroads

Shohada Square

Madani St

Kesra Square

Madani St

Motahhari Ave

Faqiyeh Square

Taleqani St

17 Shahriwar Blvd

Vahdat St

Vahdat Square

Montazeri

Bazaar

Sandian

Khayyam St

Imam Ave

Besat St

M Amin Ave

Tarzi St

Basij

Bakeri St

Jantaban Ave

Danesh (Kashighari) St

Qods Square

Khayyam Ave

Enqelab Square

Kashani St

Jehad St

Fatima Mosque

Stadium

Some Minor Roads Not Depicted

Beheshti St

Shahr Chay River

Nobovvat Square

Shahr Park

WESTERN IRAN

History

Known as the 'Garden of Persia', Orumi-yeh's fruit gardens made it prosperous for millennia. Until the late 19th century it was the centre of a large Christian community in which Chaldeans, Armenians, Assyrians and Nestorians, as well as a thriving Jewish com-munity, lived undisturbed. Then overzealous Protestant and Catholic foreign missionaries arrived in force and the result was a harsh backlash against all non-Muslims. This was initially led by Kurdish groups fearing the possible loss of territory should a Christian-Armenian state be declared. The first mas-sacres came in 1880 when the Persian army stormed Orumiyeh to counterattack Kurd-ish nationalist leader Sheikh Ubayd Allah. Christians were massacred by both sides and orchards were devastated. In 1918 his-tory threatened to repeat itself in the face of an Ottoman invasion. Most of the Christian population fled Orumiyeh, Salmas and Khoy – a sensible precaution given the butchery that had just befallen the Armenians in eastern Turkey. Most of those who stayed were slaughtered, but the escapee Christian com-munity returned when the Turks retreated. Today they constitute around one-third of the population, probably the highest propor-tion in any Iranian town.

Orientation & Information

Although it's a big city, Orumiyeh has only the gentlest of slopes and it's possible (if somewhat exhausting) to get around the most central areas on foot. The main com-mercial streets are Imam Ave and Kashani St which intersect at busy but attractive Enqelab Sq. The narrower lanes directly to the west are relatively pleasant.

Bank Melli (☎ 223 6774; Kashani St) Changes major currencies, but not Turkish lira.

Espoota Travel (☎ 345 5555; espoota@espootatravel .com; Beheshti St; 🕑 8am-7pm Sat-Thu, 8am-noon Fri)

Hotline (Bakeri St; Internet per hr IR6000; 🕑 10am-9pm)

ITTO(☎ 222 7722; 2/38 Danesh (Kashtghar) St, 2nd fl; 🕑 7.30am-1.30pm Sat-Thu) Friendly but of limited use. Brochures list regional natural attractions and there's a half-hearted free city map.

Narvinet (Khayyam St; Internet per hr IR7000; 🕑 8am-10pm)

Police (Enqelab Sq) The office marked 'Administration of Foreign Affairs' could theoretically extend visas, but very rarely will. Better to try in Tabriz.

Post Office (M Amiri Ave) Shared taxi from Enqelab Sq.

Telephone Office (Imam Ave; 🕑 8am-midnight) Help-ful and efficient.

Yahoo (Tarzi St; Internet per hr IR7000; 🕑 7am-8pm)

Sights

Orumiyeh's most commonly depicted view is the 1932 European-style **city hall** (Enqelab Sq). However don't be tempted to take photo-graphs as the police station is nearby and at best you'll lose your camera. The **bazaar** is interesting and it's fun to hunt for the hid-den entrance of the large brick-domed **Jameh Mosque** (partly Seljuk era). Don't confuse the latter with the much more visible onion-domed **Azam Mosque** nearby. The Qajar-period **Sardar Mosque** (Imam Ave) has a tri-lobed cornice of pastel tile-work above the entrance and a beautifully brick-vaulted interior. Tucked away in a quiet mini-park the two-storey AD 1115 **Seh Gonbad** tomb tower might have started life as a Sassanian fire temple or an early type of lookout. None of the various churches are architecturally gripping. How-ever, **St Mary's** (Kalisa-ye Maryam-e Moqaddas; Khayyam St) is claimed to be the last resting place of one of the magi (three wise men) who trot-ted across to Bethlehem to greet the infant Jesus (inventing Christmas presents in the process). Magi were the pre-Islamic Persian priestly class whose mesmerising ceremonies give us the English term 'magic'. **Orumiyeh Museum** (☎ 224 6520; Beheshti St; admission IR20,000; 🕑 9am-2pm Tue-Sun) is a low-rise marble-clad building whose best exhibits are two stone rams, left outside and visible for free.

Sleeping

Orumiyeh has dozens of hotels, mostly mid-range. The following are handily central.

Reza Hotel (☎ 222 6580; Besat St; s IR50,000, tw 80-90,000; **P**) Large, dowdy-looking but ex-cellent value, the Reza has a gregarious Eng-lish-speaking owner. The neat if sometimes noisy rooms have Western loo and good hot showers with soap and towels.

Tak Setareh (☎ 223 1861; Sardar Camii Ln; s/tw IR30,000/50,000) Great-value mosaferkhuneh with a basic shower and squat.

Guds Hotel (Qods Hotel; ☎ 222 2596; Imam Ave; s/tw IR35,000/45,000) Clean and cosy by mosa-ferkhuneh standards, but shared facilities.

Khorram Hotel (Horem; ☎ 222 5444; Sardar Camii Ln; s/tw IR70,000/100,000) Tucked quietly behind the Sardar Mosque, it looks smarter than the Reza, but its rooms are no better.

Darya Hotel (☎ 222 9564; fax 222 3471; Tarzi [Chamran] St; s/d/tw US$20/30/30) Pleasant and quiet, but not worth over double the price of the Khorram.

Urumia Tourist Inn (Orumiyeh Grand Inn, Meh-munsara Jahangardi; ☎ 222 3080; fax 224 3202; Kashani St; s/d US$30/40) Completely renovated to international business standards, the Tourist Inn is now superb value, if lacking any real atmosphere.

Ana Hotel (☎/fax 345 3314; 77 Kashani St; s/d/tw IR180,000/280,000/280,000) Rooms are less attractive than you'd expect from the rather up-market new entrance. Curiously there's a 15% discount if you have a tourist visa.

For a beach-ball experience with a twist you could stay instead at nearby Bandar-e Golmankhaneh on Lake Orumiyeh (p131).

Eating

Flamingo (☎ 346 1177; Kashani St; meals IR30,000; ☺ noon-3pm & 5-10pm) This is the best city-centre restaurant. Head downstairs through a smoked-glass door with red script to find succulent kebabs and a salad bar (IR4000). Décor is restrained with solid wooden benches, lanterns and etched mirrors.

Bonab (☎ 222 5741; Bakeri St; meals IR10,000-15,000) One of several reasonably priced kababis on Bakeri (Bakerry) St featuring bread fresh from the *tandir* oven.

Pizza 69 (☎ 344 9169; Kashani St; pizzas IR15,000-22,000; ☺ noon-3pm & 5-10pm) Almost directly above Flamingo this cosy place has gentle mood-lighting.

Pizza 81 (☎ 346 1177; Kashani St; pizzas IR15,000-19,000; ☺ noon-11pm) A bright, pleasant fast-food style eatery with an English menu and generously heaped if somewhat anaemic pizzas.

Gorba (Kucheh Berg; meals IR800; ☺ lunch) Uncompromisingly down-market this hole-in-the-wall serves cheap, very sheepy *dizi* (see the boxed text 'Getting Dizi', right).

Ostad Shahriya (Khayyam St; qalyan IR5000; ☺ 10am-11pm) This is a carpet-decked tea-house, upstairs near the church, that's wonderfully friendly – if male dominated.

Nogleh Homa (Janbazan Ave; ☺ 10am-9pm) The local speciality *noqleh* (white sugar-coated nuts) is made here using big copper coating vessels which are on display.

Cakes, fruit juices and baked potatoes are to be found around the bazaar entrance on Imam Ave.

GETTING DIZI

Known alternatively as *abgusht* (or as *piti* in Azerbaijan) *dizi* is a cheap Azari meal named for the earthenware pot in which it's served. Don't just dig in. The first stage is to drain off the soupy broth and soak it up with bread. Then turn to the main ingredients. The chickpeas, potatoes, tomatoes, onions and soft boiled mutton should be accompanied by a large chunk of fat. It looks rather unappetising, but tastes delicious. When correctly mashed into a paste using the curious pestle device provided the typical design looks like a stylised toilet plunger.

Shopping

Shayestan Handicrafts (Imam Ave) stocks Esfahan-style inlaid boxes. **Iran Handicrafts Organisation** (Imam Ave) has a wide range of curios, carvings and rugs.

Getting There & Away

AIR

There are two flights daily to Tehran (IR207,000), best purchased at English-speaking Espoota Travel (p129).

BUS, MINIBUS & SAVARI

All long-distance buses leave from the bus station on Haft-e Tir Blvd, but companies TBT, Seiro Safar and Iran Peyma have handy booking offices on Imam Ave. Vangölu has a daily service to Van, Turkey ($10, eight hours) at 9.30am, but you will spend half of the journey time waiting at the border.

Use TBT for Kermanshah (IR26,500, 11 hours) at 6.30pm and 7.30pm or Ahvaz (IR46,000, 19 hours) at 3.30pm, Seiro Safar for Sanandaj (IR23,100, nine hours, several) and Iran Peyma for Esfahan (IR50,000, 19 hours) at 4pm. For Maku, Taavoni 9 goes direct (IR9500, five hours) at 8.30am, 10am, 2pm and 4pm or you could make minibus/savari hops via Salmas and Khoy. Taavoni 11 has one or two buses hourly to Maraqeh (IR8850, four hours) with the last at 4.30pm. Tabriz buses (IR10,800, 4½ hours) leave every half-hour and circle around via Tasuj, but it's much more interesting to use savaris (IR25,000, 3½ hours), which take a causeway and ferry combination across Lake Orumiyeh's narrow waist.

In summer minibuses and savaris (IR2000, 20 minutes) leave frequently to Bandar-e Golmankhaneh from the corner of Valiasr and Haft-e Tir Blvds; in winter, you might need to charter a taxi.

For Sero most locals use a taxi (IR30,000 to IR50,000), though savaris (IR10,000) are occasionally to be found outside Orumiyeh's Sero terminal (off Raja'i Blvd). From that terminal many minibuses head up to villages of the Gonbadchay Valley. These cost very little and take you almost to Sero, turning north 6km before the border. It's a gamble to hope for a waiting taxi service at that turning and no public transport covers the last section to the frontier, but hitching is feasible if the police post permits.

Getting Around
A taxi to the airport costs only IR20,000 (20 minutes). The most useful shared-taxi routes run from Faqiyeh Sq, either along Imam Ave then down Kashani St or up Taleqani St to the bus station.

LAKE ORUMIYEH & AROUND
دریاچه ورمیه
A Unesco Biosphere Reserve since 1976, Lake Orumiyeh is huge (6000 sq km), but shallow (maximum seasonal depth 16m). Its super-salty waters are therapeutic for rheumatism but don't make for great swimming and support only very primitive life forms, such as the artimasalenya worm. However, this is enough to attract plenty of migratory birds, notably flamingos in spring, which are most conveniently viewed from Bandar-e Golmankhaneh, near Orumiyeh.

Hulagu Khan, grandson of Genghis Khan and founder of Iran's Ilkhanid Mongol dynasty, had his treasury on **Kabudi Island** in the middle of the lake. His burial there in 1265 was accompanied by the wholesale sacrifice of virgins, as demanded by the custom of the day. Archaeologists are still examining the site, but for now it's inaccessible and generally closed to tourists.

The lake's hard-to-access **eastern coastline** is starkly barren; the vivid blue waters contrast with jagged, sun-blasted rocks and parched mud-flat islands. A great way to glimpse this otherworldly landscape is to take a shared taxi (*not* a bus) between Tabriz and Orumiyeh, which involves a picturesque little ferry ride across the lake's pinched waistline.

The western coast is greener but the orchards stop short of the shore.

A perfectly feasible, if rather underwhelming day trip (taxi IR250,000), loops south from Orumiyeh to Mahabad, Miyando'ab, Bonab and Maraqeh. While physically possible in minibus hops, you might need to stop one night in Mahabad or Miyando'ab, whence it's possible to cut southeast to Takht-e Soleiman.

Bandar-e Golmankhaneh   بندر گلمانخانه
☎ 0443
The most accessible lakeside from Orumiyeh (17km) is a 2km strip of mud flats with a few scattered houses, a lonely windswept jetty and two 'resorts', but no village per se. Beyond the headland is the popular Kashtiban picnic area. In spring, ornithologists flock to Bandar-e Golmankhaneh for flamingo-watching. The area becomes a melee of holiday-makers in summer, but is eerily atmospheric and lonely on a stormy winter's day. **Fanous** (☎ 236 2356; apt IR200,000; ✖) has big motel-style units with one double and two single beds, kitchen, lounge and bathroom (with shower and squat). The lake is visible from the terrace. Much bigger, but nearer the water, is the holiday-camp style **Flamingo-Chichest** (☎ 236 2015; s/d 150,000/200,000; P IR10,000).

In summer, shared taxis (IR2000, 25 minutes) run from Haft-e Tir St, and sometimes Faqiyeh Sq, in Orumiyeh. In winter, you'll probably need to charter a taxi (IR20,000 return, plus waiting time).

Hasanlu   حسنلو
☎ 0443 / pop 400
Famous for a priceless 11th-century BC golden chalice found here (not displayed), Hasanlu was an important Iron-Age settlement that gradually developed into a fortified citadel over 4000 years. Mutilated skeletons found here (not shown either) suggest that the population met a barbaric end at the hands of the Urartians in the 9th century BC. Today the citadel is a muddy hillock rising behind Hasanlu village. Divided by what archaeologists take to be streets, the wall stumps of former dwellings and storehouses have recently been plastered for protection with straw-flecked adobe. There are a few standing stones which were probably gateways. Wide peaceful panoramas of

fields and hay-topped village roofs are pleasant, but 20 minutes here is ample for most nonspecialists.

The site is unfenced 8km off the Orumiyeh–Mahabad road via Mohammad Yar (the last 2km unsurfaced after Shonagar). It's further (15km), but easier, to access via Naqadeh, from which there's a good asphalt road (7km, IR15,000 taxi return). Naqadeh minibuses run when full to Orumiyeh and Mahabad.

Mahabad مهاباد
☎ 0442 / pop 123,000

Incredibly this unassuming market city was once the capital of its own minicountry. The Mahabad Republic was a Soviet-inspired independent Kurdish state, but it survived only one year (1946), collapsing once the USSR patched things up with Tehran. In the 17th century, as Savajbulaq Mokri, Mahabad had been the regional capital. Today, in the ramshackle bazaar, there's a fine if over-restored **Jameh Mosque**, with new-looking brick vaulting and soaring twin minarets. Kurdish cummerbunds and baggy trousers tell you this is somewhere different, but otherwise the town's appeal is as a base for striking out across the Kordestan mountains. The road to Saqqez via Bukan has some great views. Some 30km from Mahabad it passes close to the Ali Sadr–style **Sahulan Water Caves**.

A kilometre west of the Miyando'ab road, 9km north of Mahabad, **Fakhrigah** is a Median 'crypt' cave carved into a rock face on a hilly outcrop. It's fleetingly visible from the main road near the Bukan turn-off.

On Mahabad's unnamed main drag halfway between the bus station (900m) and bazaar, the **Hotel Kohestan** (Koystan; ☎ 233 5738; Shahid Kandi; s/tw IR75,000/105,000) has bearable rooms with rather musty shower and squat.

Minibuses are frequent to Miyando'ab (IR1000, 30 minutes) and Orumiyeh (IR4500, two hours).

Miyando'ab میاندوآب
☎ 0481 / pop 104,000

The much-touted **museum** (Imam St Park) in the large, flat market town of Miyando'ab (Miandob) has yet to open and the old **Mirza Rasoul Bridge** at the southern city limits is visible as you drive by on the Mahabad road. Thus the only compelling reason to stop is for transport connections to Takab

or Takht-e Soleiman, generally via Shahin Dezh. Nonetheless, the plush new **Hotel Berenjian** (☎ 222 4975; fax 222 7870; Imam St; tw IR110,000) is phenomenally good value and very central.

The (hidden) terminal for minibuses to Shahin Dezh (IR4000, two hours) is at the first roundabout (with four white geese) as you arrive from Tabriz. The main bus terminal is 1500m nearer town, just beyond the concrete 'clock on pincers' roundabout, where Imam St turns right towards the town centre. A single daily Iran Peyma bus runs from here at 2pm to Takab (IR6000, three hours). Mahabad minibuses (IR1000, 30 minutes) and savaris leave from a third terminal 4km away in the far southwest. Shared-taxi rides cost IR300 between the centre and any terminal.

Maraqeh مراغه
☎ 0421 / pop 135,000

A pleasantly rolling city full of plane trees and dotted with 800-year-old tomb towers, Maraqeh (Maragheh, Maraga) is a fairly easy 150km day trip southeast of Tabriz. Having destroyed the town in 1221, the Mongols changed heart and splendidly rebuilt it as their capital 35 years later, along with the world's foremost **observatory** (operational by 1262). Tragically this, along with its magnificent library, was destroyed a century later during Tamerlane's ravages. Today a new observatory (rasad-khana) rises on the old site, a windswept hill 3km to the northwest of the city centre (behind the TV station). You can't enter, but views nearby are sweeping and there are cave rooms in the cliff below.

The city centre is Mosallah Sq where Taleqani St, rising from the train station, meets commercial Armenistan St. Heading west (eventually to the observatory), the latter initially crosses Dezhban St, then a small river and busy Mo'allem Sq which is one long, diagonal block northeast of Gaz Sq. Here is the bus station; very nearby the Darya Hotel offers its guests free ultrabasic city maps.

TOWER TOMBS

Finding the tombs is the main fun because there's nothing much inside. The most interesting is the sizable **Gonbad-e Sorkh** (Red Tower). Brick with some tile remnants, the square plan is topped by a squinch-pinched octagon. Here an upper window hole is positioned with such astronomical precision that sunlight shines directly onto the inner doorway at spring equinox. Possibly it was a comparison of this light-angle with similar findings at Radkan (p332) that allowed the brilliant Iranian mathematician Nasruddin Tusi (Nasir Al-Tusi) to accurately calculate the diameter of the earth, centuries before the Western world even guessed it was round. The tower is hidden in an easy-to-miss walled yard. Identifying the unmarked door is easiest by spotting the tomb-top from the raised parking area beside **Gonbad-e Arqala** (Arg-tomb; Arqala; Mirhabib St). This is a seven-minute walk from Mosallah Sq: head down Taleqani St towards the train station. Having passed the Arya Hotel, turn left then follow the road that winds up the hill.

The **Gonbad-e Qaffariyeh** (Dezhban St) is a squat, square affair with a few blue tiles. It's in a riverside garden with a tacky trio of dolphins, 15 minutes' walk from Mo'allem Sq.

You'll need a taxi to find the not-very-blue **Gonbad-e Kabul** (Blue Dome) thought to be the tomb of Hulagu Khan's mum. It's the most ornately decorated of all the towers, but hidden away in a school yard, along with the **Borj-e Modavvar**.

Beside an old brick hammam (bath-house) in **Bonab**, 16km to the west, the active **Mehrabad Mosque** (Motahhari St) has a superb interior of carved wooden columns. Behind it is a traditional domed brick bathhouse. However, Bonab is suspected to house a nuclear research centre, so don't go poking around in the far northern suburbs.

SLEEPING & EATING
Sleeping in Miyando'ab is better value.

Darya Hotel (☎ 325 0304; www.Darya-hotel.com; Shekari Blvd; s/d/ste US$30/35/45) Two minutes' walk west of the bus station, the Darya has fully equipped tourist standard rooms, including cable TV.

Arya Hotel (☎ 222 2294; dm IR20,000) The Arya is the only alternative to the Darya. It is central, but unappealingly basic, with ropy rooms that share a squat toilet and single tap. Foreigners are not always accepted.

There are many cheap eateries around Mosallah Sq and the Darya Hotel has decent food. Or try the semi-smart riverside **Oba Restaurant** (Dezhban St), halfway between Armenistan St and the Gonbad-e Qaffariyeh.

GETTING THERE & AWAY
Iran Aseman has flights to Tehran on Tuesday and Saturday (IR180,000) from nearby Sahand Airport. To Tabriz, savaris take 1¾ hours (IR15,000); buses (IR5000, 2½ hours) leave roughly every 30 minutes. There are fairly regular buses from Orumiyeh (IR12,000) or use minibus/savari hops via Bonab, Miyando'ab and Mahabad. The train station is 400m south of Mosallah Sq, with convenient overnight services to Tehran (IR24,100, 10 hours) at 6.30pm (easiest for ticket availability), 8.16pm (most comfortable) and 10.07pm.

TABRIZ   تبریز
☎ 0411 / pop 1,220,000
Once a pretty oasis, Tabriz is now a gigantic sprawling city that's intriguing though not especially attractive. Although ethnically Azari, it had a spell as the Iranian capital and has proved extremely influential in much of recent history. For many travellers it serves as a fine introduction to Iran, thanks in part to the passionately helpful freelance guides available. Sometimes stiflingly smoggy and hot in summer, it can be freezing cold in winter – but the welcome is generally very warm any time of year. While in Tabriz don't miss an excursion to Kandovan, Iran's 'Cappadocia'.

History
Tabriz's early history is shrouded in mystery. Certain biblical clues point to the Ajichay River flowing out of the Garden of Eden, placing Tabriz at the gates of paradise. In any case, the city is believed to date back at least to the Sassanian period and had long been the regional trade and administrative hub. It came to eclipse Maraqeh as the later Mongol Ilkhanid capital of Azerbaijan until sacked by Tamerlane in 1392. It recovered remarkably rapidly and, while the rest of Iran was vassal to the Central Asian Timurids, Tabriz became the capital of a local Turkmen dynasty curiously nicknamed the Kara Koyunlu (Black Sheep). That dynasty's greatest monarch was Jahan Shah (no, *not* the Taj Mahal's Shah Jahan), under whose rule (1439–67) the city saw a remarkable flowering of arts and architecture culminating in the fabulous Blue Mosque.

Tabriz reached its zenith under Shah Ismail, the first Safavid ruler. An Azari born

WESTERN IRAN

TABRIZ

INFORMATION
ALP Tours & Travel Agency.....**1** E2
Bank Melli.....................................**2** B4
Bookshops....................................**3** B4
ITTO East Azarbaijan...................**4** C2
Jahan Seyer Travel Agency...(see 43)
Main Post Office...........................**5** C2
Pardis Clinic..................................**6** A3
Passport Office............................**7** B2
Pastor Clinic............................(see 39)
Post Office....................................**8** B4
RedNet..**9** E2
Sabs Coffeenet..........................**10** B4
Shafa Hospital...........................**11** A4
Telephone Office.......................**12** B4
Tourist Information Office.........**13** B4
Valiasr Coffeenet......................**14** F2

SIGHTS & ACTIVITIES (pp136–7)
Arg-e Tabriz...............................**15** B4
Armenian Prelacy Office............**16** A4
Azarbaijan Museum....................**17** B4
Bazaar Entrance.........................**18** B4
Blue Mosque...............................**19** B4
Constitution House.....................**20** A3
Jameh Mosque............................**21** B3
Municipal Palace........................**22** B4
Poets' Mausoleum......................**23** C1
Quran Museum...........................**24** C1
St Mary's Church........................**25** A4
Sarkis Church..............................**26** C2
Site of New Jameh Mosque.......**27** B4

SLEEPING (pp137–8)
Ark Hotel....................................**28** A4
Azarbaijan Hotel........................**29** A4
Djahannama Hotel.....................**30** A4
Ghostaresh Hotel.......................**31** D2
Golshan Hotel.............................**32** B4
Hotel Elgoli................................**33** E4
Hotel Sina.............................(see 37)
Kosar Hotel.................................**34** A4
Mamoodi Hotel..........................**35** B4
Mashhad Hotel...........................**36** B4
Morvarid Hotel...........................**37** A4
Qods Hotel..................................**38** A4

EATING & DRINKING (pp138–9)
Abdi..**39** D2
Atlashe Pizza...............................**40** B4
Balouch..**41** E2
Honarmandam............................**42** B4
Modern Tabriz Restaurant.........**43** A4
Nobar Bath-house......................**44** B4
Paduna Café................................**45** E2
Pars Restaurant....................(see 33)
Revolving Restaurant.................**46** F2
Shoko..**47** A2
Talar Bozorg Elgoli....................**48** E4
Teahouse (Valiasr)......................**49** E3

TRANSPORT (pp139–40)
Ahar Terminal..............................**50** E3
Aram Safar...................................**51** B4
Buses to Armenia........................**52** A2
City Bus 110 to Valiasr...............**53** B4
City Bus 111, 132........................**54** B4
City Bus 136 to Airport...............**55** B3
City Bus 60 to Bus Station..........**56** B4
Khoshrah....................................**57** C3
Main Bus Station........................**58** B4
Mihan Safar................................**59** B4
Osku Terminal.............................**60** B4
Seiro Safar...................................**61** E2
Shared Taxis to Abaresan Crossing..**62** A4
Shared Taxis to Abaresan Crossing..**63** A4
Shared Taxis to Bus Station.......**64** D2
Shared Taxis to Centre...............**65** A2
Shared Taxis to Centre...............**66** D2
Shared Taxis to Valiasr District..**66** D2

in Ardabil (p145), Ismail transformed the city from regional to national capital. But its glory was short-lived. After the battle of Chaldoran (p125), Tabriz suddenly seemed far too vulnerable to Ottoman attack so the second Safavid shah, Tahmasp (1524–75), moved his capital to safer Qazvin. Fought over by Persians, Ottomans and (later) Russians, Tabriz went into a lengthy decline exacerbated by disease and earthquakes: one of the world's worst-ever quakes killed a phenomenal 77,000 Tabrizis in November 1727.

During the early Qajar period, Shah Goli (now Elgoli), on Tabriz's southeast outskirts, became the residence of the crown prince and the city recovered its prosperity as the 19th century progressed. After heavy-handed Qajar attempts to Persianise the region, the 1906 constitutional revolution briefly allowed Azari Turkish speakers to regain their linguistic rights (open schools, produce newspapers etc). When the liberal constitution was promptly revoked in 1908 it was Tabriz that held out most valiantly. For its pains it was brutally besieged by Russian troops.

The Russians popped up again during both world wars and had time to build themselves a rail-line to Jolfa (then the Soviet border) before withdrawing in 1945. This left Tabriz as capital of Pishaveri's short-lived Provincial Government (autonomous south Azerbaijan) which tried to barter threats of secession for better Azari rights within Iran. The Provincial Government was crushed in December 1946 and far from encouraging the Azaris, the shah did the opposite, restricting the use of their mother tongue. Reaction against this discrimination put Tabriz in the forefront of the 1979 revolution well before the anti-Shah struggle was railroaded by more fundamentalist Muslim clerics.

Orientation

The city's central east–west axis is called Imam Khomeini St, though its west extension towards the train station is 22 Bahman St and, confusingly, its eastern end becomes 29 Bahman St after Abaresan Crossing. Traffic runs one way eastbound on Imam Khomeini St, east of Fajr Sq, returning westbound on Qods St, past the bazaar entrance. The widest choice of cheaper accommodation lies along Ferdosi St, which links the two, plus on Imam Khomeini St nearby.

If you want to see how Tabriz's other half live, continue 4km east of Abaresan Crossing to the Valiasr area. While hardly SoHo, it's the nearest Tabriz comes to an entertainment district and has the best choice of cafés, pizzerias and Internet places. Join the city's gilded youth on a nightly passeggiata around Valiasr's architecturally neutral Karimkhan (Bozorg) Sq and the pedestrianised Shahriyar St to the north, nicknamed Champs Elysées. Most major long-distance services use the main bus station in the far south; other bus stations are throughout the suburbs.

Information

BOOKSHOPS
There are several bookshops on Taleqani St, east of the Arg-e Tabriz (p137), but almost nothing is in English and maps are limited to Caspian tourist route plans.

EMERGENCY
Pardis Clinic (☎ 281 7681; Felestin St)
Pastor Clinic (☎ 334 0104; Imam Khomeini St, Abaresan Crossing)
Shafa Hospital (☎ 208 7168; Fajr Sq)

INTERNET ACCESS
RedNet (Valiasr; per hr IR8000; ☺ 9.30am-10.30pm)
Sabs Coffeenet (☎ 554 0577; Tarbeyat Shopping Mall off Imam Khomeini St; IR6000 per hr; ☺ 9am-10pm Sat-Thu, 10am-2.30pm Fri) Sabs is conveniently close to the budget hotels. It's on the ground floor of the mall near the back. There's much more choice at Abaresan Crossing and especially in the Valiasr district.
Valiasr Coffeenet (☎ 333 2952; Mokhaberat St, Valiasr; per hr IR8000; ☺ 8am-midnight)

MONEY
Bank Melli (Qods St) You can change money here or have one of the tourist helpers (p136) change it in the bazaar.

POST
Main Post Office (Artesh St) For shipping parcels you'll need this huge concrete building.
Post Office (Shohada Sq) This is the most central post office, but it does not ship parcels.

TELEPHONE
Telephone Office (Altaer System; east Miyar Miyar Alley; ☺ 8am-9pm) This office is easy to miss; it lurks in an alley near the Azarbayjan Hotel.

TOURIST INFORMATION
ITTO East Azarbayjan (☎ 541 6682; www.heydar baba.org; Pastor Ave, Artesh St; ☺ 7.30am-2.30pm

Sat-Wed, 7.30am-1.30pm Thu) Friendly, but awkward to reach. Its website is very comprehensive on local old stones, but its free city map is easier to collect from the Azarbayjan Museum ticket booth.

Tourist Information Office (☎ 525 2501; Qods St; ☻9am-3pm Sat-Thu) Upstairs in a curious building that straddles the main bazaar entrance. Excellent, if small, free maps, lots of help with organising trips around Azarbayjan, and the place to meet Nasser Khan (see following).

TOURS
Nasser Khan (☎ 555 2714, 0914 116 0149; amiconasser@yahoo.com) Nasser works for the tourist office, but also offers an incredible range of personal services. Often without charge he takes small groups or individuals on people-watching trips to the up-market Valiasr district. He can help with money exchange, get you into officially closed buildings and arrange various cultural experiences.
Hossein Ravaniyar (☎ 381 9776, 0914 413 8096; www.iranoverland.com) Delightfully eccentric ex-customs officer with endless, sometimes overpowering, enthusiasm. He can drive you around town for around US$6 per hour, which includes learned commentary.
Mansur (☎ 331 7233, 0913 416 6347) Gentle and amiable, Mansur is a soft-spoken teacher with decipherable English. He often lingers in the Hotel Sina and offers bargain-value accompanied city drives at IR15,000 per hour.

TRAVEL AGENCIES
ALP Tours & Travel Agency (☎ 331 0340; fax 331 0825; Karimkhan Sq) Skiing, rock-climbing and Friday sightseeing trips (IR40,000) to Jolfa's Church of St Stephanos. Contacting it via the Tourist Information Office saves a long trek to the Valiasr district office.
Jahan Seyer Travel Agency (☎ 555 6004; fax 553 2331; Imam Khomeini St)

VISA EXTENSIONS
Passport Office (☎ 477 6666; Saeb St; ☻7.30am-1.30pm Sat-Wed, 7.30am-11.30pm Thu) One of the best places in Iran for tourist visa extensions, possibly the same day. Go through the 'Foreign Affairs' door in a newish green-and-red framed building, push confidently past the ground-floor guard and go up two storeys.

Sights
BAZAAR
The city's greatest highlight is its magnificent labyrinthine **bazaar**. Some 35km of covered, often brick-vaulted passages contain over 7000 shops and 24 separate caravanserais and *timches* (domed halls). Construction first began over 1000 years ago, but much of what you see is from the 15th century. Upon entering one feels like a launched

pinball, bouncing around through an extraordinary colourful maze, only emerging when chance or carelessness dictates. Then it's time for a replay.

The **carpet** section has weavers, repairers, trimmers and finishers, as well as the inevitable salesmen. The spice bazaar still has a few shops selling **herbal remedies** and **natural perfumes**, though much of the area is now given over to stationery. Other quarters specialise in gold, shoes and general household goods. Further sections across the river to the north are devoted to copperware and foodstuffs. A couple of **hat shops** sell traditional grey or black *papakh* (Azari hats) made of tight-curled astrakhan wool. The better the quality, the younger the lamb sacrificed to the milliner's art. You can pick one up from around IR75,000 each. Try to track down the odd sugar-maker's shop and spot a few *tandir* ovens where *sangak* bread is baked (p74).

For such a huge construction, the bazaar is surprisingly easy to miss. Its front is hidden behind a row of ordinary-looking shops along Qods St. Easiest access is by walking north from the tourist office.

BLUE (KABUD) MOSQUE
Constructed in 1465, the **Blue Mosque** (Imam Khomeini St; admission IR20,000; ☻8am-8pm) was among the most glorious buildings of its era. Once built, artists took a further 25 years to cover every surface with the blue majolica tiles and intricate calligraphy for which it's nicknamed. It survived one of history's worst-ever earthquakes (1727), but collapsed in a later quake (1773). The devastated city had better things to do than mend it and it lay as a pile of rubble till 1951, when reconstruction finally started. The process continues to this day, with the brick superstructure now complete. However, only on the rear, main entrance portal (which survived 1773) is there any hint of the original blue exterior. Inside, rather than replacing lost tiles, the missing patterns are being painted on – some claim this is to save money, others that it's a deliberate policy to show new from old. The effect works well and complements a collection of before-and-after drawings displayed. The interior consists of two large, domed chambers. The smaller one furthest from the entrance once served as a private mosque for the shahs. Steps lead down to the tomb of its sponsor,

Kareh Koyunlu king Jahan Shah, though this is not accessible to visitors.

The Khaqani garden outside honours a great 12th-century Azari–Persian poet, Shirvani Khaqani, has a nice café and is great for meeting English-speaking students.

AZARBAYJAN MUSEUM

The **Azarbayjan Museum** (Imam Khomeini St; admission IR30,000; ⊗ 8am-5pm Sat-Thu, until 8pm summer, 8am-1pm Fri) is 50m west of the Blue Mosque. Enter through a great brick portal with big wooden doors guarded by two stone rams. Ground-floor exhibits include finds from Hasanlu (p131), a superb 3000-year-old helmet and curious stone 'handbags', which were actually symbols of wealth once carried by Azari provincial treasurers. There are cannon balls and more stone rams in a garden to the right, where stairs lead down to the toilets (women to the left!) and Ahad Hossein's disturbing sculptural allegories of life and war. The top floor displays pottery, ancient glassware, historical maps (95% Farsi) and a re-weave of the famous Chelsea carpet, thought to be one of the best ever made and so-called because it was last sold in King's Rd, Chelsea, some 50 years ago, ending up in London's Victoria & Albert Museum. The ticket booth sells postcards and booklets and has tourist city maps.

ARG-E TABRIZ

This huge brick edifice off Imam Khomeini St is the chunky remnant of an early-14th-century citadel (known as 'the Ark'). Criminals were once executed by being hurled from the top of the citadel walls. Far-fetched local legend tells of one woman so punished who was miraculously saved by the parachute-like effect of her chador.

While the Ark makes a great landmark, it is not possible (nor that interesting) to visit. The best views would be from the south, but they are obscured by shops. Meanwhile, the access track from the north is temporarily closed during the construction of a stadium-sized new **Jameh Mosque** next door.

CHURCHES

Tabriz has had a Christian community almost as long as there've been Christians. Near the bazaar **St Mary's** (Kalisa-ye Maryam-e Moqaddas) is a 12th-century church mentioned by Marco Polo and once the seat of the regional archbishop. The relatively central **Sarkis Church** (Kalisa-ye Sarkis-e Moqaddas; Kalisa Alley) is hidden in a basketball court behind high white gates. Armenian Christian affairs are directed from the staid **Armenian Prelacy Office** (☎ 555 3532; archtab@itm.co.ir; Shari'ati Ave). It's not a place for casual visitors, but the folks are very friendly if you have educated queries about the church or its pilgrimages.

OTHER ATTRACTIONS

In a walled garden near the bazaar, **Constitution House** (Motahhari St; admission IR20,000; ⊗ 9am-3pm winter, 9am-1.30pm & 4.30-7.30pm summer) is a charming Qajar-era house which is historically significant as a headquarters during the 1906–11 constitutional revolution.

Tucked away behind the bazaar, Tabriz's (old) **Jameh Mosque** off Motahhari St has two soaring new minarets and a well-restored brick-vaulted interior. Interlocking concrete arches form the **Poets' Mausoleum** (Magberatol-Shoara; Seyid Hamzeh St), built after the death of the much-loved Tabrizi poet Shahriyar. The century-old German-designed **Municipal Hall** (Shahrdari Sq) is a Tabriz icon and landmark. The large, brick Sahebalamr Mosque north of the bazaar now houses a **Quran Museum**.

Elgoli (Shahgoli) Park is popular with summer strollers and surreptitiously courting couples. The fairground surrounds an artificial lake, in the middle of which a photogenic restaurant-pavilion occupies the reconstruction of a Qajar-era palace. The park is 8km southeast of the centre. Until the tram-metro is finished, you'll need to take a shared taxi from Abaresan Crossing, probably changing halfway.

Activities

When it has a sufficiently large group, ALP Tours & Travel Agency (p136) can organise **skiing** on Mt Sahandkuh (December–April). Transport, lift pass and ski rental cost from just IR130,000 per person day return. ALP can also arrange climbing guides for Mt Sabalan (p145).

Sleeping
BUDGET

Mashhad Hotel (☎ 555 8255; Ferdosi St; dm/tw IR12,000/35,000) One of the only mosaferkhunehs to let foreigners use (five-bed) dormitories. The very clean hot shower costs IR5000 extra.

Mamoodi Hotel (☎ 554 1744; Imam Khomeini St; s/tw IR28,000/38,000) Clean, box rooms off an internal courtyard are unusually peaceful for such a central position, and shared showers are free.

Golshan Hotel (☎ 556 3760; Imam Khomeini St; s/tw IR40,000/50,000) Though not especially inviting the Golshan is decently clean and has about the cheapest ensuite rooms in town. Five renovated rooms on the 3rd floor have new, Western toilets. The hotel's mutton-scented reception area is hidden behind a shop marked 'Ark-Teb'.

Ark Hotel (☎ 555 1277; Ark Alley; s/tw IR60,000/80,000) Named after the citadel nearby, not Noah, this is a very quiet yet central, no-nonsense budget place with OK shared shower and Western toilet.

Djahannama Hotel (☎ 553 7539; Imam Khomeini St; s/tw IR30,000/50,000) Very basic, the slow renovation has yet to get far beyond the attractive foyer. There are around two dozen more very basic mosaferkhunehs along Ferdosi and Imam Khomeini Sts, some with signs in English, but mostly catering to petty traders from Iran and the ex-Soviet Caucasus (Russian is spoken in some). If allowed to stay you'll probably need to wash in a local hammam.

MID-RANGE

All these mid-range hotels have their own restaurants and rooms with private bathrooms.

Hotel Sina (☎ 556 6211; Fajr Sq; s/tw IR120,000/220,000; 🗴 limited Ⓟ) Calm, friendly and very well kept, the Sina offers great value for money if you're travelling alone.

Morvarid Hotel (☎ 553 1433; moravid_hotel@yahoo.com; Fajr Sq; s/tw IR74,000/102,000) Fairly cosy but really a budget place done up.

Azarbayjan Hotel (☎ 555 9051; fax 553 7477; Shari'ati St; s/d IR100,000/138,000; 🗴) For couples the Azarbayjan is ideal with good big double beds, choice of toilets and double glazing to reduce traffic noise.

Qods Hotel (☎ 555 0898; Terminal Sq; s/tw IR85,000/110,000; 🗴) If you can handle the dingy corridors and eerie vibe the Qods has surprisingly passable bathrooms. Not recommended for lone women.

Kosar Hotel (☎ 553 7691; fax 554 1570; Imam Khomeini St; d IR108,000; 🗴) Professionally managed and popular. Rooms have squat toilets and aren't as fresh as one might hope, but they do have double beds and BBC World TV.

Ghostaresh Hotel (☎ 334 5021; fax 334 6778; Abaresan Crossing; tw US$35; 🗴) The self-awarded four-star rating is slightly exaggerated given a hint of peeling paint, but you get decent-value, semi-international standards. Although it's located several kilometres from the bazaar, it's very handy for public transport to both the Valiasr and central districts.

TOP END

Hotel Elgoli (Tabriz Pars; ☎ 380 7820; fax 380 8555; Elgoli Park; s/d/ste US$60/88/168; 🗴 Ⓟ) Tabriz's best is 8km from the centre overlooking Elgoli Park. It has everything you'd expect from a top business hotel except for alcohol in the minibar beers. There's a stylish atrium café and a revolving restaurant.

Eating & Drinking

As in much of Azarbayjan, a popular street snack on winter evenings is *labu* (beet) sold roasted or boiled from carts around Bagh-e Golestan, on Imam Khomeini St and at Abaresan Crossing. To find some great teahouses wander the bazaar or enlist aid from Nasser at the tourist office.

CENTRAL AREA

For cheap *dizi* and kebabs explore the alleys behind the Azerbayjan Hotel.

Haji Ali (Kola Duzun Bazaar; set meal IR21,000; lunch) Within the bazaar, Haji Ali is a busy place for *chelo kabab* (kebab on rice), though not really atmospheric.

Honarmandam (Place of Artists; ☎ 553 4594; Imam Khomeini St; kebab meals IR18,000; 🕒 8am-10pm) This very curious new vaulted cavern serves a good, rich *dizi* (IR10,000). The brightly lit centrepiece is a rather lurid fake spring. Behind this is a small carpeted area where women feel more comfortable puffing on a qalyan (IR5000) than they would in a typical teahouse. It's entered down some steps across the road from Fooresh Publications.

Modern Tabriz Restaurant (Imam Khomeini St; meals IR20,000-35,000; 🕒 8am-10pm) This long-term favourite serves excellent fried trout in a large, basement dining hall. 'Modern' hardly matches the faded grandeur of its appealingly dowdy mirrored interior.

Afsahe Pizza (Imam Khomeini Ave; pizzas IR15,000; 🕒 11am-10pm) This conveniently central pizzeria has an English menu but watch out for the low ceilings.

Nobar Bath-house (Imam Khomeini St) This splendid building has just been converted to a particularly grand traditional Sofra-khaneh Sonate.

VALIASR AREA
The choice of eateries is considerable, but although there's a **teahouse** (Amir Kabir St) and a couple of Persian restaurants, the area's speciality is pizza and ice cream.

Balouch (☎ 330 0100; Shahriyar St; pizzas IR15,000; ☺ 11am-11pm) This is about the most appealing pizzeria on the 'Champs Elysées' and does OK fried chicken.

Paduna Café (☎ 331 8431; Karimkhan Sq) Much the most stylish ice-cream parlour in town, Paduna has sculpted furniture and coffee-collage table-tops.

Pars Restaurant (☎ 333 0048; Homam Tabrizi St; meals IR30,000; ☺ dinner) Follow elegant wrought-iron banisters upstairs just off Mokharberat Ave to reach this somewhat flashy up-market kebab specialist.

Shoko (Shahriyar St; ☺ 9.30am-11pm) This shop sells imported groceries, including Nutella and cornflakes.

ABARESAN CROSSING
Halfway to Valiasr, where you need to change shared taxi anyway, there is another clump of fairly nice little pizza parlours. **Abdi** (☎ 336 6245; 29 Bahman St; pizza IR15,500-20,000; ☺ 5-10.30pm) is the most noteworthy, with black décor and some English spoken.

ELGOLI
Revolving Restaurant (Hotel Elgoli, 11th fl; meals IR50,000-110,000; ☺ 8-11pm daily & 1-3pm Fri & Sat) Predictably great views in smart if somewhat garish peach-vermilion décor warrant the IR50,000 cover charge which entitles you to raid the soup-n-salad bar. Main courses include many international favourites, steaks and sturgeon (IR40,000). It's reached by a Plexiglas elevator that fires you through the Hotel Elgoli's atrium like Charlie in Willy Wonka's chocolate factory.

Talar Bozorg Elgoli (☎ 380 5263; Elgoli Park; meals IR25,000) This is a busy and surprisingly unpretentious restaurant within the mock Qajar palace, which caters mainly to local families. In summer it's one place that serves *tabrizi köfte*, a sort of giant Scotch egg typical of local home cooking; order ahead in winter.

Getting There & Away
AIR
Iran Air has direct Tuesday flights to Mashhad (IR376,000), but all other destinations connect via Tehran (IR190,000, four daily). Tickets are sold conveniently from Jahan Seyer Travel Agency (p136).

BUS, MINIBUS & SAVARI
A couple of bus companies including **Seiro Safar** (☎ 555 7797; ☺ 8.30am-midnight) have offices on Imam Khomeini St, but long-distance expresses usually depart from the huge, modern **main bus station** (☎ 479 6091), 3km south of the central area. Here, between the bus offices and the bus lanes, there's a handy **information office** (☺ 7am-8pm) in a squat, brick building. Most savaris use a different area of the bus station concourse but those for Bazargan (IR35,000) have a special hut beside the main bus stands. Important destinations served include:

Destination	Price (IR)	Duration (hr)	Departures
Ardabil	15,000	4	2 per hr 6am-6pm
Esfahan	40,000	16	5 daily 4-5.30pm
Kermanshah	30,000	11	6pm
Maku	13,500	4	6 daily
Maraqeh	8000	2	hourly 6am-6pm
Mashhad	70,000	26	2pm, 3pm & 5pm
Qazvin	30,000	8	frequent
Rasht	25,000	8	5-7pm
Sanandaj	28,000	8	8am, 2-4pm
Shiraz	55,000	24	2pm
Tehran	25,000-40,000	10	frequent

Buses also run hourly from 6am to 6pm to Orumiyeh (IR12,000, 4½ hours), but they loop north around the lake. It's faster and much nicer to take a savari using the bridge and ferry across the lake. The ferry operates 7am to 10pm daily, 7am to 7pm in Ramazan. In unusually bad weather, lights on the access road indicate if the ferry is cancelled.

Buses leave when full to Ahar (IR4500, 1½ hours) from a terminal beyond the Darvazeh Tehran. Savaris wait across the road.

For Osku (and thence Kandovan), minibuses use the Kosroshahr terminal, a handy parking lot hidden away off Felestin St.

Minibuses to Marand (whence savaris are frequent to Jolfa) use a terminal way out towards the airport.

WESTERN IRAN

INTERNATIONAL BUS

To Yerevan (Armenia) buses depart from Imam Khomeini Sq near the train station (IR200,000, 11pm Tuesday, Wednesday, Friday and Sunday), but buy tickets from the central branch of **Seiro Safar** (☎ 555 7797; Imam Khomeini Ave; ⏰ 8.30am-midnight). To both Baku (Azerbaijan) and İstanbul (via Erzerum, Turkey) there are nightly buses around 10.30pm from company offices along central Imam Khomeini St, notably **Aram Safar** (☎ 556 0597), **Khoshrah** (☎ 556 4451) and **Mihan Safar** (☎ 555 4908). All buses originate in Tehran.

TRAIN

There are two overnight trains to Tehran (12 hours) via Maraqeh (2¼ hours), Zanjan (nine hours, arriving antisocially early) and Qazvin. The 6pm service (IR52,550) has four beds per cabin, compared to six on the 7.45pm service (IR25,000). There's a slow 9am train to Jolfa (3½ hours, daily) and on Mondays and Saturdays an international service to Nakhchivan (Azerbaijan enclave) at 5pm, though it's much more sensible to get to Jolfa and walk across the border.

The **train station** (☎ 444 4419; Imam Khomeini Sq) is beyond the western end of 22 Bahman St. Shared taxis and city bus No 111 stop five minutes' walk away.

Getting Around

TO/FROM THE AIRPORT

Bus No 136 runs from Montazeri St near the Jameh Mosque to the airport every 40 minutes. A taxi should cost IR8000 to IR10,000.

BUS & MINIBUS

City buses are infrequent, but cost only IR250 per hop; buy tickets before entry. Useful routes include No 160 to the bus station, No 110 to Valiasr and No 136 to the airport via the Marand terminal. Buses No 132 and 111 run the length of 22 Bahman St so they get you close to the train station. Within the centre, distances between bus stops can be great and shared taxis are more frequent.

SHARED TAXI

A key route runs along Imam Khomeini St from Fajr Sq to Abaresan Crossing (IR600), but on returning diverts onto Jomhuri-e Eslami St which passes the bazaar. At Abaresan Crossing walk under the flyover to continue to Valiasr district (IR750). For the train station start from Qonaga Sq, and jump off at the west end of 22 Bahman St (IR600). To the bus station, both buses and shared taxis use Shari'ati St (passing near the passport office), but return to Imam Khomeini St on the far side of the Arg-e Tabriz via Taleqani St.

TRAM/METRO

Construction has started on a tram system linking Elgoli Park to the train station.

OSKU & KANDOVAN   اسکو کندوان

En route to Kandovan you'll pass through Osku. This gently attractive small town has two old brick mosques and an ancient *chinar* (giant plane tree) dividing in two the narrow lane that leads to Kandovan. That road weaves through walnut groves to **Ispanjan Village**, where two mosques share three fine minarets, then over arid rolling hills that turn grassy in spring. Although the road is paved, donkey traffic is as common as cars, men wear crumpled *papakh* (hats) and women appear to be wrapped in curtains.

While some visitors find Kandovan 'spoilt', it remains one of western Iran's most charming villages, a delightful escape just 50km from busy Tabriz. Locally pronounced 'Chandovan', it is a quaint Cappadocia-style village of fairy chimneys: troglodyte rooms hollowed out of the soft, curiously eroded rock. These are endlessly photogenic, some with little cottage-style windows, many more used for sheep pens and storerooms. The fun is scrambling the steep, narrow paths between them. An hour is ample to give you an idea of the place, drink supposedly health-giving water from springs on the far side of the canalised river and buy some delicious fresh honeycomb (IR30,000 per kg). However, staying overnight allows you to see the village without the crowds of local tourists. Kandovan sits at the base of 3707m **Mt Sahandkuh**, a convex pudding of a mountain which locals implausibly claim they can climb in two hours. That honeycomb must contain Kryptonite. More dramatically, David Rohl in *Legend* suggests that Sahandkuh, Mt Uash to the Assyrians, might have been biblical Eden's Mountain of God. It's certainly an inspiring place to hike. For skiing you're best to use the mountain's north face, accessed from Tabriz.

PAUL GREENWAY

Masuleh (p156)

Fairy-chimney home, Kandovan
(p140)

SIMON RICHMOND

SIMON RICHMOND

Hasan-e Sabbah's Fortress (Alamut Castle)
(p166)

MARTIN MOOS

Oljeitu Mausoleum, Soltaniyeh (p167)

Bazar-e Bozorg, Esfahan (p215)

MAR

Coppersmith, Imam Sq, Esfahan
(p216)

CHRIS MELLOR

فروشگاه قلمزنی حافظ
REZA HAFEZ STOR
رضا حافظ

PHIL M WEYMOUTH

Dome tilework, Sheikh Lotfollah
Mosque, Esfahan (p217)

JOHN BOF

Imam Mosque, Esfahan (p216)

Sleeping & Eating

In Kandovan, beside the straightened stream and overmanicured picnic area, a growing handful of discordant brick shophouses is appearing. Most of these offer tourists very basic unheated rooms for IR25,000. Don't expect toilets or running water. Yet. The Dairyman 'Restaurant' (four tables in a shop) and Kafe Gazakhuri Daiya (across the bridge) both offer local meals as well as beds.

Getting There & Away

From Tabriz to Kandovan a taxi will cost from IR80,000 return plus waiting time, and on summer Fridays you might find a direct minibus. Otherwise go via Osku. Minibuses (IR1300, 50 minutes) run regularly till around 6pm from Tabriz's Kosroshahr terminal; this is central but hidden in alleys off Felestin St. Minibuses from Osku to Kandovan (IR2000, 45 minutes, 25km) run only a couple of times daily so a taxi makes sense (IR20,000 return plus IR10,000 per hour waiting and IR2500 Kandovan village toll).

MARAND مرند

☎ 0491 / pop 100,000

With a tree-lined central avenue (Kashani St) and a ski-able mountain backdrop (Payam), Marand is somewhat more than just a transit point for reaching Jolfa. Heavily over-renovated, the ancient **Jameh Mosque** (Kashani St) has had previous incarnations as a church and fire temple. It doesn't look much from outside but, if the mullah will let you in, you will supposedly see a splendid interior. **Qala** (Aqzami District), meaning 'castle' in Azari, is the local name for Marand's ancient citadel. All

that remains is a large muddy mound with curious, shattered earthen spires. It's not vastly interesting but still dominates a lowrise quarter of town southeast of the centre. The **Marand Tourist Inn** (Mehmunsara Jahangardi; ☎ 37446; fax 37445; Old Tabriz Hwy; s/tw US$20/30) has shower, toilet and peeling paint in its rooms. It's well past its 1970s heyday when, as an exclusive guesthouse for the shah's entourage, it was an infamous den of iniquity. Situated 8km south of the city centre, it's mainly frequented by skiers using the nearby **Payam (Yam) ski slopes**.

Getting There & Away

The main terminal is 1km off the southern ring road, a 2km shared taxi ride from the city centre. There are frequent minibuses to Azerbaijan Sq in Tabriz (IR3000, 1¼ hours) and to the Tabriz terminal in Khoy (IR3500, 1½ hours). Minibuses to Hadiyshahr (Alamdar) are more rare (IR3000, 1½ hours), with the last one leaving at 4pm. For Jolfa, direct savaris (IR6000, one hour) leave from Istgah Jolfa, a tiny unmarked side street, 700m north of the city centre, IR2000 by taxi from the main terminal.

JOLFA جلفا

☎ 0492 / pop 14,000

Now a busy little border town, Jolfa was once a major Armenian settlement famous for its skilled artisans. So skilled, in fact, that in 1604 Shah Abbas kidnapped the entire population, whisking them off to build him a new capital at Esfahan. Their descendants still live in an Esfahan suburb called Jolfa.

Central Jolfa is focused on Ashura Sq, a sizable roundabout directly south of the immigration post. Nearby you'll find a large

---

CROSSING THE AZERBAIJAN (NAKHCHIVAN) BORDER AT JOLFA

Culfa, in Azerbaijan's disconnected Nakhchivan enclave, is a short walk across the Aras River from central Jolfa. Supposedly open 24 hours the border post is eerily quiet after 6pm.

Use up your rials before leaving Iran. Note that a 'Shirvan' means 10,000 Azeri manats, worth around US$2.

Don't hang around in Culfa. Some paranoid local police assume that all foreigners are spies. However, it's an easy 35-minute ride by taxi (US$5) or minibus (5000 manats) to Nakhchivan city, which is contrastingly relaxed and cosmopolitan with a decent range of accommodation. From Nakhchivan city there are direct buses to İstanbul (US$25 plus border bribes, eight daily) taking around 30 hours via Iğdır (US$5). However the enclave is separated from the rest of Azerbaijan by aggressively closed Armenian borders, so you'd have to fly to reach Baku (US$100, four daily) or Gäncä (US$50, four weekly).

flea market, freelance moneychangers and **No Avaram Internet Club** (Ulaifagi St; per hr IR7000; ☺ 9am-9pm Sat-Thu), completely unmarked, but just two doors from Ashura Sq.

Jolfa has little to see in itself, but makes a good low-budget base for visiting the Church of St Stephanos (below), exploring the fascinating Aras River Valley, crossing into Nakhchivan or Armenia, or looping around to Kaleybar, via some of the region's most attractively traditional villages.

Sleeping & Eating

There are a handful of basic hotels close to Ashura Sq.

Hotel Azerbaijan (☎ 302 3104; Ulaifagi St; tw IR40,000) A bright new hotel, one block east of Ashura Sq, where simple rooms share a hot shower, clean squat toilet and fridge.

Yemekhana Hatäm (☎ 302 2828; Ashura Sq; tw IR20,000) Survivable, waterless rooms available at the back of a popular central restaurant, which serves a splendid *zereshk polo ba morq* (chicken on rice made tangy with barberry fruit) dinner for IR16,000, including soup and drink.

Jolfa Tourist Inn (Mehmunsara Jahangardi; ☎ 302 4824; fax 302 4825; Eslam St; s/tw US$20/30) Tatty for an ITTIC place, this is the only option with loo. To find it walk a block south from Ashura Sq then 10 minutes diagonally right at the T-junction, passing the train station en route.

Getting There & Away

Savaris gather just north of Ashura Sq for Marand (IR6000, one hour), occasionally to Tabriz (IR15,000, 2½ hours) and Hadiyshahr (Alamdar; IR1000, 15 minutes). Minibuses to Marand (IR3000, 1½ hours) run from Hadiyshahr, but not Jolfa itself. The road to Khoy, shown on most maps, is partly mud track across almost uninhabited wilderness. It can be very hard to follow in places, but it's possible in a Paykan (IR100,000, 2¼ hours). The scenic road to Kaleybar along the Aras River is now asphalted, except for two short stretches of under 3km, but you'll need a full-day taxi charter (around IR300,000) to do it justice. The daily train from Tabriz (IR3000, five hours), which departs 10am, is cheap if painfully slow. Forget the cross-border train to Nakhchivan (5pm Monday and Saturday): walk across and take a taxi (p141).

AROUND JOLFA
West of Jolfa

Seven kilometres west of Jolfa look west across the Aras River near a police 'fort' (no photos). You will see, on the Azerbaijani riverbank, a truncated tomb and **broken bridge**. These mark the original site of ancient Jolfa. About 1km further, as you enter a spectacular **red-rock canyon**, there's a ruined **caravanserai** and, 400m beyond, a cute, minuscule **Shepherd's Chapel** (recently restored). After a 10km attractive drive turn left (inland) through vertical strata. From road's end, stroll five minutes through a stone arch and peaceful glade with 'mill' cascade to the very attractive Armenian **Church of St Stephanos** (Kalisa Darreh Sham; admission IR25,000; ☺ dawn-dusk). Well-preserved exterior reliefs include Armenian crosses, saints and angels. The earliest surviving part of the building is 14th century, but a church was first founded on the site by St Bartholomew around AD 62, just a generation after Christ himself.

GETTING THERE & AWAY

There's no public bus, but from Tabriz ALP Tours & Travel Agency (p136) runs great-value return one-day excursions on Fridays when interest is sufficient (IR40,000). A taxi from Jolfa (25 minutes each way) costs around IR50,000 return, with plenty of photo stops (but not near police posts). Note that for years travellers were required to have a permit to visit this area, issued in far-away Tabriz. At the time of research the requirement appeared to have been forgotten, but if you're coming from Tabriz it's worth playing it safe and asking the Tourist Information Office (p136) for the state of play.

East of Jolfa

For millennia the **Aras River Valley** (River Gihon in the Bible) was a major thoroughfare used by traders, armies and holy men. Only with treaties of 1813 and 1828 did Russia and Persia turn it into a border line. Several mud fortifications remain from the 18th-century conflicts that led to its division. Today the tension is east–west, not north–south. Clearly visible on the Aras' north bank are ruined villages, sad signs of the still unresolved 1989–94 Armenia–Azerbaijan war. What a difference 50m makes. It's fine to drive along the south (ie Iranian) riverbank as a casual tourist, but travelling the parallel north bank rail line (now severed) would be

CROSSING THE ARMENIAN BORDER AT NORDUZ

Norduz is a large, modern freight service centre in an otherwise unpopulated sweep of valley. Walking distance across the Aras River on the Armenian side is Agarak village. A 21-day Armenian tourist visa is available at the border (US$30). That's cheaper than in Tehran, but the application might take a couple of hours. This could be annoying if you're on one of the through buses (Yerevan–Tehran via Tabriz) which might end up leaving without you. Several travellers report that Armenian customs charges an unofficial US$2 fee and impoverished soldiers sometimes try to cadge gifts.

Change money on the Iran side: a shop just outside immigration buys and sells Armenian dram at decent rates, currently IR14,000 for 1000 dram, US$1 = 575 dram. A Jolfa–Norduz taxi should cost no more than IR40,000 (40 minutes), if you bargain. In both Agarak and nearby Meghri, a US$7/3000 dram, 15-minute taxi ride away, there are pleasant homestays (www.bedandbreakfast.am). A 7.30am minibus to Yerevan (3500 dram) departs from outside Meghri's grungy Soviet-era hotel (rooms from 2000 dram). For better accommodation continue to Kapan where the Hotel Darist (15,000 dram) is comfortable and clean.

unthinkable folly. That crosses two globally forgotten 'front lines': from Nakhchivan (Azerbaijan) to mortal enemy Armenia, on through Karabagh (Armenian-occupied Azeri territory), then back through mine-fields to Azerbaijan again. There's not been active fighting for a decade, but the guard posts and barricaded tunnels add a considerable geopolitical frisson to the Aras River Valley's great natural beauty.

Leaving Jolfa, the horizon is a gateau of red-and-white cliffs backed by snow-tickled Armenian peaks. In the middle distance is the cleft rocky beak of Nakhchivan's abrupt **Ilan Dağ** (Snake Mountain), through which Noah's Ark supposedly crashed en route to Ararat. Just beyond attractive **Marazakand**, the sinuous mud wall of Javer Castle rises on a rocky shoulder. Four kilometres further, the main road bypasses superb **Ahmadabad** village: a cubist array of mud-and-stone homes on a small riverside knoll. A side road soon after leads steeply up to the popular, if somewhat overrated, **Asiyab Khurabe** spring and picnic area, worth it for the superb valley views as you drive back down.

Further east the road passes through canyons with glimpses of spiky crested **Kuh-e Kamtal** (Tiger Mountain). Sixty kilometres from Jolfa, in a more open river bend, is **Norduz**, the sparkling new Irano-Armenian border terminal (see the boxed text 'Crossing the Armenian Border at Norduz', above). Four kilometres further east, **Duzal** village rises on a hillock dominated by a distinctive **octagonal tomb tower**. Behind the next rocky bluff the road passes through the gate towers and sturdy mud walls of the once huge **Abu Mirza**

fortress (Kordasht Castle). When viewed from the east, they frame an impressive spire of eroded rock. One kilometre further east, a lovely **historic hammam** is under renovation in **Kordasht** village, just north of the road. It's quite possible to continue to Ushtebin, Khudaferin and Kaleybar (p145).

AHAR اهر

☎ 0426 / pop 80,000

Set in on a high, windswept plain, Ahar is a mildly interesting junction, useful for exploring northern regions of Azarbayjan.

Orientation

The main road from Tabriz swings past the Tabriz bus terminal and, after 700m, arrives at Basij Sq, where a soldier statue waves his flag. Rajaei St leads one block east (right) to Police Sq, continuing thereafter as Shahid Bajlari St via Yadbud Sq to the Kaleybar savari terminal, beside a small river at the main vegetable market. The market leads a block north to the Hotel Razavi. The renovated 1906 covered bazaar is accessed by alleys northeast of Police Sq, emerging on Imam Khomeini St, which parallels Shahid Bajlari St east–west.

Sheikh Shahabdin Ahari Mausoleum

The town's main attraction, this imposing **mausoleum** (Sheikh Shahabdin St; admission IR15,000; ☺ when caretaker shows up) sits in a park 400m south of Police Sq. One of two chunky columns supporting its large exterior *iwan* (vaulted hall) retains the original blue glaze. Inside is a collection of Safavid Qurans, metalwork and *keshkul* dervish 'coconut handbags'. Ask the attendant to unlock doors to the inner courtyard to see the sheikh's simple black slab tomb.

Sleeping & Eating

The only accommodation, **Hotel Razavi** (☎ 222 2482; Imam Khomeini St; s/tw IR35,000/45,000), is simple but bright, clean and friendly. Rooms have a washbasin, TV, heater and fan. Unmarked in English, the **Golshan Restaurant** (Shahid Bajlari St; meals IR16,000), near Police Sq, is considered the best place for kebabs. **Vahid Coffee-shop** (Police Sq; pizza IR20,000; ☺ 10am-10pm) is an unexpectedly stylish, modern fast-food place with a real coffee machine. It's in a short alley just north then west of the square, and is marked 'Pineapple Classy'.

Getting There & Away

To Tabriz buses (IR4500, 1½ hours) and savaris (IR8000, 1¼ hours) leave when full from the Tabriz terminal. Around 20 minutes from Tabriz there's an attractive landscape of candy-striped pink-and-white strata. From the Kaleybar terminal savaris (only) leave to Meshgin Shahr (IR6000, 1¼ hours), passing some wonderful timeless villages, and to Kaleybar (IR6000, one hour).

KALEYBAR & BABAK CASTLE

كليبر
قلعه بابک

☎ 0427 / pop 17,000

Set attractively in a wide, steep-sided mountain valley, unassuming Kaleybar (Kaleibar) town makes one of the finest starting points in western Iran for random hikes. It also makes a good base to visit the upper Aras River Valley. By far its biggest draw, however, is the extensive crag-top ruin of **Babak Castle**, Iran's most impressive mountain fortress. Known to some as Bazz Qalasi, the castle has a unique emotional resonance for Azari people as the lair of their 9th-century national hero (see the boxed text 'Who was Babak?', below). The castle access path starts by some green camp huts 6km west of Kaleybar, from where, if you stand back a little, you can glimpse the ruins high above. Reaching the top is a fairly strenuous two-hour trek, initially through trees following a pretty stream then up dizzyingly steep stairways with fabulous views.

Orientation

Kaleybar's town plan is a convoluted curvy 'y'. The main road from Ahar (Imam Khomeini St) winds along the upper western flank. At the second roundabout (Shahrdari Sq) the main commercial thoroughfare (Mo'allem St) descends to the east, passing the diminutive bus station and bazaar, then wiggles south before eventually coiling right back to become the main lane north for Eskanlu and Khudaferin.

Sleeping & Eating

If you arrive during Babak's birthday celebrations (last week of June) bring a tent as there'll be no earthly hope of a room.

Araz Hotel (☎ 422 2290; s/d 15,000/30,000; Ⓟ) Kaleybar's cheapest option has very simple rooms in a gated courtyard 300m north off

---

WHO WAS BABAK?

On the last week of June each year, tens of thousands gather around the crag-top ruins of Babak Castle, near Kaleybar. This is a highly emotional celebration of Azari/Azeri identity supposedly marking the birthday of Babak, a 9th-century guerrilla leader once based here. But why should Babak be the greatest hero of Turkic Azarbayjan? Occupying a cultural position somewhere between King Arthur, Robin Hood and Yasser Arafat, Babak is celebrated for harrying Iran's Abbasid Arab regime between 815 and 837. But, beyond this, Babak's biography bends to fit a variety of ethnopolitical viewpoints. Was he Kurdish, Persian, Caucasian-Albanian or Azari? The latter is most unlikely, as the main Turkic (ie proto-Azari) influx didn't arrive till the 11th century. Was he Muslim? His portrait adorns many a mosque in Azerbaijan, where he's considered a pious Islamic warrior. Yet other sources recall him making faithful fraternal bonds in a Zoroastrian fire temple. Does any of this matter? Probably not. Most Azaris see little conflict between their ethnicity and their Iranian nationality, nor between their Zoroastrian roots and their Muslim faith. However, that doesn't stop a few firebrands along with Washington's divide-and-rule hawks portraying the whole celebration in terms of a political protest. The website www.cehreganli.com/english.html has video footage of the 2003 event.

Mo'allem St up the second alley east of the petrol station. It looks like a private house, but hides a big banqueting hall downstairs.

Kaleybar Grand Hotel (☎ 422 2048; fax 422 4666; Shahrdari Sq; quad IR200,000) Comfortable new rooms with shower and clean squat loo on the top floor of a small yellow-brick shopping centre. If it's not full you can pay per person (IR50,000), rather than per room.

Babak Hotel Sitting on a lonely hill above Shoza-Abad hamlet, 600m beyond the castle access path, this would make an ideal base for hiking. Temporarily closed at the time of research, it reportedly still operates, at least in summer, and has sweeping views from its café/restaurant.

Getting There & Away

Savaris are fairly frequent to Ahar (IR6000, 50km, one hour) passing Peyqam castle ruin. There's a direct bus to Tabriz (IR8000, three hours) at 8am.

AROUND KALEYBAR

Winding 70km down to **Eskanlu**, a lonely asphalt road descends through a wonderful variety of landscapes, from bald mountain passes to semidesert badlands and green agricultural oases. Some 25km out of Kaleybar it passes the dramatic triple rock-topped ridge where **Avarsian Castle** once stood. At Eskanlu swing west following the Aras River (the Azerbaijan border). At **Khudaferin**, 18km later, you'll pass two ruined **Safavid bridges**, crossing towards what is now Armenian-occupied Azerbaijan. Just beyond, a huge concrete water-diversion scheme is under construction, apparently to protect the bridges. Around 5km west of photogenically stepped **Qarachilar** village, an unsurfaced 6km side track (passable by Paykan when dry) cuts south into the forested hills to dead-end at **Ushtebin** (Oshtabin, Oshtobeyin). Famous for white pomegranates, this isolated little village snuggles tightly in a wooded valley and remains virtually unspoilt by visitors, despite being touted by local tourist offices as a 'new Masuleh'.

There's nowhere to stay or eat along this route, so bring a picnic. Taxis from Kaleybar want IR150,000 return with stops, IR200,000 from Ahar. Driving flat out Kaleybar–Ushtebin takes 2½ hours. It's easy enough to continue west to Jolfa (95km; p141) via Kordasht's Abu Mirza fortress (p142).

MESHGIN SHAHR & MT SABALAN
مشكين شهر
كوه سبلان
☎ 0452 / pop 52,000

Some 60km northwest of Ardabil, Meshgin Shahr is a busy market town set magnificently at the foot of Mt Sabalan's craggy north face. Climbers generally access the mountain from this side using a 4WD as far as **Shavil** (Shabil), hiking to a shelter at around 3500m then summitting next day. ALP Tours & Travel Agency (p136) can arrange guides. If you just want mountain views, take a taxi towards the brick-box foothill village of **Mo-il** (IR24,000 return). Behind the mosque where the road ends, two uncommercial hot spring pools are used as communal village baths.

In Meshgin Shahr itself, tucked amid homes 100m north of Darvazeh Ardabil (Ardabil savari stand) are three mud-wall remnants of **Kohna Qal'eh** (Old Castle). The central, blue-tiled new **Amir al-Mominam Mosque** (Azadi Sq) has golden spires like the crows' nests of medieval galleons. Just 30 seconds' walk north from here is the town's showerless **Mosaferkhuneh Baharestan** (☎ 522 3284; Ayatollah Meshkineh St; s/tw IR20,000/28,000).

Savaris to Ardabil (IR8000, 1½ hours) use the Darvazeh Ardabil. Savaris to Ahar (IR6000, 1¼ hours) leave from Razmandagan Sq at the westernmost end of Imam Khomeini St, along which shared taxis cost IR300 per hop.

ARDABIL
اردبيل
☎ 0451 / pop 352,000

Snow-topped Mt Sabalan rises dramatically through chilly smog to tower above this sprawling but historic city. Ardabil is a logical stopping point between Tabriz and the upper Caspian coast. The central area is pleasantly calm and the city has a fair scattering of minor sights. The magnificent Sheikh Safi od-Din Mausoleum is by far its greatest attraction.

Ardabil sits on a high plateau reached by a busy but very picturesque road from Astara. The weather is cool in summer and terrifies brass monkeys in winter. Snow is probable from November, and a new ski resort is taking shape beyond the nearby hot springs resort of Sara'eyn.

History

A military outpost for millennia, Ardabil was declared a city around AD 470. It was

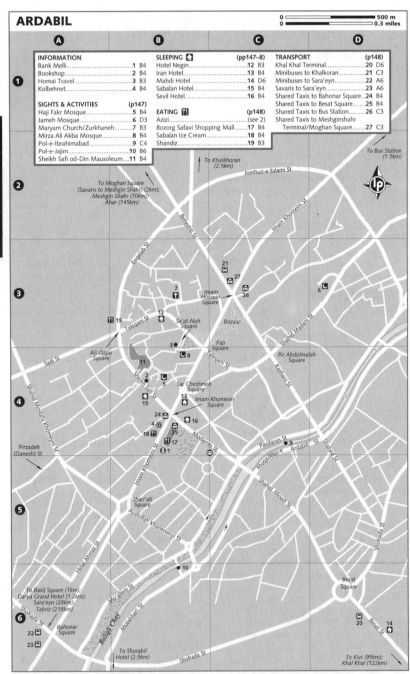

ARDABIL

0	500 m
0	0.3 miles

INFORMATION
Bank Melli.......................................**1** B4
Bookshop..**2** B4
Homai Travel..................................**3** B3
Kolbehnet.......................................**4** B4

SIGHTS & ACTIVITIES (p147)
Haji Fakr Mosque...........................**5** B4
Jameh Mosque.................................**6** D3
Maryam Church/Zurkhaneh...........**7** B3
Mirza Ali Akba Mosque..................**8** B4
Pol-e-Ibrahimabad..........................**9** C4
Pol-e-Jajim.....................................**10** B6
Sheikh Safi od-Din Mausoleum....**11** B4

SLEEPING (pp147–8)
Hotel Negin....................................**12** B3
Iran Hotel..**13** B4
Mahdi Hotel....................................**14** D6
Sabalan Hotel..................................**15** B4
Sevil Hotel......................................**16** B4

EATING (p148)
Azizi..(see 2)
Bozorg Safavi Shopping Mall........**17** B4
Sabalan Ice Cream..........................**18** B4
Shandiz..**19** B3

TRANSPORT (p148)
Khal Khal Terminal.........................**20** D6
Minibuses to Khalkoran..................**21** C3
Minibuses to Sara'eyn....................**22** A6
Savaris to Sara'eyn.........................**23** A6
Shared Taxis to Bahonar Square....**24** B4
Shared Taxis to Besat Square........**25** B4
Shared Taxis to Bus Station..........**26** C3
Shared Taxis to Meshginshahr
   Terminal/Moghan Square........**27** C3

To Bus Station
(1.5km)

To Khalkhoran
(2.5km)

Jomhuri-e Eslami St

To Moghan Square
(Savaris to Meshgin Shahr) (2km);
Meshgin Shahr (70km);
Ahar (145km)

Imam Khomeini St

Beheshti St

Enqelab St

21
27
Imam
Hossein
Square

7
6

12
Sa'at-Noh
Square

19
Taleqani St

Bazaar

Shahid Madani St

Ali Qapu
Square

11

3
8
Fajr
Square
Taleqani St

Pir Abdolmaleh
Square

Kashani St

Sadi St

Sheikh Safi St

2
5
Sar Cheshmeh
Square

15

13
Imam Khomeini
Square

24
16
Imam Khomeini St

Pasdaran St

Pirzadeh
(Danesh) St

4
18
25
17
1

Modarres St

9
Moqaddas-e Ardabili St

Shahid Moadi St

Shahed St

Shari'ati
Square

Ayatollah Khanenenyi St

Shohada St

To Basij Square (1km);
Darya Grand Hotel (1.2km);
Sara'eyn (28km);
Tabriz (218km)

Shahid Mosala Khomeini St

Hedat Atmat St

Mo'allem St

Madathan St

Besat
Square

Shohada St

Bahonar
Square

22
23

To Shurabil
Hotel (2.5km)

Shohada St

20
14
Besat St

To Kivi (95km);
Khal Khal (122km)

WESTERN IRAN

capital of Sajid dynasty Azarbayjan from AD 871 to 929, and saw independence as a khanate from 1747 to 1808. However, Ardabil is best remembered for spawning two great leaders: the Safavid patriarch and great dervish-Sufi mystic Sheikh Safi od-Din (1253–1354), plus his later descendant Ismail Safavi. The latter expanded the clan domains so successfully that by 1502 Ismail had become Shah of all Persia. His glorious Safavid dynasty was to rule Iran for over two centuries.

Orientation & Information

The central triangle formed by Imam Hossein, Imam Khomeini and Ali Qapu Sqs is manageable on foot. Beyond that the city expands in three big concentric hoops. Excellent maps are sold from a modest **bookshop** (Sheikh Safi St) opposite the Sabalan Hotel. **Bank Melli** (Imam Khomeini St) changes money. **Kolbehnet** (☎ 223 1617; Imam Khomeini St; per hr IR8000; ☯ 8am-midnight) has fast Internet connections, and some staff speak English. **Homai Travel** (☎ 223 3233; Sa'at-Noh Sq) sells air tickets.

Sights

SHEIKH SAFI OD-DIN MAUSOLEUM

The Safavid patriarch is buried on the site of his dervish monastery in a suitably splendid **mausoleum complex** (Sheikh Safi St; admission IR20,000; ☯ 8.30am-5pm winter, 8.30am-noon & 3.30-7pm summer). The central courtyard is charming if relatively petite. Its blue ceramic designs are so mesmerising that one almost forgets to enter the shrine itself. The main tomb is within an **Allah-Allah tower**, so called because the apparently geometrical motif of blue, glazed bricks is actually the endlessly repeated name of God. Inside are the beautiful wooden sarcophagi of Safi od-Din and other lesser notables. Nearby, a team of craftsmen are still working on re-creating the world-famous 1568 'Ardabil Carpet', a massive 10.7m by 5.34m masterpiece that contains nearly 30 million knots. The **Khan-e Chini** (Porcelain Museum) has a dramatic 'stalactite' ceiling and the **Candil Khaneh** (Chandelier House) has ornate plaster mouldings and silver-finished doors.

OTHER SIGHTS

Sheikh Safi od-Din's father, Sheikh Jebra'il, is buried underneath a mildly attractive 16th-century **mausoleum** (admission by donation; ☯ irregular) at Khalkhoran, a village-suburb 3km northeast of the centre. It's an active shrine, so remove your shoes before inspecting the murals and multifaceted ceiling.

Ardabil has at least five restored **Safavid bridges** across the Baliqli Chay (Fishy River). Nicknamed Yeddi Göz (Seven Eyes), the seven-span **Pol-e-Jajim** is the most famous, but the cute, three-arch **Pol-e-Ibrahimabad** is more appealing.

Stroll the back alleys to find the sweet **Haji Fakr Mosque** with its squat, Bukharan-style peppermill minaret. Nearby, the attractively brick-vaulted **Mirza Ali Akbar Mosque** (Sa'at-Noh Sq) has a blue Kufic-tiled exterior frieze. The Mongol Ilkhanid **Jameh Mosque** (Shahid Madani St) was once a truly gigantic brick edifice. Ravaged by earthquakes it lies in heftily lumpsome ruins, as it has for centuries. Nonetheless, a surviving chamber still welcomes the faithful to prayer. Off Taleqani St, the former **Maryam Church** has an unusual old stone pyramid as its central dome and now hosts a *zurkhaneh* (p45; a house of strength). The **covered bazaar** is attractive, though sliced brutally in half by Imam Khomeini St.

Sleeping

Ardabil has a reasonable choice, but if nothing suits there's loads more accommodation in nearby Sara'eyn.

Shurabil Hotel (☎ 551 3096; fax 551 3097; Shurabil Lakeside; s IR65,000-85,000, tw 80-100,000) Hurry before someone tells the Shurabil about foreigner pricing. For now it's a bargain-value, relaxingly quiet mid-range place 5km from the centre. Rooms have good hot showers and all mod cons. Some have lake views.

Sevil Hotel (☎ 224 6644; Modarres St; s/tw IR40,000/ 50,000) Of several central cheapies, this super-clean mosaferkhuneh with shared shower is by far the best deal.

Darya Grand Hotel (☎ 777 4977; Atayi St; s/d/tr/ste US$30/45/56/70; ⓟ) Near Basij Sq, the Darya is reckoned Ardabil's best. English is spoken, it's clean and pleasant, but rooms are not significantly better than the much cheaper Shurabil.

Sabalan Hotel (☎ 244 8081; Sheikh Safi St; s US$12-15, tw $20-25) Rooms vary from bright and fresh to musty but acceptable. They have bathrooms and upper back rooms have views of Mt Sabalan. Some staff speak a little English, there's a good restaurant and the position is superbly central.

Hotel Negin (☎ 223 5671; fax 223 5674; Taleqani St; s/tw IR240,000/320,000) Behind a promisingly neat, modern reception area, the quiet, strangely shaped rooms don't quite live up to expectations. Carpets are dirty but there are full, Western facilities.

Mahdi Hotel (☎ 661 2985; Besat St; s/tw US$20/30) New but jerry-built and already slightly tatty, the Mahdi's Western bathrooms nonetheless have soap and toilet paper, the windows are insulated against problematic road noise and the owner speaks fluent German. It's near the Khal Khal terminal.

Iran Hotel (Sar Cheshmeh Sq; s/tw IR26,000/37,000) A mangy stuffed bird flies over fake foliage in the Iran's time-warp dining room. Washing is limited to a basin in the somewhat tatty, basic rooms.

Eating

The best place for kebabs is the **Hotel Sabalan restaurant** (meals IR13,000-18,000) or the bright, but standard **Shandiz** (Enqelab St; meals IR18,000-24,000). Other central dining options huddle together immediately south of Imam Khomeini Sq, both in the **Bozorg Safavi Shopping Mall** (three small pizzerias) and facing it (kababis, fried chicken, a café). None are gastronomically exciting, but the curious, well-heated **Sabalan Ice Cream** (Imam Khomeini St; ✆ 9am-10pm) has moulding-and-mirror walls and serves a good fresh pomegranate juice.

For dessert try *helva siyah* (black halva), a rich local speciality reminiscent of Christmas pudding. Sold at **Azizi** (Sheikh Shafi St; ✆ 9am-11pm), and at several shops facing the mausoleum, it costs IR8000 per kilogram. For just IR500 you can try a small plateful sprinkled with coconut, grated nuts and cinnamon. Delicious. Ardabil honey is also famous.

Getting There & Away

AIR

Flights to Tehran (IR164,000) leave daily with Iran Air, Friday and Sunday only with Iran Aseman. Buy tickets from Homai Travel (p147).

BUS, MINIBUS & SAVARI

The main bus station is on Moqaddas-e-Ardabili St is 3km northeast of the centre. Buses leave hourly to Tehran via Astara (IR3000, 1½ hours), Rasht (IR10,000, four

hours) and Qazvin (IR16,000, seven hours). Equally frequent buses to Tabriz (IR5300, four hours) thunder through Sarab and Bostanabad. For the more scenic route via Ahar you'll need to make savari hops via Meshgin Shahr. Start from Moghan Sq.

For Mianeh (thence Zanjan) most people head first to Tabriz, but a nicer way is to take a Khal Khal–bound savari as far as Kivi, from which a charter taxi costs around IR200,000. Khal Khal savaris (IR12,000, 1½ hours) leave just south of Besat Sq.

Sara'eyn minibuses and savaris leave from different points near Bahonar Sq.

Getting Around

The airport is 11km away, IR10,000 by taxi. From Imam Khomeini Sq shared taxis run to Bahonar Sq (for Sara'eyn minibuses) and to Besat Sq (for the Khal Khal terminal). Others start near Imam Hossein Sq, including minibuses to Khalkhoran (IR200, 20 minutes, three per hour). In snow, consider chartering a taxi (IR12,000 per hour) to see the sights – easily arranged through hotels.

AROUND ARDABIL
Sara'eyn   سرعین
☎ 0452
Little Sara'eyn is an architecturally insensitive scar on an otherwise attractive plain that slopes up towards the mighty south face of Mt Sabalan (4811m). It's a rapidly developing hot springs resort town. The mineral cocktail in its famous water is said to cure anything from baldness to syphilis, and in summer the town is packed with miracle seekers. To find the most accessible bathing, walk five minutes to the right from the minibus terminus. The big concrete building of the relatively plush **Hydrotherapy Complex** (indoor bathing per person IR10,000) is easy to spot. Across the road the tattier, outdoor **Ghavkash-Goli hot pool** (IR2500; ✆ women afternoons, men evenings) is fun in the snow. In winter Sara'eyn is eerily empty, but that's likely to change as a new Austrian ski lift has just been installed at the **Alvares ski station**, 25km away by a new road.

SLEEPING

It's easy enough to take a day trip from Ardabil, but Sara'eyn offers virtually endless accommodation. Cheap, basic rooms are available in homes or above virtually any shop, such as the **Kareyi Reza Bakery** (☎ 222 3367; Taleqani St; per person IR30,000). Multiplying as you watch are semi-smart new apartment hotels where for US$25 to US$40 you get a kitchen, lounge and multiple beds, though often a fairly small bathroom. Competitors are under construction but for now the best hotel is the fairly grand **Laleh International** (☎ 222 2750; s/d US$76/113.50; ✷ ℗) behind Ghavkash-Goli hot pool.

GETTING THERE & AWAY

Grindingly slow minibuses (IR1500, 40 minutes) depart when full from Ardabil's Bahonar Sq (Istgah Sara'eyn) and savaris (IR6000, 25 minutes) from nearby. Sara'eyn taxis want IR40,000 return to Alvares ski station.

Khal Khal   خل خل
☎ 0452 / pop 37,000
Set in a valley of high, bald mountains Khal Khal would make a great hiking base but is itself a depressingly drab 4km strip-town. It's a possible transit stop on a scenic but little-travelled alternative Ardabil–Rasht route. From Ardabil this follows a broad valley of remarkably sparsely populated nomad territory to the almost-attractive stepped town of **Kivi** (Chivi, Kosar). Here it swerves east, approaching Khal Khal through a narrow, steep-cut rocky valley before wiggling down to the Caspian.

There's also a lovely but tough road from Khal Khal to the Zanjan–Tabriz highway. Between Hashtjin and Aqkand the asphalt is unfinished, and muddy tracks (impassable if wet) zigzag across the Qizil Owzan valley with glimpses of some incredibly isolated, inaccessible villages clinging valiantly to the distant canyon sides. The best views are just before Kejal village where there's a single tin shack *chaykhuneh* (teahouse) at the roadside.

SLEEPING

Unmarked in English on a central roundabout opposite the post office, **Hotel Iran** (☎ 423 2104; dm/tr IR25,000/35,000) is the only cheap mosaferkhuneh in Khal Khal that accepts foreigners. **Khal Khal Tourist Inn** (Mehmunsara Jahangardi; ☎ 422 5991; tw IR200,000) is up an unlikely mud track at the east end of town. The bearable, if aged, rooms have showers.

GETTING THERE & AWAY

Savaris to Ardabil (IR12,000, 1½ hours) and Rasht (IR20,000, two hours) leave from opposite ends of town. The adventure to Zanjan via Aqkand will cost at least IR200,000. Few drivers know the way; **agency** (☎ 422 2212) might have drivers who can help.

ASTARA   آستارا
☎ 018252 / pop 32,000
This small, busy if undistinguished border town is the main crossing point to Azerbaijan. With ample accommodation in all price ranges, it's an ideal place to overnight while exploring Talesh/west Caspian villages or taking the lovely mountain road to Ardabil. The only sight per se is the **Imamzadeh Gassem** (Rasht–Astara highway) with its blue twin minarets and lemon-shaped dome. This is 5km south of town, just beyond the Espinas Hotel and its attractive mountain-backed **lake**.

Orientation

Astara starts at Qods Sq, a roundabout where the highway from Rasht swings west towards Ardabil. Imam Khomeini St runs north from here passing the bus station (200m) and the Internet café (2.5km) before reaching Shahrdari Sq (3km). Here Hakim Nezami St cuts east through Mo'allem Sq, passes the Tourist Inn, and ends near the sea at a big border bazaar. To make it all the more fun, there's a confusing one-way system.

The pedestrian border crossing into Azerbaijan (Mosaferi Gumruk) is a short but less than obvious stroll from Mo'allem Sq, and a five-minute alley walk from Shahrdari Sq. Vehicles cross at Gumruk Transit (Vehicular Customs Post) somewhat further east opposite the Tourist Inn.

Information

The nearest reliable banks are in Rasht or Ardabil.
Bank Melli (Shahrdari Sq) Despite an 'exchange' sign, Bank Melli directs potential clients to freelance moneychangers in the bazaar or at the border post. When buying Azeri money note that 'one shirvan' means 10,000 manats (roughly US$2). Rates are best on the Iran side, but hardly generous.
Internet Cafe Caspian (Imam Khomeini St; per hr IR8000; ☯ 10am-11pm) Connection is way better than anything in Azerbaijani Astara.
Telephone Office (Helali Ahmer St; ☯ 9am-9pm) Phone numbers still have various lengths, but are due for rationalisation.

Sleeping & Eating

There are countless mosaferkhunehs and simple hotels around Mo'allem and Shahrdari Sqs, notably in the nearby alleys.

Espinas Hotel (☎ 7050; www.espinashotel.com; s/d/tw/ste US$79/127/127/190; ❄ P) This is one of Iran's finest hotels, with marble floors and a grand Persepolis frieze entranceway. It's 5km south of Astara town, and set in a landscaped garden with mountain views across a lake on which you can rent jet skis. Tennis courts and sauna are available.

Astara Tourist Inn (Mehmunsara Jahangardi; ☎ 22134; fax 6065; Hakim Nezami St; s/tw US$20/30; ❄ P) Set back in a yard close to Gumruk Transit, the inn has very pleasant, fresh-scented rooms. Those on the top floor have Western toilets.

Mehmunpazir Asseman (☎ 2300; dm IR40,000) This typical, bearable cheapy has a shower and tap (but no toilet) in each three-bed dorm. If alone, you might have to pay for all three beds. It's in an alley marked 'Asiman Gostinicha' in faulty Russian.

Hotel Belal (☎ 5586; Mo'allem Sq; s/d IR88,000/160,000) Easy to find, with clean if unironed sheets in rooms with fan, decent shower and Western toilet. Facing it **Hotel Seydan** (Mo'allem Sq) is similar.

There are kababis around Shahrdari Sq; stylish dining is at the Espinas Hotel's **restaurant** (mains IR18,000-35,000 +15x; ☑ 7am-10am, noon-4pm & 7.30-11pm) with views of the lake and a choice of schnitzel, trout, Persian favourites and Caspian dishes, including *mirza ghasemi* (a dish of mashed aubergine, squash, garlic and egg; see the boxed text 'Cut the Caviar', p154).

Getting There & Away

To Tehran (IR30,000, 10 hours) via Rasht (IR13,000) and Qazvin, buses depart the main terminal at 6am, 7am, 8am and 2pm then hourly 6pm to 11pm. TBT has a 3pm bus to Tabriz (IR12,500, 6½ hours) via Ardabil (IR5000, two hours).

Savaris outside the terminal charge IR10,000 to Ardabil but, especially in the snow, it's worth chartering the whole car (IR50,000) to allow photo stops in the frosted forest scenery. Savaris are also a sensible option for Rasht (IR18,000, 2½ hours) or Hashtpar (Talesh), or you could try to hail passing ex-Ardabil buses at Qods Sq.

ASTARA TO RASHT

Of all the Caspian coast the least spoilt is the stretch between Astara and Rezvanshahr skirting the Talesh region. There are no must-see sights, but even the main road has attractive moments with areas of rice paddies (notably at **Lavandevil**, **Khotbeh Sara** and **Sust**) and some lovely woodland around **Asalem**. Most accessible of the region's castle ruins is the cute little **Dezhe Sasal Fortress** (Qal'eh Lisar; Salsal St) which crowns a wooded knoll at the southern end of **Lisar** town, just five minutes' walk off the main highway. Its gate arch is intact and offers fine sea views, though the rest of the site is fenced off.

Lavandevil, **Chalvand**, **Plasy** and **Keshli** are main road villages and each has a scattering of semi-traditional tile-roofed cottages, not dissimilar from British suburban bungalows. Some (eg in **Vizneh**) have distinctive wooden porches, and there are a few thatched homes south of **Ziyabar**. However, the real highlights are remote mountain villages with quaint timber-framed houses and no easy road access, such as **Agh Oilar**, 25km up a very rough track from Hashtpar (Talesh). The track starts as Mehr Ghorbani St, along the north bank of the river, but

CROSSING THE AZERBAIJAN BORDER AT ASTARA

A narrow river divides Astara (Iran) from Astara (Azerbaijan). Crossing is allowed 8am to 6pm Iran time, 8.30am to 6.30pm Azerbaijan time. By Caucasus standards this border is particularly straightforward and friendly, with neither fees nor bribes to pay. The authors were through in under 20 minutes. By contrast international Baku–Tehran buses wait between three and seven hours while the whole bus is checked. Visas are *not* available on arrival.

Accommodation is better in Iranian Astara, but cheaper on the Azerbaijan side. Heading north an overnight sleeper train to Baku leaves Astara around 7pm for under US$4, but the station is a US$2 taxi ride from the border. It's cheaper to walk 500m straight up Azadlyq St to Azeri Astara's minibus stand, take a 1000 manat shuttle to Länkäran and catch the train from there at around 9pm.

TRADITIONALLY TALESH *Mark Elliott*

'Everyone dies young these days. I blame those things,' says my Talesh friend, Seyran, as he waves his hands dismissively at the mobile phone antennae rising above the vegetable patch where his 103-year-old grandma is bent double, busily weeding. 'Her?! 103's not old!' he scoffs. Indeed she barely looks 73. 'In her day people reckoned anything under 120 was premature.' Lovingly featured in the movies of Farhad Mehranfar *(Paper Airplanes, Tree of Life)* the beautiful Talesh ethnogeographic subregion straddles the border from Länkäran in Azerbaijan to Asalem in Iran's Gilan province. It includes many remote, relatively traditional, Talesh-speaking mountain villages including one where Shiralev Muslimov (1805–1973) supposedly lived to a phenomenal 168 years old. The *Guinness Book of Records* later dropped him as 'World's Longest-Lived Man' due to doubts over his Tsarist birth certificate. Who cares? Even if he added a sneaky decade to his tally, he still had about the best innings of anyone since the Old Testament.

---

is only passable on foot, horseback or with a tough 4WD.

Hashtpar is the Talesh area's small main town, often confusingly referred to as Talesh city. Behind the charioteer statue in its central square is an attractive Qajar-era octagonal pavilion; this is used by revolutionary guards and photographing it is unwise.

Sleeping & Eating

Graciously spared the ugly overdevelopment of the ventral Caspian strip, there are only a few scattered hotels along the main Rasht–Astara highway. A reasonable choice 2km north of Hashtpar is the **Hotel-Restaurant Talesh** (☎ 01842 2299; tw IR120,000; P), where rooms are clean and much nicer than the gloomy corridors suggest. Road noise can be disturbing.

Some 3km west of Rezvanshahr, 200m southwest of the main coast road junction, the **Hotel Punel** (☎ 0182 462 3149; Masal Road; dm from IR60,000; P) is potentially pleasant with big four- and six-bedded rooms. However, pricing is random, and it's important to establish whether you're being charged per room or per person. The area's hills and rice fields are attractive, but views are marred by a factory.

Both hotels have decent restaurants.

Getting There & Away

Hopping along the coast road in savaris is possible, but can be slow going. You'll probably change in Hashtpar and Asalem, whence occasional savaris link to Khal Khal (p149). Chartering a savari from the relevant terminals in Astara or Rasht is a fine alternative. Typically you'll pay IR90,000 for the whole route, plus around IR5000 per stop or short detour.

RASHT رشت

☎ 0131 / pop 428,000 / elevation -7m

Rapidly expanding Rasht is by far the largest city of the Shomal (Caspian littoral) region and is the capital of Gilan province. Gilan has had extended periods of independence and the lispy local Gilaki dialect remains noticeably distinct from Farsi, its reversed adjective-noun order causing much amusement for other Iranians.

Although 15km inland, Rasht is a popular weekend and holiday destination for Tehranis, for whom the greatest attraction is its 'refreshing' climate (ie lots of rain). Year-round downpours and steaming summer humidity appeal rather less to most foreign tourists. The city has precious little in the way of historical buildings, but Rasht is a useful transport hub from which to visit the lush mountain forests, rice paddies and thatched-house villages of the emerald-green Gilan hinterland, most famously at Masuleh. It's also a great place to taste the garlic-stoked, vegetable-rich Gilan cuisine, but don't drink the tap water.

History

Historically Lahijan and Fuman were Gilan's main centres. Rasht (previously Resht) developed in the 14th century, but the population was massacred in 1668 by the forces of the Cossack brigand Stepan 'Stenka' Razin who also sank Persia's entire Caspian navy. The Russians, a constant factor in the region thereafter, were back in 1723 clearing spaces in the then impenetrable forest to allow Resht's growth. In 1899 a Russian company cut the road to Qazvin, diminishing Gilan's isolation from the rest of Iran. By WWI the town boasted 60,000 inhabitants and four

WESTERN IRAN

RASHT

0 ————— 2 km
0 ————— 1 mile

A   **B**   **C**   **D**

INFORMATION
Bank Melli (Exchange)...................1 B3
Bank Melli (Visa Payments)..........2 A3
Bookshop.....................................3 B3
Central Telephone Office.............4 B3
Day..5 A3
E-Gil...6 B6
Gictic...7 B3
ITTO...8 B4
Mazarieh Telephone Office..........9 C6
Mehrpouya Currency Exchange
   Service.....................................10 B3
Police Headquarters...................11 B3
Post Office..................................12 B3
Rata...13 B6

SIGHTS & ACTIVITIES   (pp153–4)
Donna Ali Shrine........................14 A5
Gilani House...............................15 C4

Kuchuk Khan Horseman Statue.....16 B3
Kuchuk Khan Mausoleum.............17 B6
Rasht Museum.............................18 A3
Shahrdari.....................................19 B3

SLEEPING   (p154)
Bahar..20 B3
Behesht.......................................21 B3
Carvan..22 B3
Golestan.....................................23 B3
Hotel Ordibesht..........................24 A3
Kadus Hotel................................25 C6
Keyvan.......................................26 B3
Pamchal.....................................27 C6
Paradis.......................................28 C6

EATING   (pp154–5)
Babak...29 B4
BFC..(see 29)

Bijan's.......................................(see 6)
Boof...30 B4
Kourosh......................................31 A2
Kumeh..32 B5
Neshirat Cafeteria......................33 B3
Pizza Gilar..................................34 B5

SHOPPING   (p155)
Cadeau.....................................(see 35)
Farahmand..................................35 B4
Nafis...36 B4

TRANSPORT   (p155)
Bus Offices.................................37 B3
Buses to Astara & Ardabil...........38 C6
Buses to Astara & Ardebil............39 D3
Ham Safar Office........................40 A2
Iran Air Office.............................41 B4
Lahijan/Chalus Terminal..............42 D5
Main Bus Station........................43 D6
Savaris to Astara & Ardabil.........44 B2
Savaris to Qazvin........................45 C6
Savaris/Minibuses to Fuman........46 A5
Shared Taxis to Bandar-e Anzali...47 B3
Shared Taxis to Bus Station.........48 C6
Shared Taxis to Golsar................49 B3
Shared Taxis to Lahijan Terminal...50 B3
TBT Office...................................51 B3

Sahid Dabiri St

Sadi St

40 ●
31 ■   47 49 12 4
24 🏠   37 ⊙ 11
●19 ■ 16
3 🏠   *Bazaar*
35 🏠   📶 33
23 🏠
21 🏠 26 🏠
10 🏠
22 🏠   ● 51
20 🏠

Shan'ati St
Motahari St
Imam Khomeini St
A'lamol Hoda St
Shari'ati St

0 ————— 500 m
0 ————— 0.3 miles

18 🏛
Talechi St
Sabz Square
@ 5
Soleymani St
Pir Sara St
22 Bahman St
17 *Shahrivar St*
1 🏠
7 @
2 🏠
Shohada Square (Shahrdari Square)
Engelab St
Engelab Square

To Airport (3km);
Bandar-e Anzali (40km)

Valiasr Square (Istgah Anzali)
🏠 39

Deylaman Blvd
Khoramshahr Blvd
Shahid Ansari Blvd

Somiyah St
📶 30
📶 29
41 ●
36 🏠
Golsar District
Golsar Ave

Gholipar St

● 15

To Lahijan (43km);
Ramsar (119km);
Chalus (205km)

Saipa Showroom ●

● 42
8 🏠
Talebi St
Sa'di St

Shohada St   *Janbazan Square*

Shohada Square (Shahrdari Square)
Sabz Square
See Enlargement

Talechi St
14 ●
Rajai Blvd

To Fuman (25km);
Masuleh (62km)

● 46
Yakhsazi Square
Beheshti Hwy

Pasdaran Square
Chamran St
Pir Dawud St
Fredin St
Imam Hossein Square

34 📶
32 📶
Ziyabari Blvd
Taqi Eshki St
@ 13
Lakani Square
Park-e Shahr
22 Bahman St
Namju Blvd
Azodegan St
Pasdaran St
Imam Khomeini Blvd
Modarres Hwy

6 ●
28 🏠
Azadi Blvd
Azadi Square
25 🏠
9 ●   27 🏠
Mosallah (Tushuba) Square
🏠 38
43

Entezam Square
Jirdeh Rd
Shahid Nazar St
Flatekegaz Blvd
Gaz Square
Beheshti Hwy
Manzariyeh St
17 🏠

To Jirdeh (16km);
Shaft (25km)

To Rudbar (67km);
Qazvin (177km);
Tehran (325km)

48 🏠
45 🏠
Some Minor Rds Not Depicted

LP

international consulates. From 1917 it was the centre of Kuchuk Khan's Jangali ('Forest') Movement, an Islamic, Robin Hood–style rebellion. Among their grievances with collapsing Qajar Iran was the shah's perceived sellout to oil-hungry Britain. Courting the Bolsheviks who'd just taken control of Russia, Kuchuk Khan joined forces with communist-agitators and, on 4 June 1920, set up Gilan as the 'Soviet Socialist Republic of Iran'. However, radical-leftists and land-owning Muslim nationalists made very prickly bedfellows. Once Kuchuk Khan had ejected the infidel communists from his 'government', his Russian backers slipped away leaving Gilan prey to the efficient new regime of Reza Khan (later Shah Reza Pahlavi) who'd taken over Persia in a February 1921 coup. Reza Khan first dealt with Azadistan (temporarily independent Tabriz/Azarbayjan) then attacked Gilan. Most of Rasht's pretty wooden houses were burnt, Kuchuk Khan was executed and his severed head was brought to Tehran for public display.

These days any enemy of the Pahlavis has become a friend of the current Islamic Republic. Thus Kuchuk Khan has now ridden back into favour on many a horseback statue across Gilan.

Orientation

The three main thoroughfares, Shari'ati St, Sa'di St and Imam Khomeini Blvd, converge at pleasantly palm-filled Shahrdari Sq (officially Shohada Sq). Traffic can be nightmarish but budget accommodation is conveniently close. The relatively chic Golsar District in the far north is the up-and-coming centre for middle-class café society.

Information

INTERNET ACCESS
Day (☎ 222 1609; Sabz Sq; per hr IR9000; ☺ 8am-midnight) Central but slow.
E-Gil (☎ 323 1306; Namju Blvd; per hr IR8000; ☺ 10am-last customer leaves) Handy for Bijan's bistro.
Gictic (Imam Khomeini Blvd; per hr IR6500; ☺ 7am-7pm Sat-Thu; ☒) Plush, modern but painfully slow.
Rata (Ziyabari Blvd; per hr IR8000; ☺ 8.30am-1.30pm & 4.30-10pm Sun-Thu)

MONEY
Bank Melli (Enqelab Sq) Currency exchange upstairs. There is another branch for visa payments – see Visa Extensions (below).

Mehrpouya Currency Exchange Service (☎ 222 7826; ☺ 9am-1.30pm & 4.30-8pm Sat-Thu) Instant exchange for major currencies (3% less than bank rates) and Azerbaijani manats.

POST
Post Office (Shahrdari Sq)

TELEPHONE
Central Telephone Office (Shahrdari Sq) Sometimes unreliable for international connections.
Mazarieh Telephone Office (Azadi Blvd; ☺ 9am-9pm) Smaller but dependable.

TOURIST INFORMATION
Bookshop (A'lam-ol Hoda St) Sells good but outdated city maps.
ITTO (☎ 223 1306; Takhti St; ☺ 8am-2pm Sat-Thu) Helpful with specific problems, but not worth the trek for its so-so brochures.

VISA EXTENSIONS
Police Headquarters (Shohada Sq; ☺ 8am-2pm Sat-Thu) To extend your visa, apply as early as possible at room 10, upstairs. Nobody speaks English, but the success rate is high. Pay IR100,000 into the small, specific branch of **Bank Melli** (cnr 22 Bahman & 17 Shahrivar Sts). Return with the receipt, pay IR2500 to a uniformed officer and collect the extension around 1pm.

Sights

The **Shahrdari** (Municipality Building; Shahrdari Sq) is Rasht's most identifiable landmark, its colonial style tempered by a token dome-let topping a distinctive whitewashed tower. It looks great when floodlit at night. In the square opposite, palm trees grow hula skirts of ivy. The central **horseman statue** (Shohada Sq) is Kuchuk Khan, the Jangali leader of 'Soviet Iran'. At his **mausoleum** (Manzariyeh St) Kuchuk Khan's grave is sheltered by a brick gazebo with intricate wooden roof. It's in a cemetery in the far south of town and attracts a steady flow of well-wishers.

Small, but well presented in a 70-year-old house, **Rasht Museum** (Taleqani St; admission IR15,000; ☺ 9am-5pm Sat-Thu, 9am-1pm Fri) displays local crafts and attractively illustrates the Gilaki lifestyle. Amid pottery exhibits and a model of Qal'eh Rudkhan fortress, the basement displays some ancient bronzes plus the metal detector that found them.

Cute **Donna Ali Shrine** (Taleqani St) sits in the middle of the road on the site of a city gate.

Stranded in a triangle of green beside thundering Shahid Ansari Blvd is a fantastic old wooden **Gilani house** with a thatched roof. A sign says 'ITTO Tourism' but the poor, confused resident can't understand why.

Sleeping

While there are many options, you might still have trouble finding somewhere to stay in peak summer season (May to September) when the overwhelming humidity makes air-con virtually essential.

BUDGET

Most cheapies are handily central, though none are particularly impressive, or over-clean.

Bahar (☎ 222 1415; Imam Khomeini Blvd; tw/tr/quad IR39,500/43,800/50,600) Neat but very basic rooms in an old house with fans and high ceilings. A shower costs IR6000 extra.

Behesht (☎ 222 2608; Cinema Kuchuk Alley; s IR25,000-37,000) The cheapest place to take foreigners, it has no washing facilities.

Golestan (☎ 222 4915; Sady Alley; tw/tr IR42,000/55,000; P) Simple rooms with a tap and good, clean shared showers.

Carvan (Caravan, Karavan; ☎ 222 2612; Shahid Mehrban Ln; s/tw IR50,000/90,000) This backpacker favourite remains popular, though sheets are threadbare and shared facilities are no better than the Golestan.

MID-RANGE

Keyvan (☎ 222 2979; Imam Khomeini Blvd; s/tw IR110,000/160,000; ☒) Much nicer than you'd guess from its mosaferkhuneh-style sign, but a step short of the bijou boutique hotel suggested by its reception area. Rooms are simple but clean, cool and with fridge.

Hotel Ordibesht (☎ /fax 222 9210; tw US$30; ☒) Pleasantly olde-worlde, if very slightly unkempt for the price. Set well back off Shahrdari Sq, it manages to be splendidly central yet very quiet.

Paradis (Paradise; ☎ 2323 1101; fax 322 0997; Imam Khomeini Blvd; s/d/tw US$30/35/35; ☒) Once appealingly modern and stylish; carpets are now getting tatty. On the 4th floor (no lift) are curious split-level doubles. Avoid the noisy roadside rooms.

Pamchal (☎ 666 1653; 15 Khordat St; tw IR240,000; ☒) More functional than the Paradis despite the columned entry porch.

CUT THE CAVIAR

The Caspian produces 95% of the world's caviar, but don't count on seeing any – it's virtually all for export. In fact, Gilan's cuisine ignores the sea and focuses on the local wealth of fruit, nuts and vegetables. Typical dishes are packed with garlic and turmeric, rather shocking for the taste buds of central Iranian tourists. *Sirabi* is essentially fried garlic leaves, *shami Rashti* are deep-fried lentil-and-meat patties, *baghala ghatogh* are dill-and-garlic flavoured broad beans, while *anarbij* is a meatball variant of *fesenjun* (classic Persian sauce, see p75) in a walnut and pomegranate sauce. *Torshi Tareh* uses virtually every vegetable and fruit with yet more garlic and possibly pennyroyal, once considered a natural contraceptive. None of the above are particularly easy to find in restaurants but throughout the region it's worth asking for *mirza ghasemi*, a vegetarian marvel of mashed aubergine, squash, garlic and egg.

Kadus Hotel (☎ 322 3075; cadus_hotel@yahoo.com; Azadi Blvd; s/d US$50/65; ☒ P ☒) A faded 1970s international-style concrete box hotel with three restaurants, a summer-only pool and obliging staff. Rooms are acceptable, if barely memorable. The location is inconvenient.

Eating

Bijan's (☎ 323 3099; Namju Blvd; meals IR25,000; ☺ 6-11pm Sun-Fri) Here it is, a cosy Italian bistro too perfect to even dream of in provincial Iran: just four small tables and a chef who studied in Sheffield rather than Sorrento. Pasta comes with huge bowls of Parmesan, there are vegetarian options, and garlic bread is served in pizza-style rounds.

Kourosh (☎ 222 0890; Erkhtesat Ln; meals IR30,000; ☺ 9am-4pm & 6pm-midnight) Kourosh is rare in serving several typical Gilani dishes and hard-to-find *fesenjun*.

Kumeh (☎ 322 6579; Taqi Eshkil St; kebabs IR5500; ☺ 4pm-midnight) The most interesting of a huddle of restaurants in the Park-e-Shahr area, Kumeh has Irano-Hawaiian covered dining platforms outside and colourful geometric designs inside. Kebabs are served with fresh bread. Sharing a post-prandial puff on a lemon qalyan is an ideal way to meet the friendly regulars.

Pizza Gilar (☎ 322 4342; Taqi Eshkil St; pizzas IR20,000; ☽ 10am-midnight) Near Kumeh, Pizza Gilar has an English-speaking owner who has experimented with sidelines like Russian *pirozhki* (part doughnut, part spring roll).

Neshirat Cafeteria (☎ 222 5460; meals IR8000-35,000; ☽ noon-10pm) This bland, 3rd-floor self-service place has views over Shahrdari Sq from its corner tables; the food is quite unprepossessing.

There are several quite central pizza and fast-food places along Alam-ol-Hoda St and on Sabz Sq, but locals prefer the Golsar district. **Boof** (Golsar Ave; burgers IR9000; ☽ noon-3pm & 6pm-midnight) is the biggest of these with a striking grey-and-neon battleship interior. **BFC** (☎ 775 6888; Golsar Ave; chicken dinner IR17,000; ☽ 10am-3pm & 5.30pm-midnight) is a Kentucky takeoff, located nearby and you can call for delivery. One of many stylish cafés to be found in Golsar, **Babak** (Golsar Ave; cappuccino IR8000; ☽ 1pm-1am) is a green, cream and chrome coffee bar that serves sundaes and shakes.

For cheaper desserts, nuts and snacks there are **stalls** around the bazaar and at night near the Hotel Ordibesht.

Shopping
Souvenirs ranging from Gilaki wooden spoons to wonderfully tacky shell-encrusted boxes are sold at **Farahmand** (Imam Khomeini Blvd; ☽ 9.30am-9pm Sat-Thu). You will find slightly classier items at **Cadeau** (Imam Khomeini Blvd; ☽ 9.30am-9pm Sat-Thu). Or try the stylish, but much more expensive, **Nafis** (☎ 772 7308; Bastani Shoar Sq; Golsar District ☽ 9am-1.30pm & 4-10pm).

Getting There & Away
AIR
Iran Air (☎ 772 4444; Golsar Ave; ☽ 7.30am-7pm Sat-Thu, 9am-1pm Fri) has flights to Tehran (IR144,000, daily) and Mashhad (IR293,000, twice weekly).

BUS, MINIBUS & SAVARI
The main bus terminal is 300m northeast of Gil Sq, itself 2km south of Mosallah (Tushuba) Sq down Imam Khomeini Blvd. It's easy by shared taxi. Several bus companies have handy booking offices in the centre, many on Sa'di St just off Shahrdari Sq.

Destination	Price (IR)	Duration (hr)	Departures
Ahvaz	42,000	18	11am, Taavoni 11
Esfahan	26,000-40,000	12	5-6pm
Gorgan	22,000-30,000	9	7-10am & 7-9pm Ham Safar; 1pm Taavoni 8
Hamadan	16,300	9	9am Taavoni 11
Mashhad	65,000 Volvo	18	2.30pm TBT
Tabriz	30,000	9	4-8pm various
Tehran	23,000-28,000	6	frequent via Qazvin

For Qazvin, Taavoni 7 has one direct bus (IR10,800, three hours, 9am); hop on a Tehran-bound bus or use a savari (IR20,000, 2½ hours) from Mosallah (Tushuba) Sq.

Buses to Astara and Ardabil start from Tehran and pick up at both Mosallah Sq (beside a massive mosque) and Valiasr Sq (Istgah Anzali). But it's much simpler to take an Astara-bound savari from behind the Armenian church in an alley off Sa'di St.

For Bandar-e Anzali, shared taxis collect passengers from various points off Shohada Sq notably near the Kourosh restaurant.

For Caspian towns to the east, minibuses are frequent until 6pm (savaris later) from the Lahijan terminal, 500m east of Janbazan Sq. This is hidden in a yard opposite a Saipa showroom. Durations will vary according to traffic conditions, but prices for minibuses/savaris are Lahijan IR1400/3000, Ramsar IR6000/12,000 and Chalus IR7500/18,000.

For Fuman (and thence Masuleh) savaris and minibuses depart from Yakhsazi Sq.

Getting Around
For the airport you can get a taxi for around IR10,000 from Valiasr Sq (Istgah Anzali), much more from the city centre. Key shared-taxi routes from Shohada Sq run the length of Imam Khomeini Blvd, others are along Shohada St to the Lahijan terminal. Northbound, many shared taxis go up Sa'di St via Shahid Ansari Sq, where some swing left up to Golsar, others continuing to Valiasr Sq (Istgah Anzali). These return southbound down Takhti St, passing the ITTO.

AROUND RASHT
Bandar-e Anzali   بندر انزلی
☎ 0181 / pop 101,000
Bandar-e Anzali (formerly Enzeli) was developed by Russians in the late 19th century

as the harbour of the Caspian & Mercury Mail-Steamship Company. In WWI it was a malarial hellhole with a population of barely 4000, but nonetheless became the launching pad for several thrilling cloak-and-dagger operations which were to shape the history of the Caucasus. Notably it was from Enzeli that Britain's doomed Dunsterforce set out in a futile 1918 attempt to prevent Azerbaijan's oilfields falling to the Turks in WWI.

Today Bandar-e Anzali is Iran's foremost Caspian port city. Just two short, ragged blocks in the midst of a 10km-long sprawl give any architectural hint of its neocolonial history. On and immediately east of central Imam Khomeini Sq there are a few sad but potentially beautiful **Russian house facades** and a hidden **Armenian Church**; passingly interesting but hardly enough to justify the short day trip from Rasht.

Bandar-e Anzali's other potential appeal is its position on the world's largest fresh(ish) water lagoon. The **lagoon** itself isn't as attractive, but it's fun to take a motorboat ride (IR150,000 per hour) starting off by hurtling along a canal lined with vaguely Bangkok-style stilt houses. Seasonal **waterfowl** flee when they hear the roaring engines of such craft so ornithologists would be better off hitching a ride on a local fishing boat (cheap, but probably lasting all day).

Of Bandar Anzali's several hotels the most appealing is the wooden-framed **Ancient Golsang** (☎ 25500; Imam Khomeini Sq; s/tw US$18/28) All rooms have bathrooms, the helpful staff can help you find lagoon rides and the kitchen serves a particularly heavenly *mirza ghasemi* (see the boxed text 'Cut the Caviar', p154).

GETTING THERE & AWAY

Direct savaris (IR5000, 30 minutes) link Imam Khomeini Sq with central Rasht (Sa'di St or Shahrdari Sq). Don't bother with inconvenient minibuses. For Astara and the west Caspian coast there's a special savari/minibus terminal 3km west of central Bandar-e Anzali.

RASHT TO QAZVIN

Were it not litter strewn and so fearsomely busy, the Rasht–Qazvin deathtrap highway would be an attraction in itself. About 33km out of Rasht the much-revered **Imamzadeh Hashem** is plonked on a wooded knoll by the roadside. Some 25km further, where a side road to the east wiggles up onto delightfully rolling hills, 'Allah' is spelt out on a hillside in specially planted trees overlooking Rustamabad. Almost all transport stops in **Rudbar** for passengers to buy nationally famous olives and pickled garlic. Olive groves and conifers grace the grassy, rocky valley walls above town, offering attractive random rambles. Climbing steeply towards breezy **Manjil**, famous for its huge wind turbines, you pass the **Sefirud dam** and lake, at whose far, inaccessible western end lies the isolated ruin of **Shemiran Castle** and a scenic, lonely road via Gilvar to Zanjan. Passing through **Loshan** look north (left) to catch a glimpse of a sloping **Safavid bridge**. Greenery gives way to long rocky defiles for the final stretch towards Qazvin.

FUMAN فومان

☎ 0132 / pop 32,000

Gilan's main attraction is its wooded hinterland villages reached via Fuman. Formerly known as Dar-al-Emareh, and once capital of Gilan, Fuman is a leafy junction town 25km west of Rasht, its boulevards lined with date palms, plane trees and numerous rather tacky plaster-cast statues. It's the most famous place to buy *klucheh fuman,* typical Gilan cookies filled with walnut paste, available hot from the oven at several bakeries around town. Savaris to Rasht and Somaeh-Sara leave from a roundabout at the northeast edge of town, 500m from the grassy central square and bazaar. Rasht minibuses and an 8am bus to Tehran (IR22,350, 6½ hours) use a small terminal between the two. West of the bazaar, at the Shikh Restaurant, the road to Qal'eh Rudkhan branches southwest. Continue 400m west to find the savari stop for Masuleh (where the dual carriageway ends). There's no hotel.

AROUND FUMAN

Shown in many brochures, the supposedly 'typical' thatched-roof **Gilani cottages** with upper-wooden balustrades are now very rare. One accessible classic example is by the Masuleh road in **Makhlavan** (Makelun) village. Most visitors head straight for Masuleh.

Masuleh ماسوله

☎ 0132 / elevation 1050m

Previously known as both Maasalar and as Khortab, Masuleh is at least a millennium old. Reached through delightful, mist-draped mountain valleys, it is a delightful, tourist-conscious village with irregular rows of pale cream houses stacked on a double amphitheatre of wooded valley. They rise so steeply that the roof of one level forms the pathway for the level above. Despite ongoing gentrification and summer hoards, it remains a truly charming place to while away hours or days watching village life, observing traditional bread-making or just gazing across the flat roofs. In winter you'll have the place largely to yourself, if snow-drifts allow access at all. The inhabitants sell trinkets and handicrafts and friendly, young men are keen to show you attractive hikes to so-so waterfalls for a consideration.

SLEEPING & EATING

Many villagers rent out **basic rooms** from IR20,000 per bed. Several families are extending their homes to create extra apartment rooms for tourists. Fortunately this is being done in a way that blends surprisingly well with the village's architectural unity. Already operational, the unmarked **Mehran Suites** (☎ 757 3296; apt IR150,000-170,000) is great value. Each 'suite' has kitchen, shower, toilet, TV and a settee which folds out into a bed. Most have terraces with photo-perfect views over the main village. The similar **Hotel Nabi** (☎ 0913 123 5247), at the eastern end of the little bazaar, is almost complete. At the base of the village, the **Monafred Hotel** (☎ 757 3250; tw US$30) is older, but decently refurbished.

The **Mo'allem Restaurant** (☎ 757 1372; meals IR16,000-30,000; ♥ 9am-10pm) is stacked above the Monafred Hotel and does a decent *chelo mahi* (fried fish on rice). The **Masarkuh Restaurant** has a summer-only terrace under thatched parasols. In the bazaar is a marvellously down-market **teahouse** where grizzled mountain-men chew the cud.

Several country eateries line the most scenic sections of the approach road from Fuman, notably just before Lar Cheshmeh hamlet, about 5km east of Masuleh.

GETTING THERE & AWAY

From Fuman savaris (IR3000, 45 minutes) are regular in summer, but rare in winter. It's worth chartering in one direction (IR15,000) in order to make photo stops en route as the scenery is splendid. Although

the asphalt ends at Masuleh, there's a rough track leading to Khal Khal (p149), which some taxis might attempt in perfect, dry conditions for IR50,000 or so.

Qal'eh Rudkhan قلعه رودخان

One of Gilan's largest mountain fortresses, Qal'eh Rudkhan's extensive ruins are high above Qal'eh Daneh village, though you'll need a guide, stout hiking boots and much of the day to trek up there. There's an impressive scale model in Rasht Museum. Even if you don't climb to the castle, the 25-minute drive from Fuman to Qal'eh Daneh is delightful, crossing rice paddies and skirting hills with neat green-tea haircuts. At **Hajalof** village the asphalt degenerates into potholes as it follows a stream up a gentle valley passing several traditional timber homes.

Somaeh-Sara صومعه سرا
☎ 0182 / pop 30,000

Somaeh-Sara is 10km from Fuman. Come here to short-cut to the Talesh coast road, without doubling back via Rasht. The decent **Abrisham Hotel** (☎ 322 5080; fax 322 7198; Valiasr Sq; tw US$30; [icon] [P]) has neat, pleasantly functional rooms with bathroom, towels, soap and toilet paper. Its restaurant is pricey, but locally reputed for its fish dinners (IR45,000).

LAHIJAN & AROUND لاهیجان
☎ 0141 / pop 55,000

Famed for its tea, Lahijan is one of Gilan's oldest towns and retains charm in its central tree-lined streets. The alleyways around Vahdat Sq hide a few old homes with mossy, tiled roofs, a green-timbered Muslim library and the intriguing **Akbariyeh Mosque** (4th West Kashef Alley), which looks more like an old brick church. Around Vahdat Sq itself you'll find the **Jameh Mosque** with a brick missile minaret, a disused old domed bathhouse and the tile-roofed **Chahar Padeshah Mosque**. The latter's famous carved wooden doors have now been removed to Tehran's National Museum of Iran.

A kilometre further east, Kashef St starts to rise up **Sheitan Kuh** (Satan's Mountain), a tree-covered ridge fringed with tea gardens. En route it passes the austere, grey **Mausoleum of Kashef-ol-Saltaneh** (☎ 222 9980; East Kashef St; admission IR15,000; ♥ 8am-6pm Tue-Sun). This entombs the man who is credited with

WESTERN IRAN

ROOTS OF THAT CUPPA

Gilan province produces 90% of Iran's tea. The deep green, manicured tea bushes are now so emblematic that it's hard to believe they were introduced only a century ago. In fact, tea didn't reach Persia at all until the 17th century, when it became an expensive luxury. Qajar-period attempts to grow the stuff were unsuccessful until Kashef-ol-Saltaneh, an Iranian consul in India, managed to learn the secret art. Around 1900 he slipped home to Lahijan with some 4000 tea plants and the rest is history.

---

introducing tea cultivation to Iran (see the boxed text 'Roots of that Cuppa', above), and houses an underwhelming museum of tea paraphernalia, including a crusty 19th-century samovar salvaged from a Russian shipwreck. At Sheitan Kuh's northwestern base an attractive, if artificial, cascade trickles down into a landscaped urban lake. In a quiet, rural setting some 2km east is the distinctive wooden **Sheikh Zahed Mausoleum** (Boq'eh Sheikh Zahed; admission by donation). Its blue, pyramidal roof is Lahijan's architectural icon. The holy man buried here supposedly lived to the ripe old age of 116 (1218–1334), longer than the present mausoleum which was rebuilt after a devastating 1913 fire. You can catch a glimpse from the main Ramsar road east of the bypass. However, to reach it start from the Sheitan Kuh cascade and use a parallel small lane running above through tea fields. This dead-ends at the short, muddy access track where drinking Lahijan tea from a makeshift house-café is more interesting than viewing the mausoleum's typical imamzadeh-style interior.

Of several attractive villages in the appealing semi-alpine mountain hinterland, the best known is **Deilaman** (60km).

Sleeping & Eating

Lahijan accommodation is a pleasantly low-key alternative to Rasht's.

Tourist Inn (Mehmunsara Jahangardi; ☎ 333 3051; tw US$36; 🗏) This inn offers delightful rooms and a nice position on the western edge of the lake.

Fajr Hotel (☎ 222 3081; d/ste US$40/60; 🗏) The well-kept former Abshar Hotel is a 1960s block in its own tea garden, 4km east of

town off the Ramsar road. Rooms are big and well equipped.

Chaharfasi Mehmunkhuneh (☎ 222 3222; Shohada Sq; s/tw IR40,000/50,000) Clean, but very basic. Some rooms are windowless.

All three have restaurants, and there are snack bars, kababis and pizzerias along central Abdul Hasan Karimi St that links Shohada and Vahdat Sqs, perpendicular to Kashef St.

GETTING THERE & AWAY

Minibuses from Rasht (IR1400, four per hour, 45 minutes) arrive at Vahdat Sq. To Ramsar (IR3000) and Chalus (IR5000) minibuses leave from a junction 200m north of the Tourist Inn. For Deilaman take a taxi or wait for a savari and change in Siyahkal.

LAHIJAN TO CHALUS

If you stick to the main road there's little of interest, barely a glimpse of sea and none of the towns en route are particularly memorable. The mild highlights come when the mountain foothills, covered with a fuzz of tea bushes, come temptingly close to the coast between Lahijan and **Langarud** and again around Chaboksar. **Ramsar** is another place where mountains and sea conjoin fairly attractively. It's a popular holiday resort town, though the casino has long since closed and there's not much of a beach. Its **Caspian Museum** (Motahhari St; admission IR20,0000; 🕑 8am-3pm winter, 8am-1pm & 4-8pm summer) is intriguing, mainly for being housed in the 1937 summer palace of Reza Shah. Arguably more interesting, and free to snoop around, is the wonderful neocolonial-style former **Ramsar Grand Hotel**, now part of the nearby Azadi Hotel.

Continuing east you might need to change savaris at **Tonekabon**, known to most taxi drivers by the old name Shahsavar. There's a handy Internet café on the central square. At **Abbasabad** there's a turning for the scenic trip to Kelardasht.

For the most spectacular Caspian views pick a rare clear day and head for **Namak Abrud**, 14km west of Chalus. Here a long, steep **cable car** (telecabin; ☎ 0192-246 2012; return ride IR50,000; 🕑 10am-3pm winter, 9am-3pm summer) slices up through the forests. The base-station is 2km off the main Rasht highway by a toll road (IR10,000). Dress up warmly and expect the unexpected from notoriously antisocial clouds.

To get the best out of this region you'll really need to get far out into the mountains. The ideal way to do that is to hike across from Alamut (p166).

Sleeping

There are dozens of fairly up-market apartment-hotels all along the route, catering primarily to rain-addicted Iranian holiday-makers. However, few are marked in English and in summer everywhere is likely to be booked solid for months; the best advice is to ask around for ad hoc rooms. In winter, however, there are some real mid-range bargains to be had, particularly in Ramsar. There are no budget choices until Chalus or thereafter till Amol.

RAMSAR

Safardan Hotel (☎ 522 2916; ste IR240,000; ✂ P) Walking distance from the museum (east then south) in a peaceful, signed alley off Motahhari St, the Safardan has huge double beds, a great kitchen, bathroom and views.

Nazia Suites (☎ 522 4588; ste IR300,000; ✂ P) Similar, next door. In winter, rooms go as low as IR80,000.

Caspian Hotel (☎ 522 2457; Motahhari St; ste from IR120,000; ✂ P) This plush, but slightly musty, hotel varies prices daily, according to demand.

Azadi Hotel (☎ 522 3593; info@ramsarazadihotels .com; s/d/ste US$54/78/104; ✂ P) The 'old wing' is the former Ramsar Grand. Undersized rooms are atmospheric, with Edward VII chairs, bathtub and small double beds, but not quite as grand as you'd think from the gardens and classic lobby. Rooms in the concrete-box 'new wing' are 20% cheaper.

ABBASABAD

Though there's no accommodation in town, three decent hotels lie along the coast road within 5km of the Kelardasht turning. The best option is the **Gol Hotel** (☎ 462 4153; fax 462 4152; Salmashahr; tw IR250,000; ✂ P) with a rear garden, spaciously stylish common lounge, decent restaurant and good modern rooms with bathroom, though road rumbles can be annoying. Twin rooms drop to IR150,000 in winter.

NAMAK ABRUD

Near where the cable-car access road swings south, a quiet lane runs north to the seaside **Caspian Azadi Hotel** (☎ 246 2001; s/d US$77/110) Designed to look like it's falling over, this was the prerevolution Hyatt. Its rooms have been repainted but remain fundamentally 1970s in conception, albeit with the rarity of a bidet. Plexiglas elevators play crackly Kitaro music, there's no beach,

---

THE MIGHTY CASPIAN SEA

At 370,000 sq km the Caspian (Darya-ye Khazar) is five times the size of Lake Superior. That makes it by far the world's largest lake. Or does it? Despite setting up a Caspian Co-operation Organisation (CASCO), its littoral states (Iran, Russia, Turkmenistan, Azerbaijan and Kazakhstan) can't decide if the Caspian's a lake at all. Perhaps it's a 'sea'. What might sound like petty semantics is actually of enormous economic importance. In international legal terms, if it's a 'lake', the sea-bed resources must be shared equally among all littoral states. If it's a 'sea', however, each nation deserves its own territorial slice. And that's ideal for those with valuable oilfields in their sectors. The debate continues.

For all its impressive statistics the Caspian simply isn't very beautiful. Under-sea mud volcanoes and oil vents add to the industrial effluent which flow in through its tributaries, notably the great Volga River. And at 27m below sea level, there's no outlet from which pollution can escape. This is a particular worry for the slow-growing Caspian sturgeon, which produce 90% of the world's caviar but are now facing possible extinction.

Beaches are mostly grey and ugly, and for years have been disappearing as sea levels rose an astonishing 15cm to 20cm per year between 1977 and 1994, stabilising of late. Local holiday-makers don't mind too much. After all, swimming in full chador isn't much fun. When Iranians tell you how wonderful the coast is, they might mean because of all the lovely rain. Rasht incorporates rain drops into the calligraphy of its welcome sign. There are even seaside restaurants named Barun (Rain). For people from the desert plateau, the Caspian coast's regular downpours must seem exotic. Few foreigners have ever shared their enthusiasm, apart from caviar smugglers and the odd Russian agent.

WESTERN IRAN

and the pool and tennis courts look abandoned so, like local tourists, you may prefer to photograph yourself among the hotel's topiary birds then sleep elsewhere.

Getting There & Away

From a handily central airport in eastern Ramsar, **Iran Aseman** (☎ 522 4525; ◷ 7am-4pm Sat-Thu) has four flights weekly to Tehran (IR144,000).

Minibuses run the whole Rasht–Chalus route, but savaris are more frequent if you're happy to make the trip in hops. In Ramsar use Istgah Ramsar (Imam Khomeini Sq) westbound, Basij Sq eastbound. From the latter it's IR2500 to Tonekabon (Shahsavar) where you'll probably change cars at the chaotically busy Imam Sq, whence it's another IR2500 to Abbasabad or IR5000 to Chalus.

CHALUS & NOSHAHR

چالوس
نوشهر

☎ 0191 / pop 82,000

These pleasant twin towns offer a fair range of accommodation at the end of a spectacular road from Karaj (near Tehran). The road crosses a high mountain pass then slithers inexorably down through steep-cut forest valleys, which are narrow and dramatic in places though slated for brutal widening in the near future. Were it not for the hectic traffic the route's scenery would easily justify a visit to Chalus/Noshahr. However, stopping en route can be perilous and, especially in icy conditions, it's hard to focus on the scenery given the suicidal driving style of the speeding maniacs.

Noshahr (Nowshahr) is the more attractive of the two towns with palm trees, manicured gardens and a neat little bazaar around Azadi Sq.

Orientation

The main road from Karaj ends at Mo'allem Sq (Chalus) beside a tall telephone mast. To the west, 17 Shahrivar St crosses a bridge to central Chalus, becoming Imam St after a central roundabout. This continues 2km further to Azadegan Sq, where the main coast road meets the southwestern bypass. That bypass curls back to the Karaj road, which it meets 800m south of Mo'allem Sq. To the east of Mo'allem Sq, Noshahr Blvd leads east passing the Chaloos.net Internet café, the best hotels and then the airport as

it enters Noshahr (5km). Further east it divides into parallel Edalat/15 Khordat (east bound) and Abdul Karimi (westbound) Sts which, a block beyond a large mosque, rejoin at Noshahr's main Azadi Sq.

Sleeping & Eating

Hotel Malek (☎ 222 4107; Noshahr Blvd; d IR243,000; ⛶ Ⓟ) Stylishly modern rooms have pleasing décor, bathroom and good-sized double bed. Discounts for single occupancy (IR120,000) are possible in winter and the cool café section has Internet connection (IR14,000 per hour). It's on the Chalus–Noshahr border. The super-hip **restaurant** (◷ 8am-10pm), misleadingly signed 'Malek-Burger', has the most appealing dining on the Caspian with designer décor. The menu (in English) ranges from steaks, fish meals (IR25,000 to IR60,000) and chicken kiev to local specialities. Beluga caviar on toast costs IR150,000, plus 15%.

Kouvosh Hotel (☎ 222 4103; fax 222 4174; small/large tw US$20/40; ⛶ Ⓟ) Comfortable rooms have a pine-fresh interior; bigger ones away from the road are quieter. There's a garden café, billiards, Internet connection and sauna. It's the creeper-covered building across the road from the Malek.

Shahlizar Hotel (☎ 325 0001; Azadi Sq, Noshahr; tw IR150,000; ⛶) Comfortable and cosy, colourful rooms have checkerboard sheets, crimson curtains and twee, decorative paintings. It lacks the panache of the Malek, but is more conveniently positioned right at the heart of Noshahr.

If all the above are full there are other less-pleasant options along Noshahr's Abdul Karimi St, and on the main Karaj road, 3km south of Chalus.

Mosaferkhuneh Tavakuli (☎ 222 2157; s/tw IR50,000/70,000) A quiet, old place in central Chalus, with uneven floors and no shower. It's a short stroll from Mo'allem Sq in a lane off 17 Shahrivar St. Turn beside Tejarat Bank.

You will find a few snack bars on Abdul Karimi St, a block west of Azadi Sq (Noshahr). More are dotted along Imam St in Chalus, notably Pizza Toranj and the atmospheric, wood-interior **Chinika** (☎ 222 3288; fish dinner IR32,000; ◷ noon-9pm) near the NIOPDC petrol station.

Getting There & Around

With no flights operating, staff at **Iran Aseman** (☎ 322 5217; Edalat St, Noshahr) are merrily underworked. Buses to Tehran leave virtually around-the-clock from two separate terminals on the Karaj road, 900m and 1.5km respectively south of Mo'allem Sq. Savaris to Kelardasht leave from the southwest corner of Mo'allem Sq. Westbound minibuses to Ramsar, Lahijan and Rasht use an inconvenient terminal off the southwestern bypass, 300m southeast of Azadegan Sq. Eastbound savaris and minibuses to Nur and Amol depart a block east of Azadi Sq in Noshahr. Shared taxis shuttle from Mo'allem Sq to both Azadegan and Azadi Sqs till late evening.

AROUND CHALUS
Kelardasht كلاردشت
☎ 0192 / pop 5600 / elevation 1250m
Nicknamed the 'Paradise of Iran', Kelardasht is probably the most popular Caspian-side getaway for forest-loving Tehranis seeking outdoor activities. Cupped in a once-lovely, fertile depression and backed by towering, broad-shouldered peaks, the region offers trout fishing in nearby streams, cross-country skiing in winter, mountain climbing on Mt Alam and hiking trails.

Sadly the area is a victim of its own success. Once an idyllically inaccessible collection of quaint country villages, Kelardasht is now inexorably coalescing into a diffuse resort town centred on relatively built-up **Hasankeif**. The most traditional area is **Rudbarak**, 5km southwest of Hasankeif, where you can still find a few old **log-framed barns**, their slate roofs anchored down with rocks. But even here these are increasingly hidden amid all the new holiday homes. The approach from Abbasabad follows a lovely road winding up through thick, mostly **unspoilt forest** emerging abruptly into Kelardasht's grassy bowl at Makaroud. From here concrete clusters dot the hillside for the last 7km into Hasankeif, but there are several spectacular views of snow-toothed Mt Alam soaring behind. A third strand of development is sprinkled east of Hasankeif. This thins out after the minuscule bus terminal (Zibadasht) and over a pass, but resumes at **Kaleno** where an 11km part-paved road leads up to much-vaunted **Valasht Mountain Lake**. In summer the lake is a starting point for short hikes; in winter taxis struggle to reach it. Throughout Kelardasht's 'villages' are 'suites' (holiday apartments) to rent, but other services are mostly limited to Hasankeif around whose

large central square you'll find a bank, Internet connection, supermarket, a couple of eateries and the Vila Electric Shop, which sells schematic tourist maps of the area.

MOUNTAINEERING
The Alborz offers climbers a selection of 4000m peaks including **Mt Alam** which at 4850m is Iran's third tallest and most technical. An 800m near-vertical granite **wall** makes the mountain's north face a special challenge for climbers, though there are much easier alternative routes to the top. Ascents start 20km northeast from Rudbarak in Kelardasht, where you should sign in at the **Mountaineering Federation** (Federasion-e-Kuh Navardi; ☎ 262 2579; ☼ 24hr). It's on the main street at the far south end of Rudbarak.

Staff here can help arrange mules and guides, have climbing maps and are supposed to demand a US$20 peak fee from foreigners. It takes at least a day to trek to one of two base-camp huts: Hesarchal or Sarchal (3900m). Hesarchal offers the easier summit approach. To view the wall's grandeur head from Sarchal to a cwm called Alamchal (4150m). Climbing the wall is a very serious undertaking and not to be taken lightly.

From Sarchal it's also possible to climb **Mt Takht-e Soleiman**, at the other end of the main knife-edge ridge. NB This *is* the peak that Freya Stark wandered up almost by mistake in her book *Castles of the Assassins*. However, it is *not* the Takht-e Soleiman citadel near Takab.

SLEEPING & EATING
International Hotel (Hotel Beinal Melali; ☎ 262 7000; fax 262 3995; d IR700,000-900,000) Kelardasht's top option so far, the two-storey terraced house-units are fully equipped and very comfortable, though the marble-floored showers are small. Surreally suburban in style, they form a pastel yellow arc around a hobbit-house of a restaurant.

Azarbayjan (☎ 262 2678; Nasiri St; tw IR100,000) Cheap by Kelardasht standards, this slightly run-down green-and-white mansion is in an alley just off Sardar Jangal St in Hasankeif. Rooms have bathroom and fireplace. The communal dining terrace is good for meeting other guests. Some English is spoken.

Motel Jam (☎ 262 2580; fax 252 6031; huts IR450,000) Wooden cabins with double bed, kitchen, shower and squat toilet can sleep four at a pinch. Conditions are much nicer than the outside suggests. If you're coming from the Hasankeif to Rudbarak road (Pasdaran Blvd), fork left beyond Safe Burger. After 200m turn left again down a small lane until you come to a big concrete elephant.

Motel Panis (☎ 262 5330; units US$40-45) Almost next door to the Jam, the Panis has similar units with a choice of toilet styles.

Maral Hotel (☎ 262 6726; Pasdaran Blvd, Hasankeif) This smart, if chintzy, central option was nearing completion at the time of writing.

There are dozens of other options and private rooms to rent, often opening seasonally. Many new alternatives are under construction, notably in Rudbarak.

GETTING THERE & AROUND

Rahat Safar/Talayi Safar buses run to/from Tehran's west terminal at 8am and 2pm in either direction (IR17,000, five hours). The terminal is a small office marked 'Shahin Kelar', 3km east of Hasankeif. Alternatively jump off a Tehran–Chalus bus at Marzanabad, whence it's a 25km taxi hop to Kelardasht. Savaris to Chalus (IR8000, one hour, frequent via Marzanabad) and Abbasabad (IR6000, one hour, rare) depart from Hasankeif Sq, near Milli Bank. An agency taxi from Abbasabad (IR45,000) is reckoned safer than hitching the forest road alone.

Shared taxis between Rudbarak and Hasankeif cost IR1000 but, for most routes and for reaching hiking trailheads, you'll generally have to charter, which is often pricey in Kelardasht.

QAZVIN   قزوين
☎ 0281 / pop 321,000

Famed for carpets, seedless grapes and limp wrists (see the boxed text 'Butt of the Joke', below), ancient Qazvin has a fine bazaar, retains a wide scattering of religio-historic curiosities and makes the ideal base for excursions to the famous Assassins' Castles of Alamut.

History

Founded by the Sassanian king Shapur I in the 3rd century BC, Qazvin prospered under the Seljuk rulers, who erected many fine buildings. It had a second, much later burst of prominence when the Safavid shah Tahmasp I (r 1524–76) transferred the Persian capital here from Tabriz. A great patron of the arts, his ambitious architectural plan for Qazvin proved to be only a dress rehearsal for Esfahan, where his successor, Shah Abbas I, set up court in 1598.

Orientation

The city centre is Azadi Sq, widely known as Sabz Meydan. The bazaar and alleys to its southeast are the most atmospheric areas for random strolling.

Information

The small central telephone office in an alley opposite Bazaar-e Vazim can't handle international calls.

Aria.net (☎ 223 0905; Narderi St; Internet per hr IR7500; ☽ 9.30am-1.30pm & 4-9.30pm) Slow connection.

Bank Sepah (Azadi Sq) Changes major currencies.

Golpoyen Travel (☎ 332 2820; Narderi St) Can book air and rail tickets and arrange guides for the more awkward treks beyond Alamut. Some staff speak English.

ITTO (☎ 334 7407; qazvin@irantourism.org; Resalat St; ☽ 8am-2pm Sat-Thu) A backup, if the booth can't help.

Qazvin.net (☎ 223 6821; Khayyam St; per hr IR8000; ☽ 8.30am-midnight)

Tourist Information Booth (Narderi St; ☽ 8am-2pm Sat-Thu) Facing the historic Rah Kushk Gate, it has decent maps and copious leaflets, partly in English.

BUTT OF THE JOKE

'If you drop your wallet in Qazvin, don't bend down to pick it up!' Political correctness has yet to touch the Iranian sense of humour and poor Qazvin, 'where birds fly on one wing', suffers constantly from jibes of predatory homosexuality. Other regions are equally unfairly stereotyped for jocular effect. Men from Rasht are portrayed as sexually liberal and constant cuckolds, Esfahanis as mean and cunning, Shirazis as lazy and fun-loving, Turkmen as vengeful, Kurds as hot-blooded and the Loris of Lorestan as congenitally untrustworthy. In common jokes, Azaris are supposedly slow-witted yet cash-canny, with Tabrizis surly and religious but those from Orumiyeh contrastingly relaxed and open-minded. Within their loose-fitting *dishdasha* robes, Iranian Arab men are whispered to be endowed with an especially impressive set of wedding tackle.

QAZVIN

0 — 1 km
0 — 0.5 miles

Ⓐ Ⓑ Ⓒ Ⓓ

INFORMATION
Aria.net..1 B4
Bank Sepah.......................................2 B4
Golpoyen Travel............................(see 7)
ITTO...3 B3
Post Office..4 B4
Qazvin.net..5 C4
Telephone Office.............................6 B4
Tourist Information Booth................7 C3

SIGHTS & ACTIVITIES   (pp164–5)
Ali Qapu...8 B5
Amineh Khatun Shrine......................9 C5
Aminiha Hossein..............................10 B5
Amir Kabir House............................11 C5
Arasi House......................................12 B4
Bazaar (Carpet Section)..................13 B4
Chehel Sotun..................................14 B4
Copper-Sculpting Studio..................15 B3
Cushion-Maker................................16 B4
Eltofatiyeh Madraseh......................17 B4
Former Grand Hotel.........................18 B5
Furniture Makers.............................19 B6
Furniture Makers.............................20 B4

Haji Kazem Cistern..........................21 A5
Hamdollah Mustawfi Mausoleum....22 C5
Handicrafts Centre...........................23 B3
Imam Jafar Mosque.........................24 B5
Imamzadeh-ye Hossein....................25 B6
Jameh Mosque.................................26 B5
Kantur Church..................................27 C4
Metal-Beating Workshops................28 B5
Nabi Mosque....................................29 B4
Peyghambarieh.................................30 B4
Rafie Church.....................................31 C4
Rah Kushk Gate................................32 B3
Sadd Sultani Caravansarai................33 B4
Safa Hammam..................................34 B5
Sardar Big Cistern............................35 C6
Sardar Madraseh..............................36 A5
Sardar Smaller Cistern.....................37 A5
Tehran Gate.....................................38 C6
Traditional Shoemaker.....................39 C6

SLEEPING 🛏   (p165)
Alborz Hotel.....................................40 C4
Golestan...41 B4
Hotel Iran...42 B4

Khahsar Hotel..................................43 C4
Marmar Hotel..................................44 D5

EATING 🍴   (p165)
Broasted Chicken.............................45 D5
Dishlemeh..46 B3
Shabestan Teahouse........................47 D5
Yas...48 C4

TRANSPORT   (pp165–6)
Main Bus Station..............................49 D6
Minibus Station................................50 D6
Minibuses to Takestan......................51 A5
Savaris to Rasht...............................52 A4
Shared Taxis to Qaribqosh Square....53 D5
Shared Taxis to Takestan Minibus
  Stand..54 C6
Shared Taxis to the Bazaar...............55 A5
Shared Taxis to Valiasr Square..........56 D6
Shared Taxis via Ali Qapu to
  Takestan Minibus Stand.................58 B4
Transport to Zanjan, Soltaniyeh
  & Hamadan...................................59 A6

Sights

CHEHEL SOTUN

When Qazvin took its turn as Iran's capital, this attractive, colonnaded cube was Shah Tahmasp's royal palace. Built in 1510, it was greatly remodelled in the Qajar era. Set in the town's little central park it looks especially photogenic at night, with its wood-framed coloured glass windows glowing through the foliage and its floodlit delicate balustrades. Inside is a small **museum** (admission IR10,000; ☑ 8am-2pm & 4-6pm, until 8pm summer) accessed by a narrow, easy-to-miss spiral stairway at the side. There's just one room of ancient coins, tassel wear, 500-year-old doors and intriguing 19th-century animal-form padlocks.

MOSQUES & MADRASEHS

Built in 1115, but extensively remodelled in the early 17th century, the **Jameh Mosque** has impressively huge *iwans* and a fine marble mihrab. The very appealing Qajar-era **Nabi Mosque** with its Mogul-style topknots also has an impressively expansive courtyard. The **Eltofatiyeh** and **Sardar Madrasehs** are working Islamic colleges not used to tourists, but are worth a peep if you can get in. The soaring, if unrefined, brick minaret of the new **Imam Jafar Mosque** is a useful landmark, should you get lost in the back alleys.

SHRINES & TOMB TOWERS

The 16th-century **Imamzadeh-ye Hossein** is particularly pretty, with a most well-proportioned blue dome framed by fountains, although building works and a nearby container depot detract from the atmosphere. Behind is a martyrs' graveyard, beneath an aged fighter plane on a stick. Tucked away in the backstreets near the colourfully domed **Amineh Khatun shrine** is the 14th-century **mausoleum** of the Qazvin historian Hamdollah Mustawfi (1281–1350). It has a fine blue conical spire and band of Kufic script, but seems forlornly lost in a handkerchief of grass amid modern homes. The glittery central **Peyghambarieh** (four prophets shrine) has Safavid origins.

GATES

Two dinky little brick gates with colourful tiling and minaret style mini-towers are the last remnants of Qazvin's once vast city walls. The famous, attractively colourful **Tehran Gate**

(Darvazeh-e-Qadim-e-Tehran) is stranded in a traffic circle close to the bus station. **Rah Kushk Gate** (Darbe Kousht; Narderi St) is arguably more interesting, with lion tiles adorning its north face. **Ali Qapu** (Helal-e-Ahmar St) is much more powerfully massive and looks like it belongs to a missing mosque. In fact, it was the original 16th-century gateway to the royal precinct, a kind of forbidden inner city. Today it's used as a police post, so don't snap a photograph.

CISTERNS & BATHHOUSES

Qazvin has some of Iran's best-preserved and most impressive domed cisterns. Here water was stored underground and cooled by windtowers beneath buildings that look at first glance like fine, half-sunken mosques. Though none appeared to have visiting times, several have been restored. Even if one can't get in and descend to the water level, the brick domes and wide stairways of the two **Sardar cisterns** are particularly impressive. The **Haji Kazem Cistern** has an especially fine blue-glazed brick patterned portal and well-preserved windtower.

Safa Hammam (Molavi St; bath IR3000; ☑ 8am-8pm) is the best known of Qazvin's traditional subterranean bathhouses, though it's relatively small and limited to men.

HISTORIC HOUSES

Tucked away in an overgrown walled garden, the **Aminiha Hossein** (Ahemyna Hossein; Molavi St; admission by donation) is a fine, well-preserved 1773 merchant's house. It doesn't look much from outside, but has a splendid if somewhat gaudy wood, glass and mirrored interior. Getting in is hit and miss, and theoretically you'll need a paper from the tourist office, but it's worth ringing the buzzer on the unmarked green door beside Amin Close to see if the caretaker will let you in.

Tourist maps show dozens more historic homes, but few are really worth the dull alley walks required to find them. Best of the bunch are the **Amir Kabir house** and **former Grand Hotel** (both derelict) and the lived-in **Arasi house** with his-and-hers Islamic door knockers.

CHURCHES

The cute, **Kantur Church** (Borj-e-Naghus) is known for its domed 20th-century blue-brick belfry dome and its tiny Russian graveyard. The Armenian **Rafie Church** is a pyramidal-spired brick building hidden in a schoolyard. Neither is usually open.

BAZAAR & CRAFT WORKSHOPS
The covered **bazaar** is not as splendid as that of Tabriz, but amply repays idle wandering. There is a fine **carpet section** and a collection of **metal-beating workshops** in the southeast corner. Hidden behind huge blue wooden doors of Imam Khomeini St are the multiple courtyards of the wonderfully unkempt **Sadd Sultani Caravanserai**. There are **furniture makers** along the Bazaar-e Vazim and more opposite the Imamzadeh-ye Hossein, a **cushion maker** reveals his craft in an alley off Molavi St and there's a **traditional shoemaker** near Shohada Sq. The contrastingly stylish new **handicrafts centre** (Narderi St) is yet to become fully operational, but already has a fine **copper-sculpting studio**.

Sleeping
Hotel Iran (☎ 222 8877; Peyghambarieh St; s/tw IR40,000/60,000) This traveller favourite has a recently refurbished rear block where good, quiet rooms have shower and toilet. It's great value and very central. Savvy owner Karim Noruzi speaks English and offers 4WD excursions to the Assassins' Castles.

Alborz Hotel (☎ /fax 222 6631; Hotel_Alborz_q @yahoo.com; Teleqani Blvd; s/tw US$23/35; 🖳) This ideal mid-range option has small but fully equipped modern rooms, Internet access (IR24,000 per hour) and a calm coffee shop. Book ahead, especially while the **Marmar** (Blvd Ayatollah Khomenei), Qazvin's best hotel, is closed for refurbishing.

Khahsar Hotel (☎ 222 4239; Khaleqi Alley; tw IR50,000) A maudlin last resort, the Khahsar has plain, camp-bed rooms. Unappetising squat toilets are shared.

Cheap mosaferkhunehs like Golestan usually refuse foreigners.

Eating
Between the bazaar and Azadi Sq there are many places to snack, notably confectioners selling melt-in-the-mouth macaroons.

Dishlemeh (☎ 334 9265; Narderi St; meals IR20,000-28,000; 🕙 10am-11pm) Appealing Dishlemeh serves particularly succulent *kubideh* (pressed mince kebab) in an evocative beamed chamber with neo-traditional Persian décor. It's beneath the handicrafts centre, unmarked in English.

Yas (☎ 222 2853; Yasa Alley; meals IR15,000-20,000; 🕙 7am-10pm) It's worth sharing a table with strangers at this popular, crowded spot for its excellent *gheymeh nasar* (meat stew) served on fluffy barberry rice.

Broasted Chicken (☎ 333 0030; Blvd Ayatollah Khomeini; chicken & chips IR15,000; 🕙 10am-10pm) Grease-smelling, but fairly plush with a little goldfish pond inside, this is just one of many restaurants of all types that line Blvd Ayatollah Khamenei between Valiasr Sq and the Marmar Hotel. **Shabestan** almost next door is a subterranean teahouse that's fairly atmospheric, but very much male dominated.

Getting There & Away
BUS, MINIBUS & SAVARI
From the main bus station, northeast of the Tehran Gate, there are frequent buses to Tehran (IR6000 to IR9000, three hours), and a handful to Hamadan (IR12,000, 3½ hours, three daily) at 7am, 10am and 2pm, and Kermanshah (IR18,000, six hours, two daily) at 7.45am and 2.30pm. Buses for Mashhad leave at 2pm, Rasht at 7.45am and 2.45pm and Sari at 7.30am. The minibus station outside has a daily service to Gazor Khan (for Alamut) at 11.30am.

For Rasht there are frequent savaris from Enqelab Sq (Darbaza Rasht) where many through buses also pick up/drop off.

For bus pick-ups or savaris to Zanjan, Soltaniyeh or Hamadan use the busy Dorah-e Hamadan junction. Minibuses to Takestan congregate nearby. For savaris to the villages of Alamut use Qaribqosh Sq 2km east of Valiasr Sq.

TRAIN
To avoid the traffic a train to Tehran (IR5000, two hours) makes sense. Best departure times are 8.30am, 10.30am and 5.30pm. For Zanjan (IR8500, 2½ hours) handy trains leave at 8am and 5.40pm. The best sleeper train for Tabriz leaves around 9.30pm (11 hours), but tickets can be in short supply. Call ☎ 223 0001 to check the schedule.

Getting Around
City buses run both ways along the main drag (Imam Khomeini St/Taleqani Blvd), but cars and shared taxis can only use it eastbound, returning from Valiasr Sq to central Azadi Sq (Sabz Meydan) via Shahrdari or Buali Sina Sts. From the centre to the

bus station change at Valiasr Sq. From the bus station to the centre without chartering requires two shared taxis: west from Darvazeh Tehran Sq to the Takestan bus stand on Asadabadi Blvd (a short walk from Dorah-e Hamadan) then change to a bazaar-bound car, which will loop back east on Imam Khomeini St.

AROUND QAZVIN

Many fascinating, isolated sites like the **Hejib Caravanserai** (off the Saveh road) and the 1067 **Kharaqan Twin Towers** (near Hesar, an unsurfaced 30km drive off the Hamadan road) would make great day trips, but for scenery and historical intrigue it's hard to beat Alamut.

Alamut & the الموت
Castles of the Assassins
دژهای حشیشیون

Beneath awe-inspiring Alborz peaks, the shattered remnants of over 50 fortresses, collectively known as the **Castles of the Assassins** (Dezha-ye Hashish-iyun), nestle among the broad valleys and timeless secluded villages of Alamut. It's another world from Qazvin just 30km to 80km away, a scenically delightful, varied and quite undeveloped land that beckons you to hike, explore and reflect.

HISTORY
From the late 11th century these heavily fortified lairs hid the followers of Hasan-e Sabbah (1070–1124), known to the Crusaders as the 'old man of the mountains'. His heretical offshoot of Ismailism rapidly unravelled into a mercenary organisation whose much-feared followers were dispatched to murder or kidnap leading political and religious figures. They believed that their actions would transport them to paradise. The belief was cunningly cultivated by showing them beautiful secret gardens filled with equally enticing young maidens while stoned on hashish. This preparation for their homicidal assignments led to their popular name the Hashish-iyun, root of the modern English term assassin.

Their impregnable castles including the main stronghold at Gazor Khan were finally captured and demolished by Hulagu Khan in 1256. This defeat was achieved mostly by diplomacy. Only two, Girdkuh and Lamiasar,

thanks in large part to their sophisticated water cisterns, decided to put up a fight.

Among the grateful hostages liberated was the era's foremost scientist Nasruddin Tusi, who thanked Hulagu Khan by building him the medieval world's greatest observatory (p132). This was effectively the end of the Assassins, though their co-religionists continued in Syria, and Hasan-e Sabbah's successor, Buzurg Ummid, later returned to rebuild Lamiasar. It was only with Dame Freya Stark's 1930s travel diary *Valleys of the Assassins,* that the castles were brought back into public consciousness. A copy of that recently reprinted volume makes a great companion for the trip.

SIGHTS
Most of the castle sites require strenuous but delightful guided treks, possibly camping en route for several days – after all, they were designed to be inaccessible. None are more than rubble, but the views, superbly varied countryside and delightful villages of the region, are the real attractions. Roads are improving all the time and it is now relatively easy (snow permitting) to approach fairly near to two of the most famous ruins by vehicle. **Lamiasar** (aka Lambuserd, Lamsar) might have slightly more stones, but Hasan-e Sabbah's fortress at **Gazor Khan** (popularly if imprecisely known as Alamut Castle) is more famous, more beautifully set and has great views from on top.

ACTIVITIES
Tempting trek options are limitless in the Alamut area, but you'll need a tent and a local guide (even they get lost). It's worth hiring mules, too, to carry your bags. A great idea is to strike north through flower-filled meadows, across the Alborz highlands then down towards the Caspian (not uphill in reverse). One such five-day route starts at Hir, 10km northeast of Razmian, passes through the lovely Darja Valley, offers stunning vistas across the forested Caspian littoral, then descends to Jawardeh from where there are savaris to Ramsar (p158).

SLEEPING & EATING
Fortunately near the foot of the castle crag in Gazor Khan is the spotless and charming **Hotel Koosaran** (☎ 554 004; dm IR20,000). This is basically a family home where guests sleep

on cotton mattresses on the floor of shared rooms. The owner speaks a little English, there's a lovely roof terrace and reasonably priced meals are available, if you call ahead. If you're not just heading to Gazor Khan, a tent might prove useful.

GETTING THERE & AWAY
The easy way to get around is to rent a taxi or join a group from the Hotel Iran (p165), which charges around US$30 for a day return in a 4WD, though that should get you to Lamiasar and Gazor Khan. By public transport you'll need to stay a night or two in Alamut which is part of the pleasure.

To Gazor Khan
Occasional savaris from Qaribqosh Sq in Qazvin take the 73km paved road to Mo'allem Kalayeh, also known confusingly as Alamut village (Alamut also being the general term for the area).

Gazor Khan is 21km beyond Mo'allem Kalayeh on an unsurfaced road passable by taxi in dry weather. To reach the access path for Hasan-e Sabbah's Fortress (Alamut Castle) turn right through Gazor Khan village square. A stepped path to the ruins takes roughly half an hour each way.

One daily direct minibus (IR8000, three hours) to Gazor Khan leaves Qazvin at 11.30am in winter, later in summer. This gives you about enough time to stagger up to the castle before dusk. The minibus returns from Gazor Khan next morning at 7am.

To Lamiasar
Some 30km from Qazvin, Razmian village is accessed by a spur of unsurfaced road branching northwest off the Mo'allem Kalayeh road after crossing the Siyahdasht River. You might find savaris from Qaribqosh Sq. Lamiasar Castle is roughly an hour's walk north of Razmian, a 15-minute scramble above the nearest 4WD track. With a guide it's a relatively easy hike between Lamiasar and Evan Lake, half an hour by four-wheel drive from Mo'allem Kalayeh/Alamut village.

SOLTANIYEH   سلطانیه
☎ 0242 / pop 6500
The appealing village of Soltaniyeh ('Town of the Sultans') was a purpose-built Mongol town constructed in the early 14th century. It lasted only a few decades, being largely destroyed by Tamerlane in 1384, but retains three fine monuments. By far the largest and most dramatic of these is the magnificent Oljeitu Mausoleum now a Unesco World Heritage site. This alone is worth the trip from Zanjan or Qazvin.

Sights
OLJEITU MAUSOLEUM (GONBAD-E SOLTANIYEH)
This unique **mausoleum** (admission IR20,000; ⊙ 8am-4pm, until 8pm summer) dominates the entire horizon for miles around with the world's tallest brick dome, 48m high and almost 25m in diameter. Originally it was conceived to rehouse from Najaf (now Iraq) the remains of Imam Ali, son-in-law of the Prophet Mohammed. That would have made it Shiite Islam's holiest pilgrimage site. However, the grandiose plan was abandoned when its sponsor, Mongol sultan Oljeitu Khodabandeh, inconveniently converted to Sunni Islam. The sultan modestly earmarked the vast unused mausoleum for himself and was buried here in 1317.

One approaches across low, partly rebuilt stubs of fortress wall. Inside the mausoleum the renovators' scaffolding still obscures photography, but can't hide the enormity of the enclosed space. A ground-floor exhibition of photos, historical pictures and plans shows views before and after restoration. Spiral stairs within the hugely thick walls lead up to an inner mid-level and an outer upper terrace with panoramic views.

In the precinct behind the mausoleum there's an atmospheric but easy-to-miss subterranean teahouse.

OTHER SIGHTS
From the upper terrace of the Oljeitu Mausoleum it's easy to spot the lonely blue-domed **Mullah Hasan Kashi tomb** in semidesert, a dusty 20-minute walk south towards the mountain skyline. The more interesting **Khanegah Dervish Monastery** is right beside the Katalekhor Rd, 10 minutes' walk west of the mausoleum. Newly renovated it should soon open as a museum.

Until recently Soltaniyeh itself was an extremely picturesque patchwork of low-rise mud-walled homes. Very visible gentrification is now under way with many old houses bulldozed for a needlessly wide new access boulevard. Nonetheless, for now it's still possible to see shepherds herding their flocks at sunset right past the great mausoleum.

Getting There & Away

Soltaniyeh is 5km south of the main Zanjan–Qazvin road, but *not* accessible from the new motorway that swings further north. Buses using the former can drop you at the junction whence taxis whisk you into the village. From Zanjan (Honarestan Sq) it's easier to use the frequent direct savaris (IR3000, 30 minutes) or irregular minibuses (IR1000, 50 minutes). These drop you at a roundabout an obvious 10-minute walk north of the mausoleum.

ZANJAN زنجان

☎ 0241 / pop 304,000

Hidden in tiny alleys behind its modern facade, Zanjan retains some attractive mosques, a fantastic bazaar, a plethora of knife-grinders, two delightful teahouses and a brilliantly renovated caravanserai restaurant. The city is a logical base for visiting the impressive Soltaniyeh mausoleum and, now that the road via Dandy is paved, makes a good staging point to reach Takht-e Soleiman.

Zanjan city's moment of infamy came in 1851 with a bloody siege ordered by Persian prime minister Amir Kabir. The resulting massacre was part of the relatively successful campaign to crush the nascent Baha'i religion. Baha'i-ism had only broken away from Islam three years before, but was spreading much too rapidly for Tehran's liking.

Orientation & Information

The main commercial centre is Enqelab Sq. **Bank Melli** (Sabz Sq) and **Bank Tejarat** (Imam St) can change money. Charming Parvis Golbazi, an employee in the latter, speaks English and is keen to help foreigners. **Aftabomahtab.Net** (Zand Alley; per hr IR6000; ⏱ 8am-midnight) has excellent Internet connection. There's a **telephone office** (⏱ 7am-10.30pm) on Sabz Sq. All-Farsi city maps (IR8000) are sold from a **bookshop** (Sa'di St) near Enqelab Sq.

Sights

Built in 1926 but looking considerably older, the curious **Rakhatshor-Khaneh** (Rakhatshor-Khaneh Ln; admission IR20,000; ⏱ 8.30am-5pm Tue-Sun) is a dome-and-column subterranean hall whose water channels were provided as a public laundry. Now almost unique, if somewhat overrestored, it's dotted with wax washerwomen to remind you how life was before Electrolux and Zanussi. Enter through an unmarked door, dodge the grouchy policeman and cross a courtyard of amphorae guarded by a stone ram.

The long, narrow, mostly brick-vaulted **bazaar** is inspiring and surrounding alleys hide half-a-dozen historic mosques. At the ungentrified eastern end is the inspiringly decrepit yet still-active **Dokhtar Caravanserai** and modest but appealing **Motahhari Mosque**. Grandly tiled, the dome and minarets of the **Rasul-Ullah (Sai-ini) Mosque** peep above Enqelab Sq. Madraseh cells line the inner courtyard of the sizable 1826 **Jameh Mosque**, accessed through a spired portal on Imam St. **Imamzadeh Mosque** is similarly extensive. The dinky **Khanum (Women's) Mosque** has a commonly photographed pair of squat pepper-pot minarets. The 1851 Baha'i massacres were perpetrated in lanes behind where you now see philosopher **Soravardi's bust** (Sa'di St) on a library wall. Of three Safavid bridges the easiest to see is **Pol-e-Sardar**, in marshland to the west of the Bijar road.

Sleeping

Amir Kabir (☎ 322 4922; Imam St; tw IR38,000) Amir Kabir is unusually clean for a mosaferkhuneh and very handy for the bazaar. Rooms have heaters and big fans. Clean toilets are shared. Please remove your shoes upstairs or they might revert to refusing foreigners. It's above a decent restaurant.

Sa'di (☎ 322 2528; Imam St; tw IR25,000-38,000) Similar to the Amir Kabir, if not quite as fresh.

Park Hotel (☎ 332 2228; fax 332 6798; Imam St; s/tw IR192,000/288,000; 🖳) A friendly, modern place at Azadi Sq whose rooms, though already somewhat worn, have Western toilets.

Sepid Hotel (☎ 322 6882; Imam St; s/tw US$30/45; 🖳) Overpriced but with bathroom and very central right at Enqelab Sq.

Hafez (☎ 322 2740; Enqelab Sq; s/tw IR50,000/ 80,000) Depressingly gloomy rooms have a basic squat toilet and shower cubicle.

Eating

Karavansara Sangi (☎ 326 1266; Beheshti St; meals IR18,000-25,000; ⏱ 11am-4pm & 6-11pm) It would be madness not to dine at this splendid, reasonably priced 400-year-old vaulted caravanserai. It is entered via a small private

ZANJAN

INFORMATION
Aftabomahtab.Net........................1 F1
Bank Melli...................................2 E2
Bank Tejarat...............................3 F2
Bookshop....................................4 F2
Telephone Office..........................5 F2

SIGHTS & ACTIVITIES (p168)
Dokhtar Caravanserai.....................6 F2
Imamzadeh Mosque.......................7 F2
Jameh Mosque.............................8 E2
Khanum (Women's) Mosque............9 E2
Motahhari Mosque.......................10 F2
Pole-e-Sardar..............................11 B4
Rakhatshor-Khaneh.....................12 F1

Rasul-Ullah (Sai-ini) Mosque..........13 F2
Soravardi Bust............................14 F2
Station Gateway..........................15 F3

SLEEPING (p168)
Amir Kabir.................................16 E2
Hafez.......................................17 E3
Park Hotel.................................18 D3
Sa'di..19 F2
Sepid Hotel................................20 F2

EATING (pp168–70)
Haji Dadashi...............................21 E2
Karavansara Sangi........................22 F3
Sofrakhane Sonate Abache............23 F2

SHOPPING (p168)
Knife Shop.................................24 E3

TRANSPORT (p170)
Bus Pick-up Area for Tehran...........25 F3
Bus Station................................26 E4
Buses to Tehran, Qazvin & Tabriz....27 E3
Eastbound Shared Taxis.................28 F2
Minibuses & Savaris to Soltaniyeh...29 F4
Minibuses to Dandy, Bijar & Takab...30 E3
Savaris to Bijar & Sanandaj............31 E3
Westbound Shared Taxis................32 E2

Some Minor Roads
Not Depicted

See Enlargement

To Maneh (130km);
Tabriz (291km)

22 Bahman (Bypass)

Asia
Hotel

Esteqlal
Square

15 Khordad
Square

Azadi
Square

To Dandy (100km);
Bijar (136km)

To Soltaniyeh (44km);
Qazvin (170km)

Honarestan
Square

Shilat
Square

Train Station

Beheshti St (Khayyam St)

Khoramshahr Blvd

Imam St

Ferdosi St

Engelab
Square

Enelab St

Sa'di St

Khagani St

Zeinabieh St

Shohada St

17 Shahinat St

0   1 km
0   0.5 miles

0   500 m
0   0.3 miles

car park behind metal-railed gates. Sit at tables or on carpeted platforms, order great *bademjun* (eggplant paste with tahini and lemon) and, some evenings, enjoy live traditional music.

Haji Dadashi (☎ 322 2020; bazaar; meals IR12,000-20,000; ☾ 11am-11pm) This subterranean, family-orientated tea-cavern also oozes great character, especially in its carpet-draped front cellar. Enter through an unmarked heavy wooden door in the main bazaar. *Dizi sangi* comes with a plate of fresh herbs to fine-tune the flavour.

Sofrakhaneh Sonate Abache (Bostani Bashkah; ☎ 323 7250; Bashkah Alley; ☾ 10am-8pm) Decorated with old samovars, portraits and peacock feathers this single octagonal domed cellar is ideal for tea and qalyans, though it's rather male dominated. Look for the black door with brass knobs and knockers.

Getting There & Away

The huge but eerily empty bus station is a five-minute walk south of Shilat Sq with services to Esfahan (IR24,000, 6.30pm), Rasht (IR18,500, 8.30am) and Tehran (fairly frequent). However, many buses on the Tehran–Qazvin–Tabriz route use Beheshti St and pick up/drop off more conveniently near the train station. One block beyond the train station are savaris to Bijar (IR6500) and Sanandaj, with rare minibuses for Bijar, Takab and Dandy in between.

To Soltaniyeh, minibuses (IR1000, 50 minutes) and frequent savaris (IR3000, 30 minutes) leave from Honarestan Sq.

The train station is beyond a Dali-esque gate of winged-wheels. Best-timed departures for Tehran (IR13,120, four hours) are at 6.20am and 8.22am. Tickets for the midnight sleeper to Tabriz (IR16,200, 8½ hours) via Maraqeh (five hours) sell fast.

Getting Around

Eastbound shared taxis (IR600) run to Honarestan Sq from Enqelab Sq, passing near the bus station. Westbound they start at Sabz Sq and terminate at Esteqlal Sq, 300m short of the Asia Hotel.

TAKHT-E SOLEIMAN تخت سلیمان

In a high, lonely bowl of mountains ringed by 1500-year-old fortress walls, **Takht-e Soleiman** (Throne of Solomon; admission IR30,000; ☾ 8am-sunset) is a Unesco World Heritage site and one of the most memorable sights of western Iran. Known as Azergoshnasb, this was the spiritual centre of Zoroastrianism in the 3rd century AD. The site was perfect for the state religion of Sassanian Persia which had by this stage incorporated many Magi-inspired elements, including the veneration of earth, wind (plenty here), water and fire. The fire was provided thanks to a natural volcanic gas vent. The gas, channelled through ceramic pipes, would have sustained an 'eternal flame' in the **fire temple** or *ateshkadeh*, whose walls are partly preserved. Water (albeit undrinkably poisonous) was provided in abundance by the mysterious, limpidly beautiful **crater lake**, which forms the centre of the site. This still pours forth 90L per second and would have been channelled through an Anahita-style water temple (p180).

The site has no historical link to Old Testament King Solomon. The name was a cunning 7th-century invention by the temple's Persian guardians in the face of the Arab invasion. Realising Islam's reverence for biblical prophets they entirely fabricated a tale of Solomon's one-time residence to avert the site's certain destruction. The ruse worked, the complex survived and the name stuck.

In the 13th century, Takht-e Soleiman was used by the Mongol Ilkhanid khans as a summer retreat before falling into decay. The remnants of their hunting palace, once the site of a Sassanian original, is now covered with a discordant modern roof. It forms a museum displaying amphora, unlabelled column fragments, photos and a couple of ceramic sections of ancient gas pipe.

Don't expect impressive buildings or Persepolis-style carving. There are chunky wall segments and the odd arch, but it's the magnificent setting that's the real attraction. A guide is often available or navigate using an IR1500 map/brochure, which is sold – but not on display – at the ticket booth.

Takht-e Soleiman is 2km from the delightful mud-and-haystack village of **Nostrabad**, probable site of the as-yet unexcavated historical city of Shiz. Here the minuscule Sadaghat Kababi feeds a few hungry tourists in season, but the nearest accommodation is 42km away in Takab.

Getting There & Away

An ideal way to visit is by chartering a taxi for a day from Zanjan: take the gorgeous mountain route via Dandy (two hours), continue beyond Takab and get dropped off in Bijar (around IR200,000, full day with stops) or Miyando'ab (for better accommodation). Take your time en route as you'll pass through some of western Iran's more picturesque villages.

By public transport there's only one minibus (around 9am) from Zanjan to the mining town of Dandy. From Dandy's **taxi stand** (☎ 0242 352 2566) you'll still have to charter a ride for the last, but most scenic, 50km to Takht-e Soleiman. See around Takht-e Soleiman (below) for some of the sights en route.

It's much easier and still attractive to approach from Takab. Occasional shared taxis (IR3500) and very rare minibuses (IR1500) run to Nostrabad, with rather more frequent services to Ahmadabad-Ohlea, a somewhat bigger village 5km further from the ruins. However, if you're not prepared for long walks and longer waits in the middle of nowhere, seriously consider taking a taxi (IR30,000 return, plus IR12,000 per hour waiting time) and visit a few villages on the way.

AROUND TAKHT-E SOLEIMAN

For utterly stunning views scramble up **Zendan-e Soleiman** (Solomon's Prison), the very obvious conical peak which dominates the valley landscape, 1.5km west of Nostrabad. Once it too had a fortified, magical crater lake, like Takht-e Soleiman's, till one side of the cone collapsed. Be careful on the crater edge.

The entire area is aching to be explored on foot or by donkey. Even if you stick to the (very quiet) road there are some fabulously timeless villages. Among the loveliest is **Qaravolkhana**, 10km beyond Takht-e Soleiman towards Dandy, located just after a lurid, metallic-green igloo-shaped Sirchalebi Shrine. The bucolic meadowland behind offers great hikes and the possible ascent of **Mt Belqeis**, topped by fragmentary ruins of a Sassanid line-of-sight fortress. In summer this is also accessible by 4WD on a track from near the Angoran mine. **Shikhlar**, 30km towards Dandy, is another picturesque village, backed by the pyramidal peak of **Tozludagh** (Dusty Mountain).

TAKAB   تکاب
☎ 0482 / pop 85,000

Not unpleasant, this hilly market town is the closest access point for Takht-e Soleiman and has the nearest accommodation, albeit limited and overpriced. The traffic lights at the crossroads of Imam and Enqelab Sts mark the commercial centre. Signed 'Pensiun', 150m to the southeast, is the ultrabasic, showerless **Mehmunpazir Takht-e-Jamshid** (☎ 522 2119; Imam St; tw IR60,000). A kilometre uphill from the crossroads, the only other choice is **Rangi Hotel** (☎ 522 3179; Upper Enqelab St; s/tw/tr/quad with breakfast US$25/32/40/45). It's acceptable with shower and squat toilet. The friendly English-speaking management can arrange 4WD trips to minor local curiosities, such as the 3000-year-old **Qom Choqa** fortress ruins or the **Karaftu Caves** (25km southwest) which have some Greek inscriptions.

Getting There & Away

For Miyando'ab (which has connections to Maraqeh or Orumiyeh) head first to Shahin Dezh. Both savaris (IR10,000) and minibuses (IR3300, hourly) depart from 9am to 3pm at the **Taavoni 10 garage** (☎ 552 2218; Imam St); look for blue gates just beyond the Jameh Mosque.

Near Galem Sq, 600m further west along Imam St, is the pick-up point for very rare savaris to Takht-e Soleiman (IR3500).

Taavoni 16 (☎ 522 2136) has buses to Tehran via Soltaniyeh and Qazvin (IR19,900) at 6am and 10am. It also has a 6am service to Zanjan (IR10,600) and roughly hourly minibuses to Bijar (IR3900, one hour) from 7am to 1pm. The office is near the bazaar, across a stream, 200m east of the Mehmunpazir Takht-e-Jamshid. Savaris to Bijar (IR8000) leave from outside, the last one around 6pm.

BIJAR   بیجار
☎ 0872 / pop 51,000

Few travellers bother lingering in this diffuse junction town, but for budget travellers visiting Takht-e Soleiman, Bijar's two central, if slightly grubby, mosaferkhunehs are much cheaper than the Takab equivalent. The town centre is Taleqani Sq, a mini-roundabout where Tohid St (the old Zanjan–Sanandaj main road) crosses Taleqani St in front of the **Mosaferkhuneh Golshan** (☎ 424 3172; Tohid St; s/tw IR20,000/23,000).

The **Mosaferkhuneh Moqadam** (☎ 422 3260; Shahid Ardalon St; s/tw 20,000/30,000) is an Escheresqe maze of stairways. It's between Milli Bank and the small brick-vaulted bazaar on a quiet tree-lined street off Tohid St, two blocks east of Taleqani Sq. Both charge IR5000 extra for a shower. Apart from the mosaferkhunehs the only restaurant is the unappealing **Kordestan** (☎ 424 4798; Tohid St) 2km towards Zanjan. However, 1200m up Taleqani St the kitschy but atmospheric teahouse **Sofrakhaneh Sahel** (☎ 424 6632; dizi IR12,000; ⏱ 7am-9pm) is a great place for a qalyan and cinnamon tea. In a valley 18km further northwest towards Takab, look right to catch a glimpse of a fine, rebuilt **Safavid bridge**.

Getting There & Away
Just 30m up Taleqani St from Taleqani Sq, a tiny terminal yard has hourly minibuses to Takab (IR3700). Sign a passenger list in the office before taking one of the regular savaris to Sanandaj or Zanjan from outside.

SANANDAJ   سنندج
☎ 0871 / pop 320,000 / elevation 1520m
Even by Iran's super-hospitable standards, Sanandaj is a remarkably friendly city. It's the capital of Kordestan province and a great place to learn more about Kurdish history and culture. You'll see plenty of men wearing traditional cummerbunds and baggy Kurdish *shalvar* (trousers). Yet it's a modern, noticeably prosperous city with a large, fashionable population of students ever anxious to try out their English. From Sanandaj you can venture further into the Kurdish heartland, though beyond Marivan getting into the astonishing Howraman valley can be something of an adventure.

History
Originally known as Senna, the city was of major importance in the Middle Ages but withered to nothing in the chaotic post-Chaldoran era. A *dej* (fortress) was built here in the early 18th century and Senna-dej slowly developed into Sanandaj. It became the seat of the powerful Ardalan emirs who, from 1169 to 1867, ruled the last autonomous principality of Iranian Kurdistan. Under the Ardalans the town developed many fine 19th-century buildings, though most have since been lost to rapacious 20th-century development.

Orientation & Information
Busily commercial Ferdosi St links the twin centres Enqelab and Azadi Sqs. From the latter, Abidar St slopes up into the caress of a rocky ridge that was the city's historic defence and is today the pleasant **Abidar mountain park**. Detailed, but dangerously outdated, Gita Shenasi city maps are sold from a small **bookstall** (Imam St). To change money use **Bank Melli** (Taleqani St), but not the big branch on Azadi Sq. Internet is available in the plush shopping malls of Pasdaran St, but the best connection is at **Wireless Kafenet** (☎ 323 8727; Seyid Qotb St; per hr IR7000; ⏱ 9.30am-midnight). The website www.sanandaj.com has a wide range of city photos to send as e-postcards. Travel agency **Kia Parvaz** (☎ 222 7770) is in a side alley off Imam St.

Sights
The **fortress site** (Imam St) is firmly closed for military use, the **covered bazaar** is cruelly bisected by Enqelab St and new Kordestan Blvd cuts ruthlessly through formerly interesting areas of late Qajar brick homes. Nonetheless, several fine historic mansions have been spared. The well-renovated Lutfulla Sheikh-al-Islam Mansion is now the **Regional Museum** (Habibi Ln; admission IR20,000; ⏱ 8.30am-12.30pm & 2.30-5pm Tue-Sun). Even if you don't appreciate the rich regional collection of extraordinarily old pottery and metalwork treasures, the acoustically engineered fountain-cellar is fun, with its bare-breasted nymphs turned modestly away from the viewer to avoid offending religious mores. The multicoloured *orosi* were built for hygiene as well as beauty: supposedly they disorientate mosquitoes.

Perhaps the most attractive mansion is the brilliantly restored **Asif Divan** (Imam St; admission IR20,000; ⏱ 8.30am-12.30pm & 2.30-5pm Tue-Sun), now a relatively interesting museum of Kurdish life. Some of the distinctive tribal costumes displayed are still worn in nearby villages. A guide pamphlet sold at the reception shows many more historic (but often derelict or inaccessible) buildings around Sanandaj including the collapsing trefoil-topped **Moshir Divan**, hidden through a walled garden off Shohada St: ring the speaker phone and hope. Once approached by a grand avenue, the fine **Khorosabad Mansion**, around 2km west of the centre between Abidar Ave and Blvd Shebli, has an impressive central courtyard

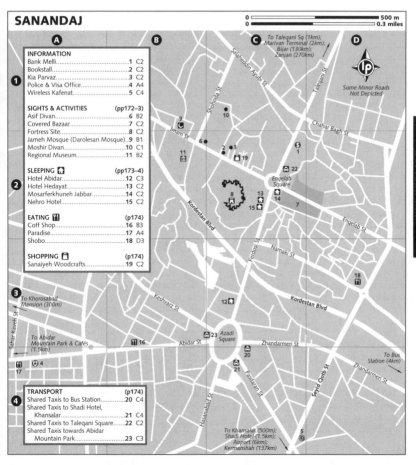

SANANDAJ

WESTERN IRAN

and was once the palace of Ardalan emir Amonulla Khan. Ideas to renovate it as a hotel don't seem to be progressing. In 1813 Amonulla Khan also sponsored the fine **Jameh Mosque** (Darolesan Mosque; Imam St), with tiled twin minarets and 32 interior domes. He was so pleased with the result that he had the architect blinded to prevent its repetition for any other patron.

Sleeping

Shadi Hotel (☎ 662 5112; Pasdaran St extension; tw/tr IR194,000/240,000; P) This is the best accommodation for hundreds of miles around. For a mid-range price you get full four-star facilities down to the shoeshine kit and (alcohol-free) minibar. Owner Amjet speaks

fluent English, there's Internet access and a decent but inexpensive restaurant serving great Turkish coffee. The main drawback is its out-of-town position beyond Mellat Park, but shared taxis from Azadi Sq pass outside.

Nehro Hotel (☎ 225 5170; Ferdosi St; tw IR58,000) Great-value clean new rooms above a shopping centre, have shower and squat.

Mosarferkhuneh Jabbar (☎ 323 6584; Enqelab Sq; tw IR35,000) Acceptable if basic rooms have a tap and TV. There's a communal shower. Look for a yellow sign in Farsi.

Hotel Hedayat (☎ 226 7117; Ferdosi St; s/tw IR40,000/ 50,000) Similar to the Jabbar, except that you'll pay IR6000 to use the shared shower.

Hotel Abidar (☎ 324 1645; Ferdosi St; s/tw IR78,000/ 156,000) Rooms with bathroom are quiet, but the furniture is disturbingly soiled. It's much worse than the Nehro for three times the price, yet this is where most taxis want to bring you.

Eating
Typical kababis and fruit-juice squeezers are scattered along Ferdosi St but for more atmosphere you'll need to venture away from the centre.

Khansalar (☎ 662 351; Pasdaran St; meals from IR20,000; ☺ 11.30am-3pm & 5.30-10pm) Great kebabs and oodles of old Persian style. Get off a shared taxi from Azadi Sq, opposite the university when you see Moravid, an amusingly blatant McDonald's lookalike.

Shobo (☎ 324 1179; Shahid Namaki St; ☺ noon-10pm) This stylish yet reasonably priced new place serves Kurdish favourites such as the regional favourite *dokhwa* (try it if they haven't sold out) and a preposterously rich *ash* (yogurt and barley soup; IR9000), which would feed the 5000. Stir very well to make it palatable. The ground floor has trendy Western décor while downstairs there's a neotraditional basement.

Paradise (☎ 0913 971 1040; Abidar Ave; pizzas IR15,000-18,000; ☺ 10am-2pm & 4-11pm) This is the most appealing of several trendy pizzerias and cafés dotted for 1km up Abidar Ave from Azadi Sq.

Coff Shop (Abidar Ave) A fairly stylish, ill-spelt coffee shop.

In Abidar mountain park there are a few more basic cafés with city views.

Shopping
Sanaiyeh Woodcrafts (☎ 226 5170; Imam St) sells regional crafts, musical instruments including *tars* (local lutes) and inlaid *nard* sets (a form of backgammon), which are made in a small workshop seven doors up the road.

Getting There & Away
Travel agency Kia Parvaz (p172) sells tickets for the weekly Sanandaj–Tehran flight on Iran Aseman (IR162,000, Wednesday).

To Bijar, Saqqez and Marivan, savaris (and rare minibuses) leave from the far northern edge of town, but inbound often drop passengers at Taleqani Sq, 1km further south. For other destinations you'll need the main bus station, 4km east of the centre. Fortunately several bus companies have handy ticket offices around Enqelab Sq, such

as Taavoni 4 for Orumiyeh (IR24,000, nine hours) at 7.30pm and Tabriz (IR25,000, nine hours) at 9pm and useful Taavoni 7 for Ahvaz via Andimeshk (IR28,100, 13 hours) at 5.30pm, Borujerd (IR12,500) at 2pm, Rasht via Qazvin (IR25,600) at 4.30pm and Esfahan via Saveh (IR29,000) at 5.30pm. For Kermanshah and Hamadan (via Qorveh), savaris are more convenient.

Getting Around
Often insufficient for the demand, fast-filling shared taxis from Enqelab Sq run east (for the bus station) and north (for Taleqani Sq). From Azadi they run in all six directions, notably down Pasdaran St to the Shadi Hotel and up Abidar St to the edge of Abidar mountain park (15 minutes' walk from the cafés).

MARIVAN   مريوان
☎ 0875 / pop 70,000
The main tourist draw of this bustling Kurdish market town is **Zarivar Lake**, 3km to the west. Backed by low, rolling mountains and fronted by marshlands it is idyllically peaceful, except on summer weekends when invaded by pleasure boats. Even if you're staying at one of Marivan's cheap central mosaferkhunehs it's worth the IR10,000 in taxi fares to visit the **ITTIC Tourist Inn** (Mehmun-sara Jahangardi; ☎ 322 1626; bungalows with bathroom IR230,000), especially if you dine at its brilliantly positioned terrace restaurant that looks directly over meditationally still waters.

The route from Sanandaj passes through the mid-sized stepped village of **Negel**, incongruously dominated by a modernist mosque and **Quran museum**. However, for more impressive Kurdish scenery continue south into Howraman.

Getting There & Away
Savaris for Sanandaj (IR15,000, 1¾ hours) use a terminal 2km east of the centre. Shared 4WDs into Howraman are sometimes available from Jomhuri St, but there's a better chance from Biya Kaya, a roadside junction market 20km towards Sanandaj.

HOWRAMAN   هورامان
Caught at the intersection of powerful empires, the Kurds have had their homes destroyed so regularly in recent history that, by the 18th century, a sizable part of society had foregone villages altogether

and resorted to nomadism and brigandry. An important exception, thanks to its impenetrable mountain-hemmed position, was the Howraman (Oruman) valley. This remains one of Iran's least known and most spectacular areas. In colder months you'll still see Howraman men wearing *kolobal*, brown-felt jackets with distinctive shoulder 'horns'. There is plenty of age-old stone terracing and the villages are stacked Masuleh-style, one house's roof forming the next one's yard. The Howrami Kurdish language is quite distinct from the Kurmanji Kurdish, which replaced it in Sanandaj, though Howrami was once the dialect of choice for all regional Kurdish poets. *Ju-an* means beautiful, *wazhbu* means thank you.

The road from **Biya Kaya** near Marivan takes you through a dramatic narrow canyon, over a high pass and into the valley at very picturesque **Kamala** where the asphalt ends abruptly. That's a slushy 5km short of austere **Howraman-at-Takht** (Oruman-Takht), the valley's biggest and most famous stepped village, if not its most beautiful. Below the track at the very far end of Howraman-at-Takht is the diminutive **Pir Shaliar shrine**, where a Mithraic midwinter festival is still held on the Friday nearest to 4 February. Some suggest that this is a cultural relic from pre-Zoroastrian 'angel' worship, albeit with an Islamic overlay.

The slippery mud road onwards to Paveh (72km, 4½ hours) is 90% hairpins: marvellously scenic but spine-jarringly exhausting, and impossible if wet or snowy (ie most of the winter). The best views are around **Habasawa** with grandeur reminiscent of the Karakoram Highway. Asphalt returns at Ura, 21km from Paveh.

Sleeping

There's no formal accommodation en route, but if you are invited to stay you might find hospitality so overwhelming that a polite quick 'escape' is hard to arrange.

Getting There & Away

Kamala would make a delightful, relatively easy taxi day trip from Marivan (or even Sanandaj). Morning shared 4WDs run between Biya Kaya and Howraman-at-Takht (IR10,000, 1¾ hours, 50km), but you can't be sure of finding a ride back again the same day. If you want to reach Paveh within a day

the best bet is to engage a 4WD at Biya Kaya. Prices vary enormously (IR50,000 to IR500,000) according to vehicle, driver and what other co-passengers you can find for intermediate points. The author paid IR120,000 plus various tips.

PAVEH & AROUND   پاوه
☎ 0832 / pop 17,000

If you can't get into Howraman, the bigger, more developed town of Paveh is an attractive, accessible introduction to the sort of thing you're missing. It has a fine setting, high up a fold of mountainside valley. Views of Paveh's most characteristic stepped area are best from the Ferris wheel in Kazemi Park. Also look south (away from Paveh) from here: the pronounced rocky knob on the mountain top across a deep valley was once Sassanian Persia's second-greatest Zoroastrian temple complex (after Takht-e Soleiman). A track leads most of the way and makes a great two-day hike if you have a tent.

The **Ghuri Gahleh Cave** (Goori Gala Qar; admission IR4000; ⏰ 9.30am-5pm) claims to be Asia's longest, but the marketing photos show formations well beyond the tourist-ravaged first 500m that is all you'll get to see. If you're keen, it's beside the main road between Paveh and Ravansar. Inside, the narrow path is paved but slippery, wet and often crowded.

Sleeping & Eating

Until a planned hotel is built, Paveh's only accommodation is in little dormitories at the **Ostad Khanim Mo'allem** (School Hostel; Molui St; dm IR20,000). It's supposedly for women only, but the caretaker (who speaks no English) usually accepts foreign men if they're suitably polite. Totally unmarked, it's down a flight of steps on the main street. Nearby, across the road is the town's only eatery, the minuscule **Ostad Hossein Amini** (Molui St) where kebab-with-bread (IR7000) is the only choice.

Getting There & Away

From the terminal 3km east of central Paveh, Kermanshah minibuses (IR5000) and savaris (IR12,000, 1¾ hours) fill slowly so it's often quicker to go via Javanrud (IR6000, 45 minutes) or, more directly but less conveniently, via Ravansar (IR6000, one hour) where you'll need to change terminals.

From either, minibuses leave every few minutes to Kermanshah.

KERMANSHAH   كرمانشاه
☎ 0431 / pop 800,000

By far the largest and busiest city in central west Iran, Kermanshah developed in the 4th century AD astride the Royal Road to Baghdad. Its strategic position has caused both prosperity and attack. Most recently it suffered missile damage during the Iran-Iraq War. Briefly renamed Bakhtaran in the 1980s, the city is a melting pot of Kurds, Lori and other Iranians. Its backdrop of glowing red-rock mountains is impressive and, if you're passing through, don't miss Taq-e Bostan.

Orientation
Kermanshah is bewilderingly vast. The main street changes names (Kashani–Modarres–Beheshti–Sheikh Shoodi) as it stretches over 10km from the busy commercial centre (the southern third) to the foot of the magnificent rocky Parom Mountain massif. Here the Taq-e Bostan carvings, ringed by parks and outdoor restaurants, form the city's foremost attraction. Cheap accommodation is found south of the mammoth Azadi Sq which has a mini Dome-of-the-Rock in its midst. Another key junction is 15 Khordat Sq (Meydan Panzdah Khordad), commonly known as Labab or simply 'Meydan'.

Information
Bank Melli (Modarres St) The big branch on Azadi Sq won't change money, but this main office opposite the mosque will.
Emperator (Modarres St; Internet per hr IR6000; ☼ 9am-9pm) Two floors up for Internet service. Handy for Azadi Sq.
Farah Andish (Kashani St; Internet per hr IR5000; ☼ 9am-7pm) Internet access can be found here, opposite the Bisotun Hotel.
ITTO (☎ 822 3801; fax 822 3800; Beheshti St; ☼ 7.45am-3pm Sat-Thu) Very helpful and offers free postcards and basic tourist maps.
Malekseyr Travel Agency (☎ 729 2112; Kashani St; ☼ 8am-8pm)
Tagh Bostan Travel (☎ 824 6222; Vila St; ☼ 8am-6pm Sat-Thu, 10am-1pm Fri)

Sights
TAQ-E BOSTAN
Kermanshah's star attraction is **Taq-e Bostan** (admission IR25,000; ☼ 8am-sunset), where the

city ends in a cliff inscribed with a series of extraordinarily well-preserved **Sassanian bas-reliefs**. These are in and around a pair of **carved alcoves**. The finest tableau shows Shah Ardeshir II (r AD 379–383) trampling a defeated enemy and receiving a crown of blessing from Zoroastrian God Ahura Mazda. Meanwhile Mithras sneaks up behind pretending to be Luke Skywalker with a light sabre.

Surrounding open-air restaurants remain popular late into the evening. Even though the reliefs-complex is closed, sympathetic lighting means a golden glow emanates warmly from the alcoves, attractively half visible through trees across a little pond.

HOSSEINIEHS
Distinctively Shiite, Hosseiniehs are shrines commemorating the martyrdom of Imam Hossein at Karbala (AD 680). These places come to life during the commemorative period of Moharram, famous for the self-flagellation of mourners. The 1913 **Takieh Mo'aven ol-Molk** (Hadad Abil St; admission IR30,000; ☼ 8am-noon & 4-8pm summer, 2.30-5.30pm winter) is a particularly impressive late-Qajar Hosseinieh that accepts tourist visits. Although marked 'Ethnographical Museum', the shrine is very much active, with pilgrims kissing the doors and looking genuinely moved by the blue ceramic 'footprint of Ali' in the rear courtyard. It's a copy of a Mashhad original, set amid tiles depicting a wacky gamut of images. These include Quranic scenes, pre-Islamic Gods, Shahnameh kings, European villages and local notables in 19th-century costumes. One panel depicts dervishes with all their paraphernalia. The central covered chamber shows the great battle at Karbala.

The **Takieh Biglar Begi** is a lesser-known Hosseinieh down a tiny alley marked 'Dentiste Okhovat'. At present it's not open to drop-in visitors, but the tourist office might be able to get you in.

OTHER SIGHTS
The fine **Jameh Mosque** (Modarres St) has a beautiful, Yazd-styled twin minaret. The extensive, much restored **covered bazaar** sloping up from Modarres St is well worth exploring with a couple of dilapidated old caravanserai courtyards at the western end. **Ehmad Dohla Mosque** (Jewellery Bazaar), entered through an attractive tiled portal, has a peaceful courtyard with

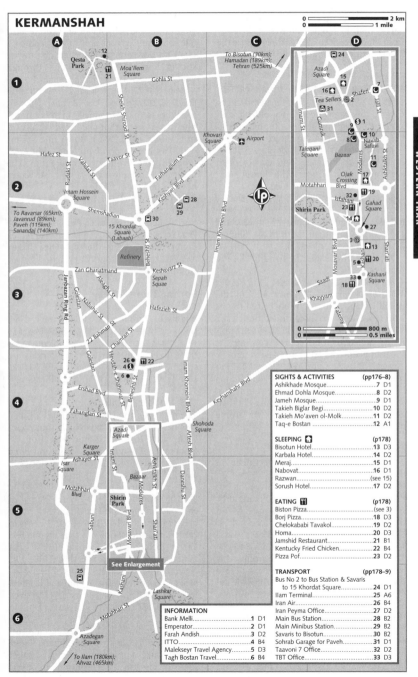

KERMANSHAH

0   2 km
0   1 mile

Qesta Park

12

Moa'llem Square

21

Gohla St

Sheikh Shroodi St

Hafez St

Taavor St

Rudaki St

Vahdat St

Khovari Square

Fahandum St

Airport

To Bisotun (30km);
Hamadan (189km);
Tehran (525km)

24

Azadi Square

15

16

Tea Sellers 2

31

7

Shafen St

Gurniak

9

8

1

10

Navab Safavi St

Ashkalih St

Imam St

Taleqani Square

Bazaar

Modares

11

17

Ojak Crossing Blvd

Isfahani St

32

19

Motahhari

Shirin Park

23

14

Gahad Square

27

Mosavar Blvd

Sahbani

3

13

5

20

Saadi

33

18

Khayyam

Fatemy

Kashani Square

0   800 m
0   0.5 miles

Imam Hossein Square

To Ravarsar (65km);
Javanrud (89km);
Paveh (115km);
Sanandaj (140km)

Shemshadian

Kchyari Blvd

28

29

30

15 Khordat Square (Labaab)

Refinery

Behesti St

Imam Khomeini Blvd

Zan Ghariatmand

Keshavarz St
Sepah Squae

Janbazan Ring Rd

Golestan

Alesgha St

Nabahar St

Hafezieh St

22 Bahman

Chaman St

Colestan

26

4

6

22

Ershad Blvd

Heydar-e Shahrivar St

Beheshti St

Imam Khomeini Blvd

Keyhanshahr Blvd

Fahanglan St

Azadi Square

Ashkalih St

Modares St

Daneshu St

Shohoda Square

Artesh Blvd

Karger Square

Isar Square

Ashayer St

Imam St

Bazaar

Modares

Mosavar Blvd

Shariati St

Motahhari Blvd

Shirin Park

Sabun

See Enlargement

25

Kashani

Lashkar Square

Azadegan Square

Motahhari St

To Ilam (180km);
Ahvaz (465km)

SIGHTS & ACTIVITIES (pp176–8)
Ashikhade Mosque	**7** D1
Ehmad Dohla Mosque	**8** D2
Jameh Mosque	**9** D1
Takieh Biglar Begi	**10** D2
Takieh Mo'aven ol-Molk	**11** D2
Taq-e Bostan	**12** A1

SLEEPING (p178)
Bisotun Hotel	**13** D3
Karbala Hotel	**14** D2
Meraj	**15** D1
Nabovat	**16** D1
Razwan	(see 15)
Sorush Hotel	**17** D2

EATING (p178)
Biston Pizza	(see 3)
Borj Pizza	**18** D3
Chelokababi Tavakol	**19** D2
Homa	**20** D3
Jamshid Restaurant	**21** B1
Kentucky Fried Chicken	**22** B4
Pizza Pof	**23** D2

TRANSPORT (pp178–9)
Bus No 2 to Bus Station & Savaris to 15 Khordat Square	**24** D1
Ilam Terminal	**25** A6
Iran Air	**26** B4
Iran Peyma Office	**27** D2
Main Bus Station	**28** B2
Main Minibus Station	**29** B2
Savaris to Bisotun	**30** B2
Sohrab Garage for Paveh	**31** D1
Taavoni 7 Office	**32** D2
TBT Office	**33** D3

INFORMATION
Bank Melli	**1** D1
Emperator	**2** D1
Farah Andish	**3** D2
ITTO	**4** B4
Malekseyr Travel Agency	**5** D3
Tagh Bostan Travel	**6** B4

WESTERN IRAN

Qajar-era clock tower. An area of derelict, part-demolished older houses leads down from Modarres St to the **Ashikhade Mosque** (Jalili St), now curiously stranded in a roundabout.

Sleeping

Bisotun Hotel (☎ 722 3792; fax 723 7037; Kashani St; s/d IR240,000/360,000; 🐱) Kermanshah's nicest option, this renovated, classy old building is set in a delightful garden. Rooms have all the trimmings including choice of toilet.

Karbala Hotel (☎ 727 5999; Parking Shaderi; s/d US$15/23; 🐱) This characterless concrete box offers acceptable, no-frills rooms with shower, squat and fridge. Towels are provided.

Sorush Hotel (☎ 722 7001; Motahhari Blvd; s/d IR200,000/240,000; 🐱) Rooms with Western toilets and bathtubs have no towels and are poorer value than the Karbala. Slightly dilapidated and very 1970s.

A gaggle of cheapies lie handily close to Azadi Sq.

Nabovat (☎ 823 1018; Modarres St; s/d/tw IR35,000/55,000/60,000) Marked 'A home an Inn' the friendly Nabovat has sensibly priced rooms with tap. Sheets are discoloured, but clean.

Razwan (☎ 823 1627; s/tw IR30,000/40,000) Similar to the Nabovat but less welcoming, the Razwan is entered from a car-park track.

Meraj (☎ 823 3288; s/tw US$10/15) Next door to the Razwan, this grown-up mosaferkhuneh has small shower booths in the rooms, but shared squat toilets. The foyer has stuffed animals, ceiling mouldings and an aroma of silver polish.

Eating

There are snack stalls and confectioners in the northwest corner of Azadi Sq and on Motahhari Blvd around Ojak Crossing, but the greatest concentration of restaurants, cafés and open-air teahouses are around the Taq-e Bostan carvings.

Jamshid Restaurant (☎ 424 4185; Shah Shoodi St; meals IR20,000-35,000; 🕙 noon-3pm & 8-9.30pm) Though blatantly aimed at tour groups, this large mock fortress remains the classic Taq-e Bostan choice. A stream runs through the dining room surveyed by a gigantic bronze eagle and huge samovar. Waiters wear Laurel-&-Hardyesque Bakhtiyari hats.

Chelokababi Tavakol (☎ 722 7184; Modarres St; meals IR11,000; 🕙 11.30am-3pm & 5.30-9pm) This would be the backpacker meeting place, if there were any backpackers. Once a grand

old bathhouse it's now a cheap, slightly gone-to-seed kababi that offers *ghorme sabzi* (stewed beans, greens and mince) and eggplant for vegetarians. The charming owner speaks English. Go downstairs through white doors with coloured glass panels.

Homa (☎ 723 4246; Kashani/Dabir Azam Sts; meals IR23,000-32,000; 🕙 noon-11pm) A chandelier-lit fountain is the centrepiece of this atmospheric new restaurant decorated with irises in Chinese vases. Wash down fine kebabs with tea from porcelain pots, or acidic *dugh* (yogurt drink) from earthenware jugs. The manager and amusingly camp head waiter have an inkling of English.

Borj Pizza (☎ 728 9741; Shahid Ashrafi St; pizza IR20,000; 🕙 9am-2pm & 5-10pm) Fairly stylish, Borj is better than **Biston Pizza** (Kashani St) or **Pizza Pof** (Mohammad Isfahani St) which also serves döner kebabs. A fake **Kentucky Fried Chicken** (Beheshti St) opposite Iran Air even has its own Colonel Sanders lookalike.

Getting There & Away

AIR

Flights to Tehran (IR161,000) leave three times daily on **Iran Air** (☎ 824 8610; Beheshti St; 🕙 7.30am-2.30pm Sat-Thu, 7.30am-1pm Fri), plus four times weekly on Iran Aseman. Tickets are sold by Tagh Bostan Travel (p176), Malekseyr Travel Agency (p176) and others.

BUS, MINIBUS & SAVARI

The main bus and minibus stations are side by side. Get there on bus No 2 from Azadi Sq or walk 10 minutes northeast from 15 Khordat Sq. For advance tickets Iran Peyma and Taavoni 7 have offices on Modarres St and TBT has one off Kashani St.

Frequent buses to Tehran (IR20,000 to IR42,000, nine hours) pass close to Hamadan en route, though for Hamadan itself you'll need to take a minibus (three hours), or savari (via Kangavar). Several companies serve Tabriz (including Gity Safar; IR30,600, eight hours) at 6am and 8pm. For Ahvaz (IR21,500, 10 hours) TBT, Taavoni 7 and others have buses at 8am and between 7pm and 8.30pm. Iran Peyma has a 5pm bus to Orumiyeh (IR26,500, 12 hours) and TBT serves Esfahan (IR23,100, 10 hours) at 7.30pm.

To Khorramabad, Taavoni 7 has a direct bus at 8am (IR22,400, five hours). Alternatively take a minibus to Harsin, 30km south of Bisotun. Then continue by savari to Nurabad on an acceptable unpaved road with lovely scenery, followed by another minibus to Khorramabad.

If you're heading for Iraq use the quite separate Ilam Terminal (Rah-e-Karbala Terminal, Sabuni St) in the southwest corner of Kermanshah. For the Khosravi border take Qasr-e-Shirin minibuses (IR6300, three hours) or savaris (IR25,000, two hours) which are frequent till 5.30pm. For Mehran use Ilam savaris (IR20,000, 2½ hours).

For Paveh there's a special taxi garage **Sohrab** (☎ 823 3462; Gumruk St) close to Azadi Sq. For Bisotun savaris start from 15 Khordat Sq.

TRAIN

There's no railway, but Tagh Bostan Travel (p176) can procure advance train tickets for travel from any major Iranian station.

Getting Around

Bisotun-bound shared taxis from 15 Khordat Sq pass the airport gates, or take a private taxi (IR10,000 to IR15,000). City buses usefully drive the 'wrong way' (northbound) up Modarres St while shared taxis have to wind around the one-way system. Bus No 2 handily links Azadi Sq with the bus station, though shared taxis are more frequent – at least as far as 15 Khordat Sq, where you might need to change for Taq-e Bostan.

AROUND KERMANSHAH
Bisotun   بیسوتون
☎ 0832
Awesome dry cliffs line the north flank of the busy, partly industrialised Kerman-

shah–Hamadan road. These climax 2km west of Bisotun town in a series of historic **bas-relief carvings** opposite a decorative pond. Some steps and rusty scaffolding lead up to the nearest viewpoint of the key grouping in an inaccessible but obvious cleft. Here a well-preserved 480 BC Darius receives supplicants while a *farohar* (winged Zoroastrian 'angel') hovers overhead. Though hard to make out from ground level, the scene is surrounded by cuneiform inscriptions expounding upon Darius' greatness in three 'lost' languages (Elamite, Akkadian and Old Persian). Bemusing the locals, eccentric British army officer Henry Rawlinson spent much of 1835 dangling over the abyss to make papier-mâché casts of the text. It's hard to know how his superiors gave him the time off to attempt so life-threatening an eccentricity, nor why Rawlinson didn't just tootle up to Ganjnameh (p185) and copy those inscriptions instead. Nonetheless, his transcriptions later allowed the deciphering of the cuneiform scripts, a thrilling breakthrough for ancient historians that renders Bisotun as significant as the Rosetta Stone to Egyptologists. At the time of research the site was open without any gates or admission fee, but this is unlikely to last.

To reach the carvings jump out of a savari from Kermanshah at Bisotun's first roundabout then walk seven minutes west through a car park following the mighty cliffs. You'll pass a loose-headed, club-wielding **Hercules statue** from AD 148 sitting on a rocky ledge and a very eroded **Parthian relief of Mithrades II**, partly overwritten by a 17th-century inscription of Sheikh Alikhan in Arabic script.

CROSSING THE IRAN–IRAQ BORDER

Local pilgrims head in unending streams to Karbala and Najaf, the great Shiite shrine cities where Imam Hossein and Imam Ali respectively are entombed. Thus from almost any town in the region there's likely to be a direct pilgrim bus to Iraq. If you're a Muslim you might be allowed to come along.

Although there are three main crossing points, the most popular route is via **Mehran**. To get there independently head first to Ilam then swap savaris. Amid the melee, Westerners don't seem to be given any special hassles on the Iran side. However, once in Iraq the fact that you've come from Iran at all can lead to suspicion and hours or days of random detention and interrogation. The idea of backpacking this way has yet to be fully understood and it's certainly not something to undertake lightly. The **Khosravi** border (bus to the oasis town of Qasr-e-Shirin then savari) has recently been allowing travellers across but suspicions seem even worse there. The **Piranshahr** border southwest of Orumiyeh is open to locals but foreigners without specific authorisation from Iraq's autonomous Kurdish authority might have difficulties. Everything is in flux and the best tool for checking the latest situation is the Thorn Tree at www.lonelyplanet.com.

WESTERN IRAN

Some 200m beyond the main site, past a small café, is the huge, smooth **Farhad Tarash** rock face, cleared in the 7th century BC but never inscribed. Today this is popular with climbers who consider it among Iran's greatest challenges. If you forgot your clips and ropes, contact the **Kermanshah Climbers' Club** (☎ 824 7711), which can also show you the vertical shafts of **Paroh Qar**, 12km away, said to be the world's deepest.

Walk back through Bisotun town to see a 115m Safavid-period **bridge**, which was partly built from cannibalising Sassanian stone structures.

GETTING THERE & AWAY
Savaris (IR2500, 25 minutes) are frequent from Kermanshah's 15 Khordat Sq. For Kangavar (and thence Hamadan) flag down passing buses or cross Bisotun town (3km) and take a savari first to Sahneh.

Kangavar كنگاور
☎ 0837 / pop 58,000
The pleasant town of Kangavar isn't worth a special detour, but as it conveniently straddles the Kermanshah–Hamadan road it's easy to get a quick glimpse of the famous **Anahita Temple Ruins** (admission IR20,000; ◷ 8.30am-6pm) as you pass through. The once-fabulous complex was already a ruinous wreck when Robert Byron saw it in 1933, and wasn't helped by a 1957 earthquake.

Though the site is expansive, the only visually impressive section is a 5m-tall section of dressed stone wall topped with stubby columns. This is very easily viewed for free as you walk up Raja'i St from Araqi St (the main Hamadan road). Raja'i St culminates in the quietly attractive bazaar area where there's a basic mosaferkhuneh.

The savari terminal for Hamadan (direct or via Asadabad) is 2km east of the ruins. For Kermanshah, flag down a passing bus or use the Nahavand terminal at the western end of town and make savari hops via Sahneh and Bisotun.

HAMADAN همادان
☎ 081 / pop 420,000 / elevation 1830m
Looking at bustling Hamadan's architectural ordinariness, it's hard to believe that this was classical Ecbatana, once one of the ancient world's greatest cities. Pitifully little of antiquity remains, though large parts of the city centre are given over to excavations and there are a few historical curiosities. Sitting on a high plain, Hamadan is graciously cool in August, but snowy and freezing cold from December to March. The air is often hazy, but on a rare, clear spring day there are impressive glimpses of snowcapped Mt Alvand (3580m) preening itself above the ragged neocolonial cupolas of Imam Khomeini Sq. A popular summer retreat, Hamadan's main draw card for Iranian visitors is its proximity to the vastly overrated Ali Sadr Caves (p185).

History
Valuable finds from the ancient city continue to come to light, but the lower layers of settlement remain mostly unexplored and much is beneath the presently inhabited modern centre. Thus Hamadan's ancient history (pre 1000 BC) has yet to be fully pieced together.

According to ancient Greek historians, Ecbatana was fortified as the opulent capital of the Median empire around 650 BC. Its massive walls were said to have had seven layers, the inner two coated in gold and silver, the outer one as long as that of classical Athens. Yet within a century it had fallen to the Achaemenid Persians, and King Cyrus was using it for his summer court. Known as Hagmataneh (Meeting Place) in Old Persian, it controlled the Royal Road to Babylon and was then, as now, a major trade crossroads.

A 521 BC return of the Medes was reversed within six months by Darius who was so pleased with himself that he recorded his achievements in stone beside the Royal Road at Bisotun (p179) and at Ganjnameh (p185).

After centuries of wealth and pre-eminence under Parthian and Sassanian dynasties alike, Ecbatana/Hamadan faded somewhat after the Arab conquest in the mid-7th century AD, but it became the regional capital under the Seljuks for some 60 years in the late 12th century. Despite the usual devastations by Mongols (1220) and Tamerlane (1386), Hamadan only hit a major decline in the 18th century following a Turkish invasion. It began to recover in the mid-19th century and was totally redesigned to a modern city plan in 1929 by German engineer Karl Frisch.

HAMADAN

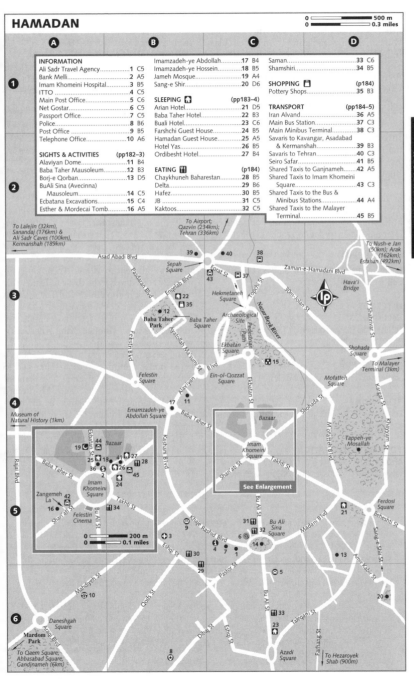

0 — 500 m
0 — 0.3 miles

INFORMATION
Ali Sadr Travel Agency.................**1** C5
Bank Melli.................................**2** A5
Imam Khomeini Hospital..........**3** B5
ITTO..**4** C5
Main Post Office.......................**5** C6
Net Gostar................................**6** C5
Passport Office..........................**7** C5
Police......................................**8** B6
Post Office................................**9** B5
Telephone Office.....................**10** A6

SIGHTS & ACTIVITIES   (pp182–3)
Alaviyan Dome.........................**11** B4
Baba Taher Mausoleum...........**12** B3
Borj-e Qorban.........................**13** D5
BuAli Sina (Avecinna)
     Mausoleum.........................**14** C5
Ecbatana Excavations..............**15** C4
Esther & Mordecai Tomb.........**16** A5

Imamzadeh-ye Abdollah...........**17** B4
Imamzadeh-ye Hossein............**18** B5
Jameh Mosque.........................**19** A4
Sang-e Shir.............................**20** D6

SLEEPING   (pp183–4)
Arian Hotel..............................**21** D5
Baba Taher Hotel.....................**22** B3
Buali Hotel..............................**23** C6
Farshchi Guest House...............**24** B5
Hamadan Guest House.............**25** A5
Hotel Yas................................**26** B5
Ordibesht Hotel.......................**27** B4

EATING   (p184)
Chaykhuneh Baharestan...........**28** B5
Delta......................................**29** B6
Hafez.....................................**30** B5
JB...**31** C5
Kaktoos...................................**32** C5

Saman.....................................**33** C6
Shamshiri................................**34** B5

SHOPPING   (p184)
Pottery Shops..........................**35** B3

TRANSPORT   (pp184–5)
Iran Alvand.............................**36** A5
Main Bus Station......................**37** C3
Main Minibus Terminal.............**38** C3
Savaris to Kavangar, Asadabad
     & Kermanshah.....................**39** B3
Savaris to Tehran.....................**40** C3
Seiro Safar..............................**41** B5
Shared Taxis to Ganjnameh.......**42** A5
Shared Taxis to Imam Khomeini
     Square.................................**43** C3
Shared Taxis to the Bus &
     Minibus Stations...................**44** A4
Shared Taxis to the Malayer
     Terminal.............................**45** B5

WESTERN IRAN

WESTERN IRAN

Orientation

Frisch's masterplan is a cartwheel design with six avenues radiating from the circular hub of Imam Khomeini Sq, which mostly retains its early-1930s architecture and corner domes, albeit in great need of repair. The wheel distorts to the northeast around the lumpy hill of Tappeh-ye Mosallah and the ongoing excavation site of old Ecbatana.

Information

BOOKSHOPS

A small but interesting selection of multilingual books are sold at the Buali Hotel. Detailed, if outdated maps, are available at the reception of the Baba Taher Hotel. The best place for postcards is the giftshop at the BuAli Sina Mausoleum, but you'll be charged the entry fee to reach it.

EMERGENCY

Imam Khomeini Hospital (☎ 825 2438; Eshqi St)
Police (☎ 827 4986; Dibaj St)

INTERNET ACCESS

Net Gostar (☎ 252 9929; BuAli Sq; ☺ 8am-8pm Sat-Thu, 10.30am-1pm Fri) Good connection, English spoken.

POST

Main Post Office This is on a lane off BuAli St. There's another small office on Khaje Rashid Blvd.

TELEPHONE

Telephone Office (Mahdiyeh St) Take a shared taxi down Shari'ati St.

TOURIST INFORMATION

Ali Sadr Travel Agency (☎ 824 9611; alisadr-mehr@yahoo.com; 40 Khaje Rashid Blvd; ☺ 9am-12.30pm & 4.30-7.30pm, until 10pm summer) Although a commercial agency, the staff are super-friendly and happy to answer general questions. Some speak great English.
ITTO (☎ 827 4773; fax 826 6026; Khaje Rashid Blvd; ☺ 8.30am-2.30pm Sat-Thu) Third floor above a shop beside the passport office. Staff are helpful and some speak English. Passable free maps and colourful brochures are available.

VISA EXTENSIONS

Passport Office (Gozannameh; ☎ 826 2025; Khaje Rashid Blvd; ☺ 8.30am-2.30pm Sat-Thu) A forbidding blue-walled building with armed sentries. Applications for visa extensions are very rarely granted.

Sights

ESTHER & MORDECAI TOMB

Behind a 400kg granite door, this vaguely Tolkeinesque **tomb tower** (Aramgah-e Ester va Mordekhay; ☎ 252 2285; 12 Zangeneh Ln; admission IR20,000 plus donation, preferably a pen; ☺ 8am-noon & 3-6pm Sun-Fri) contains two graves much more ancient than its 13th-century dome. These are traditionally considered to be those of Esther (for whom a book in the Bible's Old Testament is named) and her cousin/guardian Mordecai (who possibly wrote it). Jewish orphan Esther married Xerxes I (Biblical King Ahasuerus) who'd ditched his first wife, Vashti, for being too much of an early feminist. Esther's better-honed feminine wiles are later said to have saved the Jews from a massacre planned by Xerxes' commander (and Mordecai's enemy) Haman. With names eerily reminiscent of Babylonian Gods, Esther (Ishtar?) and Mordecai (Morduk?) are probably largely allegorical. The tomb is more likely to be that of Jewish queen, Shushan-Dokht, who persuaded her husband, Yazdgerd I (r AD 399–420) to sanction a renewed Jewish

---

BUALI SINA

Better known to the west as Avicenna, the great philosopher and physician BuAli Sina ('bu' means 'son of') was born near Bukhara (now Uzbekistan) in AD 980. Having practised medicine virtually from childhood, he left Bukhara at the age of 22 and spent several years as a traveller, before settling in Hamadan and becoming vizier to the ruling emir whose ailments he had successfully treated. Unfortunately, when his patron died, Avicenna was caught out conspiring with a rival to the new emir and was thrown into prison. Eventually he managed to escape and fled to Esfahan where he spent the next 14 years working for the shah.

By the end of his life BuAli Sina had produced 250 books, including a widely respected medical encyclopaedia *(Canon Medicinae)* which was published in Europe and continued to be used in universities until the 17th century. His works showed the influence of both Greek and Islamic philosophers, and included several volumes of poetry. He eventually returned to Hamadan where he died and was buried in 1037.

colony at Hamadan. Either way, for centuries the tomb was Iran's most important Jewish pilgrimage site. Now largely forgotten, some of the Hebrew inscriptions inside have been repainted so often by those who evidently couldn't understand them, that they have become stylised beyond readability.

OTHER MAUSOLEA & TOMB TOWERS

Although dating from only 1954, the concrete tower of the **BuAli Sina (Avicenna) Mausoleum** (Aramgah-e Buali Sina; ☎ 826 1008; admission IR30,000; 8am-6pm summer, 8am-4pm winter) has become Hamadan city's icon. A rare triumph of modernist design, it is loosely modelled on the 1000-year-old Gonbad-e Kavus tower near Gorgan, itself built in BuAli's lifetime. The best view is from the west, but there's little reason to pay the entry fee unless you really want to see the single-room **museum** of Avicenna memorabilia, his tombstone and a small library. Inside there's also a little bookshop and herbal remedy stall.

Architecturally less successful is the heavily buttressed **Baba Taher Mausoleum** (Aramgah-e Baba Taher; admission IR15,000), which looks like a failed prototype for Thunderbird 3.

The **Alaviyan Dome** (Gonbad-e Alaviyan; Shahdad Ln) is now a misnomer as the 12th-century green dome, immortalised in a Khaqani reference, has long since been removed. The dome-less brick tomb tower remains famous for the whirling floral stucco added in the Ilkhanid era. This ornamentation enraptured Robert Byron in *Road to Oxiana*, but is frankly ugly. In the crypt, reached by a spiral staircase, are the Alaviyan family tombs. The tower is in the playground of a school, accessed through the first metal door on the right as you walk from Alaviyan Blvd. You might be charged an admission fee of IR25,000 should anyone notice you wandering in.

Currently being expanded, the unremarkable, mirror-domed **Imamzadeh-ye Abdollah** (Imamzadeh Sq) is a useful landmark but the 1883 **Imamzadeh-ye Hossein** is more appealing, tucked behind the Hotel Yas in a little courtyard with an ancient mulberry tree. The 13th-century **Borj-e Qorban**, a classic 12-sided, pointy-roofed tower tomb, looks out of place in its dowdy housing-estate setting.

ECBATANA EXCAVATIONS

The ancient Median and Achaemenid **city site** (☎ 822 4005; admission IR30,000; 9am-1pm

& 3-5pm, until 8pm summer) is slowly being excavated on an extensive plot of land, just north of the town centre. Small items found here and elsewhere in Hamadan are on display at the **museum** in the centre of the site, but most are in the National Museum of Iran in Tehran. As excavations progress so the site is becoming more interesting, but there are no signs to explain what you're looking at and it's easy enough to get an idea of the 9m thick ramparts from the free footpaths outside.

OTHER ATTRACTIONS

Entered through a vaulted passage in the bazaar, the large Qajar-era **Jameh Mosque** (admission free) has some 55 columns and six minarets, four of which are blue-tiled. Feverish excavations in its central courtyard are in the process of revealing what might have been a very ancient mill.

The 2300-year-old **Sang-e Shir** is the only surviving monument from the ancient city of Ecbatana whose gates it once guarded. Possibly carved at the behest of Alexander the Great, it was supposedly a stone lion but is now eroded beyond any possible recognition.

Primarily designed for students, the quirky **Museum of Natural History** (Mozeh-e Tarikh Tabi-i; ☎ 252 1054; Keshervazi Agricultural College; admission IR8000; 8am-5pm) has an extensive collection of stuffed animals, pinned insects, dinosaur models, geological samples, bottled foetuses and (live) fish in tanks. This is the closest you are likely to get to the huge, horned Alborz red sheep. The museum is unmarked, a 5km taxi ride from the city centre. Where Azadegan Blvd narrows abruptly into a quaint country lane, go through the green gates on the left then look for the building with a faded mural and new fauna-tiled doorway.

Sleeping

BUDGET

There are several cheap mosaferkhunehs conveniently close to central Imam Khomeini Sq.

Hamadan Guest House (☎ 252 7577; Ekbatan St; r IR60,000; P) Upstairs in a two-storey building with no English sign, this large, institutionally basic place is the most accustomed to foreigners. Rooms are four- or six-bed dorms for which locals pay IR10,000 to

IR15,000 per person. Foreigners must rent the whole room, even when alone. There's a communal hot shower, but it's a fairly long walk to the shared toilets whose doors don't lock. The fairly atmospheric café-teahouse offers cheap meals.

Farshchi Guest House (Mosaferkhuneh-ye Farsi; ☎ 252 4895; Shohada St; tw IR40,000) Cosier and with cleaner toilets than the Hamadan Guest House, the Farshchi is upstairs opposite the Hotel Yas.

Ordibesht Hotel (☎ 252 2056; Shohada St; s/tw/tr IR70,000/85,000/95,000) Tidy, clean and relatively new, this mosaferkhuneh has no-frills shared facilities.

Hotel Yas (☎ 252 3464; Shohada St; tw US$20) Simple if clean rooms have old but functioning shower and Western toilet. The building is marked in English. Reception is on the 3rd floor.

MID-RANGE

Arian Hotel (☎ 826 1266; Takhti St; s/tw US$25/30) This is an ideal, modern mid-range choice. Small but impeccably clean rooms with bathroom are fully equipped in the style of a European Ibis Hotel.

Buali Hotel (☎ 825 0856; buali-hotel@hotmail.com; BuAli St; tw US$73) Rooms with fridge and TV (showing BBC) are comfortable, though no more than one would expect for the price.

Baba Taher Hotel (☎ 422 6517; fax 422 5098; Baba Taher Sq; s/tw US$45/85) Welcome to a dazzlingly garish festival of Las Vegas kitsch. Thankfully the well-appointed rooms are more subdued than the mirror-tiled lobby. It's pleasant enough if the Arian is full.

Eating

Hezaroyek Shab (1001 Nights; ☎ 822 7569; local mains IR19,000-35,000, European dishes IR40,000) Owner Pari Bakhtiyari speaks fluent English and with a day's notice she can supplement the already wide menu with virtually anything you might dream of including Persian classics like *fesenjun*. It's 2km south of the centre on the southern continuation of Fahrang St. Book ahead.

Chaykhuneh Baharestan (☎ 254 2777; Shohada St; dizi IR7000; ☺ 6am-7pm) This atmospheric, if decidedly down-market, teahouse is adorned with metalwork, sepia photos and Quranic murals. It's ideal for a greasy fried egg breakfast, cheap lunch or a puff on the qalyan, and is populated by photogeni-cally haggard old white-beards. To find it, head upstairs through a partly illustrated doorway opposite a small branch of Bank Maksan.

Kaktoos (Buali Sq; meals IR20,000-30,000; ☺ noon-3pm & 7-10pm) Down easy-to-miss stairs, Kaktoos is the most atmospheric of several middle-class kebab restaurants, with more character than **Hafez** (☎ 826 0962; Eshqi St; meals IR25,000) or similar **Delta** (Eshqi St).

Shamshiri (Imam Khomeini Sq; meals IR14,000-18,000) Conveniently central this is a bright but unremarkably standard kababi.

Saman (☎ 825 3352; BuAli St; pizzas IR11,500-18,000; ☺ 11.30am-2.30pm & 5-10.30pm) The most appealing of almost a dozen fast-food places along BuAli St, Saman is a spacious basement around a diving-bell shaped central fireplace with real beer mugs for your IR3000 Delster. The owners speak Danish and English.

JB (BuAli St; burgers IR8000-10,000) Looks like a McDonald's conceived by Mondrian.

Buali Hotel restaurant (☎ 825 0856; BuAli St; mains IR30,000-46,000) The menu in English includes steaks, schnitzels and decent-sized Gulf shrimps in a 'sauce' that's more like a mild salsa. From June to August it's possible to eat in the garden. In winter the rather upmarket dining-room is pleasant, if spookily quiet.

Shopping

Hamadan region is famous for its carpets, leatherwork, wooden inlay and ceramics. The ITTO tourist office has a booklet listing workshops and can put you in touch with the **Union of Carpet Co-operatives** (☎ 252 8622) if you can't find what you want in the rather tatty bazaar. There are several **pottery shops** (Baba Taher Sq) selling locally famous ceramics made in nearby Lalejin. Much of it is tawdry.

Getting There & Away

AIR

The only scheduled flight is on Caspian Airlines to Dubai (Mondays). Tickets cost IR1,200,000 one way, and are sold by Ali Sadr Travel Agency (p182).

BUS, MINIBUS & SAVARI

Bus services from the main bus station, which is 300m north of Hekmetaneh Sq, include:

Destination	Price (IR)	Duration (hr)	Departures
Ahvaz	26,500	9	6-7pm
Bijar	9900	3	Taavoni 9, 8.30am
Esfahan	17,500	8	8-10am, 8.30-10pm
Qazvin	10,800	3½	Seiro Safar 2.15pm
Orumiyeh via	34,900	12-14	Taavoni 2, 7.30am,
Sanandaj			Iran Peyma 1.30pm
Rasht via Qazvin	21,000	6	Taavoni 9, 9.30am
Tehran	14,500	5	frequent 24hr
Zanjan	13,000	4	Taavoni 5, 3.30pm

Well-connected local bus company Iran Alvand has a handy ticket office below the Hamadan Guest House; Seiro Safar has an office near the Hotel Yas.

Tehran buses take either the expressway via Takestan or the more direct road via Saveh but very few go via Qazvin. Expect delays after fresh snow.

The main minibus station is on Zaman-e-Hamadani Blvd. Minibuses leave when full for Kermanshah (via Bisotun; IR6300), Kangavar (via Asadabad), Lalejin and Qorveh (for Sanandaj; IR2200). This station also has rare minibuses to Gol Tappeh (for Ali Sadr), but you're better off using a taxi: in summer listen for shouts of 'Qar, qar' (Cave, cave).

For Khorramabad there's one direct Taavoni 9 bus at 6pm (main bus station) but it's easy enough to make savari or minibus hops via Malayer and/or Borujerd from the Malayer terminal, 600m east of Hossein Sq on the east edge of town.

Savaris to Tehran (IR60,000), Asadabad, Kangavar and Kermanshah (rare) leave from relevant points on Sepah Sq.

Getting Around

Shared taxis run along the spokes of Hamadan's cartographic wheel for IR250 (one block), IR500 per normal hop. Shared taxis to the bus station and minibus station leave from near the Farshchi Guest House; change at Shohada Sq for the Malayer terminal. To avoid chartering into town from the main bus station walk one minute northwest towards Sepah Sq where you'll find shared taxis to Imam Khomeini Sq.

AROUND HAMADAN
Ganjnameh   گنج نامه

At Hamadan's westernmost extremity, some 8km from the centre via the popular Mar-

dom Park fairground, is **Ganjnameh** (Treasure Book). It's so named because for years its **cuneiform rock carvings** were thought to be cryptic clues to help find caches of mythical Median treasure. Belatedly translated, the texts turn out instead to be a rather immodest thank you to the Zoroastrian God Ahura Mazda from the Achaemenian monarch Xerxes (486–466 BC) for making him such a very, very good king. To emphasise the point the message is repeated in three languages (Old Persian, Elamite and Neo-Babylonian) on rock faces some 2m high. A second panel similarly commemorates Darius, his dad. The carvings are a very obvious two-minute stroll from the shared taxi drop-off circle, passing a row of tatty teahouses and snack bars. Just beyond is a 9m-high waterfall which becomes a popular ice-climbing spot when frozen in winter. The whole site can get crowded with local weekenders and messy with their detritus, but several long-distance paths lead directly up the fore-slopes of Mt Alvand making for relatively convenient yet bracing **hikes**.

Continue 4km up the Abbasabad Valley to Tark Dare (no public transport) to reach the main **skiing** area where new chairlifts are under construction.

GETTING THERE & AWAY

Shared taxis (IR1000) take 20 minutes from Shari'ati St outside the Esther & Mordecai Tomb. They're fairly frequent at weekends, but midweek you'll probably have to charter (from IR15,000 return).

Ali Sadr Caves   غار علیصدر
☎ 0812

These highly commercialised **caves** (Qar Ali Sadr; ☎ 553 3440; www.alisadr.com; admission IR80,000; ☒ 8am-4pm winter, 8am-8pm spring & autumn, 8am-midnight summer) were discovered 40 years ago by a local shepherd out looking for a lost goat. They rise to a maximum internal height of 40m with a river up to 14m deep flowing through the middle. For most Iranians Ali Sadr is simply western Iran's greatest tourist attraction. You might not agree. The visit, which will take about two hours, both starts and ends with a 20-minute trip down the underground river in roped-together paddle boats. The boat route is colourfully lit, though the big central cavern has many more steps than geological superlatives. In summer the caves feel cool so bring a light sweater. In winter it's refreshingly warm compared with the snow-bound exterior.

SLEEPING & EATING

Close to the cave entrance the ITTO's **Ali Sadr Hotel** (Mehmunsara; ☎/fax 553 3312; tw US$30; ⛄ Ⓟ) has reasonable rooms with bathroom. Out of season it charges only $18 a twin and would make a delightfully peaceful getaway and possible hiking base. In summer it will be bustling and you'll need to book. There are also some **bungalows** (known confusingly as 'suites') and picnic huts.

Stalls around the cave entrance sell cold drinks and pots of tea, the hotel has a decent restaurant and there is even a **teahouse** just inside the cave.

GETTING THERE & AWAY

At 8am on summer Fridays there's a direct bus to the caves from Ali Sadr Travel Agency in Hamadan (p182). A public minibus to Ali Sadr village supposedly leaves Hamadan's minibus terminal at 4pm returning next day at 7am, but can't be relied upon. Taxis from Hamadan want around IR80,000 return, plus IR12,000 per hour waiting time (minimum two hours to see the caves). It can work out cheaper to hire one way then ask the hotel to arrange a car back to Hamadan for you (IR50,000 one way, 70 minutes). En route stop briefly to admire the remarkable mud walls of fortified farm village Mihamlar Ohlea, right beside the road.

A budget alternative is to use very rare minibuses to Gol Tappeh (even more rare Bijar buses/savaris pass here too). This windswept little township is a 14km hike from the caves: finding a taxi will require a fair bit of asking around.

Parking at Ali Sadr costs IR10,000, unless you're a hotel guest.

Malayer   ملایر
☎ 0851 / pop 148,000

Pronounced ma-loy-a, you might need to change transport here between Hamadan and Borujerd. Malayer's main sight is an ancient beehive-domed **Yakhchad-e Mirfattah**, 2km from the centre near the Borujerd road. The medieval equivalent of a deep freezer, ice put inside in winter would stay frozen well into summer.

Near Shushab village, some 20km northwest, is **Nush-e Jam**, a fortified Median settlement site in the 8th to 6th centuries BC. Excavations have revealed what was possibly Iran's earliest fire temple, though the steel-girder covering-shed is far from picturesque. **Mosaferkhuneh Moghadam** (☎ 222 5160; Imam Sq) near the bazaar won't necessarily let foreigners stay.

To Hamadan minibuses (IR3000) and savaris (IR10,000) leave from Beheshti Blvd. For Arak they leave from Esteqlal Sq and for Borujerd from Besat Blvd, 1km west of the main Tehran terminal on Besat Sq.

Tyuserkan   تویسرکان
☎ 0852 / pop 39,000

This ancient city has a covered bazaar and a 17th-century **madraseh** (totally rebuilt in 1991) but the main tourist attraction is **Gonbad-e-Hayaquq-Nabi.** Try saying that with your mouth full of Tyuserkan's famous walnuts. It's an eight-sided brick tower with a clamshell-grooved conical roof. It sits in a garden on the west edge of town beside Rud Avar hill, 500m off Shahid Ashraf Esfahani Blvd. The tower is considered to be the tomb of Jewish prophet Habakuk who possibly came here after Darius released the Jews from Babylonian exile in 538 BC. Other sources date him much earlier (700–650 BC).

From Hamadan, minibuses (IR3800) and savaris (IR10,000) use the Malayer terminal, looping right around via Hosseinabad rather than using the scenic mountain road via Shahrestan and Oshttoran, which both have mud-walled fortresses nearby. There's a 17th-century caravanserai off the Tyuserkan–Kangavar road.

Nahavand   نهاوند
☎ 085232 / pop 67,000

Apart from a column fragment plonked in a shopping centre, there's no sign of the 193 BC Seleucid temple that once graced a local hill. If you ask a taxi driver for the temple site he's likely to whisk you off to Kangavar. Otherwise there's the 1852 **Hammam-e Haji Agha Torab**, a mural-filled 1852 bathhouse now being renovated, and the central, eye-catching if architecturally unremarkable **Sardab Mosque**. Its gilt-tipped, octagonal, blue minaret is visible as you shuttle between the Borujerd terminal (south) and the main northern bus terminal (for Kangavar, and for Hamadan via Malayer).

KHORRAMABAD   خرم آباد

☎ 0661 / pop 300,000

Khorramabad (Khorram Abad) is the capital of Lorestan. Little visited, yet scenically appealing, the province straddles the glorious Zagros Mountains and its Lori (Lurish) people have their own language and culture.

Khorramabad lies in a long gorge sandwiched by dry, impressive crags in which have been found at least five Palaeolithic cave-dwelling sites. The most accessible are now lairs of local junkies, so avoid them. Historians disagree whether Khorramabad was the site of Shapurkhast or of Samha. Both are ancient 'lost' cities which had advanced irrigation and milling systems 1500 years ago judging from archaeological clues like the Gerdab-e-Sangi cistern.

In the Middle Ages a fortified central citadel was built here by the Atabegs, the powerful clan who ruled Lorestan from the 12th century until subjugated by Shah Abbas around 1600. The citadel later became the residence of the Persian governors who developed it into a classical fortress that soared so impressively that it became known as Falak-ol-Aflak (Heaven of Heavens). In the 1830s, when they felt a little safer, the governors moved into the mansion at the castle's base (now a military academy) and the fortress became a prison. It's now an interesting museum. In the local Lori language thank you is *dast-darg nakoneh*, delicious is *tomdara*.

Orientation

Around the fortress, narrow central streets are attractively lined with *chinar* (plane) trees, but driving is awkward thanks to an infuriating one-way system. Bypassing the melee, busy Shari'ati St (the main Ahvaz–Hamadan highway) hosts the bus offices and most of the hotels. Note that locals call Imam Hossein Sq 'Meydan Shaqayeq' (a type of local orchid), 22 Bahman Sq is 'Kyo' while Imam Khomeini and Alavi are interchangeable names for the same street.

Information

Bank Melli (Imam Khomeini St) Money exchange upstairs.
ITTO (☎ 221 3317; Shafian Ln; ◷ 8am-2.30pm Sat-Thu) In the third lane off Alavi St from Imam Sq walk upstairs

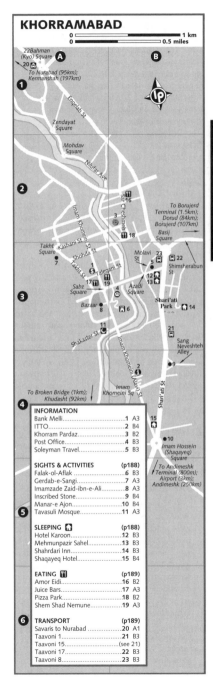

KHORRAMABAD

0 —————— 1 km
0 —————— 0.5 miles

through an unmarked green door. They might give you a colourful Lorestan pamphlet, but they speak no English and have no city maps, so it's not really worth the trek. Hotel Karoon has photos of regional attractions and on request gives favoured guests a detailed Farsi-only city map featuring some as-yet only imagined roads.

Khorram Pardaz (☎ 220 5671; Kashani St; Internet per hr IR10,000; ☻ 10am-1.30pm & 4.30-8pm) Upstairs then left beside a patisserie.

Post Office In a yard off the castle access lane.

Soleyman Travel (☎ 220 0600; Muhajadine-e Islam St; ☻ 8am-1pm & 4-6pm Sat-Thu)

Sights
FALAK-OL-AFLAK

Dominating the city centre from a 40m-high rocky promontory, the impressive **Falak-ol-Aflak** (☎ 220 4090; www.lorestanmiras.org; admission IR20,000; ☻ 9am-noon & 3-5pm, later in summer) is unmissable.

It's worth climbing to the entrance ramp to see the views. For even better views, walk inside past an incredibly deep (43m) grating-covered **well** to the crenellated battlements. Rooms around the rear courtyard form a very well-presented **ethnographic museum** showing vignettes of Lurish life, including the weaving of black canvas for traditional *siyah-chador* (nomad tents). There's a superb knob-topped tombstone from Alishtar, but as yet the rooms containing priceless Lurish bronzes remain closed for renovation (see the boxed text 'The Lorestan Bronzes', below).

OTHER SIGHTS

A 20m-high pale brick tower called **Manar-e Ajon** (Ajon Minaret; Imam Hossein Sq) was probably not a minaret at all but a 900-year-old signalling point for caravans. In the otherwise unremarkable bazaar is the colourfully tiled **Imamzadeh Zaid-ibn-e-Ali**. The **Tavasuli Mosque** (Shakaster St) is also appealing. **Gerdab-e-Sangi** (Takht Sq) is a curious, if rather dull, Sassanian stone reservoir that once powered the city's ancient watermills. It now contains stagnant mud. Beside thundering Shari'ati St, forgotten in a dirty stone-edged circle, is an **inscribed stone** (Sang Neveshteh Alley) from around AD 1150, apparently setting out details of local grazing rights. The rather impressive **broken bridge** (Pol-e-Eshkesseh) is stranded in a field off the Khudasht road. It's visible across the river, from the edge of a new housing estate, 1km directly east of the Andimeshk terminal.

Sleeping

Hotel Karoon (☎ 220 5408; Shari'ati St; s/tw/tr US$15/20/24) The management is obliging and rooms are acceptable, if unlovely, with showers and bizarre piggy-back toilet contraptions. Water supply can be dodgy.

Shahrdari Inn (☎ 220 2227; s/tw US$20/30; ☒ ℗) Tucked quietly away behind Shari'ati Park, potentially great views of the fortress are mostly hidden by the trees. Rooms are pleasant enough and have bathroom, but are somewhat musty and past their prime.

Shaqayeq Hotel (☎ 420 2648; Shari'ati St; s/tw US$20/30) Incredibly tatty for the price.

Mehmunpazir Sahel (☎ 220 3260; Shari'ati St; s/tw IR50,000/70,000) The dismal dive next door to the Karoon has no showers and just one shared squat toilet.

THE LORESTAN BRONZES

In 1931 the valiant Freya Stark risked brigands, bandits and police ire as she sneaked about in the 'wastes of civilisation'. Lorestan had lapsed into lawless nomadic 'backwardness' after centuries of wars which had wiped out virtually all settled agriculture. Alishtar (off today's Nurabad road) had been a major city before Tamerlane's 14th-century ravages, but in the 1930s all that remained was a nervous garrison of Persians huddled insecurely within a mud-walled fortress, in fear of the wild tribes beyond. Yet millennia before, ruled from around 1800 BC by the hazily documented Kassites, the region had been at the forefront of technology. These horse-breeding warriors later expanded southwards becoming rulers of a great Mesopotamian empire till toppled by the Elamites around 1155 BC. In their glory years the polytheistic Kassites perfected bronze making, casting exquisite items whose fine decoration belies their often mundane purposes. It was in search of Kassite, and later bronze work buried in ancient graves, that adventurers like Ms Stark risked their saddles. Today exploring is much safer. However, until the treasury in Khorramabad's Falak-ol-Aflak reopens, your best hope of seeing Lorestan bronzes is in Tehran (at the National and Reza Abbasi Museums) or for sale on a dozen Internet sites.

Eating

A gaggle of juice bars line Imam Khomeini St north of the bazaar.

Shem Shad Nemune (☎ 220 5235; Taleqani St; 8am-3pm & 6-10pm) Local scenes adorn the walls and there's great fried trout (IR18,500), but mind those bones. Upstairs is glitzier with chandeliers, stucco mouldings and thumping music.

Amor Eidi (Sar Cheshmeh St; meals IR12,000-16,000; 24hr) Standard kebabs are served with delicious bread straight from the oven. It's clustered with three others, all small but tastefully semimodern.

Pizza Park (☎ 220 5888; Sar Cheshmeh St; pizzas IR15,000-18,000; 9am-9pm) The nicest central pizzeria.

Getting There & Away

AIR

Tickets to Tehran (IR147,000, twice weekly) are sold by helpful Soleyman Travel (p188). The airport's 3km south of Imam Hossein Sq.

BUS

Long-distance buses leave from the relevant company offices found along Shari'ati St. Most have morning and evening services to Esfahan (IR17,500, seven hours) and Tehran (IR21,500, eight hours via Qom). Taavoni 15 has services to Orumiyeh (IR55,000, 16 hours) at 3pm and to Sanandaj (IR19,000) via Hamadan. For Kermanshah, Taavoni 17 (Pekesaba) has a direct bus at 2pm (IR12,400, 3½ hours) or make savari hops via Nurabad and Harsin (attractive, but partly unsurfaced). Taavoni 1 and 15 have night buses to Ahvaz (from IR17,000, six hours), antisocially passing Andimeshk and Shush before dawn.

Minibuses arriving from Andimeshk (IR9000, 4½ hours) thoughtfully drop you off at Imam Hossein Sq, but depart from a terminal 800m further south.

The terminal for savaris to Nurabad (IR8000, 90km) and Kermanshah (IR20,000, 190km) is at 22 Bahman Sq.

Savaris and minibuses for Borujerd (IR4000, 100km) and Dorud (IR3800, 80km) use a terminal 1.5km up Shimsherabun St from Basij Sq.

Getting Around

Handy shared-taxi routes run both ways along Shari'ati and Enqelab Sts to and from Basij Sq. Northbound others run straight up Imam Khomeini St then up Kashani to Takht Sq, returning by wiggling through traffic jams around the back of the bazaar.

DORUD   دورود

☎ 0665 / pop 49,000

This unexciting light industrial town is a useful base for excursions into deepest Lorestan. It's also the starting point for climbing Mt Oshturan, which would be visible from town but for the dusty haze pumped out by a satanically vast cement works. The town's new (and only) hotel, **Shahrdari Dorud** (☎ 423 0020; Beheshti Blvd; tw US$30), has a big concrete-columned portico and very comfortable rooms. It's a real bargain if the friendly staff let you pay the local price (IR80,000). Great photos of local beauty spots grace the decent restaurant, which serves outstanding *qizil arla* (special local fish) barbecued for IR30,000 on request.

From the bus station, 4km west of the centre, are minibuses (IR4000, two hours) and scorchingly fast savaris (IR11,000, 50 minutes) to Khorramabad. To Borujerd, minibuses (IR1800) and savaris (IR6000) are also frequent.

Esfahan-bound buses pick up passengers around midnight from Taavoni offices on Beheshti Blvd.

Incoming trains are met at the station by savaris for both Khorramabad and Borujerd. The 2pm day train to Andimeshk (8½ hours) is sheer mayhem, but between the endless tunnels you'll spy some of the most remote, roadless parts of beautiful Lorestan.

AROUND DORUD

Inaccessible by road and nestled in a thick glade of plane and fig trees, the tiny village of **Bisheh** (Bishehpuran) hides one of Iran's prettiest **waterfalls**. It cascades in 30m chutes off a tree-topped gully then trickles in rivulets into the river below. In summer many local tourists make the scenic day trip from Dorud (rail only), but by autumn only their litter remains and you'll have the village to yourself, the entire population of children following you Pied Piper–style. Although you can scramble down to the falls in 10 minutes (with a guide) the best view is from across the river. This requires a long but pleasant loop: walk along the rail tracks for a couple of kilometres south (not north across the viaduct), descend before the first tunnel to the footbridge, then walk back up the opposite bank.

Six stations south of Bisheh there's another, even more isolated waterfall at **Talezang**.

An outrageously overfull, but effectively free, train trundles out of Dorud at 2pm taking half an hour to Bisheh. En route see fabulous glimpses of ziggurat-shaped Mt Parvis. You'll have an ample 4½ hours in Bisheh before the 7pm northbound train back to Dorud. That continues all the way to Tehran (IR9000, 10½ hours), via Qom.

The highest peak in the Zagros Mountains at 4070m, **Mt Oshturan**'s main attraction is beautiful **Lake Gahar**, famed for its succulent *qizil arla* fish. The outbound hike takes four to five hours (less back) from a trailhead at Haft Cheshmeh, a lonely yellow guide hut/emergency refuge 23km from Dorud. Here there's a car park, toilet, freshwater spring and, in summer, the possibility of engaging a guide (IR120,000, not really necessary). Bring your own food and tent. Even if you don't hike, great views make the access journey worthwhile, at least as far as the mud-house village of **Darb-e-Astaneh** (taxi IR40,000 return, 18km). Beyond there's a IR10,000 road toll, but less to see.

BORUJERD   بروجرد
☎ 0622 / pop 237,000

This big town has limited charm, but the mountain backdrop looks great in its snowy winter wear. Unlike Dorud there is top-range and budget accommodation plus an **Internet café** (Takhti St). The main sight is the 900-year-old **Imamzadeh Jafar** (Imamzadeh Ln), an active shrine just 50m off Jafari St. It has a mirrored entry portal and is famed for intricately carved, if slightly slapdash, Indian-style wooden doors. Walk around to the cemetery behind for the best view of its unique conical spire. Also well worth a look are the Seljuk blue-domed **Jameh Mosque** (Jafari St) and the fine Qajar-era **Soltani (Imam) Mosque** (Safa St) with four pale brick-and-tile *iwans* surrounding an attractive courtyard.

Sleeping & Eating
Zagros Hotel (☎ 350 4901; www.zagros-hotel.com; tw/ste US$82/99) On a pronounced hill northwest of the centre, this upscale hotel is a local tourist attraction in itself. Fully international-standard rooms have sparse, Scandinavian-style pine interiors with the

best mountain views from rooms 202 to 207 or from the creaky glass elevators. The surprisingly unpretentious restaurant (meals IR20,000 to IR28,000) does a reasonable chicken schnitzel.

Hotel Behroz (☎ 262 3533; Azadi Sq; s/tw IR22,000/ 28,000) Right by the bazaar entrance, the Behroz's rooms look like prison cells and are almost as cheap. Mosaferkhunehs Navid and Moghadan on Shohada Sq should be slightly better, if you can talk your way in.

Steghlal Hotel (☎ 262 4017; Khashani St; tw US$20) Rooms are musty and overpriced, and mixed-sex couples might be asked to show marriage certificates.

Getting There & Away
The savari/minibus terminal for Dorud and Khorramabad is at the far southeast edge of town. The terminal for most other destinations is equally inconvenient, 1km northwest of the Zagros Hotel. The latter has savaris to Kermanshah (IR18,000), Hamadan (IR18,000 direct or via Malayer) and Nahavand (IR6000), where you'd change terminals for Kangavar.

ANDIMESHK   اندیمشک
☎ 0642 / pop 138,000

Though pleasant enough, travellers generally only visit Andimeshk for its useful transport connections, heading swiftly on to much more intriguing Shush or Shushtar. The town's thoroughfare is Enqelab St diverging from the big ring road at Azadegan Sq but mimicking its northeasterly arc. It forms a 4km-long banana around the centre to the Khorramabad terminal, 500m beyond, where it rejoins the ring road to strike north. Tucked into the protective curve, the town centre is Imam St, which heads diagonally north off Enqelab at Beheshti Sq (1.5km north of Azadegan). Passing the bus station and Hotel Rostan, Imam St crosses Taleqani St at Clock (Sa'at) Sq after two blocks.

Sleeping
If you're stuck the town has two hotels.

Hotel Rostan (☎ 424 1818; Imam St; s/tw IR80,000/ 100,000) A block north of the bus station, the Rostan has recently repainted rooms with simple squat toilet and shower. Rooms have fans and some also have old air-conditioners.

Hotel Bozorg (Andimeshk Grand; ☎ 422 2100; fax 422 9295; s/d IR155,000/220,000; 🗱 ℗) This is a sensibly priced, relatively up-market edifice on the southern bypass just east of Azadegan Sq. Towels, but no toilet paper, are provided.

Getting There & Away
BUS, MINIBUS & SAVARI
The **main bus station** (☎ 422 5831; Imam St) looks more like a shop. Useful destinations include Esfahan (IR25,000), departing 3.30pm and 7.30pm, and Kermanshah (IR20,000, seven hours), at 3pm and 7pm. Helpful Mr Faribors speaks English. For more long-distance choices flag down buses ex-Ahvaz at Basij Sq or at other key roundabouts on the ring road. For Khorramabad, minibuses (IR9000, 4½ hours) fill slowly at a special terminal 2km north of the centre on Enqelab St, with savaris faster and more frequent. They travel via Pol-e-Dokhtar (Virgin Bridge) which is both a town and a separate chunky brick arch straddling the road in a canyon further north.

Across the road from the main bus station is a minibus/savari stand for Dezful (IR500, 20 minutes). For Shush, minibuses (IR1300, one hour) leave frequently from a nearby point on Enqelab St just south of Beheshti Sq.

TRAIN
The station (Taleqani St) is handily central, one short block west of Clock Sq. A slow, uncomfortable, overcrowded but fascinating 5am day train takes 8½ hours to Dorud via Bisheh and through some of Lorestan's roadless, rarely visited valleys. Four faster, more comfortable sleeper trains run nightly to Tehran (14 hours). Tickets are easiest to find on the 9pm service, which originates in Andimeshk. Once weekly there's a train to Mashhad.

SHUSH
شوش
☎ 0642 / pop 67,000
Now a pleasantly small, relatively new town, Shush (Susa) was once among the greatest cities of ancient Persia. A vast archaeological site remains which might be less visually arresting than Choqa Zanbil but is dominated by a splendid 19th-century guardian castle. With its enigmatic Tomb of Daniel, a bustling market and a great-value hotel, Shush makes the ideal regional base as long as you can get a room.

History
Though best known as an Achaemenid capital, Shush was in fact a prehistoric settlement from at least the 4th millennium BC, and an important Elamite city from about the middle of the 3rd millennium. Around 640 BC, it was burnt by the Assyrian king Ashurbanipal, but regained prominence in 521 BC when Darius I set it up as his fortified winter capital. At that time it was probably similar in grandeur to Persepolis.

The palace survived the city's fall to Alexander the Great in 331 BC, but was sacked eight years later. Still prosperous in the Seleucid and Parthian eras it re-emerged as a Sassanian capital. During Shapur II's reign (AD 310–379) it became an important centre of Christianity, as well as a Jewish pilgrimage site. Evacuated in the face of Mongol raids Shush disappeared into the sands of time, only re-emerging after 1852 when the British archaeologist WK Loftus became the first to survey the site. His work was continued by the French Archaeological Service from 1891 more or less continuously until the Islamic Revolution of 1979.

Ancient City
Entered from a roundabout two blocks east of the hotel, the **archaeological site** (admission IR30,000; dawn-dusk) occupies the whole southern flank of modern Shush. To the right as you enter it is dominated by the **Chateau de Morgan**. This crenellated Omani-style desert fortress sits on the site of an Elamite acropolis but was actually built by the French Archaeological Service between 1897 and 1912 to defend researchers from raids by local Arab and Lurish tribesmen.

Previously used as a museum, the castle is now closed pending structural repairs. Most of the key finds are in Tehran (National Museum) and Paris (Louvre) anyway. However, you can still admire a cuneiform-inscribed brick which has been incorporated into the castle's doorway and is thus more accessible than the equivalents at Choqa Zanbil.

Turning left at the top of the site's main entry ramp you can walk through the site of the 521 BC **Palace of Darius**. It's now just a muddy rise on which a 30cm-high labyrinth of brick-and-wattle wall fragments marks the former room layout. At the north rim are the massive stone bases of what was once an **Apadana**, with six by six 22m-high columns topped with animal figures. A couple of the double-horse capitals are partly preserved on the paved terrace. Here Darius, just like recent visitors, could only dream how perfectly the views and blazing heat would be complemented by an ice-cold gin and tonic.

To the east, beyond the partly paved **Royal Gate**, the **Royal City** is a misleadingly interesting name for barren, lonely undulations stretching to the far horizon. It's more sensible to loop back towards the castle amid muddy gullies, pottery shards and thorn thickets alive with darting desert foxes. At the western side of the castle there's an earthen watchtower above ancient caves and niches.

Tomb of Daniel

As in any typical imamzadeh, Muslim pilgrims crowd the glittery interior of the **Tomb of Daniel** (Aramgah-e Danyal), kissing the metal grate around a green-draped grave slab. Here, however, this behaviour is particularly intriguing given that Daniel has at best tangential relevance to Islam. In fact, he's a semi-mythical Jewish figure who supposedly served as a faithful *satarap* (administrator) to Darius (522–486 BC). Dubiously recorded as having 'tender love with the prince of the Eunuchs' (Daniel 1, 9) he is best remembered for unenviable ordeals in lions' dens. These exploits were already over 300 years old when recorded in the Bible's Old Testament (Daniel 6, 16–23).

Whatever the real provenance of the Daniel relics, for over a millennium they brought an extremely lucrative flow of Jewish pilgrims from right across the Middle East. Great wealth accrued to the townsfolk living nearby, but those living across the Shahur River were missing out on the bonanza and wanted a share of the pilgrims' shekels. A comical compromise was arranged whereby Daniel's bones would spend alternate years on either riverbank, bringing prosperity to both communities. In the 12th century, travellers reported that an even more fanciful arrangement had left the holy remains dangling in a crystal coffin suspended from a metal bridge across the middle of the river.

What happened to them during the Mongol destruction is not recorded, but the present structure with its distinctive, pine-cone faceted spire, so typical of Khuzestan tombs, was only built in 1871.

Almost more photogenic than the shrine itself are the Belfast-style revolutionary propaganda murals in the courtyard urging assorted 'pious' actions, from female modesty to the 'liberation' of Jerusalem.

The shrine complex is easy to find in the bazaar area, a short walk from the hotel and ancient city entrance. It remains open late into the evening, and a donation is appropriate.

Sleeping & Eating

Shush has only one hotel, the **Apadana Hotel and Restaurant** (☎ /fax 522 3131; s/tw IR80,000/ 120,000; ✖ P) but it's comfortable, central, friendly and excellent value. Pleasant rooms have heaters, bathrooms and towels, though water pressure can be rather low in the upper rooms. Note that often when the restaurant is closed, the staff temporarily lock the hotel section. This has left a few guests stranded both inside and out, so it's wise to mention to the manager if you're planning a midnight stroll.

The hotel restaurant is the best place to eat, although there are plenty of **snack bars** and **kababis** scattered around the bazaar area.

Getting There & Away

Long-distance buses en route to Ahvaz can often be persuaded to drop passengers off on the main highway, 2km east of town. Shared taxis shuttle from this point into the centre, but not necessarily at 2am when most buses go by. Heading out of Shush, you'll usually need to go first to Andimeshk or Ahvaz.

Halfway between the highway and the town centre, minibuses to Andimeshk (IR1200, 38km) are frequent, to Dezful (for Shushtar) and Ahvaz, much more occasional, each from a separate but nearby terminal. The hotel can call you a sensibly priced taxi to get you to Choqa Zanbil and/ or Shushtar (IR80,000).

CHOQA ZANBIL & HAFT TAPPEH

The ideal way to visit the world's foremost Elamite sites is by taxi from Shush. Visit Haft Tappeh first as the museum is a good primer for Choqa Zanbil. In reverse you'd find Haft Tappeh's lumpy ziggurats rather an anticlimax. If the new road is open it's a brilliant idea to continue from Choqa Zanbil to Shushtar.

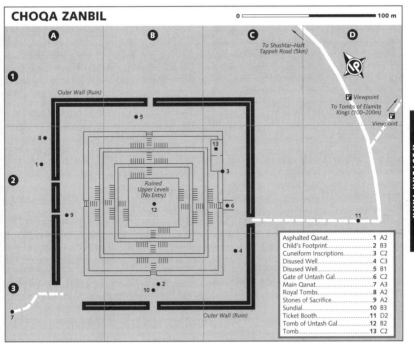

CHOQA ZANBIL

0 — 100 m

To Shushtar–Haft Tappeh Road (5km)

Outer Wall (Ruin)

• 5

8 •
1 •

13
• 3

Ruined
Upper Levels
(No Entry)
• 12

• 9

• 6

Viewpoint
To Tombs of Elamite Kings (100–200m)
Viewpoint

11

• 4

10 •   • 2

7

Outer Wall (Ruin)

Asphalted Qanat	1 A2
Child's Footprint	2 B3
Cuneiform Inscriptions	3 C2
Disused Well	4 C3
Disused Well	5 B1
Gate of Untash Gal	6 C2
Main Qanat	7 A3
Royal Tombs	8 A2
Stones of Sacrifice	9 A2
Sundial	10 B3
Ticket Booth	11 D2
Tomb of Untash Gal	12 B2
Tomb	13 C2

WESTERN IRAN

Haft Tappeh

هفت تپه

The name of this 3000-year-old city site means 'seven hills'. In fact there are dozens of little hill-mounds in this otherwise flat oasis, and at least three are thought to have been ziggurats. They're not mind-blowingly exciting, and are currently under excavation, but you're free to wander around. Beside the site set in a lovely garden of roses, hibiscus, bougainvillaea and soaring palms is a Unesco-sponsored **museum** (admission IR20,000; 8am-2.30pm Sat-Thu;) which has a selection of archaeological finds, a curious black sarcophagus and photo-rich explanations of the excavation, restoration and partial reconstruction of Choqa Zanbil (25km away).

The museum and site is 3km off the Ahvaz–Andimeshk highway on a road signed to the big Haft Tappeh sugar refinery. A little to the east after crossing the rail tracks there's a 1km unpaved short cut south to the Choqa Zanbil road.

Choqa Zanbil

چغازنبیل

One of Iran's Unesco World Heritage sites, Choqa Zanbil's magnificent brick **ziggurat**

(admission IR30,000; guarded 24hr) is the best surviving example of Elamite architecture anywhere. Even if you're not a fan of ancient ruins, the great bulk and splendid semidesert isolation of Choqa Zanbil will impress.

HISTORY

The ancient inhabitants of proto-Iran attached great religious importance to mountains. Where they had no mountains, they made their own. This was the origin of distinctive pyramidal, tiered temples known as ziggurats. Choqa Zanbil's ziggurat was the *raison d'être* of the town of Dur Untash, founded by King Untash Gal in the mid-13th century BC. Dur Untash bloomed especially in the early 12th century BC when it had a large number of temples and priests. The town was eventually sacked by Ashurbanipal around 640 BC and, incredibly, remained 'lost' for more than 2500 years. It was accidentally rediscovered during a 1935 aerial survey by the Anglo-Iranian Oil Company, the forerunner of BP.

THE ZIGGURAT

The ziggurat was dedicated to Inshushinak, the chief god of the Elamite pantheon and patron of Shush. As the area was then fertile and forested, it was built on a slightly raised base to guard against flooding. It has a square plan with sides measuring 105m. The original five storeys were erected vertically from the foundation level as a series of concentric towers, not one on top of another as was the custom in neighbouring Mesopotamia. At the summit (now lost) was a temple accessible only to the highest elite of Elamite society. Even now the taboo remains and you're not allowed to climb the remnant stairways that rise on each of the four sides.

The structure is made of red bricks so well preserved that one might think they're brand new. However, if you look very closely on a brick-wide strip at around eye-level, they're intricately inscribed in **cuneiform**, the world's spiky first alphabet that looks like a spilt box of tin-tacks. The inscriptions are not easy to make out unless you cross the rope cordon. Permission to do so is the only apparent advantage of tipping the 'guide'. He speaks not a word of English, but gesticulates with gruesome clarity as to the purpose of the **sacrifice stones**. Also easy to spot is an ancient **sun dial** and, beside it, a strangely moving **footprint** of an Elamite child, accidentally preserved for three millennia.

AROUND THE ZIGGURAT

The ziggurat was surrounded by a paved courtyard protected by a wall. At the foot of the northeastern steps would once have been the **Gate of Untash Gal**, two rows of seven columns where supplicants would seek the pleasure of the king. Around the wall were originally a complex of **tomb chambers**, tunnels and **qanat** channels which, as the site's climate became drier, brought water an incredible 45km from ancient rivers. Vestiges are still visible. Outside were the living quarters of the town and 11 temples dedicated to various Elamite gods and goddesses. Little of this remains.

Walk a couple of minutes east of the main asphalt access road towards an isolated lamppost to find some more, excavated **Elamite royal tombs**. There's little to see here, either, though steep ancient steps lead down into (unlabelled) **tomb number five**. Descend-ing is unwise as the pit stinks of toiletry misdemeanours... especially bad when the temperature hits 45°. Nonetheless, it's still worth strolling up the slight nearby rise to see the ziggurat from a particularly photogenic angle.

GETTING THERE & AWAY

The Apadana Hotel in Shush can arrange a taxi for no more than you'd pay on the street. Typical cost via Haft Tappeh is IR65,000 return (or IR80,000 if you continue one way to Shushtar), plus IR15,000 per hour waiting time. There's no public transport whatever.

SHUSHTAR شوشتر

☎ 0612 / pop 105,000

Scrappy but perversely fascinating, the historic city of Shushtar lies strategically where the last contoured red ridges of the expiring Zagros Mountains fade into the endless flat watermelon fields of southern Khuzestan. Its *raison d'être* for millennia was controlling the irrigation of those plains, and the town's most famous attraction is a set of 700-year-old **'watermills'** (Shari'ati St; admission IR30,000; ⊙ 7am-10pm). Actually, these aren't buildings at all but an impressive arc of cascading water chutes marking where key mills and irrigation systems must once have been. Entrance is down steps beside the cutely ragged **Seyid Mohammad Haref Imamzade**, but you can see almost as well by simply peering over the parapet of the Shari'ati St bridge.

Beneath the initially unexciting surface of today's low-rise cityscape, there's loads more to discover including no less than 14 imamzadehs. Many are grand, but the most eye-catching is **Imamzadeh Abdullah** with a white pine cone of a central tower, reminiscent of Daniel's tomb in Shush. Along with the high arch of the ancient **Aletayeb Bridge**, it's visible from the bus as you arrive from Ahvaz. A short walk south of the bus station, the partly 9th-century **Jameh Mosque** (Masjed Jameh Ln; ⊙ noon-1pm & 5-7pm for prayers) has a truncated, gently leaning minaret and sits in a quiet tree-filled quadrangle of fruit-sellers. About 400m west of the bus station at Bateni Sq, a substantial ruined **ancient bridge** parallels the new one on the Dezful Rd. A barred alley wiggles from Bateni Sq around to the sweet little **museum** (admission free; ☎ 8am-2pm), which has no exhibits per se but occupies a delightful heavy-doored building with palm-tree courtyard facing the river.

Sleeping & Eating
The cheap **Shushtar Hotel** (☎ 622 3288; Taleqani St) is presently closed, but the new **Hotel Jahangardi** (☎ 622 1690; Taleqani St; s/tw/tr/quad IR180,000/230,000/280,000/300,000; ✳ P) has clean, reasonably comfortable rooms with bathroom. It's in a wonderful, quiet position where east Taleqani St dead-ends in a curl of river near an ancient octagonal stone 'light house'. Fine views look across the river's ancient Sassanid weir to the blue-domed Seyid Mohammad Golabi Shrine. The hotel has Shushtar's best restaurant. The simple kababi **Tak** (17th Shahrivar Sq) has a friendly English-speaking owner.

Getting There & Away
Shushtar's single, handily central bus terminal is between Almas and Sheikh Sts. Very regular buses run to Ahvaz (IR3500, 1½ hours) and Dezful (IR2000, one hour), where you can transfer for Shush or Andimeshk. A small gated lane between Shushtar and Haft Tappeh passes within 5km of Choqa Zanbil. There's no public transport. Taxis should know if the road is open.

DEZFUL   دزفول
☎ 0641 / pop 261,000
Lively Dezful, which claims to have built the world's first bridge, is a big, low-rise university city. It suffered horribly in the Iran-Iraq War. There are three weekly Iran Aseman flights (IR169,000) from Tehran, but most tourists only pass through in transit to/from Shushtar. Minibuses from Shushtar drop off at Yakoub Lays Sq. From there it's a 2km, IR500 shared-taxi ride to Dezful's central Imam Sq. You'll need another shared taxi to reach the separate Andimeshk and Shush terminals. From Haji Moradi Sq open-top pickups run as savaris through citrus gardens to **Muhammad Bin Djafar Tayyar Shrine** (Bin Jafar village), with its attractive 10-sided blue-cone spire.

AHVAZ   اهواز
☎ 0611 / pop 1,040,000
Abu Nuwas ('Father of Curls') is perhaps the only Muslim poet celebrated for writing homoerotic drinking songs *(khamriyyat)*. He was born in AD 756 in Ahvaz, but got out as soon as he could. You'll probably

want to do the same. But hopefully not (as Abu was) sold as a sex slave to a Yemeni drug dealer.

Ahvaz today is a sprawling, featureless, industrial city serving the Masjed-e Soleiman oilfields (discovered in 1908). Unremitting Iraqi bombing during the Iran-Iraq War didn't beautify it and subsequent redevelopment has failed to offer much inspiration. April to October temperatures regularly top 50°C, making an air-conditioned hotel room the greatest attraction. Use the good transport connections, then hurry on to much nicer Shush or Shushtar.

Information
Bank Melli (Azadegan St) Changes money.
Iran Handicrafts (☼ 9am-1pm & 5-10pm) Sells pamphlets and a detailed, but dangerously outdated, city map. Opposite the Fajr Grand Hotel.
ITTO (☎ 222 4024; Shahid Atangari St; 7am-2pm Sat-Thu) Bemused to actually meet tourists. They have no maps, but speak English and can help with specific questions and problems. Just off Azadegan St, behind Farhad Turbo motor spares shop.
Main Post Office (Felestin St) Across Moalleq Bridge.
PishgamanISP.com (☎ 222 5183; Taleqani St; ☼ 9am-1pm & 4.30-9pm Sat-Thu) Fast Internet connection above Boof Hamburgers, entered from Hafez St.
Post Office (Azadegan St) Small, but central.
Tayareh Travel Agency (☎ 222 9849; fax 222 6108; Azadegan St)
Telephone Office (Shari'ati St) Tiny private place; handily central for international calls.

Sights & Activities
Boatmen beneath Moalleq Bridge can take you for a little punt on the river. Bring sunscreen. For strolling, the least unpleasant stretch of riverbank is near Mellat Park. June to September you could cool off at the **swimming pool** at the Fajr Grand Hotel (nonguests IR10,000). Several new mosques are cladding themselves in attractive blue tiles including the **Jezari Mosque** (Behbahani Hwy) built right beside a roller-coaster (a spiritual metaphor?). Generally it's better to leave Ahvaz and go somewhere interesting instead.

Sleeping
Fajr Grand Hotel (☎ 222 0091; fax 221 8677; Karun Riverbank; s/tw/d $65/95/95; ✳ ▣) Much the best in town, the Fajr's comfortable international-standard rooms and (summer only) pool are the best reason to stay in Ahvaz.

AHVAZ

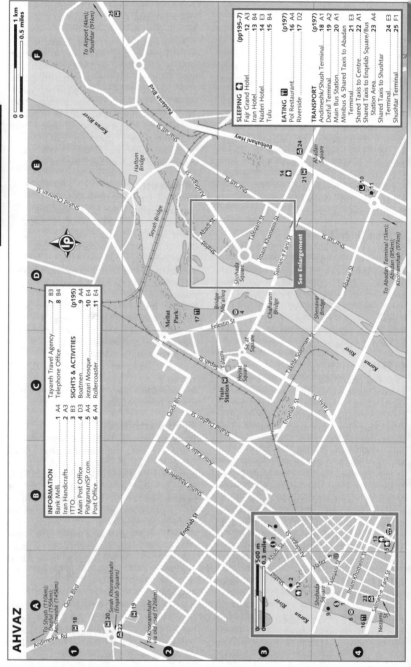

INFORMATION
Bank Melli	1 A4
Iran Handicrafts	2 A3
ITTO	3 B3
Main Post Office	4 D3
PishgamanISP.com	5 A4
Post Office	6 A4
Tayareh Travel Agency	7 B3
Telephone Office	8 B4

SIGHTS & ACTIVITIES (p195)
Boatmen	9 A4
Jezair Mosque	10 E4
Rollercoaster	11 E4

SLEEPING (pp195-7)
Fajr Grand Hotel	12 A3
Iran Hotel	13 B4
Naderi Hotel	14 E3
Tulu	15 B4

EATING (p197)
Pol Restaurant	16 A4
Riverside	17 D2

TRANSPORT (p197)
Andimeshk/Shush Terminal	18 A1
Dezful Terminal	19 A2
Main Bus Station	20 A1
Minibus & Shared Taxis to Abadan Terminal	21 E3
Shared Taxis to Centre	22 A1
Shared Taxis to Enqelab Square/Bus Station Area	23 A4
Shared Taxis to Shushtar Terminal	24 E3
Shushtar Terminal	25 F1

Iran Hotel (☎ 221 7200; Shari'ati St; s/tw IR150,000/ 250,000; 🛜) Better than the uninviting foyer suggests, the Iran's acceptable mid-range rooms have OK bathrooms and only a little peeling paint.

Naderi Hotel (☎ 222 9000; fax 222 2610; Imam Khomeini St; small/big d $30/45; 🛜) A slight step up from the Iran, if only because they won't rent you their cheaper rooms.

Tulu (☎ 222 2221; Shari'ati St; tw IR60,000) The Tulu is no bargain but it is nonetheless Ahvaz's cheapest central option. Don't be fooled by the posh-looking ceilings; without air-conditioning you'll do more sweating than sleeping, adding your own gallons of perspiration to the contents of already unsavoury mattresses.

Eating
There are fast-food places along Taleqani St, and sandwich shops around attractively palm-filled Hejirat Park near the train station. Apart from those in the hotels, decent restaurants are surprisingly hard to find.

Pol Restaurant (☎ 222 6279; meals IR17,000-27,000; ⏲ noon-3pm & 7-10pm) Lurking under Chaharom Bridge this is a central, if hardly exotic, place for kebabs.

Riverside (Rudkenar; ☎ 333 2421; meals IR20,000-40,000; ⏲ noon-3pm & 7-10.30pm) Though a little ragged, the Riverside has river views and serves shrimp and fish dinners (by weight).

Getting There & Away
AIR
Iran Air, Caspian Airlines and Kish Air all fly daily or more to Tehran (IR196,000). There are other flights to Kuwait (IR1,060,000) on Saturday, Dubai (IR960,000) on Wednesday, Esfahan (IR144,000), Mashhad (IR369,000, twice weekly), and Shiraz (IR169,000) on Friday.

BOAT
From Khorramshahr, 125km south, **Valfarje-8 Shipping** (☎ 336 7116) sails to Kuwait ($112 one way, US$200 return, six hours, four weekly).

BUS, MINIBUS & SHARED TAXI
From the big main bus station you can get virtually anywhere. Useful services include:

Destination	Price (IR)	Duration (hr)	Departures
Bandar-e Abbas	35,000-51,500	19-21	7.30am-4pm
Esfahan	35,000-54,000	14	8.30-9am, 4-9pm
Hamadan	30,000 Volvo	9	2pm
Kermanshah via Eslamabad	21,500-35,000	9	8-9pm
Khorramabad	17,000-30,000	6½	10pm, 11pm
Shiraz	23,000-40,000	10	8am, 7pm
Tehran	35,000-50,000	15	mostly 6-9am

For Buhshehr (IR17,000 to IR35,000, seven hours) Tavoni 5 has regular departures 8am to 2pm, Seiro Safar at 4pm and 5pm.

Minibuses run regularly to Andimeshk (IR4000, 2½ hours) and more rarely to Shush from a separate nearby yard/terminal that's so well hidden that taxi drivers deny it exists. Dezful minibuses use yet a different yard off Enqelab St (IR4000).

For Abadan and Khorramshahr use the Abadan terminal on Behbahani Hwy, 4km south of Abadan Sq.

The terminal for buses to Shushtar (IR3500, 1½ hours) is halfway to the airport on Pasdaran Blvd, some 3km northeast of Abadan Sq. There are no tickets. Instead your name is written down and there's a roll call when the list is full.

TRAIN
Overnight trains to Tehran leave at 12.30pm (IR16,700, 17½ hours) stopping all stations, 3.40pm (IR30,750 to IR49,300) and 5pm (IR103,400, 15½ hours) air-conditioned.

Getting Around
Shared taxis from Abadan Sq pass within 1km of the airport or pay IR5000 by taxi. Also from Abadan Sq you can reach Abadan terminal by minibus and Shushtar terminal by shared taxi. The handiest shared taxis run from the bus station area, Serah Khorramshahr (Enqelab Sq), to Sa'at Sq (for the train station, IR1000) and on down Narderi (Salman-e-Farsi) St to 'Chahrah' (IR1500) near the flyover at Shari'ati St. To the drivers raising three fingers means 'to Enqelab Sq', four fingers means 'to the centre'.

WESTERN IRAN

Central Iran
ایران مرکزی

CONTENTS

CENTRAL IRAN

Ever since Cyrus the Great's dramatic rise from provincial overlord to ruler of the largest empire on earth, central Iran has been something of a showcase for the region's greatest civilisations. The unrelenting splendour and majesty of Esfahan, the refined elegance of Shiraz and the mud-brick antiquity of Yazd, Abyaneh and Kharanaq are a fascinating contrast representing the fusion over 2500 years of myriad cultures and starkly different terrains. Then, of course, there's that monumental expression of artistic harmony commissioned by Darius I – Persepolis.

With so much on offer, it's no surprise that the towns of Iran's central provinces are where you'll probably spend the most time. But it's not just about ticking off the undoubtedly impressive popular sights. Central Iran has many a hidden gem. Kashan, with its splendid mosques, gardens and magnificently restored traditional houses, is one. And for those prepared to go way off the beaten track, there's Garmeh, the oasis village between the harshest stretches of Iran's two great deserts, the Dasht-e Kavir and the Dasht-e Lut.

Central Iran's people are also surprisingly diverse, from the religious conservatives of Qom to the reform-minded Esfahanis, while Yazdis have long sought to keep the peace in their precarious position at the edge of the desert. Often you will experience the region's cultural richness and physical beauty in combination – sitting in the garden of Hafez's tomb discussing the ways of the world with a Shirazi medical student, perhaps. Or drinking tea with a carpet-weaver in Esfahan's Imam Sq. Whatever it is you happen upon, central Iran is a place you'll remember for a long time.

CENTRAL IRAN

HIGHLIGHTS

- Watch the sun set over Esfahan's many-splendoured **Imam Sq** (p216) from the rooftop **Qeysarieh Tea Shop** (p226)
- Sit on the hill behind the sublime **Persepolis** (p252), just soaking it all up
- Climb the Hosseinieh, or anything else, in **Yazd's old city** (p233) around sunset
- Wander through the charmingly lethargic **bazaar** (p205) at Kashan en route to the city's magnificent **traditional houses** (p205)
- Take the desert detour to a bygone time at the simple, silent **Garmeh** (p229)
- Haggle over a carpet or kilim in the vaulted arcades of Esfahan's **Bazar-e Bozorg** (p215) or **Imam Sq** (p216)
- Treat yourself to a dose of Safavid-era luxury in the wonderfully restored **Caravanserai Zein-o-din** (p240)
- Sleep! Yes, drifting off in history in one of the great old city hotels in Yazd – **Malek-o Tojjar** (p237) is a standout

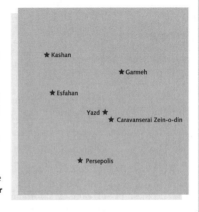

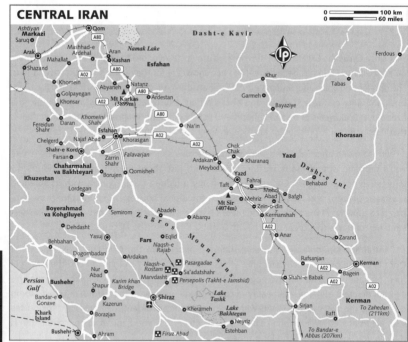

CENTRAL IRAN

QOM   قم

☎ 0251 / pop 270,000

Iran's second-holiest city after Mashhad, Qom (Ghom) is home to both the magnificent Hazrat-e Masumeh shrine and the hardline clerics who have ruled the country since 1980. The genesis of the 1979 revolution can be credited to Qom, from where clerics had railed against the shah's regime since well before Ayatollah Khomeini was exiled from the city in 1964. Today it remains one of the most conservative places in the country. Shiite scholars and students come from across the world to study in the madrasehs of Qom.

Despite the ever-present scaffolding, the shrine is indeed magnificent. Unfortunately, if you don't make fast friends with some pilgrims you'll have to admire it from afar, as non-Muslims are not permitted to enter. Still, if you are not going to Mashhad and have an interest in the devotion that is a hallmark of Shiism, then Qom is worth a visit.

The 'peoplescape' of Qom is absorbing in its contrasts. Mullahs and religious students mix with a steady flow of pilgrims, and everywhere you look women wear the head-to-toe chador. But even Qom is seeing some change, and the odd figure-hugging manteau and made-up face. Still, travellers should be discreet and dress conservatively, particularly around the Hazrat-e Masumeh. The best place to sit and watch all this is at **Astane Sq**, behind the shrine.

Very little English is spoken in Qom. Note too that the tap water is salty – bottled water is readily available.

Orientation

Almost everything is located around the Hazrat-e Masumeh shrine and neighbouring **Qom River**. The 'river', however, is so dry that it has been concreted over and is now used as a car park, market and late-night raceway by some of Qom's more-daring motorcyclists.

Information
INTERNET ACCESS

SabaCenter (☎ 774 8034; Mar'ashi Najafi St; per hr IR5000; ☻ 8am-2am) Fast machines.

Waroone (☎ 774 8853; Mo'allem St; per hr IR8000; ☻ 24hr) Very stylish.

MONEY

Bank Melli (Mar'ashi Najafi St) Slow as a wet week; change money in Tehran or Kashan instead.

Sights

HAZRAT-E MASUMEH

At the physical and spiritual centre of Qom is the **Hazrat-e Masumeh**, the burial place of Imam Reza's sister Fatemeh, who died and was interred here in the 9th century AD. Much of what you see today was built under Shah Abbas I and the other Safavid kings who were anxious to establish their Shiite credentials and provide a counterweight to the sect's shrines at Karbala and Najaf (in modern-day Iraq), then under Ottoman occupation. The magnificent golden cupola of the shrine was an embellishment built by Fath Ali Shah, and today's 'shahs', the Ayatollahs of Qom, have embarked on a massive project to expand the complex.

Unfortunately, if you're not a Muslim you won't be allowed into the complex. If this is the case, the enormous tiled dome and ever-growing number of exquisite minarets can be viewed from outside. However, several readers have reported being escorted around by clerics keen to practise their English.

KHAN-E KHOMEINI

Surprisingly little fanfare surrounds the simple brick former **residence** of Ayatollah Khomeini southeast of Shohada Sq. It was here that Khomeini lived – before being forced

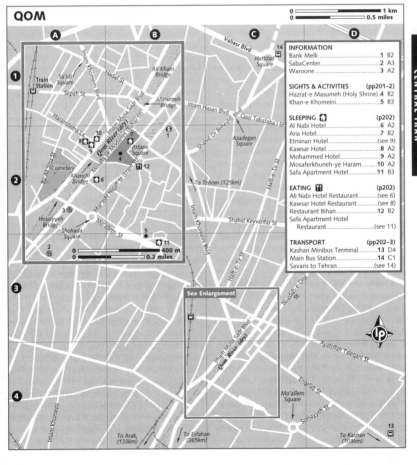

QOM

| 0 | 1 km |
| 0 | 0.5 miles |

INFORMATION
Bank Melli..............................1 B2
SabaCenter...........................2 A3
Waroone................................3 A2

SIGHTS & ACTIVITIES   (pp201–2)
Hazrat-e Masumeh (Holy Shrine)..4 B2
Khan-e Khomeini....................5 B3

SLEEPING 🛏   (p202)
Al Nabi Hotel...........................6 A2
Aria Hotel................................7 B2
Etminan Hotel.....................(see 9)
Kawsar Hotel..........................8 A2
Mohammed Hotel...................9 A2
Mosaferkhuneh-ye Haram........10 A2
Safa Apartment Hotel.............11 B3

EATING 🍴   (p202)
Ali Nabi Hotel Restaurant...........(see 6)
Kawsar Hotel Restaurant...........(see 8)
Restaurant Bihan....................12 B2
Safa Apartment Hotel
   Restaurant...........................(see 11)

TRANSPORT   (pp202–3)
Kashan Minibus Terminal........13 D4
Main Bus Station....................14 C1
Savaris to Tehran..................(see 14)

To Tehran (125km)

To Arak (133km)

To Esfahan (265km)

To Kashan (103km)

into exile – and built his power base among conservative clerics. Apart from the standard mural of him alongside Ali Khamenei, there's little to distinguish this house. It is not open to visitors and is of purely historic appeal.

Sleeping

Safa Apartment Hotel (☎ 773 2499; fax 773 2574; Mo'allem St; d/ste US$30/40; P 🞬) Easily the best in town, the rooms are spotless and have bathroom and satellite TV – top-end quality at mid-range prices. The location's not so central, but it's still an easy walk to the shrine.

Aria Hotel (☎ 774 8450; www.aria-hotel.com; Astane Sq; s/tw/apt US$23/38/70; 🞬 💻) In a super location overlooking Astane Sq, these rooms become very good value in winter, when prices are slashed.

Al Nabi Hotel (☎ 774 4270; fax 774 4600; Bahar St; s/d IR180,000/250,000; 🞬) A stone's throw from the shrine, Al Nabi offers clean, comfortable rooms and friendly service.

Budget travellers should head straight to Haramnema Lane, a small alleyway just north of the Ahanchi Bridge.

Kawsar Hotel (☎ 660 9571; fax 661 8969; Haramnema Ln; r with breakfast IR200,000; 🞬 P) The best option in this part of town, Kawsar's rooms are spacious and comfortable with shower but no toilet. They are better value in winter, when prices fall to IR120,000. The restaurant is not bad.

Etminan Hotel (☎ 664 9640; Haramnema Ln; s/d IR80,000/120,000) These small but functional rooms with bathroom are good value, especially if you want to wake up to a view of the holy shrine. However, the rooms with a view are among the noisiest in Iran, so you're guaranteed to wake early. Guests can use the kitchen.

Mohammed Hotel (☎ 661 4861; hotelmohammad@noavar.com; Haramnema Ln; r per person IR70,000) Next door to Etminan, Mohammed is quieter when it's not full of pilgrim families. Rooms have a simple bathroom.

Mosaferkhuneh-ye Haram (Haramnema Ln; r per person IR45,000) Probably the cheapest and brightest place in town. English isn't spoken here, nor is there an English sign, but there is an especially friendly atmosphere. The rooms are simple, have shared bathrooms and are popular with families. It's a good choice for lone women travellers, and guests can use the kitchen.

If these places are all full, head further down the alley or along Imam Musa Sadr Blvd to the next alley for more budget options. Do not confuse the unfriendly Safa Hotel on Imam Musa Sadr Blvd with the Safa Apartment Hotel.

Eating

Fine dining is not exactly an option in Qom. Hotel restaurants, which are all open for breakfast, lunch and dinner, are probably the best but still have fairly uninspired menus. **Safa Apartment Hotel** (☎ 773 2499; Mo'allem St) is the best, with options such as chicken schnitzel (IR27,000) and, somewhat surprisingly, chelo trout (IR33,000). **Al Nabi Hotel** (☎ 774 4270; Bahar St) and **Kawsar Hotel** (☎ 660 9571; Haramnema Ln) are reasonable, with meals for about IR25,000.

There are plenty of kababis around town and several restaurants on Mar'ashi Najafi St opposite the southeastern entrance to the shrine, of which **Restaurant Bihan** (☎ 774 3433; meals IR26,000; 🕑 11am-3pm, 6.30-11pm) is among the best.

One thing you must try is the sinfully delicious pistachio-and-ginger brittle known as *sohun*, produced locally and available on almost every street in Qom.

Getting There & Away

Travelling to Qom on a Friday, and on any holy day, will mean your transport is packed.

BUS & MINIBUS

Qom's main bus station is comprised of groups of touts and potential passengers milling around the edge of a huge roundabout called Haftdad Sq in the north of town. There is an actual station nearby, but most of the dozens of buses that come through here to or from Tehran don't drive into it. Most services are frequent, and prices on Mercedes buses include: Tehran (IR5000, 1½ hours), Hamadan (IR11,000, five hours), Esfahan (IR14,000, six hours), Kermanshah (IR16,500, eight hours) and Yazd (IR18,500, eight hours) and Shiraz (IR34,000, 13 hours). As many buses are full, competition for seats can be fierce – your best bet is the morning or late afternoon. If you have no luck and are heading anywhere north, just jump on any bus to Tehran and go from there.

For Kashan, most locals use the regular minibuses (IR5000, two hours) from the Terminal-e Kashan at the eastern end of Enqelab St.

SAVARI

Savaris leave from Haftdad Sq, the main bus station and, if you're going to Tehran, from the end of the Ahanchi Bridge opposite the holy shrine. However, this stop is less than official so it's wise to check this before carting your luggage down there.

TRAIN

You'd want to be really keen to use the train from Qom. There are only two services a week to Tehran (2nd class IR3850, 2½ hours), departing at 11.30pm Tuesday and 6.20pm Friday.

Getting Around

Most things to see in Qom are easily reached on foot. To get to or from Haftad Sq or the Terminal-e Kashan, shared taxis run frequently from the corner of Imam Khomeini Blvd and Hadaf St for about IR1000 per person. The whole car should cost about IR5000.

KASHAN   کاشان

☎ 0361 / pop 170,000

Kashan and its surrounds have been home to human settlements since at least the 4th millennium BC. However, much of what is known of Kashan's history is interwoven with legend (see the boxed text 'A Sting in the Tail', below). What *is* known is that Kashan was destroyed at least twice by the inconsiderate hordes of invading armies. The city walls were rebuilt, and it became prominent during the Seljuk period (AD 1051–1220), famous for its textiles, pottery and tiles.

Some of the most impressive surviving architecture is from the Qajar era, when the mansions of the rich and powerful were embellished with incredible stucco panels, coloured glass and lofty *badgirs* (windtowers), all set around a series of interlinked courtyards.

Shah Abbas I was so enamoured with this delightful oasis city on the edge of the Dasht-e Kavir that he insisted on being buried here rather than in Esfahan. Spend a couple of days wandering through the bazaar and pale brown history of the place, and it's easy to see why.

If anything, Kashan is more beautiful today than during Abbas's time. It is home to several of the best traditional houses in the country, some beautiful gardens and various splendid Islamic buildings.

The covered bazaar is deceptively large and has an enchantingly lethargic atmosphere that serves as the perfect counterfoil to the frantic bustle of Tehran and the sightseeing intensity of Esfahan.

While accommodation options are quite limited, you still need a very good excuse for skipping Kashan – it just might well be one of the unexpected highlights of your Iranian trip.

Note that phone numbers were due to be changed in Kashan soon after we visited.

Orientation

The centre of town is **Kamal-ol-Molk Sq**, from where most of Kashan's sites can be reached on foot. For sites along the road to Baghe Tarikhi-ye Fin (Fin Gardens) – variously known as Fin Rd and Amir Kabir Rd – you'll probably need to take a taxi.

A STING IN THE TAIL

While there is no written history of Kashan before the Seljuk period, there is an entertaining oral history. One story has the Bible's 'Three Wise Men' setting out from Kashan to pay their respects to the newborn Christ, an event that is distinctly possible given the 'Wise Men' were almost certainly magis (Zoroastrian priests), hence the 'Adoration of the Magi'.

Another legend tells of Abu Musa al-Ashari's novel method of taking the city during the Arab invasion of the 7th century AD. When the Arab general found the city's walls impregnable, he ordered his men to gather (somehow?) thousands of scorpions from the surrounding deserts. Armed with these stingers, he attacked the city by having them thrown over the walls. According to the tale the poor Kashanis, who could never have expected such a deviously genius attack, soon capitulated.

KASHAN

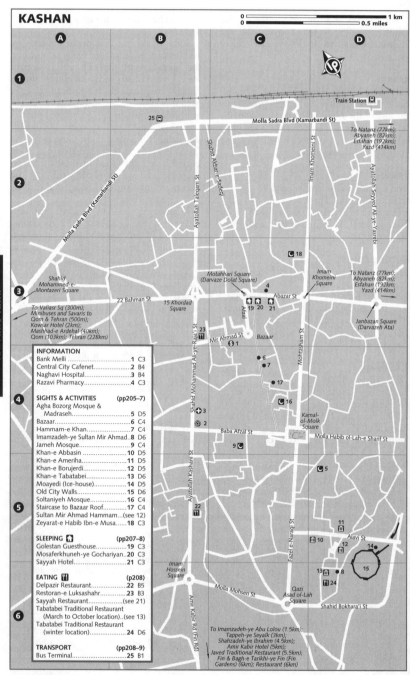

0 _____ 1 km
0 _____ 0.5 miles

Train Station

Molla Sadra Blvd (Kamarbandi St)

To Natanz (77km);
Abyaneh (82km);
Esfahan (192km);
Yazd (414km)

Molla Sadra Blvd (Kamarbandi St)

Shahid
Mohammed-e-
Montazeri Square

To Valiasr Sq (300m);
Minibuses and Savaris to
Qom & Tehran (500m);
Kowsar Hotel (2km);
Mashhad-e Ardehal (40km);
Qom (103km); Tehran (228km)

22 Bahman St

15 Khordad
Square

Motahhari Square
(Darvaze Dolat Square)

Abazar St

Imam
Khomeini
Square

To Natanz (77km);
Abyaneh (82km);
Esfahan (192km);
Yazd (414km)

Janbazan Square
(Darvazeh Ata)

Mir Ahmad St

Bazaar

Baba Afzal St

Kamal-
ol-Molk
Square

Molla Habib ol-Lah-e Sharif St

Imam
Hossein
Square

Alavi St

Molla Mohsen St

Qazi
Asad ol-Lah
Square

Shahid Bokhara'i St

To Imamzadeh-ye Abu Lolou (1.5km);
Tappeh-ye Seyalk (3km);
Shahzadeh-ye Ibrahim (4.5km);
Amir Kabir Hotel (5km);
Javed Traditional Restaurant (5.5km);
Fin & Bagh-e Tarikhi-ye Fin (Fin
Gardens) (6km); Restaurant (6km)

INFORMATION
Bank Melli	1 C3
Central City Cafenet	2 B4
Naghavi Hospital	3 B4
Razavi Pharmacy	4 C3

SIGHTS & ACTIVITIES (pp205–7)
Agha Bozorg Mosque & Madraseh	5 D5
Bazaar	6 C4
Hammam-e Khan	7 C4
Imamzadeh-ye Sultan Mir Ahmad	8 D6
Jameh Mosque	9 C4
Khan-e Abbasin	10 D5
Khan-e Ameriha	11 D5
Khan-e Borujerdi	12 D5
Khan-e Tabatabei	13 D6
Moayedi (Ice-house)	14 D5
Old City Walls	15 D6
Soltaniyeh Mosque	16 C4
Staircase to Bazaar Roof	17 C4
Sultan Mir Ahmad Hammam	(see 12)
Zeyarat-e Habib Ibn-e Musa	18 C3

SLEEPING (pp207–8)
Golestan Guesthouse	19 C3
Mosaferkhuneh-ye Gochariyan	20 C3
Sayyah Hotel	21 C3

EATING (p208)
Delpazir Restaurant	22 B5
Restoran-e Luksashahr	23 B3
Sayyah Restaurant	(see 21)
Tabatabei Traditional Restaurant (March to October location)	(see 13)
Tabatabei Traditional Restaurant (winter location)	24 D6

TRANSPORT (pp208–9)
Bus Terminal	25 B1

Information
EMERGENCY
Naghavi Hospital (☎ 22021; Shahid Mohammad Ali-ye-Raja'i St)
Police (☎ 110)
Razavi Pharmacy (☎ 444 554; Abazar St) Opposite Sayyah Hotel.

INTERNET ACCESS
Central City Cafenet (☎ 0912 261 0911; Shahid Mohammad Ali-ye-Raja'i St; per hr IR20,000; ☺ 8am-11pm)

MONEY
Bank Melli (Mir Ahmad St)

TOURS
Ahmad Pourseyedi (☎ 30321; outside Bagh-e Tarikhi-ye Fin) 'Charming old rogue' is probably the best way to describe English-speaking septuagenarian Ahmad, who makes delightful company as he recalls anecdotes while driving sedately around the Kashani hinterlands. Tours to Abyaneh, with a picnic lunch, cost about IR200,000 for the day. If you can't find him, ask around at Fin Gardens – he lives nearby.

Sights
BAZAAR
Kashan's **bazaar** (☺ Sat-Thu) is one of the most enjoyable in Iran. Busy but not hectic, traditional but with a wide variety of goods, large enough to surprise but not to get lost in, it is a great place to wander for a couple of hours in the morning. The domed roof of the bazaar dates from the 19th century, but the site has been the centre of trade in Kashan for much longer. If you step off the main thoroughfare you'll find yourself in ancient caravanserais, mosques or the refreshingly ramshackle **Hammam-e Khan** (☎ 442 4282; ☺ 9am-9pm), which actually operates as a teahouse and is a great place to stop and meet the locals; it's down a few stairs off the main bazaar (look for the sign).

But the best way to really appreciate the extent of the bazaar is to climb to its roof. There are tiny staircases throughout and it's fun to ask a *bazari* (bazaar shopkeeper) to lead you up. Alternatively, when you reach the open space where a makeshift teahouse sits under a large dome, head for the stairs in the southwestern corner. If the staircase is locked, ask the man selling tea.

TRADITIONAL HOUSES
Hiding behind the very high mud-brick walls of Kashan are hundreds of once-grand traditional houses. Most have long since been carved up or are literally turning to dust, but recently a few have been restored and many others are being slowly and meticulously revived. All four of the houses open to the public at the time of research are on or just off Alavi St in the south of town.

Khan-e Borujerdi
Originally built as a private residence in the early 19th century, the **Khan-e Borujerdi** (adult/student IR20,000/10,000; ☺ 7.30am-dark, until 8pm summer) has a lovely courtyard flanked by summer and winter houses. At the southern end of the courtyard, the splendid motifs above the arched entrance to the summer house indicate this was the home of a rich merchant of handicrafts. The summer guest room has beautiful stalactite work (elaborate stepped mouldings used to decorate recesses), faded murals and sunken doorways, while one of the smaller adjoining rooms has a carpet design carved in relief on the ceiling.

If you ask nicely you might be allowed to climb to the roof for views over the courtyard and the distinctive six-sided domed *badgirs*, for which the house is famous.

To get here, walk east along Alavi St, turn right up a small incline opposite the Khan-e Ameriha and walk about 80m.

Khan-e Tabatabei
Built in 1834 by Seyyed Ja'far Tabatabei, a wealthy carpet merchant, the **Khan-e Tabatabei** (☎ 422 0032; adult/student IR20,000/10,000; ☺ 7.30am-dark, until 8pm summer) is renowned for its intricate relief designs carved into stone, its fine stuccowork and its wonderful mirror and stained-glass work; photographers will love it. All the windows open onto the main courtyard and the house is entirely concealed from the street. Larger than the Borujerdi house, it covers 4700 sq metres, has 40 rooms and over 200 doors. It consists of three sections – the *andaruni* (internal area), where family members lived; the *biruni* (external area), used for entertaining guests; and the *khadameh* (servants' quarters).

From March to October it's worth making the Khan-e Tabatabei your last stop for the day so you can enjoy tea or dinner in Tabatabei Traditional Restaurant, which sets up in the main courtyard from 6pm (p208).

WHO'S THAT KNOCKING AT MY DOOR?

As you wander around the narrow streets of Kashan look carefully at the doors. Most have two knockers, one round and fat, the other long and thin. These were designed to give off different sounds so that whoever was in the house would be able to tell whether a man or woman was knocking and so decide who should open the door to them; vital in a society where women lived in purdah (in seclusion or behind a veil).

To get here, walk south past the Khan-e Borujerdi towards the blue conical tower of the **Imamzadeh-ye Sultan Mir Ahmad**, turn right and walk through the courtyard away from the shrine. As soon as you've left the courtyard, turn left and you've made it. In winter, the teahouse moves to an indoor setting. To reach it, continue past the main entrance and turn left (southeast) and walk about 75m.

Khan-e Ameriha

As the home to Kashan's powerful Qajar-era governor Agha Ameri, it will come as little surprise that the **Khan-e Ameriha** (adult/student IR20,000/10,000; ☉ 7.30am-dark, until 8pm summer) is perhaps the finest of all the traditional houses. Slightly older than the others, it has two exquisitely embellished *hammams* (bathhouses) that Agha Ameri would open to the public at regular intervals. Narrow stairways lead to the undulating roof where photographers will get especially excited looking over the city or down into the courtyards of this house and those of several others being restored nearby; the various *badgirs* and domed vents make a wonderful foreground!

Khan-e Abbasin

Famous for its ground-breaking design, the **Khan-e Abbasin** (adult/student IR20,000/10,000; ☉ 7.30am-dark, until 8pm summer) is a bewildering complex of six buildings spread over several levels. Unusually, the numerous courtyards are designed to enhance the sense of capaciousness by becoming larger as they step up, culminating in an open courtyard on top. The high porticos and reception halls are decorated as extravagantly as you'd expect, with the usual plaster reliefs, fine

mirror work and exceptionally beautiful and detailed stained-glass windows.

SULTAN MIR AHMED HAMMAM

A few metres from the entrance to the Khan-e Borujerdi, **Sultan Mir Ahmad Hammam** (☎ 422 0038; Alavi St; admission IR20,000; ☉ 10am-3pm & 7-11pm) is a superb example of an Iranian bathhouse, though sadly it's no longer used for that purpose. Instead, in order to see the glorious tile and low-relief plasterwork that adorns the walls and vaulted ceilings you must pay to enter what is an atmospheric but expensive teahouse. If you have tea and a qalyan the manager might drop the cover charge.

OLD CITY WALLS

As one of the few remnants of the ancient city of Kashan, these walls are worth a quick look if you're visiting the traditional houses in the area.

AGHA BOZORG MOSQUE & MADRASEH

Arguably the finest Islamic complex in Kashan, the **Agha Bozorg Mosque & Madraseh** (admission IR25,000; ☉ 8am-noon & 2-4pm Sat-Thu, until 5pm summer) was built in the 19th century and is famous for its austere dome and large sunken courtyard. It also has a fine portal and mihrab (niche indicating the direction of Mecca) at the back. The imposing dome is flanked by two squat minarets adorned with beautiful tiles and geometric designs. The fine Quranic inscriptions and mosaics throughout stand out against the sand-coloured brick used for much of the construction. The wooden door at the entrance is said to have as many studs as there are verses in the Quran. Above the entrance are, unusually, two four-sided *badgirs*.

ZEYARAT-E HABIB IBN-E MUSA

The revered Shah Abbas I would be disappointed with the comparative size of his unimpressive tomb, the **Zeyarat-e Habib Ibn-e Musa** (Imam Khomeini St). For all his empire-building efforts, surely Abbas deserves better. Admittedly, the building is getting a face-lift and should be impressive once finished.

SOLTANIYEH MOSQUE

Lost in the midst of the labyrinthine bazaar is the **Soltaniyeh Mosque**, dating back to the Seljuk period. The current structure was built in 1808 by Fath Ali Shah and now houses a madraseh, which is not open to women.

IMAMZADEH-YE ABU LOLOU

Just off the the road from Kashan to Fin, **Imamzadeh-ye Abu Lolou** (Amir Kabir Rd; ☉ 9am-4pm) probably dates back to the Mongol period, although it has been heavily renovated many times since. The shrine is notable for its fine, slender dome and is visible from the road.

SHAHZADEH-YE IBRAHIM

The delightful **Shahzadeh-ye Ibrahim** (Amir Kabir Rd; ☉ 9am-4pm) shrine was built in 1894 and boasts beautiful tiles, two colourful minarets and a pretty courtyard. The conical, tiled roof over the dome is distinctive to this part of the country and chances are you'll have seen it on posters long before you arrive. It's clearly visible from the main road to Fin. Although chartering a taxi in combination with a visit to the gardens at Fin is the easiest way to get here, it's easy to use the minibuses that service this road.

TAPPEH-YE SEYALK (SIALK)

This is one of the oldest and richest archaeological sites uncovered so far in central Iran, the **Tappeh-ye Seyalk** (Sialk, Seyalk Mound; off Amir Kabir Rd; ☉ 8am-3pm Sat-Thu) has given up a plethora of interesting pottery, metal tools and domestic implements made from stone, clay and bone dating from as early as the 4th millennium BC. More significantly, perhaps, is the structure itself – what is emerging from the dust is clearly a ziggurat, and some Iranians are claiming this predates those of the Mesopotamians.

It is still a working dig and while visitors are welcomed, there are few facilities. Most finds have been moved to various institutes and museums, including the National Museum of Iran in Tehran (p93) and the Louvre in Paris. There's no charge, but if you are shown around a tip is appreciated.

Seyalk is 4.5km to the northwest of Fin, on the northern side of the road from Kashan.

BAGH-E TARIKHI-YE FIN

Designed for Shah Abbas I, **Bagh-e Tarikhi-ye Fin** (Fin Garden; Amir Kabir Rd; admission IR30,000; ☉ 8am-5pm, until 7pm summer) is a classical Persian vision of paradise. It has always been prized for its natural springs, which flow into several pools and water the garden's orchards. The garden contains the remains Abbas' two-storey palace and other Safavid royal buildings, though they have been substantially rebuilt. Others were added in the Qajar period.

Perhaps the most interesting thing to see in the gardens is the bathhouse in which Iranian nationalist hero Amir Kabir was murdered. Amir Kabir served as prime minister under Nadir al-Din from 1848 until his untimely end in 1851. He is remembered as a moderniser who instituted significant change, especially in the fields of education and administration. However, his popularity proved unpopular in the royal court, and the shah's mother eventually persuaded her son that he had to go. He was imprisoned in the Bagh-e Tarikhi-ye Fin and, having been presented with a fait accompli, was asked to choose how he wanted to die. Amir Kabir is believed to have opted to slash his wrists, but the reconstruction you see in the bathhouse seems to show him sitting back calmly while the villain is about to plunge the knife into his wrist. The bathhouse is not always open and if you find the doors closed it's well worth asking someone to open them.

There is also a mildly interesting museum containing archaeological items from Tappeh-ye Seyalk and Choqa Zanbil – though it's not worth the additional IR10,000 entrance fee – and a picturesque teahouse.

The gardens are in the village of Fin about 8km southwest of central Kashan at the end of Amir Kabir St. You can get here by shared taxi (IR1000), private taxi (IR5000) or minibus (IR350) from central Kashan.

Sleeping

The cheapest of Kashan's few sleeping options can be found around Motahhari Sq (Darvaze Dolat Sq) near the entrance to the bazaar.

Golestan Guesthouse (☎ 446 793; Motahhari Sq; s/d IR50,000/80,000) The friendly and helpful owner and his son, who both speak some English, make this the best of the cheapies. The small rooms are clean and some have vaulted ceilings and windows looking down on the bazaar. The shared bathrooms are adequate, but if you like soft beds, look elsewhere.

Mosaferkhuneh-ye Gochariyan (☎ 445 495; Abazar St; s/d IR50,000/80,000) Between Sayyah

Hotel and the bazaar entrance, there's little English spoken at Gochariyan and the rooms are even simpler than those at Golestan Guesthouse.

Kowsar Hotel (☎ 560 322; fax 560 323; Qotb-e Ravandy Blvd; apt IR450,000; P 🞈) This new apartment hotel offers the best-equipped and most comfortable rooms in town – you'd need a basketball team to fill the beds in each apartment. Unfortunately, it's 3km west of town on the road to Tehran. Prices are very negotiable.

Sayyah Hotel (☎ 444 535; www.sayyahhotel.com; Abazar St; s/d with breakfast US$20/25; r without shower US$15; P 🞈) Sayyah is well located and has pleasant, if rather small, rooms with fridge and TV. Some readers have found the service less than enthusiastic.

Amir Kabir Hotel (☎ 30091; fax 30338; Amir Kabir Rd; s/tw US$35/53; P 🞈) Way out near Fin Gardens, this hotel has pretensions to luxury but the rooms are ageing badly and overpriced; even the most timid should have no trouble knocking down the price here. Minibuses to town run past the front door (IR250) or a taxi will cost about IR5000.

The management of the Delpazir Restaurant (below) was planning to open a mid-range hotel; it might be worth asking about it.

Eating

Delpazir Restaurant (☎ 455 322, 0913 161 0350; Ayatollah Kashani St; meals IR40,000; 🕓 lunch & dinner) Delpazir's reputation as the best place to eat in Kashan is well founded. It has one of the most extensive and varied menus in Iran, with starters including the light but tasty *bademjun* (eggplant served in various styles). The excellent main dishes include three types of *khoresht* (any kind of thick, meaty stew made with vegetables and chopped nuts and served with rice), steak and kebabs, and this is one of the best places in Iran to try *fesenjun* (a sauce of pomegranate juice, walnuts, eggplant and cardamom served over roast chicken and rice). There's also 'a selection of dishes' for vegetarians. Delpazir is managed by Englishwoman Jane Modarresian, who is happy to swap any novels you've finished with and can organise tours of the surrounding area.

Restoran-e Luksashahr (☎ 454 745; Shahid Mohammad Ali-ye-Raja'i St; meals IR30,000; 🕓 noon-midnight) Luksashahr is popular with locals. It serves pizzas (about IR18,000) and the usual kebabs as well as a few dishes that sound vaguely familiar, including 'kentaki chicken'.

Tabatabei Traditional Restaurant (☎ 422 6106; Khan-e Tabatabei; meals IR30,000; 🕓 6-11pm) Sitting in the courtyards of this wonderful house as the sun goes down, the stars come up and water bubbles out of the fountains will give you a pretty good idea of how rich Kashanis lived 200 years ago. And it ain't bad. The food is cheap but OK, with *dizi* (a soup-stew combination) just IR10,000. During winter, the restaurant moves indoors.

Javed Traditional Restaurant (Amir Kabir Rd; meals IR40,000; 🕓 6pm-midnight) This is one of several garden restaurants in the kilometre before Bagh-e Tarikhi-ye Fin. Water from the spring runs through the middle of the eating area – very soothing, especially in summer. Meals here consist mainly of kebabs, one of which resembles King Arthur's longsword jam-packed with lamb.

Sayyah Restaurant (☎ 444 535; Abazar St; meals IR25,000; 🕓 7am-9pm) Attached to the hotel of the same name. It's had mixed reviews, but none of them has criticised the size of the meals.

There are also several kababis along Abazar St.

Getting There & Away
BUS, MINIBUS & SAVARI
As with Qom, most buses that pass through Kashan are going to or from Tehran. Buses usually stop at the new **bus terminal** (Molla Sadra Blvd) north of the city centre and go regularly to Esfahan (IR8000, 4½ hours) and Tehran (IR8000, 3½ hours). You'll also find frequent services to Yazd, and most buses to Esfahan go through Natanz.

Minibuses to Qom (IR5000, two hours) leave from the southwestern corner of Valiasr Sq (Madkhal Sq, it's the one with the new-age ziggurat in the middle) about every hour. You might also find savaris to Tehran here.

TRAIN
There are three trains a day between Kashan and Tehran (IR13,500, 3½ hours, 217km), but they generally pass through here in the middle of the night.

There are also daily trains to Esfahan (four hours, 270km) Yazd (six hours, 475km) and Kerman (10 hours, 711km), but all leave between about midnight and 3am. Mercifully, the daily train to Bandar-e Abbas (19 hours) passes through Kashan at about 7.30pm, *in sha'Allah* (if God wills it).

The **train station** (☎ 460010) is within walking distance of the city centre, to the north.

Getting Around

A shared taxi from the centre of town to Bagh-e Tarikhi-ye Fin costs IR2000, or if you go *dar baste* (closed door) it will cost about IR8000. Cheaper is the minibus that runs at regular intervals between 15 Khordad Sq and the gardens (IR250, 20 minutes).

Shared taxis run from 15 Khordad Sq to the bus terminal for about IR800.

AROUND KASHAN
Mashhad-e Ardehal   مشهد اردهال

About 40km west of Kashan is a magnificent **Seljuk tomb**. It has two courtyards and two balconies, built for Ali ibn Mohammed Bagar on the slope of a hill. The village of Ardehal (more often called Mashhad by the locals) is famous for its annual carpet-washing ceremony.

Abyaneh   ابیانه
☎ 0362

One of the most fascinating villages in the country has to be Abyaneh. Its twisting, climbing lanes of mud and stone pass predominantly ochre-coloured houses with lattice windows and fragile wooden balconies. There are some magnificent views across the valley. Recognised by Unesco for its antiquity and uniqueness, the village provides the perfect antidote to the bustling cities – there are barely any cars.

Serenely situated at the foot of **Mt Karkas** (3899m), Abyaneh is cool in summer and frightfully cold for the rest of the year. The village faces east for maximum sun and was built high to minimise the effects of floods and howling gales in winter. The houses were built in a huddle to increase their security against frequent raids by marauders and are on the rocks rather than on valuable farmland. Most of the homes were built from mud brick and clay and many lanes and the front yards of some homes are built on the roofs of homes below.

Although Abyaneh is best appreciated by just wandering, look for the 14th-century **Imamzadeh-ye Yahya** with its conical, blue-tiled roof, and the **Zeyaratgah shrine** with its tiny pool and views of the village. Probably the most beautiful building is the 14th-century **Jameh Mosque** with its walnut-wood mihrab and ancient carvings. On top of the rocky hills are the remains of a couple of **castles**. By following the steep paths between the houses up the hillside, it is possible to reach one of these small castles, which have spectacular views onto the town and across the valley – a great place for a picnic.

SLEEPING & EATING

Abyaneh Hotel Restaurant (☎ 436 2223; bed per person with breakfast US$20; meals IR40,000; P   ✗) There's only one hotel and restaurant in Abyaneh, and this is it. Located on a bend in the road as you come downhill into Abyaneh, it's a work in progress, and while Abyaneh village would be a great place to chill out for a night or two, the four- or six-bed rooms were not worth the money when we visited. Better rooms were, however, due to open imminently. Bargain hard. The restaurant is huge and fairly quiet apart from in summer. There are no set meal times. The *fesenjun* (IR23,000) is not bad.

GETTING THERE & AWAY

Abyaneh is 82km from Kashan, and not easy to reach. The cheapest way is to take a regular minibus from Kashan towards Natanz (make

---

THE CARPET-WASHING CEREMONY OF ARDEHAL

In the first week of October every year, the *qali shuran* is held at Ardehal. Dating from about 1200 years ago, the ceremony commemorates the legend of an imam's son from the holy city of Medina. The imam's son, who lived in Ardehal, had a premonition in his sleep that a local governor planned to assassinate him. He and his supporters thwarted the initial assassination attempt, but he was later killed while praying on a mat. His followers placed the body on the carpet, and washed it in accordance with tradition before burying him.

On the anniversary of his murder, thousands of locals, joined by visitors from Kashan, Qom and as far away as Yazd, carry the same carpet (or what's left of it) from the shrine, beat it to symbolise their hatred of the murderers, and then wash it in a local stream.

sure the bus is not taking the road to Na'in) and get off at the signposted turn-off. Then wait for another lift from whatever is passing for the remaining 22km. There are allegedly minibuses (IR5000) running directly between Abyaneh and Kashan, but even the locals don't know what times they leave (your best bet is the afternoon). Or you could always try hitching from outside the hotel.

Alternatively, chartering a taxi for a day from Kashan should cost about IR170,000, or IR120,000 for half a day. Ahmad Pourseyedi is a good option – see Tours (p205). If you're in your own transport or cycling, be sure not to loiter too long around the military facility you'll see about halfway there. It's apparently part of Iran's nuclear program and foreign visitors aren't welcome.

Natanz نطنز

☎ 0362 424

The attractive town of Natanz, on the lower slopes of Mt Karkas, is a good place to chill out in a place unused to tourists. Its two main attractions, the **Jameh Mosque** (admission IR10,000; 8am-noon & 2-5pm, until 7pm summer) and **Imamzadeh-ye Abd al-Samad**, are next to each other in what was an important early Islamic complex. The tomb belongs to a renowned local Sufi mystic of the 11th century; the mosque is believed to date from the early 14th century. The beautiful portal of the (now closed) shrine has some unusual turquoise ceramics and sparing use of calligraphy while the entrance to the mosque has an intricately carved wooden door.

Hotel Saraban (☎ 2603; fax 2602; r US$30; P) This is Natanz's only accommodation and when we passed it was quieter than a small-town mortuary. The rooms are pleasant enough, with bathroom, fridge and balcony, but the pursuit of a lower (and fairer) price will likely be exhausting. There's a restaurant in the hotel, and others nearby. The hotel is on the main road into town from Esfahan, on the left.

Most buses between Esfahan (IR5000, two hours) and Kashan (IR3000, one hour) pass through Natanz – wait outside the hotel.

ESFAHAN اصفهان

☎ 031 / pop 1,598,000

Esfahan is Iran's masterpiece, the jewel of ancient Persia and one of the finest cities in the Islamic world. The exquisite blue mosaic tiles of Esfahan's Islamic buildings, its expansive bazaar and it's gorgeous bridges demand as much of your time as you can spare. It's a city for walking, getting lost in the bazaar, dozing in beautiful gardens, and drinking tea and chatting to locals in the marvellous teahouses. More than anything else, though, Esfahan is a place for savouring the high refinements of Persian culture most evident in and around Imam Sq – the Imam Mosque, Sheikh Lotfollah Mosque, Ali Qapu Palace and Chehel Sotun Palace. Such is Esfahan's grandeur that it is easy to agree with the famous 16th-century half-rhyme *Esfahan nesf-e jahan* (Esfahan is half the world). Robert Byron was slightly more geographically specific when he ranked 'Isfahan among those rarer places,

ESFAHAN IN...

Two days

Start by taking the '**Half the World' Walking Tour** (p222), which should take up most of your first day. On the second day, head back to **Imam Sq** (p216) in the morning for a more leisurely look around and to suss out the **carpet shops** (p226) for something that might look good on your floor (or wall). After lunch at a place you didn't eat at last night, wander down to the **Zayandeh River** (p220) for a bridge-appreciation walk, stopping for tea and qalyan in the bridges as you go.

Four days

On the third day, take the bus out to **Manar Jomban** (Shaking Minarets; p221), then walk up to the **Ateshkadeh-ye Esfahan** (p221) for a (hopefully clear) view over Esfahan. Walk back into town along the riverbank, watching the clothmakers drying their wares on the riverbed and stopping for tea with the locals. Get back to **Jolfa** (p220) in time to see the striking frescoes of **Vank Cathedral** (p220), then spend the evening eating in the Armenian quarter.

On day four, just chill out in the square, on a bridge, in the garden around the **Hasht Behesht Palace** (p219) or in your favourite teahouse with a book, or renew your visa.

like Athens or Rome, which are the common refreshment of humanity'.

That said, there is quite a lot of heavy industry on the outskirts, and the city also suffers that problem felt by 'half the world' – air pollution and traffic congestion.

History

Esfahan did not rise to national prominence until the early 1500s when the first rulers of the Safavid dynasty drove the Mongols from the country. When Shah Abbas I (also revered as Shah Abbas the Great) came to power in 1587, he extended his influence over rivals within the country and then pushed out the Ottoman Turks who had occupied a large part of Persia. With his country once more united and free from foreign influence, Shah Abbas I set out to make Esfahan a great city. However, its period of glory lasted little more than a century. An invasion from Afghanistan hastened the decline and the capital was subsequently transferred to Shiraz and later Tehran.

The power and breadth of Shah Abbas' vision is still very much in evidence. During his rule, Esfahan produced some of the most beautiful and inspiring architecture, art and carpets seen anywhere in the world.

Orientation

The main street, Chahar Bagh (Four Gardens), was built in 1597, and was once lined with many palaces. Although it's over 5km long, most travellers base themselves along the middle section of the street, called Chahar Bagh Abbasi St, between Si-o-Seh Bridge (Pol-e Si-o-Se) and Takhti Junction. Most of the sights, shops, offices and hotels are within easy walking distance from this part of Esfahan and it's a pleasure to wander along the tree-lined avenues; Chahar Bagh Abbasi St has a pedestrian boulevard in the middle of the road. The few outlying attractions are easily visited by shared or private taxi.

The Zayandeh River starts in the Zagros Mountains, flows from west to east through the heart of Esfahan, and then peters out in the Dasht-e Kavir. It separates the older and low-rise northern part of the city from the Armenian quarter in Jolfa, southwest of Si-o-Seh Bridge, and the fast-growing southern part of town.

For details on how to get to/from the airport, see p228.

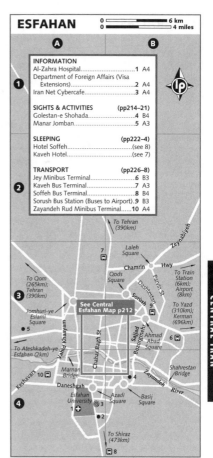

ESFAHAN

0 — 6 km
0 — 4 miles

INFORMATION
Al-Zahra Hospital..............................1 A4
Department of Foreign Affairs (Visa
  Extensions)...................................2 A4
Iran Net Cybercafe...........................3 A4

SIGHTS & ACTIVITIES   (pp214–21)
Golestan-e Shohada.........................4 B4
Manar Jomban..................................5 A3

SLEEPING   (pp222–4)
Hotel Soffeh..................................(see 8)
Kaveh Hotel..................................(see 7)

TRANSPORT   (pp226–8)
Jey Minibus Terminal.........................6 B3
Kaveh Bus Terminal..........................7 A3
Soffeh Bus Terminal.........................8 B4
Sorush Bus Station (Buses to Airport).9 B3
Zayandeh Rud Minibus Terminal......10 A4

MAPS

A large, unwieldy but largely accurate map of Esfahan from Gita Shenasi is available in bookstores for IR7000. The **Tourist Information Office** (Map p216; ☎ 222 8541; Imam Sq) produces a basic but useful map with descriptions of the city's highlights in English, French, German, Italian and Spanish.

Information
BOOKSHOPS

Chehel Sotun Palace Bookshop (Map pp212-13; Ostandari St) Decent range of books, and great posters!
Kowsar International Hotel (Map pp212-13; ☎ 624 0230; Mellat Blvd) In the foyer.
Naqshe Jahan Bookshop (Map p216; ☎ 0931 310 7901; Imam Sq; ☽ 9.30am-1.30pm & 4.30-9.30pm) A few

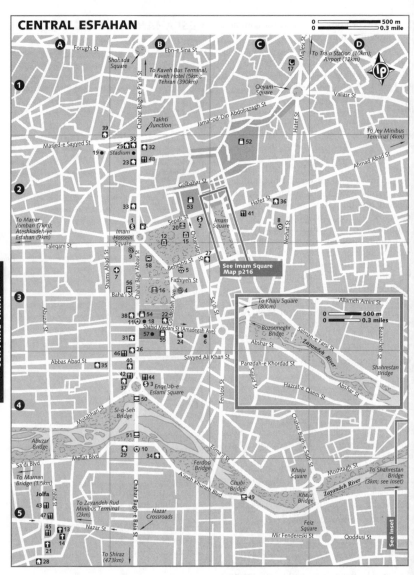

CENTRAL ESFAHAN

0 — 500 m
0 — 0.3 mile

Forughi St

Shohada Square

Ebn-e Sina St

To Train Station (10km); Airport (12km)

Qeyam Square

Valiasr St

Chahar Bagh-e Palm St

To Kaveh Bus Terminal, Kaveh Hotel (5km); Tehran (390km)

Takhti Junction

Jamal-od-Din Abdolrazagh St

To Jey Minibus Terminal (4km)

Masjed-e Sayyed St

Stadium

Ahmad Abad St

To Manar Jomban (7km); Ateshkadeh-ye Esfahan (9km)

Talegani St

Shams Abad Blvd

Chahar Bagh Abbasi St

Imam Hossein Square

Golbahar St

Sepah St

Imam Square

See Imam Square Map p216

Hafez St

Neshat St

Oktari St

Benebshi St

Fathiyeh St

Sa'di St

Baha'i St

To Khaju Square (800km)

Allameh Amini St

0 — 500 m
0 — 0.3 miles

Bozorgmehr Bridge

Salman-e Farsi St

Zayandeh River

Abshar St

Sheikh Sadaqa

Golzesteh Ave

Shabid Medani St (Amadegah Ave)

Panzdeh-e Khordad St

Shahrestan Bridge

Abshar St

Sayyed Ali Khan St

Hazrat-e Qaem St

Abbas Abad St

Enqelab-e Eslami Square

Ferdosi St

Motahhari St

Si-o-Seh Bridge

Abuzar Bridge

Mellat Blvd

Sa'di Blvd

To Marnan Bridge (1.5km)

Jolfa

Chahar Bagh-e Baia St

To Zayandeh Rud Minibus Terminal (2km)

Nazar Crossroads

Nazar St

To Shiraz (473km)

Ferdosi Bridge

A'ineh Khuneh Blvd

Chubi Bridge

Esma'il St

Chahar Bagh-e Sadr St

Khaju Square

Khaju Bridge

Zayandeh River

Moshtagh St

To Shahrestan Bridge (3km; see inset)

Feiz Square

Mir Fendereski St

Qoddusi St

See Inset

---

doors north of Ali Qapu Palace, with Esfahan's best range of English-language books and postcards.

EMERGENCY
Ambulance (☎ 229 2222 or 115)
Tourist Police (24hr ☎ 668 0046/7) English-speaking officers can be found at the booths in the middle of the following streets: Chahar Bagh-e Abbasi St (Map pp212-13; outside the Madraseh-ye Chahar Bagh; ☎ 221 5983); Chahar Bagh-e Baia St (Map pp212-13; southern end of the Si-o-Seh Bridge).

INTERNET ACCESS
Esfahan's coffeenets seem to open and close faster than the door of a filthy squat toilet. The pokey places around Enqelab-e Eslami Sq are slow. More-established coffeenets include:

Central Library of Esfahan (Map pp212-13; ☎ 222 3698; Goldasteh Ave; per hr IR5000; ⏰ 8am-8pm Sat-Thu) Friendly, English-speaking staff and loads of fast terminals.

Iran Net Cybercafe (Map p211; ☎ 668 1868; Chahar Bagh-e Baia St; per hr IR9000; ⏰ 9am-9pm) Opposite Esfahan University.

Rose Internet (Map pp212-13; ☎ 221 1222; Imam Hossein Sq; per hr IR10,000; ⏰ 9am-9pm) Right on the corner and up the stairs.

Several carpet shops around Imam Sq will let you check your email for nothing more than the opportunity to bend your ear about carpets and kilims; the best of these are **Nomad Carpet Shop** (Map p216; ☎ 221 9275; Imam Sq) and **Aladdin Carpets** (Map p216; ☎ 221 1461).

MEDICAL SERVICES

Al-Zahra Hospital (Map p211; ☎ 669 2180; Soffeh St) Best hospital in Esfahan, but not that central. English-speaking doctors.

Dr Hosseini Pharmacy (Map pp212-13; ☎ 222 3511; Shahid Madani St; ⏰ 24hr) Central and well stocked.

Esfahan Hospital (Map pp212-13; ☎ 223 0015; Shams Abadi) Convenient and recommended.

MONEY

The following central bank branches will change money. Many hotels and shops (particularly those around Imam Sq) will also gladly change money.

Bank Mellat (Map pp212-13; Imam Hossein Sq)

Bank Melli (Map pp212-13; Sepah St) In an office upstairs. English is spoken.

Bank Tejarat (Map pp212-13; Enqelab-e Eslami Sq)

POST

DHL (Map pp212-13; ☎ 222 4568; Shahid Medani Ave; ⏰ 8am-5pm Sat-Wed, 8am-1pm Thu) Upstairs in the complex opposite Abbasi Hotel.

Main Post Office (Map pp212-13; Neshat St) East of Imam Sq, come to this post office if you're trying to post anything big – like a carpet.

Post Office (Map pp212-13; Imam Sq) For postcards and the like, try here or the post office on Enqelab-e Eslami Sq.

TELEPHONE

Central Telephone Office (Map pp212-13; Beheshti St; ⏰ 24hr)

TOURIST INFORMATION

Tourist Information Office (Map p216; ☎ 222 8541; fax 661 8660; Imam Sq; ⏰ 8am-noon & 5-7pm) Under the Ali Qapu Palace, the helpful English-speaking staff have maps and can arrange guides in several languages for about IR120,000.

TOURS

Few travel agencies offer tours in and around Esfahan for budget travellers, possibly because many carpet shops and hotels offer these services. Among these, the following have been recommended by readers. They can all arrange overnight trips to nomad communities in the surrounding countryside (spring and autumn are the best times).

Aladdin Carpets (Map p216; Imam Sq; ☎ 221 1461)

Amir Kabir Hostel (Map pp212-13; Chahar Bagh Abbasi St; ☎ 222 7273; mrziaee@hotmail.com)

Nomad Carpet Shop (Map p216; ☎ 221 9275; nomadshop@yahoo.com)

TRAVEL AGENCIES
Iran Travel & Tourism Tour (Map pp212-13; ☎ 222 3010; irantravel1964@hotmail.com; Shahid Medani St) Found opposite Abbasi Hotel, this efficient agency has some English-speaking staff and can book tickets for international and domestic flights, local trains and even Persian Gulf ferries. Local tours and car hire can be arranged (per day with driver and guide IR280,000). It represents the Touring & Automobile Club of Iran.

VISA EXTENSIONS
Esfahan is the best place in Iran to get your visa extended. The **Department of Foreign Affairs office** (Map p211; ☎ 668 8166; Chahar Bagh-e Baia, 2nd Lane; ☉ 7am-1.30pm Sat-Wed, 7am-noon Thu) is located down a lane and usually looks rather daunting with all those people milling around. Enter and head to the office with the words 'Department of Foreign Affairs' on the glass. The friendly staff (who appreciate your English-language magazines) will even take your money – no need to queue at Bank Melli. As a result, the visa is issued almost immediately; in our case, it took just 10 minutes. To get here take a shared taxi south from the southern end of Si-o-Seh Bridge (IR1500) and start looking for a pedestrian overpass once you pass the enormous Azadi Sq roundabout – 2nd Lane is 50m south of this overpass. For details on extending visas, see the boxed text 'More Time, Please' (p362).

Dangers & Annoyances
After countless scams involving bogus police who rob unsuspecting tourists, Esfahan's real police have cracked down and many of the pretenders have apparently found themselves a cell in the big house. Unfortunately, the occasional tourist is still stung, so be aware (see Scams, p346). If you are targeted, ignore the 'police' and contact the Tourist Police (see Emergency, p212).

You are far more likely, however, to be annoyed by touts in Imam Sq. There's no real danger here beyond you buying something you don't want. These guys are pretty soft-core on the world tout scale. They will take no for an answer.

Sights
These sights are listed roughly in order of north to south.

JAMEH MOSQUE
A veritable museum of Islamic architecture. Within a couple of hours at the **Jameh Mosque** (Masjed-e Jameh or Friday Mosque; Map p215; admission IR30,000; ☉ 8-11am & 1.15-4.30pm, 8am-noon & 2-6pm summer) you can see and compare 800 years of Islamic design, with each example near to the pinnacle of its age. The range is quite stunning: from the understated elegance of the Seljuks, through the Mongol period and on to the refinements of the more baroque Safavid style. Although more sober in its decorations than the Imam Mosque or Sheikh Lotfollah Mosque, the Jameh Mosque provides a fascinating bridge between some of the most important periods of Persian history. At more than 20,000 sq metres, it is also the biggest mosque in Iran.

Religious activity on this site is believed to date back to the Sassanid Zoroastrians, and the first sizable mosque was built by the Seljuks in the 11th century. Of this, the two large domes above the north and south *iwans* (rectangular halls opening onto a courtyard) have survived intact, with most of the remainder destroyed by fire in the 12th century. The mosque was rebuilt in 1121, with later rulers making their own enhancements.

In the centre of the main courtyard, which is surrounded by four contrasting *iwans*, is an attractive **ablutions fountain** designed to imitate the Kaaba at Mecca; would-be haj pilgrims would use it to practise the appropriate rituals. The two-storey porches around the courtyard's perimeter were constructed in the late 15th century.

The **south iwan** is the most elaborate, with Mongol-era stalactite mouldings, some splendid 15th-century mosaics on the side walls, and two minarets. The **north iwan** has a wonderful monumental porch with the Seljuk's customary Kufic inscriptions and austere brick pillars in the sanctuary.

On the western side of the courtyard, the **west iwan** was originally built by the Seljuks but later decorated by the Safavids. It has mosaics that are more geometric than those of the southern hall. The courtyard is topped by a *maazeneh*, a small raised platform with a conical roof from where the faithful used to be called to prayer.

To fully appreciate this mosque you must go into the fine interior rooms. The **Room of Sultan Uljaitu** (a 14th-century Shiite convert)

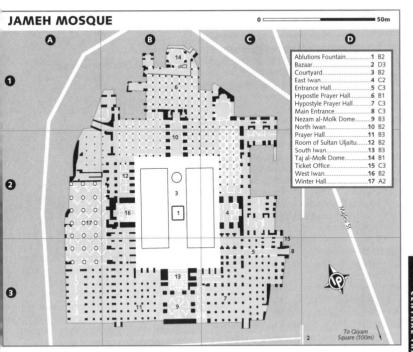

JAMEH MOSQUE

0 _____ 50m

Ablutions Fountain	1 B2
Bazaar	2 D3
Courtyard	3 B2
East Iwan	4 C2
Entrance Hall	5 C3
Hypostle Prayer Hall	6 B1
Hypostyle Prayer Hall	7 C3
Main Entrance	8 C3
Nezam al-Molk Dome	9 B3
North Iwan	10 B2
Prayer Hall	11 B3
Room of Sultan Uljaitu	12 B2
South Iwan	13 B3
Taj al-Molk Dome	14 B1
Ticket Office	15 C3
West Iwan	16 B2
Winter Hall	17 A2

Majlesi St

To Qiyam
Square (100m)

is home to one of the mosque's greatest treasures – an exquisite stucco mihrab awash with dense Quranic inscriptions and floral designs. Next door is the Timurid-era **Winter Hall** (Beit al-Sheta) built in 1448 and lit by alabaster skylights, though the excessive neon spoils the effect.

The room beneath the grand **Nezam al-Molk Dome** and the Seljuk-era hypostyle **prayer halls** either side just breathe history, while at the other end of the complex the **Taj al-Molk Dome** is widely considered to be the finest brick dome ever built. While relatively small, it is said to be mathematically perfect, and has survived dozens of earthquakes with nary a blemish for more than 900 years. To reach it you walk through a forest of imposing pillars. These domes are among the oldest parts of the mosque.

If you don't want to buy a ticket, come during the lunch hours and you'll be able to wander around the courtyard without problem. However, if you want to see the interior rooms, go to the **ticket office** at the **main entrance** and once you've paid admission the gatekeeper will summon an English-speaking guide to show you around. It's worth paying, because the rooms at the northern and southern end of the complex are quite breathtaking.

BAZAR-E BOZORG

Esfahan's **Bazar-e Bozorg** (Great Bazaar; Map pp212-13; ☸ Sat-Thu) is one of the highlights of Esfahan, linking Imam Sq with the Jameh Mosque, several kilometres away. The covered bazaar, one of the largest and most labyrinthine in the country, was mostly built during the early 16th century, although some of it dates back almost 1300 years.

The bazaar can be entered at dozens of points along its winding route, but the main entrance is via the **Qeysarieh Portal** at the northern end of Imam Sq. The high gateway is decorated with tiles and, higher up, frescoes by the great Reza Abbasi, depicting Shah Abbas' war with the Uzbeks. These paintings have deteriorated over the centuries and were being restored when we passed.

In the bazaar itself, the distinctive domed and vaulted ceilings usually culminate in an opening, sometimes star-shaped, allowing

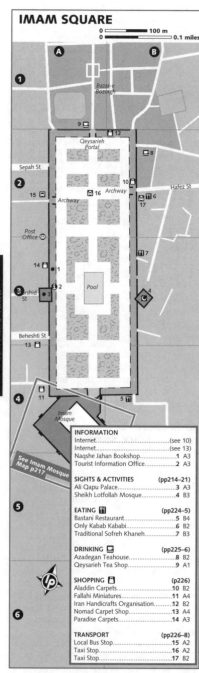

IMAM SQUARE

INFORMATION
Internet	(see 10)
Internet	(see 13)
Naqshe Jahan Bookshop	1 A3
Tourist Information Office	2 A3

SIGHTS & ACTIVITIES (pp214–21)
Ali Qapu Palace	3 A3
Sheikh Lotfollah Mosque	4 B3

EATING 🍴 (pp224–5)
Bastani Restaurant	5 B4
Only Kabab Kababi	6 B2
Traditional Sofreh Khaneh	7 B3

DRINKING 🍷 (pp225–6)
Azadegan Teahouse	8 B2
Qeysarieh Tea Shop	9 A1

SHOPPING 🛍️ (p226)
Aladdin Carpets	10 B2
Fallahi Miniatures	11 A4
Iran Handicrafts Organisation	12 B2
Nomad Carpet Shop	13 A4
Paradise Carpets	14 A3

TRANSPORT (pp226–8)
Local Bus Stop	15 A2
Taxi Stop	16 A2
Taxi Stop	17 B2

shafts of light to spill in on the commerce below. Trade is busiest in the mornings and you'll find souvenirs nearer to Imam Sq.

IMAM SQ (NAQSH-E JAHAN SQ)

When French poet Renier described Esfahan as 'half of the world' in the 16th century, it was the myriad wonders of the square called Naqsh-e Jahan that inspired him. The description wouldn't be out of place today, because while it is now known as **Imam Sq** (Meydan-e Imam; Map p216) it is still the home of arguably the most majestic collection of buildings in the Islamic world.

Naqsh-e Jahan means 'pattern of the world', and it's a world that owes much to the vision of Shah Abbas the Great. Begun in 1602 as the centrepiece of Abbas' new capital, the square was designed as home to the finest jewels of the Safavid empire – the incomparable Imam Mosque, the supremely elegant Sheikh Lotfollah Mosque and the indulgent and lavishly decorated Ali Qapu Palace and Qeysarieh Portal. At 512m long and 163m wide, this immense space is the second-largest square on earth – only Mao Zedong's severe Tiananmen Sq is bigger.

The square has changed little since it was built. The upper levels of the many-arched arcades that surround the square are empty these days, though currently being restored as a museum of Esfahan's history. The open space has been reconstituted several times, most recently by the Pahlavis, who added the fountains. At either end of the square, you can still see the marble goal posts used in regular polo games 400 years ago. You'll see these polo games depicted on miniatures for sale around the square.

The square is best visited in the late afternoon and early evening when local families flood in to outnumber the Iranian and foreign tourists. This is also when the fountains are turned on, the light softens and the splendid architecture of the perimeter is illuminated; you can't beat the **view** from the Qeysarieh Tea Shop (p226).

Imam Mosque

The **Imam Mosque** (Masjed-e Imam; Map p217; admission IR30,000; ⏰ 8am-5pm, until 7pm summer, closed Friday morning) is one of the most beautiful mosques in the world. The richness of its blue-tiled mosaic designs and its perfectly proportioned Safavid-era architecture form

IMAM MOSQUE

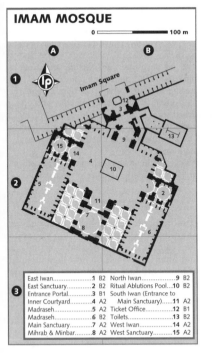

0 ━━━ 100 m

East Iwan	1	B2	North Iwan	9	B2
East Sanctuary	2	B2	Ritual Ablutions Pool	10	B2
Entrance Portal	3	B1	South Iwan (Entrance to		
Inner Courtyard	4	A2	Main Sanctuary)	11	A2
Madraseh	5	A2	Ticket Office	12	B1
Madraseh	6	B2	Toilets	13	B2
Main Sanctuary	7	A2	West Iwan	14	A2
Mihrab & Minbar	8	A2	West Sanctuary	15	A2

a visually stunning monument to the imagination of Shah Abbas I. The sumptuous decoration of the mosque perfectly complements the architectural elegance.

Work started on the magnificent entrance portal in 1611, although it took four years to finish – look for mismatches in its apparent symmetry, intended to reflect the artist's humility in the face of Allah. It was not until 1629, the last year of the reign of Shah Abbas, that the high dome, and therefore the mosque, was completed. Although minor additions were later made, most of what remains dates from that 18-year period. Although each of the mosque's parts is a masterpiece, it is the unity of the overall design that leaves a lasting impression.

The original purpose of the **entrance portal** had more to do with its location on the square than with the mosque's spiritual aims. Its function was primarily ornamental, providing a counterpoint to the Qeysarieh Portal at the entrance to the Bazar-e Bozorg. The foundation stones are of white marble from Ardestan and the portal itself, some 30m tall, is decorated with magnificent geo-

metric designs, floral motifs and calligraphy by some of the most skilled calligraphers of the age. The splendid niches contain complex stalactite mouldings in a honeycomb pattern, each panel with its own intricate design.

Although the portal was built to face the square, the mosque is angled to point in the direction of Mecca. A short corridor leads into the **inner courtyard**, which has a pool for ritual ablutions in its centre and is surrounded by four **iwans**. The walls of the courtyard contain the most exquisite sunken porches, framed by mosaics of deep blue and yellow. Each *iwan* leads into a vaulted sanctuary. The **east** and **west sanctuaries** are covered with particularly fine floral motifs on a blue background.

The **main sanctuary** is entered via the **south iwan**. Find yourself a quiet corner in which to sit and contemplate the richness of the domed ceiling, with its golden rose pattern (the flower basket) surrounded by concentric circles of busy mosaics on a deep blue background. The interior ceiling is 36.3m high, although the exterior reaches up to 51m due to the double-layering used in construction. The hollow space in between is responsible for the loud echoes heard when you stamp your foot on the black paving stones under the centre of the dome. Although scientists have measured up to 49 echoes, only about 12 are audible to the human ear – more than enough for a speaker to be heard throughout the mosque. The marble **mihrab** and **minbar** are also beautifully crafted.

The main sanctuary provides wonderful views back to the two turquoise **minarets** above the entrance portal. Each is encircled by projecting balconies and white geometric calligraphy in which the names of Mohammed and Ali are picked out over and over again. Each is topped by an elegant dome.

To the east and west of the main sanctuary are the courtyards of two madrasehs. Both provide good views of the main **dome** with its tiles every shade of turquoise. Cameras are welcome.

Sheikh Lotfollah Mosque

This mosque is the perfect complement to the overwhelming richness of the larger Imam Mosque, and is probably the most fabulous mosque in Iran. **Sheikh Lotfollah Mosque** (Masjed-e Sheikh Lotfollah; Map p216; admission IR30,000; 8.30am-4.30pm, until 7pm summer) is

SHAH IN A HURRY

When the Imam Mosque was begun Shah Abbas the Great probably didn't think it would be 25 years before the last of the artisans left the building. He was already 52 when work began, and as he grew older he also grew evermore impatient to see his greatest architectural endeavour completed. Stories tell of Abbas repeatedly demanding corners be cut to hasten the progress.

Legend has it that these orders included one insisting work on the walls be started despite the foundations having not yet set. His architect, Ali Akbar Esfahani, was having none of it. He flatly defied his boss, and then decided to make himself scarce until Abbas calmed down. After all, Abbas had killed two of his own sons and blinded another, so Esfahani was understandably nervous. He eventually returned to the court, and because the wisdom of his defiant decision had been demonstrated, he was welcomed back with a royal pardon.

Other innovative time-saving techniques were employed: rather than covering the entire complex with millions of individual mosaic tiles, larger prefabricated patterned tiles were created – a first in Iran.

a study in harmony and can be found on the eastern side of the square.

It was built between 1602 and 1619, during the reign of Shah Abbas I. The ruler dedicated it to his father-in-law, Sheikh Lotfollah, a revered Lebanese scholar of Islam who was invited to Esfahan to oversee the king's mosque (the Imam's Mosque) and theological school.

The pale dome makes extensive use of delicate cream-coloured tiles that change colour throughout the day from cream to pink (sunset is usually best). The signature blue-and-turquoise tiles of Esfahan are evident only around the dome's summit.

The pale tones of the cupola stand in contrast to those around the **portal**, where you'll find some of the best surviving Safavid-era mosaics. The exterior panels contain some wonderful arabesques and other intricate floral designs; those displaying a vase framed by the tails of two peacocks are superb. The portal itself contains some particularly fine stalactite work with rich concentrations of blue and yellow motifs.

The mosque is unusual because it has neither a minaret nor a courtyard, and because steps lead up to the entrance. This was probably because the mosque was never intended for public use, but rather served as the worship place for the women of the shah's harem. The **sanctuary** or prayer hall is reached via a twisting **hallway** which, although purely functional in purpose, is itself attractive with its subtle shifts of light.

You should stop in the sanctuary to marvel at the complexity of the mosaics that adorn the walls and ceiling, which is extraordinarily beautiful with its shrinking, yellow motifs drawing the visitor's eye into the exquisite centre. The shafts of sunlight that filter in through the few high, latticed windows produce an interplay of light and shadow.

The mihrab is one of the finest in Iran and has an unusually high niche; look for the calligraphic montage that names the architect and the date 1028 AH.

Photography is allowed but flashes are not. Bring a tripod.

Ali Qapu Palace

Built at the very end of the 16th century, the majestic six-storey **Ali Qapu Palace** (Map p216; admission IR30,000; ☾ 8am-sunset) was to serve as a monumental gateway (Ali Qapu means the 'Gate of Ali') to the royal palaces that lay in the parklands beyond. It is widely believed that it was also built as a residence of Shah Abbas I.

The highlight of the palace is arguably the **elevated terrace** with its 18 slender columns. The terrace affords a wonderful perspective over the square and one of the best views of the Imam Mosque. If you look up, you'll see an attractive wooden ceiling with intricate inlay work and exposed beams, reminiscent of the nearby Chehel Sotun Palace.

Many of the valuable murals and mosaics that once decorated the small rooms, corridors and stairways were destroyed during the Qajar period and since the 1979 revolution. However, some remain in the **throne room**, which leads off the terrace.

On the upper floor, the **music room** is definitely worth the climb. The plaster ceiling is riddled with the shapes of vases and other household utensils cut to dramatic, almost eerie effect. This distinctive craftsmanship, considered by some to be one of the finest examples of secular Persian art, is said to have enhanced the acoustics.

CHEHEL SOTUN PALACE

Standing in a pretty garden, this palace is another of the highlights of Esfahan – its frescoes are as beautiful as any you'll see. **Chehel Sotun** (Map pp212-13; Ostandari St; admission IR30,000; 8am-4pm, 8am-noon & 2-8pm summer) was undoubtedly built as a pleasure pavilion and reception hall, using the *talar* (columnar porch) style that dates from Achaemenid times. There are historical references to the palace dating from 1614, however, an inscription uncovered in 1949 says it was completed in 1647 under the watch of Shah Abbas II. Either way, what you see today was built after a fire in 1706.

The palace is entered via the elegant *talar* terrace, which perfectly bridges the transition between the Persian love of gardens and interior splendour. Its slender, ribbed wooden pillars rise to a superb wooden ceiling with crossbeams and exquisite inlay work.

The Great Hall contains a very rich array of frescoes, miniatures and ceramics. The upper walls are dominated by **historical frescoes** on a grand scale, sumptuously portraying court life and some of the great battles of the Safavid era. From right to left, above the entrance door, the armies of Shah Ismail do battle with the Uzbeks; Nader Shah battles Sultan Mahmud (astride a white elephant) on an Indian battleground; and Shah Abbas II welcomes King Nader Khan of Turkestan with musicians and dancing girls.

On the opposite wall, also from right to left, Shah Abbas I presides over an ostentatious banquet; Shah Ismail battles the janissaries of Sultan Suleiman; and Shah Tahmasp receives in his court Humayun, the Indian prince who fled to Persia in 1543.

These extraordinary works of art survived the 18th-century invasion by the Afghans, who coated the paintings with whitewash to show their disapproval of such extravagance. Even more surprisingly, a fresco showing a man kissing the foot of a half-naked dancing girl – in an adjoining room – survived the 1979 revolution, thanks to the palace caretakers who stood heroically between the masterpieces and fundamentalists intent on their destruction.

There is a small teahouse serving ice cream, and a bookshop near the entrance. Early morning is the best time for photos (flashes are banned inside).

MUSEUMS

Near the entrance to the Chehel Sotun Palace are three museums. The **Decorative Arts Museum of Iran** (Map pp212-13; Ostandari St; admission IR20,000; 7am-2pm Wed-Mon) is the pick. It contains some wonderful miniatures, lacquer work, ancient Qurans, calligraphy, ceramics, brass work, woodcarvings and traditional costumes. Photos are not allowed.

The other two – the **Natural History Museum** (Map pp212-13; Ostandari St; admission IR3000; 8am-1pm & 2-5pm; 4-9pm summer), and the **Museum of Contemporary Art** (Map pp212-13; Ostandari St; admission IR6000; 9am-noon & 4-7pm, 5-8pm summer Sat-Thu) – are probably not worth your time.

HASHT BEHESHT PALACE

Once the most luxuriously decorated in Esfahan, the interior of the small **Hasht Behesht Palace** (Map pp212-13; admission IR20,000; 8am-5pm, until 7pm summer) has been extensively damaged over the years. However, it retains a seductive tranquillity that comes from its setting amid the tall trees of the surrounding garden. The Hasht Behesht ('Eight Paradises') blends perfectly into the garden, with the soaring wooden columns on its open-sided terrace seeming to mirror the trees in the surrounding park.

Built in the 1660s, the inside boasts some impressive mosaics and stalactite mouldings, but the palace is famous for its garden setting and the ceilings cut into a variety of shapes. Most of this can be seen by walking around the outside, so unless you're desperate to get upstairs, save your money.

MADRASEH-YE CHAHAR BAGH

Part of an expansive complex built at the very end of the Safavid dynasty, the **Madraseh-ye Chahar Bagh** (Madraseh-ye Mazadar-e Shah or Theological School of the Shah's Mother; Map pp212-13; Chahar Bagh Abbasi St; admission IR30,000; 8am-9pm Thu only) has an imposing wood-and-silver door that's mostly closed to visitors. However, if you come here on Thursday you'll find a large courtyard with many trees, surrounded by two-storey porches leading to the rooms of the students. It is beautiful and restful. Built between 1704 and 1714, the whole complex contains a prayer hall with a lovely mihrab, two of the finest Safavid-era minarets in Esfahan, some exquisite mosaics and a particularly attractive dome.

ZAYANDEH RIVER BRIDGES
There are few better ways to spend an afternoon than strolling along the **Zayandeh River**, crossing back and forth using the fairytale old bridges, stopping in their cosy teahouses and just relaxing with the Esfahanis. Such a stroll is especially pleasant at sunset and early evening when most of the bridges are illuminated. In total, 11 bridges (six are new) cross the Zayandeh, and all but one of the historic crossings lie to the east of Chahar Bagh St. The exception is the shorter **Marnan Bridge** (Pol-e Marnan; Map p211). Like most of the bridges, it was built in the Safavid period.

Si-o-Seh Bridge
The 298m-long **Si-o-Seh Bridge** (Pol-e Si-o-Seh, Bridge of 33 Arches or Allahverdi Khan Bridge; Map pp212–13) was built by Allahverdi Khan, a favourite general of Shah Abbas I, between 1599 and 1602 to link the upper and lower halves of Chahar Bagh St. It served as both bridge and dam, and is still used to hold water today. The teahouses at either end of the bridge, both accessed through the larger arches underneath, are great places to stop.

Chubi Bridge
Nearly 150m long, with 21 arches, **Chubi Bridge** (Map pp212–13) was built by Shah Abbas II in 1665, primarily to help irrigate palace gardens in the area. Chubi and the two parlours within were for the exclusive use of the shah and his courtiers. Today, however, anyone can stop in at the cosy teahouse (p225), which some consider the best in the city.

Khaju Bridge
The finest of Esfahan's bridges, the **Khaju Bridge** (Map pp212–13) was built by Shah Abbas II in about 1650 (although a bridge is believed to have crossed the waters here since the time of Tamerlane). It also doubles as a dam, and has always been as much a meeting place as a bearer of traffic.

Its 132m length has two levels of terraced arcades; the lower containing locks regulating water flow. If you look hard, you can still see original paintings and tiles, and the remains of stone seats built for Shah Abbas II to sit on and admire the views. In the centre, a pavilion was built exclusively for his pleasure. It was a teahouse, but hadn't been open for some time when we passed.

Shahrestan Bridge
This is the oldest of Esfahan's bridges (Map p211). Most of the 11-arched stone and brick structure is believed to date from the 12th century, although it stands on the foundations of a much earlier Sassanian bridge. Although it's about 3km east of Khaju Bridge, it's a pleasant walk from there.

ARMENIAN QUARTER
The Armenian quarter of Esfahan is **Jolfa** (Map pp212–13). It dates from the time of Shah Abbas I, who transported this colony of Christians from the town of Jolfa (now on Iran's northern border, see p141) en masse, and named the village 'New Jolfa'. Abbas sought their skills as merchants, entrepreneurs and artists – a look at the walls of Vank Cathedral reveals what he was after. The Armenian Christians had their religious freedom respected, but they were restricted to one area and kept away from the Islamic centres.

Today there are 13 Armenian churches and an old cemetery scattered around Jolfa, serving a Christian community of about 7000. It's worth heading out here (it's not far) in the evening for the village atmosphere – a very liberal village, by Iranian standards. Many of the residents speak English and the eating is good (p224).

Vank Cathedral
Built between 1606 and 1655 with the encouragement of the Safavid rulers, **Vank Cathedral** (Kelisa-ye Vank; Map pp212–13; Kelisa St; adult/student IR30,000/15,000; 8am-12.30pm & 2-5.30pm, until 6.30pm summer) is the historic focal point of the Armenian church in Iran. The church's exterior is unexciting, but the interior is richly decorated and shows the curious mixture of styles – Islamic tiles and designs alongside Christian imagery – that characterises most churches in Iran. The frescoes are truly

magnificent, if sometimes gruesome. There's a detached **bell tower**.

The attached Vank Cathedral **museum** contains more than 700 handwritten books, including what is claimed to be the first book printed in Iran, and other ethnological displays relating to Armenian culture and religion. There's even a small drawing by Rembrandt.

Other Churches

The frescoes on the walls and ceilings of the **Church of Bethlehem** (Kelisa-ye Bethlehem; Map pp212-13; Nazar St), built in 1628, are arguably more intricate and impressive than those in Vank Cathedral. The interior of the high dome is decorated with swirling black motifs on a golden background, while the base is surrounded by paintings of Biblical scenes. The **Church of St Mary** (Kelisa-ye Maryam; Map pp212–13) is the least impressive of the three, but does have some nice frescoes. These churches are often closed so you might have to seek help from the people at the cathedral to get the doors open.

MANAR JOMBAN (SHAKING MINARETS)

In Kaladyn (about 6km west of the city centre) is the tomb of Abu Abdollah, a revered dervish of the 14th century. The tomb is

---

A SHAKE TOO FAR?

Ask guides why the shaking minarets shake and they are likely to embark on a lengthy explanation of vibration theory. It's a bit of a disappointment, therefore, to find out that a mundane building error may really be responsible for this astonishing phenomenon.

Geologists now suggest that the wrong kind of sandstone was used to build the minarets. This sandstone contains felspar, which dissolves over time and leaves the stone flexible and liable to shake. In support of their argument, geologists point out that there are no historic references to the minarets shaking.

Luckily for romance, not everyone agrees with this theory. One expert points out that other buildings in the city were constructed from the same sandstone and yet they show no propensity to shake.

---

normally known as **Manar Jomban** (Shaking Minarets; Map p211; admission IR30,000; 8.30am-4pm, until 8pm summer) because if you lean hard against one minaret it will start to sway back and forth, followed by its twin. Although by no means unique, these Safavid-period shaking minarets are probably the most famous of their kind. If you visit on a Friday you might have to wait for a while before you can climb to the top.

However, concern that the minarets were being shaken too hard, too often has led to a 'crackdown' on shaking. The result is that the minarets are closed frequently, but with no apparent timetable.

Almost every bus (IR250, 20 minutes, 4km) that heads west along Bahai St from near the corner of Chahar Bagh Abbasi St runs past Manar Jomban; the man in the ticket booth will point you to the right one. Chartering a taxi for an hour to include the nearby Ateshkadeh-ye Esfahan fire temple is another alternative (IR15,000).

ATESHKADEH-YE ESFAHAN

Dating from Sassanian times, the crumbling mud bricks of the **Ateshkadeh-ye Esfahan** (Esfahan Fire Temple; Map p211; admission IR20,000; 8.30am-5pm, until 7pm summer) stare out over the Zayandeh River and the city from a low hill on its outskirts. This really ancient fire temple is an energetic 10-minute scramble up the low hill, and it is well worth the effort on a clear day. It's about 2km west from the Manar Jomban, along the same road.

GOLESTAN-E SHOHADA

This one of Iran's many cemeteries for those who died in the Iran-Iraq War. **Golestan Shohada** (Rose Garden of Martyrs; Map p211) has rows and rows of photographs on the tombstones, which are an unforgettable sight and a powerful testament to the futility of the war. By the entrance there is also a modern, domed mausoleum to Ayatollah Shams Abadi, said to have been assassinated by the last shah's secret police shortly before the 1979 revolution.

The cemetery is about 1.5km south of the Khaju Bridge. To get here take a shared taxi from the southern side of the bridge to Basij Sq, and then walk east for about 400m.

CENTRAL IRAN

'Half the World' Walking Tour

Starting on the southeastern side of Takhti Junction, head south along Chahar Bagh Abbasi St for about 200m, where a small lane leads east, away from the clamour of modern Esfahan and into the quiet, attractive lanes around the bazaar. Winding your way east, you'll come to the **Hakim Mosque (1)**. This is Esfahan's oldest mosque, but only the beautiful portal, which is on your route, has survived from the Buyid-dynasty structure; the rest is far more recent.

Continuing east, you'll pass through the quieter alleys of the **Bazar-e Bozorg (2**; p215) where Esfahanis buy their household goods. The bazaar veers northeast and becomes busier, with domestic goods' shops, mosques, madrasehs, teahouses, banks, bathhouses and even the occasional garden.

The bazaar veers right but keep going straight for about 40m to get to the **Madraseh-ye Nimurvand (3)**, where the students normally welcome visitors. Rejoin the main bazaar and follow it across Jamal-od-Din Abdolrazagh St to the imposing **Jameh Mosque (4**; p214).

From the mosque skirt around Qiyam Sq, stopping for a look at the **bird market (5)**, and head down Haruniyeh St. You'll soon see the

attractive, 48m-high **Minaret of the Mosque of Ali (6**; Manar-e Masjed-e Ali). Inside the mosque, which was rebuilt in 1522, are some impressive Safavid paintings that were hidden under Qajar-era decoration, until recently. Opposite the mosque is the 16th-century **Mausoleum of Harun Vilayet (7**; Bogh-e Harun Vilayet), in which some high-quality frescoes remember the son of the 10th, or perhaps the 11th, Shiite Imam (no-one is quite sure).

Rejoin the main bazaar and wander southwest through the shafts of sunlight and spice-filled air towards Imam Sq. En route, the **Madraseh-ye Sadr (8)** has a large green courtyard that can provide momentary respite from the call of cajoling traders. After entering **Imam Sq (9**; p216) through the grand **Qeysarieh Portal (10**; p215), your first stop should be **Qeysarieh Tea Shop (11**; p226) which overlooks the square, to get your bearings and some liquid refreshment. Launch into the square by either following the covered bazaars that circle the square behind the façades or by setting off to explore the jewels of Esfahan: the **Imam Mosque (12**; p216), the **Sheikh Lotfollah Mosque (13**; p217) and the **Ali Qapu Palace (14**; p218).

When you can finally tear yourself away from the splendour, turn off Sepah St to the **Chehel Sotun Palace (15**; p219) entrance between the two museums on Ostandari St. With the shadows getting longer, head back to Imam Sq to watch the light play softly over this wonderful place, either from one of the many stone benches or the comforts of the Qeysarieh Tea Shop (yes, there's no better viewing spot!). With the sun gone and the fountains of the square glowing (it's not bad, this, is it?) round off the day with a meal at either **Azadegan Teahouse (16**; p226) or **Bastani Restaurant (17**; p224).

Sleeping

Esfahan has a pretty good range of accommodation, most of which is within walking distance of Imam Sq. Anything on Chahar Bagh Abbasi St is likely to be noisy, so ask for a room away from the street. Prices listed here are for the high (summer) season and tend to fall dramatically in winter, especially in the mid-range.

BUDGET

Amir Kabir Hostel (Map pp212-13; ☎ 2227273; mrziaee@ hotmail.com; Chahar Bagh Abbasi St; dm/s/tw IR25,000/

> **WALKING TOUR**
> Distance: about 7km
> Duration: four to seven hours, depending on how often you stop and for how long

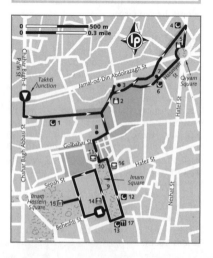

8,000/70,000;) Esfahan's only real backpacker hang-out, so if you're craving Western company, this is for you. The rooms are
basic and the shared bathrooms not good
at all. While the Ziaee brothers have been
accused of being too businesslike by some
readers, they speak good English and have a
cheap laundry, an enlightening guest book, a
bus ticket-booking service, reasonably priced
tours, and an adjoining restaurant. It's worth
booking ahead in peak times.

Shahrzad Hostel (Map pp212-13; /fax 336 3610;
Masjed-e Sayyed St; s/tw IR50,000/70,000;) The
rooms are small and simple but it's hard to
argue with the price in this homely place. The
clean bathrooms are shared, and guests can
use the kitchen. The front rooms are noisy.

Persia Hotel (Map pp212-13; /fax 222 3274;
Chahar Bagh Abbasi St; s/d IR120,000/160,000;) Close
to Takhti Junction, this family-run place
comes recommended by several travellers.
The rooms are clean have bathroom, fridge
and TV, and you can phone home from your
room for IR3000 a minute. Great value!

Shad Hotel (Map pp212-13; 221 8621; fax 220
4264; Chahar Bagh Abbasi St; r IR68,000) A good-value,
central option, with small, clean two- and
three-bed rooms and shared bathrooms.
The elaborate ceiling in the reception area
suggests this place was once a lot grander.

Sahel Hotel (Map pp212-13; 222 1702; fax 220 2994;
Chahar Bagh Abbasi St; s/tw IR100,000/180,000) Rooms
have bathroom and aren't bad. The beds
are rock hard, but extra padding is provided
on request. The teahouse upstairs (see Bame
Sahel Teahouse, p226) is a local favourite.

Other reasonable choices along Chahar
Bagh Abbasi St include **Pars Hotel** (Map pp212-
13; 221 9072; Chahar Bagh Abbasi St; s/tw US$15/20;
), which has rooms that can be rather
noisy, with TV, fridge and bathroom; and
friendly **Tous Hotel** (Map pp212-13; 222 1599;
toos@yahoo.com; s/d IR90,000/160,000;), with
English-speaking staff and nice, airy rooms.

MID-RANGE
All the rooms in this range have bathrooms
and air-con, and most will have a TV and
fridge as well.

Sadaf Hotel (Map pp212-13; /fax 223 6692; www
.sadafhotel.com; Hafez St; s/d US$45/65;) A really
top location, professional management and
impressive rooms make this Esfahan's best
mid-range option. All the rooms are crystal
clean and have satellite TV and fridge, and

CENTRAL IRAN

THE AUTHOR'S CHOICE

Aria Hotel (Map pp212-13; 222 7224; fax
233 2441; Shahid Medani St; s/d with breakfast
US$15/20;) This is really a great place to
come home to after a long day pounding
the streets, squares and bridges of Esfahan.
The staff are super-friendly and the rooms,
while ageing, are large with soft beds, a
fridge and TV, and bathrooms that work
(some even have baths, with plug!). Breakfast is taken in a small cafeteria, and guests
are welcome to make use of the kitchen. The
snug communal area is popular with travellers. It's ideally located between Imam Sq
and the river and rooms are relatively quiet.
For the money, this is Esfahan's best deal.

it's less than five minutes' walk to Imam Sq.
The rooftop restaurant is a delight in summer.
Big discounts are available in the low season.

Pol and Park Hotel (Map pp212-13; 661 2785; fax
661 2788; A'ineh Khuneh Blvd; s/d US$20/30;) This
place could do with a face-lift, but with half
the rooms sporting a balcony overlooking
the Si-o-Seh Bridge, you could do far worse.
Even better, prices are eminently negotiable.

Safir Hotel (Map pp212-13; /fax 221 9931; www
.safirhotel.com; Shahid Medani St; s/d US$45/60; ）
This is a busy but welcoming place with
modern rooms and a handy café, and is in a
great location. Several languages including
English and French are spoken, and management is most obliging.

Julfa Hotel (Map pp212-13; 624 4441; fax 624 9446;
Hakim Nezami St; s/d US$24/36;) For something
different you could stay in the Armenian
quarter, around the corner from Vank Cathedral. This welcoming hotel has petite but
clean and functional rooms. Downstairs is
the excellent Khangostar Restaurant (p225).

Saadi Hotel (Map pp212-13; 220 3881; saadi_
hotel@yahoo.com; Abbas Abad St; d/tr IR185,000/215,000;
) The best part about Saadi is its quiet
location. Staff are helpful and guests can use
the kitchen.

Some solid but generally drab mid-range
options:

Hotel Ali Qapu (Map pp212-13; 222 7929;
www.aliqapuhotel.com; Chahar Bagh Abbasi St; s/d
US$54/78 plus 17% tax;) Has nice rooms and
a men-only pool.

Piroozy Hotel (Map pp212-13; 221 4354; hotel-
piroozy@yahoo.com; Chahar Bagh Abbasi St; s/d US$45/65;

P 🕃) Should (and probably will) afford you a sizable discount for its rather startling 1970s décor.

Azady Hotel (Map pp212-13; ☎ 220 4011; fax 220 3713; Masjed-e Sayyed St; s/tw US$36/54; P 🕃) Near Takhti Junction, it offers decent rooms and a restaurant downstairs.

Pardis Apartment Hotel (Map pp212-13; ☎ 220 0308; fax 222 7831; Takhti Junction; apt for 2 IR250,000; 🕃) Suitable for longer stays. Pardis has spacious suites that sleep up to five, and friendly service.

If you're arriving late by bus, **Hotel Soffeh** (Map p211; ☎ 668 6462; soffe@isfahan.org.ir; s/d US$20/30; P 🕃) is upstairs in the Soffeh bus terminal, while in the north it's **Kaveh Hotel** (Map p211; ☎ /fax 442 5540; s/d US$20/30; P 🕃), upstairs at the northern end of the Kaveh terminal.

TOP END

There are surprisingly few top-end options in Esfahan considering it is such a tourist drawcard, so it's worth booking ahead.

Abbasi Hotel (Map pp212-13; ☎ 222 6010; www .abbasihotel.com; Shahid Medani St; s/d US$91/141; P 🕃 🖳 🕭) In the shell of the caravanserai built to help fund the neighbouring Madraseh-ye Chahar Bagh (p219), Abbasi should be one of the most romantic hotels in Iran. It's not. While the setting, around a gorgeous garden in what was once the caravanserai's courtyard, is undoubtedly sublime, the rooms are surprisingly ordinary and the service can leave you feeling more like a sheep than a shah. If you do stay, be sure you ask for and get one of the doubles overlooking the courtyard – booking ahead is safest. Guest or not, it's worth visiting to see the extravagance of the decorations, or just to linger over a pot of tea in its teahouse (see Abbasi Hotel Teahouse p226). There's a decent bookshop in the foyer, and the pool is open to nonguests for IR50,000.

Kowsar International Hotel (Map pp212-13; ☎ 624 0230; info@hotelkowsar.com; Mellat Blvd; s/d US$65/95 plus 17% tax; P 🕃 🖳 🕭) Overlooking the Si-o-Seh Bridge and the rest of Esfahan, the refurbished rooms here are as luxurious as you'd expect, but cheaper. Be sure to ask for a room on a high floor at the front.

Hotel Apartments Mehr (Map pp212-13; ☎ /fax 222 2625; hotelmehr@yahoo.com; Ostandari St; apt for 4 US$80; P 🕃) These modern, luxurious apartments are ideally located a couple of hundred metres from Imam Sq and include a kitchen, spacious sitting room and bedrooms. The price is very negotiable. Good value!

Eating

There is a reasonable selection of eateries in Esfahan, though less variety than you'd expect for such a tourist centre. The rooftop teahouse in Imam Sq is an obvious highlight here, and there are several other teahouses around town (and under bridges) worth visiting. Try also to make time for an evening in Jolfa, where the atmosphere is subtly but distinctly different and there are several decent eating options. All places are open for lunch and dinner unless otherwise stated.

FAST FOOD & KABABIS

Esfahan has no shortage of places selling fast food. You certainly won't go hungry along Chahar Bagh Abbasi St, where the greatest concentration of places selling pizza, sandwiches, burgers, ice cream and, occasionally real kebabs is around the intersection with Sayyed Ali Khan St.

Elsewhere, **Only Kabab Kababi** (Map p216; Hafez St) just east of Imam Sq, is recommended.

For an Iranian breakfast experience (at any time of day) head for **Fereni Hafez** (Map pp212-13, Hafez St; ☼ 8am-midnight), where you can enjoy a delicious bowl (or two) of *fereni*, made of rice flour, milk, sugar and rose-water for IR1000; look for the red sign. Continuing the Iranian budget-food theme, stop for lunch at the all-day **ash-e reshte place** (Map pp212-13; Chagh Bagh Abbasi St; ☼ 7am-9pm), a few metres south of Amir Kabir Hostel; you'll know it by the huge pot of *ash* (a type of soup made from yogurt and barley) inside the doorway. A bowl of *ash* with bread is IR4000.

RESTAURANTS

Bastani Restaurant (Map p216; ☎ 220 0374; Imam Sq; meals IR30,000) Off the southeastern corner of Imam Sq, this place is undoubtedly geared towards tourists, but don't let that put you off. The setting is spectacular, in the shadow of the minarets of the Imam Mosque, and the food is good and surprisingly cheap. Even the service is good. The usual range of kebabs is complemented with several dishes to excite the vegetarian in you – squash, quince and aubergine *khoreshts* (IR12,000 to IR18,000) among them.

Traditional Sofreh Khaneh (Map p216; ☎ 221 9068; Imam Sq; meals IR35,000) It's actually a modern-traditional restaurant (no qalyans here), but the running water, stained glass and live music nights give it a pleasant atmosphere.

The Esfahani biriani (IR12,500) is recommended. Look for the unsightly blue neon sign (head out of the square and turn left up the stairs).

Restoran-e Sa'di (Map pp212-13; ☎ 222 0237; Chahar Bagh Abbasi St; meals IR20,000) Down the mirrored staircase opposite Amir Kabir Hostel, this place is popular with locals and is cheap; kebabs are about IR16,000 and *khoresht* less than IR10,000.

Nobahar Restaurant (Map pp212-13; ☎ 221 0800; Chahar Bagh Abbasi St; meals IR25,000) A good, solid cheapie. The food here is better than the surroundings, but not exactly inspirational. Some readers have had problems with the service and, to be fair, it's not great. The *khoresht* (IR10,000) is a decent option.

Maharaja Restaurant (Map pp212-13; ☎ 222 4985; Enqelab-e Eslami Sq; meals IR40,000) The Maharaja should be atmospheric, but it's not. The curry we had was not bad, and vegetarians should enjoy the daal (IR12,000).

Restaurant Shahrzad (Map pp212-13; ☎ 220 4490; Abbas Abad St; meals IR50,000) One of Esfahan's best restaurants. The beautiful period wall-paintings, stained-glass windows and mirror work certainly give it a look of Qajar-era opulence, and the food doesn't disappoint. The *fesenjun* (IR22,800) is mouthwatering.

The village of Jolfa is home to a few restaurants.

Pizza Jolfa Armenian Restaurant (Map pp212-13; Kelisa St; meals IR25,000; 🕑 6.30pm-midnight) Right outside Vank Cathedral, the enthusiastic young guys running this place serve pizzas and pastas (from IR15,000) as well as Armenian *dolmehs* (rice wrapped in vine leaves) and *zabon* (about IR20,000).

Khorshid (Map pp212-13; ☎ 624 7536; Khorshid St; meals IR35,000) Located under the Apache pizza joint, this Modern Iranian restaurant is not bad and appeals to the upwardly mobile young Esfahani.

Restoran-e Khayyam (Map pp212-13; Nazar St; meals IR17,000) Cheap, popular and justafiably busy.

HOTEL RESTAURANTS

Most hotels have a restaurant (some better than others).

Sadaf Hotel (Map pp212-13; ☎ 223 6692; Hafez St; meals IR35,000) This is a good option, especially between June and October, when you eat on the rooftop. There's steak with mushroom sauce (IR25,000), tomato soup (IR8000) for a change, and tasty kebabs (about IR20,000).

Khangostar Restaurant (Map pp212-13; ☎ 627 8989; Hakim Nezami St; meals IR45,000) Located inside Julfa Hotel, some say this is the best restaurant in Esfahan. That's a big call, but the food is pretty good, from vegetable kebab (IR12,000) to chicken cordon bleu (IR32,000) and beyond.

Chehelsotoun Restaurant (Map pp212-13; ☎ 222 0611; Shahid Medani St; meals IR70,000) Located at Abbasi Hotel. If the food here was as impressive as the surrounds, it would be the best dining option in Iran. It's not. And, as several readers have complained, the service is worse, which makes paying the 15% service on top of the already high prices particularly galling.

TASTY TREATS

Many places along Chahar Bagh Abbasi St serve ice cream; others sell delicious fruit shakes for about IR3000 for a small cup – try **Iseman** (Map pp212-130; Chahar Bagh Abbasi St) for one of the best.

Esfahan's famous speciality is *gaz*, a delicious kind of nougat usually mixed with chopped pistachios or other nuts. It isn't generally served in restaurants, but you can easily pick it up in the confectionery shops along Chahar Bagh Abbasi St or around Imam Sq.

Drinking

There are few things more enjoyable than sipping a pot of tea in the teahouses underneath the bridges of Esfahan. It is very easy to spend an entire morning or afternoon sauntering along the riverbank, stopping every few hundred metres for a chay (tea) and a qalyan. In summer most of the teahouses have limitations on how long you can stay, sometimes just 15 minutes.

Si-o-Seh Bridge (Map pp212-13; 🕑 8am-11pm) There are outdoor teahouses underneath both ends of the bridge. The northern end also serves some food, including breakfast. You'll quite often hear people reciting Hafez here; it's far more of an Esfahani atmosphere than a tourist scene.

Chubi Bridge (Map pp212-13; 🕑 8am-8pm) Once the exclusive hang-out of shahs and their cronies, this intimate little teahouse is idyllic. Sitting in the window, drinking tea, smoking qalyan and talking with the locals – travelling doesn't get much better than this.

The Khaju Bridge teahouse had been closed for some time when we passed.

The bridges don't have a monopoly on ambience...

Qeysarieh Tea Shop (Map p216; Imam Sq; ☺ 8am-11pm) Sitting at the outdoor tables here is the perfect place to soak up this beautiful 'half of the world', especially when the colours and moods of the square change in the late afternoon. And despite its position, it's often pretty quiet. It's up a steep staircase to the left of the Qeysarieh Portal. There are other teahouses in the bazaar.

Azadegan Teahouse (Map p216; Chaykhuneh-ye Azadegan; ☎ 221 1225) In a lane off the northeastern corner of Imam Sq, local men and their qalyans line either side of this tavernlike place, which houses an astonishing collection of old weapons, photographs and other memorabilia. The atmosphere is *much* better if you don't come as part of a group.

Bame Sahel Teahouse (Map pp212-13; Chahar Bagh Abbasi St; ☺ 8am-11pm) On the top of Sahel Hotel, Bame Sahel is a bit rough around the edges and all the better for it. Escape the traffic for tea, or enjoy a good *dizi* dinner (IR12,000).

Abbasi Hotel Teahouse (Map pp212-13; Shahid Medani St; ☺ 4-10pm) Just up the street but at totally the other end of the spectrum from Bame Sahel, this teahouse is everything you'd expect of the Abbasi.

Shopping

Esfahan has probably the widest selection of handicrafts anywhere in the country. The best buys are carpets (from all over Iran), hand-painted miniatures on camel bone (many of the artists run the stores themselves and are happy to give demonstrations) and intricate copper work. You can also pick up locally produced, hand-printed tablecloths and bedspreads and other metalwork (brass and silver). Esfahan can be more expensive than elsewhere but there's more choice and it's certainly more pleasurable to shop here than in Tehran. For gold, head directly to **Bazar-e Honar** (Map pp212-13; Chahar Bagh Abbasi St; ☺ 8.30am-1pm & 4-9pm Sat-Thu).

A good place to get an idea of prices is **Iran Handicrafts Organisation** (Map p216; ☎ 222 9333; northern end of Imam Sq; ☎ 222 0916; opposite Abbasi Hotel).

There are plenty of handicrafts shops in the **Bazar-e Bozorg** (Map p212–13) and in the arcades around the square. Competition is fierce (and sometimes nasty) among the various carpet shops in particular, so don't pay too much attention to what one shop owner says about his competitor down the lane. Although some places employ high-pressure sales tactics, most are friendly and willing to chat over a chay without twisting your arm too much. It can actually be quite enjoyable as long as you remember that you don't *have* to buy anything. Nevertheless, bargain hard wherever you go (see the boxed text 'What A Bargain', p358).

A few Imam Sq shops recommended by readers:

Aladdin Carpets (Map p216; ☎ 221 1461; Imam Sq) You'll almost certainly meet the Aladdin men in the square; they're more aggressive than at Nomad, but not too bad.

Fallahi Miniatures Shahid Medani St (Map pp212-13; ☎ 220 4613; ☺ 8.30am-12.30pm & 3-7.30pm); Imam Sq (Map p216; ☎ 220 4613; ☺ 8.30am-12.30pm & 3-7.30pm) The charming Hossein Fallahi's works have been exhibited around the world. They're a cut above most miniatures.

Nomad Carpet Shop (Map p216; ☎ 221 9275; nomadshop@yahoo.com; Imam Sq) Has a well-earned reputation for its almost-comatose approach to selling, free Internet access and wide range of good-quality carpets and kilims. Carpets can be posted home from here.

Paradise Carpets (Map p216; ☎ 220 4860; Imam Sq) Under the Ali Qapu Palace, this father-and-son operation is worth a look.

Getting There & Away

AIR

The **Iran Air office** (Map pp212-13; ☎ 222 8200; www.iranair .com; Shahid Medani St; ☺ 7am-7pm Sat-Thu) is in the shopping complex opposite Abbasi Hotel. As well its domestic services listed below, Iran Air has two flights a week to Dubai (IR720,000 one way) and a weekly flight to Kuwait City (IR750,000).

Destination	Price (IR)	Frequency
Ahvaz	144,000	daily
Bandar-e Abbas	267,000	3 per week
Bushehr	167,000	weekly
Kerman	197,000	weekly
Mashhad	281,000	4 per week
Shiraz	144,000	daily
Tehran	144,000	several daily
Zahedan	302,000	weekly

BUS

There are two main bus terminals – the **Soffeh bus terminal** (Map p211; ☎ 668 8341/2) in the far south, and the **Kaveh bus terminal** (Map p211; ☎ 441 4375) in the north. Both the terminals are clean and well organised. There are no bus company offices in town so you must go to the stations to buy tickets, or do so through **Amir Kabir Hostel** (Map pp212-13; ☎ 222 7273; Char Bagh Abbasi St), which takes about IR3000 in commission – money well spent to save the hassle. Both terminals have buses to most destinations outside Esfahan province, although the Kaveh terminal is more convenient from the centre of town and has slightly more bus company offices. There are no buses to Kashan from Soffeh.

DOMESTIC SERVICES
From Kaveh, buses leave Esfahan several (often many) times a day to the following places. Prices are for Mercedes/Volvo buses:

Destination	Price (IR)	Duration (hr)
Ahvaz	35,500/54,000	14
Bandar-e Abbas	35,500/57,000	18
Hamadan	30,000/17,500	8
Kashan	8000	4½
Kerman	24,000/35,000	12
Kermanshah	23,000/38,000	10
Mashhad	75,000	22
Rasht	26,400/40,000	12
Shiraz	18,000/30,000	8
Tabriz	37,400/50,000	16
Tehran	17,500/30,000	7
Yazd	11,500/22,000	5
Zahedan	42,200/65,000	21

Buses to Yazd also leave from the Jey minibus terminal (below).

Services to more far-flung destinations, such as Zahedan, might not be so frequent, so book ahead. For most major destinations you shouldn't have to wait longer than an hour or so; just go from office to office until you find a bus going your way.

For the Kaveh terminal take a shared taxi north along Chahar Bagh St for IR2000; to get to Soffeh, take one from just south of the Si-o-Seh Bridge (IR2500). A private taxi to either terminal will cost around IR10,000. If you're budget is really tight, look for bus No 301, which runs along Chahar Bagh St en route between the two terminals for IR500.

International Services
If you have a deep-seated masochistic streak, or you're right out of time, you might want to take a bus direct to Ankara or İstanbul. Services leave (in theory) everyday, cost IR260,000 and take at least three days to reach İstanbul. In practice, the bus' departure depends on demand. Either way, *khoda hafez!*

MINIBUS & SAVARI
For destinations around Esfahan there are two minibus terminals. For Shahr-e Kord (IR3500, two hours, 107km), head for the **Zayandeh Rud minibus terminal** (Map p211; ☎ 775 9182), from where minibuses leave when full, usually every hour or so. To get to Zayandeh Rud terminal, take a shared taxi west from just south of the Si-o-Seh Bridge (IR3000).

From the **Jey minibus terminal** (Map p211; ☎ 521 6607), there are at least five departures each day to Yazd (IR10,000, six hours, 316km). Minibuses also go to Na'in (IR3500, three to four hours, 138km) and Ardestan (IR4000, 132km). To get to the Jey minibus terminal, take a shared taxi from Takhti Junction (IR1500).

Savaris leave from outside the terminals far more frequently than minibuses but for about four times the price, such as Shahr-e Kord (IR12,500, one hour and 20 minutes).

TRAIN
There is a daily train between Esfahan and Tehran (IR30,300, seven hours, 487km) that leaves at 9.50pm and stops at Kashan. Your money buys you a bed in a six-berth compartment. All trains from Esfahan go north towards Tehran. To get to Kerman or Bandar-e Abbas you'll have to change in Kashan or Ardakan.

The **Raja Trains ticket office** (Map pp212-13; ☎ 222 4425; Enqelab-e Eslami Sq; ☷ 8am-4pm Sat-Thu) is wedged between the Bank Mellat and Bank Tejarat buildings; look for the stylised blue train. Alternatively, try a travel agency.

The **train station** (Map p211; ☎ 668 8001) is way out to the east of the city. To get here, catch a bus from outside Kowsar International Hotel; ask for the *istgah-e ghatah* and you'll be put on the right bus. Be at the bus stop well over an hour before your train is due to depart. A private taxi (IR25,000) can cost almost as much as the train ticket to Tehran. Alternatively, take a shared taxi from Qods Sq (Map p211).

CENTRAL IRAN

Getting Around

Esfahani taxi drivers have a bad reputation, but in reality they're not much worse than taxi drivers anywhere else in the universe – if they see someone fresh off the plane, train or automobile, they'll try to take you.

Still, it pays to be wise to a few standard tricks. If you want a shared taxi, avoid empty vehicles. If you do get an empty car, tell the driver you want to share ('*nah dar baste!*' usually works), otherwise the driver will assume you do want it *dar baste* (closed door) and charge you accordingly. You're most likely to get stung arriving at Kaveh bus terminal, where drivers operate as a virtual cartel. They will ask for IR30,000 to take you to one of the hotels on Chahar Bagh Abbasi St. You should laugh at this and offer IR10,000. Eventually one driver will sidle up to you and agree to the price, but you absolutely *must* have settled on the price before getting in. Alternatively, take a shared taxi – traffic passing on the terminal-side of the road is heading south into town.

TO/FROM THE AIRPORT

The airport (Map p211) is way out of town (northeast) and there isn't an airport bus service. To get here, take any bus (IR250) heading east along Jamal-od-Din Abdolrazagh St from Takhti Junction. Get off the bus at Ahmad Abad Sq where the small Sorush bus station (Map p211) has buses to the airport (IR300). From the airport, ask around for any shared taxis heading into the city, from where you might need to get another to your hotel. A private taxi in either direction will cost about IR30,000.

BUS & MINIBUS

Buses and minibuses leave the local bus station, near Chehel Sotun Palace, to every direction every few minutes. Just ask – and keep asking – for one heading your way. Elsewhere in town simply jump on any bus going your way and jump off when it deviates. Rides cost IR250 or IR500 depending on the distance. You buy tickets at the booths along or just off Chahar Bagh Abbasi St.

The No 301 bus links the Kaveh and Soffeh bus terminals (IR500).

PRIVATE TAXI

Depending on the distance – and your negotiating skills – a fare in a private taxi

around town costs from IR5000 to IR7000, although getting to the terminals, train station or airport will cost more. Luckily there are so many taxis that it's easy to negotiate by threatening to find another one. Unless you're desperate, avoid the taxi drivers who hang around Imam Sq as they can spot tourists a mile off.

To hire a private taxi for an hour costs between IR15,000 and IR20,000 within the city limits, depending on your bargaining form. It's a very good way to see the Ateshkadeh-ye Esfahan and Manar Jomban.

SHARED TAXI

The long Chahar Bagh St is the city's main thoroughfare, and every couple of seconds a shared taxi goes *mostaghim* (straight ahead) for about IR1000. To outlying destinations such as the transport terminals, look for taxis heading in the right direction from the following places: Laleh, Qods and Ahmad Abad Sqs (for anywhere to the east); Imam Hossein and Shohada Sqs (for the north); and the southern side of Si-o-Seh Bridge and Azadi Sq (for the south and west).

SHAHR-E KORD شهر کرد
☎ 0381

Nestled between two mountain ranges, this sleepy provincial capital is pretty laid-back. The major sight of interest is the **Atabakan Mosque**, but there is little else. When Isabella Bird travelled around this region in 1890, she painted a picture of a wild and inhospitable terrain inhabited by fiercely independent and warlike tribespeople (principally Lors and Bakhtiyaris) governed by feudal chieftains. It's a lot more hospitable these days.

Sleeping & Eating

Shahr-e Kord Azadi Hotel (☎ 333 6791; fax 333 6790; r/ste US$49/64; P ⊗) The best place in town. Big rooms are pretty good and the views very good. It's way out of town on a hill. Otherwise, the ITTIC's **Shahr-e Kord Inn** (☎ 222 1077; fax 222 9892; Dr Shariati St; r US$25; P ⊗) is not bad.

Hotel Mohammad (☎ 222 2197; s/tw IR40,000/ 60,000) The unmarked Mohammad is noisy but it's the cheapest option. It's beside the Imamzadeh shrine in the centre of town; ask for the mosaferkhuneh.

There are plenty of kababis and hamburger joints along the main street. One reader described the **Ferdosi** (Ferdosi Sq; lunch & dinner Sat-Thu), in an old bathhouse, as 'one of the most pleasant traditional restaurants in the whole of Iran'.

Getting There & Away
To and from Esfahan, minibuses (IR3500, two hours, 107km) leave about every hour until 7pm, while savaris (IR12,500, 80 minutes) travel between the Zayandeh Rud terminal in Esfahan and the Terminal Esfahan, southwest of Shahr-e Kord town centre. Shared taxis (IR1000) run into town from the terminal at regular intervals.

NA'IN نائين
☎ 0323
Slumbering Na'in is an important transit point at the geographical centre of Iran and the start of the road that runs through the deserts to Mashhad. The town is known for its carpets, and the 10th-century **Jameh Mosque**. This mosque has no *iwan* and is especially notable for its fine mihrab and innovative yet simple use of stucco decoration, which is remarkably well preserved. Watch out also for the restored **traditional houses** dotted around town.

There are two options on the sleeping front: the ITTO's excellent **Na'in Tourist Inn** (Jahangardi Inn; ☎ 225 3665; fax 225 3665; r IR280,000; P), with its stylish split-level rooms; or **Imamzadeh Soltan Said Ali** (IR35,000; P), where the caretaker will offer you a pilgrim's minimalist room with a mattress (no showers).

Keliza Pizza, underneath a carpet shop on Imam Sq, and **Torans Coffee Shop** are good places to sit, eat and contemplate your next move.

To get to Na'in, take any bus travelling from Esfahan or Kashan to Yazd or Kerman, and hop off en route. There is also a direct minibus from Esfahan's Jey minibus terminal (IR3500, 138km, three to four hours). To get to Khur, for Garmeh, walk around to the junction (roundabout) a few hundred metres from Imamzadeh Soltan Said Ali, where you can try to hitch or wait for the 5pm Mashhad bus, which stops in Khur (IR12,000, four hours).

GARMEH گرمه
☎ 0324 / pop about 200 plus a few camels
The tiny oasis village of Garmeh is everything you'd imagine an oasis village to be. More than 50 varieties of date palm spread out from a small spring, and where the palms finish the mud-brick village, which is *very* old, begins. In the midst of this village is **Ateshoni** (☎ 443 3356, in Tehran 021-273 1983; www.ateshoni.com; per person US$15), where Tehrani artist Maziar Ale Davoud has fled the fumes to renovate the home that has been in his family for 400 years. The US$15 per night also includes all the food (such as wonderful dates and pomegranates) you can eat and is all you will spend in Garmeh – there is literally nothing to buy here. It's a bargain!

Part of the beauty of Garmeh is its total, overwhelming silence. When you're not chilling out in the quiet, Maziar can take you **hiking** to a hot-water spring or, for a few extra dollars, **camel riding** or on a trip to the nearby salt desert. Accommodation is in

INTO THE ZAGROS
There are several peaks in the Zagros Mountains that, while not all that technically challenging, could be climbed or skied. If you're interested, the Esfahan office of the **Mountaineering Federation** (Map pp212-13; Shams Abadi St) is the place to get information, though as little English is spoken you'll need to find a translator. The Ziaee brothers from **Amir Kabir Hostel** (Map pp212-13; ☎ 222 7273; mrziaee@hotmail.com) have an arrangement with the federation; they will be willing to help you to organise the trip. Unfortunately, the only effective way of contacting the Mountaineering Federation before you arrive is through Amir Kabir Hostel; email your questions to them.

The guys at the Mountaineering Federation know their way to the best climbs (you can look at their photo album to see what takes your fancy), and can arrange insurance and a guide; rent or sell you equipment; and keep you out of trouble in a region where police are unused to foreigners walking unaccompanied through their hills.

An example of a four- to seven-day tour (depending on your level of fitness) would be climbing or skiing on one of several mountains near the Zagros town of **Chelgerd**. For about US$50 per person per day, you'll get transport, food, basic equipment (tent etc) and transport to Chelgerd.

the traditional style, with basic mattresses unfolded on the floor of your room.

Maziar speaks very little English and a little French. His French-Iranian wife, Ariane, speaks both languages well, so if you can coordinate your visit with one of hers (she is a teacher in Tehran), then it will be much more rewarding. Ateshoni usually closes during summer – it's just too hot. It's a good idea to call or email ahead, especially if you are coming with more than one person.

Getting There & Away

Getting to Garmeh is not easy. From Na'in, you can hitch or take the 5pm Mashhad bus (IR12,000, four hours) to Khur, 38km to the north of Garmeh on the Na'in to Tabas road. Alternatively, buses come direct from Tehran's Terminal-e Jonub to Khur (IR45,000, 14 hours) on Sunday and Wednesday. On other days, the bus to Birjand stops in Khur. From Esfahan, the daily bus to Mashhad leaves the Kaveh bus terminal between about 11am and 1pm and takes about six hours to get to Khur.

Khur is pretty quiet, but even at 9.30pm you will probably be able to find someone to drive you out to Garmeh. Just say 'Garmeh, Maziar'. Expect to pay about IR25,000 for the trip. From Garmeh, there are two buses a week to Yazd via a very quiet desert road – ask Maziar for details.

TABAS طبس
☎ 0353 / pop 32,000

An oasis between two deserts (the Dasht-e Lut and the Dasht-e Kavir), Tabas is the only town of any size for hundreds of kilometres in any direction, and no visitor can fail to appreciate its special relationship with the desert. When you arrive at Tabas with its palm trees, paved roads, bazaar and public gardens, you'd be forgiven for thinking you had stepped into a mirage.

The city is one of the more attractive towns in the Iranian desert, and none of its fertile land is wasted. The **Bagh-e Golshan**, with its lush variety of tropical trees, pools and cascades, and its utter defiance of the desolate conditions at its edge, is quite amazing. The ruined 11th-century citadel, the **Arg-e Tabas**, is also worth a look.

Hotel Bahman (☎ 422 5951-4; apt IR120,000; P 🕸), on the street leading east from the Imamzadeh Hossein Nebn Musa, has ancient

apartments that were due to be renovated (when we visited they desperately needed it).

Getting There & Away

Tabas is not exactly a bus hub. Daily services leave to Yazd (IR20,000, eight hours, 419km) and Mashhad (IR24,000, 10 hours, 521km). Alternatively, flag down any bus heading your way – there aren't many, so it's best to go to the bus station beside the huge Imamzadeh Hossein Nebn Musa to see what time buses leave or pass through.

YAZD یزد
☎ 0351 / pop 450,000 / elevation 1230m

With its winding lanes, windtowers and mud-brick old town, Yazd is one of the highlights of any trip to Iran. Wedged between the northern Dasht-e Kavir and southern Dasht-e Lut, Yazd boasts the best old – and still inhabited – city in the country. It is home to Iran's largest community of Zoroastrians. The combination of an ancient desert city and a multireligious heritage gives Yazd its distinctive relaxed atmosphere. The proliferation of tree-lined streets doesn't hurt, either.

Yazd can be quite cold in winter, but is very hot in summer. The city has always been a great weaving centre, known for its silks and other fabrics even before Marco Polo passed through along one of the Silk Routes in the late 13th century. Yazd is also famous for its *badgirs*, the windtowers designed to catch and circulate the merest breath of wind, which dominate the city's roofscape (see the boxed text 'The Badgirs of Yazd', p233).

History

Although Yazd dates from Sassanian times (AD 224–637), its history is fairly undistinguished. It was conquered by the Arabs in about 642, and subsequently became an important station on the caravan routes to Central Asia and India, exporting its silks, textiles and carpets far and wide. When Marco Polo passed this way in the 13th century, he described Yazd as 'a very fine and splendid city and a centre of commerce'. It was spared destruction by Genghis Khan and Timur, and flourished in the 14th and 15th centuries, yet its commercial success and stability were never translated into political status. Like most of Iran, the town fell into decline after the end of the Safavid era and remained little more than a provincial

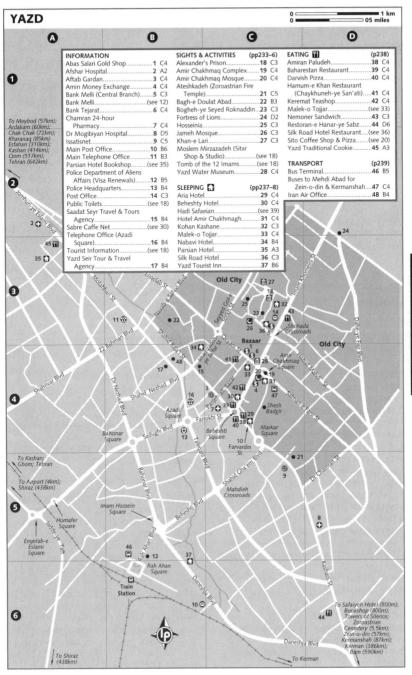

YAZD

0 — 1 km
0 — 05 miles

INFORMATION
Abas Salari Gold Shop..............1 C4
Afshar Hospital.........................2 A2
Aftab Gardan............................3 C4
Amin Money Exchange............4 C4
Bank Melli (Central Branch)......5 C3
Bank Melli............................(see 12)
Bank Tejarat.............................6 C4
Chamran 24-hour
  Pharmacy..............................7 C4
Dr Mogibyan Hospital...............8 D5
Issatisnet..................................9 C5
Main Post Office.....................10 B6
Main Telephone Office...........11 B3
Parsian Hotel Bookshop.......(see 35)
Police Department of Aliens
  Affairs (Visa Renewals)........12 B5
Police Headquarters...............13 B4
Post Office.............................14 C3
Public Toilets.....................(see 18)
Saadat Seyr Travel & Tours
  Agency...............................15 B4
Sabre Caffe Net..................(see 30)
Telephone Office (Azadi
  Square)...............................16 B4
Tourist Information.............(see 18)
Yazd Seir Tour & Travel
  Agency...............................17 B4

SIGHTS & ACTIVITIES   (pp233–6)
Alexander's Prison..................18 C3
Amir Chakhmaq Complex.......19 C4
Amir Chakhmaq Mosque........20 C4
Ateshkadeh (Zoroastrian Fire
  Temple)...............................21 C5
Bagh-e Doulat Abad...............22 B3
Bogheh-ye Seyed Roknaddin..23 C3
Fortress of Lions.....................24 D2
Hosseinia...............................25 C4
Jameh Mosque........................26 C3
Khan-e Lari.............................27 C3
Moslem Mirzazadeh (Sitar
  Shop & Studio).................(see 18)
Tomb of the 12 Imams........(see 18)
Yazd Water Museum..............28 C4

SLEEPING   (pp237–8)
Aria Hotel..............................29 C4
Beheshty Hotel.......................30 C4
Hadi Safaeian....................(see 39)
Hotel Amir Chakhmagh..........31 C4
Kohan Kashane.......................32 C3
Malek-o Tojjar........................33 C4
Nabavi Hotel...........................34 B4
Parsian Hotel..........................35 A3
Silk Road Hotel.......................36 C3
Yazd Tourist Inn......................37 B6

EATING   (p238)
Amiran Paludeh.......................38 C4
Baharestan Restaurant............39 C4
Darvish Pizza...........................40 C4
Hamum-e Khan Restaurant
  (Chaykhuneh-ye San'ati)....41 C4
Keremat Teashop....................42 C4
Malek-o Tojjar.....................(see 33)
Nemoner Sandwich.................43 C3
Restoran-e Hanar-ye Sabz.......44 D6
Silk Road Hotel Restaurant....(see 36)
Sito Coffee Shop & Pizza.....(see 20)
Yazd Traditional Cookie..........45 A3

TRANSPORT   (p239)
Bus Terminal...........................46 B5
Buses to Mehdi Abad for
  Zein-o-din & Kermanshah....47 C4
Iran Air Office.........................48 B4

To Meybod (57km);
Ardakam (60km);
Chak Chak (72km);
Kharanaq (85km);
Esfahan (310km);
Kashan (414km);
Qom (517km);
Tehran (642km)

Jomhuriye Eslami Blvd

Old City

Mizbahi St
Engelab St
Navab-e Safavi Blvd
Seyyed Gole
Sorkh St
22 Bahman Blvd
Shahid Rajai St
Imamzadeh
-ye Jafar St
Qiyam St
Imam Khomeini St
Daneshye Fahadan Blvd

Bazaar
Old City

Amir
Chakhmaq
Square

Shohada
Crossroads

Shahrivar Blvd
Dr Nezhad Blvd
Shahid Nezhad Blvd
Panjeh-ali Bazar
Sahnan-e Farsi St
Hazrat Mahdi St

Azadi
Square
Fartokhi St
Beheshti
Square
Markar
Square
Shesh
Badgir

Bahonar
Square
Sadughi Blvd
Bahonar Blvd
Talegani Blvd
Shahid Cha'em Blvd
Beheshti Blvd

To Kashan;
Ghom; Tehran

Farvardin St

Mahdieh
Crossroads
Dr Chamran St

To Airport (4km);
Shiraz (438km)

Imam Hossein
Square

Homafer
Square
Jadde-ye Taft

Engelab-e
Eslami Square

Kashan St

Rah Ahan Blvd
Daneshju Blvd

Rah Ahan
Square

Train
Station

To Shiraz
(438km)

Daneshju Blvd

To Kerman

To Safaiyeh Hotel (800m);
Bookshop (800m);
Towers of Silence;
Zoroastrian
Cemetery (5.5km);
Zein-o-din (57km);
Kermanshah (87km);
Kerman (386km);
Bam (590km)

CENTRAL IRAN

outpost until the last shah extended the railway line to Yazd.

Orientation

Yazd is laid out on a very loose northeast–southwest grid, the centre of which is Beheshti Sq. If you stay within walking distance of this square, most sights and restaurants can be visited on foot. To the north lies the old city, bisected by the main Imam Khomeini St. Expect to get hopelessly lost when walking around the old city – when you want to get out just ask for directions or orient yourself by climbing until you can see the minarets of the Jameh Mosque.

The airport is on the western fringe of the city (for details on how to get to/from the airport, see p239), while the train station and bus terminal are about 2.5km southwest of Beheshti Sq. Plans to move the bus terminal to a space near the airport might come to fruition during the lifetime of this book.

Information

BOOKSHOPS

Shops in the following hotels sell the usual range of coffee-table books in English.

Parsian Hotel (☎ 525 3111; Meysam St)
Safaiyeh Hotel (☎ 824 2812; Shahid Timsar Fallahi St)

EMERGENCY

Afshar Hospital (☎ 525 5011; Jomhuri-ye Eslami Blvd) For less-urgent ailments.
Dr Mogibiyan Hospital (☎ 624 0061; Kashani St) For urgent problems.
Police Headquarters (☎ 110; Azadi Sq)

INTERNET ACCESS

Aftab Gardan (☎ 626 8470; Shahid Raja'i St; per hr IR5000; ⊠ 9am-2pm & 5-11pm; closed Fri) Kinda psychedelic inside, but with only three terminals.
Issatis.net (☎ 623 1425; www.issatis.net; Kashani St; per hr IR6000; ⊠ 9am-1.30pm & 5-9.30pm Sat-Thu) Efficient, friendly and informative manager Saman Soujoudi offers international calls, and scans, and can download pictures and write them to CD. He also sells pre-paid Internet access and international phonecards.
Sabre Caffe Net (☎ 622 3505; Imam Khomeini St; ⊠ 9am-10.30pm Sat-Thu) Central, stylish, slow.

INTERNET RESOURCES

Yazd City (www.yazdcity.com) In six languages, this site covers sights as well as services.
Yazd.com (www.yazd.com) Check out what's happening in Yazd.

MEDICAL SERVICES

Chamran 24-hour Pharmacy (☎ 626 6900; Farrokhi St)

MONEY

Unusually, the banks in Yazd take a commission of about US$2 on exchanges.
Amin Money Exchange (☎ 626 0745; Imam Khomeini St) Just south of Amir Chakhmaq Sq, it has its fair share of paperwork.
Abas Salari Gold Shop (Qeyam St) This green cornerstore is the least formal and fastest option.
Bank Melli (Shohada Crossroads) Exchange is upstairs.
Bank Tejarat (Qeyam St) Also upstairs.

POST

Main Post Office (Ghasem Abad St; ⊠ 7.30am-2pm) It's out of town but you'll have to come here if you're looking to turn your rug into a flying carpet.
Post Office (Imam Khomeini St) Near Bank Melli.

TELEPHONE

The usual IR1597-per-minute international calls are available at:
Main Telephone Office (Motahhari St)
Telephone Office (Taleqani Blvd) More conveniently located than the main office.

TOURIST INFORMATION

Yazd has some excellent guides and a decent tourist office.
Tourist Information Office (☎ 621 6542-5, 0913 351 4460; yazdguide@yahoo.com; Ziaee Sq; ⊠ 8am-1pm & 3.30-6pm, 8.30am-1.30pm & 4.30-7pm summer) Manager Mohsen Hajisaeed is a wonderful young guy who has plenty of maps and brochures and can arrange all of the tours mentioned below. Email for a quote. The office is opposite Alexander's Prison and also sells handicrafts, postcards and drinks.

TOURS

The following guides all speak good English and can arrange tours to anywhere you'd like to go in Yazd province. The most commonly taken tour is the Kharanaq–Chak Chak–Meybod loop (about US$40 for three or less people, US$55 with breakfast and lunch), which is totally impossible on public transport. Prices vary, but not spending an extra couple of dollars on a guide would be a great shame. Other options include camel tours (about US$25 per person for a half-day, US$75 overnight, more for groups comprised of fewer than five people) and desert walks (one day and one night about US$20 per person). Old city tours are also popular.

Recommended guides:

Hadi Safaeian (☎ 523 8037, 0913 353 1894; hadiinyazd@hotmail.com; Beheshti Sq) Hadi is keen, has a surprisingly detailed knowledge of Yazd's history for one so young, has boundless enthusiasm, has great 'contacts', and can open almost any door – in short, a great guide. Hadi also operates the Tourist Information office at the airport and arranges the usual trips plus mountain walks with 72-year-old 'mountain coach' Saeed Hasan, 4WD desert tours and, *in sh'Allah*, a ballooning trip over Yazd – *that* would be something. His office is next to the Baharestan Restaurant.

Hossain Bagharian (☎ 0913 352 0370) Also a manager of Silk Road Hotel, Hossain is very experienced and can arrange almost any tour, often for less money. His caravanserai-to-caravanserai camel safaris are reported to be pretty good.

TRAVEL AGENCIES

The following are good for plane and train tickets.

Saadat Seyr Travel & Tour Agency (☎ 626 6599; saadatseyr@pishgaman.com; 21/1 Imamzadeh-ye Ja'far St; ☼ 7.30am-8pm Sat-Thu, 9am-noon Fri)

Yazd Seir Tour & Travel Agency (☎ 724 5116; www.yazdseir.com; Motahhari St; ☼ 7.30am-8pm Sat-Thu, 9am-noon Fri)

VISA EXTENSIONS

For visa extensions, visit the **Police Department of Aliens Affairs** (Rah Ahan Blvd; ☼ 7am-2pm Sat-Wed, 7am-noon Thu) two days before your visa expires. It's in a large building opposite the entrance to the bus terminal. From the entrance foyer take the second door on the left. You'll be pointed to the preferred branch of Bank Melli in a building next door – see the boxed text 'More Time, Please' (p362) for details.

Sights

OLD CITY

With its *badgirs* poking out of a baked-brown labyrinth of lanes, the **old city** of Yazd emerges like a phoenix from the desert – a very old phoenix. Yazd's old city is one of the oldest towns on earth, according to Unesco, and is the perfect place to get a feel for the region's rich history. Just about everything in the old city is made from sun-dried mud bricks, and the resulting brown skyline is dominated by the tall *badgirs* on almost every rooftop (see the boxed text 'The Badgirs of Yazd', below). The residential quarters appear almost deserted because of the high walls, which shield the houses from the narrow and labyrinthine *kuches* (alleys) crisscrossing the town.

Follow the walking tour (p236) or just wander around; you'll doubtless discover simple courtyards, ornate wooden doors and some lovely adobe architecture. In the meantime you'll be discovered by countless children who will help lead you out of the maze when you are ready. Be sure not to miss the **Hosseinieh** (follow directions in the walking tour, p236), the roof of which has fine views over Yazd and the desert fringe.

Jameh Mosque

The magnificent **Jameh Mosque** (Masjed-e Jameh St) dominates the old city. Its remarkably high, tiled entrance portal, flanked by two magnificent 48m-high minarets and adorned with an inscription from the 15th century, is simply superb. The beautiful mosaics on the dome and on the mihrab are also exquisite, while the tiles above the main western entrance to the courtyard are particularly stunning.

THE BADGIRS OF YAZD

Any summer visitor to Yazd can hardly fail to appreciate the need for cool air and for the proliferation of *badgirs* (windtowers), constructed to fulfil that need. These ancient systems of natural air-conditioning, which can also be seen in the towns and villages of the Persian Gulf coast, are designed to catch even the lightest breeze and direct it to the rooms below.

All but the simplest towers – which range from standard two-sided models to the more elaborate six-sided variety – consist of at least four parts: the body or trunk that contains the shafts; air shelves that are used to catch some of the hot air and prevent it from entering the house; flaps which redirect the circulation of the wind; and the roof covering. The currents that enter the house do so above a pool of cool water, thereby cooling the air, while the warm air continues its circular path, redirected upwards through a different shaft.

If you stand directly beneath a *badgir*, the air is appreciably cooler, and while not quite as cold as modern air-con, it's a whole lot healthier.

THE QANAT

Iranians have been digging underground water channels called *qanats*, to irrigate crops and supply drinking water, for at least 2000 years. To build a *qanat* you first need to find an underground water source, which might be more than 100m deep but must be at a higher level than the point at which the water is to be collected. Then you dig a tunnel just wide and tall enough to crawl along to carry the water across a very shallow gradient. Narrow wells are dug down to the tunnel at regular intervals for ventilation and to dispose of the excavated soil – you'll see the piles of soil regularly in this part of Iran.

Because of the hazards and expense of constructing a *qanat*, complex laws govern every aspect of their use and maintenance. Iran is thought to have more than 50,000 *qanats*. Although modern irrigation projects now take priority, *qanats* and other traditional methods of supplying water are still very important, and the highly skilled, well-paid *qanat* builders of Yazd (which is where they traditionally come from) won't be picking up redundancy cheques for many years yet.

For the lowdown on *qanats*, head for the impressive **Yazd Water Museum** (☎ 626 8340; Amir Chakhmaq Sq; admission IR10,000; ⊙ 8am-7pm), located in a restored mansion that happens to have a *qanat* or two underneath. The displays are clear and in English.

The mosque was built on the site of a 12th-century building believed to have itself replaced an earlier fire temple. In the courtyard of the mosque there is a stairwell leading down to part of the Zarch Qanat, used these days for ritual ablutions. For a small tip, the caretaker will allow you down.

If you're around on a Friday morning you might see a traditional matchmaking ceremony. Women wearing padlocks on their scarves climb to the top of the minarets, from where they throw the keys into the courtyard of the mosque. If a man picks up her key, the woman will go down to the courtyard, allow him to open the lock and offer him sweets. Locals believe (though we're not sure how strongly) that the couple will marry.

Bogheh-ye Seyed Roknaddin

The beautiful blue-tiled dome that marks the **Bogheh-ye Seyed Roknaddin** (Mausoleum of Seyed Roknaddin; off Masjed-e Jameh St; ⊙ 7.30am-7pm Sat-Tue & Thu), the tomb of local Islamic notable Seyed Roknaddin Mohammed Qazi, is visible from any elevated point around the city. It forms the perfect complement to the tall minarets of the nearby Jameh Mosque. The door is often closed but a knock should bring the caretaker.

Khan-e Lari

The 150-year-old **Khan-e Lari** (⊙ 7am-4pm Sat-Thu) is one of the best-preserved houses of its kind, with traditional doors, stained-glass windows,

elegant archways and alcoves as well as *badgirs*. It was once the home of a rich merchant family, and was sold to the government. Restoration work has yielded results, and the building is now home to architecture students and cultural heritage officers. The house is not signposted and is hidden behind a mud wall. See the walking tour on p236 for directions.

Alexander's Prison

This 15th-century domed school is known as **Alexander's Prison** (admission IR10,000, incl entry to the Tomb of the 12 Imams; ⊙ 7.30am-dark) because of a reference to this apparently dastardly place in a Hafez poem. Whether the deep well in the middle of its courtyard was in fact built by Alexander the Great and used as a dungeon is open to speculation, and you'll probably hear conflicting stories from local guides. Now renovated, it is worth a visit for the building itself and for the small display on the old city of Yazd, the clean toilets and the studio/shop of sitar-maker and player **Moslem Mirzazadeh** (☎ 621 0075; moslemmirzazadeh@yahoo.com). It is next to a garden in the old city.

The early-11th-century brick **Tomb of the 12 Imams** is almost next door to Alexander's Prison. The once-fine inscriptions inside boast the names of each of the Shiite Imams (see the boxed text, 'The 12 Imams', p49), none of whom are buried here.

Amir Chakhmaq Complex

The stunning three-storey façade of the *takieh* (a building used during the rituals to ommemorate the death of Imam Hossein) in the **Amir Chakhmaq Complex** (admission IR15,000; 8am-12.30pm & 4-7.30pm Sun-Fri) is one of the most recognisable and unusual buildings in Iran. Its rows of perfectly proportioned sunken alcoves are at their best around sunset when the light softens and the towering exterior is discreetly floodlit to spectacular effect. The complex contains a small set of buildings at ground level behind the façade, including a lacklustre **bazaar**. In front of the *takieh* look out for the huge wooden palm *nakhl*, an important centrepiece for the observance of the Shiites' passionate Ashura commemorations in the month of Moharram.

Bagh-e Doulat Abad

Once a residence of former ruler Karim Khan Zand, **Bagh-e Doulat Abad** (admission IR30,000; 7.30am-5pm, until 6pm summer) was built in about 1750 and consists of a small pavilion set amid quiet gardens. The interior of the pavilion is superb with intricate latticework and exquisite stained-glass windows throughout. It is also renowned for having the loftiest *badgir* in town, standing over 33m high.

The entrance can be reached from the western end of Shahid Raja'i St, taking one of the narrow lanes and then following the direction of the tallest *badgir* you can see, though it might be moving to Navab-e Safavi Blvd.

ZOROASTRIAN SITES

Yazd is the heartland of an Iranian Zoroastrian community that's becoming ever-smaller in this Islamic stronghold. See Zoroastrianism (below).

Ateshkadeh

Zoroastrians come from around the world to visit this **Ateshkadeh** (Sacred Eternal Flame; nominally 7-11am & 5-7pm Sat-Thu), which is said to have been burning since about AD 470. Visible through a window from the entrance hall, the flame was transferred to Ardakan in 1174, then to Yazd in 1474 and to its present site in 1940. The priests regularly stoke the flame with dry and durable wood (apricot or almond is preferred).

Above the entrance you can see the symbolic bird-man symbol of Zoroaster.

ZOROASTRIANISM

Zoroastrianism was the main religion across the Iranian plateau until the Arab Conquest brought Islam to the fore. Zoroastrians are followers of Zoroaster (Zartosht, Zarathustra), who was probably born about 550 BC at Mazar-e Sharif in what is now Afghanistan. Zoroastrianism was one of the first religions to postulate an omnipotent, invisible god, which is represented as an 'eternally' burning flame in Zoroastrian temples.

Very little of what Zoroaster wrote has survived, though the teachings in the Avesta (sometimes referred to as the Zoroastrian bible) are attributed to him. The core lesson is dualism: the eternal battle of good and evil. Zoroaster believed in two principles – Vohu Mano (Good Mind) and Ahem Nano (Bad Mind), which were responsible for day and night, life and death. These two opposing 'minds' coexisted within the supreme being, Ahura Mazda, and in all living things.

Since Zoroastrians believe in the purity of the elements, they refuse to bury their dead (because it pollutes the earth) or cremate them (because it pollutes the atmosphere). Instead the dead were exposed in 'towers of silence', where their bones were soon cleaned up by the vultures. Nowadays, deceased Zoroastrians are usually buried in graves lined with concrete to prevent 'contamination' of the earth.

Many Zoroastrian temples are adorned with bas-relief winged figures, with the layers of feathers on the wings symbolising purity of thought, word and action. These can also be seen at other sites around Iran, such as Ferdosi's Tomb in Tus (p330) and at Persepolis (p252).

Of the 150,000 or more Zoroastrians in the world, the number in and around Yazd has dwindled to just 5500. Zoroastrian women can be recognised by their patterned headscarves and embroidered dresses with predominant colours of white, cream or red colours. They never wear chadors, but do follow the strict hejab laws governing women's dress.

Zoroastrianism is also known as Mazdaism from the name of its supreme god, Ahura Mazda, and as Magism from the name of its ancient priests, the magi. The Three Wise Men of the Bible are believed to have been Zoroastrian magi, hence the Adoration of the Magi.

CENTRAL IRAN

One hand holds a ring, which symbolises loyalty, while the other hand is held up to indicate respect. The wings have three layers of feathers, reflecting the Zoroastrian belief that you should think, speak and act decently.

Enter via a small gate in an alleyway off Kashani St. Hours here are inconsistent, but if you can get the caretaker to open the gate he will appreciate your small donation.

In the northeast of Yazd, the **Fortress of Lions** (Ghal'eh-ye Asadan) houses another Zoroastrian eternal flame. It is usually closed, and to get in you'll need permission from the caretaker at the Ateshkadeh.

Towers of Silence

Set on two lonely, barren hilltops on the southern outskirts of Yazd are the evocative Zoroastrian **Towers of Silence** (Dakhmeh-ye Zartoshtiyun). In accordance with Zoroastrian beliefs about the purity of the earth, dead bodies were not buried but left in these uncovered stone towers so that vultures could pick the bones clean. A priest would sit with the bodies, which were placed in a sitting position, and watch to see which eye the vultures plucked out first: the right eye and the soul faced a good future; the left and the future looked grim. Such towers have not been used since the '60s.

At the foot of the hills are several other disused Zoroastrian buildings, including a defunct well, a water cistern and two small *badgirs*, a kitchen and a lavatory. The modern **Zoroastrian cemetery** is nearby.

The easiest way to get here is by chartering a private taxi for about IR17,000 return, including waiting time of 45 minutes or so. Ask for Dakhmeh-ye Zartoshtiyun.

Get Lost In Yazd Walking Tour

Start at the **Amir Chakhmaq Complex** (**1**; p234), and check out the nearby **Amir Chakhmaq Mosque** (**2**), and, on the opposite corner, the **Yazd Water Museum** (**3**; see the boxed text 'The Qanat', p234).

From here, head up Imam Khomeini St, take a quick look at the **Hazireh Mosque** (**4**), and turn left up Masjed-e Jameh St. Before you reach the remarkably high *iwan* of the Jameh Mosque, turn down a lane to the right to see the stunning portal of the turquoise-domed **Bogheh-ye Seyed Roknaddin** (**5**; p234).

You could now head around the corner for an Indian lunch and a fine view from the **Silk Road Hotel** (**6**; opposite), or continue into the grand **Jameh Mosque** (**7**, p233). Exit the mosque through the northeastern door (near the *qanat*), turn right, then left, and keep straight for about 75m until you come to a distinctive junction with several arches and open ceilings. Turn left here and you'll reach an open space with a playground. Stay on the right (eastern) side and keep heading northeast. After about 250m on Fazel St a small lane leads off to the right, where a **water reservoir (8)** surrounded by four *badgirs* stands next to a shaded park.

Head back to Fazel St and keep going northeast a few metres then turn left (northwest) on Mirzazadeh St. Walk past Ziaee Sq and keep straight for about 150m. Turn right

WALKING TOUR

Distance: about 5km
Duration: three to five hours, depending on how often you get lost

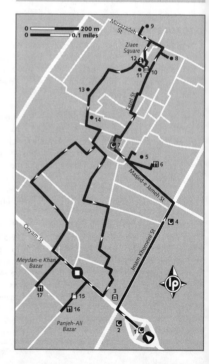

down a small alley that has several arches and on the right side is the entrance to the **Khan-e Lari** (**9**; p234). Head back to Ziaee Sq and turn right. Ahead is the dome of **Alexander's Prison** (**10**; p234) – which has a clean bathroom – and just beyond is the **Tomb of the 12 Imams** (**11**; p234). You can stop for a drink or directions at the **Tourist Information Office** (**12**; p232) opposite.

From the tomb, turn left and follow a sweeping bend until it comes to a dusty space with a concrete table-tennis table. Then head left (southwest) under a domed passage for about 70m until you come to a square with a three-storey façade on the left. Through an arched entrance opposite is the **Hosseinieh (13)**, and a battered wooden door to the right of the archway leads to the roof and quite splendid views of the old city – a great place for sunset pictures.

Coming down from the roof, turn right (south) and walk about 100m. On your left is the domed roof of the now-closed **Madraseh-e Kamalieh (14)**.

Keep along the same lane and you'll see the minarets of the Jameh Mosque. Using these as a guide, you're now on your own. Wend your way through the old city, heading roughly southwest, until you reach Qeyam St. Cross into the **Panjeh-ali Bazar (15)** and head for either **Malek-o Tojjar (16**; p238) or the **Hamum-e Khan (17**; p238) for some well-earned sustenance.

Sleeping

Yazd is becoming one of the best places in Iran in which to stay in a traditional Iranian home. Several properties in the old city have been, or are in the process of being, converted into mid-range hotels, so this is a great place for a splurge. A couple of these places cater to budget travellers, with comfortable dorms.

BUDGET

Hotel Amir Chakhmagh (☎ 626 9823; Amir Chakhmaq Sq; r per person IR30,000; ⚇ 💻) There is nothing fancy about the Amir but its easygoing atmosphere and communal lounge make it the most popular choice for budget travellers. The rooms can be noisy and the shared bathrooms a bit grubby but you forget this when waking to spectacular views over the Amir Chakhmaq complex. In summer the roof is a good place for tea at sunset. Cheap

THE AUTHOR'S CHOICE

Malek-o Tojjar (☎ 626 1478; Panjeh-ali Bazar, Qeyam St; s/d/tr US$35/45/55; ⚇) The walk through a narrow, lamplit passage from the Panjeh-ali Bazar to this Qajar-era home-cum-hotel is like stepping into the decadent days of yore. You'll soon be lying around drinking tea, eating fine food and smoking the qalyan. Staying at Malek-o Tojjar would be arguably the best hotel experience you'll have in Iran. The rooms are not huge and the bathrooms tiny, but the tinkle of water from the fountain and smell of food from the courtyard restaurant (p238) easily compensate for this. Even if you don't stay, you should try to eat here at least once. To find it, enter the Panjeh-ali Bazar from Qeyam St and look for the sign and small doorway on the left.

'tours' to Chak Chak, Kharanaq and Meybod are offered, but your 'guide' will likely be little more than a driver.

Aria Hotel (☎ 626 0411; 10 Farvardin St; s/tw IR50,000/70,000; r with bathroom IR80,000; ⚇) The service and the state of the air-conditioning here have come in for criticism from some readers, while others have praised the communal kitchen and clean, quiet rooms around a small internal courtyard. However, avoid the room right next to reception, where the TV blares 24/7. No English is spoken.

Beheshty Hotel (☎ 626 5517; Imam Khomeini St; s/d IR40,000/50,000; ⚇ 💻 Ⓟ) If you're driving, stay here for the parking. Bathrooms are shared except for one triple room (IR100,000).

MID-RANGE

In a similar vein to Malek-o Tojjar are the following two places.

Silk Road Hotel (☎ 625 2730; touristicplace@yahoo.com; Masjed Jameh Ave; s/d €15/25; Ⓟ ⚇ 💻) Less than 100m from the Jameh Mosque in the heart of the old city, rooms in this beautifully restored home are set around a courtyard with fountain. The roof affords a great view of the Bogheh-ye Seyed Roknaddin and the Jameh Mosque, and you can eat on the roof in summer (see Eating, p238). The open-minded managers, Ali and Hossain, are happy to discount in the low season and can arrange bus, train and air tickets.

Kohan Kashane (☎ 621 0928; off Imam Khomeini St; dm IR35,000, s/d with breakfast US$16/22; ⚇ 💻)

Similar to the Silk Road except harder to find, owner Taslim has renovated his family home and work was being completed when we passed. Each of the seven rooms has bathroom, fridge and satellite TV, as does the dorm. There are plans for a restaurant. To get here, head northeast on Imam Khomeini St, past Masjed-e Jameh Ave, and look for a small sign pointing along a lane on your left a few hundred metres along.

Yazd Tourist Inn (Jahangardi Inn; ☎ 671 3437; yazd@ittic.com; Daneshju Blvd; s/d US$30/60; P ⛌) The location is not good, but rooms here are attractive, the management is friendly and there's a coffee shop and a gift shop in the lobby. Doubles have fridge and TV. Prices halve in winter.

Nabavi Hotel (☎/fax 662 0677; s/d IR180,000/ 200,000; ⛌) If you're looking for a bit more room in your room the doubles here aren't bad. The singles are overpriced. The hotel is in a quiet lane off Imamzadeh-ye Ja'far St.

TOP END
There are no genuinely top-end places in Yazd, but here are the best:

Safaiyeh Hotel (Shahid Timsar Fallahi St; r US$80; P ⛌ 💻) Has a motel-style sheltered garden setting, and good rooms with satellite TV and fridge.

Parsian Hotel (Azadi, Enghelab Hotel; ☎ 525 3111; Meysam St; s/d US$35/60; P ⛌ 🏊) Male guests can use the pool for free, while nonguests pay IR10,000. Rooms are adequate, but it's a long way from the old city.

Eating

Yazd has some atmospheric restaurants that serve first-rate food, which only adds to the city's allure.

These are Yazd's highly recommended atmospheric options.

Malek-o Tojjar (☎ 626 1478; Panjeh-ali Bazar, off Qeyam St; meals IR35,000) Even if you don't stay at the hotel, come for a meal or, at least, tea and a qalyan. There's a good range of Iranian dishes (a couple of them vegetarian), which are very reasonably priced considering the classic surrounds. Romantics take note – this is the place for you.

Silk Road Hotel Restaurant (☎ 625 2730; Masjed Jameh Ave; meals IR40,000) The Indian and Persian food here has had good reports, and the views from the rooftop tables (in summer), looking over the dome of the Bogheh-ye

Seyed Roknaddin and the minarets of the Jameh Mosque, are unbeatable.

Hamum-e Khan Restaurant (Chaykhuneh-ye San'ati; ☎ 627 0366; meals IR40,000; ⏰ 9am-10.30pm) Deep in the heart of the old city, this elegantly restored underground *hammam* is entered via a lovely staircase underneath mud-brick arches, while the interior of the restaurant itself has tranquil pools and attractive tiles, but too much neon. It's in the Meydan-e Khan Bazar, off Qeyam St (follow the signs).

Restoran-e Hanar-ye Sabz (☎ 32 824; Mazari Lane; meals IR40,000) Housed in an old henna grinding mill in the southeast of town, the food here is pretty good and the setting is charming. It's off Kashani St, and a taxi will bring you here for IR5000; ask for *'hanar sayeh sar'* (henna-grinding mills).

For a tasty breakfast (IR6000), a pot of tea and/or a qalyan, head straight for **Keremat Teashop** (Imam Khomeini St) recognisable by, of all things, a picture of Donald Duck enjoying the qalyan. Women are expected to sip their tea away from the men here.

The area around Beheshti Sq is crowded with places selling Iranian-style hamburgers and kebabs. The **Baharestan Restaurant** (Beheshti Sq; meals IR20,000) is down-to-earth and the food is reasonable, and fairly priced. Nearby, **Darvish Pizza** (☎ 626 9767; Imam Khomeini St) is popular with locals; as is the **Sito Coffee Shop & Pizza** (☎ 622 0888; Amir Chakhmaq Sq; pizzas IR16,000; ⏰ 5pm-midnight, closed Fri), where the pizzas aren't as good but the rooftop views (in summer) are worth it. Other interesting local fare includes camel burgers (IR5000) at the **Nemoner Sandwich** (⏰ Sat-Thu), which is opposite the camel butchery; **Amiran Paludeh** for a bowl of *paludeh* (a type of sorbet made of rice flour, grated fruit and rose water), a fantastic local dessert (IR1000 a bowl); and the **Yazd Traditional Cookie** (☎ 525 3673; Jomhuri-ye Eslami Blvd; ⏰ 8am-4pm), which must be one of the best sweets shops in Iran – they will happily let you try the myriad offerings, we liked the pistachio-flavoured *loze peste* best.

Shopping

The many bazaars in the old city are probably the best places in Iran to buy silk (known locally as *tirma*), brocade, glassware and cloth – products that brought the town its prosperity in centuries past. Finding the best places to buy these in the old city can be difficult – try to take an Iranian friend with you. If you have a sweet tooth, don't forget to try some of the *pashmak* sweets (a kind of fairy floss), renowned in Yazd and available in many shops around Beheshti Sq.

Getting There & Away

AIR

The **Yazd airport** (☎ 199) is not the busiest in Iran, but Hadi Safaeian does run a helpful **Tourist Information Office** (☎ 523 8037, 0913 353 8914) near the baggage collection area. **Iran Air** (☎ 622 2080; Motahhari St; ⏱ 7am-6pm Mon-Thu, 8am-noon Fri) only flies to Mashhad, (IR237,000, 80 minutes, twice-weekly) and Tehran (IR186,300, 70 minutes, twice-daily), leaving for Tehran at 8am and 7pm.

BUS & MINIBUS

All buses leave from the **main bus terminal** (Rah Ahan Blvd), about 3km southwest of the town centre, accessible by shared taxi from Beheshti and Azadi Sqs.

Prices on Mercedes buses to the following destinations are:

Destination	Price (IR)	Duration (hr)
Bam	20,000	9
Bandar-e Abbas	28,000	11
Esfahan	11,500	5
Kerman	13,150	6
Mashhad	45,000	16
Shiraz	16,400	7
Tabas	17,850	8
Tehran	24,800	10
Zahedan	31,400	14

Buses to Tehran, Esfahan, Bandar-e Abbas and Kerman leave frequently. For Shiraz, there are buses at 8am, 2pm and 8.30pm. For Zahedan there is always a 4pm service, and usually a few others. The 4pm gets you to the border just as it opens. Any bus to Zahedan will drop you in Bam.

TRAIN

There are three trains daily from Yazd to Tehran (2nd/1st class IR23,600/38,500, eight hours), via Kashan and Qom, which leave at 9.55pm, 11.10pm and 2.10am. From Tehran, trains leave at 6.20pm and 9.10pm. For Kerman (2nd/1st class IR15,000/25,000, five hours) the train stops here at about

2.20am. For Bandar-e Abbas (1st class only, IR48,200, 9½ hours) there is a daily train at midnight, and on Monday, Wednesday and Friday at 7.10pm.

The **train station** (☎ 139; 8am-1.30pm & 7-11pm) is next to the main bus terminal. Get here by shared taxi from Beheshti or Azadi Sqs. Train tickets can be bought in advance at the travel agencies in Yazd (p232).

Getting Around

TO/FROM THE AIRPORT

Take a shared taxi from Enqelab-e Eslami Sq to the airport for about IR2000, or a private taxi for IR15,000.

TAXI

The standard fare in a shared taxi anywhere around town is about IR1000. For private taxis, the fare will be about IR6000 to the bus and train terminals. Taxis can be chartered for around IR18,000 per hour.

AROUND YAZD

Kharanaq, Chak Chak, Meybod and Ar-dakan are best seen as part of a looping day trip from Yazd. It's a long day (about 7am to 6pm) and you can either hire a taxi from the street (about IR250,000) or, much more rewarding but more costly, take a guided tour (p232). Minibuses run to Meybod or Ardakan from the main bus terminal in Yazd, but there's no public transport at all to Chak Chak.

Kharanaq   خرانق

The virtually deserted and crumbling village of Kharanaq, on the side of a hill about 85km north of Yazd, is a captivating place to wander around. Parts are believed to be more than 1000 years old, and it's been occupied in some form for more than 4000 years. The Qajar-era **mosque**, 17th-century **shaking minaret** and **caravanserai** on the edge of town have all been restored. You'll need a key to get into these, however, and you'll need a guide to arrange that.

Many of the buildings are falling down and at least one tourist has fallen through the roof here, so be careful where you step. From the village you can walk about 250m down the valley below to an ancient aqueduct, built to irrigate the surrounding fields. Photographers will love the shots of the village through the arches of the bridge.

CENTRAL IRAN

Chak Chak

چک چک

This is the most important Zoroastrian pilgrimage site in Iran. About 72km northwest of Yazd on the southern fringes of the Dasht-e Lut, many of the buildings are modern and uninspiring. However, the **Pir-e-Sabz fire temple** cut into the cliff-side at the top has a wonderful brass door that's embossed with the likeness of Zoroaster, and the location and views are suitably dramatic.

Chak Chak attracts thousands of pilgrims for an annual festival between June 14 and 18. Legend has it that after the Arab invasion in AD 637 the Sassanian princess Nikbanuh fled to this site. Short of water, she threw her staff at the cliff and water began dripping out – *chak, chak* means drip, drip.

Meybod

ميبد

About 52km north of Yazd, Meybod boasts a thoroughly restored **old post office**, a **caravanserai** (🕐 8am-11pm) with a splendid covered *qanat*, and a Safavid-era **ice house** nearby in the west of town. **Narein castle** (admission IR10,000; 🕐 8.30am-3.30pm), in the centre of town, is worth a quick look.

As you enter town be sure to stop at the bizarre circular **bird tower**. It was once used to house up to 4000 pigeons whose guano was collected as fertiliser. The tower has been meticulously restored and today about 100 pigeons swing from strings in a crude testament to the taxidermist's art. Avoid taking anything mind-altering before coming here...

Ardakan

اردکان

In the middle of the desert, about 60km northwest of Yazd, Ardakan is a regional agricultural centre, courtesy of the amazing *qanat* irrigation system (see the boxed text 'The Qanat', p234). Ardakan's desert setting, rather than any buildings, makes it worth a detour on the way back to Yazd from Chak Chak. There are some attractive old lanes and *badgirs* around the **Jameh Mosque**. Ardakan is famous for its camels, so for a distinctive taste, try a delicious **camel kebab** from the store that's about 150m south of the mosque.

Zein-o-din & Kermanshah

زین الدین کرمانشاه

Zein-o-din and Kermanshah are two stops on one of the more-southerly branches of the Silk Road. There is a caravanserai at each site, but there the similarity ends. The

Caravanserai Zein-o-din (🕿 0351-823 1886; per person US$50; 🅿) is a classic small caravanserai built on the orders of Shah Abbas I, who is reputed to have constructed 999 such hostels to promote trade. This one has been lovingly and faithfully renovated and turned into a fine hotel where you can relive the experience of travelling on the Silk Road.

The rooms at the caravanserai are as they would have been; covered in carpets on raised brick floors and curtained off from the hallway. The bathroom is shared, but very nice. Your US$50 (US$30 in winter) buys accommodation and superb food; camel meat and bread baked on the spot are regulars, and vegetarians are well catered for. In summer you can eat on the roof, which surrounds a courtyard and fountain. There's a hot spring about a 6km walk away at the foot of the mountains, and camel treks can be arranged.

In sharp contrast is the **Kermanshah caravanserai** 30km south (one day's travel for a Silk Road caravan), which is almost identical structurally but the only guests it sees are shepherds and their flocks. If you don't mind sleeping rough (and smelly) this is a great way to get in touch with history. It is often locked, so speak with Ali at the Silk Road Hotel (p237) to organise for it to be opened, or take a chance on finding a shepherd.

Both of these (and several other) caravanserais are on the main road leading south towards Kerman. You can get transport from Yazd's Abuzar Sq towards Anar and get off at Zein-o-din (60km) or Kermanshah (90km), or take the daily bus to Mehdi Abad (IR3000) from behind the Amir Chakhmaq Complex at about 1pm. A private taxi to Zein-o-din will cost about IR40,000 (more to Kermanshah).

Abarqu

ابرقو

This historic town on the road between Yazd and Shiraz is a good off-the-tourist-trail stop. There are several attractions, including a huge **ice house**, the 11th-century **Gonbad Ali dome**, the Jameh Mosque and a 4000-plus-year-old **cypress tree**. The main draw, however, is the **Khan-e Aghazadeh**, a Qajar-era mansion that is being slowly restored into a hotel; look for the distinctive two-storey *badgir*.

The good-value **Hotel Pouya Tourist** (🕿 0352-682 1030; s/d IR100,000/176,000; 🅿 💥 💻), on the left as you come into town from the east, also has a decent restaurant.

SHIRAZ شیراز

☎ 071 / pop 1,206,800 / elevation 1491m

Shiraz is a city of sophistication and has always been celebrated as the heartland of Persian culture. In its heyday, the city was given the epithet of Dar-ol-Elm (House of Learning) and became synonymous with education, nightingales, poetry, roses and wine. It was also one of the most important cities in the medieval Islamic world and was the Iranian capital during the Zand dynasty (AD 1747–79), when many of its most beautiful buildings were built or restored.

In his 1893 book *A Year Amongst the Persians*, Edward Browne described Shirazis as '...amongst all the Persians, the most subtle, the most ingenious, the most vivacious'. Shiraz is still a city of poets, and one that is home to the graves of Hafez and Sa'di. There are the usual Iranian traffic issues, but Shiraz's agreeable climate, set as it is in a fertile valley once famed for its vineyards, makes it a pleasant place at most times of year. Its splendid gardens, exquisite mosques and whispered echoes of ancient sophistication reward those who linger longer than it takes to visit nearby Persepolis.

The attractions of Shiraz range from exquisite mosques to mausoleums of great historical significance to tranquil gardens. No visit will be complete without joining the thousands – literally – of locals in the very modern Friday night ritual of strolling and picnicking along the western reaches of Dr Chamran Blvd.

History

There was a settlement at Shiraz at least as early as the Achaemenid period, and it was already an important regional centre under the Sassanians. However, it did not become the provincial capital until about AD 693, following the Arab conquest of Estakhr, the last Sassanian capital (8km northeast of Persepolis, but now completely destroyed). By 1044 Shiraz was said to rival Baghdad in importance and grew further under the Atabaks of Fars in the 12th century, when it became an important artistic centre.

Shiraz was spared destruction by both the Mongols and Tamerlane's rampaging armies when the rulers of the time saw the wisdom of offering tribute to their potential executioners. Having avoided calamity, the Mongol and Timurid periods became among the most successful eras in Shiraz's development. The encouragement of enlightened rulers, and the presence of Hafez, Sa'di and many other brilliant artists and scholars helped Shiraz to become one of the greatest cities in the Islamic world throughout the 13th and 14th centuries.

While Shiraz remained a provincial capital during the Safavid period, even attracting several European traders who exported its famous wine, it then fell into nearly a century of decline. This was worsened by several earthquakes, the Afghan raids of the early 18th century, and an uprising led by Shiraz's governor in 1744, which was put down in typically ruthless fashion after a siege by Nader Shah.

At the time of Nader Shah's murder in 1747, most of Shiraz's historical buildings were damaged or ruined, and its population had fallen to 50,000, a quarter of what it had been 200 years earlier. However, Shiraz soon returned to prosperity under the enlightened Karim Khan, the first ruler of the short-lived Zand dynasty, who made Shiraz the national capital in 1750. Master of virtually all Persia, Karim Khan refused to take any higher title than *vakil* (regent). He was determined to build Shiraz into a worthy capital, the equal of Esfahan under Shah Abbas I.

Karim Khan founded a royal district in the area of the Arg-e Karim Khani and commissioned many fine buildings, including the preeminent bazaar in Persia. However, Karim Khan's heirs failed to secure his gains and the vengeful Qajars destroyed the city's fortifications. In 1789 they moved the national capital – and the remains of Karim Khan – to Tehran. Although reduced to the rank of provincial capital, Shiraz managed to remain prosperous due to the continuing importance of the trade route to Bushehr.

The city's role in trade greatly diminished with the opening of the trans-Iranian railway in the 1930s, as trade routes shifted to the ports in Khuzestan. Much of the architectural inheritance of Shiraz, and especially the royal district of the Zands, was either neglected or destroyed as a result of irresponsible town planning under the Pahlavi dynasty. Lacking any great industrial, religious or strategic importance, Shiraz is now largely an administrative centre, although its population has grown considerably since the 1979 revolution.

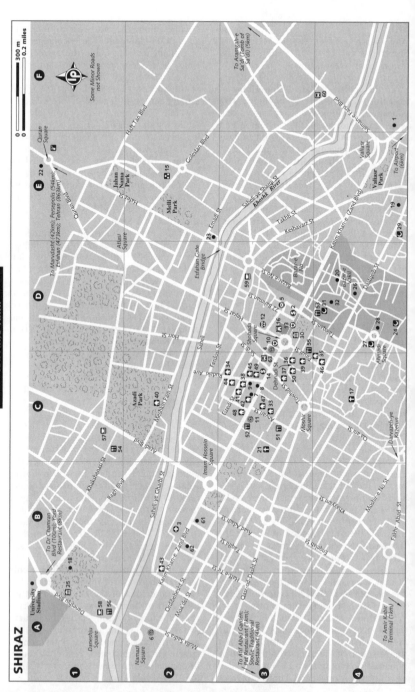

SHIRAZ

0   300 m
0   0.2 miles

Some Minor Roads
not Shown

Orientation

The main street of Shiraz is the wide, tree-lined Karim Khan-e Zand Blvd (often shortened simply to Zand). This boulevard runs about as far east and west as you would want to go without leaving Shiraz. Most of the things to see, and nearly all the hotels, are along here or within walking distance, so this is a street you'll keep coming back to.

The old city and the commercial centre of Shiraz are south of the Khoshk River, while the smarter residential areas are to the north. The modern university buildings and dormitories are on a steep hill in the northwest of town. The city centre is Shohada Sq (still widely known as Shahrdari Sq), on Zand.

For details on how to get to/from the airport, see p252.

Information

BOOKSHOPS

Bookshop (Bazar-e Vakil) This good bookshop is in a branch of the bazaar southeast of Serai Mushir.
Armagh-e Hafez Bookshop (🕙 9am-5pm) Probably the best bookshop in Shiraz.
Persepolis Bookshop (☎ 233 8200; Rudaki St) Opposite the Sadra Hotel, a good range of posters.

EMERGENCY

Shiraz is famous for its medical training, so it's a good place to get sick. Ask at your

hotel which of the dozens of hospitals best suits your ailment.
Dr Faqihi Hospital (☎ 235 1091; Zand Blvd) The most central hospital.
Police Headquarters (☎ 236 4998; Shohada Sq)
Tourist police (Karim Khan-e Zand Blvd) Outside the Arg-e Karim Khani. There's rarely anyone here outside peak season.

INTERNET ACCESS

Ferdous Internet (Park Hotel Ln; 🕙 Sat-Thu) Fastest service in Iran when we visited. Very busy.
Max Coffee Net (☎ 628 6081; Mollasadra Passage, Molla Sadra St; per hr IR9000; 🕙 9am-10pm Sat-Thu) Fast connections. In a small complex of computer stores 50m south of the western end of Zand.
Shiraz Net Cafe (☎ 233 7989; Karim Khan-e Zand Blvd; per hr IR20,000; 🕙 9am-1.30pm & 5-9.30pm Sat-Thu) Overpriced for an average service.

MONEY

The central branches of the major banks have foreign exchange facilities. However, the exchange offices along Zand are simple, safe and your best option.
Bank Melli (Karim Khan-e Zand Blvd) Next to the Arg-e Karim Khani.
Chahtoosi Exchange (☎ 222 2580; Park Hotel Ln) Same rates as the banks, no commission, fast, longer hours.
Zand Exchange (☎ 222 2854; Karim Khan-e Zand Blvd; 🕙 9am-8pm Sat-Thu) As above.

CENTRAL IRAN

PHOTOGRAPHY
Pardis Photo Gallery (☎ 233 1095; ☼ 8am-10pm Sat-Thu) Best place for processing and buying film, including Kodak E100VS slide film.

POST
DHL (☎ 627 6771; 2nd fl, Mollasadra Passage, Molla Sadra St)
Main Post Office (Taleqani St) Behind the central branch of Bank Melli.

TELEPHONE
There are two offices with cheap international calls:
Telephone Office (☼ 8am-10pm; Park Hotel Ln) Found beside Ferdous Internet. It's often very busy.
Telephone Office (Hejrat St; ☼ 8am-1am)

TOURIST INFORMATION
Tourist Information Office (Karim Khan-e Zand Blvd; ☼ 8am-8pm) Outside the Arg-e Karim Khani. Helpful English-speaking staff will give you a free map and/or directions.

TOURS
A lot of travellers choose to hire a taxi or driver to get to Persepolis, or to visit other attractions around Shiraz. See the Persepolis section for further recommendations (p252):
Park Taxi Service (☎ 222 5544) Found in a lane just off Zand Blvd near Shohada Sq. It's relatively expensive but is on call 24 hours and has been recommended.
Pars Tourist Agency (☎ 222 3163; www.key2persia .com; Karim Khan-e Zand Blvd; ☼ 9am-9pm Sat-Thu) Pars runs a range of daily trips to places such as Persepolis (per person US$8), Pasargadae (per car US$35), Firuz Abad and all manner of other places within Fars province and elsewhere (check out its website for more information). All the here drivers speak English and, if you give them some some notice, Pars can arrange knowledgeable and interesting guides in German-, French-, Italian- and Japanese-speaking incarnations.

TRAVEL AGENCIES
Mohajeri & Co International Travel & Tours (☎ 222 7427; www.mohajeri.com; 6 Karim Khan-e Zand Blvd; ☼ 8am-7pm Sat-Thu) Reliable service for air tickets, both domestic and international.
Pars Tourist Agency (see above) This is one of the best and most professional agencies in Iran. It runs a range of daily trips and also rents out bikes (per day US$4), offers Internet access, can help with visa extensions and bus tickets or, in the event of an emergency, can be contacted to help sort things on ☎ 0917 111 8514. Highly recommended.

VISA EXTENSIONS
Shiraz is the second-best place in Iran, after Esfahan, to extend your visa. The efficient staff at the **Aliens Office** (Valiasr Sq; ☼ 7.30am-1.30pm Sat-Wed, 7.30am-noon Thu) are used to foreigners, and tourist visas are commonly extended by a month, all of which takes only a few hours. Walk or take a shared taxi (about IR800) along Zand to Valiasr Sq, where it's on the southeast corner. The appropiate Bank Melli is also on Valiasr Sq, not far from the Aliens Office. For full details on extending visas see the boxed text 'More Time, Please' (p362).

Dangers & Annoyances
There's not too much that's dangerous or annoying about Shiraz. You have to be aware of the usual bogus police scam (p346), though it seems less prevalent here than in Tehran.

Sights
ARG-E KARIM KHANI
Dominating the city centre, the imposing structure of the **Arg-e Karim Khani** (Citadel of Karim Khan; ☎ 222 1423; Shohada Sq; admission IR30,000; ☼ 8am-4pm, until 7pm summer) served as a prison in Pahlavi times. This well-preserved fortress with four 14m-high circular towers was, in the time of the Zand dynasty, part of a royal courtyard that Karim Khan hoped would rival that of Esfahan.

The sign inside proclaims that 'The exalted stature of the Karim Khani citadel amuses every new traveller for a long time who arrives in Shiraz'. The courtyard is filled with citrus trees, but it's arguable whether it, plus a private prayer room and bathhouse, are worth your money. If you do enter, be sure to check out the model of Shiraz. The austere and squat exterior of the fortress is perhaps of more interest, particularly the disturbing slope of the tower on the southeastern side – experts from as far away as Pisa in Italy have given up efforts to correct the slope.

PARS MUSEUM
The future of the **Pars Museum** (☎ 222 4151; Karim Khan Zand Blvd) is in doubt after its most prized exhibit, an ancient and valuable Quran, was stolen by a cunning burglar. It was closed when we visited. If it does reopen, the building itself is of some interest.

REGENT'S MOSQUE

The beautiful **Regent's Mosque** (Masjed-e Vakil; admission IR15,000; 8am-noon, 3.30pm-sunset Sat-Thu) was built in 1773 by Karim Khan at one of the entrances to his bazaar. The mosque has two vast *iwans* to the north and south, a magnificent inner courtyard surrounded by beautifully tiled alcoves and porches and a wonderful vaulted mihrab with 48 impressive columns. Don't miss the remarkable 14-step marble minbar – the enormous block of marble from which it was cut was carried all the way from Azerbaijan. Most of the tiling, with its predominantly floral motifs, was added in the early Qajar era.

The mosque was being renovated when we visited and opening times were more random than suggested. Women do not need a chador, but should have a manteau that reaches below the knee, and a dark scarf.

BAZAR-E VAKIL

Shiraz's finest bazaar is one of the most atmospheric in Iran and has been described as the most architecturally impressive in the country. It was constructed by Karim Khan as part of a plan to make Shiraz into a great trading centre. The vaulted brick ceilings ensure that the interior is cool in summer and warm in winter. In the best traditions of Persian bazaars, the **Bazar-e Vakil** (Bazar-e Vakil; dawn-dusk Sat-Thu) is best explored by wandering without concern for time or direction, soaking up the atmosphere in the maze of lanes.

Chances are you'll stumble across **Serai Mushir**, off the southern end of the main bazaar lane coming from Zand. This tastefully restored two-storey caravanserai is a pleasant place to gather your breath and do a bit of souvenir shopping.

The bazaar's Zand-era bathhouse, the **Hammam-e Vakil**, has been converted into one of the country's most impressive traditional teahouses (p250).

MARTYR'S MOSQUE

One of the largest ancient mosques in Iran, the rectangular courtyard of the **Martyr's Mosque** (Masjed-e Shohada; Ahmadi Sq) covers more than 11,000 sq metres. Founded at the start of the 13th century, the mosque has been partially rebuilt many times, and now has very little in the way of tiling or other decorations, though it does boast some impressive barrel vaulting. It lives under acres of unsightly corrugated fibreglass and is seldom open – your best bet is Friday, when it is still used for prayer. Entry is through a gate off Ahmadi Sq.

MAUSOLEUM OF SHAH-E CHERAGH

The remains of Sayyed Mir Ahmad (a brother of Imam Reza) who died in Shiraz in AD 835 are housed at the famous **Mausoleum of Shah-e Cheragh** (Mausoleum of the King of the Lamp or Bogh'e-ye Shah-e Cheragh; Ahmadi Sq; 2222158; 7am-6pm, until 9pm summer). A mausoleum was first erected over the grave in the mid-14th century and it has been an important Shiite place of pilgrimage ever since.

The expansive courtyard is a great place to sit and discreetly observe the moving climax to what is an important religious rite for Shiites. Non-Muslims should ask for permission before entering – if you are polite and well presented, you'll be allowed in. The multicoloured reflections from the countless minute mirror tiles inside the shrine are quite dazzling and the golden-topped minarets above it are superb.

Women must put on a chador if they plan to enter the shrine itself; you can borrow one from the bookshop outside the complex. Cameras are forbidden inside the shrine but permitted in the courtyard.

Hidden away in the northwestern corner of the courtyard is a small **museum** (admission IR500; 7am-6pm, until 9pm summer), which houses a few old Qurans and, more interestingly, photos and belongings of some of those who died during the Iran-Iraq War.

At the southeastern corner of the courtyard is the **Mausoleum of Sayyed Mir Mohammed** (Bogh'e-ye Sayyed Mir Mohammad; 7am-6pm, until 9pm summer). It was built for the brother of Mir Ahmad, who also died in Shiraz. The shrine has intricate mirror tiling and some inscriptions in the dome, but it is less interesting than the Shah-e Cheragh mausoleum.

JAMEH-YE ATIGH MOSQUE

In an alley reached through the southeastern entrance to the Shah-e Cheragh courtyard, the ancient **Jameh-ye Atigh Mosque** was first built in AD 894. Most of what you see dates from the Safavid period onwards. What looks like an extensive refurbishment was underway when we visited.

The mosque is mainly of interest for the rare turreted rectangular building in the centre of the courtyard. Known as the **Khodakhune** (House of God), it was built in the mid-14th century to preserve valuable Qurans, and is believed to be modelled on the Kaaba at Mecca. Although most of it was very skilfully rebuilt in the early 20th century, the House of God still bears an original and unique inscription in raised stone characters on a tiled background.

MADRASEH-YE KHAN
In 1615, Imam Gholi Khan, governor of Fars, founded the serene **Madraseh-ye Khan** (Dastqeib St) theological college for about 100 students. The original building has been extensively damaged by earthquakes and only the impressive portal at its entrance has survived; watch for the unusual type of stalactite moulding inside the outer arch and some intricate mosaic tiling with much use of red, in contrast to the tiles used in Yazd and Esfahan. The training college (still in use) has a fine stone-walled inner courtyard set around a small garden.

The building can be reached via a lane off Dastqeib St. The madraseh is often closed but if you get lucky the caretaker will open it; a tip is appreciated (locals also pay to have the door opened). If you can get in, make sure you ask to be shown to the roof for wonderful views over the bazaar.

NASIR-OL-MOLK MOSQUE
Further down the bazaar from the Madraseh-ye Khan, **Nasir-ol-Molk Mosque** (off Dastqeib St; admission IR15,000; ☺ 8am-1pm & 3.30-6.30pm, until 8pm summer) is one of the most elegant mosques in southern Iran. Built relatively recently, at the end of the 19th century, its coloured tilings (an unusually deep shade of blue) are exquisite. There is some particularly fine stalactite moulding in the smallish outer portal and in the northern *iwan*, but it is the stunning stained glass and exquisitely carved pillars of the winter prayer hall that are most eye-catching. Photographers should come between about 10.30am and 2pm for the best shots of the prayer hall.

The structure has survived numerous earthquakes, due in part to its construction using flexible wood as struts within the walls – look for the wooden bricks in the *iwan* columns. The small **museum** is worth a

quick look (entry to the mosque also grants entry to the museum).

CHURCHES
The **Anglican Church of St Simon the Zealot** (Kelisa-ye Moqaddas-e Sham'un-e Ghayur), built by R Norman Sharp in 1938, is very Iranian in character and even contains stone tablets with biblical stories incised on them in cuneiform, probably by Sharp. According to local tradition, St Simon was martyred in Persia together with St Thaddeus, another of the 12 Apostles. The great metal door bearing a Persian cross is usually closed; just ring the doorbell to be let in.

The 17th-century **Armenian Church** (Kelisa-ye Aramaneh), in an alley off Qa'ani St, is worth a quick look if you just happen to be in the area.

IMAMZADEH-YE ALI EBN-E HAMZE
This tomb of the nephew of the seventh Shiite Imam has a bulbous dome that's quite stunning. The interior of the **Imamzadeh-ye Ali Ebn-e Hamze** (☎ 222 3353; Hafez St; ☺ dawn-dusk) has mirror work as dazzling as you'll see anywhere, as well as beautiful stained-glass windows and an intricate, ancient wooden door. The tombstones around the courtyard, for which families of the deceased paid a small fortune, are also interesting; some date back to the 19th century. Virtually all the original 10th-century structure has disappeared, after several earthquakes and significant repairs and extensions, but unless you managed to see the original you're unlikely to be disappointed.

ARAMGAH-E HAFEZ
Iranians have a saying that every home must have two things: first the Quran, then Hafez (see p65). And many would reverse that order. Hafez the poet is an Iranian folk-hero – loved, revered and as popular as any a modern pop star. Almost every Iranian can quote his work, bending it to whichever social or political persuasion they ascribe to. And there is no better place to try to understand Hafez's eternal hold on Iran than here, at **Aramgah-e Hafez** (Tomb of Hafez; Golestan Blvd; admission IR30,000; ☺ 8am-9.30pm), his tomb.

Set in a charming garden with its two pools, the whole scene is very restful, despite the ever-present traffic noise. The marble tombstone, engraved with a long verse from the poet's works, was placed here, inside a small shrine, by Karim Khan in 1773. In 1935, an octagonal pavilion was put up over it, supported by eight stone columns beneath a tiled dome. Plan to spend a couple of hours sitting in a discreet corner of the grounds, at sunset if possible, to watch the way Iranians react to what is, for many, a pilgrimage to his tomb.

You might see people performing the *faal-e Hafez*, a popular ritual in which you seek insight into your future by opening a volume of Hafez – the future is apparent in his words. Around the tomb itself, this deep respect for the greatest of Persian poets comes to life, with Iranians strolling through the gardens reading from his poetry in groups or alone and approaching the tomb with great reverence. After the sun sets, with the tomb floodlit and sung versions of the poetry of Hafez piped quietly over the public address system, it is difficult not to feel transported back to the magic of ancient Persia.

There's a wonderful teahouse in the private, walled garden inside the grounds (see Aramgah-e Hafez Teahouse, p250) and an excellent bookshop.

To get here you can take a shared taxi from Shohada Sq or bus No 2 from Sa'di St (IR200). A private taxi from the centre of town should cost no more than IR4000.

ARAMGAH-E SA'DI
The natural spring at the foot of a hill, and the fish pond fed by a *qanat*, make the garden at the **Aramgah-e Sa'di** (Tomb of Sa'di; Bustan Blvd; adult/student IR30,000/15,000; 🕑 9.30am-8.30pm, until 10pm summer) a tranquil place. The plain marble tomb with its Farsi inscription dates from the 1860s and is surrounded by an octagonal stone colonnade, inscribed with various verses from Sa'di, supporting a tiled dome (see p65 for more on Sa'di). There is an underground teahouse set around a fish pond, which is atmospheric if slightly smelly.

The useful bus No 2 (IR300) leaves from the city centre and stops at a terminal about 50m from the entrance to the tomb. There are plenty of places to buy food and drink near the entrance, so you can enjoy an impromptu picnic in the gardens.

BAGH-E NARANJESTAN
This is a worthy, if rather smaller rival to the Bagh-e Eram (p247). The main pavilion of the **Bagh-e Naranjestan** (Orange Garden; Dastqeib St; admission IR30,000; 🕑 9am-6pm, until 8pm summer), the **Naranjestan-e Ghavam**, was built between 1879 and 1886 as a reception hall for visitors, and was also used as the Governor's Residence during the late Qajar period.

Inside the pavilion is a dazzling mirrored entrance hall, while the surrounding rooms have a breathtaking combination of intricate tiles, inlaid wooden panels, and beautiful stained-glass windows. The façade also has some mock Persepolis bas-reliefs.

The gardens are behind a pale, sandstone, walled compound, about 300m beyond the Nasir ol-Molk Mosque.

BAGH-E ERAM
Famous for its cypress trees, the delightful **Bagh-e Eram** (Garden of Paradise; Daneshju Blvd; admission IR40,000; 🕑 8am-noon & 2-5pm, until 7pm summer) is the place where any budding botanist should head. Alongside a pretty pool is the charming 19th-century Qajar palace, the **Kakh-e Eram** (Eram Palace). Unfortunately, visitors cannot enter the palace.

The gardens are easy enough to reach by taking any shared taxi going along Zand towards the university. The best time for photos is early morning.

DARVAZEH-YE QURAN
On the outskirts of Shiraz is the **Darvazeh-ye Quran** (Quran Gateway; Quran Sq). Some say it was built in the 9th century, but it is known that Karim Khan added a room at the top of the gateway to house a holy Quran. An ancient Persian tradition, still observed by some, requires that all travellers pass underneath a Quran before undertaking any journey. Unfortunately, the room is home only to pigeons these days. The gateway is lucky to exist at all. It was pulled down 70 years ago to make way for the road, but was reassembled five years later by outraged local businessmen.

Those with good leg muscles might want to look for some **bas-reliefs** further up the hill, from where the views of Shiraz are breathtaking. There are two teahouses, one of which offers superb views of the city at sunset, interrupted only by the immense hotel being completed nearby.

CENTRAL IRAN

Getting a shared taxi to the gateway is not easy, but you could combine it with a visit to the tomb of Hafez (see Aramgah-e Hafez, p246), which is within walking distance – just head back up Hafez St.

Sleeping

Shiraz has probably the best range of hotels, in the most confined space, in all of Iran. They are almost all within a short walk of Zand, and tend to be clustered by price range, making comparisons a breeze. The only drawback is that hotels right on Zand can be noisy, so ask for a room away from the street. Competition is keen so most managers will be happy to knock a few rial off the price out of season.

BUDGET

Most budget places are concentrated in the neighbouring Dehnadi and Piruzi Sts.

Anvari Hotel (☎ 233 7591; Anvari St; d/tr IR90,000/ 130,000; 🔀) At the 'luxury' end of the budget range, with affable staff and a welcoming atmosphere. All of the large rooms have a bathroom (in the triple, the bathroom is enormous), and for a little extra you'll get a TV and fridge. Negotiation will be rewarding in winter. Travellers with vehicles can park opposite the hotel. There is a kitchen for guests, and breakfast (IR8000) is good.

Esteghlal Hotel (☎ 222 7728; Dehnadi St; tw without/with bathroom IR50,000/65,000; 🔀) The Esteghlal is probably the most popular place with budget travellers, which is due more to the savvy manager than to the quality of the small rooms. Not that they're bad; most are pretty quiet and if you get a room with a toilet as well as a shower (they cost the same, so ask specifically) it's great value. Tours to Persepolis cost US$10, or US$15 to include Pasargadae as well. If you have trouble communicating at reception, ask for English-speaking Fallah, the manager.

Zand Hotel (☎ 222 2949; Dehnadi St; tw IR55,000; Ⓟ) This place has had some good reviews from travellers, especially overlanders in need of parking space. Rooms with a basic bathroom are adequate, and there's a kitchen guests can use.

Toos Hotel (☎ 224 7261; Rudaki Ave; d/tr IR50,000/ 70,000; 🔀) Rooms here have basins, but bathrooms are shared. They're clean, service is friendly and the location is good. Fair value.

THE AUTHOR'S CHOICE

Shiraz Eram Hotel (☎ 230 0814; www.eram hotel.com; Karim Khan-e Zand Blvd; s/d/tr with breakfast US$30/40/50; Ⓟ 🔀 ▣) It's the guys at reception who make the difference at this mid-range hotel. Speaking excellent English, they are smiling fonts of knowledge on most things Shiraz and they understand good service. The rooms are not exactly luxurious, but they are huge and come with fridge, satellite TV and enormous beds. There's a 24-hour coffee shop in the foyer and the Sarve Naz Restaurant (p250) is very good, as is the breakfast. The front-desk guys can arrange trips to Persepolis, and will probably drive you themselves.

There are a stack of noisy but decent cheapies competing for business along Piruzi St. Most are pretty basic but with so much on offer, you should find something that suits:

Darya Hotel (☎ 222 1778; s/tw IR45,000/65,000; 🔀) Among the best; the clean rooms with attached shower and shared toilet have been enjoyed by several readers.

Saadi Hotel (☎ 222 5126; s/tw/tr IR45,000/70,000/ 90,000) Not far behind Darya in quality, with especially clean rooms with shower.

Hashemi Guest House (☎ 222 5271; s/d IR40,000/ 57,500) This place is rudimentary, no more.

MID-RANGE

Rudaki Ave and the adjoining Eizedi St are the best place to start looking for mid-range options. There are several new places and when we visited prices were mostly very reasonable. Bargaining at any of mid-range places should bear fruit.

Aryo Barzan Hotel (☎ 224 7128; www.aryohotel.com; Rudaki Ave; s/d with breakfast US$37/50) This new hotel is top-end quality for a mid-range price. The tasteful and comfortably furnished rooms have a sort of mini-bath, which would submerge about half of a normal person, and are set around an atrium. The Aryo has been recommended by several readers, who report that significant discounts are possible. If you book ahead they will collect you from the airport for nothing.

Jaam-e-Jam Suite Hotel (☎ 230 4002; jaam-e-jam-shiraz@nasiran.com; Eizedi St; d/q apt with breakfast US$50/70; Ⓟ 🔀 ▣) These sprawling, tastefully decorated new apartments are about the best value in town, especially if you're part of a small group or family. The location is quiet, management are professional and facilities include a sauna and spa that men and women can use (separately, of course). It might not last, but healthy discounts were available when we visited.

Sasan Hotel (☎ 230 2028; sasanhotel@shiraz sport.com; Anvari St; s/d IR120,000/160,000; 🖳) At the bargain basement end of the mid-range, the rooms here aren't flash but with TV and clean bathroom they're more than adequate. The manager could talk the leg off a billiard table, but he's friendly enough. Note that there's no air-con.

Ghane Hotel (☎ 222 5374; fax 224 9037; Towhid Ave; US$24/37; 🍴) In a quiet location, this place is best visited in winter, when prices for the pleasant rooms fall to US$15/20. It's set around a courtyard full of citrus trees.

Parsian Hotel (☎ 233 0000; www.parsian-hotel.com; Rudaki Ave; d US$55; Ⓟ 🍴 🖳) This government-run place is not bad, but the semi-luxurious rooms are small and the discounts (for multiple nights only) not big enough.

The following are reliable lower mid-range options:

Kowsar Hotel (☎ 230 0207; kowsarhotel@shirazsport .com; Karim Khan-e Zand Blvd; s/d with breakfast US$20/ 30; Ⓟ 🍴 🖳) Has good rooms with satellite TV. The restaurant is only open for breakfast.

Roodaki Hotel (☎ /fax 222 9594; Rudaki Ave; s/d with breakfast US$20/30 plus 15% tax; Ⓟ 🍴) Nice enough but doesn't look so good with all the new places around.

Top End

Hadish Hotel (☎ 235 1988; hadishhotel@ny.com; Rudaki Ave; s/d/tr apt with breakfast US$70/80/110; Ⓟ 🍴 🖳) This new apartment hotel has huge suites (the kitchens here could probably sleep about six) fitted with all the gear. Staff are friendly, professional and, in low season, happy to discount (we were offered a single for US$42 after about 30 seconds' bargaining).

Pars International Hotel (☎ 233 6380; shirazpars hotel@yahoo.com; Zand Blvd; s/d/ste with breakfast US$65/ 95/150 plus 17% tax; Ⓟ 🍴 🖳) This new four-star hotel is more convenient than the Homa, though not quite as plush. Rooms are well equipped and those on the upper floors have great views. Popular with businesspeople.

Homa Hotel (☎ 222 8000; shiraz@homahotels.com; Meshkin Fam St; s/d/ste US$72/112/162 plus 17% tax; Ⓟ 🍴 🖳) A recent refurbishment means the Homa is probably worth the money. The rooms are very nice indeed, but be sure to ask for one overlooking the city – the view is great.

Eating

Shiraz is noted as a culinary capital but you'd sometimes wonder. There are a few quite good restaurants, but also an incredible number of crap eateries. You can rely on getting good fruit juices here, though sadly the world-famous Shiraz (Syrah) grape is no longer made into the wine that inspired Omar Khayyam to poetry.

FAST FOOD

Shiraz might just be the pizza capital of the world. Since 2001 more than 60 new pizza joints have opened in this city. The pizzas are usually pretty dire – there's that whole lack-of-tomato thing – but most also sell a range of burgers, hot dogs, saucis (sausage) sandwiches and other such delicacies. Zand is the place to go. Among the better options is **Nikan** (☎ 222 9365; Karim Khan-e Zand Blvd; 🕙 11am-11pm), where you can choose your own toppings (sorry, no tomato) and the pizza (IR11,000) will arrive at something approaching the speed of sound. Around the corner, **110 Hamburgers** (Anvari St; 🕙 11am-midnight) is very popular with Shirazis, who come like moths to its neon flame (two glowing palm trees). The burgers and pizzas are of dubious quality, but the shwarmas (meat sliced off a spit and stuffed in a pocket of

THE AUTHOR'S CHOICE

Yord Restaurant (☎ 625 6774; meals IR40,000; 🕙 lunch & dinner, dinner only in winter) On a patch of open land beside a stream about 8km northwest of the city centre, the Yord is a chance not only to enjoy some fine nomad food, but also to experience a fast-disappearing culture. These Qashqa'i nomads have set up a huge yord (tent). Inside the welcome is warm, the food is good and relatively cheap, and the live traditional music will carry you away. It's almost impossible to reach by public transport, so ask your hotel to write the name in Farsi and get a taxi (about IR18,000); it is also worth paying the taxi to wait for you (about IR50,000 total) as taxis out here are rare indeed. **Pars Tourist Agency** (☎ 222 3163; Zand Blvd) can also help with directions.

pita-type bread with chopped tomatoes and garnish; IR8000) are pretty good.

RESTAURANTS

There might not be much culinary variety in Shiraz, but there are some excellent Iranian restaurants.

Hammam-e Vakil (☎ 222 6467; off Taleqani St; meals IR40,000; 🕙 11am-11pm) Found in the wonderfully restored baths of the Bazar-e Vakil, this teahouse and restaurant is highly esteemed. The violin echoing through the vaulted ceilings makes up for the inconsistent service, and the food is pretty good – *dizi* (IR12,000) and bakhtiyari kebab (lamb and chicken pieces on a sword; IR20,500) are both recommended, and the salad bar isn't bad. Note that food is only served at lunch and dinner, the latter no earlier than 8pm; outside these times you'll have to settle for tea and sweets.

Shater Abbas Restaurant (☎ 227 1612; Azadi Blvd, Khakshenasi St; meals IR40,000; 🕙 lunch & dinner) Popular with middle-class locals, this cosy place is traditional but with modern touches; it has an open-sided kitchen where they bake their own (delicious) bread. Try the larry kebab (a meaty speciality of southern Iran; IR28,000). The restaurant isn't signed in English, but look for the flame torches outside.

Haji Baba Restaurant (☎ 233 2563; Zand Blvd; meals IR35,000; 🕙 lunch & dinner) It's not exactly atmospheric, but the Iranian food here is very good and it's a great place when you want to be fed with a minimum of fuss – like after a day at Persepolis.

Restaurant Hatam (☎ 222 1809; Piruzi St; meals IR25,000; 🕙 11am-9pm) Down the food chain, so to speak, is this no frills cheapie with a limited range of decent Iranian food. It's underneath the Hashemi Guest House. Along a little is an unnamed **subterranean restaurant** (Piruzi St; meals IR15,000; 🕙 11am-9pm) that serves kebabs and a couple of good *khoreshts*.

Other recommendations:

Pat Restaurant (Paramount Sq; meals IR55,000; 🕙 lunch & dinner) The live music is good – the prices are not.

Soofie Traditional Restaurant (☎ 661 573; Afif Abad St; meals IR55,000; 🕙 lunch & dinner)

Teen Restaurant (☎ 229 6472; Saheli-ye Gharbi St; meals IR40,000; 🕙 lunch & dinner) A modern Iranian place where the only teenagers likely to be waiters.

HOTEL RESTAURANTS

Almost every hotel mid-range or above has a restaurant.

Sarve Naz Restaurant (☎ 230 0814; 1st fl, Shiraz Eram Hotel, Karim Khan-e Zand Blvd; meals IR35,000; 🕙 breakfast, lunch & dinner) You come here for good food, service and price, but not atmosphere. The Caucasian kebab (small, tender pieces of marinated meats with onion and capsicum) is recommended, and the salad bar and steaks are good. Readers have raved about the cheap buffet breakfast.

Apadana Restaurant (☎ 224 7128; Rudaki Ave; meals IR45,000) A smart establishment in a smart hotel (Aryo Barzan Hotel), with a good range of fish and Western dishes to go with the usual Iranian fare.

Other good-value options on the Rudaki Ave strip, all of pretty good value:

Narenjestan Restaurant (☎ 233 000; Parsian Hotel)
Sadra Hotel Restaurant (☎ 222 4740)
Roodaki Hotel Restaurant (☎ 222 9594)

Drinking

There are some cracking teahouses in Shiraz, and a few decent cafés too.

TEAHOUSES

Towhid Teahouse (Ferdosi St; 🕙 7.30am-midnight) This tiny, unpretentious place is your classic workers' 'pub'. The owner is gruff, the (almost exclusively male) patrons banter animatedly, and the food (eg *dizi* for IR6000 or kebabs grilled on the pavement) is good and super-cheap. It's great for tea and a qalyan, after dinner, but it's best to come in small groups.

Aramgah-e Hafez Teahouse (Golestan Blvd; 🕙 8am-9.30pm) This delightful garden teahouse is in perfect harmony with its surrounds at the tomb of the poet Hafez. The great man would no doubt approve of the relaxed atmosphere, often accompanied by music, though he'd probably have preferred a glass of Shiraz to a cup of chay. Pots of tea cost IR3000 (more when a band is playing), *dizi* IR12,000 at lunchtime, or you could try the local Shirazi speciality, *faludeh*, a refreshing vermicelli-type ice cream drowned in either lemon juice or rose-water.

You may stumble across a few other teahouses around the Bazar-e Vakil, and the ones at the Darvazeh-ye Quran (p247) and the Afif Abad Gardens are charming.

CAFÉS

Shiraz's cafés are good places to meet young, English-speaking locals.

Jazireh Coffee Shop (☎ 229 9761; Daneshju Sq; ⏰ 10am-9pm) A tiny taste of Europe with a wide variety of coffees, milkshakes and even desserts. It makes a good stop en route to or from Bagh-e Eram (p247).

Ghoroob Coffee Shop (☎ 229 8027; Azadi Blvd; ⏰ 9am-11.30pm) Stylish Ghoroob, overlooking Azadi Park, is busy between 8pm and 10pm.

Shopping
Good buys in the Bazar-e Vakil include metalwork and printed cottons, especially tablecloths and rugs woven by Fars nomads. Shiraz can be a good place to buy kilims and *gabbehs* (traditional rugs), though the selection is not as great as in Esfahan. For handicrafts, head to Serai Mushir in the Bazar-e Vakil, where you'll find some excellent shops and a great atmosphere. Along the streets off Zand, there are plenty of places to stock up on dates and pistachios.

Getting There & Away
AIR
It's easy to start or finish a trip to Iran in Shiraz. **Gulf Air** (☎ 230 1962; Zand Blvd) has twice-weekly flights to Bahrain, from where connections can take you to just about anywhere in Europe, Asia or the Middle East.

Iran Air flies between Shiraz and Dubai (one way IR660,000, twice-weekly), Doha (IR620,000, weekly), Bahrain (IR570,000, weekly) and Kuwait (IR720,000, twice-weekly). All flights take under 90 minutes.

The airport has a handy **flight information number** (☎ 721 8888; ⏰ 8am-9pm), and the busy **Iran Air** (☎ 233 0041; cnr Zand Blvd & Faqihi St) has some charming English-speaking staff. Iran Air flies from Shiraz to the following destinations within Iran:

Destination	Price (IR)	Flights
Ahvaz	169,000	1 weekly
Bandar-e Abbas	171,000	2 weekly
Bandar-e Langeh	157,000	4 weekly
Bushehr	144,000	1 weekly
Esfahan	144,000	daily
Kish	150,000	2 weekly
Mashhad	319,000	5 weekly
Tehran	232,000	several daily

Iran Aseman (☎ 230 8841; Zand Blvd; ⏰ 8am-8pm Sat-Thu) has daily flights (except Tuesday) to Tehran (IR233,000).

Kish Airlines has several flights a week to Kish; see a travel agency (p244) for tickets.

BUS & MINIBUS
The main bus terminal is the **Carandish bus terminal** (Terminal-e Bozorg; ☎ 730 1654; Salman-e Farsi Blvd), which handles all long-distance destinations. Buses and the occasional minibus leave regularly for the following destinations. Prices are for Mercedes/Volvo buses.

Destination	Price (IR)	Duration (hr)
Ahvaz	22,250/40,000	10
Bandar-e Abbas	24,000/40,000	10
Bandar-e Langeh	29,000/45,000	12
Bushehr	12,000/20,000	5
Esfahan	18,250/30,000	8
Hamadan	31,250/44,000	15
Kerman	21,000/30,000	8
Kermanshah	39,000/60,000	18
Tabriz	50,000/75,000	24
Tehran	33,500/40,000	13-18
Yazd	16,500/26,000	7
Zahedan	60,000	17

Buses to larger centres such as Tehran and Esfahan leave pretty frequently, and there are buses almost hourly to Bushehr until about 5pm. But for places such as Bandar-e Langeh (usually early morning), Kerman (infrequent, one at 10.30am and in the evening), and Zahedan, you're strongly advised to check the options ahead of time. To do this, you could go to Carandish, which is not far from town, but it's easiest to check and buy your ticket from the **Iran Peyma** (Taavoni No 1; ☎ 222 3888; Zand Blvd) office near the corner Sa'di St, or the nearby **Pars Tourist Agency** (☎ 222 3163; Zand Blvd).

Buses to towns closer to Shiraz leave from the Amir Kabir Terminal on the southern outskirts. Buses for Kazerun (IR7,000, three hours) depart regularly throughout the day. There are also buses to Bushehr (IR11,000, five hours); note that if you're arriving from Bushehr, you might be dropped here.

SAVARI
Savaris for regional towns such as Kazerun, Firuz Abad and Marvdasht (for Persepolis) go from outside the Carandish terminal on a semi-regular basis (see the relevant sections later in the chapter for more details).

Getting Around
TO/FROM THE AIRPORT
Bus No 10 leaves from the airport and will drop you off at Valiasr Sq, which is not really convenient. You're better off taking a private taxi – to or from the city centre should cost about IR10,000.

BUS & MINIBUS
Shared taxis are generally more useful in Shiraz although one very handy bus is No 2 (with Roman numerals, and sometimes marked 'Sa'adi' in English). It leaves from near the corner of Zand Blvd and Sa'di St and passes the corner of Golestan and Salman–Farsi Blvds (from where you can walk to the Carandish bus terminal), Hafez's tomb and finishes outside Sa'di's tomb. Bus tickets cost IR200 for a short trip, IR300 for the longest trip around the city, and in a first for Iran, you don't need to buy a ticket in advance, just pay once you are on board the vehicle.

TAXIS
Shared taxis ply the streets for IR500 to IR1000 per trip. Chartering a taxi will cost from IR3000 to IR5000 depending on the distance.

PERSEPOLIS   پرسپولیس
This magnificent site embodies the greatest successes of the ancient Achaemenid Empire (see History, p26). The monumental staircases, exquisite reliefs, immense columns and imposing gateways leave you in no doubt that this was indeed the finest jewel in the empire's crown.

Persepolis (Takht-e Jamshid; admission IR30,000; ☺ 8am-5pm Nov-Mar; 6am-6pm Mar-Jun, Sep & Oct, to 8pm Jul & Aug) is a result of the vast body of skill and knowledge gathered from throughout the nations the empire ruled; Persian in ideology and design but truly international in its superb architecture and artistic execution.

This multicultural concoction is alone in the ancient world, and is undoubtedly the greatest surviving masterpiece of the ancient Near Eastern civilisations. Be prepared to compare it with the better-known Pyramids of Giza, the Colesseum in Rome or Angkor Wat in Cambodia.

As Arthur Upham Pope, a respected scholar of Persian architecture, wrote in *Introducing Persian Architecture* (published by Tuttle in 1982):

> Humane sentiments found expression in the nobility and sheer beauty of the building: more rational and gracious than the work of the Assyrians or Hittites, more lucid and humane than that of the Egyptians. The beauty of Persepolis is not the accidental counterpart of mere size and costly display; it is the result of beauty being specifically recognised as sovereign value.

Work on Persepolis began under Darius I (the Great) in about 518 BC. Some historians believe that the site was chosen by Cambyses II, son of Cyrus the Great. It was added to by a host of subsequent kings, including Xerxes I and II, and Artaxerxes I, II and III, over a period of about 150 years.

The ruins you see today are a mere shadow of Persepolis' former glory. But their very existence is due in part to the fact the ancient city was lost for centuries, totally covered by dust and sand. It wasn't until the 1930s that extensive excavations revealed its glories to the world once again.

Tours
Just about every hotel in Shiraz organises 'tours', with prices which are directly proportional to room rates. However, a real tour – one with a knowledgeable guide – costs a bit more.

Pars Tourist Agency (☎ 222 3163; www .key2persia .com; Karim Khan-e Zand Blvd, Shiraz) Pars organises daily trips (not tours) to Persepolis for US$8 per person. The highly professional drivers from this agency speak passable English. Also, if you give them some notice, Pars are willing to arrange very knowledgeable and interesting guides who can speak German, French, Italian and Japanese.

The following speak good English and charge about IR150,000 for a half-day trip and IR250,000 for a full day. However, they are not guides.

Ali Kooroony (☎ 0917 314 2702)

Morteza Mehrparvar (☎ 0917 314 6124) Morteza has been recommended by readers. Negotiation is possible.

Shiraz Eram Hotel (☎ 230 0814; Karim Khan-e Zand Blvd, Shiraz)

PERSEPOLIS RECONSTRUCTED

In its heyday the city spread over an area of 125,000 sq metres and was the place where all the peoples of the empire came over No Ruz (New Year) to pay homage to the kings; at other times of year it was probably deserted. For a city that stood at the heart of such a great empire, Persepolis was rarely mentioned in foreign records, fuelling speculation among some archaeologists that the existence of the city was kept a secret from the outside world. In the records that remain, attention is focused on the other Achaemenid cities at Shush and Babylon.

Persepolis stands on the slopes of Mt Rahmat and in places it is 18m above the level of the surrounding plain. Its original name was Parsa; the first known reference to it by its Greek name of Persepolis – meaning both City of Parsa (City of Persia) and Destroyer of Cities – came after its sacking by Alexander the Great's army.

Persepolis was burned to the ground during Alexander's visit in 330 BC. If you're wondering how a palace built almost entirely of stone could be burned to the ground, the explanation lies in the roof. The ceilings of most buildings are believed to have been made from huge timber beams, and as these burned they heated, then melted, the iron and lead clamps that held it all together. The result was catastrophic.

The Persepolis Complex

ENTERING THE CITY

From the outside, much of the city is obscured by its high walls. Entry to the site is, as it was during the days of Achaemenid Persia, via the monumental **Grand Stairway**, carved from massive blocks of stone but with shallow steps so Persians in long elegant robes could walk gracefully up into the palace.

Whenever important foreign delegations arrived, their presence was heralded by trumpeters at the top of the staircase (amazingly, fragments of these bronze trumpets are on display in the museum). Acolytes then led the dignitaries through **Xerxes' Gateway**, also known as the **Gate of All Nations**, which is still a wonderfully impressive monument.

The gateway was built during the time of Xerxes I and is guarded by bull-like figures that have a strong Assyrian character. Above these, look for a cuneiform inscription in the Persian, Babylonian and Elamite languages. It declares, among other things, that 'I am Xerxes, Great King, King of kings, King of lands, King of many races...son of Darius the King, the Achaemenid...Many other beautiful things were constructed in Persia. I constructed them and my father constructed them'.

PALACE OF 100 COLUMNS

Visitors from nations of lesser importance were sometimes led to the Palace of 100 Columns, where the king would receive them. As you follow in their footsteps through the **Court of Apadana**, look for the **Unfinished Gate**, the **Hall of 32 Columns** and an impressive array of griffins.

The Palace of 100 Columns was the largest of the palaces at Persepolis; here delegates from subject nations came to restate their loyalty and pay tribute in a ritual reassertion of the power of the Achaemenid Empire. Light was provided by lamps placed in alcoves around the walls.

APADANA PALACE & STAIRCASE

Important Persian and Median notables were more likely to be ushered to the **Apadana Palace** to the south. Constructed on a terrace of stone by Xerxes I, the palace was reached via another staircase. Although it can be difficult to picture the grandeur of the palace from what remains, the bas-reliefs along the northern wall evocatively depict the scenes of splendour that must have accompanied the arrival of delegations to meet with the king.

Most impressive of all, however, and among the most impressive historical sights in all of Iran, are the bas-reliefs along the **Apadana Staircase** of the eastern wall, which can also be reached from the Palace of 100 Columns. The northern panels recount the reception of the Persians in their long robes and the Medes in their shorter ones, and the three tiers of figures are amazingly well preserved. Each tier contains representations of the Imperial Guard or the Immortals. On the upper tier, they are followed by the royal procession, the royal valets and the horses of the Elamite king of chariots, while on

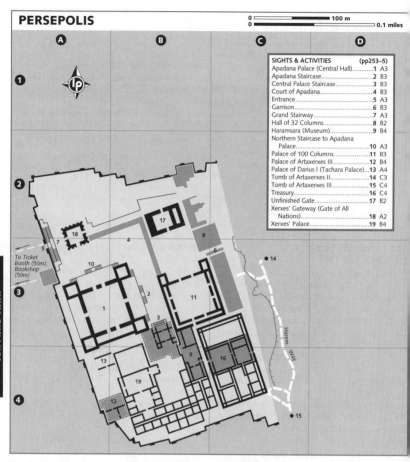

PERSEPOLIS

0 ———— 100 m
0 ———— 0.1 miles

To Ticket
Booth (50m);
Bookshop
(50m)

Harem Way

the lower two tiers they precede the Persians with their feather headdresses and the Medes in their round caps. The stairs themselves are guarded by Persian soldiers.

The central panel of the staircase is dedicated to symbols of the Zoroastrian deity Ahura Mazda, symbolised by a ring with wings, flanked by two winged lions with human heads and guarded by four Persian and Median soldiers; the Persians are the ones carrying the indented shields. An inscription announces that the palace was started by Darius and completed by Xerxes and implores God to protect it from 'famine, lies and earthquakes'.

The panels at the southern end are, for many visitors, the most interesting, showing

23 delegations bringing their tributes to the Achaemenid king. This rich record of the nations of the time ranges from the Ethiopians in the bottom left corner, through a climbing pantheon of, among various other peoples, Arabs, Thracians, Indians, Parthians and Cappadocians, up to the Elamites and Medians at the top right. Of all the panels, those on the staircase's southern face most strongly evoke the great power of the Achaemenid Empire.

ROYAL PALACES

The southwestern corner of the site is dominated by the palaces attributed to each of the kings. The **Palace of Darius I** (Tachara or Winter Palace) is probably the most striking, with its impressive gateways and bas-reliefs and cuneiform inscriptions around the perimeter. The palace opens onto a royal courtyard, which is also flanked by the unfinished **Palace of Artaxerxes III** and **Xerxes' Palace**.

CENTRAL PALACE

This palace is also referred to as **Xerxes' Hall of Audience** (the Triplyon), and stands at the heart of Persepolis. Its location enabled the king to receive his notables in an area shielded from outside view and it was here that many important political decisions were made. On the columns of the eastern doorway are reliefs showing Darius on his throne, borne by the representatives of 28 countries; the crown prince Xerxes stands behind his father. The 28 have their arms interlinked, representing a union of nations.

HAREMSARA (MUSEUM)

Immediately to the east of the Central Palace lies the **Haremsara** (admission IR30,000; 8am-5pm, 6am-8pm summer), which houses the museum. Despite the depictions around the door of the king defeating evil, the original purpose of this structure is not known, though it is thought by some to have been the harem of Xerxes. The museum contains a stone foundation tablet and a range of artifacts discovered during excavations; alabaster vessels, cedar wood, lances and arrow tips. Note the highly polished walls; almost every wall in Persepolis was finished in this expensive, labour-intensive fashion. If you're on a tight budget, you'll probably prefer to look in from the door.

TREASURY & TOMBS

The southeastern corner of the site is dominated by Darius' **Treasury**, where archaeologists found stone tablets in Elamite and Akkadian detailing the wages paid to the unsung (and underpaid) labourers who built Persepolis. When Alexander looted the Treasury it is reported that he needed 3000 camels to cart off the contents. The foundations of hundreds of columns are all that remain. On the hill above the Treasury are the rock-hewn **tombs** of Artaxerxes II and Artaxerxes III, each with Zoroastrian carvings. The view from the tombs over Persepolis is quite beautiful.

SOUND & LIGHT SHOW

A sound and light show takes place intermittently, and only in summer, at around 8.30pm. Ask before you leave Shiraz whether it will be on, and remember that if you leave the site you might have to pay another IR30,000 to get back in for the show.

Eating

There are no sleeping and few eating options at Persepolis. The best food is found at **Parsian Restaurant** (☎ 0917 128 2942; meals IR35,000; dinner; lunch & dinner in summer), about 2km south of the entrance to Persepolis on the road to Shiraz. Its faux-grotto style is a bit cheesy, but the food (including *bademjun* and the interesting sounding Bulgarian BBQ) is good, portions large and it's all for a reasonable price. About 1km before Naqsh-e Rajab, **Laneh Tavvus Restaurant** (☎ 0917 128 0058; meals IR30,000; 11am-10pm) is not bad.

TATTERED HISTORY

Outside the entrance to Persepolis, through the pine trees, are the remains of a luxurious tent city built by Mohammed Reza Pahlavi in 1971 to celebrate the 2500th anniversary of Persian monarchy. The tents played host to a lavish and incredibly expensive party, attended by dignitaries including 60 monarchs or heads of state, but few Iranians. Food was flown in from Maxims in Paris, and many of the VIPs were put up in luxury tented apartments, complete with marble bathrooms and three rooms. They were arranged on five streets, each representing a geographical area – Europe, Oceania, Asia, Africa and America – that came together to form a five-pointed star.

The celebration, meant to instil in Iranians a nationalistic pride and love of their monarch, was a public relations disaster. Opponents quickly pointed to the unnecessary extravagance, and some believe the party was a turning point from which the Shah never recovered. The irony is unavoidable – here, at the greatest monument to imperial power in Iran, saw the beginning of the end of Iranian monarchy.

Today, scraps of faded purple cloth flap from the steel frames, but the marble is long gone. The main tents are weather beaten, but it's not hard to imagine the gala event in all its glory.

Getting There & Away

BUS & SHARED TAXI

It is possible to reach Persepolis by public transport. Take a minibus from the southern side of the Carandish bus terminal in Shiraz to Marvdasht (IR2000, 42km, every hour or so). From the last stop, walk about 1km along the main road to Imam Khomeini Sq, from where you should be able to find a shared taxi to Persepolis (IR2000, 12km). If not, a private taxi should cost about IR10,000.

Returning from the site, there are always plenty of vehicles lurking outside the entrance – either hitch a ride or take a taxi back to Marvdasht.

PRIVATE TAXI

The easiest way to get to Persepolis is to charter a taxi from Shiraz that will also allow you to visit the other sites of Naqsh-e Rostam (below) and even Pasargadae (below). Expect to pay about IR120,000 for a six-hour trip to Persepolis, and IR220,000 for an 11-hour day seeing all four sites.

NAQSH-E ROSTAM نقش رستم
& NAQSH-E RAJAB نقش رجب

Definitely worth visiting as part of a trip to Persepolis are the sites of Naqsh-e Rostam and Naqsh-e Rajab. The rock tombs of **Naqsh-e Rostam** (admission IR20,000; 7.30am-5pm, until 7pm summer) are magnificent. Hewn out of a cliff high above the ground, the four tombs are believed to be those of Darius I, Artaxerxes I, Xerxes I and Darius II (from left to right as you look at the cliff) although historians are still debating this. The tombs of the later Artaxerxes above Persepolis were modelled on those at Naqsh-e Rostam. The openings in the massive tombs lead to the funerary chambers, where bones were stored after the vultures had picked them clean. The reliefs above the openings are similar to those at Persepolis, with the kings standing at Zoroastrian fire altars supported by figures representing the subject nations below.

The eight Sassanian **stone reliefs** cut into the cliff beneath the façades of the Achaemenid tombs depict scenes of imperial conquests and royal ceremonies.

Facing the cliff is the **Kaba Zartosht**, which is believed to be an Achaemenid fire temple, although the walls are marked with inscriptions cataloguing Sassanian victories.

The tombs of **Naqsh-e Rajab** (admission IR10,000; 7.30am-5pm, until 7pm summer) are directly opposite the turn-off to Naqsh-e Rostam on the Shiraz–Esfahan road and are worth a quick look on your way between Persepolis and Naqsh-e Rostam. Four fine Sassanian bas-reliefs are hidden from the road by the folds of the cliff-face and depict various scenes from the reigns of Ardeshir I and Shapur the Great. A man called Rajab once had a teahouse here, hence the name.

GETTING THERE & AWAY

Both Naqsh-e Rostam and Naqsh-e Rajab can be easily combined with a trip to Persepolis (p252). If you don't have a vehicle, you could walk the 6km from Persepolis to Naqsh-e Rostam, stopping off at Naqsh-e Rajab en route. The latter is about 2km from Persepolis on the main highway. From here, follow the turn-off to Naqsh-e Rostam (signposted in English) for another 4km. If you're planning on doing this trip in summer, take plenty of water.

PASARGADAE پاسارگاد

Begun under Cyrus the Great in about 546 BC, the city of Pasargadae was quickly superseded by Darius I's magnificent palace at Persepolis. Some travellers have questioned whether **Pasargadae** (admission IR20,000; 8am-5pm, 7am-6pm summer) is worth the effort of getting here – it is 50km north of Persepolis. The site is certainly not as well preserved as Persepolis, however, these ruins are beautiful in a lonely kind of way.

The first structure you'll come across is the six-tiered **Tomb of Cyrus**. Standing proudly on the windswept plain, this impressive stone cenotaph was originally much taller than it is now and is still the best preserved of the Pasargadae ruins. Legend has it that when Alexander the Great arrived at Pasargadae, he was greatly distressed by the state of the tomb and ordered its restoration.

Within walking distance of the tomb are the insubstantial remains of three **Achaemenid Palaces** – the Entrance Palace, the Audience Palace and Cyrus' Private Palace; the ruins of a tomb on a plinth, known as the **Prison of Solomon** (Zendan-e Soleiman); a large stone platform on a hill known as the **Throne of the Mother of Solomon** (Takht-e Madar-e Soleiman); and two **stone plinths** that originally formed part of a pair of altars within a sacred precinct. Some local historians believe that the references to Solomon date from the Arab conquest, when the inhabitants of Pasargadae renamed the sites with Islamic names to prevent their destruction. In both the Audience Palace and in Cyrus' Private Palace there is a cuneiform inscription that reads: 'I am Cyrus, the Achaemenid King'.

By far the easiest way to get here is to charter a taxi from Shiraz; see Persepolis Getting There & Away (opposite) for options.

If travelling by public transport, you can take a bus (IR8000) from the Carandish bus terminal in Shiraz to Sa'adatshahr (also known as Sa'adat Abad), but from here you'll have to take a taxi or a very occasional minibus the remaining 30km or so. Even better, jump on any bus heading towards Yazd or Esfahan (you may have to pay full fare) and get out at the turn-off to Pasargadae that's signposted in English. From there, it's an 8km walk or hitch with any vehicle heading down the road.

FIRUZ ABAD   فیروز آباد
☎ 0712

Two places often missed by those in a rush to get to Persepolis are the remains of the old cities of Firuz and Gur, dating from the Sassanian period. If you are here around April or May, you will see plenty of Qashqa'i nomads crossing the Zagros Mountains.

About 6km before Firuz, along the road from Shiraz, you'll see a chairlift, with cables stretching across the road, leading to the **Qal'eh-e Doktar** (Maiden's Palace). This is a three-storey fort with a courtyard, probably built by Ardeshir I. Sadly, the chairlift doesn't work, so you'll have to scramble up the rocky hill to see the remains of the palace. The views from the top are worth the effort. There are several **Sassanian bas-reliefs** in the area, not all of them easy to find.

About 4km further on, towards Firuz, an unsigned rocky trail leads to the best of the ruins of ancient Firuz – what was thought to be a fire temple, but is probably the ruins of Ardeshir's **palace** (admission IR20,000; 🕒 8am-4pm, until 5pm summer), with the remains of a small fire temple beside it. Architecture buffs will be interested in what are thought to be the earliest examples of the squinch (what the dome rests on) and *iwan*.

In a taxi you'll have to take a lengthy 20km detour to avoid the Tang-Ab River. Alternatively, if the water is not flowing too

fast stride across the river, then walk about 800m along the rocky trail.

Sleeping & Eating

The only place to stay in Firuz is the ITTO's **Firooz Abad Tourist Inn** (☎ 622 2105; fax 622 3699; s/d US$25/35; Ⓟ 🏠). It's better to take a day trip from Shiraz.

There are plenty of hamburger joints and kababis in town, but taking food and drink from Shiraz, and having a picnic by the tiny lake at the fire temple, is a great idea. Firuz is famous for the quality of its *dugh*, a sour-milk drink.

Getting There & Away

There is at least one bus every day from Shiraz to Firuz (ask to get off where the broken chairlift crosses the road), but make sure you find out when it returns. Savaris run back to Shiraz but space in them is limited, or you might get lucky with a hitch. To see most of the remains of both ancient cities, it's best to charter a taxi, which you can do either from Shiraz or Firuz, or take a tour with Shiraz's Pars Tourist Agency (p244).

KAZERUN &   کازرون
SHAPUR   شاپور

Just off the main road between Shiraz and Bushehr are the small but fascinating ruins of another two ancient cities: Kazerun and, about 25km to the west, Shapur. At **Kazerun** (the name comes from an ancient word meaning 'people who wash cotton clothes'), there are some mildly interesting **bas-reliefs** from the Sassanian period, though they are most interesting to archaeologists for their unique inscriptions.

Shapur (admission IR25,000; 🕒 8am-4pm, until 5pm summer) is more interesting to the casual visitor. The remains of this fortified Sassanian city are spread out across a few hectares, and include the **Palace of Shapur** and **Anahita's Temple**, the largest structure on the site where a stairway leads underground to a now-dry pool around which the faithful once walked and prayed.

Along both sides of the river there are some excellent **bas-reliefs** (admission IR20,000) that commemorate, among other historical moments, the victory of Shapur citizens over Roman invaders. To see the best reliefs, on the opposite side of the bridge to ancient Shapur, you need to pay yet another entrance fee and it's arguable whether it's worth it. If you do go in, you'll see a deep groove running right through the reliefs. This was caused by a powerful flood in the 1960s; the groove marking the high-water mark.

The **Tang-e Chogan** (Shapur Cave) contains the 7m-high **Statue of Shapur I**, one of the most impressive archaeological sites in Iran, in our view. To get to the cave is easiest on a taxi tour, but you could walk the 5km or so from Shapur. On the same side of the bridge as the city of Shapur, take the road that follows the river for about 4km. When you reach a village on your left, head down to it. One of the friendly villagers will probably offer to lead you up the very steep ascent to the cave, which you can see from the roadway. A tip is appreciated.

The trip to this part of Fars province is pretty and worth dedicating a day to. Chartering a taxi is the easiest way (at least IR180,000 from Shiraz), but with an early start, it can be done by public transport.

Take the bus to Kazerun from the Amir Kabir terminal in Shiraz (IR7000, 2½ hours) or from Bushehr, or a savari. From Shiraz, keep an eye out en route for the 15-arch **Karim Khan Bridge**, an ancient bridge built in the Zand period; it's about 40km west of Shiraz. After the bus turns off the Shiraz–Bushehr road, it's about 7km to the ruins, which are on the right-hand side of the road.

The best alternative is to get three people together and take a tour with the excellent guides from **Pars Travel Agency** (☎ 222 3163; Zand Blvd); they bring a traditional picnic breakfast and make the experience that much richer for being able to tell you about the sights.

FROM SHIRAZ TO KERMAN

If you have your own transport and are heading from Shiraz towards Kerman or even Bandar-e Abbas, the route south round Lake Bakhtegan (periodically home to thousands of flamingos) from Kherameh to Neyriz is well worth considering. The scenery is often stunning and the road relatively quiet. Parts of the road are quite mountainous, and the 70km-stretch along the southern shore of Lake Bakhtegan is unseal

Persian Gulf
خلیج فارس

CONTENTS

Whether you're watching the sun set over the Gulf, scrambling over the ruins of the Portuguese castle at Hormoz, or just dropping down several gears to the ultra-relaxed pace at which this part of the world operates, you can't escape the fact that the Persian Gulf offers a different experience to the rest of Iran. There's the geographical contrast – the coast and islands of the Gulf itself – but the major difference comes from the variety of people who live here.

The history of the Gulf is tied inextricably to trade. Africans, Arabs, Indians and Europeans as far back as Alexander the Great have passed by this way, some finding business so good they've set up shop and stayed. The result is a rich hybrid of ancient Persia and 'Arabia' across the water, and is best seen today in Bandari communities such as Bushehr, Hormoz and Minab. These communities are distinctly different to the rest of Iran, with most Bandaris being Sunni Muslims and having an even more laid-back approach to life than normally found. They're known as Bandaris because they live in ports – *bandars*. In the tiny fishing village of Laft on Qeshm Island, sitting with tea, qalyan and the locals as the sun sets over the forest of *badgirs* (windtowers) and dhows (traditional wooden boats) is almost alone worth the trip to the coast.

Unfortunately, travelling the coast is not easy, with bus services infrequent and inconveniently timed. It's also a long way from most of Iran's other tourist destinations. This combination keeps many travellers away. Should you make the trip, think twice – and then think again – before visiting in summer. While winters are often blessed with clear 25ºC days, the diabolically hot, humid and very long summer days regularly reach 50ºC.

PERSIAN GULF

HIGHLIGHTS

- Take the speedboat and a picnic lunch to **Hormoz Island** (p279), where you can eat in the serene silence of the **Portuguese Castle** (p278)

- Watch the sun set from the roof of the old stone water cistern that is **Ghavam Restaurant** (p264) in Bushehr then go downstairs for an excellent meal

- Pick out your supper in the seaside fish market at **Bandar-e Abbas** (p274)

- Cycle around Kish Island on the wonderfully flat **cycle path** (p267), stopping for a swim at the '**Exclusive Swimming Beach**' (p267)

- Delight in the traditional culture and charming atmosphere of Qeshm Island's **Laft** (p277)

- Take in Minab's **Thursday Market** (p280), where you're most likely to encounter women wearing the elaborate **Bandari burqas** (p270)

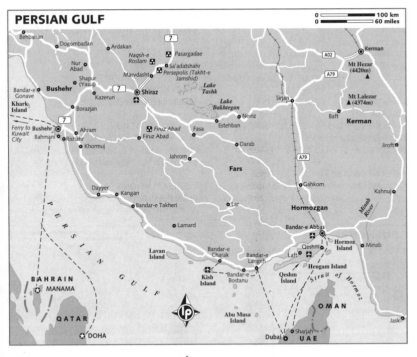

PERSIAN GULF

BUSHEHR

بوشهر

☎ 0771 / pop 200,000

The old city of Bushehr, with its elegant Bandari architecture, twisting mud-brick lanes and peninsular situation, is a place that has elicited strong emotions in some readers. Visitors tend to rave about or revile the old city, which has variously been described as 'a living museum' and a clapped-out ruin resembling 'Grozny after the third Russian war'. In truth, both are partly accurate.

The modern town is not a bad place for a day or two, lacking the frantic bustle of Bandar-e Abbas but mostly free of the lethargy of Bandar-e Langeh. The Bushehris like to talk to foreigners and there's a good chance you'll end up sipping tea in one of their homes.

History

Much of Bushehr's history lies in the town of Rishahr, 12km to the south, which dates back as far as the Elamite era. Rishahr was one of the chief trading centres of the Persian Gulf from the 7th to the 16th century, but it dwindled in importance after

Bandar-e Abbas was established in the early 17th century.

In 1734, Nader Shah chose the site of Bushehr, then a village, to become Persia's principal port and naval station. Its prosperity was assured when in 1759 the British East India Company, then the power in the Persian Gulf, moved its base to Bushehr after the French destroyed its factory at Bandar-e Abbas.

In the mid-19th century Bushehr became the seat of the British political residency on the Persian Gulf. However, Bushehr's long, slow decline began in the 1930s when it was bypassed by the trans-Iranian railway in favour of the ports in Khuzestan province. The British moved the political residency to Bahrain in 1946, and their consulate closed in 1951. The town was an important naval base during the Iran-Iraq War, but most of its commercial activities collapsed and were relocated to the less-exposed Bandar-e Abbas.

Orientation

The Old City is in the northern tip of Bushehr, while the town centre is Enqelab Sq. Bushehr is small and manageable enough to explore on foot, and no matter where you are you're never too far from the waters of the Persian Gulf. Most of the attractions and the hotels, restaurants and bus station can be found in the northern part of Bushehr, which is circled by Khalij-e Fars St (the esplanade).

Information

EMERGENCY
Police Headquarters (☎ 252 3035; Qods Sq) Ask for English-speaking Saeed Iranzad.
Main Hospital (☎ 252 6591; Siraf St) Only if very sick.

INTERNET ACCESS
Coffeenet Baharrayanehlian (☎ 252 1505; Leyan St; per hr IR6000; ☷ 8am-midnight) In an arcade opposite Bank Melli; look for the red sign.

MONEY
Bank Melli (Leyan St) Some English spoken on 1st floor.

POST
Post Office (Valiasr St)

TELEPHONE
Telephone Office (Valiasr St)

TRAVEL AGENCIES
Setar-e Bandar Travel Agency (☎ 252 8878; fax 252 0313; Imam Khomeini St) Handles domestic and international air tickets. For information on boat tickets, see p264.

VISA EXTENSIONS
Police Headquarters (Qods Sq; ☷ 8am-2pm) It's possible to extend visas here, but if the colonel is not

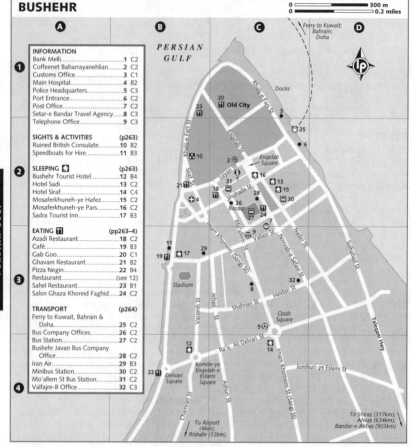

BUSHEHR

0	300 m
0	0.2 miles

PERSIAN GULF

INFORMATION
Bank Melli....................................**1** C2
Coffeenet Baharrayanehlian........**2** C2
Customs Office.............................**3** C1
Main Hospital..............................**4** B2
Police Headquarters....................**5** C3
Port Entrance..............................**6** C2
Post Office...................................**7** C2
Setar-e Bandar Travel Agency.....**8** C3
Telephone Office.........................**9** C3

SIGHTS & ACTIVITIES   (p263)
Ruined British Consulate.............**10** B2
Speedboats for Hire....................**11** B3

SLEEPING 🏠   (p263)
Bushehr Tourist Hotel.................**12** B4
Hotel Sadi...................................**13** C2
Hotel Siraf..................................**14** C4
Mosaferkhuneh-ye Hafez............**15** C2
Mosaferkhuneh-ye Pars...............**16** C2
Sadra Tourist Inn........................**17** B3

EATING 🍴   (pp263–4)
Azadi Restaurant.........................**18** C2
Café..**19** B3
Gab Goo.....................................**20** C1
Ghavam Restaurant.....................**21** B2
Pizza Negin.................................**22** B4
Restaurant...............................(see 12)
Sahel Restaurant.........................**23** B1
Salon Ghaza Khoreid Faghid......**24** C2

TRANSPORT   (p264)
Ferry to Kuwait, Bahrain &
Doha..**25** C2
Bus Company Offices..................**26** C2
Bus Station.................................**27** C2
Bushehr Javan Bus Company
Office......................................**28** C2
Iran Air......................................**29** B3
Minibus Station..........................**30** C2
Mo'allem St Bus Station.............**31** C2
Valfajre-8 Office.........................**32** C3

Docks

Old City

Enqelab Square

Bazaar

Stadium

Qods Square

Komite-ye Enqelab-e Eslami Square

Delvari Square

Ferry to Kuwait; Bahrain; Doha

To Airport (4km); Rishahr (12km)

To Shiraz (317km); Ahvaz (634km); Bandar-e Abbas (903km)

around you'll have to wait for him to come back, and that could take days. If you desperately need a visa, ask here for the helpful English-speaking Saeed Iranzad, who has been known to organise 30-day extensions within a day. If he's not around you'll only get two weeks, if anything. Shiraz is a better option (p244). For full details on extending your visa, see the boxed text 'More Time, Please' (p362).

Sights & Activities
OLD CITY
Whether or not you are enchanted by decaying Bandari buildings and winding *kuches* (alleys), Bushehr's **old city** is a rarity among the ports of the region in that it offers glimpses of a fast-disappearing way of life. There is little of the traffic and noise found in Bandar-e Abbas, for example, and it is possible to lose yourself in the old city only to be found by a family willing to invite you into their home for chai (tea) and oranges. Most of the old houses are still inhabited and many women dress in the traditional, brightly coloured layers of clothing unique to the Persian Gulf.

The densely packed wooden struts that overhang some of the narrow lanes are only found in Bushehr. Of particular interest are the door knockers shaped like human hands in the northwestern quarter of town. Also check out the pillars and white façade of the **mansion** on the waterfront facing west – it was once home to a rich merchant and more recently a museum.

The crumbling seaside ruins of the **British consulate** are worth a look; they reveal a hint of its former grandeur.

SPEEDBOAT RIDES
On Thursday and Friday afternoons one of the best things to do in Bushehr is join the local youth to hoon about the Gulf in a speedboat; boats leave from anywhere along the waterfront and you'll pay about IR10,000 for 10 minutes.

Sleeping
One of the main hassles when visiting Bushehr is in persuading cheap accommodation to let you have a bed. All three mosaferkhunehs are reluctant to take foreigners who don't have a letter from the police permitting them to stay. To get such a letter, head along to the police headquarters as early in the day as possible and ask for Saeed Iranzad. A reader reports that the

police might call your desired place of lodging rather than write you a note.

The three cheap options are near to Enqelab Sq, not far from the bus station.

Hotel Sadi (☎ 252 2605; Nader St; tw IR30,000) This is easily the best of the budget options, and so is worth the effort of getting a permit. Rooms are small but clean enough and have their own bathrooms!

Mosaferkhuneh-ye Pars (Enqelab Sq; tr IR40,000; dm IR10,000) This open-sided rooftop 'general house', aka dorm, is a great place from which to people watch, and a cheap place to sleep in summer if you have nothing valuable. However, the glass walls don't cut out much light or noise. The rooms themselves are reasonable. If these are unavailable, try simple **Mosaferkhuneh-ye Hafez** (☎ 0917 171 1204; Nader St; r IR36,000).

Hotel Siraf (☎ 252 7171; sirafhotel@yahoo.com; Imam Khomeini St; d US$30; ✷) Formerly Hotel Reza, the large rooms here aren't bad but it's arguable as to whether they're worth the non-negotiable US$30. The restaurant serves breakfast for IR10,000 and decent dinners for about IR30,000. The other mid-range option is tired **Sadra Tourist Inn** (☎ 252 2346; fax 252 2410; cnr Valiasr St & Khalij-e Fars Sts; d US$30; P ✷)

Bushehr Tourist Hotel (Delvar Hotel; ☎ 252 6342; fax 252 6881; Komite-ye Enqelab-e Eslami Sq; tw/ste US$70/119; P ✷ 💻) Rising like a modern-day ziggurat out of central Bushehr, this is definitely the best place in town, with prices to match. Most of the semiluxurious rooms have views of the Gulf, and the restaurant is quite good.

Eating & Drinking
Bushehr boasts several seaside eateries of varying quality and price. Food at the unnamed café opposite Sadra Tourist Inn is pretty standard fare – Iranian-style hamburgers, cold drinks and ice creams. But it's a great place for people-watching, especially on a Thursday or Friday evening when the whole of Bushehr seems to be promenading along the waterfront.

Salon Ghaza Khoreid Faghid (☎ 252 5755; Novvab-e Safavi St; meals IR15,000-25,000; ☽ lunch & dinner) There isn't an English sign and there's zero in the way of frills at this little place but the fish dishes are good; try the local speciality *ghalye mahi*, a richly flavoured fish stew.

Gab Goo (Enqelab St; meals IR6000-15,000; ☽ lunch & dinner) Popular with the local youth, this place serves reasonable Iranian-style hamburgers

THE AUTHOR'S CHOICE

Ghavam Restaurant (☎ 252 1790; Khalij-e Fars St; meals IR25,000-50,000; ✓ lunch & dinner) Once a cistern used to store Bushehr's water, Ghavam is now one of the best places at which to eat on the Persian Gulf coast. The underground location offers relief from the heat in summer, while the vaulted ceilings and live traditional music on Thursday and Friday create a great atmosphere. The usual range of kebabs is enhanced with a tasty fish kebab, and the surprisingly spicy *dizi* (lamb stew) is very good. Sipping tea and puffing on a qalyan are the activities of choice for the roof, from where the sunset is spectacular.

(IR8500), sandwiches, fried chicken and kebabs.

Pizza Negin (☎ 252 5818; Delvari Sq; large pizzas IR22,000; ✓ 7pm-midnight) You can't miss this trendy place, housed inside a concrete ferry 'sailing' along the paved seaside esplanade.

Also recommended are **Azadi Restaurant** (Shohada St; meals about IR15,000; ✓ lunch & dinner), with cheap, simple meals, and **Sahel Restaurant** (Khalij-e Fars St; meals IR10,000-25,000; ✓ lunch & dinner), where the Gulf-side location makes it a good place to interrupt your Old City wanderings. There isn't a sign in English. Of the hotels, the restaurant at **Bushehr Tourist Hotel** (☎ 252 6342; Komite-ye Enqelab-e Eslami Sq; meals IR30,000-75,000; ✓ lunch & dinner) has a decent menu of Western food and good Iranian dishes.

Getting There & Away

AIR

Iran Air (☎ 252 2041; Valiasr St; ✓ 7.30am-6pm Sun-Thu, 7.30am-noon Fri) has flights between Bushehr and Tehran (IR225,000, 90 minutes, twice daily except Monday), Shiraz (IR144,000, one hour, weekly) and Esfahan (IR167,000, 70 minutes, weekly). Bushehr also has an international connection: Iran Aseman flies to/from Dubai in the United Arab Emirates (UAE; one way US$113 plus IR90,000 departure tax, one hour, five days a week). Contact Setar-e Bandar Travel Agency (p262) for tickets.

BOAT

Apart from enterprising fisherman, there are no domestic boat services from Bushehr.

However, the Valfajre-8 shipping company operates to international ports, with services following a fairly haphazard timetable but averaging about two per month to each port. The ports, and one-way prices for passengers, are Qatar (US$64, 24 hours, 252km); Bahrain (US$45, seven to eight hours, 357km); Kuwait (US$64, seven to eight hours).

For information on impending departures go to the **Valfajre-8 Office** (☎ 252 2188; www.vesc.net; Ali Delvari St; ✓ 7am-5pm) or visit its website.

BUS & MINIBUS

The bus station is easy to reach on foot and there are a few bus company offices scattered around the station. For Kazerun (IR10,000), take any bus to Shiraz; for Kangan, **Bushehr Javan** (☎ 253 0930; Novvab-e Safavi St) has a dedicated bus daily at 10am. Buses are Mercedes except from Bandar-e Langeh and Tehran which are Volvo.

Destination	Price (IR)	Duration (hr)	Departures
Ahvaz	30,000	7	7am, 3.30pm
Bandar-e Abbas	36,600	16	3am, 4pm
Bandar-e Langeh	35,000	9	4.30pm
Esfahan	28,200	16	3.45am, 3.30-6pm
Shiraz	11,500	5	6-9am, 12.30-5pm, 11pm
Tehran	70,000	19	10.30am, 1-3pm

Getting Around

TO/FROM THE AIRPORT

A private taxi from Bushehr airport into town will probably cost you IR10,000 (they will ask for IR30,000). But to get to the airport the trip shouldn't cost more than IR5000. Alternatively, you could try taking a shared taxi from Komite-ye Enqelab-e Eslami Sq for about IR1500.

BUS & TAXI

You're unlikely to need the local buses unless you're heading to Rishahr. If so, head for the bus station at the northern end of Mo'allem St. You could also try the minibuses that leave from Nader St. Shared taxis cost IR500 or IR1000 depending on the trip, or IR4000 for any trip *dar baste* (private hire of a taxi).

AROUND BUSHEHR

Rishahr   ريشهر

Very little remains of the ancient trading city of Rishahr, built during the Elamite and Sassanian eras. What is left might not be for much longer if Israel carries out its threat to destroy the nearby nuclear reactor before it becomes fully operational. Extensive exploration and photography of the ruins is, to put it mildly, discouraged.

Rishahr can be reached by bus from the Mo'allem St bus station in Bushehr.

FROM BUSHEHR TO BANDAR-E LANGEH

There are some charming towns dotted along the long, quiet road that skirts the Persian Gulf coastline. About 250km southeast of Bushehr, **Kangan** is a pretty fishing village that's well worth exploring. **Bandar-e Taheri**, a little further southeast, boasts the ruins of an 18th-century sheikh's fortress; the views from the badgir over the Gulf are superb and the town itself is quite picturesque. Nearby on the rocky coastline are the ruins of the ancient town of **Siraf**, with some well-preserved stone graves. **Bandar-e Bostanu**, 18km west of Langeh, has some great *badgirs*.

Without a vehicle this area is difficult to fully explore. Most traffic just races by and there are no hotels. However, unless you arrive during the long summer siesta you'll probably get a warm welcome from the locals, who are unlikely to have seen another tourist for quite some time. If you are not found by someone who insists on putting you up for the night, your best bet is the mosque in whatever town you stop.

Getting to these towns sounds easy – just get off any bus between Bushehr and Bandar-e Langeh. The problem is that those buses often ply this route at night, and finding accommodating souls at 3am can be tough. Moving on can also involve long waits.

KISH ISLAND   جزیره کیش

☎ 0764 / pop 16,500

'Oh, but have you been to Kish? You absolutely must go.' You are likely to hear this many times while travelling in Iran. And when you ask what is so special about Kish, you're told: 'But Kish is wonderful; everything works there. It is clean, shopping is cheap, you can swim...and there are no Paykans!'

Yes, all of this is true. Kish, the desert island that the last shah started transforming into a playground for the rich and famous during the 1960s, is now looked upon by Iranians in the same way that Americans view Hawaii; more than one million flock here every year. But for foreigners who are used to being able to swim with their partners at any beach and have no interest in duty-free DVD players, the attractions are less obvious.

However, there are good reasons to visit Kish. The diving here is not bad and relatively cheap. Cycling around the island on the coastal bike path is a great way to spend a day. And if you are prepared to work through the bureaucracy you might even be able to indulge in the hedonistic pleasures of sharing a (foreigners-only) beach with members of the opposite sex.

More than anything else, though, it's the relaxed atmosphere that appeals to Iranians, many of whom treat the island as something of a mental health break – it's not a bad approach to take.

History

Kish Island is first mentioned in the memoirs of Nearchus, the Greek sailor commissioned by Alexander the Great to explore the Persian Gulf in 325 BC. Nearchus described 'Araracta' (Kish was then known as Arakata) as having 'several parks and abundant palm groves'.

In the Middle Ages Kish became an important trading centre under its own powerful Arab dynasty, and at one time supported a population of 40,000. The main town was Harireh, which is believed to be the town referred to by poet Sa'di in his famous work, *Golestan* (Rose Garden).

The island was known for the quality of its pearls; when Marco Polo was visiting the imperial court in China, he remarked on the beauty of the pearls worn by one of the emperor's wives and was told they had come from Kish. In the 14th century Kish fell into decline and remained obscure until the 1970s. It was then developed as a semi-private retreat for the shah and his privileged guests, with its own international airport, palaces, luxury hotels and restaurants, and even a grand casino. Shortly after the revolution, the new government established Kish as a duty-free port.

KISH ISLAND

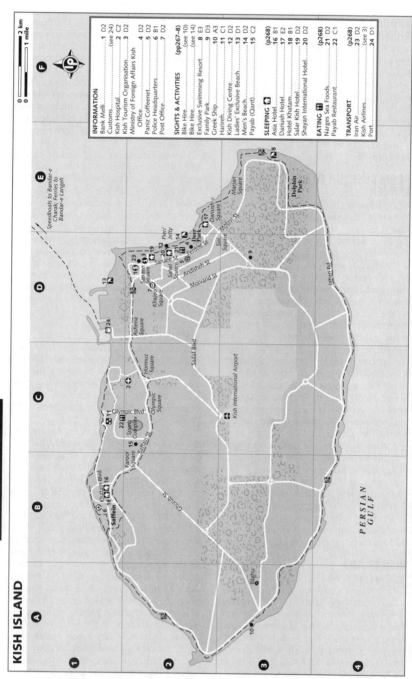

0   2 km
0   1 mile

Speedboat to Bandar-e
Charak; Ferries to
Bandar-e Langeh

Dolphin
Park

Marjan
Square

Dariush
Square

Pier/
Jetty

Deer
Park

Sanaee St

Sina
Square

Sadaf St

Midvar St

Erdos St

Andisheh St

Morvarid St

Sanaee
Square

Khajo
Square

Sadat Blvd

Kish International Airport

Jahan Rd

Athena
Square

Hormuz
Square

Olympic Blvd

Olympic
Square

Sports
Complex

Sina St

Faroor
Square

Ghods St

Khatam Blvd

Saffein

Baghu

PERSIAN
GULF

PERSIAN GULF

Orientation

There's no real centre to Kish Island, despite signs in English indicating a 'City Centre'. The Arab settlements are the town of Saffein, on the northern coast, and the small oasis village of Baghu, in the southwest of the island. Most people live near the main roads along the northern and eastern coasts, and many of the offices, banks, shops and hotels are between Sanaee and Siri Sqs in the northeast.

Information

CUSTOMS REGULATIONS
Customs (☎ 422 2577) Buying duty-free goods on Kish Island can be more trouble than it's worth as the customs paperwork at the boat terminal or airport can be tedious in the extreme. Call to check the latest rules before deciding to buy.

EMERGENCY
Kish Hospital (☎ 442 3711; Hormuz Sq)
Police Headquarters (☎ 442 2143)

INTERNET ACCESS
Paniz Coffeenet (☎ 442 0083; Paniz Bazar; per hr IR10,000; ☼ 9.15am-1pm & 4-11.30pm)

MONEY
Bank Melli (Sanaee St; ☼ 8.30am-2pm) Changes money with less paperwork than normal.

POST
Post Office (Khajoo Sq)

TOURIST INFORMATION
Kish Tourism Organisation (☎ 442 2434; Sanaee Sq; ☼ 7.30am-5pm Sat-Thu) Maps and brochures in English and French; English-speaking staff are on the 2nd floor.

VISAS
Kish is the only place in Iran that foreigners can visit without needing a visa. If you're flying in from outside Iran, your passport will be stamped allowing you to stay up to 14 days on the island. So is this a back door into Iran? According to officials on the island, the **Ministry of Foreign Affairs Kish office** (☎ 442 0734; Ferdous Villas, Complex 2, Ferdosi St) can grant tourist visas 'within 48 hours' to those who want to visit the mainland. But we have not heard from anyone who has done this.

Sights & Activities

Kish is more about doing than seeing; however, the remains of the ancient city of Har-
ireh and the restored *qanat*-like *payab* (water reservoir) are both worth a look. Otherwise, the Greek ship that ran aground here on a clear night in 1966 lures photographers at sunset.

Kish is one of the very few places in Iran where swimming is actively encouraged. There are sandy, uncrowded beaches around most of the coast, but the authorities request that female swimmers use the **Ladies' Exclusive Beach**, while men have to use the **Men's Beach**. In an effort to attract foreigners without allowing them to pollute the local culture, the Kish authorities have opened the **Exclusive Swimming Resort**. It is for the exclusive use of foreigners, but in order to be allowed in you'll first need to take your passport to the **Kish Tourism Organisation** (☎ 442 2434) and get a permit that confirms you are indeed a foreigner.

The bike track (see Cycling, following) and diving are both rightly popular, and others activities include glider flights, horseback riding, glass-bottomed boats, and several 'theme' parks, such as **Deer Park** and grand **Dolphin Park**.

CYCLING
It's almost worth coming to Kish just for the Special Bicycle Route that circles the island. It's a great way to spend a day. Bikes can be hired from near the pier on the Men's Beach and also, inconveniently, at the Greek ship, though at IR10,000 an hour they're not cheap. Otherwise, ask at your hotel. This is obviously better done during the cooler times of the year from November to March.

DIVING & OTHER EXCURSIONS
Kish is the only place in Iran that has a diving centre, and some of the reefs around the island are very well-stocked with fish. **Kish Diving Centre** (☎ 442 2757; ☼ 7am-sunset), found outside Shayan Hotel, has English-speaking instructors and charges IR300,000 for a one-hour dive with equipment. A four-day PADI open water course costs IR1,800,000 (about US$215) – when you're shooting the shit with divers in Indonesia or the Caribbean, you'll be one of very few able to say: 'Where did I learn to dive? Iran!' The centre also offers paragliding, jet-skiing and underwater photography (cameras supplied).

Ask around the boat terminal to see whether you can hire a boat to the **turtle** colony *(daste-ye lak-e poshte abi)*, off the southern coast.

Sleeping & Eating

There are 43 hotels on Kish (and counting) and you can expect to pay Western prices for most of them. If you arrive with nothing booked, discounts can be found, though anywhere remotely cheap is likely to be full of people from the Gulf states renewing their visas.

Hotel Khatam (☎ 443 1520; khatamhotel@hotmail .com; Khatam Blvd; tw IR200,000; **P** **❄**) These comfortable rooms with TV, bathroom and fridge are pretty good value for Kish. **Asia Hotel** (☎ 443 0774; Saffain St) around the corner has similar rooms for a similar price.

Shayan International Hotel (☎ 442 2771; Sahel Sq; s/d with breakfast US$80/110, cabana US$75; **P** **❄**) The sea of sprayed concrete is evidence that this is one of the oldest hotels on the island. It's no longer the best, but is holding up fairly well; the rooms with balcony are very god.

Dariush Hotel (Dariush Sq) This monument to Achaemenid styles and modern luxury will be the island's best when it's finished. The over-the-top Persian motifs almost give it a Vegas feel.

Salar Kish Hotel (☎ 442 0111; fax 442 2378; Sanaee Sq; dm IR55,000; **❄**) This place caters almost exclusively to visa runners, so if you're prepared to share an apartment with a couple of migrant workers, this is about the cheapest place in town.

There are a few small restaurants in a plaza off Ferdosi St opposite Paniz Bazar, including **Narges Sea Foods** (☎ 442 0633; ☺ lunch & dinner), which serves an excellent grilled fish and rice for IR15,000.

Payab Restaurant (☎ 0914 769 1213; Olympic Blvd; meals IR55,000; ☺ dinner) Located underground in a *payab*, this is a romantic place in the evening that serves good traditional food.

Getting There & Away

As long as you start very early, day trips are possible by *pik-up* (pick-up; utility with a canvas cover) from Bandar-e Langeh to Bandar-e Charak and then by speedboat to Kish Island (p270).

AIR

Tickets to and from Kish can be difficult to obtain, so book your onward ticket before you arrive.

Kish Airlines (☎ 442 3922; Sanaee Sq) flies to Bandar-e Abbas (40 minutes, three times a week); Tehran (one way IR334,000, 90 minutes, several daily); Esfahan (IR430,000, one hour, daily) and Shiraz (IR150,000, 45 minutes, two weekly) and has occasional flights to Mashhad.

Iran Air (☎ 442 2274; Sanaee Sq) has regular flights to Shiraz, Esfahan and Tehran for the same prices as Kish Airlines, and Mahan Air flies twice a week to Kerman.

Kish Airlines also flies to Bahrain, Sharjah and Abu Dhabi.

BOAT

Valfajre-8 sails daily between Kish and Bandar-e Langeh (IR65,000). Its catamaran Firuze takes about two hours, but the bigger Ro Ro boats (usually the Hormoz 24) take close to five hours. In theory, the Firuze is supposed to depart Langeh at 8am and return from Kish at 2pm from Saturday to Wednesday, and just one way from Kish on Thursday, and back on Friday. However, don't rely on these times. Tickets are bought at the port.

The alternative is to take the speedboat from Bandar-e Charak, an easy ride from Bandar-e Langeh in a *pik-up* (IR8000, 1½ hours, 89km). The *pik-up* will take you to the beach at Charak, where most of your fellow passengers will pile into a speedboat (IR30,000). To visit Kish in one day, start from Langeh at about 6am, and allow enough time to get back. Last boats leave about 4pm. Note that if the wind gets up the speedboats stop.

Getting Around

TO/FROM THE AIRPORT

You will probably have to charter a taxi from the airport for about IR10,000.

BICYCLE

For information on cycling around the island, see p267.

MINIBUS & TAXI

Excellent air-con minibuses (IR1000) cruise the northern and eastern roads. Standing is not allowed.

From the boat terminal, you can crowd onto a local minibus or take a private taxi. Chartering a taxi will cost you about IR40,000 per hour.

BANDAR-E LANGEH   بندر لنگه

☎ 0762

Bandar-e Langeh (or 'Langeh' to the locals) is an infectiously lethargic place. It is also an excellent introduction to the mixed Arab and Persian communities of the southern Persian Gulf. The population is both Sunni and Shiite and Arabic and Farsi are spoken. This diversity is reflected in the hybrid architecture and clothing of the locals (p270).

Langeh makes a pleasant overnight stop en route to or from Kish Island, or, if your bus is passing at a reasonable hour, a good place to stop between Bushehr and Bandar-e Abbas.

Orientation

The main streets are Imam Khomeini Blvd (the coastal road and esplanade) and Enqelab St, which heads to Bandar-e Abbas. This is not a town where foreigners are expected; few signs are in English but it would be hard to get lost.

Information

MONEY

Bank Melli (Shahrdari St) Don't arrive without any rials because Bank Melli won't change money, and rates in the bazaar are low.

INTERNET ACCESS

Graph Internet (☎ 224 1606; Enqelab St; per hr IR8000; ☼ 8am-2pm & 4-8.30pm) The friendly women at this computer studies school will let you online. It's also the best place in Langeh to meet English speakers.

Sights

During the day, especially in summer, there's little to do except observe the obligatory five- or six-hour siesta. By late afternoon, however, it's a lovely place to wander when the setting sun turns the town pale yellow. Sights include several pale-stone mosques, with single mina- rets decorated in the Arab style, and a few old and largely derelict Bandari buildings made of mud brick with huge, squat *badgirs*.

Sleeping & Eating

The sleeping situation in Langeh has taken a turn for the worse recently, with two of the three budget options closing down.

Hotel Amir (☎ 224 2311; Enqelab St; r IR45,000) Found not far from the port, the staff at the Amir are friendly and the simple rooms are aging relatively gracefully, making them good value.

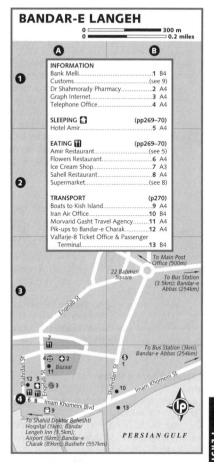

Bandar Langeh Inn (Mehmar Sara Jahangardi; ☎ 222 2566; d US$30; ⛶ Ⓟ) This is Langeh's only other hotel. Rooms are pleasant enough and most have sea views. It's 1.5km west of town down a lonely sideroad and its posi- tion, literally on the water's edge, means you can sip tea in the garden with your toes in the Persian Gulf. The restaurant isn't bad, either.

Gourmets are unlikely to find inspiration in Langeh. A few kababis, a surprisingly well-stocked supermarket and an oh-so- welcome ice-cream shop compete for busi- ness along Enqelab St near the port.

Amir Restaurant (☎ 224 1370; Enqelab St; meals IR30,000-35,000; ☼ lunch & dinner) A few doors south of the hotel of the same name, this

PERSIAN GULF

> ### BANDARI BURQAS
>
> In southern Iran, and in Minab and Bandar-e Langeh, you might see Bandari women wearing a burqa. This inflexible mask differs depending on the region; in Langeh it is usually a metal frame jutting out from the face and hiding very little of the face itself – reminiscent of the structure of Darth Vader's mask, but without the black. In Minab it is often bright red with multicoloured stitching along the border, covering all of the face that's not already hidden by the chador (except two tiny slits for the eyes). Ethnologists do not believe these masks have any religious links, but are a fashion accessory dating back to the period of Portuguese rule. Bandari women also wear distinctive colourful pants under their outer garments. Often red or green, the pants are tight around the ankle and usually have elaborate gold patterns stitched above the hem. Women in burqas will almost never agree to being photographed by a stranger.
>
> If you think your mother-in-law might look good in one of these, head for the market in Minab and ask around. The locals will think you're mad, but a burqa could make an 'interesting' gift.

no frills place serves the best food in the centre of town. The *ash e sabzi* (green vegetable soup) and rice (IR15,000) and *meigu* (battered prawns, IR20,000) are both good. A door leads through to a cosy teahouse where the manager is happy to store your bags...as long as you don't mention his resemblance to Saddam Hussein.

Opposite the port gate, **Flowers Restaurant** (☎ 222 4180; Imam Khomeini Blvd; meals IR15,000-20,000; ☻ lunch & dinner) and **Sahell Restaurant** (Imam Khomeini Blvd; meals IR15,000-20,000; ☻ lunch & dinner) sell cheap sandwiches and kebabs.

Getting There & Away
AIR
Looking at the size of the huge **Iran Air office** (☎ 222 2799; Imam Khomeini Blvd; ☻ 7.30am-1.30pm & 5.30-8.30pm Sat-Thu, 8am-noon Fri) you'd think you were in Tehran or Esfahan, but the sometimes sleepy service will soon bring you back to reality. Iran Air offers four flights a week to Tehran (IR342,000, 75 minutes) via Shiraz (IR157,000, 30 minutes). You could also try **Morvarid Gasht Travel Agency** (☎ 222 3345; Enqelab St) for tickets.

BOAT
Langeh has daily ferries (IR65,000, two to five hours depending on the boat) to Kish Island, the duty-free hot spot in the Persian Gulf, though the times are variable and ferries are often cancelled due to rough seas. Tickets can be bought at the **Valfarje-8 office** (☎ 222 1689; Imam Khomeini Blvd; ☻ 7am-2pm & 3-6pm Sat-Thu, 7.30am-1.30pm Fri).

The quicker alternative is to take an open speedboat (IR30,000, 45 minutes) from Bandar-e Charak (89km west of Langeh). If you want to return to Langeh by nightfall you'll need to leave early, taking a 6am *pik-up* from Shahrdari St. However, be sure to check the sea conditions before heading to Bandar-e Charak, lest you get there and find the boats are not running.

Valfajre-8 also runs a passenger-only catamaran to Dubai (US$52, 4½ hours) on most, but not all, Sundays.

BUS & SAVARI
The bus station is about 3km east of town and is easy to miss – it's behind a wall on the right just before a large square. Buses (IR10,000, four hours, 255km) and savaris (Pakyan IR30,000, 3½ hours; Peugeot IR40,000, 2½ hours) to Bandar-e Abbas leave about every hour between 6am and 8pm. Several buses a day leave for Bushehr (IR25,000, nine hours, 656km). There are occasional buses to Shiraz, although you'll probably need to get a connection from Bandar-e Abbas or Bushehr.

Coming from Bushehr there's a good chance you'll arrive at about 2am. Although such an ungodly arrival time can be disorienting, if you ask to be dropped at the port entrance (other locals will get out here), it's easy to find your way up the main street opposite; the driver might even drop you near Bandar Lengeh Inn as he drives into town, if that's where you want to stay.

Getting Around
From the airport, you can take a shared taxi or *pik-up* (IR3500) to the bazaar. A taxi *dar baste* to or from the airport will cost IR12,000. Shared taxis around town are cheap, but you're unlikely to need one.

BANDAR-E ABBAS   بندر عباس
☎ 0761 / pop 380,000

For a city founded by one of Persia's greatest kings, Shah Abbas I, and named in his honour, almost nothing of historical interest remains in the bustling 'Port of Abbas'. Strategically positioned overlooking the Strait of Hormoz and the entrance to the Persian Gulf, the city, known to most Iranians simply as 'Bandar', is the country's busiest port. Smuggling is big business – everything from cars to carpets circumnavigates the customs inspectors in these parts. Needless to say, if you're walking along the seafront at night and notice boxes being hurriedly unloaded from a dark-coloured speedboat, it would be unwise to offer help with the haulage.

Bandar's fast-growing population is a mix of Persian Bandaris, Arabs and Africans, with a large Sunni minority. There is also a small but long-established Hindu community. Depending on your perspective, Bandar-e Abbas is either delightfully seedy with the audible whispers of smugglers, or a stepping-off point for the more languid nearby islands.

History
The rise, fall and rise again of Bandar-e Abbas over the last five centuries has been directly linked to the role of meddling European powers. Once a tiny fishing village called Gamerun, it was chosen as Persia's main southern port and naval dockyard after the Portuguese were kicked off nearby Hormoz Island in 1622 (p279). The British East India Company was granted a trading concession, as were Dutch and French traders, and by the 18th century Bandar had become the chief Persian port and main outlet for the trade in Kermani carpets.

The port went into decline following the end of the Safavid dynasty and the withdrawal in 1759 of the British East India Company. By 1793 the port had fallen into the hands of the Sultan of Oman, who controlled it until 1868. Its role remained peripheral until the Iran-Iraq War, when the established ports at Bushehr, Bandar-e Imam Khomeini and Khorramshahr were either captured or became too dangerous for regular shipping. It hasn't looked back.

Orientation
Bandar-e Abbas is stretched along a narrow coastal strip. The main east–west thorough-

fare changes its name from Beheshti Blvd (in the eastern suburbs), to Imam Khomeini St (through the centre of town), ending as Pasdaran Blvd (towards the docks to the west). The city is well signposted in English. Apart from the top-end options, most of the accommodation is on or just off Imam Khomeini St, between Velayat Sq and Abuzar Sq – all within an easy walk of the boats to Hormoz and Qeshm. The airport is about 8km east of the bazaar (for details on how to get to/from the airport, see p275).

Information
EMERGENCY
Emergency Clinic (☎ 553 1001; cnr Jomhuri-ye Eslami Blvd & Amir Kabir St)
Police Headquarters (☎ 27 676; 17 Shahrivar Sq)

INTERNET ACCESS
Coffee Net Sorena (17 Shahrivar Sq; per hr IR9000; ☼ 5-9pm Sat-Thu) On the 3rd floor; look for the sign near the Persian Restaurant.
Net Cofe Yahoo (☎ 0917 161 2915; Imam Khomeini St; per hr IR8000; ☼ 8am-11pm Sat-Thu)

MONEY
The bazaar has a black market in UAE dirhams and other Gulf State currencies.
Bank Melli (17 Shahrivar Sq) The only bank to change money officially. Avoid at lunchtime.
Morvarid Money Exchange (☎ 222 7446; Imam Khomeini St; ☼ 8am-1pm & 4.30-9pm Sat-Thu) Good rates and no hassle. In an arcade just west of 17 Shahrivar Sq.

POST
Main Post Office (Shahrivar St) About 50m north of 17 Shahrivar Sq.

TELEPHONE
Telephone Office (Mahan Alley; ☼ 7am-9pm) Down an alley about 30m east of 17 Shahrivar Sq.

TRAVEL AGENCIES
Bala Parvaz Travel Agency (☎ 222 4500; fax 222 2519; Imam Khomeini St) Helpful staff who speak some English book domestic and some international flights. The train ticket office is upstairs.
Gameron Air Travel Agency (☎ 222 0274; fax 222 9021; Taleqani Blvd) Sells tickets for all domestic and some international airlines. Little English is spoken, however.

VISA EXTENSIONS
It's 'possible' to get your visa extended at the **police headquarters** (17 Shahrivar Sq) but that

PERSIAN GULF

BANDAR-E ABBAS

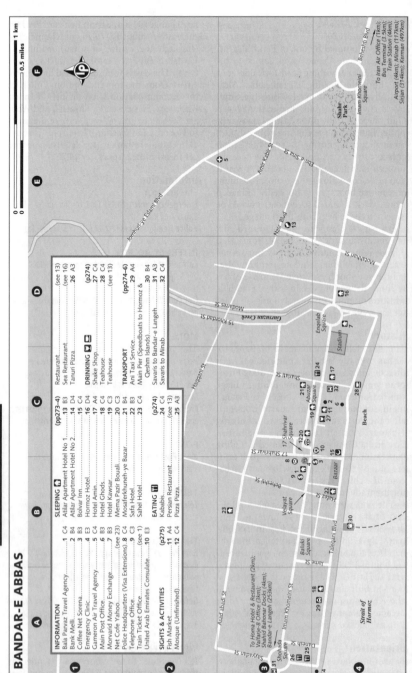

INFORMATION
Bala Parvaz Travel Agency.............1 C4
Bank Melli...................................2 B4
Coffee Net Sorena........................3 B3
Emergency Clinic..........................4 E3
Gameron Air Travel Agency..........5 C4
Main Post Office...........................6 B3
Morvand Money Exchange............7 B3
Net Cofe Yahoo...................(see 23)
Police Headquarters (Visa Extensions).8 C4
Telephone Office..........................9 C3
Train Ticket Office....................(see 1)
United Arab Emirates Consulate....10 E3

SIGHTS & ACTIVITIES
Fish Market................................11 A4
Mosque (Unfinished)...................12 C4

SLEEPING 🏠
Atilar Apartment Hotel No 1........13 C4
Atilar Apartment Hotel No 2........14 B4
Bolvar Inn..................................15 C4
Hormoz Hotel.............................16 E3
Hotel Amin.................................17 A4
Hotel Ghods...............................18 B3
Hotel Kawsar..............................19 C3
Mema Pazir Bouali.......................20 C3
Mosaferkhuneh-ye Bazar.............21 B4
Safta Hotel.................................22 B3
Sahel Hotel.................................23 C4

EATING 🍴
Kababis......................................24 C4
Persian Restaurant..................(see 13)
Pizza Pizza.................................25 A3

Restaurant.............................(see 13)
Sea Restaurant.........................26 (see 16)
Tanuri Pizza...............................26 A3

DRINKING 🍸 🍷
Shake Shop...............................(pp274)
Teahouse....................................27 C4
Teahouse....................................28 C4
Teahouse...............................(see 13)

TRANSPORT   (pp274–6)
Ani Taxi Service...........................29 A4
Main Pier (Speedboats to Hormoz &
  Qeshm Islands)..........................30 B4
Savaris to Bandar-e Langeh..........31 A3
Savaris to Minab.........................32 C4

To Homa Hotel & Restaurant (2km);
Valfaje-8 Office (3km);
Shahid Bahonar Dock (4km);
Bandar-e Langeh (253km)

To Iran Air Office (1km);
Bus Terminal (3.5km);
Train Station (4km);
Airport (4km); Minab (117km);
Sirjan (314km); Kerman (497km)

Strait of Hormoz

Gazorsan Creek

Shahr Park

Imam Khomeini Square

Enqelab Square

Stadium

Shohada Square

Baluki Square

Velayat Square

Ahuzar Square

Shahrivar Square

doesn't mean it will happen. The officers would really prefer that you go somewhere else – and it would be a very good idea to oblige them.

Most travellers won't need a visa for the UAE, but if you do, the **UAE consulate** (☎ 222 4229; Nasr Blvd; ♥ 8.30am-3pm Sat-Thu) is friendly and the consul speaks English. A one-month visa can take three days to issue and you'll need a sponsor. Costs vary.

Sights

A pleasant walk heading east along Taleqani Blvd takes you from the busy beach, past the bustling bazaar to the morning and evening fish market (p274). Work on the huge mosque a few metres east of the bazaar has stopped; some locals say the engineering is not up to the standard required in what is a major earthquake zone. If it is finished it will have one of the tallest *iwan*s (rectangular halls opening onto a courtyard) in Iran.

Sleeping

Bandar is another place where budget travellers might need to confront the beast that is Iranian bureaucracy and get a letter of introduction from the police headquarters in order to stay in a mosaferkhuneh. However, these letters are being requested less often, so try your luck at the mosaferkhuneh first. Alternatively, you could join the growing number of travellers opting to stay in Qeshm (p277) or Minab (p280). Most of Bandar's accommodation is fairly centrally located, a short walk from Velayat Sq. In summer don't even think about staying anywhere that doesn't have a working fan.

BUDGET

Mema Pazir Bouali (☎ 222 2516; Shariati St; dm IR15,000, r IR50,000) The faded-yellow awning and anonymous staircase don't promise much, but for atmosphere this friendly, family-run place is the best in Bandar. Women travellers will feel comfortable here and mother and daughter will be happy to practise their English with you. The simple rooms and shared bathroom are a bit noisy.

Mosaferkhuneh-ye Bazar (☎ 222 2303; cnr Taleqani Blvd & Hafez St; dm/s/d/tr IR12,000/30,800/41,800/49,600) Located above the bazaar, this is the cheapest place in town. In summer, beds on the covered rooftop (just IR10,000) afford wonderful views of the smugglers and sunset over

the Persian Gulf. The rooms and shared bathrooms are pretty clean, but security is relaxed. Not recommended for women.

Hotel Kawsar (☎ 222 6250; s/d IR100,000/150,000; 🕸) At the top of the budget range, this place has big, spotless rooms that are cleaned daily – the shared bathrooms more often. Rooms come with TV and fridge. It can be hard to find; head along an alley about 40m east of Velayat Sq and turn right.

Three other budget options are fair-value **Sahel Hotel** (☎ 222 2304; fax 222 2603; Imam Khomeini St; tw IR107,000; 🕸), basic **Bolvar Inn** (☎ 222 2625; Abuzar St; r IR75,000; 🕸), and **Safa Hotel** (☎ 222 2651; Asad Abadi St; s/d IR38,000/56,000).

MID-RANGE

Hotel Ghods (☎ /fax 222 2344; Imam Khomeini St; s/d IR300,000/500,000; 🕸 💻) The Ghods is a well-run place with all the facilities you'd expect in a mid-range hotel (fridge, satellite TV etc) but none of the personality you'd like. The rooms are big and you can choose to squat or sit in the bathroom, though some of the thrones we saw were sans seat. Food in the downstairs restaurant is both ordinary and overpriced.

Atilar Apartment Hotel No 1 (☎ 222 7420-5; info@atilar-hotel.com; Imam Khomeini St; apt from US$60; 🕸) Down a lane near Velayat Sq, No 1 does not look much from the outside – until you walk into the opulent foyer. The apartments, with at least a large bedroom, sitting room, kitchen and bathroom, are somewhere between these two extremes. You should have little trouble knocking down the price, perhaps as far as the Iranian price of IR256,500.

Atilar Apartment Hotel No 2 (☎ 334 0926; info@atilar-hotel.com; Imam Khomeini St; apt US$90; 🕸) Found near Enqelab Sq, No 2 is newer and better than No 1 – the views of the coast and Hormoz Island are spectacular. If money is no object, head for the penthouse apartment.

Hotel Amin (☎ /fax 224 4305; Taleqani Blvd; r with breakfast US$32; 🕸) On the seafront west of the bazaar. We don't know what they're thinking with the price – it's way too much for these small rooms.

TOP END

Hormoz Hotel (☎ 334 2201-5; www.hormoz-hotel .com; Enqelab Sq; s/d/ste US$70/105/165 plus 17% tax; 🅿 🕸 💻 📡) It's fair to say the 'stars' have aligned at the Hormoz and it deserves all five of them. Rooms are luxurious and most have a balcony; some with Gulf views, others with Gulf glimpses. There are five restaurants and an indoor pool that women can't use.

Homa Hotel (☎ 555 4080; Meraj St; bandarabbas@ homahotels.com; s/d/ste US$60/80/150 plus 17% tax; P ✷ 🖵 🞩) Out on the westerly edge of town, off Pasdaran Blvd, Homa has all the top-end amenities: tennis court, swimming pool, café and the signature 8ft-long model of an Iran Air 747.

Eating

If you like 'modern Iranian' cuisine such as pizzas and hamburgers then you'll like Bandar. If you're looking for something more traditional, you'll struggle.

Persian Restaurant (Imam Khomeini St; meals IR20,000; ☽ lunch & dinner) A few metres from 17 Shahrivar Sq, this place does good, cheap Iranian food, specialising in – you guessed it – kebabs. The chicken is also good, the service friendly and the atmosphere relaxed.

Sea Restaurant (☎ 334 2205; Hormoz Hotel, Enqelab Sq; meals IR70,000; ☽ 5.30-11pm) With an excellent range of fish dishes and a patio location overlooking the sea, this is a great place to come at sunset. European dishes are also available.

The restaurants at **Homa Hotel** (☎ 555 4080; Meraj St) and **Atilar Apartment Hotel No 1** (☎ 222 7420-5; Imam Khomeini St) have also been recommended by readers, with the latter serving a good version of the local speciality, *chelo meigu* (battered prawns or shrimps with boiled rice).

There are plenty of kababis along Imam Khomeini St, particularly around Abuzar Sq. But for that 'modern Iranian' experience you really should wander along to Sayyadan St, where more than a dozen eateries line the street. Most of these sell pizzas and burgers: **Tanuri Pizza** (☎ 224 1988; pizzas IR18,000; ☽ 9am-2pm & 5pm-midnight) is the most popular and employs real mozzarella – there's even a vegetarian option; **Pizza Pizza** (☎ 557 6221; pizzas IR19,000; ☽ lunch & dinner) is also pretty busy. You'll find similar varieties of pizzas at similar prices all along the strip, and you'll probably also find plenty of English-speaking students – another good reason to head down here.

Self-caterers should head straight for the **fish market** (cnr Taleqani Blvd & Sayyadan St; ☽ 6am-9am, 6-9pm) for all the ingredients for a great fish meal: prawns; all manner of the Gulf's finest fish, filleted if you ask; and fresh lemons, garlic, spring onions, limes, coconuts and potatoes. If you can convince your hotel that you'll clean up the fish scales, they might even let you use their kitchen.

Drinking

Instead of atmospheric subterranean teahouses, the local Bandaris have found the perfect antidote to the heat by turning the sea wall into a long seat. Here you can relax with a cup and a pipe in the (relative) cool of the evening. Tea and qalyan can be bought along the waterfront from just before sunset. Alternatively, there is a permanent **teahouse** (Taleqani Blvd; ☽ 11am-11pm) on the waterfront near the end of Shariati St – it's the one that looks like a giant concrete fire hydrant wearing a hat.

During the day the teahouse in **Atilar Apartment Hotel No 1** (☎ 222 7420-5; Imam Khomeini St) is as good a place as any to escape the Bandar heat.

For the best banana shake (IR3500) on the coast head for the unnamed shake shop on Imam Khomeini St, opposite and slightly west of Hotel Ghods.

Getting There & Away
AIR
Domestic Flights
Bandar is, mercifully, fairly well connected by air. The **Iran Air office** (☎ 333 7170; Beheshti St; www.iranair.com; ☽ 7am-7.30pm Sat-Thu & 7am-noon Fri) is inconveniently located east of the centre; it's better to use one of the agencies in town (p271). Flights from Bandar-e Abbas include:

Destination	Price (IR; one way)	Flights (weekly)
Ahvaz	292,000	2
Esfahan	267,000	3
Mashhad	347,000	2
Shiraz	171,000	3
Tehran	356,000	20

Mahan Airlines (www.mahanairlines.com) flies to Tehran (IR356,000, daily except Thursday).

International Flights
Iran Aseman flies the short hop to Dubai five times a week (one way IR440,000, 30

minutes); Mahan Airlines makes the same trip for a similar price twice a week. Mahan Airlines also flies to Colombo in Sri Lanka twice a week (40 minutes). Iran Air flies twice a week to Sharjah (one way US$60, one hour). For tickets, see Travel Agencies (p271).

BOAT
Domestic Services
Boats from Bandar to the nearby islands of Hormoz and Qeshm leave from the *eskele* (main pier), near the bazaar. For Qeshm, you can do the 23km trip in an open fibre-glass speedboat (IR10,000, 45 minutes) or a covered but less-frequent launch with padded seats (IR15,000, 25 minutes).

If the seas are too rough for the small boats you could try the ferry (IR20,000, 50 minutes, daily). It leaves at 7.30am from the chaotic Shahid Bahonar docks, 5km west of the town centre. Tickets can be bought at travel agencies or the **Valfarje-8 office** (☎ 555 5590; www.vesc.net; Eskleh Shahid Bahonnar Blvd), about 1km east of the docks.

The speedboats to Hormoz Island (IR8000, 30 minutes) leave every 15 to 20 minutes in the morning from the docks 20m closer to shore than boats to Qeshm. As the day wears on, they take longer to fill. There are no tickets; simply pay the owner of the boat.

If taking one of the open fibreglass boats in summer, take a hat and something to sit on to prevent a seriously scalded bottom.

International Services
To UAE Valfajre-8 runs high-speed cata-marans between Bandar-e Abbas and Dubai (US$55/52 1st/2nd class, four hours) and a car ferry to Sharjah (US$38, 12 hours, 233km). Schedules are inconsistent; check the website (www.vesc.net).

BUS
Buses leave Bandar for almost every city in Iran. However, heavy truck traffic, poor facilities along the roads and punishing temperatures can make it an extremely arduous journey.The bus station is in the far east of town and is chock-full of locals who wish they could afford to fly. To join them you'll need to take two shared taxis; one to the turn-off to the bus station and another to the bus station itself. A taxi *dar baste* (IR8000) is a better option.

Iran Peyma (Taavoni No 1) has the most buses from Bandar. The following is a rough guide to its services:

Destination	Price (IR)	Duration (hr)	Departures
Bam	17,000	8	5.30pm
Bandar-e Langeh	10,000	4	hourly 6am-7pm
Bushehr	37,000	16	early morning & 3.30pm
Esfahan	35,500	18	frequent
Kerman	28,500	8	3pm, 4pm & 5pm
Shiraz	25,000	10	frequent
Sirjan	15,000	5	6 daily
Tehran	52,500	20	frequent
Yazd	28,000	11	6 daily
Zahedan	42,000	17	5.30pm

SAVARI
There are a few buses to Minab, but most people travel by savari (IR13,000, 90 minutes, 97km). They leave from just south of Abuzar Sq throughout the day. Savaris for Bandar-e Langeh (Peugeot IR40,000, two hours; Paykan IR30,000, three hours) leave from the southwestern corner of Shohada Sq.

TRAIN
The train starts its 1483km-long journey to Tehran daily at 3pm, taking a minimum of 20 hours (IR80,600). It travels via Sirjan (IR29,600, five hours) and Yazd (IR48,200, 9½ hours) among other places, and your money buys a bed in a six-berth couchette. Note that an entirely different train goes to Esfahan (IR60,050, Tuesday, Thursday and Saturday), leaving at 5pm and arriving at an unusually civilised hour of 8.30am – *in sh'Allah*!

The train station is 8km away in the far north of town. As it's not on the way to anywhere else, you'll probably have to charter a private taxi (IR12,000) to get here. Fortunately, there is a ticket office in town, upstairs in the **Bala Parvaz Travel Agency** (☎ 222 4500).

Getting Around
TO/FROM THE AIRPORT
It is easy enough to charter a taxi to or from the airport for about IR12,000. A shared taxi (which is harder to find to the airport) will cost about IR2000.

BUS

Local buses crisscross the town; tickets cost IR200 to IR300 depending on the distance.

TAXI

Shared taxis are easy to find and cost a reasonable IR500 around town. To places like the bus terminal, train station and airport, it's far easier to charter one, especially in summer. For a private taxi, don't pay more than IR8000 to the bus station or the Shahid Bahonar docks from the centre of town.

The professional **Ani Taxi Service** (☎ 555 5539; Taleqani Blvd; ☼ 8am-8pm) has air-con Peugeots for which it charges IR25,000 per hour (including driver) within Bandar-e Abbas. For a half day beyond the city limits (eg Minab), expect to pay IR210,000.

QESHM ISLAND
جزیره قشم
☎ 0763

Qeshm is by far the largest island (1335 sq km) in the Persian Gulf, with a rocky coastline that protects a mountainous and often beautiful interior. The coast is dotted with villages and small towns but there are few settlements of any size in the interior. The village of Laft is particularly charming; a day trip here via the bizarre boat-building yards found in the middle of nowhere could be one of the best days you spend in Iran.

Qeshm Island is a duty-free area – a sort of poor man's Kish.

History

Qeshm Island was referred to briefly in documents from the Achaemenid period, and has for many centuries been a centre of trade with India. The island was mentioned by Marco Polo, and later marked out for potential colonisation by Vasco da Gama. However, Qeshm lacks the historical status of the smaller Hormoz Island and very little is known of its early development. In more-recent times, Qeshm came under the sway of the Dutch, French, Germans and British before being brought back firmly under the control of Iran shortly after WWI.

Orientation

Qeshm is the largest town on the island. The main north–south road begins at Pasdaran Sq, 150m east; it then becomes Montazeri Ave, then Valiasr Ave and finally Imam Golikhan Blvd, passing by several uninspiring duty-free malls.

Outside the entrance to Sangi Pier, from where speedboats operate to Bandar-e Abbas, is a taxi stand where shared taxis are available. Alternatively, follow the small lane directly opposite the gate to Imam Khomeini Ave and the bazaar area; three hotels are within an easy walk of Sangi Pier. The infrequent large ferries leave from Bahonar Port, not far from Qeshm International Hotel.

Qeshm International Airport is about 43km southwest of Qeshm town (for details on how to get to/from the airport, see p278).

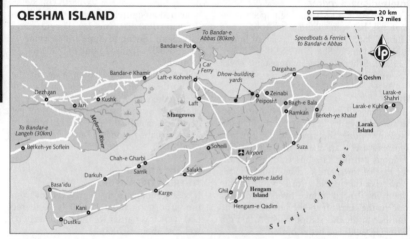

QESHM ISLAND

Information
There isn't a tourist office but the website www.qeshm.ir is good. You can change money at **Bank Melli** (Pasdaran Sq).

Sights & Activities
The village of **Laft**, at the end of the road that continues west from Qeshm town, is the highlight of any trip to the island. Only here is it possible to catch a glimpse of the fast-disappearing traditional cultures of the Persian Gulf fishing villages. The roofscape of Laft is a breathtaking forest of *badgirs*, and old dhows sit anchored offshore in the channels of the mangrove swamps. Climb the hill above the town for marvellous views. You might also come across some activity in the dhow-building yards as you enter town from the east, although there are larger yards on the barren coastline north of Zeinabi, accessible by dirt track off the main road.

If you've ever had a hankering to fly in a **glider**, Qeshm town is the place to do it. The runway is right in the middle of town and a 15-minute flight costs a bargain IR50,000! Gliders definitely fly on Fridays, but there's no guarantee on other days.

Sleeping & Eating
Even though Qeshm town is pretty much a plain Jane among Iranian urbania, it can be a good place to stay while you explore the rest of the island at a leisurely pace. Three hotels are within a short walk of the Sangi Pier on Imam Khomeini Ave; the rest are a couple of kilometres further into town and you'll most likely need a taxi to reach them.

Qeshm International Hotel (☎/fax 255 4905; 22 Bahman Blvd; s/d/tr US$30/35/50; P ✖ 🖳) This is Qeshm's finest and one of the best-value places in Iran. The service is very good and the restaurants are not bad, either. The only drawback is its location, at the southern end of Qeshm town.

Two recommended mid-range options are on a hill with spectacular views over the town and Hormoz Island, and while both were being renovated when we visited, they should be open when you come here and are worth checking out. To get here head west along Imam Khomeini Ave as far as Jahadsazandegy Sq, then take Sayadan Blvd up to the top of the hill and follow the road to the right for about 200m. Rooms in **Qeshm Hotel** (tw/tr/q US$22/30/35; P ✖) had fridges, TVs

and windows that would afford magnificent views if they weren't so small. Government-run **Qeshm Tourist Inn** (Jahangardi Inn; ☎ 522 8232; fax 522 5557; P ✖) is next door and will have similar furnishing and prices.

The budget options, all with shared bathrooms, aren't great. **Hotel Sahel** (☎ 522 4723; Imam Khomeini Ave; tw IR70,000) is quite handy for the pier and has passable twin rooms. A few doors along is **Khalija Fars Hotel** (Imam Khomeini Ave; r IR60,000; ✖), but it's not as good as Sahel. In town, **Mehmunsara Sittare** (☎ 522 3061; Valiasr Ave; r per person IR25,000; P ✖) is simple but clean, though not as well located.

Straight down the lane from the speedboat, **Golestan Apartment Hotel** (☎/fax 522 7707; Imam Khomeini Ave; tr/q apt IR250,000/300,000; ✖) is well located but overpriced.

Bany (☎ 522 8901; Imam Gholi Khan Blvd; meals IR50,000; 🕑 lunch & dinner) Qeshm's best and probably most expensive restaurant overlooks the sea at the southern end of town. The food here is very good and the grilled prawns (IR52,000) are worth the money.

Otherwise, there are plenty of snack bars and kababis along the main streets, particularly around the bazaar, and the hotel restaurants are generally pretty decent.

Getting There & Away
When arriving and departing, you may be searched for smuggled duty-free goods, though foreigners are usually waved through.

AIR
Mahan Air (www.mahanairlines.com) flies to Tehran (80 minutes, six times a week), Sirjan (45 minutes, twice weekly) and direct to Dubai (one hour, six times a week). **Naderi Travel Agency** (☎ 522 5155; Shahid Bahonar Blvd) can help with tickets.

BOAT
There are two types of regular speedboats (open/closed IR10,000/15,000, 40/25 minutes) between Qeshm's Sangi Pier and Bandar-e Abbas. There is also at least one ferry everyday from Bahonar Port, usually at 7pm (IR10,000, one hour).

If you have a vehicle, Qeshm is a good place to lose a few days wandering around the quiet roads. To get a vehicle to the island take a cheap and fairly quick car ferry from Bandar-e Pol to Laft-e Kohneh. Departure times depend on demand.

PERSIAN GULF

Getting Around

Shared taxis, vans and *pik-ups* take passengers along the coastal road. The fare between Qeshm and Dargahan is about IR3500 per person. For Laft (51km from Qeshm), you may have to charter your own taxi for about IR90,000 for half a day. A taxi from the airport will cost about 50,000, depending on your negotiating skills.

HORMOZ ISLAND   جزیره هرمز
☎ 0763 / pop 7000

Just 30 minutes from Bandar-e Abbas, this delightfully sleepy 42-sq-km island is a world away from the frantic bustle of the regional capital. When your speedboat rounds the sea wall and the captain kills the motor you'll be engulfed by something almost completely unheard of in Bandar – pristine, relaxing silence.

The only settlement is tiny Hormoz village, with a wonderful Portuguese castle on its northern edge. The rest of the island is virtually uninhabited, its interior hilly and infertile, the forbidding peaks seared by centuries of fierce Persian Gulf sun.

History

The island was, until the 14th century, known as Jarun Island, while Hormoz was the name of a long-established commercial town on the mainland, probably on the Minab River. Around 1300, the damage caused by repeated Mongol raids made the 15th Amir of Hormoz shut up shop and move. He took many of his subjects with him and together they briefly stopped on Kish Island before finally settling on Jarun Island.

This new Hormoz soon became the grand emporium of the Persian Gulf, attracting immigrants from the mainland, and traders from as far away as India and Africa. Visitors to Hormoz described it as heavily fortified, bustling and opulent. European traders arrived, most notably the Portuguese (opposite). After the Portuguese were forced out in the early 17th century, Shah Abbas I selected the small mainland fishing town of Gamerun to be the new outlet for Persian trade, changing its name to Bandar-e Abbas. Within a few years much of the splendour of Hormoz was reduced to ruins.

Today, Hormoz is still an impoverished outpost where foraging goats and barefoot children are rarely disturbed by traffic.

Sights
PORTUGUESE CASTLE

Some 750m to the north of Hormoz beach is the famous **Portuguese castle** *(ghal'e-ye Portoghaliha)*, without doubt the most impressive colonial fortress in Iran. The elements have taken a heavy toll and much of the original structure has crumbled into the sea but it is still hauntingly beautiful.

From the port, walk along the waterfront until you reach the castle walls then follow them anticlockwise as far as you can go. You'll come to a pair of rusting cannons and the low arched entrance right on the tip of the cape.

The archway opens onto a wide courtyard facing the sea. On the right as you enter is the ancient armoury. In the middle of the courtyard is a partially underground church, which has some splendid, if simple, vaulted ceilings. Before following the path marked by stones up onto the ramparts, you can visit the ground-floor room of the watchtower if the door is open. Higher up is another door to the submerged 'Water Supply', a surprisingly deep and impressive cavern circled by an elevated, interior walkway amid the pillars.

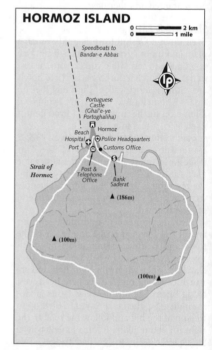

HORMOZ ISLAND

0 — 2 km
0 — 1 mile

THE PORTUGUESE ON HORMOZ

In 1507, talented Portuguese admiral and empire builder Afonso de Albuquerque (also known as Afonso the Great) besieged and, after a battle, conquered Hormoz in an attempt to establish a network of Portuguese bases. The castle of Hormoz, which he started the same year, was completed in 1515.

With Hormoz Island as their fortified base, the Portuguese quickly became the major power on the waters of the Persian Gulf. Virtually all trade with India, the Far East, Muscat (Oman) and the Gulf ports was funnelled through Hormoz, to which the Portuguese, under an administration known for its justice and religious tolerance, brought great prosperity for over a century.

But Portugal's stranglehold over vital international trading routes could hardly fail to arouse the resentment of Persia and the other rising imperial powers. In 1550, Ottoman forces besieged the fortress of Hormoz for a month but failed to take the island.

Early the next century, Shah Abbas I granted the British East India Company trading rights with Persia through the port of Jask to the southeast of Hermoz Island, thus enraging the Portuguese. Abbas, who had no naval power with which to challenge the Portuguese, cunningly detained the company's silk purchase in 1622 until the English agreed to send a force to assist him in liberating Hormoz. The Portuguese put up a brave defence, but ultimately were forced off the island.

From the ramparts the views back over the village and island are spectacular. The village, punctuated by palm trees and the pale-stone minaret of the Sunni mosque, is surrounded by the blue waters of the Persian Gulf with the starkly beautiful backdrop of the mountains of Hormoz; it's the perfect place to sit, soak up the silence and let your mind wander back a few hundred years.

There is no gate or entrance fee and, if you're lucky, the old caretaker might let you into the locked doors of the tower and water supply – a tip is appreciated.

HORMOZ VILLAGE

This pleasant little **village** is interesting, though there's nothing much to do except ramble through the maze of kuches. In the northern-most part of Hormoz village is the small Sunni **Jameh-ye Imam Shafe'i mosque**.

There is nowhere to stay or eat on Hormoz Island. The small grocery stores on the road between the castle and the port sell bottled water, soft drinks, biscuits and ice creams. It's well worth bringing a picnic, as lunch at the castle overlooking the sea is wonderfully relaxing.

Getting There & Away

The only way to get to Hormoz is by speedboat (IR8000, about 30 minutes) from the main jetty in Bandar-e Abbas. In summer, Hormoz is witheringly hot so start your journey as early in the day as possible. Boats leave whenever they have their full complement of about 18 passengers – every 15 or so minutes in the morning and less often later.

Getting Around

There's not much in the way of roads on Hormoz, not that you're likely to need them; the village and castle are easily explored on foot. If you wish to see the bone-dry interior, you could persuade one of the locals to take you on their motorcycle or, more creatively, you could charter a boat from the port to circumnavigate the island (IR130,000) or drop you around the uninhabited southern shores. If you choose to do the latter, be wary of tides and leave a detailed explanation of your plans with the police. You should also be self-sufficient in food and water and understand that the only trails are those left by shepherds.

MINAB   میناب

☎ 0765 / pop 55,000

A growing number of travellers is finding Minab to be one of those places you visit for one night and end up staying five. Wedged between a line of rocky desert hills and luxuriant date palm plantations, the town was once the biggest in the region. But that was a very long time ago. Today it has a mañana feel except on Thursday, when the famous weekly **market** draws merchants and shoppers from far and wide.

Bandari, Arabic and Indian influences are to be found everywhere. Women wear

---

THE THURSDAY MARKET OF MINAB

If possible, arrange your visit to coincide with Minab's Thursday market (panjshambe bazar). The market, one of the most colourful in the country, is held on a patch of open ground along the banks of the seasonal river 500m west of the main bridge. It's famous throughout the region, attracting buyers and sellers from outlying villages, even as far afield as Bandar-e Abbas. You'll see many women wearing the burqa (p270), as well as bright headscarves and pants.

The panjshambe bazar is actually three separate markets. In the main one you'll find a motley array of makeshift stalls selling everything from fresh fruit, vegetables and clothing to the distinctive zaribafi – a range of items made from local palm leaves including mats, fans, brooms and baskets – and the brocaded strips of cloth used by local women to adorn their clothing. There's even a father-and-son strongman show. Nearby is a livestock market, which is especially interesting early in the morning when the serious bargaining is done; and a small market for indigenous arts and crafts that is tucked away in the permanent bazaar.

Whether you're there to buy or not, arrive as early as possible to soak up the atmosphere – a cross between the colour and vibrancy of an African market and the discreet smiles of an Iranian bazaar.

---

shamat instead of the more common black chador. The shamat is made of a finely patterned, gauze-like fabric that comes in pale blues, orange, cream and pink; it's draped Indian-style around the body and head. As one reader put it: 'A truly intoxicating sight after the oppressive uniformity of black "tents" elsewhere.'

The approach to Minab from Bandar-e Abbas is quite dramatic. As you enter town you'll see the crumbling but picturesque **Hazareh Castle** competing for space on a hill with hundreds of mud-brick houses. It is believed that Minab was built by two sisters, Bibi Minoo and Bibi Nazanin, and the castle is known locally as Bibi Minoo. Bibi Nazanin's castle long ago returned to dust. Traditional custom has couples from the town walk once around this fortress, in the company of their families, before taking their marriage vows. Photographers will be well rewarded by a walk in these hills at sunset.

Sleeping & Eating

Sadaf Hotel (☎ 5999; r IR110,000; 🔀) Even before you start the easy job of negotiating down the price, these clean, comfortable rooms with TV, fridge and bathroom are excellent value. The staff are friendly and some speak English, and there is a decent restaurant attached that has been recommended for its range of fish dishes. Sadaf is well signposted on the left about 500m before the main bridge into Minab.

Minab Inn (☎ 2263; fax 5322; r IR285,000; 🅿 🔀) Inside a shady park about 2.5km past the main bridge as you come from Bandar, the location is probably not enough to justify the price for these rooms. The pleasant restaurant is reasonable value and is open to guests and the public.

There are plenty of sandwich shops and kababis around, and the ice cream in Minab is exceptional.

Getting There & Away

Savaris (IR13,000, 75 minutes, 97km) to and from Bandar-e Abbas operate from Imam Khomeini Sq, at the bazaar-end of the bridge into town; just stand on the street and someone will soon pick you up.

Big buses leave Minab for Bandar-e Abbas, Shiraz, Yazd and anywhere else en route, but it's important to book in advance at the **bus office** (🕙 10am-4pm), opposite and about 200m north of Sadaf Hotel. Even with a ticket, arrive early because services are oversold and competition for seats and luggage space is fierce.

Savaris to Minab leave from Bandar from 50m south of Abuzar Sq throughout the day. If you've been staying in Minab and want to avoid Bandar, ask to be dropped at the roundabout with the replica sailing ship as its centrepiece about 10km east of Bandar; buses pass this way en route to Sirjan, Kerman and Yazd although your choice of seats will be limited.

Southeastern Iran
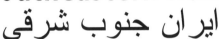
ایران جنوب شرقی

CONTENTS

Southeastern Iran is frontier territory, and on this frontier the exotic is never too far away. The region stretches from Kerman, on the cusp of the cultural divide that separates the ethnic Persians of the central plateau and the more eastern-oriented Baluchis, across the Dasht-e Lut and into the remote Sistan va Baluchestan province, where smugglers criss-cross the deserts and borders and the rule of law is tenuous, at best.

For travellers, the Bam earthquake has changed things in the southeast. While still an awesome sight, the Arg-e Bam, the famous mud-brick citadel, is not the draw it was. Work on restoring the Arg has tentatively begun, but it will be years before the town or the citadel itself approach anything like their pre-quake glory.

Bam's soothing date groves and strong tradition of hospitality will still reward a visit, but you'll want to see a few 'new' places on the way. Rayen is probably the pick of these, with the 15 towers of its adobe Arg-e Rayen and luxuriously relaxed atmosphere. Desert excursions and visits to nomads, be they by camel or 4WD, are growing in popularity. And if you head for the den of smugglers that is Zabol you'll be amply rewarded with a visit to Kuh-e Khajeh, which is almost spiritual in its lonely, ancient position in the middle of a desert lake.

HIGHLIGHTS

- Check out the 'new Arg' at picturesque **Rayen** (p292)
- Marvel at the gardens and mausoleum of **Mahan** (p290)
- Lunch in Kerman's **Chaykhaneh-ye Vakil** (p289)
- Watch the sunset over the **Kaluts** (p292), then pitch a tent
- Blaze a trail to the ancient and imposing **Kuh-e Khajeh** (p300)

★ Kaluts
Kuh-e Khajeh ★
★ Kerman
★ Mahan
★ Rayen

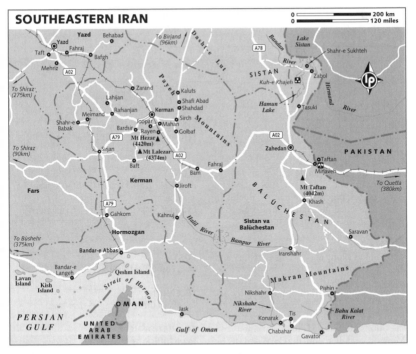

SOUTHEASTERN IRAN

SIRJAN
سيرجان

☎ 0345

Sirjan is probably not really worth a detour, but it's a useful place to break a journey from Kerman to Bandar-e Abbas or Shiraz. If you do stay you might want to see the **Mir-e Zobair**, which contains some ancient calligraphy, and the ancient **Firuz Fire Temple**.

Sleeping & Eating

There is not a great choice here. The only cheap hotel is the basic **Hotel-e Kasra** (☎ 422 5172; s/tw IR35,000/40,000), down a lane between the main branches of Bank Mellat and Bank Melli, in the centre of town. Alternatively, the mid-range **Sirjan Tourist Inn** (Jahangardi Hotel; ☎ 27878; s/d IR92,000/111,000; P ✖) didn't seem to have a foreigner price, making it great value.

For food, take your choice of kababi.

Getting There & Away

Sirjan is easy to get to by shared taxi (IR12,000) from Kerman's Azadi Sq, or by direct bus from Kerman, Yazd, Shiraz or Bandar-e Abbas. There is no bus station, and the individual bus companies are spread all over town. It is best to take a private taxi and ask, for example, for the *terminal-e Yazd* (or wherever you want to go). There's a train to Tehran, leaving midmorning.

AROUND SIRJAN

If you've made it to Sirjan, or are driving between Kerman and Yazd or Sirjan, it's well worth taking the route via Shahr-e Babak and diverting 27km northeast to **Meimand**, a pretty village with houses carved out of the hillside, similar to Cappadocia in Turkey, albeit on a small scale. The scenery en route certainly warrants a day trip, if you have some time up your sleeve. It's usually deserted in summer and there's nowhere to stay.

To get here, you will have to take a shared taxi from Shahr-e Babak, accessible by bus from Kerman (IR6000); or you can charter a taxi from Kerman or Shahr-e Babak. To leave, jump in any savari or bus going your way, or hitch.

SOUTHEASTERN IRAN

KERMAN

کرمان

☎ 0341 / pop 508,000 / elevation 1754m

The desert city of Kerman is sheltered from the vast Dasht-e Lut by the barren Payeh Mountains and is a pleasant place to visit, even in summer. With Bam no longer the tourist draw it was, some have asked whether Kerman is worth the trip. Well, yes. Kerman and the towns scattered through the surrounding semidesert are yet another distinctive aspect of Iran and the physical and cultural differences are well worth exploring. The city is something of a melting pot, mixing the more-European style of the Persians and the clearly subcontinental Asian philosophies of the many Baluchis in town. The small but significant Zoroastrian population only adds to the mix.

History

Kerman has a long and turbulent history and has only enjoyed short spells of simultaneous peace and prosperity. Believed to have been founded in the early 3rd century AD by Ardeshir I, founder of the Sassanian dynasty, from the 7th century it was ruled in turn by the Arabs, Buyids, Seljuks, Turkmen and Mongols, and then until the Qajar dynasty by a further succession of invaders and regional despots. Kerman obtained security under the central government in Tehran during the 19th century, but its relative remoteness has continued to deny it prosperity.

For many centuries the livelihood of Kerman depended on its place along the Asian trade routes, but from about the beginning of Safavid times it has relied more on the production of carpets. In view of its barren nature, the city and the province to which it gives its name are very dependent on *qanats* (underground water channels; see the boxed text 'The Qanat', p234), built many centuries ago.

Orientation

The two main squares in Kerman are Azadi Sq to the west and Shohada Sq to the east. Most of the important offices and things to see are on or close to the road between these two squares, or in the bazaar near Shohada Sq. Be on the lookout for that Iranian traffic hazard, the contraflow bus lane along which buses hurtle in the *opposite* direction to the rest of the traffic, particularly along Dr Beheshti St.

Information

EMERGENCY

Bahonnar Hospital (☎ 223 5011-8; Shahid Qarani St) The most central and easiest hospital to find.

Police Headquarters (☎ 110 or 211 3068; Adalat St)

INTERNET ACCESS

Alpha Cafe Net (☎ 226 7270; Valiasr Sq; per hr IR10,000; ☼ 8am-10pm, closed Fri) Easily the best option, with webcams, mics, XP for picture uploads.

Coffeenet Day (☎ 244 4917; Azadi Sq; per hr IR12,000; ☼ 8am-2pm & 4-9pm, closed Fri)

MONEY

Bank Melli Central Branch (Adalat St) Nightmare on Adalat St...five signatures, 25 minutes.

Exchange Shops (Felestin St) The two small exchange shops near the corner of Dr Shariati St are easily the best and quickest places to change money. Otherwise, try your hotel.

POST

Main Post Office (Adalat St)

TELEPHONE

Telephone Office (Tohid Sq; ☼ 7am-10pm)

TOURIST OFFICES

Tourist Office (☎ 221 0635; ☼ 7.30am-2pm, closed Fri) Has helpful and obliging staff and is worth a visit for its maps, postcards and brochures.

TOURS

Both of these guys are highly recommended.

Jalal Mehdizadeh (☎ 271 0185, 0913 142 3174; jalalguesthouse@yahoo.de) Also the manager of the Jalal Guesthouse (p288), Jalal can arrange tours throughout the province, but his speciality is the waterfall tour, taking in several waterfalls around Kerman.

Vatan Caravan Tours & Travel Agency (☎ /fax 223 7591, 0913 343 5265; vatan_caravan@yahoo.com; Ganj Ali Khan St) Hossein Vatani is a charismatic guide who speaks good English and has a deep knowledge of and enthusiasm for the region around Kerman. Hossein offers a range of tours, including cultural tours of Kerman; overnight trips to nomad encampments in the desert; 4WD and camel treks. Prices are very reasonable, and modes of transport depend on your means (one reader wrote of enjoying a trip in which Hossein improvised a series of hitches). Travellers can check their email in his office.

TRAVEL AGENCIES

Kerman Gasht Travel Agency (☎ 226 0217; Ferdosi St) Elham Vakili does the usual ticket-selling thing and also offers tours of Kerman and surrounds from a woman's

KERMAN

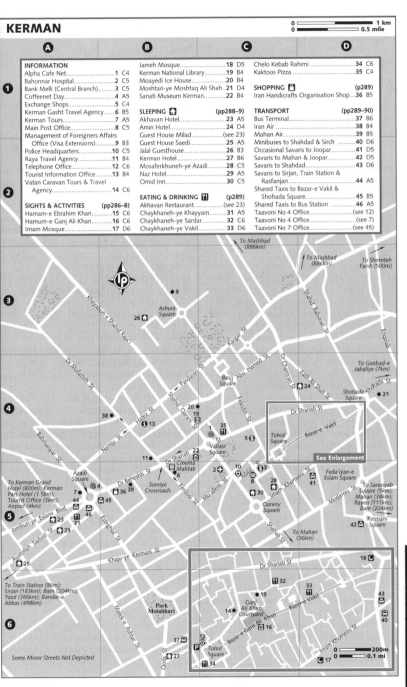

0 — 1 km
0 — 0.5 mile

INFORMATION
Alpha Cafe Net..........................1 C4
Bahonnar Hospital.....................2 C5
Bank Melli (Central Branch)........3 C5
Coffeenet Day............................4 A5
Exchange Shops..........................5 C4
Kerman Gasht Travel Agency.......6 B5
Kerman Tours.............................7 A5
Main Post Office.........................8 C5
Management of Foreigners Affairs
  Office (Visa Extensions)............9 B3
Police Headquarters...................10 C5
Raya Travel Agency...................11 B4
Telephone Office.......................12 C5
Tourist Information Office...........13 B4
Vatan Caravan Tours & Travel
  Agency.................................14 C6

SIGHTS & ACTIVITIES (pp286–8)
Hamam-e Ebrahim Khan...........15 C6
Hamum-e Ganj Ali Khan...........16 C6
Imam Mosque...........................17 D6

Jameh Mosque..........................18 D5
Kerman National Library............19 B4
Moayedi Ice House....................20 B4
Moshtari-ye Moshtaq Ali Shah...21 D4
Sanati Museum Kerman.............22 B4

SLEEPING (pp288–9)
Akhavan Hotel..........................23 A5
Amin Hotel...............................24 D4
Guest House Milad................(see 23)
Jalal Guesthouse.......................25 A5
Guest House Saedi....................25 A5
Kerman Hotel...........................27 B6
Mosaferkhuneh-ye Azadi...........28 C5
Naz Hotel................................29 A5
Omid Inn................................30 C5

EATING & DRINKING (p289)
Akhavan Restaurant...............(see 23)
Chaykhaneh-ye Khayyam..........31 A5
Chaykhaneh-ye Sardar.............32 C6
Chaykhaneh-ye Vakil................33 D6

Chelo Kebab Rahimi..................34 C6
Kaktoos Pizza...........................35 C4

SHOPPING (p289)
Iran Handicrafts Organisation Shop..36 B5

TRANSPORT (pp289–90)
Bus Terminal............................37 B6
Iran Air...................................38 B4
Mahan Air...............................39 B5
Minibuses to Shahdad & Sirch....40 D6
Occasional Savaris to Joopar.......41 D5
Savaris to Mahan & Joopar........42 D5
Savaris to Shahdad...................43 D6
Savaris to Sirjan, Train Station &
  Rasfanjan..............................44 A5
Shared Taxis to Bazar-e Vakil &
  Shohada Square.....................45 B5
Shared Taxis to Bus Station........46 A5
Taavoni No 4 Office...............(see 12)
Taavoni No 4 Office.................(see 7)
Taavoni No 7 Office...............(see 45)

perspective, without taking you to more than you want to see. The tours are cheap at US$15 a day.

Kerman Tours (☎ 245 0465; fax 245 1299; Bahmanyar St)

Raya Travel Agency (☎ 245 4602; Ferdosi St)

VISA EXTENSIONS

The **Management of Foreigners Affairs Office** (☎ 272 5798; ◷ 7am-1.30pm, closed Fri) is relatively efficient, though it generally only issues two-week extensions, and you have to go all the way back to the Bank Melli central branch to deposit your cash. The office is in **Police Building No 14** (Abbas Pour St), about 300m north of Ashura Sq; look for the pale-green guard-house on the right-hand (eastern) side of the road. Go to the office one or two days before your visa expires and if you get there early you should have the extension the same day.

Dangers & Annoyances

Three overland cyclists were unfortunate enough to get caught up in Iran's long-running war on drugs (see the boxed text 'Drug-Running Dromedaries', p286) in late 2003, being kidnapped by smugglers while riding between Kerman and Zahedan. The smugglers, obviously seeking some compensation after a shipment reportedly worth about €5 million was seized by police, promptly demanded just that amount in ransom for the two Germans and an Irishman. The three were held for about three weeks before being released a couple of days after the Bam earthquake. Apparently, no ransom was paid. Unlike a similar incident in 1999, there were no stories this time of how relaxing it can be being held by the mostly hospitable opium smugglers.

But seriously, while these are isolated incidents, it's worth keeping an ear out for major successes or seizures by the authorities, especially if you're heading to Pakistan by bike. They could provoke a reaction.

Sights

BAZAR-E VAKIL

The **Bazar-e Vakil**, which runs between Tohid Sq and the Jameh Mosque, is not as large or confusing as many bazaars but it's got a vivacity about it that should keep you interested, especially in the morning and late afternoon. Although the entire 1km-long bazaar is called the Bazar-e Vakil for the sake of simplicity, each section dates from a different historical period. The area around the pretty **Ganj Ali Khan Courtyard** is known as the **Bazar-e Ganj Ali Khan** and was built in the Safavid period; the courtyard is partially surrounded by the **Coppersmith's Bazaar**.

Leading west from the courtyard, the section known as **Bazar-e Ekhtiari** runs into the Bazar-e Vakil, which extends to the back gate of the Jameh Mosque. Both of these bazaars are around 150 years old. Running outside the southern wall of the mosque to Shohada Sq is the open-air **Bazar-e Mosaffari**, the oldest of Kerman's bazaars at over 700 years old, although there is little evidence of such antiquity.

One of the less-frequented minor bazaars is the **Gold Bazaar** (Bazar-e Zargaran), which runs from the northeastern corner of the Ganj Ali Khan Courtyard. Take the first lane to the left and after about 50m, you'll reach a small square with an attractive portal leading to an old (and now closed) madraseh.

DRUG-RUNNING DROMEDARIES

Camels. They're unassuming, a bit thick and no-one seems to care where they go or what they do...sounds like the perfect description for undercover work. And so it is that these ships of the desert have been recruited, well, trained, to ship drugs. The camels are walked for several days from somewhere near the border to a predetermined place beyond Kerman, where the police and military surveillance is much less vigilant than in the border regions. The process is repeated, with the camels being fed each time they arrive to build an attachment to the destination. When they know where they're going, their humps are stuffed with kilograms of opiates and they're off. Even the government's US$400 million annual war on drugs cannot account for every wandering camel in the desert.

It's a war that's been running for more than 20 years, and in that time almost 3000 soldiers have died in battles with the heavily armed drug lords. Iran has erected electric fences, desert ditches (to dissuade after-hours motorcyclists) and has 30,000 men on the Afghan border, but still an estimated 85% of all Europe's opiates come through Iran from Afghanistan and Pakistan.

Follow the steps down into the **Hamam-e Eb-ahim Khan** (⏰ 7am-5pm, until 7pm summer), one of the few traditional bathhouses where men, but sadly not women, can still be rubbed, scrubbed and beaten, all for the fun of it – such a service costs IR20,000. However, one intrepid woman traveller reported that the friendly, English-speaking manager gave her a guided tour of the place – once he'd checked with the bathers, of course.

JAMEH MOSQUE
The well-preserved and restored **Jameh Mosque** (off Shohada Sq) sits beside the bazaar and is definitely worth a quick look. With its four lofty *iwans* (rectangular halls opening onto a courtyard) and shimmering blue tiles, it was built in 1349 and extensively modernised during the Safavid period and later. At the main entrance there is a useful explanation in English. The back entrance leads directly into the bazaar.

MOSHTARI-YE MOSHTAQ ALI SHAH
The attractive **Moshtari-ye Moshtaq Ali Shah** (Shohada Sq), mausoleum to a renowned Sufi mystic, dates from the Qajar period, although some parts of the structure are from the Mongol era. The stuccowork and the blue-and-white-tiled roofs are beautiful and visible from Shohada Sq), though the compact interior courtyard, with its gardens and octagonal pool, was looking a little neglected when we passed.

HAMUM-E GANJ ALI KHAN
Once Kerman's most important bathhouse, the **Hamum-e Ganj Ali Khan** (☎ 222 5577; Gang Ali Khan Sq; adult/student IR30,000/15,000; ⏰ 8.30am-6pm, until 7.30pm summer) has been meticulously restored and transformed into a museum. Once through the entrance, with its wonderful frescoes of people and animals, you'll see a collection of wax dummies illustrating the workings of a traditional bathhouse. The reception area, for example, was divided so men practising different trades could all disrobe together. The hammam was originally built for Ganj Ali Khan, the governor of Kerman, in 1631. The entrance, signposted in English, is off Ganj Ali Khan Courtyard.

IMAM MOSQUE
The quadrangular, domed **Imam Mosque** (Imam Khomeini St) dates from the Seljuk period, and

> ### JAMEH MOSQUES
> Although every Iranian town has several mosques, the most important one is the so-called Jameh or Friday Mosque *(masjed-e jameh)*. This is where men gather for prayers at noon every Friday and where they will listen to the Friday prayer leader preach. In small towns he may be a simple imam (prayer leader) but in the bigger towns he may be an *hojattol-Eslam* or even an ayatollah, a religious expert who may have studied the Quran for 20 years or more.

includes the remains of the original Seljuk mihrab and minaret, though much of the building has since been rebuilt. The mosque has been under restoration for some years, but the painstaking work is revealing some splendid reliefs, particularly in the rooms high above the main *iwan*. Much of the *iwan*'s outer tilework has been given a heavy-handed restoration – it's gone.

SANATI MUSEUM KERMAN
This **museum** (Dr Shariati St), in a Qajar-era building set around an attractive courtyard, was being renovated at the time of writing. Works by local artist Sayyed Ali Akhbar Sanati, known for his expertise in stone inlay, might be worth a look when it's completed, as might the promised teahouse.

MOAYEDI ICE HOUSE
The Safavid-era **Moayedi Ice House** (Abu Hamed St) must be one of the weirdest 'tourist attractions' in Iran. The stepped sides of this cone-shaped building, originally dating from the Safavid period, have been renovated so well they look new. But while it is undoubtedly an impressive-looking structure, it's what awaits you inside that is a bit of a freak-out. Currently used by the Kerman Centre for Intellectual Development of Children, the pool in which ice was once stored is today carpeted and filled with plastic balls. If you poke your head in, kids will likely encourage you (with adult assent) to leap in while they throw balls at you. All good fun, certainly, but wait until you look up. Swinging from the neck from the domed ceiling is an effigy of Mohammed Reza Pahlavi, complete with a hat decorated with the stars and stripes...demonstrative education, perhaps?

KERMAN NATIONAL LIBRARY

The **Kerman National Library** (Shahid Qarani St; 7am-midnight) is worth a look because both the inside and outside are a particularly harmonious example of Qajar-era architecture. It's hard to think, with the forest of columns supporting vaulted ceilings, that this was once a textile factory – if only Manchester had been so blessed. There is an Internet café inside.

SHEKETEH FARSH

Set up to preserve the traditional carpet-weaving techniques, the **Sheketeh Farsh** (Bausteny Piroozy Blvd; 8am-4pm, closed Fri) carpet factory is a fascinating example of carpet-weaving in action. However, only a few of the huge looms are still operating and cameras are banned. The centre is in the northeast of town; you'll need to get a taxi.

GONBAD-E JABALIYE

Just beyond the eastern edge of Kerman is the double-domed **Gonbad-e Jabaliye** (Mountain of Stone). It's of unknown age or purpose and the Kerman Tourism brochure sums it up: 'A big, strange dome in the eastern part of Kerman'. Quite. It's thought to predate the 2nd century AD and might have been a Zoroastrian building. It is remarkable because it's constructed of stone rather than the usual brick.

It's a fair way to come just to see two domes but the setting, at the foot of the Payeh Mountains, is picturesque. To get here, try to find a shared taxi from Shohada Sq, but you will probably have to charter one for about IR15,000 return, including waiting.

Sleeping

BUDGET

Kerman is not blessed with an abundance of good budget options.

Jalal Guesthouse (271 0185, 0913 142 3174; jalalguesthouse@yahoo.de; 11 Imam Reza St; per person with breakfast US$12;) Local guide Jalal Mehdizadeh (p284) has made his home into a genuine traveller's stop and the best budget option in town. There are only three rooms, but the bathroom is spotless and guests can use the kitchen, washing machine and watch the satellite TV. Jalal speaks English and German.

Omid Inn (222 0571; Shahid Qarani St; s/tw/tr IR35,000/50,000/70,000;) Set around a courtyard

(which is ideal for overlanders), the Omid is spartan but welcoming. The manager speaks English and the rooms (with kettle), shared bathroom and kitchen are clean. Unfortunately, lone women are not welcome.

The next two are a longer walk into town, but good value.

Guest House Milad (245 0617; Ayatollah Saduqi St; s/tw IR20,000/40,000;) The clean rooms and shared bathrooms are good value in this friendly place. Guests can use the kitchen.

Guest House Saedi (252 0802; Ayatollah Saduqi St; s/tw IR35,000/60,000;) Another friendly choice with simple, quiet rooms and a good, cheap restaurant attached. The twin rooms have bathrooms, but singles (with fan) don't. No English is spoken here.

If you're desperate, the seedy **Mosaferk-huneh-ye Azadi** (222 7007; Felestin St; r IR40,000) is above the Paykan showroom; there are no showers. Women, especially, should look elsewhere.

MID-RANGE & TOP END

Akhavan Hotel (244 1411-2; akhavanhotel@yahoo .com; Ayatollah Saduqi St; s/d with breakfast US$24/34;) Possibly the best-value hotel in Iran. The helpful Akhavan brothers are happy to negotiate on even these very reasonable rates and in all but the busiest times you can knock at least US$10 off the price of a modern, semiluxurious room. They can arrange tours, bus, train and plane tickets and assist with visa extensions, faxes and international phone calls. The parking is secure and you can camp out back and use their showers for US$1 per person per day. The restaurant is also good (p289). Highly recommended.

Amin Hotel (222 9464; aminhotel@yahoo.com; Dr Chamran St; tw/ste IR140,000/170,000;) Near the bazaar, this place has been recommended by travellers but was being renovated at the time of writing.

Kerman Hotel (251 5065; Qods St; s/d US$20/25;) Near the bus station, this homely place has spacious yet pricey rooms.

Naz Hotel (244 6786; fax 245 0498; Ayatollah Saduqi St; tw with breakfast IR200,000;) It's opposite the Akhavan Hotel but is bad value by comparison. Its rooms are large, but plain.

Kerman Pars Hotel (211 9301; kerman @pars hotels.com; Jomhuri-ye Eslami Blvd; d/apt with breakfast US$90/230;) This 200-room behemoth is easily the best hotel in Kerman.

The range of rooms is as impressive as the foyer, and the rooms themselves quite luxurious. There's a gym, sauna and three restaurants. The pool is open to nonguests for IR35,000.

Kerman Grand Hotel (☎ 244 5203; fax 244 4087; Jomhuri-ye Eslami Blvd; s/d/ste US$54/60/84; P ⊠) One reader described this place as 'the worst hotel in Iran'. That's a bit harsh, and once the renovations are complete it should be reasonable value. There are several restaurants but the swimming pool is open to children only.

Eating & Drinking

For cheap eats, there are kababis, ice-cream and fruit-shake places, and a pizza place or two on Dr Beheshti and Dr Shariati Sts, particularly around the squares. The **Chelo Kebab Rahimi** (Tohid Sq; meals IR15,000; ☺ 11am-3pm & 5-9pm) is a no-frills place true to its name and also offers a decent *khoresht* (thick meaty stew with rice). **Kaktoos Pizza** (☎ 223 5300; Dr Shariati St; pizzas IR16,000; ☺ 4pm-midnight) does refreshingly thin crusts.

Chaykhaneh-ye Vakil (☎ 222 5989; Bazar-e Vakil; admission IR5000; meals IR30,000; ☺ 8.30am-5pm Sat-Thu, until 7.30pm summer, 8.30am-2pm Fri) This architecturally magnificent subterranean teahouse and restaurant is easily the most atmospheric dining option in Kerman. It's better known for its elegant arches and superb vaulted ceilings than its food, though it's not bad. There is live music most days.

Chaykhaneh-ye Sardar (☎ 226 4016; meals IR45,000) This place is more popular than Chaykhaneh-ye Vakil with Kermanis, who enjoy lolling around on the cushions and carpets in the garden while live traditional music (extra IR5000) is played from about 8.30pm each night. You should consider the local speciality, *borsgone*. This dish is a do-it-yourself mixture of *dizi* and *kashke bademjun*, an eggplant dish cooked in a milky sauce to a souplike consistency; the combination is spectacular. It can be difficult to find. Head east along the main Bazar-e Vakil. About 50m after the Chaykhaneh-ye Vakil, take the first lane on the left; look for the Bank Sepah sign. Follow the lane to an open parking area, veer left across the yard and then right; the restaurant is on the right before the main road.

Chaykhaneh-ye Khayyam (☎ 245 1417; Ayatollah Saduqi St; meals IR35,000; ☺ 11am-11pm, closed Fri)

Near Azadi Sq, this expansive restaurant is more faux traditional than anything, but they bring it off relatively well and, more importantly, the food is absolutely delicious.

Akhavan Hotel & Restaurant (☎ 244 1411-2; Ayatollah Saduqi St; meals IR30,000) The downstairs restaurant isn't too atmospheric but the food is good and the quantities large. The menu is relatively varied, and they are happy to feed you in your room, if you're staying.

Shopping

Kerman is a good place to buy carpets for a bit less than in Esfahan or Tehran. This is also the only place you're likely to see the beautiful Kerman *pate*, a brightly coloured square of cloth with intricate embroidered designs that is unique to Kerman. The **Iran Handicrafts Organisation shop** (☎ 244 7074; Dr Beheshti St; ☺ 8am-12.30pm & 4-8.30pm, closed Fri) is worth a look, but you'll get better prices in the bazaar.

Getting There & Away

AIR

Iran Air (☎ 245 8871; Dr Mofatteh St) has flights to Esfahan (IR197,000 one way, weekly); Tehran (IR269,000, daily); and Zahedan (IR152,000, weekly). **Mahan Air** (☎ 245 0542; Dr Beheshti St) also flies to Tehran (IR269,000) twice daily except Friday.

BUS, MINIBUS & SAVARI

The bus station is in the southwest of Kerman but Taavonis Nos 4 and 7 have offices on Azadi Sq, and No 4 also has an office on Tohid Sq. Services are on Volvos and include:

Destination	Price (IR)	Duration (hr)
Bam	12,000	3
Bandar-e Abbas	28,500	8
Esfahan	35,000	12
Mashhad	65,000	16
Shahr-e Babak	10,000	4
Shiraz	30,000	8
Tehran	60,000	15
Yazd	26,000	6
Zahedan	30,000	7

For services to Shahr-e Babak, go first to Taavoni No 4; for Bandar-e Abbas, No 7. Minibuses to Mahan (IR750) leave from around Kermani Sq, though it's worth asking around near Shohada Sq as well.

For Shahdad, take a minibus or savari (IR10,000) from Imam Khomeini St, just south of Shohada Sq.

Savaris to Bam (IR22,000) and Rayen (IR15,000) leave from Sarasiyab Sq (about 5km east of Kermani Sq), and to Sirjan from Azadi Sq for IR20,000. Savaris to Mahan (IR3000) leave from Kermani Sq and occasionally from Azadi Sq. Occasional savaris to Joopar (IR4000) run from just south of Kermani Sq.

TRAIN

The 1106km line from Tehran will be extended to Bam during the life of this book. The daily train to Tehran (1st/2nd class IR57,400/36,150, 13 hours) leaves at 6.20pm and stops at Yazd, Kashan and Qom, but not Esfahan.

Train tickets can be bought from **Kerman Tours** (☎ 245 0465; Azadi Sq) or arranged through Akhavan Hotel (p288), saving you the trip to the **train station** (☎ 211 0762), 8km southwest of town. Shared taxis (IR2000) leave from Azadi Sq, but you may have to charter a taxi for about IR10,000.

Getting Around
TO/FROM THE AIRPORT

There is no airport bus. You can take a shared taxi along Jomhuri-ye Eslami Blvd from Azadi Sq, or a taxi *dar baste* (closed door) for about IR10,000.

BUS & MINIBUS

Buses travel between Azadi Sq and Shohada Sq for IR200.

TAXI

Shared taxis use Azadi and Shohada Sqs. From Azadi Sq, shared taxis run to the bus station (IR800), Bazar-e Vakil and Shohada Sq (IR500; for a private taxi, expect to pay IR5000). Prices are similar from Shohada Sq. Taxis all to yourself cost IR6000 to most destinations around town and IR15,000 per hour.

AROUND KERMAN

There are some great places to visit in the vicinity of Kerman. Not all, however, are well served by public transport, so it's worth considering a taxi for the day. Depending on how far you go, you can expect a half-day to cost about IR100,000, and a full day

about IR180,000. Some drivers might want to charge you by the kilometre – the going rate was about IR700 at the time of writing, but by now will have probably risen with petrol prices.

Mahan   ماهان
☎ 0342 622

Some travellers choose Mahan, southeast of Kerman, as a base from which to explore the region. And when you visit this relaxed place it's easy to see why. Apart from the pleasant, tree-lined streets, Mahan attracts visitors for its fine mausoleum, and beautiful palace and gardens.

ARAMGAH-E SHAH NE'MATOLLAH VALI

The splendid dome over the **Aramgah-e Shah Ne'matollah Vali** (admission IR20,000; ⏱ 8am-5pm, until 8pm summer), the mausoleum of a well-known Sufi dervish, is one of the most recognisable images of eastern Iran. The mausoleum dates from the early 15th century, when it was built by an Indian king who was an adherent of the shah's teachings. However, many of the other religious buildings in the complex around it were built during the reign of Shah Abbas I or in the 18th century. The mausoleum is renowned for its tiles, and for the seven Indian doors throughout the building, some inlaid with ivory. Don't miss the small, tranquil prayer room where the dervish is thought to have stayed on frequent visits; it's adorned with wonderful hand-painted Quranic verses and symbols such as the double-edged sword of Imam Ali.

The entrance ticket allows you into a small but interesting **museum** and then up to the roof. The views from here are superb – photographers will be rather excited walking around beside the vast (and dented) Safavid cupola and Qajar minarets, which can be climbed. There is a **bookshop** in the courtyard, and also a **teahouse**.

The mausoleum is in the middle of Mahan, and minibuses (IR1750) and shared taxis (IR3000) from Kerman will take you straight to it.

BAGH-E SHAHZADE

Arriving at the handsome **Bagh-e Shahzade** (admission IR30,000; ⏱ 9am-6pm, 8am-11pm summer) gardens is like being beamed onto a different planet. One second you're in the

DOMES & MINARETS

The development of the dome was one of the greatest achievements of Persian architecture. The Sassanians (AD 224–642) were the first to discover a satisfactory way of building a dome on top of a square chamber by using two intermediate levels, or squinches – the lower octagonal and the higher 16-sided – on which the dome could rest. Later domes became progressively more sophisticated, incorporating an inner semicircular dome sheathed by an outer conical or even onion-shaped dome. Externally the domes were often encased in tiles, with patterns so elaborate they had to be worked out on models at ground level first.

The minaret started life as an entirely functional tower, from the top of which the muezzin called the faithful to prayer. However, during the Seljuk period (AD 1051–1220) minarets became tall, tapering spires, which were far more decorative than practical. Since it is feared that someone standing atop a minaret can look into the private family areas of nearby houses, Shiite mosques often have a separate hutlike structure on the roof from where the muezzin makes the call to prayer *(ezan),* though these days it's more likely to be a tape recording. A light in the top of the minaret acted as a beacon to direct people coming from the fields to the town to pray.

arid semidesert, the next it's all flowing water and tall green trees. The beautifully maintained grounds, built in 1873, contain a series of split-level fountains leading to a large palace that was once the residence of Abdul Hamid Mirza, one of the last princes of the Qajar dynasty. To the left of the palace there is a well-preserved bathhouse, which the caretaker will open for you; a tip is appreciated.

The palace itself has been converted into a **restaurant** (meals IR35,000), which serves a decent lunch and drinks. As the sun disappears, the fountains and palace are floodlit – a wonderful sight. The small handicrafts store just inside the entrance sells attractive *pate,* the local silks. Occasional music festivals are held in the grounds.

The gardens are a 5km walk up the main road through the village from the mausoleum, and the turn-off is signposted in English.

It is easy to get a private taxi between the two main attractions in town.

SLEEPING & EATING

Staying in Mahan makes a lovely alternative to Kerman.

Mahan Inn (☎ 2700; Gharani Sq; d/ste US$15/25; **P** ❉) This place is excellent value. Its big, tidy rooms have a bathroom and Western toilet, and the staff are friendly. There's also a good restaurant. The hotel is at a roundabout, a couple of blocks west of the mausoleum and public transport from Kerman takes you past the hotel.

Hotel Garden Shahzadeh (☎ 2103; 4-bed r IR100,000) This hotel, inside the walls of the

gardens, would be among the most romantic places in Iran if it wasn't so hard to get into one of its traditional rooms surrounding the garden. Apparently there are a couple of rooms with bathroom for IR150,000, but – and here's the problem – if you don't call in advance, you probably won't be able to even see a room let alone stay. It's best to get a Farsi-speaker to call.

GETTING THERE & AWAY

About every hour, savaris (IR3000) and minibuses (IR800) travel the 38km between Kermani Sq in Kerman (they can also occasionally be found at Azadi Sq) and Ne'matollahi Sq in Mahan, located right in front of the mausoleum.

Joopar جوپار

A visit to Joopar, 30km south of Kerman, is also worthwhile. The main attraction is the **Imamzadeh-ye Shahzade Hossein** (☾ 5.30am-10pm), built in the Safavid period for one of Imam Reza's many brothers, and similar in design to the mausoleum in Mahan. The mirrored ceiling inside the room containing the shrine is exquisite. The *zarih* (gilded, latticed 'cage' that sits over a tomb) was moved here from Mashhad, where it had encased Imam Reza. It's possible to stay in the basic **pilgrims' quarters** downstairs for a contribution of about IR20,000.

Occasional savaris to Joopar (IR3000) run from Kerman, just south of Imam Khomeini St and a minibus (IR1000) leaves from near Kermani Sq every hour or so. It's easier to charter a taxi from Mahan or Kerman. The mausoleum is off the main roundabout in the village.

Shahdad & Around شهداد

Shahdad is a quiet oasis town northeast of Kerman wedged between the Payeh Mountains and the southwestern fringe of the Dasht-e Lut. Shahdad is fiercely hot in summer, but its oranges (harvested in October) are reputedly the best in Iran.

Shahdad is mainly of interest as an entree to the desert, although there is an impressive Safavid-era mausoleum, the **Imamzadeh-ye Mohammed Ebn-e Zeid**, and to the east of town two prehistoric archaeological sites: the **Tappeh-ye Kohne**, which is believed to have been settled about 5000 years ago; and 1km further the **Shahrak-e Kotuluha** (City of the Little People) – the name refers to a local Lilliputian legend but its origin is unknown. There's not much to see.

Shafi Abad, an oasis village a few kilometres north of Shahdad, has an impressive mud-brick **caravanserai**, where you could feasibly camp or park-up if you so desired. You'll see the four corner towers and grand gatehouse long before you get there. Be sure to look in the lodgings along the northern wall, where rooms are linked by a long, arched corridor.

If you keep heading north along the new sealed road to Birjand, after about 28km you'll come to an area of stunning desert known as **Kaluts**, where wind and water have carved out the greatest 'sand castles' you're ever likely to see. These stretch for about 145km northwest to southeast, and make a spectacular sight, especially around sunset.

There is nowhere to stay out here so you'll have to come from Kerman for the day or take a desert tour with Vatan or Jalal (p284). Semiregular minibuses and savaris travel between Shahdad and Imam Khomeini St, just south of Shohada Sq, in Kerman, but there is no public transport to Kaluts.

RAYEN راین
☎ 0342

With the demise of Bam, several other ancient adobe structures are challenging for the title of the 'new Arg'. The pick of them is the **Arg-e Rayen** (☼ 8am–noon & 2–6pm) in the tranquil town of Rayen, which sits in the lee of Mt Hezar, 111km from Kerman.

On a hill overlooking the town, the Arg-e Rayen is about a quarter of the size of its

Bam cousin. The hotchpotch of architectural styles suggests it is well over 1000 years old, though its exact age is unknown. The Arg has been abandoned for about 150 years; restoration began in 1996. The imposing **outer walls** are 3m thick at the base and 1m thick at the top, and support most of the Arg's 15 towers.

The entrance leads straight onto the **bazaar** and from the gatehouse you can climb a narrow staircase to the **ramparts**, from where the views are spectacular. Coming back down, turn right and you'll come to the **'main walkway'**. About halfway along a door on the left leads to the remains of some **public houses**, some of which stood three storeys high and would have been home to several families.

A few metres along on the opposite side is the **barracks**. Cross the square towards the northwest and you enter what was the wealthier part of town; look for the crumbling **chimneys** built into the outer wall.

Inside the inner walls is the **governor's complex**. A veer to the right as you enter leads to the governor's house, which has been restored with a fairly heavy hand, but it does give you an idea of the relative luxury in which the governor and his family lived. The three others khans in here were also the property of the gov, but their exact function is unknown. Climb up a couple of crumbling staircases to the ramparts of this inner wall for great views of the rest of the town and mountains behind.

Turn right out of the governor's complex and you'll soon be at a restored building that might have been a storeroom, stables or a mosque; no-one really knows. Covered *kuches* (lanes) weave their way through the rest of the town, and at several points you can climb to the **outer ramparts**, though be warned that they are fairly narrow.

Hamid Reza (☎ 662 3644) is the caretaker and he'll unlock the various doors for you. He is also a sword maker, with his simple workshop just inside the main gate. If you arrive and can't get in, give him a call. There was no entrance fee when we visited, and Hamid Reza appreciated the IR10,000 tip.

SLEEPING & EATING
Restaurant Arg (☎ 662 3931; meals IR30,000) It serves tasty food in large portions and also has a few simple rooms with bathroom for IR30,000

per bed, though this is negotiable if you have three or more people. It's about 30m down the hill from the Arg, opposite a park.

GETTING THERE & AWAY

Rayen is 23km south of the Kerman–Bam road, the turn-off being 88km from Kerman. Buses (IR5000) leave from Kerman bus station every hour or so; Taavonis Nos 3 and 16 are your best bet. Savaris (IR15,000) are probably more frequent, leaving from Kerman's Sarasiyab Sq and dropping you at a square in Rayen about 1km from the Arg, from where they also return to Kerman. Alternatively, a taxi will cost about IR150,000 for a half-day trip from Kerman.

BAM   بم

☎ 0344

Having been all but flattened by a massive earthquake (see the boxed text 'Down, But Not Out', p294), Bam is obviously not the tourist attraction it once was. However, travellers continue to visit this historic city, and the information here will hopefully be enough. Of course, with the author having been in Bam before rebuilding began, these details are highly susceptible to change.

Orientation

Bam's bus station is in the south of the city near Arg Sq and unless you're packing light you'll need a taxi to get you to any of the lodgings. Once in town, Bam is easy enough to walk around. What remains of the ancient Arg-e Bam is about 2km from the centre of town, which is Imam Khomeini Sq.

Information

As you'd expect after a major earthquake, things were in a state of flux when we were in Bam. However, the **main post office** (Pasdaran St) was due to reopen, the **telephone office** (Dr Beheshti St) was expecting to resume international calls and the petrol stations were busy. **Bank Sepah** (Shahid Sadoqi St) was changing cash. By the time you visit expect to see at least one travel agency, shops and the police station to be back up and running.

To get an idea of what's happening in Bam, speak with Panjali Akbar at Akbar Tourist Guest House, the staff at the Azadi Hotel or **Mohammad Ali Dastres** (☎ 0913 144 4405; madastres@yahoo.com), a personable, engaging and oft-recommended guide who now describes

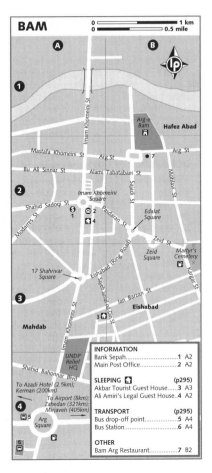

BAM

INFORMATION
Bank Sepah..........................1 A2
Main Post Office....................2 A2

SLEEPING (p295)
Akbar Tourist Guest House.....3 A3
Ali Amiri's Legal Guest House..4 A2

TRANSPORT (p295)
Bus drop-off point.................5 A4
Bus Station...........................6 A4

OTHER
Bam Arg Restaurant..............7 B2

himself as a 'widower' – he used to say he was 'married to the Arg'. If you are interested in tours to the desert, or even in other parts of Iran, he is worth contacting. He also acts for Arg-e-Jadid Travel (p381) in Tehran.

Arg-e Bam

The ancient mud city of Bam was one of the jewels in Iran's tourism crown, and for many visitors the most memorable of all the country's sights. Dating from at least as far back as the Sassanian period, the city was a staging post on the trade routes between India and Pakistan at one end and the Persian Gulf and Europe at the other. Visitors included Marco Polo and countless others who were awestruck by the city's 38 towers, huge mud walls and fairy-tale citadel – the **Arg-e Bam** (Arg means a citadel surrounded by fortified walls).

Today, it remains memorable, but for different reasons. Scrambling up the crumbling remains of the 9th-century walls to the shattered mud-brick and clay ramparts, the ancient city is undoubtedly still an impressive site. The pure scale of the brown lanes, bazaar and the citadel above it are striking,

and as one overlander said as we looked into the mess, people get excited about buildings that are far more badly damaged.

So what now for the Arg? In the immediate aftermath of the earthquake many promises were made about rebuilding. A member of the Iranian Cultural Heritage Organisation (ICHO), which oversees historical buildings such as the Arg, told me that rebuilding would go ahead using tradi-

---

DOWN, BUT NOT OUT *Andrew Burke*

Arriving in Bam on 27 December 2003, was like stepping into a scene from hell. It was about 30 hours since an earthquake measuring 6.8 on the Richter scale had shaken the city. Death was everywhere. Having donned my newspaper reporter's hat, I began speaking with the Bamis. One man, still plainly in a state of shock, described in monotone the loss of most of his family and his escape. 'After this house collapsed,' he said, pointing to a pile of rubble that was once his home, 'five people were dug out without any injury. But 15 or 16 members of my [extended] family are dead.'

A few metres away, a woman wailed as another body was carted past in a blanket and loaded onto a pink suburban bus: 'My brother is dead. My flower is gone,' she keened. The scene was repeated across Bam. Women wailing and beating themselves; men scrambling through broken concrete in an effort to extract the dead – for even then few held out hope of finding anyone alive.

That day, and the next, Bam buried most of the more than 26,000 people who had been killed when the earth shook at 5.30am that bitterly cold morning. With about 80% of the ancient town levelled, and those buildings still standing being unsafe to enter as regular aftershocks hit, those Bamis who could began moving into canvas Red Crescent tents to keep out the notoriously cold winter nights.

At the popular Akbar Tourist Guest House, manager Panjalizadeh Akbar wept as he described the frantic scenes that followed the quake. Travellers and family members had dug with their bare hands to free several people buried under the rubble. 'The English lady and German man, they were so helpful,' Akbar told me. The woman he was describing, Ruth Millington, is now raising money for Bam's orphans (see the boxed text 'How You Can Help...', p295). Sadly, their efforts were not enough to save two travellers and his son's best friend. In the face of it all, Akbar was defiant. 'We will stay and rebuild, *in sh'Allah*. Bam is our home, we cannot leave...'

When I returned 40 days later, Akbar's family had settled into their two-tent home on the street outside the destroyed guesthouse about as well as you could reasonably expect. The drama and short-term uncertainties had been replaced by a restless boredom. With the city reduced to rubble few people had jobs to go to and there was no word on when relief money would arrive, let alone reconstruction work begin. Frustration was setting in. For Akbar, however, some progress was being made.

Two Dutch couples driving towards Pakistan had parked up outside the guesthouse and offered to help. In between unloading relief supplies from Europe, Coen, Karin-Marijke, Gert and Miranda started clearing tonnes of rubble from Akbar's yard, and within a couple of days a tent donated by a departing British aid group had become 'the first room in my new guesthouse', as Akbar described it.

I tracked down Mohammad Ali Dastres, a local tour guide who had described himself as being 'married to the Arg' until he became a 'widower' on 26 December. Like several guides from Kerman, he had been working with the Red Crescent and other NGOs as a translator since the day of the quake. We went to the famous Arg-e Bam and were escorted by soldiers to the crumbling ramparts. Surprisingly amid all the destruction, enough of the arches, supporting walls and pure scale of the great citadel remained that much of its majesty had survived. Looking out to the citadel, Mohammad Ali summed up the scene: 'It might take a long time and no, it won't be exactly the same, but Bam will come back and so will the Arg'.

HOW YOU CAN HELP...

Quake survivor Ruth Millington has been made the director of a newly established charity called **Action For Orphans** (www.actionfororphans.com). Together with a group of concerned Iranians in Kerman and the UK, Action For Orphans is building an orphanage for 20 of the estimated 2500 Bami children who lost their parents. It's a job that's all-the-more urgent, she says, because the state has been less than proactive in establishing care, and some children are being abused.

tional methods to maintain the integrity of the structure. Those methods involve using the trunks of palm trees to reinforce walls made of mud and straw. The rebuilding job would take about five years, the representative said. This seems wildly optimistic. Even though the building materials are already on-site – mud-bricks turned to dust can easily enough be returned to mud-bricks – and there are mountains of plans and photos to draw on, you can expect to see rebuilding work going on for many years.

The best-case scenario for the next few years was outlined by a World Bank expert I met who had just visited Bam. He said that work to clear debris from the main entrance to allow people to actually enter the site was a priority. A set of photos could be established inside the Arg, and on a section of the ramparts, allowing visitors to compare the before and after. A few buildings within the ancient city were not destroyed, and it's possible they will be opened in due course. Eventually, the 2km of ramparts that surrounded the city will be restored enabling people to once again walk around the city. But that is a long way off...

Sleeping & Eating

Only a couple of places were left standing after the quake.

Akbar Tourist Guest House (☎ 231 4843; mr_panjali@yahoo.com; Sayyeh Jamal od-Din St) Akbar's guesthouse was completely destroyed in the earthquake, and it was only through the heroics of guests and staff that only three of the 14 people sleeping there died (see the boxed text 'Down, But Not Out', p294). Within three days Akbar, the former English

teacher who with his family had turned this into one of the most popular budget places in Iran, was accommodating guests in his new home, a tent on the street. Akbar has promised to rebuild and reopen, and has urged travellers to keep coming to Bam. Even if lodgings are no more than a tent, Akbar's hospitality will be unforgettable.

Ali Amiri's Legal Guest House (☎ 231 4481, 0913 144 1094) Once a popular backpacker haunt, Ali's was one of the few buildings left standing in the centre of town. Ali had taken his family to Kerman when we passed, and his brother was unsure of whether he planned to reopen. It's located off Pasdaran St.

Azadi Hotel (☎ 222 2097-9; r/ste US$65/75; P ❄) Its size, and its location 6km from the centre of Bam, meant the Azadi was left cracked and battered but still standing and welcoming guests. It's on the left of the main road into Bam from Kerman and the rooms should be back to their four-star standard by the time you arrive. The restaurant here was about the only sit-down-and-eat option when we passed.

The **Bam Arg Restaurant**, in the palm-filled garden opposite the Arg, survived the quake and might reopen, though when we visited it was being used as headquarters for ICHO.

Getting There & Away
AIR
Iran Aseman has one scheduled flight a week (on a Thursday) between Tehran and Bam's small airport to the east of town.

BUS & SAVARI
Bam's bus station is just south of Arg Sq, but it was out of commission when we visited and Arg Sq itself was acting as the terminal. Buses to Kerman (Mercedes/Volvo IR8000/12,000, three hours, 204km) leave frequently, usually at least every hour. If your destination is further north, or to Bandar-e Abbas, it's easiest to go to Kerman and change. The few regular services from Bam include Esfahan (IR45,000/60,000, 11 hours, 703km) at 2.30pm and Tehran (IR75,000, 21 hours, 1258km) at 3.30pm. For Zahedan (IR16,000/25,000, four hours, 321km), scheduled services depart at 6.30am and 4.30pm, though you should be able to find something going this way in between times.

Savaris to Kerman (IR22,000, two hours) leave from Arg Sq several times an hour.

SOUTHEASTERN IRAN

ZAHEDAN
زاهدان

☎ 0541/ pop 534,000

Zahedan is capital of the desolate and near-lawless Sistan va Baluchestan province. While it has few attractions of its own (like, very few!), its proximity to the only legal crossing point between Iran and Pakistan makes it a reasonable place to break the long journey if travelling to or from Pakistan, or to stop for a visa. It's also the place from which to make a day trip to Zabol (p299) and Kuh-e Khajeh (p300). Keep an eye out for **camel races** *(mosabagheh-ye shotor-e davani)*, a traditional Baluchi activity. They can be difficult to track down but at least one important race meeting is held here each year. Unless you're invited by a Baluchi, you're more likely to see races on television – they receive nationwide coverage.

Orientation

Zahedan is a flat, dusty, featureless town. Though the main offices are spread all over the place, most visitors will only worry about getting from the airport or bus station to their hotel and back, which is easy to do. Although the whole of Zahedan seems to be one huge marketplace with no particular focus, Bazar-e Ruz is best considered the centre of town.

Information

EMERGENCY
Khatam Hospital (☎ 322 7067) Just east of the train station.

Police Headquarters (☎ 322 2092) Next to the bazaar, but hard to find, so ask for directions.

INTERNET ACCESS
Esteghlal Grand Hotel Internet Cafe (Azadi Sq; per hr IR14,000; ☺ 8am-11pm) Fastest service in town.
Institute for Internet Services (☎ 321 4180; Azadi Sq; per hr IR7000)

MONEY
Bank Melli Central Branch (Azadi St) Changes US dollars.

If the bank is closed, someone in the bazaar will happily change your money. For Pakistani and Afghan currency, the bazaar is the only option. The Taftan bus station on the Pakistani side of the border offers the best rates for Pakistani currency.

POST
Main Post Office (Dr Shariati St) Sending parcels from here can turn into a protracted nightmare. Better to use the Kerman office.

TELEPHONE
International Phone Office (Taleqani Sq; ☺ 7am-11pm)

TRAVEL AGENCIES
Daz Tour & Travel (☎ 323 7674; www.dazagency.com; Azadi Sq) In the Esteghlal Grand Hotel, this is undoubtedly the best (and one of the most expensive) travel agencies in town. The delightful French- and English-speaking Maryam Mabadi can arrange the usual flights etc, as well as tours throughout the province.

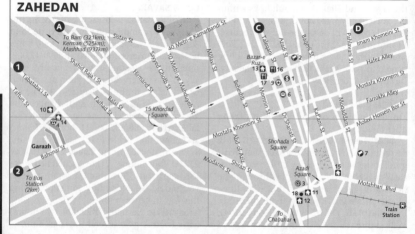

VISA EXTENSIONS

The **Police Department of Alien Affairs** (☎ 323 1182; Motahhari Blvd; ☺ 7am-2pm, closed Fri) is just outside the entrance to the airport. Downstairs is the preserve of Afghans and Pakistanis; visa extensions are handled in greater serenity on the 1st floor. Extensions of a month are not uncommon and should be sorted in two hours. You must deposit your fee at the Bank Melli central branch in Azadi St.

Some travellers have reported getting help here with recently expired transit visas, but *do not* rely on this. For details on extending your visa, see the boxed text 'More Time, Please' (p362).

VISAS FOR INDIA & PAKISTAN

Indian Consulate (☎ 322 2337; ☺ 8.30am-1pm & 2.30-5pm Sun-Thu) Visas issued in five days for about IR370,000. It's located off Imam Khomeini St.

Pakistan Consulate (☎ 325 2266; Pahlavani St; ☺ 9.30am-2.30pm Sat-Wed) At the time of writing this was the best place in Iran to get a Pakistan visa. Unlike Tehran, the problematic letter of introduction from your own embassy is not required here. Several travellers reported getting visas the same day. You need two passport photos, a copy of your passport, and about IR210,000 (depending on nationality).

Dangers & Annoyances

Because there's so much drug smuggling in the area, it is a little unsafe around some parts of Zahedan at night, and you don't see many people out on the streets after dark. Car theft is also a problem so if you have a vehicle, it's a very good idea to find a secure place to leave

it overnight. Do not venture west of Zahedan in the area known as the Black Mountains – these are the jagged hills that are visible from Zahedan – unaccompanied or on foot; gun law is in force there and they're not known as the Black Mountains for their colour alone.

Sleeping

Zahedan has a range of reasonable options to suit most budgets. The cheapest places to stay are around the bazaar or the grimy area in the west of town where the bus station used to be; if you're staying longer than overnight, the centre of town is much more pleasant.

Hotel Momtzahirmand (☎ 322 2313; Bazar-e Ruz; s/tw IR30,000/40,000; ☒) Right in the bazaar, this is the best in the budget range. Most rooms have a sink, and the shared showers and toilets are clean. The hotel is a little hard to find: head north along Dr Shariati St from the corner with Imam Khomeini St; the hotel is 80m along the first lane on your left.

Abuzar Hotel (☎ 451 2132; 40 Metri-e Kamarbandi St; r IR30,000; ℗ ☒) Excellent-value cheapie, with clean, simple rooms, shared bathrooms and a decent restaurant downstairs. Directly opposite is the similar **Islami Hotel** (☎ 451 2932; r IR40,000; ℗).

Kavir Hotel & Restaurant (☎ 323 2150; Motahhari Blvd; s/d IR90,000/130,000; ℗ ☒) The pick of the mid-range, this bright-as-a-bordello hotel has reasonable rooms, though the bathrooms could be cleaner. The restaurant downstairs is pretty good; and the secure parking has a fairly high clearance.

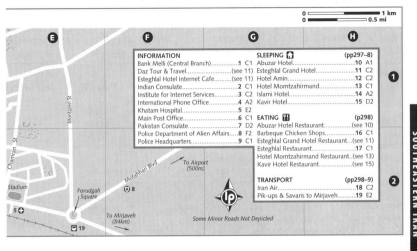

0 — 1 km
0 — 0.5 mi

To Airport (500m)

To Mirjaveh (84km)

Some Minor Roads Not Depicted

Montazeri St

Chaman St

Stadium

Forudgah Square

Motahhari Blvd

SOUTHEASTERN IRAN

FROM 'THIEVES' TO 'ASCETICS'... & BACK

Not so long ago Zahedan (meaning 'Ascetics') went under the far less-inviting name of Dozda (Thieves). The locals offer several explanations for the original name. The more obvious of the two is that the village of Dozda first developed as a place where bandits came to rest, but the more romantic version has it that rain used to soak straight through the soil, thereby effectively 'stealing' it. Passing through one day, Reza Shah was astonished that, despite its name, the town appeared no more full of thieves than its neighbours. At once he had the name changed to Zahedan in a nod of recognition to the more conspicuous collection of straggly bearded, ascetic-looking men living there.

However, Zahedan's bad reputation seemed fully justified in the days following the Bam earthquake (see the boxed text 'Down, But Not Out', p294). No sooner did truckloads of aid arrive than much of it disappeared on *pik-ups* going east. Rightly or wrongly, the Baluchis of Zahedan were blamed for stealing as many as 90,000 Iranian Red Crescent tents earmarked for the needy of Bam. And these figures came straight from the government in Tehran. So it's best to be cautious about ostentatious displays of wealth in Zahedan.

Hotel Amin (☎ 323 9892; Momnin St; s/tw US$30/40; P ⌘) These decidedly average rooms are not worth the money. The parking is low-clearance, and not for 4WDs.

Esteghlal Grand Hotel (☎ 323 8088; fax 322 2239; Azadi Sq; s/d IR497,344/706,483; P ⌘ 🖥) The best place in town by a desert mile, the Esteghlal is well worth a splurge if you're en route to or from Quetta. The rooms are quite splendid, with satellite TV, fridge and spotless bathroom. Worth every single rial.

Eating

There are several good barbecue chicken places on Dr Shariati St, with a whole bird, salad and chips for IR30,000. Other than that and a few kababis, head for the hotels. The **Abuzar Hotel** (☎ 451 2132; 40 Metri-e Kamarbandi St) is good, as are the **Hotel Momtzahirmand** (☎ 322 2313; meals IR20,000), and the **Esteghlal Restaurant** (☎ 322 2250; Imam Khomeini St; meals IR15,000), which does good *khoresht*. The **Kavir Hotel & Restaurant** (☎ 323 2150; Motahhari Blvd; ☽ dinner only) is also good, but the restaurant at the **Esteghlal Grand Hotel** (☎ 323 8088; Azadi Sq; meals IR40,000) is the best.

Getting There & Away

AIR

Given Zahedan's isolation, flying makes a good alternative to long hours of overland travel. It's also a good idea for northward journeys to Mashhad.

Iran Air (☎ 322 0813/4), near Azadi Sq, flies from Zahedan to Chabahar (IR168,000, five times weekly), Esfahan (IR302,000, weekly), Kerman (IR152,000, twice-weekly), Mash-

had (IR257,000, twice-weekly) and Tehran (IR353,000, once- or twice-daily).

Mahan Air flies to Tehran daily except Friday, but it means getting on a Tupolev. On Friday the Tupolev goes to Dubai, in what is Zahedan's only international flight. You'll need to use a travel agency to get a ticket (see Travel Agencies, p296).

BUS

If you really want to get off the beaten track, you can head north all the way to Mashhad. A more interesting and manageable day trip is to Zabol (p299) and Kuh-e Khajeh (p300). Most travellers, however, are only interested in roads east to the Pakistan border and west to Bam and Kerman.

The sprawling new bus station (terminal) in the west of Zahedan is from the same mould as almost every other bus station in Iran; large, clean and chaotic in an organised fashion. Buses leave from Zahedan several times a day for the following destinations:

Destination	Price (IR)	Duration (hr)
Bam	16,000	5
Bandar-e Abbas	42,000	17
Esfahan	42,200	21
Kerman	30,000*	7
Mashhad	65,000*	15
Shiraz	60,000*	17
Tehran	60,000	22
Yazd	31,400	14
Zabol	7000	4

* Volvo; all other buses Mercedes

If you're heading to Bam, it might be easier to take any bus heading west (to Kerman or Yazd) and get off at Bam.

To/From Pakistan

There are frequent buses (IR4000, 1½ hours) and minibuses (IR5000, 1½ hours) from Zahedan to Mirjaveh (96km). Most buses leave from the bus station. The easiest way, however, is to get a savari (IR10,000, one hour) from Forudgah Sq in the far east of town. Drivers will undoubtedly ask much more, but IR10,000 is the price.

The Iran–Pakistan border is 15km further east of Mirjaveh village, so clarify whether your vehicle is going to the village or border. It is easy enough to get something between the village and border. Cross the border on foot and take whatever transport is heading your way on the other side. For details see the boxed text 'Crossing the Pakistan Border at Mirjaveh/Taftan', p301.

CAR & MOTORCYCLE

Drivers who are travelling between Turkey and India often describe the trip between Zahedan and Quetta, across the vast Baluchestan desert, as the worst leg of their journey. The road from Quetta to the Iranian border is barren and lonely, with virtually no facilities and a risk of bandits; consider driving in convoy once on the Pakistan side.

The clearly signposted road between Zahedan and Kerman is good but short on facilities. Take plenty of water with you if you are driving, and make sure your vehicle is in good order or risk a long and unpleasant wait for repairs. Petrol is available in Mirjaveh (20L maximum), Zahedan and Fahraj (between Zahedan and Bam).

TAXI

Between Zahedan and the border, a private taxi shouldn't cost more than IR50,000 and is a good way to avoid the log jam at the checkpoint between Mirjaveh and the border.

TRAIN

The new line linking Kerman and Zahedan had not quite reached Bam at the time of writing. There is a chance, though no more than that, it will be completed all the way to Zahedan (and hence Pakistan) during the life of this book. Check **Raja Trains** (www.rajatrains.com) for updates.

To/From Pakistan

There *is* a train between Zahedan and Quetta, but you'd have to be an almost obsessive trainspotter to even consider taking it. On the other hand, you're absolutely guaranteed to end up with a story you'll tell until you die, but even with such an incentive you'd need to be brave to take this trip.

Considering the train only leaves every second Sunday at 8.30am, *in sh'Allah*, you'd need to plan ahead. The not-exactly-overworked stationmaster in Zahedan's attractive **train station** (☎ 322 4142) found time to tell us the trip takes 24 hours, but then it is his job to be optimistic about the train. With border delays, it will likely take at least 36 hours, and in summer, when sand blows across the tracks, it has been known to take several days!

If, despite all this, you make this journey, take plenty of food and water, something warm in winter, and do not consider leaving without a sleeper. You pay in rial to Taftan (1st/2nd class IR12,000/17,000), and in rupees from Taftan to Quetta (1st/2nd class Rs990/345).

Alternatively, you could get yourself across the border and get on the train in Taftan. We suggest you call ahead (in the morning for an English-speaker) to check ticket availability.

Getting Around
TO/FROM THE AIRPORT

A private taxi between the airport and town should be no more than about IR5000 for a single passenger. Bargain hard!

TAXI

Vans and private cars often duplicate the services of the official (orange) taxis and buses in Zahedan. You'll be lucky to get a private taxi for less than about IR3000, and from the bazaar to the station expect to pay IR5000. Shared taxis are available along the main roads for about IR1000 a trip.

ZABOL   زابل
☎ 0542 / pop 128,000

North of Zahedan, this dusty frontier town is sufficiently close to the Afghanistan border – and far enough away from Tehran –

that it's full of smugglers, illicit goods, big-bearded Afghans and the ever-present suggestion of drugs (see the boxed text 'Drug-Running Dromedaries', p286).

As you wander through the bazaar it becomes clear this is no ordinary town. There are all manner of smuggled goods for sale, and around just about every corner is the pungent smell of opium smoke, wafting in great clouds from behind curtained-off sections of stall.

Combined with a trip to Kuh-e Khajeh (opposite), Zabol makes a good day trip from Zahedan, though be very sure to check the current security situation before setting off. Maryam Mabadi at **Daz Tour & Travel** (☎ 323 7674; Esteghlal Grand Hotel, Azadi Sq) in Zahedan knows what's going on and doesn't seem prone to excessive caution.

They don't see many foreigners out here (like, none!), so if you're fair-haired and/or a woman try to blend in as much as possible.

Sleeping & Eating

For a bed, the family-run **Hotel Amin** (☎ 222 2823; Mostaha Khomeini St, aka Ferdosi St; r IR75,000; P), near the bazaar, is a good option. English isn't spoken here (and there's no English sign) but the manager is obliging with maps and happy for you to use the kitchen. It's about 400m east of Imam Khomeini St, on the northern side of the street – look for the green front of the attached restaurant and a small yellow sign.

There's the usual range of kababis and **burger joints**. Keep an eye out for the **Green Hovel Customary Roust** as you walk into town from near the bus station; it's true to its name.

Getting There & Away

Mahan Air flies between Zabol and Tehran via Mashhad on Fridays. Buses leave from Zabol's bus station in the southwest of town for Mashhad (IR46,000, 14 hours), and all manner of other places, including Tehran. From Zahedan, you're far better off taking a savari (IR20,000, two hours, 216km) if you want to be back in a day. Savaris leave from Zahedan for Zabol every half-hour or so from 50m west of the Abuzar Hotel. You must bring your passport; if you don't the driver won't take you. There was only one checkpoint when we went and it was passed without trouble.

KUH-E KHAJEH   کوه خواجه

The flat-topped mountain that is **Kuh-e Khajeh** can be seen for miles as it rises out of a wide, brown waste of Sistan that, in spring and summer, fills with water to become the attractive Lake Hamun. On the side of the mountain are the remains of an ancient town, the crumbling mud-brick dwellings stepping steeply up the side all the way to the peak. Wandering through the arches and squares you'll almost certainly be alone in what is one of the only surviving remnants of the Parthian era, 2000 years ago.

The views from the top are not bad at all, but there's a radar station in the middle of the mountain so don't head too far in, and refrain from taking pictures of this installation – they could become very unhappy snaps indeed. When the lake is full the area is frequented by almost 200 species of birds; don't be surprised to see a pelican lumbering by.

If you come on the minibus from Zabol, you'll be dropped in Kuh-e Khajeh village and have to walk the last 4km along a flat, straight road that turns into a causeway at the edge of town. You're unlikely to be troubled by traffic. The minibus runs every hour or so, takes about 30 minutes and leaves from Mir Hosseini St, just south of the junction with Kargar Blvd – if you came to Zabol by savari, it's on the opposite side of the road and a bit south of where you were dropped. If you don't fancy Zabol, ask the savari from Zahedan to drop you at the turn-off to Kuh-e Khajeh – it's on the left about 6km south of Zabol, just before a bridge.

MIRJAVEH   میرجاوه
☎ 0543

If you're travelling between Iran and Pakistan by road or train, you'll pass through the Iranian village of Mirjaveh. It's a typical border settlement with nothing much to interest travellers, but you can stay overnight if you arrive late or need to re-energise after the trip from Quetta.

Sleeping & Eating

The only place to stay is the ITTO-run **Mirjaveh Tourist Inn** (Hotel Ali; ☎ 322 2486; s/tw IR35,000/70,000; P ☒). One reader described this place as looking 'like a ghost hotel', it was so quiet. The rooms aren't that bad, but

JOHN BORTHWICK

Imam Mosque, Esfahan (p216)

Reflecting pool, Chehel Sotun Palace,
Esfahan (p219)

SIMON RICHMOND

PHIL M WEYMOUTH

Sheikh Lotfollah Mosque, Esfahan (p217)

PHIL M WEY

Bagh-e Eram, Shiraz (p247)

CLINT LUCAS

Regent's Mosque, Shiraz (p245)

Aramgah-e Hafez, Shiraz (p246)

PHIL M WEY

PHIL M WEYMOUTH

Arg-e Karim Khani, Shiraz (p244)

CROSSING THE PAKISTAN BORDER AT MIRJAVEH/TAFTAN

Crossing the border between Iran and Pakistan at Taftan is a relatively painless process – the painful part is the trip to Quetta. Getting to the border from Zahedan (p296) or Mirjaveh (p300) is simple enough, but be aware that Pakistan is either 30 minutes or 1½ hours ahead of Iran, meaning the border closes at 4.30pm (Iranian time) in winter, sometimes earlier (1½ hours before sundown). The border usually opens around sunrise Iranian time (about 7am).

There is more paperwork on the Iranian side, but you will get preferential treatment as a foreigner from both sets of officials; the whole process shouldn't take longer than an hour. Women entering Iran should, of course, have their heads covered (see Entering the Country, p365). American travellers might have to undergo a brief but polite interview about their itinerary in Iran. People with vehicles have reported a similarly smooth crossing, with customs on both sides being less than pedantic in their searches.

To change money you will probably have to deal with one of the sharks who circle around both sides of the border; be sure to check the rates online before you arrive or ask someone crossing in the other direction.

Taftan has been described, not unfairly, as hell on earth, especially in summer. So it's fortunate that you'll probably only have to wait an hour or two for one of the regular buses from Taftan to Quetta (617km), which cost Rs250 (Pakistani rupees) – about US$5. They often leave from right outside the border post, most frequently in the early morning, stopping in nearby Taftan before embarking on 15 to 20 hours of bumpy road. A Toyota taxi makes the same trip in 12 to 15 hours for Rs3000, or Rs750 a seat (about US$15). If you are coming from Quetta, most buses leave for the border between about 2pm and 6pm.

Coming into Iran, once the paperwork is finished a free shuttle bus will drop you at the edge of the large border compound, from where you wait for any form of transport (usually a *pik-up*) to fill up and leave for Mirjaveh or Zahedan.

If you get stuck at the border for a night, the basic Taftan Hotel will provide a bed on the Pakistani side, and there's the Mirjaveh Tourist Inn (p300) in Iran. One traveller did report, however, being put up in 'a hotel-restaurant in the Iranian border camp. We paid IR43,000 for a basic double room, no hot shower available, and IR17,000 for a good meal'.

---

only one has a locking door – the rest of the keys are lost. You can use the kitchen, and buy your groceries from shops along the main street. Overlanders can park up in the yard, which has a gate, for IR40,000.

Getting There & Away

From Mirjaveh, there is always something about to go to the border or to Zahedan, from where you will probably need another connection if continuing west.

ایران شمال شرقی

NORTHEASTERN IRAN

CONTENTS

Sandwiched between the vast desert emptiness of the Dasht-e Kavir and the hostile steppe-tribes of Central Asia, northeastern Iran has a central spine of mountains that become more lushly forested as you head west. East of Minudasht the wilderness has been declared the Golestan ('Paradise') National Park. More grand forests and the high Alborz Mountains form the hinterlands that rise above the dismally overdeveloped Caspian coast. A trio of major roads and the quite remarkable Tehran–Sari railway take you across that dramatic range but nowadays you'll need time and some perseverance to get into the more remote, unspoilt zones.

Historically, the area developed as Khorasan ('Where the [Iranian] Sun Rises') and Tabarestan (the southeastern Caspian littoral). Millennia of culture reached a zenith here around 1000 years ago, producing many of the era's great scientists (Nasruddin Tusi) and poet-philosophers (Ferdosi and Omar Khayyam). The 13th- and 14th-century ravages of first the Mongols and then Tamerlane were particularly destructive, so complete that Tabarestan's settled civilisation was virtually wiped out. Even now the sites of once prosperous cities are mere undulations in the steppe. A few marvellously overengineered tomb towers, most astonishingly at Radkan and Gonbad-e Kavus, are the last witnesses of former glories.

The 16th-century Safavid regime's move towards formal state Shiism was a major factor in the growth of Mashhad from a small shrine-village to the region's foremost city. Its focus, the grand tomb of Imam Reza, is Iran's holiest site. For travellers Mashhad is also the logical staging point for visiting Afghanistan or Turkmenistan, but rather than face the bureaucratic hassles of the latter, you can do worse than explore northeastern Iran's own extensive culturally Turkmen areas, notably north of Bojnurd and Kalaleh.

HIGHLIGHTS

- Get an incredible Caspian panorama as you wind up through mountain forests towards a 'secret valley' that hides the great **West Radkan Tower** (p310)
- Sleep in a Turkmen öy (yurt) tent on a unique stud farm at **Gharra Tappeh Sheikh** (p315)
- Witness the high emotion of pilgrims at the **Holy Shrine of Imam Reza** (p324), Shiite Islam's holiest site in Iran
- Ask yourself if a forerunner of NASA didn't help to build the incredible, 1000-year-old **Mil-e Gonbad** (p313) in Gonbad-e Kavus
- While away an afternoon smoking qalyan and eating at one of the garden restaurants in **Torqabeh** (p330)
- Switch-back across the Alborz Mountains on the dramatic **Tehran–Sari railway** (p309)
- Climb through the mountain redoubt of **Kalat** (p333), an impregnable natural fortress used by Nader Shah

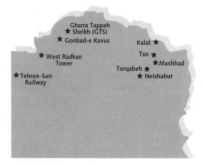

NORTHEASTERN IRAN

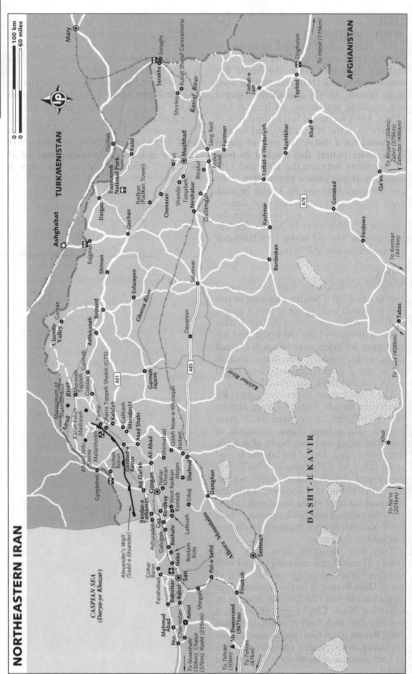

0   100 km
0   60 miles

TURKMENISTAN

Ashgabat

AFGHANISTAN

CASPIAN SEA
(Darya-ye Khazar)

DASHT-E KAVIR

Mary

Saraghs
Sarakhs
Robat Sharaf Caravanserai

Tobat-e
Jam
Taybad

Dughargan
To Herat (115km)

Shorlooq
Kanju River

Sang Bast
Fariman

Tus
Mashhad

Dushak
Kalat
Tandoureh
National Park
Radkan
(Radkan Tower)

Quchan
Dargaz
Chenaran

Shandiz
Neishabur   Torqabeh

Malek
Abad

Toqabe Heydariyeh
Roshtkhar

Khaf
Kashmar
Khaf

Qa'en
To Birjand (20km);
Zabol (378km);
Zahedan (486km)

Gonabad

A78

Ferdows
To Kerman
(441km)

Bajgiran
Shirvan
Bojnord
Ashklaneh
Garmab
Chalak
Valley   Garkaz

Esfarayen

Gharra Tappeh Sheikh (GTS)
Kalaleh
Minudasht

Garmeh
Jajarm

Oldamghan

Bardeskan

Davarzan

A83

Kalshur River

To Yazd (408km)
Tabas

To Na'in
(220km)

Khur

Mausoleum of
Makhdumkuli
Atrak River

Maraveh
Tappeh
Goklan

Tamar

Azad Shahr
Gonbad-e
Kavus

Aq Qaleh
Incheh
Borun
Gyrysletek

Kazum Eslah
Madraseh
Khalid Nibi
Shrine

Golidagh

Gharsu River

Gala Jam

Sabzevar
Binalud
Neishabur

Qaleh Now-e-Kharaqan
Bastam

Shahrud
Shirinabad

Nahar
Khoran
Kordkuy
West Radkan
Mojen

Dibaj
Damghan

Gorgan

Bandar-e
Torkaman
Ashuradeh
Galugah
Beshahr
Neka

Gohar
Baran
Farahabad

Babolsar
Babol
Amol

Sari
Rostam
Kola

Shirgah

Latkueh

Kondab

Pol-e Sefid

Alborz Mountains

Firuzkuh
Semman

To Tehran
(47km)

Mahmud
Abad
Nur
Chamestan

Mt Damavand
(5671m)

Alexander's Wall
(Sadd-e Eskander)

To Nowshahr
(30km); Chalus
(37km); Rasht (235km)

To Tehran
(30km)

To Tehran
(47km)

AMOL آمل
☎ 0121 / pop 172,000

Amol offers a half-hearted welcome to the lush east Caspian province called Mazandaran. If you've taken the hectic but wonderfully scenic Haraz mountain road from Tehran, Amol's characterless sprawl is a crushing anticlimax. At least at first glance. Amol succeeded Sari as the capital of Tabarestan in the 9th century, and became renowned for a distinctive style of glazed earthenware pottery that reached its peak of popularity between the 10th and 13th centuries. It was once a picturesque town, and although that can no longer be said, there are around a dozen historical curiosities – towers, minarets and two former fire temples – hidden away in Amol's dispiriting ugliness. The old bridge (Pol Darvazeh Cheshmeh) is also still in use.

Sights
None of the following warrants a special visit to Amol but if you have an hour or two here it's worth seeking out at least a couple of them. Although almost all are within walking distance of the old bridge and bazaar, each is hidden away in a web of small alleys, so keep asking directions. Tourists are so rare that an enthusiastic local might adopt you and show you around.

The biggest, most impressive sight is **Mir Qarameddin Marashi** (Gonbad Mir Bozorg; admission free; ⊙ 8am-2.30pm), a restored 1623 mausoleum with a huge dome, remnants of colourful tiling and fragments of a Kufic inscription band. Part of the interior is used as an office for archaeologists who'll open the central chamber upon polite request. Sadly, the setting is a letdown. It's in the backyard car park of the unrefined, circus-sized Mosallah Amol brick mosque, which is off Mofateh St after it curves 90 degrees just west of the bazaar.

Two tiny mosques have very cute, stubby Mazandarani minarets topped with wooden frame and octagonal 'hat'. One of them, **Abbas Mosque**, is on the southern edge of the bazaar; you can find the mosque by following 'Sock City' signs. However, a few minutes' walk further south, the **Hasan Askiri Mosque** (Hasan Askiri Lane) is much more appealing, with cypress patterns and two of four original sides of its old courtyard intact.

Similar motifs appear in **Imamzadeh Gassem**, a small but relatively ornate octagonal tomb tower sheltered within the courtyard of 19th-century **Andisheh Mosque** (Chaksar Lane), one block west of the river and Beheshti St.

You'll need a guide to find the charming **Mir Heydar Amoli**, a pointy tomb tower picked out with blue glaze details, and the two **ateshkadeh** (fire temples). The latter are Zoroastrian but look pretty much like other local tomb towers. The more complete of the two is leaning alarmingly and set in a scraggy suburban garden; the other is bricked-up and derelict in a nettle patch.

Sleeping
In stark contrast to the relatively upmarket apartment hotels that dot the nearby coast, Amol's accommodation is all ultra-basic.

Hotel Sadaf (☎ 222 4563; 17 Shahrivar Sq; s/tw IR20,000/30,000) This is Amol's best place to stay. It's hidden upstairs in a shopping mall and has surprisingly clean, simple rooms with both fan and tap. However, there aren't any showers.

Mehmunpazir Farhangi (☎ 222 3528; 17 Shahrivar St; s/tw/tr IR40,000/50,000/60,000) Dismal and very noisy, but worth a try if Hotel Sadaf is full.

If you're heading for Chalus (p160) there are several roadside hotels en route. Some 45km west of Amol in Nur, the **Noor Hotel** (☎ 0122-622 3338; fax 622 3416; winter s/tw US$20/25) is a handy place for those without wheels, as it's just a few seconds' walk north of Nur's main junction where you may have to change savari anyway. From the vaguely picturesque tree-lined market street walk 200m towards the sea. While the Noor is ageing noticeably, the small rooms with bathroom are bearable and the owner speaks unusually good English. Ask nicely and he just might help you arrange some interesting excursions into the hills behind the town.

Getting There & Away
Buses from Tehran take an attractive if busy mountain road skirting Mt Damavand, Iran's Mt Fuji. They arrive at a bus station at the city's far southern end, 3km from the centre. For Babol, savaris (IR2800, 25 minutes) use Hezar Sangat Sq, way out at the eastern end of Imam Reza St. For the coast, savaris depart from Istgah Mahmudabad on Talib Ahmoli St.

BABOL   بابل
☎ 0111 / pop 171,000

Founded in the early 16th century on the main east–west route through the Caspian provinces, Babol was and still is a busy commercial centre.

Sights

Babol has just a handful of few isolated ancient buildings, but if you're passing through it's worth a quick peep into **Babol Museum** (Modarres St; admission IR1500; ☺ 8.30am-12.30pm & 3-5pm, 8pm summer). Housed in an attractive colonial-style mansion, the building is more appealing than the limited exhibits, though there's an interesting series of aerial photos showing Babol's considerable growth over 50 years. Behind the museum is a fountain and garden backed by a typical Mazandarani courtyard house, as yet unrestored. Head for the toilets and you'll get to see it.

You might also want to visit **Gonbad Darvish Qeil** (Amol Hwy), a pointy-topped brick tomb tower incongruously nestled amid car repair yards beyond the Istgah Amol minibus stand.

In the village of **Soltan Mohammad Taher**, 4km beyond Babol's eastern city limits on the Chiakola road, is a famous tomb tower, the eponymous, pencil-shaped 15th-century **Maqbareh-ye Soltan Mohammed Taher**. Its exterior features a simple arched frieze beneath a polygonal tiled dome with shallow arched recesses on each outer wall. The tomb is an active shrine and the classic carved wooden sarcophagus (1470), for which it is most famous, is hidden modestly beneath a green cloth.

Babol's Caspian port, the city of **Babolsar** (20km north), attracts Iranian tourists, but is not really worth the detour.

Sleeping

Marjan Hotel (☎ 225 0433; fax 225 2188; Keshvari Sq; s/d $20/30) This high-quality new hotel has sensibly priced full-facility rooms. Despite its position on eastern Babol's most traffic-blighted roundabout, most rooms are set well back to reduce road rumble.

Babol Hotel (☎ 222 3650; 17 Shahrivar St; tw IR30,000) The Babol is very simple and antiquated (no shower) but is handily central in Babol's small old quarter. Walk two short perpendicular blocks from the museum down Ayatollah Sayidi St, passing a few houses with tiled roofs and some mouldering stucco shopfronts.

Getting There & Around

Savaris to Amol leave from the Istgah Amol on the Amol Hwy, around 2km west of the centre. Westbound minibuses use the Sari terminal on Qa'emshahr Blvd, but after this closes (around 6pm) savaris instead start from the eastern edge of massive, traffic-clogged Keshvari Sq.

SARI   ساری
☎ 0151 / pop 210,000

Sari is a large but manageable and gently attractive town. For much of the 1st millennium AD, Sari was the capital of Tabarestan, as Mazandaran was then known, the last part of Iran to yield to Islam following the Arab invasion. Later losing ground to Amol, it returned to prominence with the building of the railway from Tehran and became the provincial capital in 1937.

Orientation

The town's focus is little Haft-e Tir Sq, generally known as Sa'at (Times) Sq because of the whitewashed clock tower that sits in the middle. The tower looks particularly cute when floodlit at night. The most interesting remnants of old Sari are to be found in nearby lanes, with the bazaar to the northwest and a few traditional tiled and gabled *sofal* houses to seek out, notably to the southeast.

MAPS
Dana Stationery (Farhang St; ☺ 8am-1pm & 5-8pm Sat-Thu) sells very useful city maps (IR5000).

Information
EMERGENCY
Fatima Zahara Hospital (☎ 222 3023; Artesh Blvd) There are also dozens of medical centres along Qaren St, southeast of Sa'at Sq.

INTERNET ACCESS
Dadehrestan (Maziyar St; per hr IR9000; ☺ 8am-2pm & 4-10pm Sat-Thu) Handy if waiting for a train.
Gostar Danesh (Taleqani St; per hr IR10,000; ☺ 9am-midnight) Particularly fast connection. Type to the sound of fizzing neon. If full, it has a second basement room around the side beneath a camera shop.
Sufanet.com (per hr IR7000; ☎ 9.30am-11pm) Along with two others on Sa'at Sq, this place is handy but slow.

NORTHEASTERN IRAN

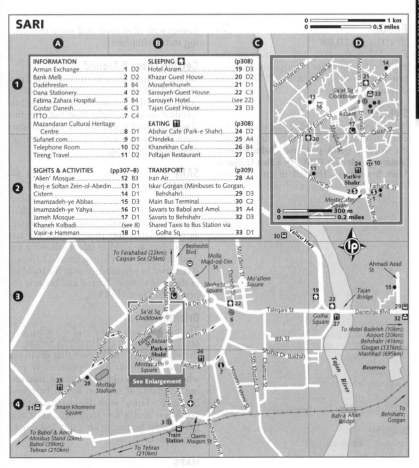

SARI

| 0 | 1 km |
| 0 | 0.5 miles |

INFORMATION
Arman Exchange.....................1 D2
Bank Melli..............................2 D2
Dadehrestan..........................3 B4
Dana Stationery......................4 D2
Fatima Zahara Hospital............5 B4
Gostar Danesh........................6 C3
ITTO......................................7 C4
Mazandaran Cultural Heritage
  Centre................................8 D1
Sufanet.com...........................9 D1
Telephone Room...................10 D2
Tireng Travel........................11 D2

SIGHTS & ACTIVITIES   (pp307–8)
'Alien' Mosque......................12 B3
Borj-e Soltan Zein-ol-Abedin...13 D1
Cistern................................14 D1
Imamzadeh-ye Abbas............15 D3
Imamzadeh-ye Yahya............16 D1
Jameh Mosque......................17 D1
Khaneh Kolbadi..............(see 8)
Vasir-e Hamman...................18 D1

SLEEPING   (p308)
Hotel Asram.........................19 D3
Khazar Guest House..............20 D2
Mosaferkhuneh.....................21 D1
Sarouyeh Guest House...........22 C3
Sarouyeh Hotel................(see 22)
Tajan Guest House................23 D3

EATING   (p308)
Abshar Cafe (Park-e Shahr)....24 D2
Chindeka.............................25 A4
Khanekhan Cafe...................26 B4
Poltajan Restaurant..............27 D3

TRANSPORT   (p309)
Iran Air...............................28 A4
Iskar Gorgan (Minibuses to Gorgan,
  Behshahr)..........................29 D3
Main Bus Terminal................30 C2
Savaris to Babol and Amol......31 A4
Savaris to Behshahr...............32 D3
Shared Taxis to Bus Station via
  Golha Sq............................33 D1

MONEY
Arman Exchange (Farhang St; ☽ 9am-1.30pm & 4-7pm Sat-Thu) No-fuss moneychangers open long after the bank has closed.
Bank Melli (Mostaz'afin Sq) Changes money.

TELEPHONE
Telephone Room (Enqelab St; ☽ 8am-10.30pm) Tucked between Bank Tejarat and Tak Pizza, this is a small subterranean room for making international and local calls.

TOURIST INFORMATION
ITTO (☎ 324 6007; Hossein Fatemi St; ☽ 7.30am-2.15pm Sat-Thu) It's unprepared for drop-in visitors, but the staff are responsive if you have specific problems to solve.
Mazandaran Cultural Heritage Centre (Khaneh Kolbadi, Ab-Anbarno Alley; ☽ 8am-2pm Sat-Thu) Staff

here are friendly, and can recommend lesser-known sights. It has a small gift shop selling guide pamphlets (albeit mostly in Farsi).

Sights
TOMB TOWERS
Sari has three famous 15th-century brick tomb towers, all active places of worship. Two of these are tucked behind the bazaar. **Imamzadeh-ye Yahya** is round with a Rhenish appearance, beautifully carved wooden panels and doors, and fairly monstrous chandeliers hanging over a glassed-in sarcophagus. Right beside it, **Borj-e Soltan Zein-ol-Abedin** has a square plan and more impressive exterior but little to see inside. A handful of old homes survive in the

mostly concrete alleys, behind where you can play table football with the local kids. **Imamzadeh-ye Abbas**, just over 2km east of central Sari, has fine wooden inner doors, a wooden sarcophagus and an attendant who sprinkles you with rose-water.

OTHER SIGHTS

The Mazandaran Cultural Heritage centre occupies the **Khaneh Kolbadi** (Ab-Anbarno Alley; 7.30am-2.15pm Sat-Thu), a most splendidly restored 120-year-old building reminiscent of an 18th-century khan's palace. Thick walls kept the lower floor warm in winter while the light, bright upper floor could be opened to through drafts for hot summers. Its *orosi* windows (wood-framed puzzles of multicoloured glass) supposedly disorientated mosquitoes. The building is unmarked through a stern, guarded portal leading to a small, attractive courtyard. Although not a museum, the staff are generally happy to show around visitors who are polite and enthusiastic. Behind is the historic **Vasir-e Hammam** (bathhouse) whose restoration is nearing completion.

The **Jameh Mosque** is in the second lane off Enqelab St coming from Sa'at Sq. It's a large courtyard complete with traditional Mazandarani tiled roofs. Another central **mosque** (Modarres St) looks like a green-skinned alien creature. The ancient stone steps off 18 Dei St lead down to a classic water **cistern**.

Sleeping

Sarouyeh Guest House (☎ 324 5600; Danesh St; s/tw IR70,000/80,000) About the best budget choice. Its clean, plain rooms have a bathroom and fridge.

Sarouyeh Hotel (☎ 324 3340; Danesh St; s/tw IR200,000/250,000; P) Attached to the Sarouyeh Guest House, this hotel offers comfortable, but somewhat worn, apartments with kitchenette.

Hotel Asram (☎ 325 5090; fax 325 5092; Valiasr Hwy; s/tw IR240,000/320,000; X) This is a relatively modern concrete tower with fairly comfortable rooms. Attached bathrooms have tub, towels and loo-roll for the ageing toilets. There's a decent café-restaurant, and some staff speak English. At night the exterior is lugubriously floodlit in red and green.

Mosaferkhuneh (Modarres St; s/tw/tr IR35,000/45,000/50,000) Upstairs, just off Sa'at Sq, this is a rough and ready, unnamed mosaferkhuneh.

You'll be hard pressed not to be dragged into watching football with the inquisitive all-male crowd who never seem to leave the reception-cum-lounge area. Most rooms are reasonably clean and have a tap.

Khazar Guest House (☎ 2227231; Jomhuri-ye Eslami St; tr IR48,000) You don't even get a tap in your room here, though it's a central place and there's a fan. It's set back in a courtyard.

Tajan Guest House (☎ 325 1791; Golha Sq; tw/tr IR95,000/100,000; P) A shared taxi ride away from the centre, Tajan has unremarkable rooms with serviceable squat toilets and shower, at least in the better triple rooms.

Hotel Badeleh (☎ /fax 422 2548; Gorgan Hwy, Angilasam; s/tw $52/75; X P) Some 10km towards Gorgan, this almost smart hotel has pleasant if unexceptional rooms with small, new bathroom, soft minibar and TV showing BBC World. There's an Internet connection but at IR30,000 per hour it's cheaper to take a taxi to Sari (see Internet Access, p306) and pay the driver's waiting fee.

Eating

There are several very downmarket kababis on Jomhuri-ye Eslami St, southwest of the bazaar, with a few nicer restaurants a kilometre further on along Ferdosi St and Azadi Blvd.

Chindeka (☎ 222 3730; Azadi Blvd; meals IR40,000; 8am-10.30pm) This is the best restaurant on Azadi St. It has a schizophrenic décor: one dining room has banqueting tables in a Western pseudo-palatial style, while next door there's a curious cave effect with dangling lanterns and pottery. There are typical, good-quality kebab meals here.

Khanekhan Cafe (☎ 222 3562; Farhang St; pizzas IR18,000; noon-10pm Sat-Thu, 6-10pm Fri) Above a musical instrument shop, this is the best of several pizzerias on Farhang St. It does good banana shakes and in summer there's a roof terrace.

Abshar Café (Park-e Shahr; sandwiches IR5000; 8am-8pm) This simple, sunny snack bar is ideal for a fresh pomegranate juice while watching the fountains. The goofy Mr Bean portrait makes for fun photographs.

Poltajan Restaurant (☎ 325 4483; Taleqani St; meals IR18,000; 8am-8pm & 6-11pm) In summer this somewhat tatty restaurant has a covered outdoor terrace with mildly pleasant river views; however, conversation is drowned by traffic noise.

Getting There & Away

AIR

Iran Air (☎ 226 9400; Azadi Blvd; ⏱ 7.30am-5pm Sat-Thu, noon Fri) uses Sari as a stopover on thrice-weekly flights between Tehran (IR144,000, 55 minutes) and Mashhad (IR204,000, 80 minutes). Tickets are also conveniently sold by friendly, English-speaking agency **Tireng Travel** (☎ 222 7973; Tabarsi St; ⏱ 8am-6pm Sat-Thu).

BUS & MINIBUS

The main terminal on the northeastern ring road has fairly frequent buses to Rasht (IR18,000, seven hours) and Tehran (IR10,250 to 13,000, five hours). Most services to Mashhad (IR27,000, 12 hours) depart from 7am to 8am and 5pm to 7pm.

For Babol and Amol savaris leave conveniently from Imam Khomeini Sq. Much less convenient minibuses leave from a yard 2km further west (Babol Hwy, southern side near the green-glass Mazand Noor building). A taxi fare to reach this point would cancel out any saving.

The Istgah Gorgan, nearly 1km east of Tajan bridge, has minibuses/savaris to Gorgan (IR4000/15,000), Behshahr (IR1500/5000, 45 minutes) and other villages to the east.

TRAIN

The route from Tehran winds dramatically across and down from the Alborz Mountains. Building the line was one of the most incredible engineering achievements of the 1930s, as much a political statement by Reza Shah as a means of transport. Trains from Tehran (2nd class IR17,500, seven hours) now travel down by day (departing 9.40am), so you can enjoy the views. However, returning to Tehran they struggle back up overnight, departing at 7.50pm and arriving at 3.30am.

Getting Around

Travel to/from the airport, 15km northeast, costs at least IR10,000 by taxi.

Shared taxis start from relevant points around Sa'at Sq. For the bus station, use eastbound cars that swing north at Golha Sq. For the train station, you'll generally have to jump out at the southern end of Artesh Blvd where southbound vehicles usually swing left.

BEHSHAHR & AROUND   بهشهر
☎ 0152

The strip town of Benshahr (population 78,000), once known as Ashraf, straddles the busy Sari–Gorgan highway. It was a favourite R&R getaway for the Safavid Shah Abbas I, for whom the town's main landmarks were constructed around 1612. In the quietly pleasant **Bagh-e-Shahr** (Shah's Garden) at the town's centre, the attractive town hall claims Safavid parentage. It's an easy stroll through gates down a pedestrianised avenue of fountains and orange trees.

Dominating the town's forested southwestern approach from flat-topped Kakh Hill is the Abbas's perky little **Safiabad Palace** (Kakh-e Safi Abad). This is now used by the military, so it's out of bounds. This hardly matters as the great Safavid's finest legacy is the delightful **Abbasabad**, a lovely landscaped area of wooded hills around a lake. In the middle stands an arched brick platform from which the Shah's wooden pavilion has long since disappeared. Abbasabad is 8km up a steeply winding access lane that starts from the eastern edge of town. In December the whole area is a riot of autumnal colours. It's an understandably popular place for Friday picnics and hikes, and is graced with a surprisingly decent restaurant. There are fine views over the Gorgan Gulf as you return.

Archaeologists might find some interest in seeking out **Qar-e-Hotu** and other overgrown caves 3km east of Behshahr in Torujan-e Bala village. Some 12,000-year-old pottery fragments have been unearthed here though there's little to see now.

Otherwise unprepossessing **Rostamkola village**, around 10km west of Behshahr, has one of the region's most accessible traditional Mazandarani homesteads. This small but beautifully preserved **Farahi Hosseinieh** retains its original *orosi* and carved wooden ceilings. It's hidden away in the Farahi family's private yard but is open to tourists on request (if you can find it). Turn south off the Sari highway into Rostamkola's palm-lined central avenue. Where this ends at a communication tower, turn right (west), then right again into the short dead-end just beyond the joyously kitschy **Goldast Mosque** with its green-spiralled and gold-tipped minarets. Knock on the end gates.

Sleeping & Eating

Miankaleh Hotel (☎ 5222150; Imam Khomeini Ave; s/tw IR160,000/240,000) Behshahr's most convenient accommodation, the Miankaleh virtually faces the entrance to Bagh-e Shahr. Rooms are old but clean, there's paper provided in the attached toilets and in summer it opens a roof-terrace café restaurant.

Hotel Behshahr (Gorgan Hwy; s/tw $20/30) This disorganised hotel is less convenient than the Miankaleh and is rather noisy.

Mosaferkhuneh Ashrafi was temporarily closed at the time of research, but should be a cheaper option when it reopens.

Getting There & Around

Savaris to Sari (IR5000, 45 minutes) and to Gorgan (1¼ hours) leave from opposite ends of the town. Even after these have stopped running, there's a reasonable chance of hopping aboard a passing bus from the same points.

BEHSHAHR TO GORGAN

The high forest escarpment that rises above the fast new Sari–Gorgan road is most impressive above **Kordkuy**. You'll enjoy the west–east trip much more by using the slow, parallel 'old road' that runs a couple of kilometres to the south (by taxi, no public transport) between **Galugah**, **Gaz** and Kordkuy. Savaris run between Kordkuy and Gorgan (20 minutes) and Galugah and Behshahr (15 minutes) frequently until late.

West Radkan (Roodkhan) Tower

کزب رادخان قلمه

An awkward, arduous but highly rewarding 4WD trip takes you right across the near-vertical mountain ridge behind Kordkuy on a seemingly unending ladder of hairpin bends. Views are fabulous from scruffy Drazno village at the top, and continue as you wind back down out of the forests into a secret valley of traditional mud-and-timber hamlets. **Kondab** and **Latkueh** villages, each re-quiring a slight detour, are especially quaint. Eventually you find **Mil-e-Radkan**, sitting upon an astoundingly lonely knoll, wistfully gazing at the cliff-sided valley. In English it's usually called West Radkan Tower to differentiate it from the better-known Rad-kan Tower near Quchan (p332). It was built for a military commander in AD 1020 by the Bavend dynasty of Tabarestan, and has been lovingly restored. Along with a small band

of Arabic inscriptions it has some stylised Pahlavi letters – virtually the last known use of that ancient script in Iran. Otherwise, the tower is relatively unadorned but nonethe-less impressively large and delightfully set, and just getting here is a great thrill.

The valleys beyond would make for great random hiking if you had a tent and a few days. While not always 100% accurate, the generally reliable Golestan map sold in Gorgan provides some tempting clues for tracks that could lead you right across to Dibaj or Mojen. From there you could link respectively to Damghan or Shahrud on the Mashhad–Tehran highway.

GETTING THERE & AWAY

Spunky and humorous, if vaguely manic, **Ali Fagoni** (☎ 0913 171 3484) is one Kordkuy resident with a vehicle strong enough to get you to West Radkan – a gloriously growling 1958 Simorg truck. He also has the neces-sary gung-ho attitude, screeching animal noises and recitations of poetry as he goes. If all goes perfectly the return trip is just about possible in four hours. Seven hours is a more realistic estimate by the time an assortment of hitching villagers and their livestock have been transported to their diverse destinations en route. We paid IR180,000 return, includ-ing a priceless memorable village dinner.

Bandar-e Torkaman

ترکمن بندر

☎ 0173 / pop 44,000

This flat, low-rise market town is architec-turally tedious and despite the vibrant col-ours of the Turkmen costumes, the famous Monday morning **market** is just a glorified car-boot sale. Nonetheless, the tiny **port** (eskele) has picturesque views over the Gorgan Gulf from its ultra-basic jetty-side teahouse. From here an occasional motor-boat speeds across to the fishing village of **Ashuradeh** on what is either an island or a long spit depending on the mood of the Caspian. The eskele is 4km west of central Bandar-e Torkaman, behind some oil stor-age tanks following old train tracks. Taxis cost IR10,000 return with a tea stop.

GETTING THERE & AWAY

From Gorgan, minibuses (IR1100, 40 min-utes) are frequent. They terminate just behind central Kariya Sq, with its copper-coloured statue of Turkmen poet Makhtumkuli.

Minibuses to Kordkuy (IR500, 20 minutes) leave from the southern edge of town, a IR250 shared taxi from Kariya Sq. There is little transport between Bandar-e Torkaman and Behshahr, but Behshahr to Gorgan transport will drop you in Kordkuy where you could connect with Bandar-e Torkaman.

GORGAN

گرگان

☎ 0171 / pop 214,000

Gorgan sits where the forested Alborz Mountains stoop to meet the northeastern steppe. It's a large but appealing city with a colourful, ethnically mixed population, and was the birthplace of the 'eunuch-king' Aga Mohammad who founded the expansionist Qajar dynasty (1779–1925). Gorgan's remnant architectural heritage dates from that period. There's not that much to see, thanks to the usual teamwork of earthquakes and concrete-block expansion. Nonetheless, as a gateway to the Turkmen steppes, backed by appealing forest villages and with some of northern Iran's best budget accommodation, Gorgan is a fine place to base yourself for some off-the-track explorations.

Orientation

The city's old commercial centre is Vahdat Sq, unanimously known as Meydan Shahrdari (Shahrdari Sq). The lanes around the bazaar to its northwest are the best area to discover tiled-roofed Mazandarani houses with wooden balconies. From Park-e Shahr/ Valiasr Sq, relatively upmarket Valiasr St continues some 6km southeast to Nahar Khoran, an appealing forest-park area with a scattering of restaurants and two hotels where the Alborz foothills start to climb.

MAPS

Beheshti Bookshop (Imam Khomeini St; ☯ 7am-9.30pm Sat-Thu, 7am-2pm Fri) sells a useful 1:300,000 scale map of Golestan province for IR4000.

Honar Stationery (☯ 7am-9.30pm Sat-Thu, 7am-2pm Fri) sells detailed city maps of Gorgan.

Information

INTERNET ACCESS

Ryaneh-Hooshmand (☎ 222 0474; Valiasr St km3; per hr IR6000; ☯ 9am-3.30pm & 5.30-10.30pm) Near Edalat 45th St.

MONEY

Bank Melli (Shahrdari/Vahdat Sq) Changes money.

TELEPHONE

Telephone Office (Beheshti 2nd Alley; ☯ 7am-10pm Sat-Thu, 8am-2pm & 4-10pm Fri) On a pedestrianised alley, just southeast of Shahrdari/Vahdat Sq.

TOURIST INFORMATION

ITTO (☎ 222 7099; www.golestanitto.org.ir; ☯ 7.30am-2pm Sat-Thu) Just off Molaghaty Sq, the ITTO is three minutes' walk from the Beheshti St shared-taxi routes.

Sights

Built around a quadrangle in the bazaar, the 15th-century **Jameh Mosque**, off Aftab 27th Lane, has a traditional sloping tiled roof, courtyard and distinctive Mazandarani-style capped minaret.

Imamzadeh-ye Nur, accessed via Aftab 15th Alley, is a 15th-century brick tomb tower of relatively minor interest but finding it is a great excuse to poke around the most interesting old alleys, where the magnificent **Mazandarani Mansion** is currently under reconstruction at the angle of Taqavi Lane.

Gorgan Museum (☎ 222 2364; Mozeh St; admission IR25,000; ☯ 8am-6pm) has limited, dusty ethnological exhibits, and displays sparse finds from local archaeological sites such as Jorjan (Gonbad-e Kavus) and Turang Tappeh (22km north of Gorgan). In a garden around the corner, the immense **Imamzadeh Abdollah** (Shohada Sq) has a glorious, blue dome and fine minarets.

If you don't have time to get into the mountain villages behind the city, the forest paths of **Nahar Khoran** offer an easy clean-air alternative, albeit crowded with weekenders and adorned with litter. A forest lane winds on to an imamzadeh 11km beyond.

Sleeping

BUDGET

Side by side, a minute's walk from Shahrdari Sq in a lane off Panzdah Metri 2nd Alley, are two delightful mosaferkhunehs, both friendly, super-clean and surprisingly peaceful. **Hotel Pars** (☎ 222 9550; s/tw/tr IR40,000/50,000/ 60,000) has a pleasant courtyard of orange trees and owner Ali speaks great English, and **Hotel Razi** (☎ 222 4613; s/tw IR50,000/60,000) has a shower in each room, though squat toilets remain shared. The top sheets arrive fresh in their laundry bags.

Hotel Khayyam (☎ 222 4924; Aftabab 15th Alley, Imam Khomeini St; tw IR59,000) This is a fallback if Hotels Pars and Razi are full. Its rooms have

attached showers, but is not quite as clean as the mosaferkhunehs, although it smells of solvents. Sometimes foreigners have to pay IR100,000.

MID-RANGE

Almost all the mid-range options could use some redecoration.

Hotel Tahmasebi (☎ 442 2780; fax 442 0575; Jomhuri-ye Eslami St; tw IR200,000; ✷) The staff is friendly and a much needed repainting is underway. Rooms are acceptable, with fan and fridge, though the reasonable attached bathrooms have a squat toilet and the old air conditioners rumble discontentedly.

Hotel Maroof (☎ 442 5591; Jomhuri-ye Eslami St; s/d US$15/20) Tattier than Hotel Tahmasebi,

but each room does have a new fridge and Western toilet.

Hotel Shahrdari (☎ 552 4077; Nahar Khoran; s/tw US$20/30) In a woodland setting 6km east of the centre, Shahrdari has a faint grandeur. However, stairways are unkempt and although rooms have been redecorated, only six of them have a bathroom and a Western toilet. Absurdly, there's no discount for the other, older rooms.

Tourist Inn (☎ 552 0034; fax 552 2279; Nahar Khoran; tw US$36) A further 300m into the forest from Shahrdari, Tourist Inn's prices are the same for a cabin or a hotel room. Both are a little musty, with attached squat toilets.

Hotel Azin (☎ /fax 442 3004; Sari Hwy; s/tw US$45/65; ✷ Ⓟ) Gorgan's best hotel has perfectly appointed if over-colourful modern rooms and a 6th-floor roof terrace with super views. Unfortunately, the position is hopelessly inconvenient beyond the westernmost city limits; even the thick double-glazing can't stop the Richter-scale vibrations of all-night truck-traffic.

Eating

There are plenty of snack bars and eateries on Shohada St, north of Shahrdari Sq.

Atlas (☎ 222 8579; Sar Khajeh St; meals IR15,000-20,000; ❤ 11.30am-9pm) Between 10th and 12th Alleys, this is about the only notable restaurant in the central area. Despite reasonable prices it's a top-range kababi overzealously decorated with chandeliers, peaches-and-cream stucco mouldings and plenty of mirror tiles.

Café Heyla (Park-e Shahr; ❤ 9am-11pm) An unsophisticated place for tea and a light snack in the park, with some hope of local music from an itinerant musician/customer.

For a wider range of restaurants head to the southern reaches of Valiasr St (from km4) or all the way to Nahar Khoran, where there are many outside teahouses and terraced kababis, some nicer restaurants and the particularly eccentric **Guri** (☎ 552 4891; Valiasr St km5; kebabs IR15,000; ❤ 4pm-1am). Its main building is shaped like a giant samovar and topped with a big concrete teapot. Eat inside or sit at cup-and-saucer tables in the attractive willow landscaped grounds. Book ahead.

Getting There & Away

AIR

Iran Aseman (☎ 224 4501) has daily flights to Tehran (IR156,000).

BUS, MINIBUS & SAVARI

The big main bus terminal is off the northeastern corner of Enqelab Sq. Among the destinations served are:

Destination	Price (IR)	Duration (hrs)	Departures
Esfahan	35,000 (Volvo)	16	2-3pm
Mashhad	20,000	10½	6-10am & 6-10pm
Rasht	20,000-22,000	9	7-8am & 7-9pm
Tabriz	60,000 (Volvo)	14	3pm
Tehran	12,500-17,500	8	Frequent
Zahedan	42,500	26	6am

Many more through-buses to/from Mashhad don't bother with the bus station and instead drop off and pick up passengers at Enqelab Sq and/or just east of Mofateh Sq. Savaris to Aq Qal'eh also leave from Enqelab Sq. A well-organised minibus station directly east of the bus terminal has frequent as-full services to Aq Qal'eh, Bandar-e Torkaman (IR1100, 40 minutes), Behshahr, Kordkuy (for West Radkan) and Sari (IR12,000, two hours).

Minibuses for Minudasht, Aliabad and Gonbad-e-Kavus (IR2750, 1½ hours) leave from the Istgah Gonbad on Blvd Jorjan at the eastern edge of town. Savaris from the same point are nearly twice as fast.

TRAIN

The train station is off the northern ring road, walking distance west from the bus station. The Gorgan-Tehran services (1st/2nd class IR36,150/15,600, 11 hours) travel overnight both ways, missing the remarkable glimpses of view; for these you'd do better taking the Tehran to Sari service.

Getting Around

The city is large, but convenient shared taxis (IR500) run from predictable points near Shahrdari/Vahdat Sq: north to the bus station, west to Mofateh Sq and east along Beheshti Rd to Istgah Gonbad. For Nahar Khoran (IR1500) and upper Valiasr St, longer-run shared taxis start from just south of Valiasr Sq.

AROUND GORGAN

The Turkmen town of **Aq Qal'eh**, 20km north of Gorgan, has a Wednesday morning **market**, which is one of the best in the region as well as a 400-year-old, five-span **bridge** (Pol-e Safavi), 5km south of town. Change savaris in Aq Qal'eh for **Incheh Borun** – along the way you will pass near lakes where it's possible to see flamingos. See the boxed text 'Crossing the Turkmenistan Border at Incheh Borun', p314.

GONBAD-E KAVUS   گنبد کاوس

☎ 0172 / pop 126,000

Gonbad-e Kavus (Gonbad-e Qabus) is a predominantly Turkmen town named and famous for one magnificent building and its sponsor – the astonishing **Mil-e Gonbad tower** (admission IR15,000; ❤ 7.30am-dusk). Built for

NORTHEASTERN IRAN

CROSSING THE TURKMENISTAN BORDER AT INCHEH BORUN

The border at Incheh Borun (Iran) and Gyzyl-Etrek (Turkmenistan) was described by one traveller as having Turkmen officials who were 'utterly charming and are among my favourite immigration officers ever'. High praise, indeed! However, few people actually cross here. Occasional transport runs from Gonbad-e Kavus to the border or you could hire a taxi. Once over the border, which is open 8.30am to 6pm, you're really in the middle of nowhere. Don't count on public transport if you haven't arranged a pick-up in Advance. It's much more common to cross the Turkmenistan border at Bajgiran (p332).

---

poet/artist/prince Qabus ebn-e Vashmgir, it's so remarkably well preserved that one can scarcely believe it's almost 1000 years old. Soaring, 55m tall on 12m-deep foundations, it has the cross-section of a 10-pointed star, and looks like a buttressed brick spaceship. It was finished in 1006 and designed to last forever. This gave Qabus, ruler of surrounding Tabarestan, six years to marvel at his creation before an assassin put him in it permanently. Well, not so permanently, actually. His glass coffin, which originally hung from the tower's dome, vanished long ago. Now there's nothing to see inside, although it's worth the entry fee for the remarkable echoes. You'll find the tower in a park two blocks north of the central Enqelab Sq.

Behind the huge, ornate **Imamzadeh Yahya**, 3km west of the centre down Meyhane St, are the lumpy **excavations of Jorjan**. Once the region's most ancient city, Jorjan was utterly obliterated by the Mongol and Tamerlane rampages. On the outskirts of Jorjan, the Mil-e Gonbad was all that survived and today's Gonbad-e Kavus town eventually grew up around that.

On Friday the hippodrome at the eastern end of town holds Savar Kareh **horse races** (1pm, spring and autumn).

On hot summer days you might want to retire behind the heavy bronze doors of the swish, new indoor **swimming pool** (☎ 555 6909; Blvd Danshju; admission IR20,000; ⏰ 8am-noon & 8-10pm). Sessions alternate by gender.

There are many carpet dealers around Enqelab Sq.

Sleeping & Eating

Hotel Ferdoosi (☎ 333 0364; Chaiboi Sq; s/tw IR35,000/ 50,000) Beyond the Istgah Gorgan, at the inconvenient southernmost edge of town, Gonbad's unpretentious best has shared toilets though the twin rooms get a clunky shower in the attached bathroom. The restaurant offers standard kebab meals (IR13,000 to IR22,000).

Hotel Khayyam (☎ 222 7663; tw IR36,000) This is the most central mosaferkhuneh. It's in a lane off Imam St just south of Enqelab Sq, before Meyhane St. Rooms are reasonably clean, with a fan.

There are kababis and a pizzeria off Enqelab Sq and two more pizzerias (Gap and Fanous) towards the Kalaleh terminal. Right in front of the great tower are a trio of coffee shops and snack bars, including **Safa Café** (⏰ 7am-midnight), which offers ice-cream sundaes, floats and freshly squeezed pomegranate juice.

Getting There & Away

Istgah Gorgan is a busy terminal towards the southern end of Imam St with minibuses for Azad Shahr, Aliabad and Gorgan (IR2750, 1½ hours), though for the latter savaris (IR8000 to IR10,000) are much faster. For Minudasht and Kalaleh, savaris (IR5000, 25 minutes) leave from Basij Sq, 2km directly east of Enqelab Sq; change in Minudasht for buses to Mashhad.

AROUND GONBAD-E KAVUS

East of Gonbad, partly cultivated steppe contrasts with mountains in whose thick forests of 500-year-old trees you expect Asterix to appear at any moment. The region is indistinctly littered with clues to a once vibrant civilisation that lasted from the Neanderthal era right up until the 13th century. Then Ghengis Khan's hordes brought it all to an abrupt end.

Much of the steppe population is ethnically Turkmen so if you're lucky you'll find yourself invited to a horse milking or for tea in one of the increasingly rare reed-ringed felt öy (yurt) tents. For a hefty fee it's possible to make unique spring and autumn **horse treks** in this fascinating area; book through www.inthesaddle.com /iran.htm. For a riders' experience read www.equitrek.com.au/Iran.html. To explore independently there are OK hotels in

TURKMEN – NOT ALWAYS THE BAD GUYS

All too often smeared by historians as the 'pillaging raiders', the pastoral Turkmen are a hospitable, fiercely independent people with more than their own share of grievances. Turkmen horsemen have long roamed the steppeland of Golestan. But many more fled south after 1881 in the wake of Geok Tepe, an infamous battle in which the Russians massacred 15,000 tribesmen in their successful attempt to annex Turkmenistan. The poor Turkmen also haven't fared too well in Iran recently. Land sell-offs since the revolution mean that their traditional pasture-lands are increasingly being ploughed up by Zaboli immigrants. Turkmen villages remain some of the most disadvantaged in the country. See www.turkmensahra.com for more about their region.

Minudasht and Bojnurd, but Gharra Tappeh Sheikh (GTS; below) is a much more inspiring base.

A large area of both forest and steppe now falls within the limited-access Golestan National Park.

Gharra Tappeh Sheikh (GTS) قره تپه شیخ

In the minuscule ethnic-Turkmen village of GTS, a unique stud-farm is home to philosophical US-born Louise Firouz (nee Laylin). Famous for 'rediscovering' (ie selectively back-breeding) the miniature Caspian horse, she also rears classic Turkman horses, thought to be the genetic forerunners of the thoroughbred. She has lived in Iran for over 40 years and has an endless wealth of fascinating tales to tell.

By advance arrangement it's possible to stay on the farm in a genuine Turkmen **öy** (yurt; ☎ 0172 334 4515; firouz@pinarnet.com; per person US$40) with shared facilities. This is a unique, very personal experience and the deliberately high price is designed to keep it that way. The village's flat, steppe position gives a magnificent big-sky panorama edged with a near horizon of high woodland ridges. It's an ideal base for visiting Alexander's Wall and Khalid Nibi Shrine, and Louise can arrange transport or give ideas for dozens more intriguing but little visited marvels.

GETTING THERE & AWAY

Transport is via Kalaleh and Tamar. Savaris from Gonbad (IR5000, 45 minutes) or Minudasht (IR3000, 30 minutes) arrive at Kalaleh's Alqadir Sq but will often take you on to Ahmedi Sq from where rare Tamar-bound savaris want a pricey IR20,000 to continue to GTS (20 minutes).

Alexander's Wall سد اسکندر

Like the Great Chinese and Hadrian's equivalents, **Alexander's Wall** (Sadd-e Eskandar) was built to keep out war-like raiders from the north. For the Iranian world it marked the very real edge of civilisation. Being banished beyond was equivalent to capital punishment. Known to the Turkmen as Qezel Alam (Red Snake), it was probably built in the 6th century and not by Alexander the Great as the name romantically suggests. With regularly spaced fortresses it stretched from the Golestan Mountains over 160km, almost to the Caspian. Comprehensively cannibalised for building materials over the centuries it is now being ploughed into little more than a muddy undulation. However, a relatively recognisable section, conveniently marked by orange concrete bollards, runs along the northern side of the gravel road from Tamar to GTS. Raised some 5m above the fields, the outline of a large, square-planned wall-fort is still easy to make out at **Malaisheikh**, around 10km west of GTS.

Khalid Nibi Shrine امامزاده خالد نبی

Dramatically perched high above a breathtaking sea of badlands sit three small **mausolea** commemorating Khalid Nibi, a 5th-century Nestorian Christian. Curiously, the place now attracts Muslim pilgrims in surprising numbers during spring and early summer. From the central shrine, a fairly obvious footpath leads down then right in about 10 minutes to a grassy knoll dotted with remarkable **pagan grave-markers**. Ancient but of unknown age, there are 2m-long spindly phalluses for men and butterfly shaped rams' horns for women.

Khalid Nibi is a slow unsurfaced 30km drive (allow 90 minutes) beyond Tamar itself off the Kalaleh–Maraveh Tappeh road. Although it's possible to get here by taxi (and seasonal pilgrim bus) the last kilometre or two is too steep for weaker vehicles. If you're staying in GTS, the best and probably cheapest solution is to arrange a 4WD truck ride from there (around IR150,000 return).

Aliabad

علی آباد

☎ 0173 / pop 45,000

A short taxi ride plus a 3km hike from this sprawling, friendly but unexciting university town brings you to the attractive **Kabud Waterfall**, hidden among trees. Or drive up a lovely mountain road (asphalted for the first 30km) through the forests to **Shirinabad**. On the main road near Istgah Gonbad (where minibuses terminate), **Mehmunpazir Zarandi** (☎ 622 9239; tr/q IR60,000/80,000) is clean but basic.

Minudasht

مینودشت

☎ 0174 / pop 23,000

Of little interest itself, Minudasht is a useful transport junction between Gonbad and Mashhad. On the northern edge of town **Hotel Esteghlal** (☎ 522 2314; Mashhad Hwy; s/tw US$20/30; 🕃) has seen better days. There are mountain views from back-facing rooms but peeling paint, missing shower curtains and stained toilets don't appeal, the garden is overgrown and the eerily deserted restaurant is like a set from *The Shining*.

Other Turkmen Areas

The arid **Atrak Valley** and the much more fertile **Chandir Valley** are both home to long-settled Turkmen communities and rapidly increasing numbers of immigrants. Though quickly disappearing, a few houses and mosques in the Chandir Valley, notably in **Garkaz** and especially **Qabelqa** villages, are vividly painted with ram-horn motifs and adorned with wooden pillars whose rams' horn capitals look eerily reminiscent of Greek Ionic. Perhaps that's no coincidence given geohistorical links with the ancient Parthians and the fair-haired children in some families. Garkaz is also the home of Iranian Turkmens' spiritual leader, the Ata-Ishan, a distant descendent of Turkmenistan's classic poet Fargo Makhtumkuli (c 1770–1840). The modernist **mausoleum of Makhtumkuli** (Makhtumqoli-e-faraqi) looks like a gigantic four-stemmed concrete umbrella and rises discordantly from the steppe at **Aq Teqeh**, some 25km west of Maraveh Tappeh. Although historians disagree wildly as to when and where Makhtumkuli actually died, the mausoleum continues to attract tourists (and scorpions), mainly from Turkmenistan.

This region is about your best hope for seeing Turkmen herders' *öy* tents in use.

Beware that very few people anywhere near here speak a word of English, nor ever imagined foreign tourists trundling through. Authorities might be suspicious and it's best to make local contacts before just turning up. The well-connected, English-speaking guide **Mohsen Aghajani** (☎ 021-760 9292; www.araz.org), based in Tehran, has been recommended by readers and can organise a car with driver for US$35 per day to explore the area.

BOJNURD

بجنور

☎ 0584 / pop 140,000 / elevation 1068m

Bojnurd can act as a good jumping-off point for the Turkmen region or as a stop on the way to either Turkmenistan or Mashhad. However, apart from the psychedelically coloured Qajar-era mansion and equally loud hospital on Dochenar St, there's not much to keep you here.

The **mosaferkhuneh** (☎ 222 2219; Imam Khomeini St; s/tw IR50,000/80,000) is well located in the centre of town, but that's about as much as you can say for it. Better is the **Guest House** (☎ 225 1523; s/tw US$15/25; 🅿 🕃) on the main through road – it's green, with a huge 'Guest House' sign. You should be able to negotiate a better rate, and food in the restaurant is not bad. Other eateries and grocery stores can be found along Imam Khomeini St.

For Internet access the Nodehy brothers at **Mobtakevan Coffeenet** (☎ 224 2215; Dochenar St; 🕙 9am-11pm) are very helpful and speak good English.

Buses leave regularly for Gorgan (IR13,000, five hours), Mashhad (IR10,000, four hours), Quchan (IR5,000, two hours), Sabzavar (IR7000, three hours) and Tehran (IR50,000, 12 hours). Savaris to Mashhad cost IR20,000 but only take two hours.

DAMGHAN

دامغان

☎ 0232 / pop 58,000 / elevation 1184m

This historic town is the best place to break the journey between Tehran and Mashhad. Being on the trade route between those two cities, it's seen plenty of history since it was first settled around the 8th century. Overnight trains and buses mean there are few foreign visitors today, as they bypass the town, making the welcome even more enthusiastic than usual. The main attraction is the Tarikhuneh Mosque, which some believe to be Iran's oldest.

The centre of town is – you guessed it – Imam Khomeini Sq, where Bank Tejarat changes money. Street signs are few and in Farsi only.

Sights

Dating from about AD 760, the **Tarikhuneh Mosque** (admission IR20,000; ☺ 8am-4pm Sat-Thu, until 5pm summer) is one of the oldest surviving mosques in Iran. It's a small, four-*iwan* (rectangular hall opening onto a courtyard) affair with a square inner courtyard that in itself is not exactly breathtaking. But a guided tour from Agha Sayyed, the caretaker, makes the admission worth it as he will unlock the 25m-high **minaret** next door, and just about every other old place in town if you ask. The minaret dates from AD 1038 and affords excellent views of Damghan – as you climb the 85 very steep steps look for the gradually receding brickwork marking the way above you. The minaret is about 500m southeast of Imam Khomeini Sq.

The only remaining feature of the original Jameh Mosque is the **minaret** (Manar-e Masjed-e Jameh), probably dating from the mid-11th century. To get here, turn left outside Tarikhuneh Mosque and walk straight ahead for 300m, cross the road and turn into Kucheh-ye Masjed.

The round **Aramgah-e Pir Alamdar** tower, 100m northeast of the Jameh Mosque, dates from AD 1026. It was originally domed, and is remarkable for its innovative use of brick patterns and its Kufic inscription, visible beneath the roof level.

Sleeping & Eating

Damghan Inn (☎ 522 2070; fax 522 6800; Azadi Blvd; r US$20; P ⊠) This ITTO-operated hotel is beside pretty Park-e Shahrdari and is designed to resemble a caravanserai – at least from the outside. It's the best place in town and fair value, though don't be surprised if the rates rise.

Amir Hotel Shadcome (☎ 523 1776; s/tw IR100,000/ 150,000; ⊠ P) Found on a square south of town, Amir is a welcoming hotel. It has small, comfortable rooms with bathrooms and a very popular restaurant downstairs.

Caffe Sun City (☎ 524 4196; Imam Khomeini St; ☺ 9am-midnight) Thirty metres north of Imam Khomeini Sq, this is a great spot to escape extremes of temperature and watch Damghan float by to eastern chill-out music. The coffee's not bad, either (IR6000).

There are several pizza and burger joints opposite Damghan Inn on Azadi Blvd.

Getting There & Away

Damghan is an easy day trip by bus from Shahrud (IR2000, 75 minutes, 71km, hourly), or a little further from the regional capital, Semnan, by minibus (IR5000, three hours, hourly) or savari (IR10,000, 80 minutes). From Shahrud, get off at Imam Khomeini Sq rather than at the distant bus station. Leaving Damghan, you'll have to get a taxi to the bus station, where savaris leave from outside the gate. Long-distance buses often bypass Damghan, so you may need to get a connection in Shahrud or in Semnan for onward travel.

The train station is 2km southeast of Imam Khomeini Sq. Trains pass through regularly but it's less convenient than travelling by bus.

SHAHRUD   شاهرود

☎ 0273 / pop 120,000 / elevation 1308m

Shahrud is a sleepy but attractive town wedged between the northern fringe of the Dasht-e Kavir and the eastern Alborz Mountains. Its tree-lined streets, relatively mild climate and relaxed atmosphere make it an excellent place to break the long journey between Tehran and Mashhad. Shahrud also makes a good base for a visit to the nearby village of Bastam. You could even travel to Gonbad-e Kavus (p313) from here.

The main road through town is 22 Bahman St, which stretches from the bus station in the south to Azadi Sq in the north.

Sleeping & Eating

Hotel Nader (☎ 333 2835; fax 333 2836; s/d IR100,000/ 150,000; ⊠ P) Above a popular restaurant, this place has simple rooms with shower but toilets are shared. To find it, head south of Jomhuri-ye Eslami Sq along 22 Bahman St for about 700m, turn right at the first big road, then take your first left. It's about 250m along on the right with a blue sign in Farsi.

New Islami Inn (☎ 222 2335; s/d IR25,000/35,000; P) A few metres east of the square, this is in a handy location and was once (quite some time ago, it seems) an impressive building.

These days you'll be lucky to find a shared shower that actually works.

Near Azadi Sq in the north of town are a couple of other places. **ITTO Sharud Tourist Hotel** (☎ 222 6078; fax 222 4008; r US$35; P 😊) is overpriced but easily the best in town, while **Hotel Azadi-Sharif** (☎ 222 8454; s/tw IR50,000/80,000) off Azadi Blvd manages to cram three short beds into small, grubby rooms.

The best choice of food is on the southern side of Azadi Sq, from kababis to something a little better. **Coffee Shop Soorena** is a good place to sit and ponder your next move, although coffee-lovers shouldn't get overexcited. **Golbar Restaurant** (☎ 222 3393; meals IR30,000; 😊 noon-10pm) is popular with locals and you can point to the pictures on the wall if you're having trouble ordering; it's about 300m south of Azadi Sq (look for the green façade).

Getting There & Around

The main bus station is 5km south of Jomhuri-ye Eslami Sq; a shared taxi costs IR2500. The bus companies have convenient offices around Jomhuri-ye Eslami Sq where you can buy tickets in advance. There are several direct buses a day to Tehran (IR22,000), Gorgan (IR10,000), Mashhad (IR16,000, 10 hours) and Sari (IR13,500), as well as less-frequent buses to Rasht (IR26,300) and Esfahan (IR40,000). Hourly minibuses go to Damghan (IR2000) and Semnan (IR8500).

Buses and minibuses for Gorgan also leave from the small Terminal-e Shimal on Imam Reza Sq; ask at the bus company offices for the best departure point.

Shahrud is on the train line between Tehran and Mashhad, but nearly everyone uses the quicker and more reliable bus or minibus. The train station is about 3km southeast of Jomhuri-ye Eslami Sq.

BASTAM   بسطام

The village of Bastam is lovely and certainly worth a look. It's a pleasant place to wander around, with quiet, tree-lined streets and a crumbling caravanserai, but the highlight is undoubtedly the **Some'e-ye Bayazid Bastami monastery complex** (😊 daylight hours Sat-Thu). Dating from about the 11th century, most of what you see today was built during the early 13th century. It is decorated with some wonderful swirling stucco reliefs, especially in the mihrab, and some fine frescoes. The stone **minaret** is particularly impressive, as is

the Mongol-era circular **tower tomb** about 100m south of the main complex.

Getting There & Away

Bastam is 7km north of Shahrud, just off the main road to Gorgan. Regular minibuses run north along 22 Bahman St from Jomhuri-ye Eslami Sq in Shahrud to Bastam (IR1000, 15 minutes). They pass right outside the entrance to Bastam mosque, from where there are plenty of shared taxis also making the return journey. Alternatively, for a private taxi, pay about IR17,000 return, including waiting time.

MASHHAD   مشهد
☎ 0511 / pop 2,964,500 / elevation 1019m

The true depth of religious feeling in Iran is perhaps best displayed in this, its holiest city. Mashhad means 'Place of Martyrdom' and the city is extremely sacred to Shiites as the place where the direct descendant of the Prophet Mohammed, Imam Reza, died in AD 817. What was then a small village called Sanabad has since grown to become Iran's most important pilgrimage centre, where you can witness the tears, the wailing and the selfless devotion of Shiites from around the world as they pay their respects (and no small amount of money) to the Imam.

The population of Mashhad ballooned during the Iran-Iraq War, simply because it was the furthest Iranian city from the Iraqi border. Many stayed and the city is now huge, unwieldy and polluted. Mashhad can get very cold in winter and there is often snow on the ground for four or five months of the year.

More than 12 million pilgrims visit Mashhad each year, and around No Ruz (the Iranian New Year; about 21 March) and the height of the pilgrimage season (June to September) the population can triple in the space of a few days. If you notice a lot of lovey young couples around, that's because the city is a haven for honeymooners, who believe sharing it with the Imam will bless their marriage.

Apart from the Holy Shrine there is little to detain you in Mashhad. However, it makes a good base for exploring Iran's northeast and the city is a natural staging post if you're travelling to/from Afghanistan or Turkmenistan.

MASHHAD

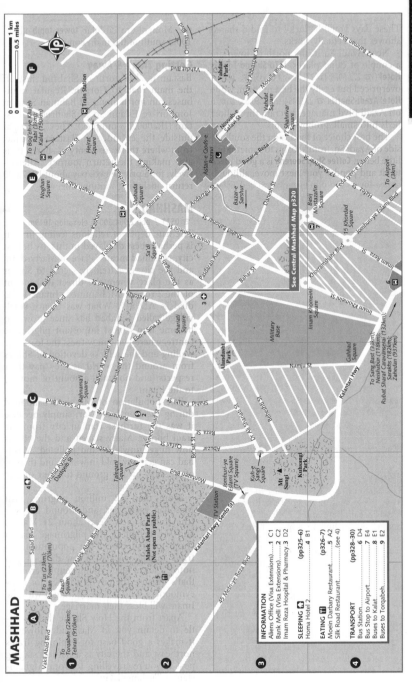

0 — 1 km
0 — 0.5 miles

INFORMATION
Aliens Office (Visa Extensions)..........1	C1
Bank Melli (Visa Extensions)..............2	C2
Imam Reza Hospital & Pharmacy 3	D2

SLEEPING (pp325–6)
Homa Hotel 2.................................4	B1

EATING (p326–7)
Moein Darbary Restaurant..............5	A2
Silk Road Restaurant.....................(see 4)	

TRANSPORT (pp328–30)
Bus Station....................................6	D4
Bus Stop to Airport.......................7	E4
Buses to Kalat...............................8	E1
Buses to Torqabeh........................9	E2

See Central Mashhad Map p320

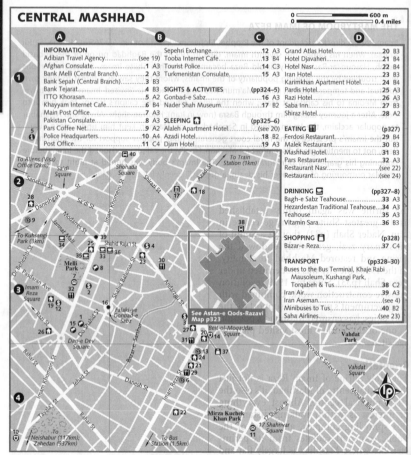

CENTRAL MASHHAD

0 —————— 600 m
0 —————— 0.4 miles

INFORMATION	
Adibian Travel Agency	(see 19) A3
Afghan Consulate	1 A3
Bank Melli (Central Branch)	2 A3
Bank Sepah (Central Branch)	3 B3
Bank Tejarat	4 B3
ITTO Khorasan	5 A3
Khayyam Internet Cafe	6 B4
Main Post Office	7 A3
Pakistan Consulate	8 A3
Pars Coffee Net	9 A2
Police Headquarters	10 A4
Post Office	11 C4

Sepehri Exchange	12 A3
Tooba Internet Cafe	13 B4
Tourist Police	14 C3
Turkmenistan Consulate	15 A3

SIGHTS & ACTIVITIES	(pp324–5)
Gonbad-e Sabz	16 A3
Nader Shah Museum	17 B2

SLEEPING	(pp325–6)
Alaleh Apartment Hotel	(see 20)
Azadi Hotel	18 B2
Djam Hotel	19 A3

Grand Atlas Hotel	20 B3
Hotel Djavaheri	21 B4
Hotel Nasr	22 B4
Iran Hotel	23 B3
Karimkhan Apartment Hotel	24 B4
Pardis Hotel	25 A3
Razi Hotel	26 A3
Saba Inn	27 B3
Shiraz Hotel	28 A2

EATING	(p327)
Ferdosi Restaurant	29 B4
Malek Restaurant	30 B3
Mashhad Hotel	31 B3
Pars Restaurant	32 A3
Restaurant Nasr	(see 22)
Restaurant	(see 24)

DRINKING	(pp327–8)
Bagh-e Sabz Teahouse	33 A3
Hezardestan Traditional Teahouse	34 A3
Teahouse	35 A3
Vitamin Sara	36 B3

SHOPPING	(p328)
Bazar-e Reza	37 C4

TRANSPORT	(pp328–30)
Buses to the Bus Terminal, Khaje Rabi Mausoleum, Kushangi Park, Torqabeh & Tus	38 C2
Iran Air	39 A3
Iran Aseman	(see 4)
Minibuses to Tus	40 B2
Saha Airlines	(see 23)

To Aliens (Visa) Office (2km)

To Train Station (1km)

Sa'di Square

Shohada Square

Sanabad St

Sa'di St

Shiraz St

Imam Khomeini St

Daneshgah

Azadi St

See Astan-e Qods-Razavi Map p323

Modares St

Shahid Raja'i St

To Kuhsangi Park (3km)

Jannat Aabi

Dr Beheshti

Melli Park

Shahid Bahonar St

Andarzgu St

Dr Pasdaran Ave

Imam Reza Square

Razi St

Falaki-ye Gonbad-e Sabz

Beit-ol-Moqaddas Square

Do Shabib St

Dan-e Dev Square

Bazaar-e Sarshur

Vahdat Park

Nowabe Safavi St

Vahdat Square

Danesh St

Imam Reza St

Jehad St

Imam Khomeini St

Tavalod St

Bahar St

Danesh St

Mosalla Blvd

To Neishabur (117km); Zahedan (937km)

To Bus Station (1.5km)

Mirza Kuchek Khan Park

17 Shahrivar St

17 Shahrivar Square

History

The history of Mashhad is inseparable from the legend of Imam Reza, heir to the Abbasid caliphate and eighth of the Shiite imams. According to popular belief, Reza was poisoned on the orders of the Caliph Ma'mun (see the boxed text 'The Martyrdom of Imam Reza', p321). Ma'mun buried him in a tower in the village of Sanabad next to the tomb of his own father, the famous Haroun ar-Rashid. The burial place began to attract Shiite pilgrims and soon became known as Mashhad.

In the centuries after it was built the shrine was destroyed, restored and destroyed again as invaders plundered the area. After the sacking of Tus in 1220, Mashhad grew to become

the capital of Khorasan and the mausoleum of Imam Reza was subsequently restored.

In the early 15th century, Shah Rokh, son of Timur, enlarged the shrine, and his extraordinary wife, Gohar Shad (p324), commissioned a mosque on the site. Mashhad did not become a pilgrimage centre of the first order until the Safavids established Shiism as the state creed in the 16th century. The most brilliant of the early Safavid rulers, Shah Esma'il I, Shah Tahmasp and Shah Abbas I, gave the city and shrine the prominence they have held ever since.

The city's location put it at constant risk of invasion, and Mashhad suffered Uzbek attacks on several occasions in the 16th and 17th centuries. In the 18th century

THE MARTYRDOM OF IMAM REZA

Imam Reza, a direct descendant of the Prophet Mohammed, was born in AD 765 in Medina (Saudi Arabia). When his father, the seventh Imam, died in 799 in the Baghdad prison of the Abbasid caliph, Haroun ar-Rashid, 35-year-old Reza became the eighth Shiite imam. Successive caliphs were troubled by the growing popularity of the imams, whom they saw as a threat to their own spiritual and temporal power. Caliph Ma'mun was no exception. He 'invited' Imam Reza to travel from Medina to his capital at Marv; when the Imam refused, the caliph's troops took him into exile. After a journey taking him through Basra (now in Iraq), Khorramshahr, Ahvaz and Neishabur to popular acclaim, the Imam arrived in Sanabad. Caliph Ma'mun kept him under close guard, but the Imam's presence at the royal court generated huge popular support for the charismatic Reza, not to mention great discomfort for Ma'mun. Finally, the caliph imprisoned the Imam before poisoning his grapes and pomegranate juice. The Imam's body was buried at night to avoid a popular outpouring of grief over his death, a grief still keenly felt to this day.

the shrine was again firmly established as the greatest Shiite pilgrimage centre in Iran. Nader Shah (p32), though a Sunni of missionary zeal, generously endowed the shrine and restored Mashhad to stability. In the 1930s the city was modernised under Reza Shah (p33). Since the 1979 revolution massive construction work, combined with the government's prominent support for the holy cities, has ensured Mashhad's position as one of the world's most visited pilgrimage sites.

Orientation

The Holy Shrine of Imam Reza is not just the spiritual centre of Mashhad, it's also the city's physical centre. Almost everything of interest is within walking distance of this sprawling complex, and most of the public transport radiates from its perimeter. Elsewhere Mashhad is largely flat and featureless. The main bus station is at the end of Imam Reza St, about 3km southwest of the shrine; the train station is at Hejrat Sq only 1.5km north of the shrine; and the airport 6km southeast of the centre. Most streets don't have signs in English, so get used to asking.

Information

EMERGENCY
Imam Reza Hospital (Map p319; ☎ 854 3031-9; Ebn-e Sina St) Probably the best and most accessible hospital, and there is a 24-hour pharmacy attached.
Police Headquarters (Map p320; ☎ 222 2001; Imam Khomeini Sq, Imam Khomeini St)
Tourist Police (Map p320; ☎ 841 8236; Beit-ol-Moqaddas Sq) This booth is handy and there's usually an English-speaking policeman nearby.

INTERNET ACCESS
Khayyam Internet Cafe (Map p320; ☎ 851 5533; Imam Reza St; per hr IR6000; ⏰ 9am-midnight) Pick of the coffeenets, with cheap international calls and fast connections.
Pars Coffee Net (Map p320; ☎ 221 5383; Daneshgah St; ⏰ 9am-10pm Sat-Thu) Nice garden; slow machines.
Tooba Internet Cafe (Map p320; Imam Reza St; per hr IR5000; ⏰ 8.30am-midnight Sat-Thu & 4pm-midnight Fri) International calls and headphones courtesy of Singapore Airlines.

MONEY
Banks with foreign-exchange counters are relatively common. They include:
Bank Melli Central Branch (Map p320; Imam Khomeini St)
Bank Sepah Central Branch (Map p320; Andarzgu St)
Bank Tejarat (Map p320; Andarzgu St)
Sepehri Exchange (Map p320; Pasdaran Ave; ⏰ 9am-6pm Sat-Wed & 9am-2pm Thu) Faster than the banks with fair rates and longer hours.

POST
Main Post Office (Map p320; Imam Khomeini St) Unmarked in English, it's opposite Bank Melli. Parcels should be sent from here.
Post Office (Map p320; 17 Shahrivar Sq) For letters, postcards, stamps etc.

TOURIST INFORMATION
ITTO Khorasan (Map p320; ☎ 726 9501; Saheb al-Zaman Ave, Molavi St; ⏰ 8am-4pm) On the 2nd floor, this office caters almost exclusively to pilgrims, but can provide a couple of maps if required. A better bet is the office full of free books, maps and brochures, some in English, at the train station.

TRAVEL AGENCIES
Adibian Travel Agency (Map p320; ☎ 859 8151; www.adibiantours.com; 56 Pasdaran Ave; ⏰ 7.30am-8pm) There are dozens of agencies in Mashhad but Adibian

is far and away the best. In addition to selling domestic and international air tickets, train tickets, and providing assistance with visa applications, it offers tours around Mashhad and further afield (see following).

TOURS

Adibian Travel Agency (Map p320; ☎ 859 8151, www.adibiantours.com; 56 Pasdaran Ave; ☼ 7.30am-8pm) Tours are with excellent guides who speak English, French, German, Spanish and Italian. The half-day city tour (US$39 per car with three passengers) or the tour of the Holy Shrine (US$30) can be pricey if you're alone. Better value considering the distances are the full-day trips to Neishabur (US$65), Kalat, Torbet-e Jam or the caravanserais of the Silk Road around Sarakhs (all US$75, although this drops if you can gather enough people). Adibian is also the representative of the Touring & Automobile Club of Iran.

VISAS

Visa Extensions

Aliens Office (Map p319; Rahnama'i Sq, Rahnama'i St; ☼ 7.30am-1pm) Travellers have reported mixed success at this office located in the northwest of Mashhad, about 4km from the Holy Shrine. The relevant **Bank Melli** (Map p319) is about 750m south along Rahnama'i St; look for the crowd of Afghans and Central Asians filling out deposit slips. See the boxed text 'More Time, Please' (p362) for more information on extending visas. If you catch a private taxi to the Aliens Office it should cost about IR5000 from central Mashhad; ask for *Edari-ye Atbareh Khariji*. Alternatively, **Adibian Travel Agency** (Map p320; ☎ 859 8151, www.adibiantours.com; 56 Pasdaran Ave; ☼ 7.30am-8pm) can take care of the process for US$10.

VISAS FOR AFGHANISTAN, PAKISTAN & TURKMENISTAN

Afghan Consulate (Map p320; ☎ 854 1653; Do Shahid St; ☼ 8am-noon Sat-Thu) Getting a visa here is refreshingly simple (forms are in English): hand over a copy of your passport, two mugshots and US$30, and two days later you'll have a 30-day visa for Afghanistan.

Pakistan Consulate (Map p320; ☎ 222 9845; Imam Khomeini St; ☼ 9am-noon Sat-Wed) The guys here like talking cricket, but aren't so keen on issuing visas – they would prefer you went to Tehran. However, some travellers have reported success.

Turkmenistan Consulate (Map p320; ☎ 345 0432; Dan-e Dev Sq, Do Shahid St; ☼ 8.30-10.30am Mon-Thu & Sat) When we visited, staff were reluctant to help. And when you consider that 'Mondays and Wednesdays are devoted to transportation companies', and the process usually takes at least 10 days, you're better off sorting it out in Tehran.

Dangers & Annoyances

Be particularly careful not to upset Muslim sensibilities in this most holy of Iranian pilgrimage sites. Dress must be conservative and clean: ideally, men should not wear short sleeves in or near the shrine, and women must wear a chador inside the Holy Shrine (borrow one from your hotel). Remember, it is a privilege for non-Muslims to visit the shrine.

Sights
ASTAN-E QODS-E RAZAVI

Almost every one of the 12 million people who visit Mashhad each year comes to see the remarkable Holy Shrine of Imam Reza and the surrounding buildings of the *haram-e motahhar* (sacred precincts), known collectively as **Astan-e Qods-e Razavi** (☼ 24hr).

The 75-hectare complex is one of the marvels of the Islamic world, with an ever-expanding number of mosques, minarets and courtyards dazzling pilgrims with their myriad coloured tiles and stunning gilded domes. But for pilgrims, visiting the Holy Shrine is as much about coming as seeing; outpourings of grief for a man who died so long ago are as common here as they are difficult for many foreigners to relate to. Witnessing the grief can be both disturbing and unforgettable.

Much of the development in this large circular walled island in the centre of Mashhad has occurred in the past 80 years or so. In 1928 most buildings within 180m of the Holy Shrine were flattened to make way for expansion. Prior to the 1979 revolution this was expanded to 320m. Since 1979 money from government and private individuals has seen constant construction work, which continues today. When historians look back on the era of the Islamic Republic, they will point to this as its greatest architectural achievement.

As well as the shrine itself, the complex contains a mosque, museums, lofty *iwans* (two of them coated entirely with gold), *madrasehs* (theological colleges), numerous courtyards, several libraries, a small post office, a bookshop, a university and many other religious and administrative buildings. Beneath the shrine complex is a vast cemetery – to be buried near the Imam is a great (and expensive) honour.

The revolution has also made the foundation that manages the shrine of Imam Reza one of the biggest business conglomerates in Iran, managing an empire with enterprises from bakers to transport companies. Most of the money comes from donations, bequests and the selling of grave sites, although the government also contributes significant amounts. The proceeds are used for the extensive charity activities of the foundation.

Information

The shrine itself is closed to non-Muslims and there are strict rules about which other parts of the complex can be visited; sadly, most of the jewels are locked away from non-Muslim eyes. Access is largely restricted to the courtyards (Sahn-e Imam Khomeini, Sahn-e Jomhuri Eslami and Sahn-e Qods),

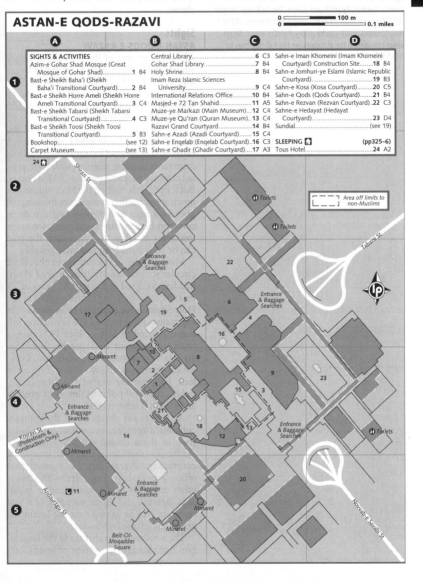

ASTAN-E QODS-RAZAVI

0 — 100 m
0 — 0.1 miles

SIGHTS & ACTIVITIES
Azim-e Gohar Shad Mosque (Great Mosque of Gohar Shad)............**1** B4
Bast-e Sheikh Baha'i (Sheikh Baha'i Transitional Courtyard)......**2** B4
Bast-e Sheikh Horre Ameli (Sheikh Horre Ameli Transitional Courtyard)......**3** C4
Bast-e Sheikh Tabarsi (Sheikh Tabarsi Transitional Courtyard).............**4** C3
Bast-e Sheikh Toosi (Sheikh Toosi Transitional Courtyard)............**5** B3
Bookshop.................................(see 12)
Carpet Museum.......................(see 13)

Central Library..................................**6** C3
Gohar Shad Library.......................**7** B4
Holy Shrine....................................**8** B4
Imam Reza Islamic Sciences University....................................**9** C4
International Relations Office..........**10** B4
Masjed-e 72 Tan Shahid.................**11** A5
Muze-ye Markazi (Main Museum)..**12** C4
Muze-ye Qu'ran (Quran Museum)..**13** C4
Sahn-e Azadi (Azadi Courtyard).......**15** C4
Sahn-e Enqelab (Enqelab Courtyard)..**16** C3
Sahn-e Ghadir (Ghadir Courtyard)..**17** A3

Sahn-e Iman Khomeini (Imam Khomeini Courtyard) Construction Site.......**18** B4
Sahn-e Jomhuri-ye Eslami (Islamic Republic Courtyard)..............................**19** B3
Sahn-e Kosa (Kosa Courtyard)........**20** C5
Sahn-e Qods (Qods Courtyard).......**21** B4
Sahn-e Rezvan (Rezvan Courtyard)..**22** C3
Sahne-e Hedayat (Hedayat Courtyard)....................................**23** D4
Sundial...(see 19)

SLEEPING 🏠   (pp325–6)
Tous Hotel....................................**24** A2

and the museums. The Sahn-e Azadi and Sahn-e Enqelab are strictly off limits, as is the shrine itself.

To put it mildly, these limits can be frustrating for travellers used to having free access to religion-inspired masterpieces elsewhere. Some have written to say the lack of access makes the long journey a waste of time. Others have said they were 'adopted' by pilgrims who accompanied them into the restricted areas – though this is unlikely to work if you're 6ft tall and fair-haired.

There are several entrances, although the most accessible are adjacent to Shirazi and Imam Reza Sts.

You may find the whole experience more rewarding if you take a guide. Some travel agencies offer tours, or you can take a free guide from the **International Relations Office** (Map p323; ☎ 221 3474; intlrela@mail.dci.co.ir; ☑ 7am-4pm Sat-Thu, 5pm summer). Whether or not you use one of its guides, all foreign visitors are required to register in the International Relations Office. The friendly, professional staff speak English and will show you a short video about the shrine. This is also the place to ask for an up-to-date map, which will reflect the dizzying pace of construction around the perimeter of the complex, or for free books on all things Shiite. Note that if you do visit this office, you might not be allowed to continue your tour without a guide.

A bombing in the shrine complex in 1994 killed 27 people and security has been significantly tighter since. No cameras are allowed inside the main gates, all bags must be left at the main entrance, and you will be frisked on the way in.

Holy Shrine

The original tomb chamber was built by the Caliph Haroun ar-Rashid in the early 9th century. In AD 944 the shrine was destroyed by the fervently Sunni Saboktagin, founder of the Qaznavid dynasty, only to be rebuilt by his son Mahmud in 1009. Both the shrine and the city were ransacked when the Mongols invaded. The present structure in the centre of the complex was built for Shah Abbas I at the beginning of the 17th century.

The actual tomb in the Holy Shrine has stunning gilt edges and is enclosed in a *zarih* (gold latticed cage). This is the fifth such *zarih* to cover the tomb and dates from

2001; it is touched and kissed in a moving climax to the pilgrimage.

The magnificent golden *gonbad* (dome) over the tomb has a circumference of 42.1m and a height of 7m, and above the tomb are some beautiful Quranic inscriptions by renowned 16th-century calligrapher Ali Reza Abbasi. The interior ceiling has some dazzling stalactite stuccowork decorated with multicoloured glass.

The two golden minarets attached to the shrine appear at first to lack symmetry. And yet, their unusual distance means pilgrims entering the complex from Imam Reza St will see the dome between two perfectly aligned minarets.

Do not attempt to enter the actual shrine unless you are a Muslim. Non-Muslims are excluded not because of their faith (or lack thereof), but because there are special cleanliness rituals and prayers to be performed before entering.

Azim-e Gohar Shad Mosque

This fine **mosque** (Great Mosque of Gohar Shad) is one of the best surviving examples of Timurid architecture in Iran. It is no longer open to non-Muslims, but the exterior can be seen as you walk around the complex. The mosque was built by Gohar Shad, one of the most remarkable women in Islamic history. She was queen of a mighty empire, wife of Timur's eldest son Shah Rokh, patron of the arts and a powerful personality in her own right. Constructed between 1405 and 1418, it has four *iwans*, two minarets and some extraordinarily beautiful stalactite mouldings, calligraphic inscriptions and exquisite floral motifs. Its blue dome and cavernous golden portal are also exceptional. The *minbar* (pulpit) next to the mihrab is, according to Shiite tradition, the place where the Mahdi (the 12th or 'hidden' Imam) will sit on the Day of Judgement.

Museums

There are three museums and all are worth visiting. The **Muze-ye Markazi** (Main Museum; Map p323; admission IR3000; ☑ 7.30am-4.30pm Sat-Thu, 7.30am-noon Fri) is the largest and is spread over three floors. On the ground floor, look for the two dazzling double-sided doors in silver and gold dating from the Qajar period and bearing a series of Quranic inscriptions. Nearby, a magnificent 18th-century prayer rug sewn with thousands of tiny pearls is very popular with women pilgrims. Other features include an intricate stone mihrab dating from 1215; a huge 800-year-old wooden door; and a one-tonne stone drinking vessel made in the 12th century.

On the 1st floor the highlight is undoubtedly the display of paintings by renowned modern artist Mahmood Farshchian, including the gorgeous *Fifth Day of Creation* and the intensely moving *Afternoon of Ashura*, which captures the grief-stricken aftermath of the martyrdom of Imam Hossein as his horse returns to camp. This floor also houses a booth selling postcards of those places deemed too holy for your eyes. The basement exhibition is a display of stamps and coins.

Due to construction work, the **Carpet Museum** and **Muze-ye Qu'ran** (Quran Museums; Map p323; admission IR3000; 8am-noon) had been combined when we visited. The Carpet Museum is home to a range of mind-boggling works, including the Carpet of the Seven Beloved Cities, which is said to have taken 10,000 weavers 14 years to make, and has a staggering 30 million knots. The hall where you enter is filled with the trophies of Ali Khamenei's presidency – this is the sort of rubbish world leaders give each other. Upstairs is a collection of more than 100 hand-inscribed Qurans.

BOQ'EH-YE KHAJEH RABI

The 16th-century Boq'eh-ye Khajeh Rabi (Map p319) is an octagonal mausoleum 4km north of central Mashhad. It contains several famous 16th-century inscriptions by Ali Reza Abbasi, one of the greatest Persian calligraphers. The mausoleum stands in the midst of a large cemetery known as **Aramgah-e Khajeh Rabi**, which contains thousands of tombstones of martyrs killed in the Iran-Iraq War. To get here take a shared taxi (IR1000) from outside the train station or just north of the Holy Shrine.

NADER SHAH MUSEUM

The huge statue of Nader Shah that looks down on the king's own mausoleum is about the most exciting thing to see here. The **Nader Shah Museum** (Map p320; 222 4888; cnr Shirazi & Azadi Sts; admission IR30,000; 7.30am-12.30pm & 2-4.30pm, until 7pm summer) is largely devoted to a collection of guns, swords and other militaria, mostly from the time of Nader Shah. Outside the museum stands

a solitary bronze Spanish cannon, dated 1591 and later inscribed in Farsi with the Persian date 1180. How it came to be here is a mystery. Save your money.

OTHER ATTRACTIONS

In the Bazar-e Bozorg, the blue dome of the 15th-century **Mosque of the 72 Martyrs** (Map p323; Masjed-e 72 Tan Shahid), previously known as Shah Mosque, can be seen from the shrine.

Gonbad-e Sabz (Green Dome; Map p320; Falaki-ye Gonbad-e Sabz) in the centre of its own small square is Mashhad's most interesting and best-preserved historical building outside the shrine. It is a small quadrangular mausoleum, once used by Naghshbandi dervishes, and originally built in the Safavid period. It contains the tomb of Sheikh Mohammed Hakim Mo'men, author of a famous book on medicine, and lots of fine metal standards, or *alamats*. Opening hours are inconsistent, but your best is to try in the morning.

Sleeping

Mashhad is bursting with hotels, most of which are bursting with pilgrims. The majority are within a few minutes' walk of the Holy Shrine. For about 10 days before and after No Ruz (about 21 March), and during the summer pilgrimage season, finding a room can be a problem. At other times, most hotels will be ripe for hard bargaining.

BUDGET

There are plenty of mosaferkhunehs around the shrine, but getting into one as a non-Muslim is not always easy. Management rarely see foreign guests and few staff speak English. All the places here have shared bathroom unless specified; all have squat toilets

Tous Hotel (Map p323; /fax 222 4385; Shirazi St; s/tw IR45,000/70,000) This is probably the pick of the budget places, with clean and surprisingly quiet rooms in a lively part of town outside the Holy Shrine. It's hard to find; walk along Shirazi St towards the Shrine until the buildings on the right open out, then turn right and it's about 25m up a lane.

Alaleh Apartment Hotel (Map p320; /fax 859 8508; Beit-ol-Moqaddas Sq; per person IR70,000) Alaleh is showing its age, but it's worth it for what is a four-bed apartment with bathroom and kitchen. It's up a small lane just to the right of Grand Atlas Hotel.

Saba Inn (Map p320; ☎ 222 3515; Andarzgu St; s/tw IR30,000/50,000) No frills to be found here, but the staff are friendly and it's well located. Note, though, that the rooms at the front can be rather noisy.

Hotel Nasr (Map p320; ☎ 854 2554; Onsori St; s/tw IR60,000/80,000) Located above Restaurant Nasr, the rooms here are small and readers report that the shared bathrooms have 'inconsistent' showers. Prices come down fast out of season.

MID-RANGE
There are dozens of mid-range hotels in Mashhad to cater for groups of pilgrims, but there is little character among them and many are decidedly mediocre. Imam Reza St has a couple of decent options, as do Azadi St and Pasdaran Ave.

Karimkhan Apartment Hotel (Map p320; ☎ 854 9407; www.karimkhanhotel.8k.com; Imam Reza St, Karbala Alley; apt IR210,000; P ☒ ☐ ☒) This stylishly decorated place with its sauna and sophisticated front-desk service represents top-end luxury at discount prices. Sadly, it's so good that you can expect the prices to go up. Its location through a courtyard blocks out most of the road noise.

Grand Atlas Hotel (Map p320; ☎ 854 5061; fax 854 7800; Beit-ol-Moqaddas Sq; s/d US$30/40, apt US$60; P ☒ ☐) Considering it's location, the value here is excellent, particularly if you can get a front upper-floor room from where you should have an uninterrupted view over the shrine. The rooms are a bit '80s, but the Grand offers more character than most of the competitors.

Razi Hotel (Map p320; ☎ 854 1122; fax 854 4099; Razi St; s/tw with breakfast US$10/20; ☒) Rooms here certainly represent value for money; they're clean, with a TV, fridge and bathroom. The trade-off is the front-desk service, which is woeful.

Hotel Djavaheri (Map p320; ☎ 859 9817; fax 854 9023; Imam Reza St; s/d/tr IR120,000/180,000/220,000; ☒) The comfortable rooms with fridge and satellite TV are reasonable value for these prices, which are about 25% lower in the low season.

Shiraz Hotel (Map p320; ☎ 841 9247; Daneshgah St; r per person IR100,000; ☒) It's a hike from the Holy Shrine, but the spacious, pleasant rooms here are cheap enough that they make up for the staff, who appeared to be in some sort of group coma when we visited.

Djam Hotel (Map p320; ☎ 859 0041-5; www.jam -hotel.com; Pasdaran Ave; s/d with breakfast US$35/45; ☐ ☒) This is one of the more professionally run hotels in town, with comfortable rooms and efficient service that make up for the fact you have to listen to a muzak version of 'Woman in Love' every time you get into the lift.

Pardis Hotel (Map p320; ☎ 222 3356; fax 222 3831; Imam Khomeini St; s/d/tr US$40/50/65; P ☒) Popular with groups, the rooms here are good and some have decent views of the city and shrine. There is an interesting collection of photos of old Mashhad in the foyer, but we couldn't find the 'licensed bar' referred to in some advertising (we tried!). Hefty discounts can be had here and the restaurant downstairs has been recommended by several readers.

Azadi Hotel (Map p320; ☎ 225 1927; www.azadi hotelmashhad.com; s/d/ste with breakfast US$30/45/50; ☒ ☐ P) Opposite Nader Shah Museum on Azadi St, this busy hotel has reasonable rooms and is popular with honeymooners.

TOP END
Surprisingly, the top end is not as well represented as you'd expect.

Homa Hotel 2 (Map p319; ☎ 761 1001; www .homahotels.com; Khayyam Blvd; s/d with breakfast US$86/120 plus 17% tax; P ☒ ☐ ☒) Easily the best hotel in Mashhad, there's all manner of good stuff here: an indoor pool, spa (both for use according to a gender-based schedule) and several restaurants – Silk Road Restaurant (p327) is the best. Of course, it wouldn't be a Homa Hotel unless it was inconveniently located on the edge of town, and so it is.

Iran Hotel (Map p320; ☎ 222 8010; www.irhotel.com; Andarzgu St; r with breakfast US$54; ☒ ☐) Homa is the best, but for location and value you can't beat this hotel. Some rooms on the upper floors have great views and the management are refreshingly welcoming for a top-end place.

Eating
Considering so many pilgrims come to Mashhad, the range of eateries is a little disappointing. There are the usual fast-food places along Imam Reza St, but because most visitors eat production-line dinners provided as part of their hotel tour package, the traditional dining options are limited. The earthenware pot known as a *dizi* originated in Mashhad, and the soupy meat stew, also

---

WORTH ITS WEIGHT

Saffron is a spice containing stigmas of the *Crocus sativus* plant, used for the natural flavouring and colouring of dishes such as Iranian *chelo* (rice), Cornish saffron cake and Spanish paella. Extracts from the plant can also help with digestive problems and nervous disorders, and there are unproven claims that saffron boosts energy and improves memory.

Over the centuries saffron found its way from Persia to many other empires, where it was used for pharmaceutical purposes, as a spice, in religious ceremonies and as a dye in the paint that decorates holy manuscripts. Cleopatra apparently used to bathe in a mixture that included saffron.

The plant is still grown extensively in southern regions of Khorasan, as well as in the Fars, Kerman and Yazd provinces. Saffron seeds are planted in May or August and the bright pink or violet flowers bloom for about three weeks from mid-October. The stigmas are separated and left to dry in sheds, or hung from the roof in special containers, and then crushed into powder. It takes a staggering 2000 to 3000 flowers to make about 15g of saffron powder.

---

called *dizi*, cooked in it is excellent here. More-pleasant garden restaurants can be found in Torqabeh (p330).

Silk Road Restaurant (Khayyam Blvd; meals IR85,000; ☼ lunch & dinner) This fancy affair serves a range of Iranian and Western food that is usually pretty good.

Pars Restaurant (Map p320; ☎ 222 5331; Imam Khomeini St; meals IR25,000; ☼ lunch & dinner) Often packed with locals, this no-frills place has tasty Iranian food at Iranian prices. The service is fast and furious.

Restaurant Nasr (Map p320; ☎ 854 2554; Imam Reza St, Onsori St; meals IR25,000; ☼ lunch & dinner) The service in this simple place is nothing if not enthusiastic. When we had difficulty with the menu, we were led to the kitchen to present the options – some decent *khoreshts* (thick, meaty stews), a range of kebabs and *bademjun* (eggplant served in various styles).

Similar to Nasr are **Malek Restaurant** (Map p320; ☎ 225 7001; Andarzgu St; meals IR25,000; ☼ lunch & dinner) and **Ferdosi Restaurant** (Map p320; ☎ 854 2884; Imam Reza St; meals IR20,000; ☼ 11am-3am), the latter serving a decent vegetarian curry, but only if you ask for it.

Moein Darbary Restaurant (Map p319; ☎ 878 5248; Kalantari Hwy (Sento St); meals IR55,000; ☼ lunch & dinner Tue-Sun) Not too many surprises on the menu, but what is there is excellent; this is considered one of the best restaurants in town. You'll need a taxi to reach it (about IR6000).

Most of the hotels along Imam Reza St have restaurants that serve good food in pleasant surroundings. Expect to pay about IR40,000 for a meal, including soup, salad and drinks. **Mashhad Hotel** (Map p320; ☎ 222

2666) is arguably the best; **Karimkhan Apartment Hotel** (Map p320; ☎ 854 9407) has also been recommended.

Drinking
FRUIT SHAKES
Vitamin Sara (Map p320; ☎ 222 7998; Shahid Raja'i St; ☼ 8am-11pm Sat-Thu) Probably the best fruit shakes in Iran! Try the shake with half a banana, ice cream, honey and crushed pistachios (IR5500) – on a hot day these are almost orgasm-inducing (well, maybe not *that* good).

TEAHOUSES
Hezardestan Traditional Teahouse (Map p320; ☎ 222 2943; Jannat Mall; meals IR45,000, tea IR6000; ☼ lunch & dinner) Hezardestan is one of the most beautiful teahouses in Iran, with carpets, samovars, antique water pipes, cushions and wooden benches surrounded by walls adorned with scenes from Ferdosi's *Shahnamah*. There is live music most nights and the food is pretty good. However, most locals come here for the tea, smoke and atmosphere; the speciality of the house is *chay khohy*, a tea said to be particularly relaxing. Look for the blue urn at the top of a discreet staircase.

Bagh-e Sabz Teahouse (Map p320; cnr Imam Khomeini & Shahid Raja'i Sts) On the 1st floor above a busy corner, this rare above-ground teahouse was closed when we passed but we subsequently heard it's still a great place to relax with a qalyan, tea and *dizi*, all while watching Mashhad's crush of people on the streets below. For a more local atmosphere, the unnamed subterranean **teahouse**

(Map p320; tea IR2000, qalyan IR5000) in a lane just off Jannat Mall (take the corner where the clothes store has 'Valiasr' on the corner) is popular with working men of all ages – several of whom spoke English when we visited.

Shopping

Mashhad used to be famous as a place to buy turquoise, although many tourists went away more sold on the sales pitch of the dealers than the quality of their turquoise. Even GN Curzon, in his 1892 book *Persia and the Persian Question*, said:

> It would be quite a mistake to suppose...the traveller can pick up valuable stones at a moderate price...I did not see a single good specimen either in Meshed or Teheran, though I made constant inquiries.

The mine at Neishabur is still one of the largest in Iran, but the real gems are invariably carted off to Tehran or further for sale. Buy only if you have a clear idea of the value and quality of what you see, rather than buying the sales pitch.

Mashhad has several bazaars and shopping arcades to tempt the pilgrims, though most of them flog modern Chinese 'treasures' rather than traditional products of Khorasan. The **Bazar-e Reza** (Map p320; ⏰ 8am-8pm Sat-Thu) is 800m long and you can buy gorgeous fabrics and rugs, as well as nuts, honey and saffron. Saffron is cheap in Mashhad; a 10g box costs about IR15,000 and makes a great souvenir (see the boxed text 'Worth Its Weight', p327). Try to resist the considerable temptation to buy an over-saturated photograph of yourself superimposed upon the Holy Shrine or a scene from the Swiss Alps.

Getting There & Away

AIR

Mashhad has regular flights to most major centres in Iran, and a few regional capitals outside the country. It's worth booking early, particularly during the summer months and around religious festivals.

Domestic Services

Iran Air flies directly from Mashhad to the following places:

Destination	Price (IR)	Flights (weekly)
Abadan	400,000	2
Ahvaz	369,000	2
Bandar-e Abbas	347,000	2
Esfahan	281,000	4
Rasht	293,000	2
Sari	204,000	2
Shiraz	319,000	5
Tabriz	376,000	2
Tehran	255,000	70
Yazd	237,000	2
Zahedan	257,000	2

The number of flights is often reduced during the quieter winter months. The efficient, English-speaking staff at **Iran Air** (☎ 225 2080; airport information ☎ 199; Imam Khomeini St; ⏰ 7.30am-6.30pm Sat-Thu, 7.30am-3.30pm Fri) should be your first port of call.

Most other domestic airlines also fly to Mashhad. **Iran Aseman** (☎ 225 8200; www.iaa.ir; Andarzgu St) flies twice daily to Tehran; Mahan Air links Mashhad with Kerman twice a week for IR256,000; and **Saha Airlines** (☎ 221 9294, saha2@isiran-net.com; Andarzgu St) flies twice-daily to Tehran in summer, and twice-weekly in winter for the same prices as Iran Air. Both flights take 90 minutes.

If you arrive in Mashhad by air, there is a useful hotel reservation counter inside the arrivals hall. Although it handles only mid-range and top-end places, it can save you driving all over town in a taxi. The airport can be pretty chaotic and there are no flight announcements in English so you must pay close attention to the departures board.

International Services

Mashhad has some handy connections, particularly to Central Asia and the Arabian Peninsula. **Iran Aseman** (☎ 225 8200) has weekly flights to Bishkek in Kyrgyzstan; three flights a week to Dubai in the UAE; two flights to Kuwait; and a handy weekly flight to Kabul.

Iran Air (☎ 225 2080) has some flights from Mashhad to Kuwait (one way IR770,000) and Bahrain (one way IR1,222,000) during peak pilgrimage season. However, seats are hard to come by as most are booked out by travel agencies in the Gulf countries.

BUS, MINIBUS & SAVARI

The chaotic **bus station** (☎ 99 001) is at the southern end of Mashhad, but easy to reach by any shared taxi (IR400) heading south along Imam Reza St.

For Tabas, it is quicker to take a bus to Yazd, although you may have to pay the full fare; similarly, you may have to pay the Tehran price even if you're only going to Shahrud.

Check the security situation before travelling overland from Mashhad to Zahedan or Kerman – the constant smuggling of drugs along the border has been known to cause problems. Expect frequent baggage searches along the way.

To catch a minibus to Tus (IR800), go to Shohada Sq. For Torqabeh (IR400), buses leave from the kerbside 100m north of Shohada Sq on Khajeh Rabi St.

Useful daily services are listed in the following table; prices are for Mercedes buses unless noted:

Destination	Price (IR)	Duration (hr)	Frequency
Esfahan (Volvo)	75,000	22	6-8pm
Gorgan	20,000	10½	6-10am & 6-9pm
Kerman (Volvo)	65,000	16	daily
Neishabur	6000 2½	114	Frequent all day
Sarakhs	6500	3	7-8am
Sari	27,000	12	6-8am, 5-7pm
Shahrud	16,000	10	Frequent
Tabas (via Birjand)	24,000	10	daily
Taybad	224	3	6am-11am
Tehran	35,000	14	Frequent
Yazd	45,000	16	daily, 6pm
Zahedan (Volvo)	65,000	15	daily

TO/FROM AFGHANISTAN & TURKMENISTAN

To get to Sarakhs from Mashhad, take a bus (IR6500, three hours) from the bus station; at the time of research, Taavoni No 10 had 17 buses daily in the morning. From Sarakhs, simply take whatever is going to Mashhad. Shared taxis from Sarakhs to Mashhad shouldn't cost more than IR17,000. For full information see the boxed texts on p332 for Bajgiran, p333 for Sarakhs and p334 for Dogharon and Afghanistan.

TRAIN

The 926km train journey to Tehran makes an excellent alternative to the plane or long hours of bus travel. The **train station** (☎ 139) is easily reached by shared taxi (IR1000 from the centre of town), and taxis from the

yellow booth outside the station cost about IR5000 to most central hotels.

This is Iran's busiest train line but tickets can still be hard to come by. Therefore, it's worth booking ahead, especially on Thursday and before public holidays. There are 11 trains daily between Mashhad and Tehran in winter and 15 in peak season. There is a wide range of prices and services, ranging from IR24,850 for a seat on the all stops, through to IR54,700 for a bunk in a six-berth compartment on the Simorgh train, and IR112,800 for dinner, breakfast and a comfortable bed in a four-berth compartment on the express Green train.

The following services go through Tehran and shouldn't be undertaken without a good book: Esfahan (IR76,650, 22 hours), leaving 10.50pm Wednesday and Saturday; Tabriz (IR75,600, 26 hours), leaving 8.30am Wednesday and Saturday; Yazd (IR89,750, 23 hours), leaving 9am Friday; and Ahvaz (IR97,850, 30 hours), leaving 9am Monday.

To/From Turkmenistan

A train runs to the border at Sarakhs, but because the gauge width changes, it goes no further. A train leaves Mashhad daily at 3.30pm, arriving at Sarakhs around 6pm, *in sha'Allah*. The train returns the following morning, leaving Sarakhs at 6am. Tickets cost IR5500.

Getting Around
TO/FROM THE AIRPORT

There is a monopoly on taxis from (but not to) the airport, so unless you jump into a Paykan lurking outside departures the trip will cost you IR15,000 to the centre of town. Far cheaper, but inconvenient if you have a lot of luggage, is the semi-regular public bus between the airport terminal and Basij Mustazafin Sq.

BUS

Most hotels are within walking distance of the shrine, so local buses are not normally needed. The following buses leave regularly from around the Holy Shrine: No 5 to the bus terminal; No 6 to Kuhsangi Park. From Shohada Sq: No 18 goes to Torqabeh; No 20 to Ferdowsi's tomb in Tus; and No 30 to Boq'eh-ye Khajeh Rabi'. Bus numbers in Iran change with annoying regularity, so ask before you climb aboard.

TAXI

Fares for shared taxis around Mashhad are reasonably low, costing about IR500 for a short ride, or IR1500 right across town. You won't get far in a private taxi for less than IR3000.

AROUND MASHHAD

You can visit most places around Mashhad by public transport, but it's worth chartering a private taxi for about IR20,000 per hour if you want to see as much as possible in one day. Otherwise, hop on a guided tour (p322).

Torqabeh   طرقبه

☎ 0512 / elevation 1333m

This pretty village with tree-lined streets is reputed to be 5°C cooler than Mashhad at any time of year and makes a quiet alternative to the bustle of the city. It is famous for handicrafts, carpets, baskets and carvings, and it's a really fantastic place to stroll around and do a bit of souvenir hunting. Although the population is small, the village stretches for several kilometres through low valleys overflowing with cherry, apple, apricot and walnut trees, the produce of which is highly sought after in Arab countries. The blossoms in spring are spectacular.

No trip to Mashhad would be complete without an evening visit to Torqabeh, especially in summer. Every night until 1am or 2am, the wonderful traditional garden restaurants for which Torqabeh is famous are filled with Mashhadis sitting under the stars, smoking qalyans in a delightfully relaxed and festive atmosphere.

The restaurants begin about 500m beyond the main roundabout and continue for almost 5km. Wherever you go the *dizi* and assorted kebabs are good. If you can't decide, the **Abshar Restaurant** (☎ 422 2755; Toroghdar Rd; ◷ lunch & dinner) serves some truly delicious kababs. Also don't leave without trying *bastani*, the local ice cream, available from the sweet shops on the main roundabout.

GETTING THERE & AWAY

Torqabeh is 25km east of Mashhad. Buses to Torqabeh (usually the No 18) leave from 100m north of Shohada Sq in Mashhad every half-hour or so.

Tus (Ferdosi)   طوس فردوسی

☎ pop / elevation 1044m

Tus (also known as Ferdosi) was an important city and a leading centre of learning until it was sacked first by the Mongols in the early 13th century, and then by Tamerlane's forces in 1389. The devastation was so great that the city was abandoned. Apart from the citadel's crumbling walls, little remains. The present-day village is best known to most Iranians as the home town of the epic poet Ferdosi, whose mausoleum lies over what is believed to be his exact place of death. It is a serene place, and an easy trip from Mashhad.

SIGHTS
Ferdosi's Tomb

Set in its own park at the edge of Tus, the pale-stone **Mausoleum of Ferdosi** (IR30,000; ◷ 8am-4pm, 7pm summer) was built in 1933 in preparation for the celebration of the 1000th anniversary of the poet's death (even though he died about AD 1020). It was rebuilt in 1934 because the first version was thought too plain, and again in 1964 after it started to sink on its weak foundations.

There has been a tomb of sorts on this site since Ferdosi died. He was supposed to be buried in the local Muslim cemetery, but it was suggested his writings were so anti-Islamic that he was not worthy of this honour. Instead he was buried in the garden of the home in which he had lived for decades. These same extreme feelings against Ferdosi resurfaced during the earliest and most violent throes of the 1979 revolution and the mausoleum was partially destroyed. Today he is revered once again, his tomb being one of Iran's most popular domestic tourism drawcards.

There is a marble statue of Ferdosi in the garden and, behind the tomb, some mud-brick remains of the city walls of ancient Tus, which are labelled in English. The small **Tus Museum** (admission IR10,000; ◷ 8am-4pm), inside the park, contains a collection of ceramics and pottery inspired by Ferdosi and a 73kg copy of the *Shahnamah*. A restaurant in the garden serves cold drinks and simple meals for lunch. For more on Ferdosi see the boxed text 'The Great Iranian Poets', p65.

Boq'e-ye Hordokieh'

The **Boq'e-ye Hordokieh'** (Gonbad-e Haruniyeh; ◷ 8am-4pm) is a 14th-century mausoleum about 1km south of Ferdosi's Tomb on the road to Mashhad. It is popularly associated with Haroun ar-Rashid, the famous Abbasid caliph whose earthly remains are, however, generally accepted to have been buried near those of Imam Reza in Mashhad. There are plenty of other theories – including that it was a prison for the killer of Imam Reza – but the only solid evidence uncovered so far is the remains of an ancient mihrab on the exterior of the northern wall, suggesting it was a mosque at some stage.

Between Ferdosi's tomb and Boq'e-ye Hordokieh', **Arg-e Tus** (the crumbling ancient citadel of Tus) is visible across the windswept plain to the west.

GETTING THERE & AWAY
Tus is 23km from Mashhad on a turn-off east of the road to Gorgan. Buses (IR600, 50 minutes) and minibuses direct to the mausoleum (IR700, 30 to 40 minutes) leave about every 20 to 30 minutes during the day from Shohada Sq in Mashhad. Shared taxis (IR4000, 20 minutes) leave from the same square in Mashhad, and hover outside Ferdosi's Tomb in Tus alongside the private taxis (IR20,000).

Mashhad to Neishabur
There are a couple of places well worth seeing on the road between Mashhad and Neishabur, and it's a good idea to hire a taxi for the trip.

SANG BAST
The Qaznavid minaret and dome at **Sang Bast** (37km from Mashhad) is worth a quick look mainly so that you can climb to the top of the single minaret, all that remains of a once grand Qaznavid-era caravanserai. It's on the old road to Neishabur, so your best bet is to see it with a taxi tour.

BINALUD
The Timurid-era **Fakhr Davood** (admission free) is unusual as far as Silk Road caravanserais are concerned – it is covered with an impressive domed roof, and has four fortified towers at its corners. Renovated in the early '90s, Fakhr Davood is one of the best examples of the Safavid-era caravanserai you're likely to see. Inside the entrance a stairway leads to the roof, which affords views of nearby Binalud village and the surrounding countryside. A caretaker lives in the caravanserai

but if he's not there ask around in the village, where you might also be invited into a home to see women weaving huge carpets.

BOQ'EH-YE QADAMGAH
This charming 17th-century octagonal **mausoleum** sits in a small, pretty garden in the otherwise dreary village of Qadamgah. The village name means 'Place of the Foot', so-called because inside the mausoleum there is a stone slab with what are believed to be the (very large) footprints of Imam Reza. Just outside the mausoleum a few steep steps lead to the source of a mountain spring, apparently created by Imam Reza himself.

This place is on the busy itinerary for pilgrims who want to see everything to do with Imam Reza – questioning aloud the authenticity of the size of the Imam's prints is not a good idea. The mausoleum and village are just north of the main road between Neishabur and Mashhad. Take a shared taxi from Neishabur (about IR6000, 38km) or get off any bus heading west from Mashhad and walk north for 1km from the main road.

Neishabur نیشابور
☎ 0551 / pop 160,000 / elevation 1209m
Due west of Mashhad, Neishabur was the earliest known capital of Khorasan. Archaeologists believe the area was first settled in the 3rd century AD, and by the Seljuk period had grown into a thriving literary, artistic and academic centre. Neishabur is now most famous as the birthplace and resting place of the poet, mathematician and astronomer, Omar Khayyam.

SIGHTS
Omar Khayyam's Tomb
The simple tombstone of Omar Khayyam (see the boxed text 'The Great Iranian Poets', p65) and the tall and narrow tiled-concrete lozenges linked above it seem vaguely out of place at the **tomb** of an 11th-century poet. However, the geometric designs, together with inscriptions from Khayyam's works, honour both his mastery of the science of mathematics and the art of poetry.

The manicured gardens surrounding the tomb, **Bagh-e Mahrugh** (admission IR 25,000; ☽ 8am-sunset), are a good place to sit around and drink tea with Neishabur's famous crystallised sugar (see p76 for more on the place of sugar in the tea-drinking ritual). As you sit you're likely to hear random Iranians breaking into verse as they recite from Khayyam's works. In the gardens is **Imamzadeh-ye Mohammed Mahrugh**, a fine 16th-century domed mausoleum. The gardens and tombs are about 1km south of Neishabur, but if you are walking here from town, you will need to ask directions.

Caravanserai

The partially restored caravanserai, on the northwestern corner of a roundabout on Imam Khomeini St between the town and Omar Khayyam's Tomb, dates back to Safavid times and is worth a quick look. It contains a couple of souvenir shops and a small **museum** (admission free; ☺ 8am-5pm, until 7pm summer).

SLEEPING & EATING

ITTO Tourist Inn (☎ 33 445; s/d US$20/25, apt US$50; ✷ Ⓟ) Also known as Neishabur Inn, this place is found next to the city park in the centre of town. The rooms are comfortable enough and the apartments seldom used. The restaurant is quite good, with meals coming to about IR35,000. There are plenty of hamburger joints and kababis along the main street.

GETTING THERE & AWAY

Several minibuses leave every morning from Mashhad to Neishabur (IR6000, 2½ hours, 114km), or you can just hop on any bus heading along the main road towards Semnan, and get off at Neishabur.

Radkan رادخان

In a field near the village of Radkan, about 75km northwest of Mashhad, the mysterious 25m-high **Radkan Tower** has baffled scientists and locals for centuries. Long believed to have been built as a tomb, or even for a coronation, Iranian archaeoastronomer Manoochehr Arian has uncovered strong evidence to suggest that it's a highly sophisticated instrument for studying the stars.

Mr Arian says the tower was built in AD 1261 by a group of astronomers led by Nasruddin Tusi (Nasir Al-Tusi; 1201–74), the man credited with finally explaining the discrepancies between the Aristotelian theory of planetary movement and Ptolemy's planetary model, a feat achieved at an observatory built at Maraqeh (p132).

The Radkan Tower was designed so that the sun would shine directly through its doors and other niches only on solstice and equinox days. Thus a 20 March visit could be quite memorable. For more on the tower, check out Mr Arian's website (www.jamejamshid.com).

To get here, turn off the main road and head for the village of Radkan. Turn right at the modern tower and go 3km down a dirt road to the tower.

CROSSING THE TURKMENISTAN BORDER AT BAJGIRAN

This mountaintop border is the most convenient to Ashghabat, the capital of Turkmenistan. Buses and savaris make frequent trips between Quchan and Bajgiran, from where a shuttle will take you the last 3km to the border. The border is theoretically open 24 hours, but 8.30am to 6pm is a safer bet as times change frequently. Once through the Iranian formalities, a shuttle will take you 5km downhill to the Turkmen immigration post. Depending on the mood of the officials, it will take between 30 and 90 minutes to clear immigration and customs, assuming you have your visa in order and (if you are coming on a tourist visa) your voucher is with the immigration officers. It's important not to lose your temper here and act as conservatively as possible. Once through, if you're not met by a guide or agent you'll take a shuttle through the remaining 25km or so of no-man's land (about US$1 to US$3) to the Yablonovka checkpoint at the bottom of the mountain, where you collect your entry/exit card. This will only be issued if a representative from the agency that arranged your letter of introduction is there to meet you and sort out the paperwork, so be sure to synchronise your watches. From here it's less than 10km to the city centre (US$1 to US$2 in a taxi). It's best to change only a little money at the border.

Crossing into Iran here, you may be lucky and find a savari going direct to Mashhad (about IR50,000, five hours). Otherwise, take whatever you can to Quchan and change.

Tomb of Darius the Great, Naqsh-e Rostam (p256)

Eagle-headed griffin statue, Persepolis (p252)

Cyrus' Private Palace, Pasargadae (p256)

BRADLEY

Azim-e Gohar Shad, Mashhad (p324)

JOHN BORTHWICK

Bagh-e Shahzade, Mahan
(p290)

Kalat (p333)

ANTHONY HAM

MARTIN MOOS

Aramgah-e Shah Ne'matollah Vali,
Mahan (p290)

QUCHAN
قوچان

☎ 0581 / pop 90,000 / elevation 1317m

People heading to Turkmenistan via the Bajgiran (Iran) and Howdan (Turkmenistan) border crossing might need to transit through Quchan and then pick up onward transportation. If you arrive too late to head on, the centrally located **Hotel Khayyam** (IR50,000) has basic rooms and a restaurant. All the taxi drivers know it.

MASHHAD TO SARAKHS
Sarakhs
سرخس

☎ 0512 / elevation 925m

The town of Sarakhs, once an important staging post along the famous Silk Road, is right on the Turkmenistan border, 185km northeast of Mashhad by road (but only 120km by train). The most notable thing to see in Sarakhs itself is the 14th-century **Gonbad Sheikh Loghman Baba**, the vast domed tomb of this famous 10th-century fableteller. However, on the way you should not miss the Rubat Sharaf caravanserai. A savari from Sarakhs to Mashhad should cost about IR17,000; otherwise, just take whatever's going in your direction. From Mashhad, take a bus (IR6500, three hours, 185km) from the bus station.

Rubat Sharaf Caravanserai
کاروانسرای رباط شرف

One of the biggest, oldest and most impressive caravanserais in Iran, Rubat Sharaf is worth making the long trip from Mashhad, even if you're not crossing the border. Built in AD 1128, this caravanserai is an exceptional *abgineh* (mirror), as it has two courtyards. The first, nearest the hill, was used by soldiers as stables, while the second was used by nobles and kings. Superb calligraphy decorates its *iwan*, either side of which are underground waterways. This is a great place just to wander around and explore; your imagination will likely be your only company, except perhaps for the odd sleeping shepherd.

For Rubat Sharaf, get off at Shorleq, about 130km from Mashhad, and follow the road south for 6km. Easier is hiring a taxi for the day or taking a tour with Mashhad's **Adibian Travel Agency** (Map p320); ☎ 859 8151; www.adibiantours.com; 56 Pasdaran Ave; 7.30am-8pm).

KALAT
کلات

☎ 0512 / elevation 512m

This dramatic natural fortress, also known as Gonbad-e Kabud (Blue Dome), is legendary throughout Iran as the impregnable redoubt where Nader Shah retreated ahead of his considerable band of enemies, and one of the only places to resist the armies of Tamerlane. In a steep and beautiful 36km-long valley 150km north of Mashhad, you don't need to have commanded an army to see why Kalat became the last resort of choice for rebels on the run.

To fully appreciate Kalat's natural impregnability, ask to be let out at the entrance to the tunnel that runs beneath the towering cliffs. Follow the creek and unpaved track that twists through the 500m-long, narrow canyon, one of only two entrances to the valley. High on the cliff face to the right is an unfinished stone tablet carved with poetry praising Nader Shah. A few fortified watchtowers sit on rocky outcrops from where there are spectacular views and where a small number of troops could control access to the valley.

The modern inhabitants of the valley trace their origins to the Germanj sect of Kurdish tribes who were transferred to

---

CROSSING THE TURKMENISTAN BORDER AT SARAKHS

The border posts at Sarakhs (Iran) and Saraghs (Turkmenistan) are open from about 8am to 5pm; totally inconvenient for the trains that arrive from Mashhad at 6pm and leave for the trip back at 6am. No transport goes right across the border, so once through immigration on the Iranian side get a shuttle (about IR4000) to the Turkmen immigration post. From there, once entry formalities are complete (see the boxed text 'Crossing the Turkmenistan Border at Bajgiran', p332), buses and shared taxis run occasionally to Mary (three to four hours) or Ashghabat (six hours) from the bus/train station, though transport slows later in the afternoon. It's wise to change some manat (the currency of Turkmenistan) at the border, but save any large transactions for the cities. If you get stuck, there is a small, cheap (about IR40,000) and simple unnamed hotel on the Iranian side of the border.

Kalat during the Safavid dynasty to keep guard against northern invaders.

Spring is the best time to visit, when the countryside turns green and the tents of nomads dot the surrounding plains. It can also be beautiful in winter after a light snowfall.

From Kalat it's possible, in your own transport, to reach the Tandoureh National Park, though there are no facilities for visitors.

Sights

About 5km from the western entrance to the valley in the village of Kabud Gonbad lies the **Khorshid Palace** (Sun Palace), with its distinctive circular stone tower on an octagonal base. Set amid lush lawns, the palace is thought by local historians to have been built by Nader Shah as a mausoleum rather than a palace.

The exterior panels are decorated with intricate carvings of fruit (pineapples and pears) not found in Khorasan, suggesting they were completed by artisans Nader Shah brought with him from his Indian conquests. The magnificent interior is decorated with Quranic calligraphy and the 16 perfectly proportioned sunken alcoves are a particular feature. A small kiosk at the entrance sells drinks.

The beautiful blue dome is the highlight of the small **Kabud Gonbad Mosque**. It was built under the supervision of Nader Shah from 1736 to 1747, although there is some brickwork on the left as you enter that dates from Seljuk times.

Sleeping & Eating

Shareri Hotel (☎ 272 3298; s/tw IR100,000/140,000) This small hotel has six simple suites and a restaurant. Room prices halve in winter.

Restoran-e Khorshid does reasonably priced meals that, surprise, surprise, consist largely of kebabs and rice. It's 400m west of the Khorshid Palace on the southern side of the road. There is also a smattering of grocery stores along the main street.

Getting There & Away

The cheapest option is to take a semi-regular bus (IR6000, three hours) from Mashhad although it's a long trip that won't allow you much time to explore the valley. Buses leave from the intersection of Kamyar St and Khaje Rabi' St in the north of

---

CROSSING THE AFGHANISTAN BORDER AT DOGHARON

After 20 years, this marker on the old Hippie Trail is once again open. And it's easy. Most travellers take the bus direct from Mashhad to Herat (leaves early daily from each end). If you go solo, take any transport from Taybad for the 20km to the border, hopefully avoiding a long line of trucks. You'll be stamped out pretty quickly and moved on a few hundred metres to the Afghan border at Dogharon. Once through there (again, fairly smartly), a couple of dollars will get you into one of the vehicles waiting to take you the last 135km of brand new highway to Herat. The border is open from 7.30am to 4.30pm, though check these times at the consulate when getting your visa.

Mashhad, although the actual place seems to change so ask around.

A private taxi will cost about IR250,000 for the day but allows you to stop off and admire the rolling hills and poplar groves of Central Asia's southern steppes, and eat a picnic lunch at one of the many shady roadside streams en route. Mashhad's **Adibian Travel Agency** (Map p320; ☎ 859 8151; www.adibiantours.com; 56 Pasdaran Ave; ⏱ 7.30am-8pm) runs professional tours for US$75 per car of up to three people. The price drops considerably if you can get a group together.

TORBAT-E JAM   تربت جام
☎ 0528 / pop 70,000

On the way to the Afghanistan border, Torbat-e Jam is a sleepy town that has seldom shown up on travellers' radars. But with the border open, people are stopping to see the town's incredible **Sheikh Ahmad Jami mausoleum complex**, where 10 buildings entwine around the grave of the famous 12th-century Sunni mystic and poet.

The attractions here are the very well-preserved mosques that date from different periods. They allow you the rare opportunity to compare different architectural styles as you step from room to room. Sheikh Ahmad Jami's grave rests under a very old pistachio tree in the courtyard – his story told on two white tablets. The door in the right side of the *iwan* leads to the **Gonbad-e Safid**, dating from about 1465. Through another courtyard is the **New Mosque**, which is actually about 600 years old; look for the magnificent vaulted ceilings and octagonal columns.

Back in the courtyard, head for the far corner where, with another key, you can see more fine, high vaulting and calligraphy inscriptions. Back at the front *iwan*, a small door on the left leads to the 14th-century **Kermani Mosque**, named after Massoud Kerman who created the fantastic mihrab and calligraphy inside. To get an idea of the genius involved in such art, compare it with the restored sections. Kerman's name appears in the right panel of the mihrab; ask the gatekeeper to show you.

Through the 730-year-old wooden doors in the *iwan* is the oldest part of the complex, the so-called **Khaneh Ghe**, which was built about 1264. Inside there are seven wooden doors from India, set into walls covered with ancient graffiti. The domed ceiling is decorated with frescoes that have survived incredibly well.

If you come alone, the gatekeeper Gholam Ali Keliddar will probably direct you to the domed chamber opposite the main gate to get permission. There is little English spoken here so to get the most from a visit it's worth taking a guide – Towhid from **Adibian Travel Agency** (Map p320; ☎ 859 8151, www.adibiantours.com; 56 Pasdaran Ave; ☉ 7.30am-8pm) in Mashhad is excellent.

Sleeping & Eating

Movarid Hotel (☎ 222 0713; Al Mahdi St; s/tw IR100,000/150,000) This friendly, family-run hotel is the best option. Rooms have a TV and fridge but the bathroom is shared. Look for a three-storey white building on the main street with 'Sefid' written on the side and a billiard room underneath.

Sadaf Restaurant (☎ 222 0716; Al Mahdi St; meals IR30,000; ☉ lunch & dinner) Serves good Iranian food. Cheaper fare is not too hard to find along this street.

Getting There & Away

Buses to and from Mashhad (IR7000, 2½ hours) leave fairly frequently in the morning, less so after lunch. Savaris are also available. To get to the border, pick up any transport coming through from Mashhad or take a savari.

TAYBAD
☎ 0529

تایباد

Taybad, 224km southeast of Mashhad, is the nearest town to the border post with Afghanistan. Taybad's main attraction is the imposing 14th-century **Molana Mosque**, honouring the Sufi mystic Sheikh Zeyn al-Din (d. 1389). Otherwise, there's little reason to hang around.

There are regular buses to Mashhad (IR9,000, three hours). For the border, jump on anything going east.

Directory

ACCOMMODATION

Iran has a reasonable choice of accommodation, from tiny cells in noisy mosaferkhunehs (basic lodging houses) to luxury rooms in world-class hotels. Camping, however, is almost nonexistent, and you'll do well to find anything resembling an ecoresort.

The Orwellian-sounding Ministry of Culture & Islamic Guidance categorises most hotels and sets the prices they can charge, for both local and foreign guests. In mid-range and top-end establishments foreign guests usually have to pay between 30% and 50% more than Iranians. Managers are generally open to a bit of friendly negotiation, especially during the low season between mid-October and mid-March. Prices inevitably fall if you agree to stay for more than one night.

Prices tend to be highest and hotels busiest during the second half of March for No Ruz, and during the summer months. Many hotels consider No Ruz the beginning of the high season, and rates remain about 20% higher until around October. In places such as the Caspian Sea coast prices can rise by 50% during this time. We have provided high-season prices throughout the book.

Mid-range and top-end places tend to quote prices in US dollars to foreigners; they will, however, usually accept rials. For foreigners, mid-range and top-end places

---

PRACTICALITIES

- Electrical current is 220V AC, 50Hz. Wall sockets are the European, two round-pin type.

- Major English-language dailies available in Tehran and some other large cities include the relatively balanced *Iran Daily*; the liberal *Iran News*, which offers good international coverage; the *Kayham International*, which is somewhere to the right of Genghis Khan; and the *Tehran Times*, which is thorough, but offers the government line.

- All Iranian broadcasters are controlled by the state; however, many Iranians have access to satellite television, including several stations broadcasting in Farsi from California.

- On Iranian TV channels 1 to 4 are national, 5 and 6 province-based. Channel 4 has 15 minutes of English news at 11pm.

- Good frequencies for the BBC World Service include 11760, 15575 and 17640kHz; and for VOA 1197, 11760 and 15205kHz.

- Iran uses the metric system. A conversion chart is on the inside front cover. You may still come across ancient Persian *sir* (about 75g) and *charak* (10 *sir*) in some remote places.

prices are often quoted in US dollars. In this book, if the hotel asks for US dollars then the price we list is in that currency, however you will almost always be able to pay in rials if you prefer. Most hotels will have their official prices displayed on a wall in reception, though not always in English.

Hotels will probably want to keep your passport overnight in case the police want to inspect it. You rarely need to bring your own soap or towel to an Iranian hotel, but you'll probably need to provide your own toilet paper. Checkout time is 2pm. As you get off the beaten track you're likely to encounter heart-warming hospitality that sucks you into 'real' homestays. It's worth coming to Iran prepared with presents to express your gratitude, as paying cash for such accommodation might be inappropriate. Sending postcards and photos to your hosts once you get home will be greatly appreciated.

In this book we present accommodation options under budget, mid-range and top-end categories when appropriate, but within these headings the venues are listed in order of author preference.

Camping

Camping is not really a viable option. There are very few official camping grounds, and unless you can make yourself look like a nomad, camping anywhere else will draw unwanted attention from the authorities. If you do choose to camp rough, try to make sure you're nowhere near one of Iran's many military facilities. And remember that camping anywhere within binocular (or machine-gun) range of a border is unwise.

Long-distance trekkers and mountaineers who obviously need to camp should still discuss plans with the provincial tourist office first (p359). The office may be able to write a letter of introduction, arrange a guide or help in other ways. It can also alert you to dangers such as wild animals or security problems.

Hotels
BUDGET
As well as mosaferkhunehs, some basic one and two-star hotels have rooms that fall into the budget range, and some of them are excellent value. In these places you normally have a bathroom with at least a shower (usually hot), and often a toilet. You might even get lucky and find a telephone, television and/or fridge,

but don't expect much English. Unless you're on the Persian Gulf coast, the heating and hot water will almost certainly be working.

Prices in this range start at about IR50,000/60,000 for a single/double and go up to about IR100,000/120,000, depending on your negotiating skills. On the down side, double beds are almost unheard of in the budget range, you're unlikely to get breakfast and some places are not as fastidious as they could be, so watch out for those telltale hairs on your pillow and don't be afraid to ask for fresh sheets.

MID-RANGE
Some two-star hotels, and all three- and four-star places will have a private bathroom with hot shower and toilet, and almost certainly a phone, fridge and TV (sometimes with BBC World and Deutsche Welt). There might even be a reasonable restaurant, and breakfast will often be included. On toilet paper, the odds are about even; bath plugs are a long shot. Prices start at about US$15/20 for a single/double and go up to as much as US$50/70. Like a 40-something boxer, a lot of places in this range charge rates that reflect a more glorious past than the beaten-around present, so negotiation is a distinct possibility.

TOP END
Apart from a few exceptions, many of Iran's five-star hotels are old enough that they used to be called Sheraton or InterContinental, and the décor, like the Bee Gees, is now so old it's become retro-cool. Sadly, this character development wasn't intentional and, ironically, now that they look so cool these places will almost certainly be refitted in typically bland modern-hotel style. Old or new, these hotels have the familiar five-star range of restaurants and luxury services, and some have bookshops, private taxi services, and carpet shops. They all have swimming pools, but at the Bee Gees–era establishments the outdoor pools are empty and serve only to frustrate you on a hot day. Prices are astronomical by Iranian standards, but pretty reasonable by those of the West, starting from about US$75/95 for a single/double and rising to about US$160/200. Check that the price includes tax, which is usually about 17%.

Mosaferkhunehs
Mosaferkhunehs (literally 'travellers' houses') invariably fall into the budget range in this

book. A mosaferkhuneh can offer anything from a bed in a noisy, grotty, male-only dorm (for about IR20,000 per person per night) to a small, simple, private room, usually with just a sink, for about IR40,000. Sometimes there is not even a shared shower, and many have no sign in English.

Sadly, the police refuse to let all *mosaferkhunehs* accept foreigners. If none will have you (as is sometimes the case in Bushehr), you might be able to persuade the local police to issue a permit allowing you to stay.

We have received some thoroughly justified complaints about the cleanliness, noisiness and overall crapness of some *mosaferkhunehs*. However, until the Iranian tourism industry picks up enough for more cheapies to be built, they will continue to be the best option for those on the tightest budgets. It's worth noting, too, that some women have found the overwhelmingly male atmosphere in some *mosaferkhunehs* uncomfortable.

Suites & Homestays

Along the Caspian Sea coast and in those northwestern rural resort-villages most frequented by Iranian tourists, you'll find locals renting out rooms in their homes. In the more popular places such as Kelardasht, Ramsar, Sara'eyn and Masuleh, such options include 'suites', which are furnished, self-contained apartments or bungalows, though these can be in short supply in summer when prices rise by up to 400%. In Sara'eyn and Kandovan several shopkeepers offer more basic rooms above their stores. Cheaper but more interesting, though rarely offered on a commercial basis except in Masuleh and Gazor Khan (Alamut), are family homestays.

Some suites and almost all rooms/homestays are unmarked in Farsi let alone English so it's just a case of asking around for an *otagh* (room). Food is generally not included.

ACTIVITIES

If you love the great outdoors and can get a visa long enough to allow it, Iran has plenty of space and scenery where you can trek, climb and even ski to your heart's content.

Beach Going

Iranians are not really sun-worshippers and even if they were, the dress code (women

must swim in full hejab) and sexual segregation of the beaches takes much of the potential fun out of lying on them. A few Persian Gulf beaches at least have some golden sand. The Caspian coast is very popular for its green backdrop and damp climate but not really for the scraggy, rubbish-strewn ribbon of ugly black-sand. A few expensive hotels have their own private beaches, but even these are far from enticing: don't expect the Costa del Sol or French Riviera.

Cycling

Iran's roads are well surfaced. Main routes can be terrifyingly truck-dominated but minor country routes would be very well-suited to cycle touring. You'll find very few locals pushing the pedals but a few over-landers brave the traffic en route between Europe and Asia (p372).

SAFETY GUIDELINES FOR DIVING

Before embarking on a scuba diving, skin diving or snorkelling trip, carefully consider the following points to ensure a safe and enjoyable experience:

- Possess a current diving certification card from a recognised scuba diving instructional agency (if scuba diving).

- Obtain reliable information about physical and environmental conditions at the dive site (eg from a reputable local dive operation).

- Be aware of local laws, regulations and etiquette about marine life and the environment.

- Dive only at sites within your realm of experience; if available, engage the services of a competent, professionally trained dive instructor or dive master.

- Be aware that underwater conditions vary significantly from one region, or even site, to another. Seasonal changes can significantly alter any site and dive conditions. These differences influence the way divers dress for a dive and what diving techniques they use.

- Ask about the environmental characteristics that can affect your diving and how locally trained divers deal with these considerations.

Diving

The only recognised site for scuba diving and snorkelling is Kish Island, and it's good value for money (p265).

Mountaineering

It may come as a surprise to learn that Iran boasts several high mountains, some of them permanently snowcapped. Most can be climbed by anyone fit without special equipment, experience or a guide, but you should always check the situation before embarking on a mountain trek (see below right). The best time to climb most Iranian mountains is between early June and the end of August.

Iran's highest and best-known peak, Mt Damavand (5671m, north of Tehran) has a classic Fuji-esque profile, but reaching the summit is not of great technical difficulty for a mountain of such altitude (p117). The magnificent Alborz Mountains surrounding it contain around another 70 peaks over 4000m. At 4850m Mt Alam (p161) is Iran's most technical peak with an 800m near-vertical granite wall on its most difficult northern face: a world-class challenge. Mt Alam is climbed from Kelardasht where there's a well-informed mountaineering centre (p161).

Mt Sabalan (4811m; p145) is an elegantly soaring peak usually approached from Mishgin Shahr, though it's worth arranging guides and equipment in Tabriz before setting out.

Mt Oshturan (4070m; p190), the highest yet also about the most accessible peak of the splendid Zagros Mountains, is relatively tame from a climber's point of view but has a fine lake near the summit and is ideal for mountain walkers.

There are thousands of other mountains in Iran, but they are very seldom, if ever, climbed. If you fancy yourself as a trailblazer, you could investigate the snowcapped Mt Taftan (4042m) volcano, near the Pakistani border; Mt Hezar (4420m) and Mt Lalezar (4374m) in the Payeh Mountains, south of Kerman; Mt Zardkouh (4337m) in the Zardkouh Mountains, west of Esfahan; or the Dena Range, northwest of Shiraz, with 37 peaks over 4000m, the highest of them being Mt Gash Mastan (4460m).

Some helpful websites include www.mountainzone.ir and www.peakware.com. The latter has mountain logs for several Iranian peaks.

GUIDES & PORTERS

The cost of a guide depends on your bargaining skills, the number of climbers in the group, the equipment needed, the length of the trip and the difficulty of the route you want to undertake. You should probably assume you will need to pay about US$50 a day for an English-speaking guide and US$25 for a donkey to carry your equipment.

EQUIPMENT RENTAL & PURCHASE

There are a couple of camping shops about 200m along the walking trail that starts at the end of the ski lift at Darband, in northern Tehran (p100), which rent out a limited range of mountaineering gear. Staff speak little English.

If you want to buy, in Tehran try **Varzesh Kooh** (☎ 021-830 1037; 4th fl, cnr Enqelab Ave & Ferdosi St, Ferdosi Sq), which sells sleeping bags, backpacks, crampons, ice axes and boots; or speak with the Mountaineering Federation of Iran (p340).

MAPS

There are few trekking or mountain-climbing maps on Iran available in English, though climbing maps for the Mt Alam area are available at the climbing centre in Rudbarak (p161). Elsewhere, spend the money you saved on maps on a local guide. For hiking in the valleys behind Gorgan the commonly available Golestan Province map gives a basic outline, while Gita Shenasi (p353) in Tehran has a map of the Alborz Mountains.

TREKKING & MOUNTAINEERING AGENCIES

Some of the travel agencies listed under Tours (p371) will be able to help you organise walking and climbing holidays. For specialised advice on trekking and mountaineering trips in Iran, try contacting the following agencies:

Araz Adventure Tours (Map p98; ☎ 021-760 9292; www.araz.org; 1st fl, 1 Chahar Baradran Alley, North Bahar St, Tehran; 🕙 8am-4pm Sat-Wed, 8am-12.30pm Thu) This helpful outdoor tourism agency comes highly recommended and offers a wide range of mountaineering, climbing, horse-trekking and mountain-biking tours, notably in the Alborz region. Director and experienced climber Mohsen Aghajani speaks good English. One reader who climbed Mt Damavand wrote that 'even the cook had made it within 45 minutes of the Mt Everest summit'. Most equipment is provided.

Kassa Mountaineering & Tourism (Map pp90-1; ☎ 021-751 0463; www.kassaco.com; 9 Naghdi Alley,

Shariati St, Tehran) This private trekking agency offers a full range of trekking and climbing tours, desert expeditions and more. It is run by Ahmad Shirmohammad, an experienced climber who speaks English. Check all the tour options on the excellent website.

Mountaineering Federation of Iran (Map pp90-1; ☎ 021-830 6641; 15 Varzandeh St, Mofatteh Ave, Tehran; ☒ 8.30am-6.30pm Sat-Wed) About 200m up from the former US embassy is a side alley accommodating most of Iran's sporting organisations. The undisputed experts in anything relating to mountain climbing, and trekking, the Mountaineering Federation people are a mine of information and advice. Staff speak English, or can find someone who does.

Rock Climbing

If clambering about on rocks is more your thing, there are several excellent and accessible places to try. Closest to Tehran is Band-Yakh-Chal, one hour's drive north of Tajrish Sq. The rocks here soar to 15m and can be climbed if you have suitable bolts. They're very busy on Friday. Alternatively, 40km north of Karaj and west of the Amir Kabir Reservoir, you can go rock climbing at Pol-Khab (The Place of Good Sleeping).

Further afield, there are some awesome rocks, sink-holes, sheer cliffs and overhangs around Kermanshah. The cliffs culminate at Bisotun where, amid a collection of ancient inscriptions, Farhad Tarash (p180) rock-face is the region's classic climbing challenge. The helpful Kermanshah tourist office can put you in touch with the local climbers club for support and equipment.

The rocky canyons around Maku (p123), Bijar (p171) and Khorramabad (p187) are easy to reach and tempting to climb, although few locals seem to do so. You'd be wise to check with police or tourist offices before setting out as certain innocuous looking climbs can overlook sensitive military posts. The 800m wall of Mt Alam is a major expedition (p161). Many waterfalls become good ice-climbs in winter, most accessibly at Ganjnameh (p185), near Hamadan.

Skiing

There are at least 19 ski fields in Iran (bet you didn't know that). The season is long, the snow is often powdery and getting out on it costs next to nothing. Of the dozen or more downhill skiing areas near Tehran, only four – Darbansar, Shemsak, Dizin and Tochal – are easily accessible, and have reliable facilities and equipment for hire (p118). There is also

good downhill skiing available near Tabriz (p133) and Kermanshah (p176). New facilities are under construction at Alvares near Sara'eyn (p148). For cross-country skiing, try the Kelardasht region near the Caspian Sea, or anywhere around Mt Damavand.

The ski slopes are also some of the most sexually equal areas of Iran outside of the family home. Skiing was banned after the revolution, and after the ban was lifted in 1988 the images were of women skiing in manteaus. But with Khatami's rise to the presidency in 1997 came a considerable easing of restrictions on what you could and couldn't do on the slopes. Women must still keep their heads covered, but skiing headgear is deemed appropriate. Needless to say, skiing is very popular among the affluent young.

The season in the Alborz Mountains (where most of the slopes are located) starts as early as November and lasts until just after No Ruz, the Iranian New Year (about 21 March), although around Tabriz and at Dizin it can last until mid-May. The resorts are particularly busy around No Ruz. The slopes are packed with Iranians on Thursdays and Fridays, and with diplomats and expats on Saturdays; on other days it should be quiet.

All the resorts have upmarket hotels, which normally charge from about US$30 to US$100 for a room. Ski lifts cost as little as IR40,000 a day. You can hire full equipment (ie skis, poles and boots, but not clothes) at the resorts.

For more information, contact the **Skiing Federation** (Map pp90-1; ☎/fax 021-882 5161; www.skifed.ir; Shahid Shirodi Sports Complex, 13 Varzandeh St, Tehran). For reviews of the slopes, see www.goski.com.

Trekking

The Mountaineering Federation of Iran (p340) is also the expert in trekking. If you plan to trek without local guides be sure to get as much background information as possible from them before you set off.

SHORT TREKS

Iran offers many excellent one-day walks. Possibilities exist in northern Tehran, around Darband and Tochal; on Hormoz Island; at Kelardasht, Masuleh and Nahar Khoran in the Caspian region; and around Kerman (p284), Orumiyeh (p127) and Takht-e Soleiman (p170).

LONGER TREKS

Iran also offers several five- to seven-day hikes across mountains and through forests, a few challenging mountain climbs and a couple of full-scale expeditions for the more adventurous.

In remote regions, especially near borders, you may stumble across military/police/security areas; an Iranian guide or a few phrases of Farsi should smooth over any misunderstandings. Drinking water is often scarce, so take your own supplies in the desert regions, and purification tablets or water filters in other places.

For treks of more than a couple of days in remote areas, you should take camping equipment, including a good sleeping bag. Though some mountains have huts for climbers, these may be closed, full or inadequate, so carrying a tent is a good idea. Although you can often buy a limited range of foods at villages along the way, you might prefer to bring food and cooking equipment from town.

The Alamut area is rich in trekking options, including some taking you across the Alborz Mountains and down to the Caspian.

SAFETY GUIDELINES FOR WALKING

Before embarking on a walking trip, consider the following points to ensure a safe and enjoyable experience:

- Obtain reliable information about physical and environmental conditions along your intended route.

- Be aware of local laws, regulations and etiquette about wildlife and the environment.

- Walk only in regions, and on tracks, within your realm of experience.

- Be aware that weather conditions and terrain vary significantly from one region, or even from one track, to another. Seasonal changes can significantly alter any track. These differences influence the way walkers dress and the equipment they carry.

- Ask before you set out about the environmental characteristics that can affect your walk and how local, experienced walkers deal with these considerations.

The five-day trek from Hir to Jawardeh is one well worth investigating (p166).

Other popular trekking routes in the Caspian region include from Abyek to Abbasabad, via Mt Alam; from Garmabdar to Noshahr; and from Shahrud to Gorgan. Most of these routes will take about five to seven days, depending on how much mountain climbing you do and whether you use public transport some of the way.

DESERT TREKS

The two most difficult areas to explore are probably the Dasht-e Kavir and Dasht-e Lut deserts, but with the right preparation and an experienced guide, there is no reason why you cannot trek across at least some of the Dasht-e Kavir.

One main trekking route taking at least eight days (about 300km) heads from Varamin to Kashan, via the eastern side of Lake Namak (you can save three days' trek by taking a car as far as Mobarakiyeh). If you have a 4WD and permission from the relevant authorities – ask the Mountaineering Federation how to go about this (p340) – it's possible to drive the whole way in two to three days.

Another really awesome 20- to 30-day trek is from Varamin to Tabas; speak with the Mountaineering Federation (p340) if you are interested in such an inspiring journey.

Crossing the barren wastes of the Dasht-e Kavir desert nearly put paid to Alexander the Great, so don't even think about venturing here alone.

BUSINESS HOURS

Opening and closing times can be erratic, but you can rely on most businesses closing all day on Friday and perhaps on Thursday afternoon (the Iranian weekend). Many businesses close during the afternoon for a siesta (from about 1pm to 3pm or 4pm); along the hot Persian Gulf, this siesta stretches until about 5pm. The only thing that rarely stops during this time is public transport. The most likely time to find anything open is between 9am and noon, daily except Friday. In this book hours will accord with the following list unless stated otherwise.

Banks 7.30am to 1.30pm Saturday to Wednesday, 7.30am to 12.30pm Thursday.

Government Offices 8am to 2pm Saturday to Wednesday, 8am to noon Thursday.

Museums 8.30am to 6pm summer, 4pm or 5pm winter, with one day off, usually Monday or Tuesday.
Post Offices 7.30am to 3pm Saturday to Thursday, some main offices open until 9pm.
Private Businesses 8am or 9am to 5pm or 6pm Saturday to Thursday, until noon Thursday.
Restaurants lunch noon to 3pm, dinner 6pm or 7pm to 11pm, or whenever the last diner leaves.
Shops 9am to 8pm Saturday to Thursday, but likely to have a siesta between 1pm and 3.30pm and possibly close Thursday afternoon.
Telephone Offices 8am to 9pm, in larger towns some open 24 hours; in smaller towns they can close at 5pm.
Travel Agencies & Airline Offices 7.30am to 6pm Saturday to Thursday, 7.30am-noon Friday.

CALENDARS

Three calendars are in common use in Iran: the Persian solar calendar is the one in offi-cial and everyday use; the Muslim lunar calendar is used for Islamic religious matters; and the Western (Gregorian) calendar is used in dealing with foreigners and in some history books. As a result, Iranian newspapers have three dates along their mastheads. For example, 8 February 2004 also appeared as Bahman 19 1382 (Persian) and Zihajjeh 16 1424 (Muslim). The Zoroastrians also have their own calendar (see the boxed text 'Iranian Calendars', below).

There is no easy way of converting a date from one system to another except by referring to an Iranian diary or calendar. This is particularly important when booking public transport or extending your visa, when you will be thinking in terms of the Gregorian calendar while the clerk at the other end is thinking in terms of the Persian calendar. If

IRANIAN CALENDARS

Persian Calendar

The modern Persian solar calendar, a direct descendant of the ancient Zoroastrian calendar, is calculated from the first day of spring in the year of the Hejira, the flight of the Prophet Mohammed from Mecca to Medina in AD 622. It has 365 days (366 every leap year), with its New Year (No Ruz) usually falling on 21 March according to the Western calendar. The names of the Persian months are as follows:

Season	Persian Month	Approximate Equivalent	Season	Persian Month	Approximate Equivalent
spring	Farvardin	21 Mar-20 Apr	autumn	Mehr	23 Sep-22 Oct
(bahar)	Ordibehesht	21 Apr-21 May	(pa'iz)	Aban	23 Oct-21 Nov
	Khordad	22 May-21 Jun		Azar	22 Nov-21 Dec
summer	Tir	22 Jun-22 Jul	winter	Dei	22 Dec-20 Jan
(tabestan)	Mordad	23 Jul-22 Aug	(zamestan)	Bahman	21 Jan-19 Feb
	Shahrivar	23 Aug-22 Sep		Esfand	20 Feb-20 Mar

Muslim Calendar

The Muslim calendar, which is used to some extent in all Islamic countries, starts from the month before the Hejira, but is based on the lunar year of 354 or 355 days, so it is currently out of step with the Persian solar calendar by some 40 years. The names of the 12 months of the Muslim calendar in Farsi are: Moharram, Safar, Rabi'-ol-Avval, Rabi'-ol-Osani (or Rabi'-ol-Akhar), Jamadi-l-Ula (or Jamadi-ul-Awai), Jamadi-l-Okhra (or Jamadi-ul-Sami), Rajab, Sha'ban, Ramazan, Shavval, Zu-l-Gha'deh and Zu-l-Hejjeh.

Zoroastrian Calendar

The Zoroastrian calendar works to a solar year of 12 months of 30 days each, with five additional days. The week has no place in this system, and each of the 30 days of the month is named after and presided over by its own angel or archangel. The 1st, 8th, 15th and 23rd of each month are holy days. As in the Persian calendar, the Zoroastrian year begins in March at the vernal equinox. Except for Andarmaz, which replaces Esfand, the months of the Zoroastrian calendar are same as those in the Persian calendar.

DIRECTORY ·· Children 343

your visa extension is written only in Farsi be sure to get an Iranian to check the date on it for you and to cross-check with a calendar.

CHILDREN

In Iran, foreign children will be the source of much amusement and curiosity, which may drive them (and you) to despair after a while. Nappies (diapers), powders, baby formula, most simple medications and so on are available in the big cities, although you might want to bring your own to save having to hunt about. The hardest thing will be trying to keep children entertained in a country where journeys are often long and the attractions often rather 'adult'. Mothers would want to relate fairly clearly to their daughters aged nine or older that they'll have to wear hejab, and pray there are no tantrums.

Some of the adult attractions that children might find appealing include Persepolis (p252), where your powers of description and knowledge of history will be put to the test; Esfahan's (p210) horse-drawn carriages around Imam Sq; and the narrow lanes of Yazd, where you need to keep them within earshot. Sadly, the National Jewels Museum (p94) is not open to children under 12.

If you have small children and plan on using taxis or private hire cars, be sure to ask the agency whether they have baby seats. Chances are they won't, so you'll probably have to bring your own. Very few vehicles have seatbelts in the back seats, so it might also be worth insisting on a car that does. At least one bewildered agent we met was forced to have seatbelts fitted in the back seat of his car before driving would drive anywhere. Similarly, you won't find high chairs anywhere outside the top-end hotels; ditto for childcare agencies and nappy-changing facilities. As for breastfeeding in public, it's not a good idea.

Anyone contemplating taking children to Iran should read Lonely Planet's *Travel with Children* by Cathy Lanigan.

CLIMATE CHARTS

Because of its size, topography and altitude, Iran experiences great climatic extremes. Winters (December to February) can be unpleasantly cold, especially in the north and west, and in most of the rest of the country the nights are very cold. In summer (June to August) temperatures as high as 50°C are nothing out of the ordinary

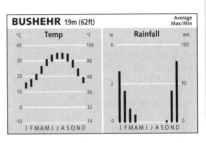

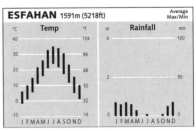

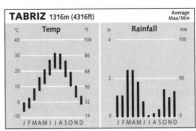

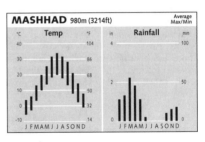

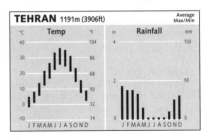

along the Persian Gulf coast and southern provinces.

Regular rainfall is more or less restricted to the far north and west – the area north of the Alborz Mountains receives an annual average of about 1300mm of rain, and year-round cloud helps keep summer temperatures more manageable. These are generally also the coldest parts of Iran. In western Iran winter temperatures are regularly well below zero and snow frequently remains until early spring. Unless you're a mad dog or an Englishman, avoid southern Iran, the deserts and the Persian Gulf coast between early May and mid-October. See also When to Go (p13).

COURSES

Even if there were more courses to sign up for, you probably wouldn't get a visa long enough to learn much. The English-language newspapers sometimes advertise courses in Farsi, but these are mainly for diplomats who don't have to fret about visa extensions.

Embassies usually have contacts for private Farsi tutors, so give yours a call. Some universities run intensive language courses, including the **Esfahan University** (Map p211; ☎ 0311-793 2039; www.ui.ac.ir/uiitems/news /persiancourse /persian.htm). To learn Farsi online, go to www.easypersian.com.

Renowned Tehran musician **Massoud Shaari** (☎ 021-879 5986; www.massoudshaari.com) offers lessons in traditional instruments, including sitar, *tar* (stringed instrument like a sitar), *santoor* (72-stringed dulcimer), *daf* (frame drum) and *zarb* (small drum). He also teaches Iranian classical music theory. Prices vary, but 10 one-hour lessons on the sitar cost IR800,000.

CUSTOMS

Contrary to popular belief, Iranian official-dom is fairly relaxed about what foreigners take into and out of the country; at airports, your bags probably won't be searched at all. However, don't take this to mean you can load your luggage with vodka, bacon and fashion mags. You are allowed to import, duty-free, 200 cigarettes and 50 cigars, and a 'reasonable quantity' of perfume.

On arrival you will be asked to fill out a fairly standard customs declaration, which you show to the customs officer, who stamps it. You *must* keep this form until you

leave; it's a big hassle if you lose it. Apart from alcohol and pork, things likely to attract interest are foreign magazines, audio cassettes and video cassettes, whether blank or not. Be careful about the books you bring in; you'll probably get away with anything, no matter how critical of the government, as long as it doesn't have too much female skin or hair visible on the cover. Visitors are supposed to declare cash worth more than US$1000. In practice few people do and the authorities aren't really interested. No more than IR200,000 in cash is allowed to be taken in or out of Iran.

On departure, if you have the customs form that you filled out on arrival you'll be very unlucky if anyone shows much interest in your bags.

Export Restrictions

You may take out anything you legally imported into Iran, and anything you have purchased, including handicrafts other than carpets or rugs up to the value of US$160 (hang on to your receipts), as long as they are not for 'the purpose of trade'. Many traders are willing to undervalue goods on receipts issued to foreigners.

You can also take out one or two Persian carpets or rugs up to a total of 20 sq metres in size, 150g of gold and 3kg of silver, without gemstones. If you want to exceed these limits, you will need an export permit from the local customs office. Officially you need permission to export anything 'antique' (ie more than 50 years old), including handicrafts, gemstones, coins and manus ique identification, so there is always a slight risk that anything vaguely 'antique' looking could be confiscated.

Until recently you were supposed to get a permit from the Ministry of Culture & Islamic Guidance before exporting a musical instrument. Although this regulation has now been relaxed, a question mark still hovers over the export of old *tars*. If you are worried that an expensive item might be confiscated, have a word with the customs office before buying. Hand baggage is rarely searched on departure.

Duty-Free Zones

The islands of Kish and Qeshm, and the port of Chabahar, are duty-free zones. However, the customs regulations can be complicated and tiresome, and that's just for taking your purchase back to mainland Iran. Unless it's a new colour TV you're after, do your shopping elsewhere.

DANGERS & ANNOYANCES
Security
'Iran? Is it safe?' It's a question you'll almost certainly be asked before you come to Iran, and often. But the perception of Iran as an unpredictable, dangerous destination couldn't be further from the truth. Violent crime against foreigners is almost unheard of, and the idea that as a Westerner you won't be welcome is plain wrong. If you do your best to fit in with local customs, you are unlikely to be treated with anything but courtesy and friendliness – that applies to Americans, too.

Of course, crime does still exist, so it pays to take the usual precautions. When travelling long distances by public transport, especially on international services, keep your passport, money and camera with you at all times. The occasional pickpocket operates in some crowded bazaars.

Theft from a hotel room is very unlikely, since the staff keep careful watch over visitors and residents. Nonresidents often have to leave their identity cards at reception if they want to go upstairs; in most places they're barred from any part of the hotel except the ground floor and restaurant. Hotels are locked or guarded at night. Most places also have a safe for guests' valuables.

If you're driving, try to avoid parking on the street overnight in Zahedan or anywhere near the Afghani, Pakistani and Iraqi borders.

The most valuable possession Westerners usually bring to Iran – and the hardest to replace – is a foreign passport. Largely because of the difficulty Iranians face in travelling to Western countries, there is a booming black market in forged and stolen foreign passports. When you're carrying it, keep your passport strapped to your body.

In 1999 and again in 2003 tourists were kidnapped in the far southeastern province of Sistan va Baluchestan. In 2003 the victims were three cyclists riding from Bam to Zahedan. The kidnapping is believed to have been in response to government successes in their war with drug smugglers who operate in the area. A reward of about

YOU'VE BEEN WARNED
For the latest travel warnings and advice you can log onto the following websites, but remember that they are usually very conservative:
Australian Department of Foreign Affairs & Trade (www.dfat.gov.au/travel)
Canadian Department of Foreign Affairs & International Trade (www.voyage.gc.ca/dest/index.asp)
Foreign and Commonwealth Office (www.fco.gov.uk/travel)
German Federal Foreign Office (www.auswaertiges-amt.de/www/de/laenderinfos/reise_warnung_html)
New Zealand Ministry of Foreign Affairs & Trade (www.mft.govt.nz/travel/)
Netherlands Ministry of Foreign Affairs (www.minbuza.nl/default.asp?CMS_ITEM=MBZ458731)
US Department of State/Bureau of Consular Affairs (www.travel.state.gov)

euro five million was demanded – similar to the value of drugs seized in a raid just prior to the kidnapping – but the three were released unharmed after being held for three weeks.

Western embassies advise their nationals to register with them on arrival, especially if you will be in Iran for 10 or more days, or plan to visit remote places.

POLICE & SECURITY FORCES
It is unlikely you'll have any problem with the Iranian police. The majority of those you'll see will be busy in a seemingly fruitless effort to improve the traffic flow, and they really have no interest in hassling foreigners.

In popular tourist destinations such as Esfahan, Shiraz and Mashhad you'll find Tourist Police in conveniently located booths. One of them should be able to speak English, or at least find someone who does.

Thankfully, the truly dreaded Komiteh (Komiteh-ye Enqelab-e Eslami; the Islamic Revolutionary Committee, or 'religious police'), who used to bail up tourists for less than rigorous adherence to Islamic dress codes, is no more. However, the Basij and Sepah religious militias do sometimes get a bit carried away (see the boxed text 'A Night With The Basij', p353).

SECURITY CHECKS

Although soldiers and policemen roam the streets and patrol the highways checking on the movements of pedestrians and road users, they rarely trouble foreigners. You can expect the usual inspections at all airports and in some public places, such as at the shrines of Imam Reza in Mashhad and Imam Khomeini in Tehran. Foreigners are expected to carry their passports with them at all times, although this can be tricky when hotels also like to hang onto them throughout your stay. In fact, you may be best off leaving your passport at the hotel so that if you're stopped by bogus police – indeed, any police – you can say you haven't got it with you.

In the eastern provinces your transport is likely to be stopped more frequently by police searching for drugs and other smuggled goods.

Political Crises

Iran is no stranger to political crises. Regardless of your nationality, it's wise to stay clear of all political gatherings – don't take photos and keep a low profile. It's a good idea to carry a short-wave radio so you can keep in touch with what's happening in Iran and elsewhere in the region.

Scams
BOGUS POLICE

Despite a concerted effort by police to crack down on such scams, we still receive a disturbing number of letters from readers who have encountered bogus police. The usual motive is theft of passports, cameras, money or whatever else you're carrying that takes their fancy. In 2003, reports of such activity mainly emanated from Tehran, though it could happen anywhere. The best advice is to ignore the 'policemen' and they'll probably leave you alone. If they are real police they will take you to the station or your hotel, otherwise they will eventually disappear. *Never* agree to hand over your passport or anything else until you are at one of these places.

Traffic

Forget religious fanatics, gun-toting kidnappers or any other threats you've asso-

ciated with Iran, you're more likely to get into trouble with the traffic than anything else. Iran has one of the world's worst road accident rates; more than 200,000 are reported every year and no-one knows how many more are not. Figures vary, but state media reported in 2004 that a staggering 13,570 people had died on the roads during the first six months of the Iranian year 1382 (beginning March 2003).

If you have travelled elsewhere in the region, Iran's traffic chaos may come as little surprise, but if you have arrived from the West, you will be horrified. No-one pays a blind bit of notice to road rules. The willingness of a car to stop at a busy intersection is directly proportional to the size of the vehicles in its path; that's right, it's survival of the biggest. Playing on this, some cunning motorists have fitted deafening air horns, usually found on trucks and buses, to their Paykans. A quick blast sees other traffic suddenly screech to a halt, fearing they've been outsized. Meanwhile, the Paykan sails through the intersection. Size (or at least the perception that you're big) matters.

Some cars and all motorbikes use the designated bus lanes that usually go in the opposite direction to the rest of the traffic. Motorbikes speed through red lights, drive on footpaths and career through crowded bazaars.

While traffic in major cities rarely goes fast enough to cause a serious accident, never underestimate the possibility of dying a horrible death while crossing the road. Vehicles never stop at pedestrian crossings and there aren't many footbridges or underpasses. You will quickly realise that there's little alternative to stepping out in front of the traffic, as the Iranians do, and hoping that the drivers will slow down. It may not be much consolation, but the law says that if a driver hits a pedestrian the driver is always the one at fault and the one liable to pay blood money to the family of the victim. Until you've got your head around the traffic, perhaps the best advice comes from one pragmatic reader: 'Cross a busy street with an Iranian person, but make sure the Iranian is closest to the approaching traffic.'

Unmarried Foreign Couples

Unmarried foreign couples used to find it very difficult to share a room while travelling

BIG JUBS

In almost every Iranian city the main streets are lined with *jubs* (canals), which originally served to distribute drinking water through the city, but now serve as rain-water channels-cum-rubbish-collecting repositories. At the best of times they're a hazard for anyone crossing a road without looking carefully, and after rain they can quickly turn into raging torrents.

If you're driving, *jubs* can be even more hazardous. In many towns the road drops straight into the *jub* without any form of kerb whatsoever. In Mashhad, we saw one reverse park go horribly wrong when the back wheel dropped off the road and into the *jub*. The anxious driver tried to drive his way out of the *jub* before his boss, whom he'd just dropped off, returned, but only managed to drop the front wheel in as well. They were still trying to lift it out three hours later.

around Iran. Recently, however, hotel staff are starting to understand the weird wishes of foreigners and don't usually ask too many questions. One way to avoid problems is to wear a wedding ring; hotel receptionists usually accept that, foreign females don't take their husbands' family name on marriage, since Iranian women don't either.

DISABLED TRAVELLERS

As long as you are healthy and come with the right frame of mind, there is no reason why disabled travellers shouldn't enjoy much of what Iran has to offer. Although special facilities for the disabled are rare, Iran is having to come to terms with more than 300,000 people left disabled by the Iran-Iraq War. As a result wheelchair ramps are starting to appear (although it will be a long time before you can depend on their presence). Only the more upmarket hotels are guaranteed to have elevators big enough for wheelchairs and European-style sit-down toilets. You should bring your own medications, and prescriptions, although medical facilities in the major cities are quite good.

So far, none of the European or American travel agencies that specialise in disabled travel are running tours to Iran. However, for general information check out the following websites:

Access-Able Travel Source (www.access-able.com)
Radar (www.radar.org.uk)
Society for Accessible Travel & Hospitality (www.sath.org)

DISCOUNT CARDS

A few sites grant a 50% discount to students with a valid International Student Identity Card (ISIC) and a smattering of relevant words in Farsi, but most don't.

EMBASSIES & CONSULATES
Iranian Embassies & Consulates

Iranian embassies and consulates abroad include:

Afghanistan Kabul (☎ 017-24700; Solh Ave, Gharar Rah Shir Pour, Kabul)
Australia Canberra (☎ 02-6290 2421; www.embassyiran .org.au; 25 Culgoa Crt, O'Malley, ACT 2606)
Azerbaijan Baku (☎ 12-92 19 32; Cafar Cabbarli 10) Opposite Nizami Metro station. This address is for visas only – the main embassy address is elsewhere.
Canada Ottowa (☎ 613-233 4726; www.salamiran.org; 245 Metcalfe St, Ottawa, Ontario K2P 2K2)
Denmark Copenhagen (☎ 39 16 00 71; www.iran -embassy.dk; Engskiftevej 6, 2100 Kobenhav)
France Paris (☎ 01 40 69 79 00; www.amb-iran.fr; 4 Ave d'Iena, 75016, Paris)
Germany Berlin (☎ 030-8419 1835; www.iranembassy.de; Podbielskiallee 67, D-14195, Berlin); Frankfurt (☎ 069-5600 0070; fax 5600 0713; Eichendorffstrasse 54; Hamburg (☎ 040-514 4060; fax 511 3511; Bebelalle 18)
Ireland Dublin (☎ 01-188 5881; fax 283 4246; 72 Mount Merrion Ave, Blackrock, Dublin)
Japan Tokyo (☎ 3-3446 8011; www.iranembassyjp.com; 10-32-3 Chome Minami Aazabu, Minato-ku, Tokyo)
Netherlands The Hague (☎ 070-354 8483; www.iranianembassy.nl; Duinweg 20, 2585JX, The Hague)
New Zealand Wellington (☎ 04-386 2976; fax 386 3065; 151 Te Anau Rd, Roseheath, Wellington)
Pakistan Islamabad (☎ 051-2276270; fax 2824839; House 222-238, St 2, G-5/1, Islamabad); Karachi (☎ 021-5874371; fax 5874633; 81 Shahrah-i-Iran, Clifton, Karachi); Lahore (☎ 042-7590926; fax 5710661; 7575650 55-A Shadman ll, Lahore); Peshawar (☎ 091-845403/4, fax 91-840305;18-C Park Ave, University Rown, Peshawar; Quetta (☎ 081-843098, fax 829766; 2/33 Hali Rd, Quetta)
South Korea Seoul (☎ 02-793 7751; Hanam Dong 726-126, Yongsan-ku, 140-210, Seoul)
Spain Madrid (☎ 6135 9642; 28016 Calle Jeres, 5 Madrid)
Syria Damascus (☎ 011-222 6459; fax 222 0997; Al-Mezzeh, Damascus)

DIRECTORY

YOUR OWN EMBASSY

It's important to realise what your own embassy – the embassy of the country of which you are a citizen – can and can't do to help you if you get into trouble. Generally speaking, it won't help if the trouble you're in is remotely your own fault. Remember that you are bound by the laws of the country you are in. Your embassy will not be sympathetic if you end up in jail after committing a crime locally, even if such actions are legal in your own country. Don't expect support for feminist or political statements you make in Iran, for example. In genuine emergencies you might get some assistance, but only if other channels have been exhausted. For example, if you need to get home urgently, a free ticket is exceedingly unlikely – the embassy would expect you to have insurance. If you have all your money and documents stolen, it might assist with getting a new passport, but you can forget a loan for onward travel.

Tajikistan Dushanbe (☎ 372-210072; Kucai Bokhtar 18 aka Tehran St)
Turkey Ankara (☎ 312-468 2195; fax 468 2823; Tahran Caddesi 10, Kavaklidere, Ankara); İstanbul (☎ 212-512 8230; fax 212-511 5219; Ankara Caddesi 1/2, Cağaloğlu, İstanbul); Erzurum (☎ 442-315 9983; fax 316 1182; just off Atatürk Bulvarı)
UK London (☎ 020-7584 8101; www.iran-embassy.org.uk; 27 Princes Gate, London SW7 IPX)
USA Washington The Iranian Interests Section is in the Pakistan embassy (☎ 202-965 4990; www.daftar.org; 2209 Wisconsin Ave, NW, Washington, 20007)

Embassies & Consulates in Iran

Embassies in Tehran generally open from about 9am to noon for visa applications and from 2 to 4pm for collecting visas, although much shorter working hours are also possible. Most embassies of Islamic countries close on Thursday afternoon and all day on Friday, although Western (and Turkish) embassies usually close on Friday and Saturday instead.

At the time of writing, the embassies of many European countries, plus the USA, Canada, Australia and New Zealand were asking travellers to register their presence by phoning in and asking for the consul. If you do, be sure to let them know when you

leave. In the event of a genuine emergency (not to ask about the embassy swimming pool), call the number listed here, wait until the message gives you the emergency number, and call that.

Afghanistan Tehran (Map p98; ☎ 021-873 5600; Dr Beheshti Ave, cnr 4th St & Pakistan St; ☼ 9am-2pm Sat-Wed, 9am-noon Thu) 30-day tourist visas cost US$30 and are issued in two days.
Armenia Tehran (Map pp90-1; ☎ 021-670 4833; emarteh@yahoo.com; 1 Ostad Shahriar St, Razi St, Jomhuri-ye Eslami Ave) Tourist visas issues in nine to 11 days for US$50, in three to five days for $80.
Australia Tehran (Map p98; ☎ 021-872 4456; www.iran.embassy.gov.au; 13 Eslamboli St, 23rd St)
Azerbaijan Tehran (Map p83; ☎ 021-233 5197; Nader Sq, 15 Golbarg St, Chizar; ☼ 9am-noon Sun, Tue, Thu) Single-entry tourist visas issued in one to two days if you have invitation.
Bahrain Tehran (Map p98; ☎ 021-877 3383; 248 Zoubin St, Afriqa Hwy; ☼ 8.30am-2.30pm Sat-Wed) Visas issued in one day.
Canada Tehran (Map p98; ☎ 021-873 2623; teran@dfait-maeci.gc.ca; 57 Sarafraz St, Motahhari Ave)
France Tehran (Map pp90-1; ☎ 021-228 0372; www.ambafrance-ir.org; 85 Nofl Loshato St)
Georgia Tehran (Map p83; ☎ 021-221 1470; Agha Bozorgi St, Fereshti St; ☼ 9.15am-1.30pm Sun, Tue, Thu) Two-week tourist visas cost US$40 and take four days (US$60 for two-day service).
Germany Tehran (Map pp90-1; ☎ 021-311 4111-14; fax 390 8474, 324 Ferdosi St)
India Tehran (Map p98; ☎ 021-875 5103-5; www.indianembassy-tehran.com; 46 Miremad Ave, cnr Ninth St & Dr Beheshti St; ☼ 9-11.30am & 4.30-5.30pm Sun-Thu); Zahedan (Map pp296-7; ☎ 0541-322 2337; off Imam Khomeini St; ☼ 8.30am-1pm & 2.30-5pm Sun-Thu) Visas issued in five days, IR370,000.
Ireland Tehran (☎ 021-222 2731/2; 8 Nahid Alley, Kamraniyeh Ave, Kamraniyeh)
Japan Tehran (Map p98; ☎ 021-871 3974; fax 886 2515; cnr Bucharest & Fifth Sts)
Netherlands Tehran (Map p83; ☎ 021-256 7005-7; 1st East Ln, 22 Sharzad Blvd, Darous)
New Zealand Tehran (Map p83; ☎ 021-280 0289; newzealand@mavara.com; 34, cnr 2nd Park Alley, Sosan St, Nth Golestan Complex, Aghdasiyeh St, Niyavaran)
Pakistan Tehran (Map p83; ☎ 021-694 4888; fax 694 4898; Block No 1, Etemadzadeh Ave, Jamshidabad, Dr Hossein Fatemi Ave; ☼ 9.30-11.30am Sun-Wed) Single-entry visas US$35 issued in two days with a letter of introduction from your embassy, pay in rial; Mashhad (Map p320; ☎ 0511-222 9845; Imam Khomeini St; ☼ 9am-noon Sat-Wed) Not so keen to issue visas;

Zahedan (Map pp296-7; ☎ 0541-223 389; Pahlavani St; ⏰ 8.30am-2.30pm Sat-Wed) As in Tehran but quicker.

Spain Tehran (Map p98; ☎ 021-878 7082 ; Afriqa Hwy; 76 Sarve St)

Sweden Tehran (Map p83; ☎ 021-229 6802; 2 Nasdaran St, Pasdaran)

Syria Tehran (Map p98; ☎ 021-205 9031; fax 205 9409; Afriqa Hwy, Arash Blvd, ⏰ 8am-noon)

Turkey Tehran (Map pp90-1; ☎ 021-311 5299; fax 311 7928; 314 Ferdosi St); Orumiyeh (Map p128; ☎ 0441-223 8970; Beheshti St); Tabriz (☎ 041-554 3134; 156 Shariati Cenubi)

Turkmenistan Tehran (Map p83; ☎ 021-254 2178; fax 258 0432; 39 Fifth Golestan St, Pasdaran Ave; ⏰ 9.30am-noon Sun-Thu) Transit and tourist visas allegedly issued in five working days with invitation.

UAE Tehran (Map p98; ☎ 021-878 1333; 355 Vahid Dastjerdi Ave); Bandar-e Abbas (Map p272; ☎ 0761-222 4229; Nasr Blvd)

UK Tehran (Map pp90-1; ☎ 021-675 5011/17; www.british embassy.gov.uk/iran; 143 Ferdosi St)

USA Tehran The **Swiss Embassy** has a US Interests Section (Map p83; ☎ 021-200 8333; Sharifi Manesh, Ela-hieh) It might be able to help in an emergency but cannot offer full consular services.

FESTIVALS & EVENTS

The majority of Iran's festivals are religious and tend to involve a lot of mourning. For a list see Holidays (right). During Dahe-ye Fajr, or the 10 Days of Dawn (1 to 10 February; 11 to 21 Bahman), which commemorates the lead-up to Ayatollah Khomeini's coming to power, there's a good chance that you'll find other festivals, as well as the film and theatre festivals described here. For details of what's on check www.tehranavenue.com.

Fajr Film Festival (www.fcf-ir.com) This is the only festival you can rely on seeing year to year. Held during the Dahe-ye Fajr, it features new Iranian and international films. They can be seen in several cinemas across Tehran, but most notably the Farhang Cinema in Golhak (p108).

Fajr Theatre Festival This is usually staged at the same time as the film festival. Contact the Tezatre Shahr (City Theatre; p108) for details.

Tehran Short Film Festival This is sponsored by the Young Filmmakers' Society of Iran, and is usually held in the second half of October.

FOOD

In our Eating sections we provide full opening hours for restaurants only when they fall outside standard opening hours (p341), otherwise we specify whether they are open for lunch or dinner. Restaurants often

add 10% or 15% to the bill in the name of service, though the waiter will rarely receive anything unless you add a further amount. In this book the 'service charge' has usually been included in the overall meal price. For more information, see also Food & Drink (p74).

GAY & LESBIAN TRAVELLERS

There are gays and lesbians in Iran, just as there are everywhere else in the world. Unlike most other places, homosexuality is not only illegal but punishable by hundreds of lashes and even death (although foreigners would probably be deported instead). Barbaric laws aside, there is no reason why gay and lesbian travellers shouldn't visit Iran. There are no questions of sexuality on visa application forms, and we have not heard of any homosexual travellers being treated badly as long as they refrained from all overt signs of affection in public.

Meeting Iranian gays and lesbians will, however, be tough. With so many cultural and legal constraints, it's no surprise that the nearest thing to a gay 'scene' are a few nervous-looking men sitting alone in Daneshgu Park in Tehran. For lesbians it's even more difficult; most Iranians would probably deny the existence of women who prefer women.

The best way to contact the gay and lesbian communities, such as they are, is through the Internet. As with anywhere, once you've made contacts all sorts of doors can be opened, and getting in touch from the safety of your computer screen makes far more sense than chancing it in the park. For gays, www.geocities.com/gay_persia has interesting articles on homosexual life in Iran plus plenty of links. Lesbians should click through to www.khanaye-doost.com.

Of course, it makes sense not to advertise that you're part of a same-sex couple. Most hoteliers will accept that you're 'just good friends', though you might find in some places that discretion is the better part of valour when seeking a double bed. In Yazd there is one smooth hotel in the old town noted for being more gay-friendly than others.

HOLIDAYS

It is vital to note the dates of the public holidays, especially if you are planning to extend your visa. Just about everything closes on a religious holiday, although not necessarily on a national holiday. Over

MOURNING DAYS *Pat Yale*

Mourning is a very big deal in Iran. Whole sections of the bazaar are devoted to the production of black flags which are hung out on public mourning days (eg on the anniversary of the death of Fatima, the daughter of the Prophet). When I asked why the flags had not come down after this anniversary I was told: 'We have 12 imams, not to mention the Prophet, and they all had families, so we're always mourning somebody'.

On mourning days, museums will close and non-Muslims will be less welcome in mosques. Such entertainment as there is in the big cities will be suspended until the mourning period is over. Traditionally, mourning lasts for 40 days; it's just as well that this period isn't observed on all these occasions or nothing in the country would ever be open.

The most intense period of mourning occurs in Moharram to commemorate the death of Imam Hossein at Karbala.

public holidays, transport will still function normally, and hotels will remain open, but only restaurants in a few hotels will stay open. See Calendars (p342).

Religious Holidays

The religious holidays listed here follow the Muslim lunar calendar, which means the corresponding dates in the Western calendar move forward by 10 or 11 days every year. They are normally celebrated with a public holiday, extended for a day or more if it falls near the Iranian weekend.

Tasua (9 Moharram)
Ashura (10 Moharram) The anniversary of the martyrdom of Hossein, the third Shiite imam, in battle at Karbala in October AD 680. This is celebrated with religious dramas and sombre parades of devout Shiite men in black shirts, some of whom whip themselves with chains until they draw blood.
Arbaeen (20 Safar) The 40th day after Ashura.
Death of the Prophet Mohammed (28 Safar)
Death of Imam Reza (30 Safar)
Birthday of the Prophet Mohammed (17 Rabi'-ol-Avval)
Anniversary of the death of Fatima (3 Jamadi-I-Okhra) Fatima was the daughter of the Prophet Mohammed.
Birthday of Imam Ali (13 Rajab)
Mission of Holy Prophet (27 Rajab)

Birthday of Imam Mahdi (15 Shaban)
Death of Imam Ali (21 Ramazan)
Eid al-Fitr (1 Shavval) The Festival of the Breaking of the Fast that marks the end of Ramazan. After sunset on the last day of Ramazan rather large meals are consumed across the country, but it's nothing like the celebration seen in some other Islamic countries.
Death of Imam Jafar Sadegh (25 Shavval)
Eid-e Ghorban (10 Zu-I-Hejjeh) Marks the day when Abraham offered to sacrifice his son. Expect to see plenty of sheep and cattle being eaten.
Qadir-e Khom (18 Zu-I-Hejjeh) Commemorates the day that the Prophet Mohammed appointed Imam Ali as his successor while returning to Mecca.

RAMAZAN

For many Muslims, the month of dawn-to-dusk fasting, known in Iran as Ramazan, is not an unpleasant ordeal but a chance to perform a ritual cleansing of body and mind. Some people, especially in cities, don't fully observe the fast, but most do for at least part of the month. Ramazan is imposed on everyone in Iran, but foreigners and non-Muslims can still eat, drink and smoke behind closed doors. Some Muslims are exempted from the fast (eg pregnant and menstruating women, travellers, the elderly and the sick), but they mustn't eat or drink in front of others who are fasting.

Ramazan can be a trying period, particularly if it falls in summer when the days are that much longer. Travellers are exempt from the fast so you don't need to worry about finding food on flights, trains or bus trips, and many hotels keep their restaurants open in the daytime, or at least allow foreigners to order food in their rooms. Other restaurants either close altogether or open only after dark. Many shops selling food remain open throughout Ramazan, so you can buy food to eat in your room.

Although you shouldn't have many problems in larger cities, you might not be able to find any food at all during the daytime in rural areas and small towns, making off-the-beaten-track travel particularly hard. Also, businesses and shops keep odd hours, tempers can flare and very little serious business gets done. Public transport continues to function, but often to reduced schedules.

National Holidays

National holidays follow the Persian solar calendar, and usually fall on the same day each year according to the Western calendar. If they fall near the Iranian weekend, an extra holiday is sometimes declared. Expect government offices are to be closed and much of the rest of the country in slow motion.

Magnificent Victory of the Islamic Revolution of Iran (11 February; 22 Bahman) The anniversary of Khomeini's coming to power in 1979.

Oil Nationalisation Day (20 March; 29 Esfand) Commemorates the day in 1951 when the Anglo-Iranian Oil Company was taken into Iranian hands.

No Ruz (21-24 March; 1-4 Farvardin) Iranian New Year.

Islamic Republic Day (1 April; 12 Farvardin) The anniversary of the establishment of the Islamic Republic of Iran in 1979.

Sizdah Bedar (2 April; 13 Farvardin) The 13th day of the Iranian New Year, when Iranians traditionally leave their houses for the day.

Heart-Rending Departure of the Great Leader of the Islamic Republic of Iran (4 June; 14 Khordad) Commemorates the death of Ayatollah Khomeini in 1989. About 500,000 Iranians flock to Tehran, Qom (where he trained and lived) and the village of Khomein (where he was born). It's worth avoiding Tehran at this time.

Anniversary of the Arrest of Ayatollah Khomeini (5 June; 15 Khordad) In 1963, Khomeini was arrested after urging the Muslims of the world to rise up against the superpowers.

Anniversary of the Death of Dr Seyed Beheshti (28 June; 7 Tir) The anniversary of the 1980 bomb blast at a meeting of the Islamic Republic Party which killed Dr Seyed Beheshti and several others.

Day of the Martyrs of the Revolution (8 September; 17 Shahrivar)

NO RUZ

Even before the Achaemenid period, the coming of spring was celebrated on a large scale throughout Persia, and today the Iranian New Year, or No Ruz, is a huge family celebration on a par with Christmas in the West. Starting on the spring equinox (around 21 March), Iranians traditionally return to their home villages and towns to celebrate the New Year with friends and relatives. March 21 and the four days following are official holidays, but most people don't actually go back to work until after Sizdah Bedar (about 2 April). This is the 13th day of the Persian New Year and Iranians traditionally avoid the bad luck associated with the number 13 by going to the countryside for a picnic. Some unmarried women pray to find a husband during the coming year, plates are sometimes

---

THE SEVEN 'S'S

The lead-up to the Iranian New Year, No Ruz, is traditionally a time for spring-cleaning. Closer to the big day, tables are specially laid according to a tradition called *haft seen*, or Seven 'S's: Seven articles must be placed on the table, the Farsi names of which all start with the letter 's'. These include seeds *(sabzi)*, apples *(sib)*, garlic *(sir)*, vinegar *(serkeh)*, a gold coin and a bowl with goldfish in it. Mothers are also expected to eat symbolic hard-boiled eggs, one for every child. During the day bonfires are also lit for people to jump over.

At the stroke of midnight, the family recites a special prayer seeking happiness, good health and prosperity, and then the serious eating and partying begins. A special No Ruz rice dish is passed around, and the older folk give presents *(eidi)* to the young. For the next two weeks, most families visit relatives and friends all over the country, placing the *sabzi* on the roof of their car as they drive off so they will blow away and thus dispel bad luck.

---

smashed, traditional food is cooked and children play games.

Finding hotel accommodation is tough from about 10 days before 21 March and 10 days after. All forms of public transport are heavily booked. Most businesses, including many restaurants (except those in good hotels), will close for about five days after the start of New Year (ie from about 21 to 25 March inclusive). If you are not visiting Iranian friends think twice before coming to Iran during No Ruz.

INSURANCE

A travel insurance policy to cover theft, loss and medical problems is a good idea. Some policies specifically exclude dangerous activities, which can include scuba diving, motorcycling, even trekking.

You might prefer a policy that pays doctors or hospitals directly rather than you having to pay on the spot and claim later. If you have to claim later ensure you keep all documentation. Check that the policy covers ambulances or an emergency flight home.

Make sure that the policy covers Iran and adjacent countries if you're travelling on. Some insurers, particularly in the USA, consider the region a 'danger zone' and either exclude it altogether or insist on exorbitant premiums. For more information, see also p383 and p376.

INTERNET ACCESS
You can get online in all Iranian cities and big towns, and a few smaller centres. In one of the ever-expanding number of Internet cafés (known as coffeenets) or a library the cost will be about IR10,000 an hour. In a hotel it will be more. The service is variable but, at the time of writing, was limited to a maximum 56kbps connection. If you plan to use a messenger service note that **Yahoo! Messenger** (www.yahoo.com) is used almost everywhere, but you'll probably have to download **MSN Messenger** (www.msn.com) yourself.

If you plan to carry a portable computer, note that the power supply can be erratic, which could damage your equipment. It's worth investing in a universal AC adaptor, which will enable you to plug it in anywhere without frying the innards. Unless you are in a top-end hotel (and even then it's not guaranteed), you'll need an adaptor to plug into the phone line. Most are unusual two-pin types that you can plug your RJ-11 into the back of, and are available in electronics stores.

Even with the adaptor, you'll still have a fair bit of work to do to get online. First, you need to find out if your hotel has a switchboard sophisticated enough to allow you to make long local calls (Many switchboards look like they've been around since Alexander Graham Bell's day). If they do, you'll then need to buy a pre-paid access card giving you a set time online. Unfortunately, most of these have access numbers for local areas only, meaning that once you've left Tehran, for example, you'll have to make a long-distance call back to Tehran to access your account. The cards are available at coffeenets and they're cheap, some as little as IR10,000, so you could, in theory, buy a new one wherever you go. You could also just use a coffeenet.

Check www.teleadapt.com or www.road warrior.com for more information on travelling with a portable computer. If you're looking for some useful websites for all things Iranian, see p15.

LEGAL MATTERS
Like most things in Iran, the legal system is based on Islamic principles, although the system is not as extreme as in places such as Sudan or northern Nigeria where various parts of one's anatomy can be lopped off for infringing the law.

Generally, the same activities that are illegal in your home country are illegal in Iran, the difference being that the penalties laid down are much harsher. For most minor crimes, foreigners will probably get deported although it is possible to fall foul of the law big time, as one German businessman found out when he was sentenced to death for having sex with an unmarried Muslim woman. The penalties for drug use and smuggling are harsh. Carrying the smallest amount of hashish can result in a minimum six-month jail sentence; don't expect assistance from your embassy, a fair trial or a comfortable cell.

There are two 'crimes' that foreigners may not be aware of. Homosexual activity is illegal and has resulted in the death penalty for some Iranians. Deliberate refusal to comply with the hejab (the Islamic dress code for women) can also result in a public flogging (although a foreigner will probably be deported).

In the unlikely event that you get arrested, it's best not to reply to, or appear to understand, any questions in Farsi (p346). If you do choose to answer questions, do so politely, openly and diplomatically. Since the primary motives for arresting a foreigner are usually curiosity, mild suspicion and the desire to appear powerful, answer your interrogators so that their curiosity is satisfied, their suspicion allayed and their sense of their own self-importance flattered. Take special care not to incriminate yourself or anyone else, especially anyone Iranian, with a careless statement, and get in contact with your embassy in Tehran as soon as possible.

In Iran, people are legally allowed to vote (for what it's worth) at age 15; can legally drive when they are 17; and can legally have sex when they're married – girls can be married when they turn 13 (it was nine until a few years ago), and boys when they 15. Premarital and gay sex are both illegal.

MAPS
The maps in this guidebook should satisfy most travellers, although people driving might need more detailed city maps to help them

A NIGHT WITH THE BASIJ *Andrew Burke*

When the first two bikes screeched to a halt we thought it was another instance of Iranian hospitality. These young guys would ask the lost foreigners looking at the map where they were going and directions would be given. But when the next two pulled up, one with a Hezbollah-style scarf around his face and a gun tucked into his pants, it suddenly looked more sinister. 'Police, police!' one of the bearded men shouted, holding aloft a tatty plastic card that for all we knew could have been his ID for the local video rental store. It was 1am on a large but very quiet Tehran street, and this had all the hallmarks of a robbery. Andrew, a fellow traveller en route from Dhaka to London, decided it was time to take his 1150cc motorbike away, but when a man snatched the keys from his bike, we were going nowhere.

For the next hour we argued by the side of the road. Uniformed police arrived, but it was the young guys in beards and black leather jackets who seemed most agitated. Our frustrated pleas that 'we are Australian tourists' were met with demands that they take the bike, and take us to separate police stations. This didn't sound like a good idea. Eventually, after one guy just rode off on the bike, we and 13 others went to the station. We were under arrest.

After two fruitless hours we were back at the hotel with some idea of what was going on. The original assailants turned out to be members of the Basij, a hard-line militia who see themselves as 'defenders of the revolution'. As Basijis argued with uniformed police at the hotel's front desk, we learned we'd been accused of being British spies and of taking pictures of sensitive sites (at 1am?), and of being on an illegal motorcycle (Iranians are limited to 200cc bikes, but as Andrew's was in transit, it was legal). The real police were as apologetic as the Basijis were enthusiastic with their allegations. Eventually, the Basijis were persuaded that we were not working for MI6, Andrew's bike was returned and we were released, promising next time to get a better map!

get in and out of the suburbs. The undisputed king of Iranian map-making is **Gita Shenasi** (Map pp90-1; ☎ 021-670 9335; www.gitashenasi.com; 15 Ostad Shahrivar St, Razi St, Valiasr Crossroads, Enqelab-e Eslami Ave) in Tehran, which publishes an impressive array of maps covering all the major cities and some of the mountain ranges. Most maps list the names of streets, suburbs and squares in English, although everything else, including the text and indexes, is in Farsi. Maps are hard to find outside Tehran, so visit this office if you need one.

Gita Shenasi's *Iran 2004* (1:2,250,000), is updated annually and is highly detailed, but too much colour makes it difficult to read. Train buffs might like their *General Map of Railways: Islamic Republic of Iran & Its Corridors*, which shows the rail system, and includes history, as well as a table of distances, in English and Farsi.

The only map widely available outside Iran is the *ITMB Iran Map* (1:2,500,000). It doesn't have anything like the detail of the Gita Shenasi map, but is a lot easier to read.

Gita Shenasi publishes climbing maps such as *Central Alborz*, *The Peaks of the Sabalan* and *Damavand and its Ridges*, but their usefulness is limited because many places are marked only in Farsi.

MONEY

The official unit of currency in Iran is the Iranian rial, but Iranians almost always talk in terms of tomans, a unit equal to 10 rials (see the boxed text 'Rials or Tomans?', p354). Throughout this book we use the abbreviation 'IR' to indicate Iranian rials.

Although there are coins for IR1, IR2, IR5, IR10, IR20, IR50, IR100 and IR250, only the latter three denominations are at all common. Indeed, so rare are IR1 coins (no longer minted) that they are considered lucky despite being utterly worthless. There are notes for IR100, IR200, IR500, IR1000, IR2000, IR5000 and IR10,000. Hang on to filthy IR100, IR200 and IR500 notes to pay shared-taxi fares. Most of the time no-one seems to care what state rial notes are in, then out of the blue someone will reject one on the grounds that it has a tiny tear or is too grubby. Banknotes are easy to read, as the numbers and names are printed in Farsi and English. However, coins are only marked in Farsi and Arabic numerals.

For all intents and purposes, Iran is a purely cash economy. No credit cards. No travellers cheques. Just cold, hard cash – preferably in US dollars or euros. Not surprisingly, the rial is the most widely accepted currency; a few hotels (p336) insist on being paid in US dollars but in most places they're happy to take rials even if the price is quoted in dollars. In this book, we've listed prices in the currency in which they are quoted. You'll obviously need to carry a mix of rials and dollars or euros – you'd need a wheelbarrow to cart around everything in rials.

When changing your dollars or euros, the rates are basically the same at the bank or on the street, so there is no longer any black market. For an idea of costs see p14; and for exchange rates see the inside front cover.

ATMs

Although Iran has a functioning network of ATMs (cashpoint machines), they can only be used with locally issued bank cards, so are useless to travellers unless you open a local account.

Banks

Although it sometimes seems as if every fourth building in Iran is a bank, only a few will change your money and then usually only US dollars, euros or, less often, British pounds in cash. Your best bet will always be the central branch of Bank Melli (BMI) in whichever town you are in. In larger cities you may also be able to change money at the central branches of the other major banks: Bank Mellat, Bank Tejarat, Bank Sepah and Bank Saderat. Banks that offer foreign-exchange facilities nearly always have the sign 'Exchange' or 'Foreign Exchange' displayed in English near the entrance. At these banks there should be someone who speaks English.

You will need to take your passport with you when changing money in a bank, and in some smaller cities a Farsi-speaker will help you to get through the mountains of paperwork – when we changed US$100 in Kerman it took 20 minutes and five different signatures.

While banks usually open at 7.30am (p341), most will not change your money until the day's rates have been faxed through from Tehran at about 9am.

Cash

In Iran, the US dollar is king, although it's being given a good run for its money (sorry) by the euro. So bring as much cash in US dollars or euros as you are likely to need. You can change these two almost everywhere, though the greenback is still the most widely accepted, especially in remote areas. A few banks and moneychangers will accept UK pounds, but you'll probably end up wasting a lot of time trying to persuade them to do so.

If you bring US dollars, the bills should be unmarked and undamaged in any way and should have been printed since 1996. Banks and moneychangers most prefer US$100 bills, and you'll get a slightly less-favourable rate when exchanging smaller notes. For euros, denominations of €100 are best.

There is a thriving business in UAE dirhams along the Persian Gulf coast. However, Turkish lira are treated with the utmost scorn everywhere except close to the Turkish border; ditto for the Afghan and Pakistani currencies. Try not to take any rials out of Iran unless you plan on using them as souvenirs.

RIALS OR TOMANS?

No sooner have you crossed the Iranian border than you will come up against the idiosyncratic local practice of talking about prices in tomans even though the currency is denominated in rials. While most travellers eventually get used to this, at first it is completely bamboozling. One toman is worth 10 rials, so it's a bit like shopkeepers in Europe asking for 10 cents whenever they wanted €1.

To make matters worse, the *bazaris*, the shopkeepers in the bazaar, sometimes say 'one' as shorthand for IR100 or even IR1000. However, when written down, prices are usually expressed in rials. It can be very confusing, but after you've been around a few days you'll understand that the two fingers the taxi driver just showed you when you told him you want go across Tehran (without picking up anyone else) mean IR20,000. Until you do, a calculator or at least a pen will be handy.

SHOW ME THE MONEY

So you've been robbed, lost your wallet, maybe bought one too many carpets in Esfahan and you're out of cash. Don't despair. What is described below is definitely not something to build into your travel plan, but if you need money sent from abroad, this system should work.

1. Go to the nearest Bank Melli (BMI) central branch, preferably in Tehran where Mr Abdollahi at counter 14 speaks English and has helped many travellers out of such situations.

2. Find an English speaker, *in sh'Allah*, and outline what you want to do.

3. Get the Swift identification code for this particular BMI branch (eg Tehran central branch is MELIIR THA060); and ask whether there is a BMI branch in your home country (these are listed at www .bmi.ir), or which bank in your country is affiliated with BMI (eg in Australia, it's Westpac bank).

4. Ask your saviour at home to go to a branch of the nominated bank (eg Westpac) with your full name, passport number and the Swift code, and deposit the money.

5. Between two and four days later, the cash should arrive at your branch in Iran.

Be warned that the charges in your home country can be high – US$60 according to one traveller. But if you're desperate, this is the least of your worries. Once you're in the money again, don't forget to pick up a decent souvenir for your saviour.

Credit Cards

The 'war on terror' and the US trade embargo mean you cannot use any credit card in Iran. You can not pay for a hotel, a plane ticket, nothing. You cannot draw cash on your credit card. This might change in future, but don't rely on it. Just file away the plastic and be sure to bring enough cash.

International Transfers

It's possible to have money transferred from overseas to a bank or an individual's account in Iran. It is best done through a branch of an Iranian bank in your home country. Most major Iranian banks have branches in Europe (mainly in the UK, France and Germany), but they are not represented in the USA or Australasia. For details, see the boxed text 'Show Me the Money', above.

Moneychangers

The quickest and easiest way to change cash is at an official money-exchange office. These can be found in several major cities – look for small shops with the words 'Currency' or 'Exchange' in English.

Changing money in an exchange shop is much safer than doing so with a street moneychanger. You're much less likely to get ripped off because you know where to find the office again and they won't want a visit from the police if you complain. Having said that, street moneychangers do operate in a reassuringly open fashion and one reader

even told of being sent out of a busy bank to change money on the street, where the moneychanger was standing next to a policeman. Demand the same rate as you'd get in the bank and expect the changer to take a IR10,000 'service fee'. Count the money carefully, and don't hand over your bill until you're sure it's correct. If you can't find a bank or exchange office, carpet shops, jewellers or someone in the bazaar should be able to help. Otherwise, try your hotel reception.

Tipping

Tipping is not a big deal in Iran, although you will be expected to leave a gratuity of about 10% if you eat in decent restaurants. This is the case even when 'service' is already included in the bill. It is also normal to offer a small tip or present to anyone who guides you or opens a building that is normally closed. If your offer is initially refused, you should persist in making it three times before giving up (see the boxed text 'Ta'arof, p40). You'll be relieved to hear there is no culture of 'baksheesh' in Iran.

Travellers Cheques

American Express. Leave home without them! Like credit cards, travellers cheques are useless in Iran. No matter what currency or who issues them, Iranian banks will not change travellers cheques. Just in case there is any confusion: *you cannot change travellers cheques in Iran!*

DUAL PRICING

The officially sanctioned practice of charging foreigners more than locals for the same service is one of the most annoying aspects of a visit to Iran. Hotels, museums and historical sites are where you will experience this most often. In all but the cheapest hotels, foreigners are routinely charged about 30 to 50% more than Iranian guests. But it is at 'tourist attractions' that the discrepancy is greatest. Unless you look like an Iranian and can buy your ticket in passable Farsi (or get an Iranian friend to buy it for you), you will be charged between five and 15 times more than the locals. For many sites, such as Persepolis or the National Jewels Museum in Tehran, you'll be happy to pay the foreign price because the site is worth those few dollars. Others, however, are not, and being asked to pay IR30,000 after the Iranian in front of you has just paid IR2000 can be particularly galling.

You can take some comfort knowing that your extra rials will, in theory, go towards the upkeep of the much underfunded building. But being told by the ticket man that you're being charged so much 'because you're rich' is irksome. Still, it's worth keeping it all in perspective – the vast majority of transactions in Iran will be perfectly fair. And there's a good chance you'll be humbled by someone for whom IR20,000 is a fortune insisting on paying your share of a meal.

PHOTOGRAPHY & VIDEO

There is no shortage of shops processing and selling film in Iran, but the range can be pretty limited. Konica, Agfa, Kodak and Fuji films are commonly available, with a roll of 36 costing about IR13,000. Decent slide film is almost impossible to find, so bring all you're likely to need. A couple of stores in Esfahan, Shiraz and Tehran stock Fuji Sensia 100 (IR45,000) and Kodak E100VS (IR60,000), but that's it, and often there are only a few rolls. Konica slide film is widely available for about IR20,000. Normal camera batteries are widely available, but lithium batteries are much harder to track down. Note that airport X-ray machines are not exactly state-of-the-art so it's worth getting the security guards to hand-check your film; they're usually happy to do so if you ask (or plead) nicely.

Most Internet cafés run the Windows XP operating system, which means you can usually upload your pictures directly to your email and send them home to your (hopefully) appreciative family.

Technical Tips

For most of the year lighting conditions during the day are good, so you can usually afford to use very slow speed film. In fact one of the main problems is that the strong sunlight throws reflections on the lens (preventable with a lens hood), casting very noticeable shadows, which can spoil an otherwise good photograph. For this reason, buildings are often best photographed with the light directly overhead. With so much reflected light it is easy to overexpose, especially during winter when the sun is shining from a lower angle. A tripod is essential if you plan to shoot inside mosques and other buildings.

Restrictions

In Iran it is especially important to avoid photographing government buildings, airports, naval dockyards, nuclear reactors, roadblocks, military installations, embassies/consulates, prisons, telephone offices or police stations, or within several kilometres of any border. When you see a 'No Photography' sign, take heed. If you're in doubt, ask.

Photographing People

Most Iranians are happy to have their picture taken provided you ask first. However, where lone women are concerned it doesn't matter how nicely you ask, the answer will almost always be no. If you point your lens at a woman without permission you can expect her to quickly disappear into her chador or scarf.

Offering to take pictures of your Iranian friends and post or email to them later is greatly appreciated – as long as you remember to post or email them. If you don't plan to keep the promise, don't make it.

POST

Postage is very cheap. The cost of sending an airmail postcard to Europe, North America and Australasia is IR1000. The cost for a normal-sized letter by airmail to anywhere outside Iran should be IR4000. The service is reliable and reasonably swift. Postcards usually reach Europe in four or five days. In contrast, the domestic postal service is reliable but slow, and sending a letter across the world is often quicker than getting it across the country.

If you're sending mail to a complicated address or to somewhere remote, try to get someone to write the address in Farsi on the envelope. Postboxes are few and far between, except outside post offices.

Poste restante is little used and, according to readers, quite unreliable. You're far more likely to receive your goods if you get them posted to a particular hotel or home.

Parcels

Sending a parcel out of Iran is an exercise in form shuffling guaranteed to take at least twice as long as you expect. Take your un-wrapped package to the parcel post counter (*daftar-e amanat-e posti*) at the main post office (*postkhuneh-ye markazi*) in a pro-vincial capital. There it will be checked, packaged and signed for in triplicate. There are three parcel services – *pishtaz* (express), *havayi* (airmail) and surface. Rates tend to vary depending on who is quoting them, but a 5kg parcel to anywhere by surface mail should cost less than US$20. The section on Customs (p344) list the customs regulations for some handicrafts and carpets, although the customs officer on duty at the head post office generally has discretion over what can be posted abroad, so be nice. You might be asked to show your passport.

SHOPPING

Iran has plenty of products that make good souvenirs, but outside of Esfahan and Shiraz they can often be difficult to find. As a re-sult of the lack of mass tourism there is also a refreshing lack of mass production. Prices are low and the quality is generally high, even at the budget end of the market. And if you are prepared to invest the time in the smaller bazaars, you should come away with not only a great souvenir but also a good story as to how you bought it. If you'd prefer to just knock it all over in a couple of hours and aren't too worried about price, the ba-zaars in Esfahan and Shiraz are for you. If you don't want to haggle at all the govern-ment-run Iran Handicrafts Organisation has fixed-price shops in most provincial capitals.

Various places in Iran specialise in specific products. Often, knowing the best place to buy something is as important as getting a good price. Export restrictions apply to some goods (p344).

In theory the best place to buy *minyaturha* (miniatures) is in and around Imam Sq in Esfahan. What constitutes a 'real' miniature is widely debated (should they be painted on paper or camel bone?), however most of what you see will be on camel bone. The better miniatures are likely to cost at least US$50. Apart from Esfahan, Manuchehri St in Tehran has some good examples. Tehran Bazaar, Khorramabad and Orumiyeh are also good for miniatures, and *qabha-ye aks* (picture frames) are good in Orumiyeh. For more on miniatures see p60.

Most cities have bookshops that sell inexpensive English-language coffee-table books about Iran with glossy photographs.

For the lowdown on the ubiquitous Persian carpet, the best and most popular souvenir investment for many travellers to Iran, see p53.

There are dozens of shops and factories selling *sefalgari* (ceramics) and *moza'i-ha* (mosaic tiles) at Lalejin, near Hamadan; Maraqeh, near Tabriz; Minab, near Bandar-e Abbas; and around Rasht and Masuleh.

Traditional clothes can make great souvenirs. *Givehs* (lightweight shoes) and *abas* (traditional coats without sleeves) are available in the Kermanshah and Khuzestan provinces. Uniquely embroidered abas from villages near Bandar-e Abbas and Bushehr are especially impressive. All sorts of beautiful garments made from a silk called *tirma* are found in Yazd province. Traditional woollen Kurdish coats and hats from Kordestan and Ilam provinces are popular, and the women of Masuleh knit fine woollen socks.

Intricate *shisheh alat* (glassware) can be bought in Yazd, Tehran and Meimand, near Kerman.

Be wary unless you know what you're doing when buying *javaher alat* (jewellery), although there is plenty of gorgeous stuff to choose from: traditional jewellery from Kordestan; turquoise from Mashhad; and silver filigree necklaces and earrings from villages in Zanjan province.

Bags made from *charmineh* (leather) from Hamadan and Yazd are popular, and Tabriz is renowned for its *abrishom* (silk).

Some interesting metalwork souvenirs to pick up include knives from Zanjan; anything made of silver or gold from Khuzestan province, Kerman or Shiraz; and *servis-ha-ye chay* (tea sets) and qalyans made from *mes* (copper) and *beronz* (bronze).

Za'faran (saffron) from Mashhad, and *hanna* (henna), particularly from Tabriz and Yazd, are readily available.

The Telephone, Post & Telegraph Ministry Museum in Tehran is of limited interest, but is the place to buy *tambrha* (postage stamps), including all manner of anti-American propaganda stamps.

Woodwork is widely available, but for carvings and *ja'beha* (inlaid boxes), it's hard to go past Orumiyeh and Esfahan. For baskets and knickknacks made from bamboo, look around Rasht and nearby villages. For *moarraq* (marquetry) try Esfahan.

SOLO TRAVELLERS

As long as you're a man, there is nowhere in Iran that can't be travelled alone. If you're a woman, solo travel is not so easy. Attitudes towards lone women travellers can be misguided, to put it lightly, and simple things like getting a room can be difficult (p362). It is certainly easier for a woman to travel with someone else, preferably a man. That said, women are visiting Iran by themselves and usually enjoying the trip.

TELEPHONE

The process of dragging the Iranian telephone system out of the dark ages is, mercifully, almost complete. With some numbers having changed four times in the previous five years, the government announced in early 2004 there would be no more changes...for five years, anyway.

Part of the great leap forward has seen dozens of new public card phones put up in cities across Iran. Cards for domestic calls come in denominations of IR5000, IR10,000 and IR20,000, but calls are so cheap that you'll need to really like the sound of your voice to get through the larger card. Local calls are just IR42 per minute, though it's more if you're calling a mobile. You can buy them in newsstands. Phonecards for international calls are also available, though much harder to find. Your best bet is to ask in an Internet café.

There are still plenty of the old-style payphones around, which take IR50 and IR100 coins. Calls are so cheap that if you

---

WHAT A BARGAIN!

While not as deeply ingrained as in Arab countries, bargaining is an important part of the shopping experience in Iran. As a general rule, the prices of groceries, transport (except private taxis) and most things with a price tag attached are fixed. On the other hand, virtually all prices in the bazaar are negotiable, particularly souvenir-type products. Especially in touristed areas like Imam Sq in Esfahan or the Bazar-e Vakil in Shiraz, if you don't bargain you'll likely end up paying well over the odds.

Bargaining can be tough if you're not used to it, so here are a couple of pointers. First, when you find something you like be sure not to show too much interest. Vendors can smell desperation a mile away. Second, don't buy the first one you see; subtly check out a few alternatives to get an idea of the price. With this knowledge, casually enquire as to the price and then make a counter-offer, thus beginning the bargaining process. The vendor will often beseech you to make a better offer: 'But I have nine children to feed'. However, having looked at the competition you know what is a fair price, so only edge up slowly. If you can't agree on a price you could try walking out of the store, but if the shopkeeper calls your bluff you'll struggle to knock the price down any further than you already have.

Remember that bargaining is not a life and death battle. A good bargain is when *both* parties are happy and doesn't necessarily require you to screw every last rial out of the vendor. If you paid more than your travelling companion, don't worry. As long as you're happy, it was a good deal. Remember too that no-one is forcing you to buy anything. Your money will stay in your pocket until you decide to take it out. And, unlike at home, if you do get ripped off in Iran the damage won't be too great.

ask nicely most hotels will let you make a few free of charge. Airports and major bus stations usually have at least one public telephone permitting free local calls.

International calls from Iran are cheap – just IR1590 per minute to anywhere in the world except Afghanistan. These rates can be had at the many small telephone offices you'll find across the country, and the few large offices that have yet to be closed down. Most of these are open from about 7.30am until 10pm, though some, such as Esfahan's main office, are open 24 hours. The process is pretty simple: give the number you want to the front desk and wait for a booth to become available. You'll be charged for a minimum of three minutes. Note that you shouldn't be put off if there are dozens of young soldiers waiting to make calls; these guys are calling girlfriends or family in Iran and the special booth for international calls will often be available. You can't make reverse-charge calls to or from Iran. Iran's country code is ☎ 98, to dial out of Iran call ☎ 00; if calling from outside Iran, drop the initial 0 from all area codes, both for fixed-line and mobile numbers.

Mobile Phones

When the authors were in Iran some mobile phone numbers changed. We think we've got them all right, but if you can't get through on a number listed here, try swapping the third and fourth digits before you give up (eg 0912 345 6789 becomes 0913 245 6789). At the time of writing you could not use foreign-registered phones on Iran's aging mobile network. Neither was renting a phone or SIM card an option. However, you will see plenty of Iranians talking into mobile phones, the use of which is growing at a staggering rate. To get an idea of how fast, consider that in the three weeks before 10 March 2004, a government sale saw 5.6 million SIM cards sold at US$520 each (the market rate is closer to US$1200), and those cards weren't due to be delivered until early 2005. If you're desperate, Thuraya satellite phones work in Iran.

TIME

Compared with some of their Middle East neighbours, Iranians are fairly punctual and will expect you to be the same.

Time throughout Iran is 3½ hours ahead of Greenwich Mean Time (GMT). Clocks go forward one hour between mid-March and mid-September. Without allowing for variations due to daylight-saving, when it's noon in Tehran it's 3.30am in New York; 8.30am in London; 10.30am in Turkey; 11.30am in Azerbaijan; noon in Afghanistan; 1.30pm in Pakistan and Turkmenistan (note this when preparing to cross these borders); and 6.30pm in Sydney. See the World Time Zones map (p389).

TOILETS

Iranian toilets are often the squat kind; even if you pay a royal US$50 for a hotel room, it might not be fitted with a throne. Almost all public toilets are squats and while some are regularly cleaned, others are very definitely not. Still, there are usually enough options that you won't have to enter anywhere that your nose tells you not to. Mosques, petrol stations, bus and train stations and airport terminals always have toilets, and they're usually fit to use.

Toilet paper is more accessible than it once was. Grocery stores in larger cities often stock it, but if you can't find any there's always the ubiquitous box of tissues. Many mid-range hotels have joined their top-end counterparts in supplying toilet paper, though sometimes you'll need to ask. Most toilets are not designed for paper and there should be a bucket next to the toilet where you place your used sheets.

TOURIST INFORMATION

The ominous-sounding Ministry of Culture & Islamic Guidance is responsible for 'cultural affairs, propaganda, literature and arts, audiovisual production, archaeology, preservation of the cultural heritage, tourism, press and libraries'. As the list suggests, tourism is not their top priority, though it does seem to be rising.

The ministry has a tourist office in every provincial capital often, but not always, called the **Iran Touring & Tourism Organization** (ITTO; www.itto.org). The ITTIC is the corporate arm of the ITTO, which runs hotels and the odd restaurant, but doesn't have much info.

Some of these are developing decent regional tourism websites. However, their offices are generally unaccustomed to walk-in visitors and although many do have brochures and maps salted away (often basic and Farsi only) they're rarely central and generally only worth the trek when you have a specific problem to solve. Possible exceptions are the very helpful offices in Kermanshah, Hamadan and Kerman. Additionally, a few local government authorities (notably Tabriz, Qazvin, Shiraz and Esfahan) run more pro-active centres where staff speak English (or can find someone that does). These usually do stock maps and brochures and are worth visiting early in your visit. There are small information booths at the main bus terminals, train stations and international airports, but staff rarely speak English.

Sadly, there are no tourist offices abroad. Beyond this guidebook, your best bet is to get online (p15).

VISAS

Perhaps the biggest reason more people don't come to Iran is that getting a visa can be unnecessarily and frustratingly difficult. There are no hard and fast rules but those that do exist tend to change with disconcerting regularity, either at the whim of the particular visa officer or as a result of words or actions in a bigger political picture. If your nation's fearless leader describes Iran as being part of an 'axis of evil', for example, you can guess that getting your visa will become that much harder. However, there is good news on the visa front. The hundreds of letters and emails we receive suggest that, on the whole, it's easier to get a tourist visa now than it was a few years ago. And when it is issued, it's more likely (but by no means certain) to be for the maximum 30 days (extensions are possible; see p362).

Turkish passport holders can get a three-month tourist visa on arrival. Everyone else will need to pay and apply well ahead of departure; to be safe that means months in the US, at least five weeks in the UK and most European countries, but only two to three weeks in Australia. Israelis (along with anyone who has an Israeli stamp in their passport) are not allowed in under any circumstances; nor are women who refuse to wear appropriate clothing. US citizens are welcome, but unless you have an Iranian sponsor or are prepared to badger the Iranian interests section in Washington for many months, you'll probably only get a visa if you join an organised tour or arrange a private guide.

Visa regulations vary greatly from one Iranian embassy to another. The same

> ### THE GOOD, THE BAD...
>
> It depends on what passport you're carrying, but feedback at the time of writing suggests that *in general* applying for a visa on your own (without an agency) in the following embassies will be smooth and efficient, even if still lengthy (Good), or a protracted nightmare with no guaranteed result (Bad). Of course, this information is particularly prone to change:
>
> **Good** Canberra, Australia; Wellington, New Zealand; Dublin, Ireland; Kabul, Afghanistan; Bishkek, Kyrgyzstan; İstanbul and Erzurum, Turkey; Amman, Jordan.
>
> **Bad** London, UK; Rome, Italy; Paris, France; Iranian interests section in the Pakistan embassy, Washington DC, USA; The Hague, Netherlands; Madrid, Spain.

embassy might be good one year then rotten the next. Check Lonely Planet's Thorn Tree bulletin board (thorntree.lonelyplanet .com) to learn from other travellers' experience. The best hand out one-month tourist visas virtually on the spot (if you've got the right passport). The worst demand you have local contacts, then after you've waited a month tell you your case is still pending. Some will only issue transit visas, which cannot be extended.

Several embassies demand that applicants have a 'sponsor' to get the tourist visa. If like most tourists you have no friends or contacts in Iran, you'll either need to apply elsewhere or use an agency.

Whether or not you have a sponsor, your application will usually need 'approval' from Tehran. Getting this approval will likely take at least two weeks. You rarely need to leave your passport at the embassy during the approval phase of application, but unless you are prepared to hang around for weeks, it is generally the best policy to apply in your home country before departure. However, once the visa is issued you must enter Iran within 90 days. Thus if you're going to be travelling for a long time before hitting Iran and want to play safe, apply (more expensively) through a specialised agency. Given a month the best agencies can get preapproval from Tehran and send the details to the embassy/consulate you designate. Thus when you show up you'll only have to wait one or two processing days to collect the visa.

Don't be put off if you're refused a visa the first time you apply. Although it won't help future applications, some travellers have been successful at a second attempt even at the same consulate, notably by using an agency.

Visa costs vary from place to place. Most Iranian embassies in Europe have websites detailing costs, how long it's likely to take and what you need to supply (p347). For example, in their home countries in 2004 Brits were being charged UK£43/47/58 for a transit visa/single/double-entry tourist visa; Canadians C$32/72/96; and Germans €29/48/57. However, sometimes you can be hit for much more than this – and for an agency you can add about US$30 to US$100 for arranging the sponsorship and visa approval. The rules about whether you need an Iranian sponsor to get a tourist visa also differ from one embassy to another. If you don't have a sponsor, ask another embassy in a neighbouring country about their rules, or use an agency.

If you are arranging your visa through a relative, travel agency or business contact in Iran, they will need your full personal details and passport information, an outline itinerary and your flight details.

After a delay that might last some weeks, your sponsor or agent will forward an authorisation number from the Ministry of Foreign Affairs in Tehran, which you use to collect your visa from the relevant embassy, submitting the usual forms, photos and money in the process. You can ask for the authorisation number to be faxed from Iran to the relevant Iranian embassy but make sure you know the number when you go to collect the visa.

Some embassies/consulates (such as the UK) require foreign women to be wearing a headscarf in the photos used for the visa application; check first. If you do need to wear a headscarf, you might also need to wear it into the embassy/consulate when you go to pick up your visa (such as in the Iranian interests section in Washington).

While we don't advocate lying on your application form, don't complicate matters unnecessarily by claiming you're something unloved like a journalist; it's better just to say you're a teacher, student or nurse. Similarly note that nobody checks whether you're following the route you supplied in

your application itinerary so choose one that sounds uncontroversial.

Whatever you do, don't overstay your visa. While this may not cost a lot to rectify, you could be stuck for up to a week sorting out the paperwork.

VISA AGENCIES

A growing number of travellers are biting the bullet and using agencies to arrange their visas. The agencies invariably have links with either the local embassy or the Ministry of Foreign Affairs in Iran, so can usually get you a visa even if you've already been rejected. They apply on your behalf and send you the approval number, as described above. Some are expensive, others very reasonable. Below are some that have been recommended by readers:

Iranianvisa.com (www.iranianvisa.com) Charges US$30 to arrange a visa number through a simple website.

Pars Tour & Travel (www.Key2Persia.com) Charges US$30 but will often drop this if you use its efficient Shiraz-based agency once you arrive.

Persian Voyages (www.persianvoyages.com) More expensive at UK£70, but reliable even when other agencies have failed.

TRANSIT VISAS

Unfortunately, Iran *no longer extends transit visas,* reversing an easy extension policy that overlanders had enjoyed for 20 years. Transit visas are usually issued for a stay of five, seven or occasionally 10 days to foreigners travelling overland through Iran (eg to anyone travelling through Iran to Turkey or Pakistan). Travellers often pick them up along the way; Turkey is usually the easiest place to apply, and from time to time getting one in Pakistan is problematic. In theory, transit visas should be issued within a few days, but it often takes two or three weeks and you might still need a (sometimes expensive) letter of recommendation from your embassy if you apply from outside your home country.

The main advantage of a transit visa is that you don't normally need a sponsor in Iran to get one. The main disadvantage? Iran is a big country and five days is a very short time.

BUSINESS VISAS

To get a two-week or one-month (extendable) business visa you must have a business contact in Iran who can sponsor your visit through the Ministry of Foreign Affairs in Tehran.

DIRECTORY

WOMEN TRAVELLERS

Travelling in Iran as a woman means stepping into a culture likely to be vastly different from your own. Accepting most of those differences as part of the experience, at least while you're in Iran, is the easiest way to deal with them.

For the most part, women travellers enjoy Iran and have few problems. Sure, there are obvious inconveniences, such as wearing hejab in the midsummer heat, being sure to never shake the hand of, or touch in any way, a man unless he's married to you and, perhaps most frustratingly, often being treated as less than your male travelling companions. If you don't take them personally, however, these will very rarely be anything more than just that – an annoying inconvenience. And, certainly, we have not heard of any woman traveller being physically abused in Iran.

In short, while you *will* be tested and frustrated on occasion by attitudes that would never be tolerated at home, the success or otherwise of your trip to Iran depends almost entirely on how you handle those situations. The best advice for most such cases is to remain calm, dignified and don't take it personally.

Attitudes towards Women

As unusual as Iranian culture is to us, Western culture is to Iranians. Possibly more so. Keeping this in mind will help you to

---

MORE TIME, PLEASE

First the good news: the uncertainties that for years have plagued the process of extending a tourist visa have largely disappeared and there is *usually* little difficulty in extending a 30-day tourist visa to 60 days, or even 90. This is how it works:

Head for the provincial police headquarters *(shahrbani)* or Foreign Affairs office, often called Aliens Bureau, in your city of choice. Take your passport, two or sometimes three mugshots of yourself, photocopies of the picture page of your passport and the page with the Iranian visa, and IR100,000 for the extension, plus about IR5000 for the processing.

Once you've filled out the appropriate form (twice) you'll be asked to deposit your IR100,000 into a specific account at a (hopefully) nearby branch of Bank Melli. When you return with your bank receipt, your passport with new visa will be handed over. This is a best-case scenario, and there are slight variations in some cities, which are listed in the relevant Visa Extensions sections where applicable. These usually involve having to wait longer once you've paid the money – from an hour to a couple of days.

Carefully choose the city where you plan to extend. In general, cities familiar with tourists are the best places: Esfahan, Shiraz, Yazd and Tabriz, are your best bets; while second-string options include Kerman, Zahedan and Rasht. Tehran's Disciplinary Force for Islamic Republic of Iran Department for Aliens Affairs is every bit the nightmare it sounds – don't go there (p000). Smaller cities often take longer to issue the extension, if at all, so you're strongly advised to choose one of the cities listed here. Timing is also important: your extension starts on the day it's issued, not the end of your original visa.

The bad news affects those with transit visas. Transit visas cannot be extended so those needing to cross the country in as few as five days can face real problems. However, if your visa is up and you've not yet made it to the border, here are a couple of tips we received from one very helpful visa official:

- A doctor's note on official stationery stating you were unwell and needed, say, two days rest will act as a quasi-extension once you get to the border, or can be used to extend for a couple of days in the nearest Aliens Bureau.

- If you are heading east and are only a couple of days over, officers at Zahedan have been known to collect a small fine and extend your visa on the spot before you leave, just to make it all legal.

It's best, of course, not to rely on these last-gasp options. All of the above is subject to sudden change so check with other travellers on the Thorn Tree (thorntree.lonelyplanet.com) before making firm plans.

understand – but not necessarily agree with – some of the attitudes you encounter as a woman travelling in Iran.

Contrary to some perceptions, many of the conservative attitudes inherent in the Iranian brand of Islam are nurtured as much by Iranian women as they are by men. If, for example, your scarf slips back a bit too far or you inadvertently expose a little too much ankle, it's far more likely to be an elderly Iranian woman who steps in to correct the situation (either literally or with a few sharp words) than a man.

Even if you're dressed appropriately, some men will look at you with an unnerving mix of curiosity, lust and hope. It will rarely go beyond just looking, or perhaps some suggestive comment in Farsi. But as one traveller put it, this could still leave you feeling like 'a piece of meat'. These distorted ideas are in part due to a perception – perpetuated largely through foreign movies – that Western women are 'easy'. They are also rooted in the fact that the traditional Iranian woman would rarely travel alone; the implication being that if you're doing so then you must be of dubious moral standing.

One other negative experience you should be aware of is that even when travelling with a man, you might find Iranian men (and Iranian women in the company of an Iranian man) will talk almost exclusively to the foreign man. This can be unsettling, especially if the conversation lasts for several hours over dinner, and you, as a woman, are rarely even acknowledged.

However, these attitudes are slowly changing and you can take heart knowing that in the overwhelming majority of situations you will be treated with courtesy and respect. As their awareness of the world increases Iranians are becoming more accepting of women travellers and more prepared to engage them. People are less wary of approaching foreigners, especially in cities.

As a foreign woman you will sometimes be considered an honorary male and be accepted into all-male preserves, such as teahouses, in a way that most Iranian women could not dream of being. You will, of course, be accepted into female society far more than any man (Iranian or foreign). It's not uncommon for foreign women to be treated with extra courtesy because of their perceived vulnerability. When it comes to finding scarce hotel accommodation or plane tickets, or lining up at places such as the visa-extension office, an unaccompanied woman is almost certainly at an advantage over a man.

Some restaurants and teahouses have separate areas set aside for women and families. Where that's the case, you will be directed straight to them.

Safety Precautions

Violence against foreign women is almost unheard of in Iran, even if the odd grope on the street or in a shared taxi or a bit of Tehran Metro frotting is not. And while there is a reasonable chance your bum will be pinched by some guy during the course of your trip, it's important to remember that not every male who speaks to you has ulterior motives. Indeed, some foreign women who have travelled through Pakistan, Turkey or Egypt say they feel more comfortable in Iran where the level of harassment is lower. In general, if you keep to the dress and social codes, most people will respect you.

Of course, you should take normal safety precautions. Always lock the door of your hotel room, for example, and when seeking accommodation it's wise to avoid the cheapest mosaferkhunehs. Look for places with women around – anywhere described in this book as family-run will probably be suitable. You shouldn't have much problem sharing a room with a foreign male companion, even if he is not your husband (p346).

Try to avoid looking men in the eye unless you know them well, as this will almost certainly be interpreted as a come-on.

If you are harassed, tell your persecutor firmly, but politely, to desist (English will do), and try to enlist the sympathy of other Iranians. If they think someone is behaving badly towards you, they will probably stop him out of shame. Try to avoid screaming blue murder; it might make the situation worse. If the problem persists, a mere mention of the police should have a sobering effect. Thanks to social constraints, you will rarely be alone with an Iranian male unless you want to be, but if it looks as if that might happen when you don't want it, it's wise to be cautious.

You might feel happier travelling in a group or with a male companion, but neither is essential. Either way, wearing a wedding

DIRECTORY

ring is a good idea even if you're not married. At times it might be sensible to say your husband is travelling with you or about to join you, but in general, Iranians understand that foreigners have different rules.

What to Wear
By law, all females over the age of nine must wear the hejab, the general term to describe the type of Islamic dress required for females in Iran. Signs in public places show two possible variants on correct hejab: The chador, an all-encompassing, head-to-toe black 'tent' (which is what 'chador' means in Farsi); or a *maqna'e* (a wimple-like scarf-shawl) with a manteau (baggy trench coat) and trousers.

These days the 'style police' are not as busy as they once were and foreign women can get away with wearing their normal clothes, provided their head, shoulders, arms, legs and body are completely covered up and the shape of their body is concealed. Even socks are no longer essential and few people bat an eyelid if you have your fringe or the front of your hair showing. On the other hand, were you to venture onto the streets with no scarf at all it would mean trouble. While the mandatory scarf is undoubtedly annoying, it can often work for you by deflecting unwanted attention.

If you're coming to Iran from Pakistan or India a *shalwar kameez*, a long loose shirt worn over baggy trousers, makes the perfect garment, provided the top is long enough to completely cover your bottom. The only times when foreign women must wear a chador are when visiting the shrines at Qom, Shiraz and Mashhad. Indeed, if you choose to wear a chador more generally you run the risk of being thought of as a try-hard by women in smaller towns and being disowned by more 'modern' women in cities such as Tehran. One traveller wrote saying she and her friend had battled with their chadors for two days (chadors have no zips or buttons so they must be constantly held closed with the hands or teeth) before a Tehrani woman asked incredulously: 'You don't wear that at home, so why are you wearing it here?' The Tehrani went on to suggest she show a bit more solidarity with her Iranian sisters and directed her to

the nearest manteau store. Another reader wrote:

> We advise the purchase soon after arrival of scarves and manteaux at the cost of between US$10 and $20. It will make the rest of the travel easier. My 18-year-old [daughter] travelled in a shortened mid-thigh manteau; the woman outfitting us stated that I, age 58, should wear a cover to my ankles (we removed the shoulder pads immediately). Wearing the barest necessities under the manteau (as long as uncovered legs don't show) would be acceptable. However, having been invited into many Iranian homes we discovered the downside of wearing the bare minimum beneath our 'covers'. A bra is not appropriate, nor is even a sleeveless scooped-neck shell, inside someone's home.
>
> *Dale Dewar*

If you are travelling in summer, light fabrics are strongly recommended. You can easily buy suitable clothes inside Iran; wearing any scarf and man's shirt several sizes too large should get you through immigration without too much trouble.

As to how to deal with Dale's summer problem of how to minimise your clothing while avoiding an embarrassing situation, this advice from an Iranian woman should help: 'Yes, we quite often go about with very little on underneath but you need to beware when you go to someone's house; often Iranian women will excuse themselves on arrival and go to the bathroom to slip on a blouse or something. It's quite useful to take a quantity of small butterfly clips or safety pins to hold together the parts of the manteau that might gape when you are just wearing a bra underneath.'

What to Bring
For most women the main difficulty when packing is to find garments in their wardrobe suitable for Iran. However, tampon-users might want to pack enough to get them through their trip. Tampons are very hard to find and, if you do manage to track them down, ridiculously expensive.

Transport

GETTING THERE & AWAY

For a country so politically insular, and one so hesitant to issue visas, there is a surprisingly large number of options for travelling in and out of Iran. Planes, trains, ferries and almost every form of road transport you can imagine crosses Iran's borders. A French woman was even crossing the country with a horse and a mule when we were there. About the only thing we haven't heard of is a unicycle (apologies to anyone whose account of their unicycle trip didn't reach us in time).

THINGS CHANGE...

The information in this chapter is particularly vulnerable to change. Check with the airline or a travel agent to make sure you understand how a fare (and ticket) works and be aware of the security requirements for international travel. Shop carefully. The details given in this chapter should be regarded as pointers and are not a substitute for your own careful, up-to-date research.

ENTERING THE COUNTRY

Arriving in Iran is usually straightforward. Assuming you have a visa, most immigration and border officials are efficient and seldom do you hear of tourists having their bags checked. You'll need to fill out a basic declaration; be sure not to lose the slip of paper they give you because you will need it on departure. If flying in, you should be negotiating with a taxi inside an hour. Land borders take longer, especially if you're on a bus or train (p368). It goes without saying that women need to be adequately covered.

Passport

Iran has issues with Israel. If you're travelling on an Israeli passport you'll be turned away at the border (and you won't even get onto a flight coming into Iran). Similarly, having an Israeli stamp in your passport will see you turned away or put on the next flight out (p360).

AIR

Airports & Airlines

Despite its political isolation, Iran has an impressive array of international flights. Most land at Mehrabad International Airport in Tehran, though as we went to press news was coming thick and fast that the vast Imam Khomeini International Airport south of the capital would finally be opened – after more than 30 years of construction (see the boxed text, p109).

Other international airports are Esfahan, Shiraz, Mashhad, Bandar-e Abbas, Ahvaz, and Hamadan, Ahvaz, Qeshm, Zahedan and even humble Shahr-e Kord. The flights are often infrequent and often on smaller regional airlines, meaning there's a dangerously strong chance you'll be on a Tupolev.

Iran Air is officially called the Airline of the Islamic Republic of Iran, and has the Homa, a mythical bird, as its symbol. As the government-owned national carrier,• it offers service with an Islamic flavour (ie no pork and absolutely no alcohol). Women flying on Iran Air used to have to wear hejab from the time they arrived at the departure airport, but this rule seems to have been relaxed. These days, as on other international

TRANSPORT

carriers, it seems to be all right to hold off on wearing the headscarf until the descent to Iran is announced. All Iran Air flights are nonsmoking.

Iran Air flies to a wide range of destinations in Asia, the Middle East and Europe and has a pretty good reputation. The prices listed in this book for Iran Air flights are for winter (October to March); in summer prices rise a little and there are more flights.

Iran Aseman, Mahan Air and Caspian Airlines operate a handful of international flights, usually to Gulf capitals, including Dubai, Bahrain and Kuwait. Mahan Air is worth investigating for flights from Asia and unusual destinations in Europe.

Airlines flying into Iran include the following:

Aeroflot (code SU; in Tehran ☎ 021-880 8480; www.aeroflot.com; hub Moscow)

Air France (code AF; in Tehran ☎ 021-670 4111; www.airfrance.com; hub Paris)

Air India (code AI; in Tehran ☎ 021-873 9762; www.airindia.com; hub Delhi)

Alitalia (code AZ; in Tehran ☎ 021-871 1512; www.alitalia.com; hub Rome)

Ariana Afghan Airlines (code FG; in Tehran ☎ 021-855 0156-60; www.flyariana.com; hub Kabul)

Austrian Airlines (code OS; in Tehran ☎ 021-875 8984; www.aua.com; hub Vienna)

British Airways (code BA; in Tehran ☎ 021-204 4552; www.britishairways.com; hub London)

Emirates (code EM; in Tehran ☎ 021-879 6786; www.emirates.com; hub Dubai)

Gulf Air (code GF; in Tehran ☎ 021-225 3284/7; www.gulfair.com; hub Bahrain)

Iran Air (code IR; in Tehran 021-880 8472; www.iranair.com; hub Tehran)

KLM (code KL; in Tehran ☎ 204 4757; www.klm.com; hub Amsterdam)

Kuwait Airways (code KU; in Tehran ☎ 021-225 3284; www.kuwait-airways.com; hub Kuwait City)

Lufthansa (code LH; in Tehran ☎ 021-873 8701; www.lufthansa.com; hub Frankfurt)

Swiss (code LX; in Tehran ☎ 021-874 8332; www.swiss.com; hub Geneva)

Turkish Airlines (code TK; in Tehran ☎ 021-874 8450; www.turkishairlines.com; hub İstanbul)

Tickets

Most tickets are for flights whose first stop in Iran is Tehran, even if the final destination is somewhere more exotic. There are a few exceptions, most notably Shiraz, Mashhad and Kish, which have flights to the Gulf

States. Iran Air usually throws in a free internal flight with an international ticket.

Asia

Iran Air flies between Tehran and Mumbai (Bombay) in India weekly for about US$350 one way. Between Iran and Pakistan, Iran Air flies between Tehran and Karachi for about US$180 one way.

Elsewhere in Asia, Iran Air flies between Tehran and Tokyo (one way/return US$860/1720, twice weekly) via Beijing; and to Kuala Lumpur for US$693/1386. Mahan Air flies to Bangkok (US$480), Manila (US$730), Delhi (US$754) and Kabul (US$611). All these prices are for return tickets.

Australia

There are no direct flights between Australia and Iran. The next best thing is to fly Malaysia Airlines to Kuala Lumpur and Iran Air to Tehran. Similar options would involve Emirates and Gulf Air.

Keep your eye on the travel pages of Melbourne's *Age* or the *Sydney Morning Herald*. Otherwise, **STA Travel** (☎ 1300 733 035; www.statravel.com.au) and **Flight Centre** (☎ 133 133; www.flightcentre.com.au) are worth approaching.

Central Asia

Flying via one of the former Soviet states in Central Asia is a fascinating way to enter or leave Iran, though flights are not frequent and are prone to change and cancellation.

Iran Air, Iran Aseman fly between Tehran and Almaty (Kazakhstan), Ashghabat (Turkmenistan), Baku (Azerbaijan), Bishkek (Kyrgyzstan), Dushanbe (Tajikistan) and Tashkent (Uzbekistan). Usually the national carrier of these countries also flies the route. If you're flying from Iran, your best bet is to just head into the nearest travel agency and ask (see the Information section for whichever town you're in).

Continental Europe

Iran Air and several major European carriers fly directly between most western European cities and Tehran. Cheaper tickets are often offered by the following European airlines: Lufthansa, Air France, Aeroflot, Alitalia, Austrian Airlines, KLM and Swiss.

Prices can be quite competitive, with prices starting at about €450, and rising steadily. Some good places to start looking include:

France
Nouvelles Frontieres (☎ 0825 000 747; www.nouvelles-fr)
OTU Voyages (☎ 0820 817 817; www.otu.fr) For students.
Voyages Wasteels (☎ 0825 887 070; www.wasteels.fr)

Germany
STA Travel (☎ 1805 456 422; www.statravel.de)

Greece
ISYTS (www.travelling.gr/isyts)

Italy
Passaggi (☎ 06 489 068 57; www.passaggi.it)

Switzerland
STA Travel (☎ 058 450 40 00; www.statravel.ch)

Middle East & Africa

Not surprisingly, most countries in the Middle East and the Persian Gulf region offer regular flights to Iran. These flights are used almost exclusively by local businessmen, local tourists and pilgrims, and there are few discounted fares, although you can save money by carefully choosing which airport you fly into.

Iran Air, Iran Aseman and the national carriers of the destination fly to and from Abu Dhabi (UAE), Bahrain, Beirut (Lebanon), Damascus (Syria), Doha (Qatar), Dubai (UAE), Kuwait, Sharjah (UAE); For the Gulf cities, a one-way ticket will seldom cost more than about US$150, often much less. It's about US$200 to Beirut and Damascus. Return fares are often exactly double the one-way fare. It's also worth checking whether there are flights to your destination from Shiraz, Bushehr, Bandar-e Abbas, or Qeshm or Kish Islands. If the distance is shorter, the fare will probably be cheaper.

The new international airports on Qeshm and Kish Islands also have flights with Iran Air and other regional airlines.

Iran Air has no services to Africa.

TURKEY

There are surprisingly few flights between Iran and Turkey. Iran Air has three flights a week between Tehran and İstanbul, while Turkish Airlines flies the same route daily. Flights leave very early and you can expect to pay at least US$500 for a return ticket, more on Turkish Airlines.

The UK

Competition out of London is fierce; for a ticket stopping in either a European or Middle Eastern capital you can expect to pay about UK£350. Airlines to look for include Gulf Air (usually the cheapest), KLM, Emirates, Lufthansa, Alitalia, Air France, Austrian Airlines and Turkish Airlines.

If you're prepared to pay a bit more you can fly nonstop from London on British Airways (twice weekly) or Iran Air (three times a week) from about UK£450; or from Birmingham on Mahan Air (weekly). For a comparison, check www.cheapflights.co.uk, which links you to agencies selling the fare of your choice. Popular travel agencies in the UK include:
Bridge the World (☎ 0870-814 4400; www.bridgethe world.co.uk)
Ebookers (☎ 020-7757 2000; www.ebookers.co.uk)
STA Travel (☎ 0870-1600 599; www.statravel.co.uk) Caters especially to young people and students.
Trailfinders (☎ 020-7628 7628; www.trailfinders.co.uk)
Usit Campus (☎ 0870-240 1010; www.usitworld.com /services/uk.htm) Caters especially to young people and students.

The USA & Canada

There are no direct flights between North America and Iran, but there are loads of indirect options and the whole process is pretty simple.

Iran Air sells codeshare seats from Boston, Chicago, Detroit, Houston, Los Angeles, Miami, Minneapolis, Montreal, New York, San Francisco, Seattle, Toronto, Vancouver and Washington. They usually involve a Lufthansa, British Airways or KLM flight linking with an Iran Air flight in the relevant capital in Europe. Those three airlines, plus a whole host of others (p365), fly direct from their home countries to Tehran. Emirates is especially worth investigating. For a rough idea, return fares from New York to Tehran start from about US$800; from Los Angeles they start at about US$950. Alternatively, scan the Internet for deals or check out the following agencies and consolidators:
Cheapflights.com (www.cheapflights.com) Compares the best offers on the web; simple to use.
Orbitz (www.orbitz.com) Not as cheap as cheapflights, but a fast link to a big range of fares.
STA Travel (☎ 800-781 4040; www.statravel.com) The best student travel service; also sells to nonstudents.

TRANSPORT

LAND

People have been crossing Iran by land for thousands of years, from the earliest merchants seeking fortunes on the Silk Road (see the boxed text 'The Silk Road', p30) through to those seeking something altogether different on the 1960s and '70s 'Hippy Trail'. The relative laissez faire of '70s travel came to an abrupt end when things got heavy, man, with the revolution in Iran and the Soviet invasion of Afghanistan, not to mention the Iran-Iraq War.

Well, the good news is that, the 'war on terror' notwithstanding, it's easier to cross in and out of Iran than it has been for 25 years. The border with Afghanistan is open; routes into Armenia, Azerbaijan and Turkmenistan are doable with varying degrees of hassle; Turkey and Pakistan are a piece of cake; and it's even possible to cross into Iraq, if not recommended.

In recognition of Iran's pivotal position in trans-Asian travel, in this book we've summarised the details of all the crossing points available to foreigners in 'Crossing the Border at...' boxes within the text. General points are given below, but for most of the specifics follow the cross-references to the relevant chapter.

Bicycle

There is no reason why you can't ride in and out of Iran at any of the land borders. There are plenty of cyclists crossing between Turkey and Pakistan, and we have had no reports of trouble at those borders, or any others.

Car & Motorcycle

To bring your own vehicle into Iran, you must be more than 18 years old and have a current international driving permit. For the vehicle, you'll need a carnet (temporary importation document), which can be obtained from the relevant international automobile organisation in your country. For further information about driving to and around Iran, contact the **Touring & Automobile Club of Iran** (☎ 021-874 0411; www.taciran.net 12 Shahid Arabali St, Khorramshahr Ave, Tehran).

Most people with vehicles have reported fairly hassle-free crossings in and out of Turkey and Pakistan. As long as everything is in order it's just a matter of following and waiting. Officials will probably note your vehicle's details in your passport to make sure you don't leave the country without it. Third-party insurance is compulsory for foreign drivers, but can be difficult to obtain outside Iran (if you do get it, make sure the policy is valid for Iran and accredited with Iran Bimeh, the Iranian Green Card Bureau). If you need it, buying the insurance in Maku is far cheaper than at the border.

Iranian oil can be of dubious quality, but the life-sized cutouts of David Beckham and Michael Schumacher should be enough to direct you to the good oil.

No-one but the police is allowed to have a motorbike over 200cc. Foreigners, however, are allowed to ride bikes of any size through Iran, so long as you take it with you when you leave. Still, big bikes are rare: expect to attract a great deal attention if you're on one.

For information about driving around Iran, see p375.

Afghanistan

The border at Dogharon, 20km east of Taybad, is open and straightforward. Daily buses between Herat and Mashhad make the trip even simpler still. For details, see the boxed text 'Crossing the Afghanistan Border at Dogharon' (p334).

Armenia

The border between Iran and Armenia is only 35km long, with one crossing point in Iran at Norduz. Visas are available at the border for US$30 (though some readers have been charged US$40) and apart from the occasional request for something to speed the process, reports suggest this border works pretty smoothly. For details, see the boxed text 'Crossing the Armenian Border at Norduz' (p143).

Azerbaijan

There are two recognised crossings along the border with Azerbaijan: between Astara (Azerbaijan) and Astara (Iran; p149), and Culfa (Azerbaijan) and Jolfa (Iran; p141), the latter leading to the exclave of Nakhchivan, from where you cannot enter Armenia and must fly to get to Baku. The Astara border is possibly one of the easiest in the region – as long as you're not on the bus from Tehran.

BUS

Everyday a bus travels from Tehran to Baku, via Astara. Taking the bus is certainly cheaper than flying, but means you must cope with the inordinate delays entailed in crossing the Astara border in any sort of vehicle – it may end up being quicker to cross the border yourself and then catch a ride on any public transport heading north or south.

Iraq

Crossing into Iraq is legal but, as you would expect from such a volatile area, it is highly unpredictable. The most popular route is via Mehran, but travellers have also reported crossing at Khosravi. Piranshahr is another option. Nervous border guards, deep suspicion and summary decisions are common, and at the time of writing there was a good chance you'd be turned away, depending on who was in charge at the time. Read the boxed text 'Crossing the Iran-Iraq Border' (p179) and check the Thorn Tree (www.lonelyplanet.com) for the very latest information.

Pakistan

Along the 830km border with Pakistan, the only recognised crossing for foreigners is between Mirjaveh (Iran) and Taftan (Pakistan). For details, see the boxed text 'Crossing the Pakistan Border at Mirjaveh/Taftan' (p301).

BUS

There is no direct bus across the Mirjaveh–Taftan border from either side; this is not a problem because you can use a combination of any conceivable type of road transport.

TRAIN

Twice a month, *in sha' Allah*, a Pakistani train putters along the track between Quetta and Zahedan. Though the train saves you changing transport midstream and is quaint (well, for the first few hours at least), taking a combination of bus, minibus and shared taxi to either side of the border and crossing it on foot is far quicker. Track is being laid between Kerman and Zahedan, but it probably won't see trains going the whole way for several years yet.

Syria

Iran and Syria have no common border, but each week several buses make the three-day journey between Tehran or Tabriz and Damascus. There is also a direct train linking the two capitals, via Turkey, costing

IR426,750 one way and taking just 65 hours, or so. According to readers you can expect up to a four-hour wait on both borders and you can't buy the ticket at the station, you must go to a travel agency. You can change any leftover rials on the train.

Turkey

There are two main crossings along the border with Turkey. The busy main one is at Gürbulak (Turkey) and Bazargan (Iran), where there are hotels, moneychanging facilities and regular transport on either side of the border. This border can be awfully congested, though these days you are usually through in a couple of hours or less. See the boxed text 'Crossing the Turkish Border at Bazargan' (p123).

Foreigners can also cross the border at Yüksekova (Turkey) and Sero (Iran), although you need to plan the timing of this crossing more carefully since there is nowhere to stay on either side of the border. See the boxed text 'Crossing the Turkish Border at Sero' (p127).

BUS

Travelling by bus you have two options. The easier is to take a direct long-distance bus to, say, Tehran or Tabriz from İstanbul, Ankara or Erzurum, although this involves lengthy delays while you wait for everyone on the bus to be cleared through customs and immigration (as a lone foreigner, you might be done and on your way in less than an hour).

Every week, several long-distance buses travel between İstanbul and Ankara and Tehran. From Tehran, tickets cost about IR200,000 to İstanbul (about 42 hours) but IR250,000 to Ankara (38 hours), which is nearer. Buses leave from both the central and eastern bus stations, and Mr Imani at **Iran Peyma** (Taavoni No 1; ☎ 021-876 3600/1) promises that if you telephone for it, you can have your ticket delivered to your hotel.

Those in the know swear it's better to take the Ankara bus, which is full of students and embassy workers, rather than the İstanbul bus, which is full of traders and therefore more likely to be taken apart at customs.

However, it is far better to break up the journey between Turkey and Iran, and enjoy some of eastern Turkey and western Iran along the way. Taking a bus to – but not across – either border will also do away with waiting for up to 50 fellow passengers to clear customs. You can cross the border between Doğubayazıt (Turkey) and Maku (Iran) in one day by bus. It's even possible to cross in one day from Erzurum (Turkey) to Tabriz (Iran), if you start early and get through the border with minimum fuss.

Expect longer than usual delays in winter as the high mountain passes near both borders are frequently snowbound.

Occasional buses for Turkey also originate in cities as far off as Shiraz, Esfahan or Tabriz.

CAR & MOTORCYCLE

Most motorists will arrive in Iran via Turkey, crossing the border between Gürbulak and Bazargan or between Yüksekova and Sero. See the boxed texts 'Crossing the Turkish Border at Bazargan' (p123) and 'Crossing the Turkish Border at Sero' (p127) for details.

TRAIN

The train from İstanbul to Tehran via Ankara and Tabriz, among others, is called the *Trans-Asia Express*. It runs weekly in either direction and, at the time of writing, trains on the 2968km journey left Tehran at 10.35pm on Thursday (IR512,550), and departed İstanbul at 6.35pm Wednesday (about US$55). It takes 70 hours and seating is in comfortable 1st-class compartments with four berths. Check www.rajatrains.com or the excellent www.seat61.com for the latest timetables and prices.

The *Trans-Asia Express* is actually two trains; an Iranian train between Tehran and Van, on the shores of Lake Van in eastern Turkey, and a Turkish train from Tatvan to Ankara and İstanbul. The train has evoked some strong feelings among readers, most notably relating to the concept of 'express'.

After some initial teething problems, recent experiences seem to have been faster and easier, though by no means free of delay. However, there is also a distinctly romantic touch to such a long train trip:

This was one of the most enjoyable trips I have made. I was the only foreigner on the train, and once this was discovered I had not nearly enough time to visit all the different compartments full of people wanting to chat (and feed me! Oh, so much food...). It is quite a spectacle to watch the (largely middle-class) female passengers switch from coats and scarves into T-shirts and hairpins as soon as you cross the border. The men, of course, fetch beer and the whole thing has a bit of a party atmosphere. I spent the days learning to sing the poems of Hafez and being pursued by the suddenly liberated single girls (Valentines apparently being in the air!). All in all, a very, very interesting trip – definitely a journey.

Joshua Smyth

Readers have said that although you need to pay for the whole trip even if you plan to get off at Ankara, the ticket is valid for six months and it's possible to make a new reservation on the same ticket for a later trip to İstanbul. They also warn that when buying your ticket in Tehran you should double-check that you have separate reservations and seat numbers for both the Iranian and Turkish trains; and you should consider taking your own food, as the choice on the train is very limited. Finally, when changing from the ferry to your new train at Van, if someone has taken your berth then just grab anything you can find.

Turkmenistan

There are three border posts open to foreigners along this 1206km-long border; Incheh Borun and Gyzyl-Etrek (p314), Sarakhs and Saraghs (p333) and Bajgiran (p332). The paperwork and organisation involved in travelling to Turkmenistan is still a big hassle; the best place for recent information is **Stantours** (www.stantours.com), which can also book you on a tour and arrange everything if the paperwork becomes too much.

BUS

No direct buses travel through the border, but you can easily take a bus or shared taxi to Sarakhs or Bajgiran from Mashhad or Quchan, cross the border yourself, and then take further transport into Turkmenistan (or vice versa).

TRAIN

Due to the small issue of inconsistent guages, trains run to but do not cross the border at Sarakhs. Departures (p329) are frustratingly inconvenient.

SEA

Iran has 2410km of coastal boundaries along the Persian Gulf, Gulf of Oman and Caspian Sea, but there are very few ways to enter or leave Iran by sea.

Persian Gulf

The main shipping agency for trips across the Persian Gulf is **Valfajre-8** (www.vesc.net), which operates car ferries and catamarans from Bushehr, Bandar-e Abbas and Bandar-e Langeh in Iran to destinations, including Dubai, Sharjah, Kuwait City and Bahrain. Services are not exactly frequent – weekly at best, possibly only monthly – and being demand driven can often be changed.

Caspian Sea

At the time of writing there didn't seem to be any regular passenger boat services on the Caspian Sea.

TOURS

Many travellers visit Iran on an organised tour, a situation likely to continue as long as visas are hard to come by. Apart from the convenience, having an English-speaking guide can be worthwhile.

Because Iran is not yet a significant tourist destination, not many foreign travel agencies bother organising regular tours. The following are some experienced and reputable agencies that offer organised tours to Iran from outside the country (for adventure tours, see p338). Unless you really want that foreign tour leader, it's usually cheaper to book through an Iran-based agency (p380).

Australia & New Zealand

Equitrek (☎ 02-9913 9408; www.equitrek.com.au) Tailor-made riding tours of the northeast in autumn and summer.
Passport Travel (☎ 03-9867 3888, www.travelcentre .com.au) A standard highlights trip, plus a more exotic tour of northwest ethnic groups.

Continental Europe

Catai Tours (www.catai.es) Ideal for Spanish-speaking travellers.
Clio (☎ 01 53 68 82 82; www.clio.fr) This company also has offices in Lyon and Marseille.
Orients (☎ 01 40 51 10 40; www.orients.com) Right up-to-date tours but not cheap.
Pars Travel (☎ 069-230882) In Frankfurt, this agency has been recommended by readers.

Middle East

Iran Discovery Tours (☎ 04-332 7662; www .irandiscovery.com) Dubai-based company with a range of group and tailor-made tours; has been recommended by readers.

The UK

Ace Study Tours (☎ 01223-835 055; study-tours.org) Occasional good study tours.
Exodus (☎ 0870-240 5550; www.exodus.co.uk) A good range of itineraries, including climbing Mt Damavand.
Imaginative Traveller (☎ 0800 316 2717; www.imaginative-traveller.com) Regular and varied tours to choose from.
Magic Carpet Travel (☎ 01344-622 832; www.magic -carpet-travel.com) Iranian-owned, with 10 different tours. Check that domestic flights aren't overly expensive.
Persian Voyages (☎ 01306-885 894; www.persian voyages.com) Organises tours to order and arranges visas.

The USA & Canada

Americans may feel more comfortable going on an organised tour, and may not be able to get a visa otherwise.
Bestway Tours & Safaris (☎ 800 663 0844; www.bestway.com) Adventurous trips often combined with various -stans.
Distant Horizons (☎ 800 333 1240; www.distant -horizons.com) Catering for senior travellers as well as others.
Geographic Expeditions (☎ 800 777 8183; www.geoex.com) Occasional tours that are a bit more physical than average.
Silk Road Tours (☎ 888 881 7455; www.silk roadtours.com) Regular package tours, plus tailor-made tours; can help with visa arrangements.

GETTING AROUND

Transport in Iran isn't as developed as it is in the West, but it's considerably better than that of most other countries in the region. Public transport is frequent, reliable and relatively safe. What's more it's unbelievably cheap. Two of the best bargains in the country are taxi fares and domestic plane fares. For planes and trains it's worth booking ahead if you're travelling on a Thursday or any public holiday, especially No Ruz, Ramazan and Eid al-Fitr. At these times bus fares can also rise sharply. For more information on holidays see p349.

AIR

Domestic air fares in Iran are cheap enough for your to consider a couple of flights even if you are normally a die-hard overlander. Zahedan is a gruelling 24-hour bus trip from Tehran, but Iran Air's flight to Zahedan is less than two hours, and it only costs IR330,000 – about US$40. Happy days! Whether you're booking with Iran Air or anyone else, using a travel agency is almost always easier, faster and only about IR1000 more expensive, if at all.

Airlines in Iran

Iran's two major internal airlines are Iran Air and Iran Aseman. Iran Air boasts an extensive network of flights to most provincial capitals, as well as to places of interest to travellers, and is worth using almost exclusively because it's far more reliable than the other airlines. Flight details are included in the relevant Getting There & Away sections that you will find throughout this book.

Iran Aseman is the most viable alternative to Iran Air. Aseman doesn't always have an office in a town to which it flies, so head for an agency.

Four other airlines fly domestically – Caspian Airlines, Kish Air, Mahan Air and Saha Air – but apart from Mahan Air it's difficult to know when or where the rest are flying. Flights are consistent only in their tardiness, and offices either don't exist, are hard to find, or are closed when you do find them. Again, use a travel agency.

Try to get to the airport a good hour ahead of domestic departures. This allows you enough time to sort yourself out at the terminal, check in your luggage, and struggle through the two or three X-ray machines, personal checks of hand baggage and frisks.

Trying to buy domestic flights from outside Iran can be difficult in some places and nigh-on impossible if the flight is on a smaller airline. None of the airlines do online bookings. However, one reader informed us that 'you can book domestic flights by calling an Iran Air office outside Iran (not London for some reason). They will give you a booking reference which you take to an Iran Air office in Iran or to Tehran domestic terminal... you pay for it then. It really does work.'

BICYCLE

Apart from summer, there will be a few people cycling across Iran at any given time. Excellent roads, friendly people and a relatively small risk of theft mean Iran sounds like an ideal cycling destination. There are, however, a few sobering points. The vast distances, dodgy traffic and hot, tedious stretches of desert road can wear thin. You will need to carry plenty of water and food to last the long stretches; camping equipment if you are not sticking to major towns; a decent map; and a phrasebook.

Bear in mind that you may arrive in a village or small town and find either nowhere to stay at all or only a hotel you can't afford. If you can't persuade the caretaker at the local mosque to take you in, you might have to load your bike on a bus or truck and head for the next big town.

The biggest drawback with cycling, as with most other activities in Iran, is the need to stay covered up. We have received varying reports from travellers: some say that it's fine to wear cycling gear when actually on the road, as long as you have clothes at hand to cover up as soon as you stop; others say that women in particular must be covered at all times.

The other snag is that finding repairers and spare parts can be tricky. There is nowhere to rent bicycles for long distances, so bring your own.

BOAT

The only places you're likely to use a boat are between the mainland and some islands in the Persian Gulf. Regular boats for Kish Island leave from Bandar-e Langeh and Bandar-e Charak. They depart less often for more remote and less interesting islands in the Persian Gulf. Numerous speedboats travel between Bandar-e Abbas and Hormoz and Qeshm Islands.

BUS

In Iran, if you can't get somewhere by bus (or minibus), the chances are that *no-one* wants to go there. More than 20 bus companies offer hundreds of services all over the country, so business is highly competitive, the fares are very cheap and, generally, there are regular departures. Most buses are comfortable, with your own cushioned seat and, except on very short trips, standing is not allowed.

Road Distances (km)

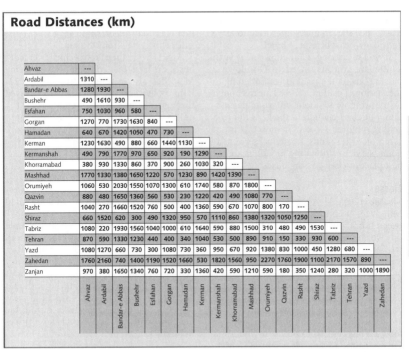

	Ahvaz	Ardabil	Bandar-e Abbas	Bushehr	Esfahan	Gorgan	Hamadan	Kerman	Kermanshah	Khorramabad	Mashhad	Orumiyeh	Qazvin	Rasht	Shiraz	Tabriz	Tehran	Yazd	Zahedan
Ahvaz	---																		
Ardabil	1310	---																	
Bandar-e Abbas	1280	1930	---																
Bushehr	490	1610	930	---															
Esfahan	750	1030	960	580	---														
Gorgan	1270	770	1730	1630	840	---													
Hamadan	640	670	1420	1050	470	730	---												
Kerman	1230	1630	490	880	660	1440	1130	---											
Kermanshah	490	790	1770	970	650	920	190	1290	---										
Khorramabad	380	930	1330	860	370	900	260	1030	320	---									
Mashhad	1770	1330	1380	1650	1220	570	1230	890	1420	1390	---								
Orumiyeh	1060	530	2030	1550	1070	1300	610	1740	580	870	1800	---							
Qazvin	880	480	1650	1360	560	530	230	1220	420	490	1080	770	---						
Rasht	1040	270	1660	1520	760	500	400	1360	590	670	1070	800	170	---					
Shiraz	660	1520	620	300	490	1320	950	570	1110	860	1380	1320	1050	1250	---				
Tabriz	1080	220	1930	1560	1040	1000	610	1640	590	880	1500	310	480	490	1530	---			
Tehran	870	590	1330	1230	440	400	340	1040	530	500	890	910	150	330	930	600	---		
Yazd	1080	1270	660	730	300	1080	730	360	950	670	920	1380	830	1000	450	1280	680	---	
Zahedan	1760	2160	740	1400	1190	1520	1660	530	1820	1560	950	2270	1760	1900	1100	2170	1570	890	---
Zanjan	970	380	1650	1340	760	720	330	1360	420	590	1210	590	180	350	1240	280	320	1000	1890

TRANSPORT

Don't be confused by the names of the destinations on a bus – it is quite common for a bus travelling between, for example, Khorramabad and Ahvaz, to have 'Tehran-İstanbul' written on the front or side in English. Similarly, phrases like 'Lovely bus' are not always a fair reflection of reality. There are no bus passes.

Bus Companies

Most bus companies are cooperatives, referred to simply as Cooperative Bus Company No X (Sherkat-e Ta'avoni Shomare X), or whatever number it is. The best cooperatives, with the most extensive network of services, are TBT (Taavoni No 15) and Cooperative Bus Company No 1 (often with the word 'Ta'avoni' or 'Bus No One' written on it).

There are also a few private bus companies, such as Sayro Safar (or Seiro Safar), which offer more luxury, for a slightly higher price. In most cases, the differences between bus companies are small. It's not worth seeking out a specific company. Just take whichever bus is going your way when you want it.

Bus Stations

With a few notable exceptions, bus stations (terminals) are way out in the suburbs of every major town, easy enough to reach by shared taxi, less so by local bus. In some cities, there's more than one bus station; if in doubt, ask someone at your hotel or charter a taxi to the relevant station – the taxi driver will know where to drop you.

Bus stations are usually well set up and easy to use, although there are rarely any signs in English or anyone speaking English at the information desk. The different bus companies have individual offices inside a building or huddled around the bus departure area. Just ask 'Shiraz?', 'Esfahan?' and someone will direct you to the right desk.

Often it's easy enough to find a tout shouting out the destination of a bus about to leave. In larger stations, they will probably approach you and (often annoyingly) guide you to the office of the company they work for. Claims that their bus is 'leaving now' should be treated with a grain of salt.

Bus stations always have somewhere to buy food and drink. Bigger stations may also have an information booth, post office, police station and somewhere to leave your bags – maybe even a hotel.

If you're leaving a junction town such as Zanjan, you may need to flag down a passing bus on the road instead of going to the station. Position yourself near enough to the window to shout out your destination, but close enough to the kerb to avoid getting run over – a combination that is not as simple as it sounds. Roadblocks, roundabouts, service stations and junctions are the best places to hail passing buses.

Classes

The boxed text 'Mercedes or Volvo?' (p374) will give you an idea of the differences between buses, but here are a couple of other tips worth noting. It probably doesn't need reinforcing, but opting for a Volvo on longer trips is well worth the extra couple of dollars it will cost, especially in summer. Chances are the air-con will work, it's less likely to break down and the chilled water on board can be a life saver. And Volvos are almost always significantly quicker – we took a Volvo bus from Shiraz to Tehran at the same time a fellow traveller took a Mercedes, telling us 'there's really not that much difference – save the money'. His bus took 19 hours, ours took 12½.

If it's a short trip or seats are at a premium, just take whatever comes. If you are travelling alone, you will often be given a single seat along one side of the bus. Try and avoid the seats at the back of the bus as they're on top of the back wheels and the engine; passengers picked up along the way also tend to congregate at the back. In summer it's *vitally important* to get a seat on the side facing away from the sun.

Apart from their retro-chic, Mercedes buses do have one edge on Volvos: many Mercedes are mercifully free of the 24-hour Bollywood movies (in Farsi) played through distorted speakers at force 11 – unlike almost every Volvo bus. Still, anyone who's been to Southeast Asia will give thanks for small mercies; Bollywood movies are far better than deafening karaoke.

Costs

At the time of writing a ticket on a Mercedes averaged out at roughly IR40 per kilometre, and about IR65 on a Volvo. Either way, it's dirt cheap. As an example of costs, the 1024km trip from Tehran to Kerman costs IR38,000/60,000 for a Mercedes/Volvo, while the 440km journey between Tehran and Esfahan costs about IR17,000/30,000. Prices in this book should be taken as a guide only – with the price of petrol due to rise repeatedly during the next few years, you can expect ticket prices to follow suit.

Reservations

You can buy tickets up to a week in advance, but most people don't bother. Between major cities such as Shiraz and Esfahan a bus is bound to be departing at least every half-hour, while in medium-sized towns such as Hamadan and Kerman, you're unlikely to have to wait more than an hour for something going your way. Only in smaller places, where there may be no more than

---

MERCEDES OR VOLVO?

At least two types of bus run on most Iranian bus routes. Depending on where you are, these are given a variety of different names, which can become very confusing. For example, in many places a 'lux' bus is an older bus, often without air-conditioning, while a 'super' is a modern coach, the likes of which you see the world over. However, in some terminals these terms can be reversed, or perhaps they'll offer you the 'super-lux' (which is normally no different to the 'super').

To try to minimise the chance of confusion, in this book we are calling the older, slower and cheaper buses Mercedes, as this is what they almost inevitably are – colourful '60s-vintage Mercedes. Some of these are in pristine condition, with air-conditioning that works to boot. Many are not. Unless specified otherwise, fares in this book are for Mercedes buses.

The bigger, faster and pricier buses we are calling Volvo. These buses often are Volvos, and if not they will probably be an Iranian joint-venture Volvo, or something similar. Either way, ticket sellers should know what you're asking for if you ask for a Volvo – the fastest and most comfortable bus.

TRANSPORT

IS THIS SEAT FREE?

Choosing where to sit on Iranian transport is fraught with difficulty. On city buses, even men and women who are married to each other are not allowed to sit together; men sit at the front of the bus, women at the back.

In contrast, on intercity buses and minibuses, seating is generally arranged so that women sit next to women and men next to men, unless they're couples or family. A woman is not expected to sit next to an unrelated man even if there's only one spare seat left on the bus, and people will move around until the gender mix is right.

If you decide to take a shared taxi you will find people hopping in and out of the front and back like yo-yos in an attempt to ensure that unrelated men and women don't end up side by side. Decide to take the Tehran Metro, however, and you'll find that anything goes. The biggest surprise comes on sleeper trains when unless you specify that you want a single-sex compartment you may find yourself assigned to a mixed one.

---

one or two buses a day to your destination, is it essential to book ahead.

Even if the bus you want to travel on seems to be full it's worth going to the bus station at the time of departure as there are often no-shows, or they might offer you the back seat. Looking desperate, helpless and lost always helps.

The tickets themselves are incomprehensible. If you don't read Farsi, you won't know if the Arabic numbers indicate the day of departure, time of departure, bus number, seat number, platform number, bus company number or fare. Be sure to double-check these details when you buy your ticket and, of course, ask the driver to make sure you're on the right bus.

The Journey

Don't count on averaging more than 60km/h on most bus journeys. Although many of them continue overnight, the buses are rarely comfortable enough to allow a good night's sleep.

On any trip of more than six hours you'll almost certainly stop every now and then at a roadside café serving kebabs, tea and cold drinks. Ice-cold water is normally available on the bus, and on Volvos they usually serve packaged cakes and biscuits and a steady stream of Zam Zam (soft drink). The bus driver will sometimes stop on the outskirts of a major town so his tachograph can be checked by the police as a precaution against speeding. Occasionally at these checkpoints (or at roadblocks along the way) a customs official or policeman may get in the bus and walk up and down, presumably looking for obvious smugglers

or dissidents. They may ask to see your passport, more out of curiosity than anything else. For foreigners there is rarely, if ever, a problem.

In places near the borders or the Persian Gulf, customs searches are more thorough. The official will often look more closely at the passengers and search hand luggage. Sometimes, everyone has to get out of the bus, identify their luggage, carry it up the road, and wait while the vehicle is searched. Very rarely will your main luggage be searched individually, and foreigners are usually waved along without problem.

Buses often arrive in a town in the early hours of the morning, which in some places can be a real hassle. Sometimes there is no option, but it's worth checking the time of arrival when you book.

CAR & MOTORCYCLE

A growing number of travellers are taking a vehicle across Iran as part of a trip between Europe and the Indian subcontinent. This naturally gives you a lot of flexibility, although you need to bear in mind that the distances are great, the scenery often monotonous and the traffic (at least in the towns) truly horrendous. Anyone considering an overland journey should check out www.go-overland.com.

Automobile Associations

The Touring & Automobile Club of Iran (p368) might be able to issue you with a carnet, if you don't already have one. They have a road service arm, though very few tourists bother to become members in order to be able to use it.

Bring Your Own Vehicle

If you are driving your own vehicle, you should always slow down and get ready to stop at roadblocks. Usually if you wind down your window, smile nicely, and give the officials your best 'I don't know what to do and I don't speak Farsi' look, you will be waved straight through. The worst that can happen is that you have to show your passport, licence and vehicle documents. As long your documentation is in order, you're unlikely to have any hassles.

You should never drive off the main road near the Pakistan, Iraq or Afghanistan borders; if you don't come across suspicious drug smugglers, you will probably come across suspicious customs and police officials instead.

Hotels with parking are marked in this book and it's recommended that you use them. Parking on the streets isn't a good idea, especially in the southeast where your vehicle might be stolen, stripped, driven across the border of Afghanistan or Pakistan and bought by a drug smuggler, before you've finished your plate of kebabs. Of course, check there is sufficient height clearance before checking in.

The maps in this guidebook are mainly designed for people using their feet and/or public transport. If you will be driving into large towns such as Shiraz, Esfahan, Mashhad or Tehran (try not to!), you'd be well advised to try and get hold of the relevant Gita Shenasi map (p353).

Driving Licence

To drive in Iran you need an international driving licence. Get one from the national automobile association in your home country.

Fuel & Spare Parts

There are large towns at least every 100km throughout the country except in the remote deserts of eastern Iran (where you should carry extra food and water), but petrol stations can be few and far between – it's as well to keep your tank topped up. Be careful: there is often nothing on the fuel pumps to indicate which is diesel and which petrol.

Diesel can be hard to find in some remote places. Readers have complained that the supply in Mirjaveh, on the border with Pakistan, is inconsistent, to say the least. Others prefer

to taunt their friends back home, telling how they filled up their 4WD tank with diesel for less than €1! That's because fuel is much cheaper than water – at the time of research about IR600 for a litre of petrol, a ludicrous IR150 for diesel! As mentioned earlier, these prices are due to rise steadily in coming years. The other downside is that the fuel is often of poor quality – dirt cheap and just plain dirty. Don't expect to get the same mileage as you would at home.

Even the tiniest settlements have repair shops, usually somewhere on the outskirts or along the main arterial roads. The price for repair work is open to negotiation but you might not have much say over the quality of the spare parts...unless you're driving a Paykan.

In the height of summer, tyre blowouts are common because of the scalding heat. The average Iranian driver needs less than five minutes to change a tyre.

Drivers have suggested that if you have a problem with your vehicle, your best bet is to talk to a truckie; many of them have been outside the country and speak a foreign language.

Insurance

Your vehicle will need a carnet and a green card, both of which you should organise before you arrive. It's possible to get into Iran without a green card from Pakistan, one reader told us, but getting into Turkey can then be problematic.

Hire

The concept of car rental barely exists in Iran, not least because without a functioning system for accepting credit cards it's hard for anyone leasing a car to be sure they can make good any damage. Instead, 'car rental' here means chartering a taxi, either privately or through a travel agency (p380) or check out particular chapters where local guides are often mentioned.

Road Conditions

Road surfaces are generally excellent, as are the dirt tracks if you're bringing a motorbike. On the other hand, driving at night is more dangerous because of occasional potholes and the risk of bumping into tractors and other vehicles crawling along the road with no lights. Strong crosswinds can be a problem for bikers keen to overtake slow-moving trucks.

Just about every road sign is in English, including directions to almost every city, town and village, the names of main roads and squares in most towns (the signs even tell you when a street is a dead end!), and general safety instructions.

Road Hazards

Iranian drivers in the cities. Camels in the deserts.

Heaven forbid that you should have any sort of accident, but if you do and you're in Tehran, ring the **Road Accident Department** (☎ 197). Elsewhere ring the local police headquarters; most have individual traffic accident departments. You should never move the vehicle from the road until the police have come to make their report. As a foreigner, you'll probably be held responsible.

Road Rules

Driving your own vehicle across Iran is not a task to be taken lightly. The major concern for anyone who hasn't driven in this part of the world before will be the appalling traffic, especially worrying for anyone on a motorbike.

In theory at least, the rule of the road is that everyone drives on the right, but even this can't be depended upon; faced with a one-way street going the wrong way, the average Iranian driver sees nothing wrong with reversing down it. The theory is that you give way to the traffic coming onto a roundabout, which seems a tad unimportant when some drivers simply drive the wrong way around it. Take 10 Iranian car drivers and an otherwise deserted open road and you can be sure that all 10 will form a convoy so tightly packed that each of the rear nine can read the speedometer of the car in front. The phrase 'optimum braking distance' is not widely known in Iran.

HITCHING

Hitching is never entirely safe in any country, and we don't recommend it. Travellers who decide to hitch should understand that they are taking a small but potentially serious risk. However, many people do choose to hitch, and the advice that follows should help to make their journeys as fast and safe as possible.

Hitching, as understood in the West, is a novel concept in Iran. Although you will often see people standing by the roadside waiting for a lift, they are actually waiting for space in a bus, minibus or shared taxi, for which they expect to pay. Occasionally drivers will offer foreigners a free ride in return for English practice or out of simple hospitality, and once they've insisted on buying you a meal, refused any payment and gone out of their way to drop you where you want to go, it's nice to have something small to thank them with.

It goes without saying that women should never hitch in Iran.

LOCAL TRANSPORT
Bus

Most Iranian towns and cities have local bus services. Because local buses are often crowded, and shared and private taxis are ubiquitous and cheap, most travellers don't bother with them.

Local buses are difficult to use unless you know exactly where they're going. Bus numbers and destinations are usually only marked in Farsi, so you need to do a lot of asking around – most will be more than happy to help (even if you don't entirely understand their reply).

Buses don't always set out and return by the same route, and services change frequently without notice. You buy your tickets in little booths along the main streets of the cities or at the bus stations – you can't buy tickets onboard anywhere except Shiraz. Depending on where you are, tickets cost between IR100 and IR250, up to a maximum of IR500 (two or more tickets).

On local buses, small children of both genders and all women have to sit at the back of the bus. This segregation can be complicated if you are travelling as a mixed couple and need to discuss when to get off. Bus travellers give their tickets to the driver either before they get on, or after they get off, depending on the local system – but women must pass their tickets to the driver while leaning through the front door of the bus, without using the steps into the front of the bus, and then board the bus using the back door.

Metro

The Tehran Metro (p114) is growing and similar systems are being built in Mashhad and Esfahan, though they are unlikely to be operational during the life of this book.

Minibus

If you think using local buses is a hassle, don't even bother trying to use the infrequent and desperately crowded minibuses. Quite often they are so crammed with passengers that you can hardly see out of the window to tell where you are going. You normally pay in cash when you get on – about IR500 a ticket. Men and women get a seat anywhere they can; there is no room for segregation. Minibuses stop at normal bus stops or wherever you ask them.

Taxi

For many Iranians and just about every foreign traveller, a shared or private taxi is the quickest and most hassle-free way of getting around a town or city.

SHARED TAXI

In most towns and cities, shared taxis duplicate or even replace local bus services. They usually take up to five passengers: two in the front passenger seat and three in the back, rarely more. A shared taxi will nearly always be a Paykan sedan, often coloured orange, or with a dash of orange somewhere. After a while you will get used to them, especially if you try them out somewhere other than Tehran first.

Shared taxis usually travel between major squares and along major roads in every town and city. They often make slight detours for passengers at no extra charge; for a longer detour, you may be charged IR500 or so extra. Shared taxis hang around places where they are most likely to get fares (bus stations, train stations, airports, major town squares), or you can hail one on the road.

Normally, getting a shared taxi goes something like this. Lean out a few metres from the kerb, far enough for the driver to hear you shout your destination but close enough to the kerb to dash back again if you have to. If the driver has a spare seat, he will slow down for a nanosecond while you shout your destination.

When you want the driver to stop you simply say *kheili mamnun* (thank you very much) or make any other obvious noise. Drivers appreciate exact change, so try and keep plenty of coins and those filthy IR200

NAH DAR BASTE!

If an empty taxi stops for you, the driver will probably think you want to hire it privately. He might ask you: *'Dar baste?'*, which literally means 'Closed door?' If you want to share, then to make your intentions clear lean in and tell him simply *'Nah dar baste,'* or 'No closed door'. He'll soon let you know if he's interested or not.

and IR500 notes handy; you normally pay when you get out.

Fares, which are fixed by the government, range from about IR500 to IR2000, depending on the distance and the city (Tehran's fares are naturally the most expensive). Always try and see what other passengers are paying before you hand over your money, though most drivers are straight enough.

If you get into an empty shared taxi, particularly in Esfahan and Tehran, it's often assumed that you want to charter it privately. Likewise, if everyone else gets out the driver might decide that you are now a private fare. Whenever possible try to take only taxis with other people in them.

PRIVATE TAXI

Any taxi without passengers, whether obviously a shared taxi or a more expensive private taxi, can be chartered to go anywhere in town. Unless it's a complicated deal, including waiting time, simply hail the vehicle, tell the driver where you want to go, and ask the price, including waiting time. Immediately offer about half what he suggests but expect to end up paying about 70% of the originally quoted price. It's hardly worth haggling over the odd IR1000.

AGENCY TAXI

Agency taxis, or 'telephone' taxis, don't normally stop to pick up passengers; you have to order them by telephone or at an agency office. There are taxi agency offices in even the smallest towns and hundreds of them in Tehran. Some of the top hotels run their own taxi services, and any hotel or mosaferkhuneh (lodging house) can order a taxi for a guest. Naturally, this is the most expensive way of using taxis, but you get a better car, the comfort of knowing there will be someone to complain to if anything goes wrong and, possibly, a driver who speaks English.

One reader wrote to say that lone women are advised to get someone to call them a taxi if they're travelling after dark, thus avoiding being hooted at or ignored by dozens of drivers as they try and hail one.

Trolleybus

Tehran boasts one environmentally friendly electric trolleybus line – even if its dedicated lane is more often used by carbon monoxide–belching buses and recalcitrant motorcyclists. The same system of paying and segregation applies as for local buses.

MINIBUS

Minibuses are often used for shorter distances to and from minor towns and villages. Sometimes they're an alternative to the bus, but usually there's no choice; just take whatever is going your way. Minibuses are particularly popular along the Caspian Sea coast, and between the Caspian towns and Tehran.

Minibuses are marginally more expensive than buses, but not enough to worry about. They are often faster than larger buses and because they have fewer passengers they spend less time dropping off and picking up. On the downside, they're not as comfortable as bigger buses and usually leave only when they're full, which can mean a long wait on less-popular routes.

Minibuses sometimes leave from a special station and sometimes from the main bus station. If in doubt, just charter a taxi and tell the driver you want to go to the *terminal-e*

Rasht, *Tehran* or wherever. Arriving in a town, they have a nasty habit of depositing you in the middle of nowhere. Luckily, hopeful taxi drivers are likely to be waiting.

PIK-UP

Occasionally, especially in southern Iran around Bandar-e Abbas, you may come across a utility with a canvas cover called a *pik-up* (pick-up). If you're tall, try to get to the *pik-up* early and negotiate a price for the front seat, which will be far more comfortable than the back. Prices are very cheap, but the comfort level is also very low.

PRIVATE TAXI

Almost every single taxi in the country is available for private hire. Needless to say, prices are open to negotiation. One excellent way to avoid getting ripped off is to ask the driver of a savari (see below) for the price per person of a certain trip then multiply it by four or five.

If you prefer to hire the taxi and driver for the whole day you are looking at somewhere between about IR150,000 and IR300,000 – depending on a long list of factors, including your ability as a negotiator, the quality of the car, the distance you plan to drive and where you are. The smaller the town, the cheaper the price. Some drivers charge by the kilometre, with IR700 being a number quoted to us on several occasions.

SAVARI (SHARED TAXI)

You can almost always find a savari for a trip between major towns less than three hours

---

THE PERENNIAL PAYKAN

The perennial Paykan, first produced in the 1960s as a replica of the Hillman Hunter (which was last produced then), is supposed to come to the end of its production line in 2004. When it does, it will mark the end of an era in which the Paykan, almost always white, has dominated the roadscape more than any other car since the Model T Ford. But while there will be a few sentimental tears, most people will be wishing this technological anachronism good riddance. While Iranians respect the Paykan's ability to get the job done – just – they are also fully aware of its diabolical impact on the environment.

To give you an idea of what you're seeing, the Paykan burns, on average, between 12L and 15L of leaded petrol per 100km. That is at least double the exhaust most modern cars pump out, and with no catalytic converter, the poisons are even greater. There are believed to be more than two million Paykans on Iran's roads, and you can be sure that they'll be around for decades yet. The 'new Paykan', as one Iranian described it, is the Kia Pride. A no-frills motor if ever you've seen one, Prides burn much less fuel and often have air-con. But before you start mourning the Paykan, note that the government promised to stop making them in 2002, as well.

apart. Savari is the term for 'shared taxi', and is usually applied to intercity versions of the species. Speed is the main advantage because savaris are generally more uncomfortable than buses. Often two people will be expected to squeeze into the front passenger seat, though for longer journeys the taxi usually leaves with four passengers.

Savaris never leave with an empty seat unless a passenger agrees to pay for it, but even so you rarely have to wait long for one to fill. Most of the time, savaris are the ubiquitous Iranian-made Paykans, but taxi drivers around the Caspian provinces use huge, battered (but sometimes lovingly restored) Mercedes Benzes, and Peugeot 404s are also becoming more popular – they might cost about 30% more than a crappy Paykan.

As a general rule, savaris cost about three times more than the Mercedes buses. This is still cheap and worth using for quick trips, especially through dull stretches of countryside. If you want to hurry up a departure, you can always pay for an empty seat; if your Farsi is

good enough, you can even arrange to pay the difference between the full fare and any fare the driver may pick up along the way.

Taxi drivers are generally honest, though it pays to be wary and agree on a clearly understood price before you start – confirming that the price is in rials or *toman* is a must, then watch what other passengers pay. For the etiquette of who to sit next to in a savari, see the boxed text 'Is This Seat Free?' (p375).

Savaris usually leave from inside, or just outside, the relevant bus terminal, or at major squares at the beginning of whichever road they're about to head down. If in doubt, charter a private taxi and ask the driver to take you to the relevant pick-up point for a savari going your way.

TOURS
Few Iranian travel agencies organise trips for foreigners within Iran: they mainly sell airline tickets or act as local operators for foreign travel companies. Furthermore, English is not usually spoken, attractions are Islamic

---

TO TOUR OR NOT TO TOUR?

In general, Lonely Planet advocates the do-it-yourself option as the best way to get to grips with a new country. However, in the case of Iran this may not always be realistic because of the difficulties with getting a visa for independent travel.

An increasing number of overseas tour operators are organising tours to Iran (p371). Usually these last for two or three weeks and take in the main highlights, including the Tehran museums, Esfahan, Shiraz, Yazd, Kerman and Bam with, perhaps, a detour to the Caspian coast, Hamadan and Mashhad. Given how cheap travelling in Iran is, most of these tours are extremely expensive, especially if you want to book a single room. You may also feel that they stop you trying cheaper restaurants and hotels, as well as excluding you from contact with local people other than the tour guide.

On the plus side, having a guide can be particularly useful when travelling in a country with such a different culture, when you are unlikely to be able to read many of the signs, and when you might arrive with preconceived ideas that don't necessarily mesh with reality. A guide will, for example, ensure you don't run aground over the dress code, which is particularly reassuring for women travellers. Some tour companies also use buses with blacked-out windows so their female clients can travel the long distances between one town and another without having to wear their scarves. If you have to travel in high summer, you will also be very grateful for the air-conditioning on tour buses.

When deciding which tour to take it's often worth looking at how many 'free days' they offer. While free days sound great in theory, in practice if yours are in Shiraz, Esfahan or Tehran it could mean you end up having to pay a lot of quite hefty admission fees yourself instead of having them included in the tour price.

A word of warning about 'extra nights' at the start and end of your tour. Many flights to Iran arrive in the early hours of the morning, before you can check into your hotel. Unfortunately tour companies often charge extortionate prices for booking 'extra nights'. You'd do well either to book directly with the hotel via fax or to wait until you arrive and book a room for the normal price on the spot.

in nature and the standard of food and accommodation may not be quite what you were expecting. Most organised tours around Iran start and finish in Tehran, with a quick look around the capital before concentrating on the must-sees: Shiraz, Esfahan and Yazd, with either Tabriz or Kerman and possibly Rayen or Mashhad thrown in.

The handful of Iranian travel companies listed here offer something different. All are well established and used to catering for foreigners. Most can organise tailor-made tours to suit particular interests and can help you get your visa. It's better not to just ring up or turn up at their office and expect to be off on a tour within the day; most need prior notice to organise a tour. Generally they can provide guides who speak English, French, German or Japanese, and sometimes Spanish or Italian. Costs depend on the length of the tour, the mode of transport, the type of accommodation and the current exchange rate. Foreigners will be expected to pay in foreign currency, usually US dollars.

Adibian Travel Agency Mashhad (Map p320; ☎ 0511-859 8151; www.adibiantours.com; 56 Pasdaran Ave) Long-established agency specialising in Khorasan province, but able to book tours of the whole country.

Arg-e-Jadid Tehran (Map p98; ☎ 021-881 1072; info@arg-e-jadid-travel.com; 296 Motahhari Ave) Highly respected among expats in Tehran.

Azadi International Tourism Organisation Tehran (AITO; ☎ 021-873 2191; www.aitotours.com; 37 AITO Bldg, 8th St, Ahmad Ghasir Ave) There are also branches in Paris and Frankfurt.

Caravan Sahra Tehran (Map p98; ☎ 021-881 1970; www.caravansahra.com; Caravan Sahra Bldg, 29 Qaem Maqam-e Farahani Ave) A big group with plenty on offer. We've had one bad report.

Iran Touring & Tourism Organisation Tehran (ITTO; Map pp90-1; ☎ 021-896 7065; irangardijahangardi@aras net.net; 154 Keshavarz Blvd) This is a quasi-government tourist bureau operated by the Ministry of Culture & Islamic Guidance, which runs many of Iran's two- and three-star hotels while acting as a travel agency as well.

Pars Tourist Agency Shiraz (Map pp242-3; ☎ 021-222 3163; www.key2persia.com; Zand Blvd) Highly professional outfit dealing purely with foreign travellers. Can arrange visas and has literally dozens of tour options.

Persepolis Tour & Travel Agency Tehran (Map pp90-1; ☎ 021-880 5266; www.persepolistour.com; 100 Nejatollahi St)

Tavakoli International Travel & Tour Tehran (Map pp90-1; ☎ 021-881 0905; tavakoli@sama.dpi.net.ir; 25 Falahpoor St, Nejatollahi St)

TRAIN

Iran's rail network is especially impressive if you consider the mountainous terrain that the tracks must often pass through: The trans-Iranian railway built in the 1930s to connect the Caspian Sea at Bandar-e Torkaman with the Persian Gulf at Bandar-e Imam Khomeini is one of the great engineering achievements of the 20th century. It's also a terrific way to meet Iranians, many of whom approach their rare train trips with some excitement.

All trains start out from Tehran, so to get from Tabriz to Kerman, for example, you would have to travel to Tehran and change. Travellers heading to Pakistan by train can

FOR TRAIN BUFFS

Most travellers end up using buses, mini-buses and shared taxis to travel around Iran, but for anyone who is interested in trains, there is much to like about Islamic Republic of Iran Railways. Here are a few facts and figures:

Track length: 6414km
Gauge: 1.435m
Locomotives: 564
Passenger coaches: 1154
Annual passengers: 12.7 million
Train stations: 352
Longest train line: Tehran to Bandar-e Abbas (1483km)

And the grand rail building program currently under way will see this network expand during the next decade or so. New lines either proposed or already being built include:

Esfahan to Shiraz via Persepolis
Kerman to Zahedan via Bam
Mashhad to Bafq via Tabas
Arak to Kermanshah
Maraqeh to Orumiyeh
Miyaneh to Tabriz

Raja Passenger Trains Company has an exceptionally good website, www.rajatrains.com. The most useful part for travellers is the three-page PDF containing a full schedule with the latest fares, departure and arrival times (though the latter shouldn't be treated as gospel) and train types. Print it out and save yourself a lot of trouble.

TRANSPORT

GETTING AROUND •• Train

only get as far as Kerman and must then continue by bus to the border, although work to extend the line was under way when we passed and it should be open at least as far as Bam sometime in 2005. Zahedan is probably still a few years off.

There are daily services to popular places such as Esfahan and Kerman but none to Shiraz – though plans to run a line from Esfahan to Shiraz are advancing. Unfortunately, departure and arrival times for anywhere other than the start and finish points of the journey are usually lousy.

However, trains are usually comfortable (at least in 1st class), fairly efficient, reasonably fast and always cheap. For overnight trips a 1st-class sleeper is a delight, and while they cost about twice as much as a Volvo bus, the comfort level is about 10 times greater. On some trains you have the added bonus of passing through striking scenery. And, of course, trains have a far better safety record than the buses.

On most 1st-class services meals are served in your compartment and aren't too bad. Long-distance trains also have a restaurant car, although the choice of food is limited. Iced water is available. Security is better than in most other countries in the region, but it's worth asking someone to look after your luggage (or chaining it to something solid) before you leave your compartment.

Classes

Most trains have two classes though a significant minority have only one. If you decide 2nd class is too crowded for you, you can often upgrade to 1st class along the way, provided there's space.

On overnight trains (usually to or from Tehran) the 1st-class carriages have sleepers with four or six bunks as in India, Pakistan and Turkey. Oddly enough, they are not all sexually segregated and one reader wrote to complain of having a man in another bunk stroking her arm in the night. Women travelling alone should make a point of asking for a single-sex sleeper. Some trains on the Tehran to Mashhad route, Iran's busiest, are very comfortable indeed. The *Simorgh*, for example, is more expensive than other 1st-class options but includes dinner, breakfast, a very comfortable bed and the mixed blessing of a TV. You can ask to be seated in a nonsmoking or single-sex compartment.

Costs

As a rough guide, a seat in 2nd class costs about the same as a Mercedes bus, and a 1st-class seat is about twice as much as a Volvo bus, depending on the class of train. For specific prices see the relevant destination in this book.

Reservations

Train ticketing is on an integrated system, so you can book tickets at stations and travel agencies around the country up to a month in advance. Especially for trains leaving on Thursday, Friday and public holidays, it's worth booking a day or two ahead.

Health <small>Caroline Evans</small>

CONTENTS

Due in part to its dryness and relative isolation, your chances of getting seriously ill with a virus or other infectious disease in Iran are fairly small. The most common reason for travellers needing medical help is as a result of accidents – the quality of Iranian cars and, more to the point, Iranian driving is dangerously low. If you are unfortunate enough to need a hospital, the good news is that Iran is home to some of the best in the Middle East. Many doctors have been trained in Europe or North America and, especially in the larger cities, you shouldn't have too much trouble finding one who speaks English. In remoter areas, medical facilities are more basic.

BEFORE YOU GO

A little planning before departure, particularly for pre-existing illnesses, will save you a lot of trouble later. See your dentist before a long trip; carry a spare pair of contact lenses and glasses (and take your optical prescription with you); and carry a first-aid kit with you.

It's tempting to leave it all to the last minute – don't! Many vaccines don't ensure immunity for two weeks, so visit a doctor four to eight weeks before depar-

ture. Ask your doctor for an International Certificate of Vaccination (otherwise known as the yellow booklet), which will list all the vaccinations you've received. This is mandatory for countries that require proof of yellow fever vaccination upon entry, but it's a good idea to carry it wherever you travel.

Travellers can register with the International Association for Medical Advice to Travellers (IMAT; www.iamat.org). Its website can help travellers to find a doctor with recognised training. Those heading off to very remote areas may like to do a first-aid course (Red Cross and St John Ambulance can help), or attend a remote medicine first-aid course such as that offered by the Royal Geographical Society (www.rgs.org).

Bring medications in their original, clearly labelled, containers. A signed and dated letter from your physician describing your medical conditions and medications, including generic names, is also a good idea. If carrying syringes or needles, be sure to have a physician's letter documenting their medical necessity.

INSURANCE

Find out in advance if your insurance plan will make payments directly to providers or reimburse you later for overseas health expenditures (in many countries doctors expect payment in cash); it's also worth ensuring your travel insurance will cover repatriation home or to better medical facilities elsewhere. Your insurance company may be able to locate the nearest source of medical help, or you can ask at your hotel. In an emergency contact your embassy or consulate. Your travel insurance will not usually cover you for anything other than emergency dental treatment. Not all insurance covers emergency aeromedical evacuation home or to a hospital in a major city, which may be the only way to get medical attention for a serious emergency.

RECOMMENDED VACCINATIONS

The World Health Organization recommends that all travellers regardless of the region they are travelling in should be covered for diphtheria, tetanus, measles, mumps, rubella and polio, as well as hepatitis B. While making preparations to travel, take the opportunity to ensure that all of your routine vaccination cover is complete. The consequences of these diseases can be severe and outbreaks do occur in the Middle East, though in Iran they are pretty rare.

MEDICAL CHECKLIST

Following is a list of other items you should consider packing in your medical kit.

- Acetaminophen/paracetamol (Tylenol) or aspirin
- Adhesive or paper tape
- Antibacterial ointment (eg Bactroban) for cuts and abrasions
- Antibiotics (if travelling off the beaten track)
- Antidiarrhoeal drugs (eg loperamide)
- Anti-inflammatory drugs (eg ibuprofen)
- Antihistamines (for hay fever and allergic reactions)
- Bandages, gauze, gauze rolls
- DEET – containing insect repellent for the skin
- Iodine tablets (for water purification)
- Oral rehydration salts
- Permethrin – containing insect spray for clothing, tents, and bed nets
- Pocket knife
- Scissors, safety pins, tweezers
- Steroid cream or cortisone (allergic rashes)
- Sun block
- Syringes and sterile needles (if travelling to remote areas)
- Thermometer

INTERNET RESOURCES

There is a wealth of travel health advice on the Internet. For further information, the Lonely Planet website (www.lonelyplanet.com) is a good place to start. The World Health Organization (www.who.int/ith) publishes

---

TRAVEL HEALTH WEBSITES

It's usually a good idea to consult your government's travel health website before departure, if one is available.
Australia (www.dfat.gov.au/travel)
Canada (www.travelhealth.gc.ca)
UK (www.doh.gov.uk/traveladvice)
USA (www.cdc.gov/travel)

---

a superb book, *International Travel and Health*, which is revised annually and is available online at no cost.

Another website of general interest is MD Travel Health (www.mdtravelhealth.com), which provides complete travel health recommendations for every country, updated daily, also at no cost.

The Centers for Disease Control and Prevention website (www.cdc.gov) is also a very useful source of traveller's health information.

FURTHER READING

Lonely Planet's *Travel With Children* is packed with useful information including pretrip planning, emergency first aid, immunisation and disease information and what to do if you get sick on the road.

Other recommended references include *Traveller's Health* by Dr Richard Dawood (Oxford University Press), *International Travel Health Guide* by Stuart R. Rose, MD (Travel Medicine Inc) and *The Travellers' Good Health Guide* by Ted Lankester (Sheldon Press), an especially useful health guide for volunteers and long-term expats working in the Middle East.

IN TRANSIT

DEEP VEIN THROMBOSIS (DVT)

Deep vein thrombosis occurs when blood clots form in the legs during plane flights, chiefly because of prolonged immobility. The longer the flight, the greater the risk. Though most blood clots are reabsorbed uneventfully, some may break off and travel through the blood vessels to the lungs, where they may cause life-threatening complications.

The chief symptom of DVT is swelling or pain of the foot, ankle, or calf, usually but not always on just one side. When a blood clot travels to the lungs, it may cause chest pain and difficulty breathing. Travellers with any of these symptoms should immediately seek medical attention.

To prevent the development of DVT on long flights you should walk about the cabin, perform isometric compressions of the leg muscles (ie contract the leg muscles while sitting), drink plenty of fluids, and avoid alcohol and tobacco.

JET LAG & MOTION SICKNESS

Jet lag is common when crossing more than five time zones; it results in insomnia, fatigue, malaise or nausea. To avoid jet lag try drinking plenty of fluids (nonalcoholic) and eating light meals. Upon arrival, seek exposure to natural sunlight and readjust your schedule (for meals, sleep etc) as soon as possible.

Antihistamines such as dimenhydrinate (Dramamine) and meclizine (Antivert, Bonine) are usually the first choice for treating motion sickness. Their main side effect is drowsiness. A herbal alternative is ginger, which works like a charm for some people.

IN IRAN

AVAILABILITY & COST OF HEALTH CARE

There are few, if any, reciprocal medical arrangements between Iran and other countries so be prepared to pay for all your medical and dental treatment. The good news is that the costs are negligible – a visit to a GP for a general ailment will probably cost only a couple of dollars. Indeed, if you fancy a nose job there is no better or cheaper place to have it done than Iran – you could tour the country while recovering, and join the legions of women (and a few men) with telltale plasters on their noses. But, seriously, medical care is not always readily available outside major cities. Medicine, and even sterile dressings or intravenous fluids, may need to be bought from a local pharmacy. Nursing care may be limited or rudimentary as this is something families and friends are expected to provide. The travel assistance provided by your insurance may be able to locate the nearest source of medical help, otherwise ask at your hotel. In an emergency contact your embassy or consulate.

Standards of dental care are variable and there is an increased risk of hepatitis B transmission via poorly sterilised equipment. And keep in mind that your travel insurance will not usually cover you for anything other than emergency dental treatment.

For minor illnesses such as diarrhoea, pharmacists can often provide valuable advice and sell over-the-counter medication. They can also advise when more specialised help is needed.

INFECTIOUS DISEASES

Diphtheria

Diphtheria is spread through close respiratory contact. It causes a high temperature and severe sore throat. Sometimes a membrane forms across the throat requiring a tracheostomy to prevent suffocation. Vaccination is recommended for those likely to be in close contact with the local population in infected areas. The vaccine is given as an injection alone, or with tetanus, and lasts 10 years.

Hepatitis A

Hepatitis A is spread through contaminated food (particularly shellfish) and water. It causes jaundice and, although it is rarely fatal, can cause prolonged lethargy and delayed recovery. Symptoms include dark urine, a yellow colour to the whites of the eyes, fever and abdominal pain. Hepatitis A vaccine (Avaxim, VAQTA, Havrix) is given as an injection: a single dose will give protection for up to a year while a booster 12 months later will provide a subsequent 10 years of protection. Hepatitis A and typhoid vaccines can also be given as a single dose vaccine, hepatyrix or viatim.

Hepatitis B

Infected blood, contaminated needles and sexual intercourse can all transmit hepatitis B. It can cause jaundice, and affects the liver, occasionally causing liver failure. All travellers should make this a routine vaccination. (Many countries now give hepatitis B vaccination as part of routine childhood vaccination.) The vaccine is given singly, or at the same time as the hepatitis A vaccine (hepatyrix). A course will give protection for at least five years. It can be given over four weeks, or six months.

HIV

HIV is mercifully rare in Iran thanks largely to the strict social taboos on extramarital sex. However, the growing use of prostitutes combined with a relaxed attitude to condoms means the HIV rate is rising. For some visa types Iran requires a negative HIV test.

Leishmaniasis

Spread through the bite of an infected sand fly, leishmaniasis can cause a slowly growing skin lump or ulcer. It may develop into a serious life-threatening fever usually accompanied with anaemia and weight loss. Infected dogs are also carriers of the infection. Sand fly bites should be avoided whenever possible.

Malaria

There is very little malaria in Iran. Still, if you are very unfortunate, it's worth knowing that malaria almost always starts with marked shivering, fever and sweating. Muscle pains, headache and vomiting are common. Symptoms may occur anywhere from a few days to three weeks after the infected mosquito bite. The illness can start while you are taking preventative tablets if they are not fully effective, and may also occur after you have finished taking your tablets.

Poliomyelitis

Generally poliomyelitis is spread through contaminated food and water. It is one of the vaccines given in childhood and should be boosted every 10 years, either orally (a drop on the tongue), or as an injection. Polio may be carried asymptomatically, although it can cause a transient fever and, in rare cases, potentially permanent muscle weakness or paralysis.

Rabies

Spread through bites or licks on broken skin from an infected animal, rabies is fatal. Animal handlers should be vaccinated, as should those travelling to remote areas where a reliable source of post-bite vaccine is not available within 24 hours. Three injections are needed over a month. If you have not been vaccinated you will need a course of five injections starting within 24 hours or as soon as possible after the injury. Vaccination does not provide you with immunity; it merely buys you more time to seek appropriate medical help.

Tuberculosis

Tuberculosis (TB) is spread through close respiratory contact and occasionally through infected milk or milk products. BCG vaccine is recommended for those likely to be mixing closely with the local population. It is more important for those visiting family or planning on a long stay, and those employed as teachers and health-care workers. TB can be asymptomatic, although symptoms can

include cough, weight loss or fever months or even years after exposure. An X-ray is the best way to confirm if you have TB. BCG gives a moderate degree of protection against TB. It causes a small permanent scar at the site of injection, and is usually only given in specialised chest clinics. As it's a live vaccine it should not be given to pregnant women or immunocompromised individuals. The BCG vaccine is not available in all countries.

Typhoid

This is spread through food or water that has been contaminated by infected human faeces. The first symptom is usually fever or a pink rash on the abdomen. Septicaemia (blood poisoning) may also occur. Typhoid vaccine (typhim Vi, typherix) will give protection for three years. In some countries, the oral vaccine Vivotif is also available.

Yellow Fever

Yellow fever vaccination is not required for any areas of the Middle East. However, the mosquito that spreads yellow fever has been known to be present in some parts of the Middle East. It is important to consult your local travel health clinic as part of your pre-departure plans for the latest details. For this reason, any travellers from a yellow fever endemic area might need to show proof of vaccination against yellow fever before entry. This normally means if arriving directly from an infected country or if the traveller has been in an infected country during the last 10 days. We would recommend however that travellers carry a certificate if they have been in an infected country during the previous month to avoid any possible difficulties with immigration. There is always the possibility that a traveller without an up-to-date certificate will be vaccinated and detained in isolation at the port of arrival for up to 10 days, or even repatriated. The yellow fever vaccination must be given at a designated clinic, and is valid for 10 years. It is a live vaccine and must not be given to immunocompromised or pregnant travellers.

TRAVELLER'S DIARRHOEA

While water is safe to drink almost everywhere in Iran, avoiding tap water unless it has been boiled, filtered or chemically disinfected can help you avoid diarrhoea. Eat only fresh fruits or vegetables if cooked or if you have peeled them yourself and avoid dairy products that might contain unpasteurised milk. Buffet meals are risky, food should be piping hot; meals freshly cooked in front of you in a busy restaurant are more likely to be safe.

If you develop diarrhoea, be sure to drink plenty of fluids, preferably an oral rehydration solution containing lots of salt and sugar. A few loose stools don't require treatment but, if you start having more than four or five stools a day, you should start taking an antibiotic (usually a quinolone drug) and an antidiarrhoeal agent (such as loperamide). If diarrhoea is bloody, persists for more than 72 hours, is accompanied by fever, shaking chills or severe abdominal pain you should seek medical attention.

ENVIRONMENTAL HAZARDS
Heat Illness
Heat exhaustion occurs following heavy sweating and excessive fluid loss with inadequate replacement of fluids and salt, and travellers will be especially susceptible during Iran's oven-hot summers, particularly if you are engaging in a greater level of exercise than you usually would. Symptoms include headache, dizziness and tiredness. Dehydration is already happening by the time you feel thirsty – aim to drink sufficient water such that you produce pale, diluted urine. The treatment of heat exhaustion consists of fluid replacement with water or fruit juice or both, and cooling by cold water and fans. The treatment of the salt loss component consists of salty fluids as in soup or broth, and adding a little more table salt to foods than usual.

Heat stroke is much more serious. This occurs when the body's heat-regulating mechanism breaks down. An excessive rise in body temperature leads to sweating ceasing, irrational and hyperactive behaviour and eventually loss of consciousness and death. Rapid cooling by spraying the body with water and fanning is an ideal treatment. Emergency fluid and electrolyte replacement by intravenous drip is usually also required.

Insect Bites & Stings
Mosquitoes may not carry malaria but can cause irritation and infected bites. Using DEET-based insect repellents will prevent bites. Mosquitoes also spread dengue fever

Bees and wasps only cause real problems to those with a severe allergy (anaphylaxis). If you have a severe allergy to bee or wasp stings you should carry an adrenaline injection or similar.

Scorpions are frequently found in arid or dry climates. They can cause a painful bite which is rarely life threatening.

Bed bugs are often found in hostels and cheap hotels. They lead to very itchy lumpy bites. Spraying the mattress with an appropriate insect killer will do a good job of getting rid of them.

Scabies are also frequently found in cheap accommodation. These tiny mites live in the skin, particularly between the fingers. They cause an intensely itchy rash. Scabies is easily treated with lotion available from pharmacies; people who you come into contact with also need treating to avoid spreading scabies between asymptomatic carriers.

Snake Bites
Do not walk barefoot or stick your hand into holes or cracks. Half of those bitten by venomous snakes are not actually injected with poison (envenomed). If bitten by a snake, do not panic. Immobilise the bitten limb with a splint (eg a stick) and apply a bandage over the site, firm pressure, similar to a bandage over a sprain. Do not apply a tourniquet, or cut or suck the bite. Get to medical help as soon as possible so that antivenin can be given if necessary.

Water
Tap water is safe to drink in most parts of Iran, though many travellers choose to stick to bottled water, which is widely available. Do not drink water from rivers or lakes as this may contain bacteria or viruses that can cause diarrhoea or vomiting.

TRAVELLING WITH CHILDREN
All travellers with children should know how to treat minor ailments and when to seek medical treatment. Make sure the children are up to date with routine vaccinations, and discuss possible travel vaccines well before departure as some vaccines are not suitable for children aged under one year old.

In hot, moist climates any wound or break in the skin may lead to infection.

The area should be cleaned and then kept dry and clean. Remember to avoid contaminated food and water. If your child is vomiting or experiencing diarrhoea, lost fluid and salts must be replaced. It may be helpful to take rehydration powders for reconstituting with boiled water. Ask your doctor about this.

Children should be encouraged to avoid dogs or other mammals because of the risk of rabies and other diseases. Any bite, scratch or lick from a warm blooded, furry animal should immediately be thoroughly cleaned. If there is any possibility that the animal is infected with rabies, immediate medical assistance should be sought.

WOMEN'S HEALTH

Emotional stress, exhaustion and travelling through different time zones can all contribute to an upset in the menstrual pattern. If using oral contraceptives, remember some antibiotics, diarrhoea and vomiting can stop the pill from working and lead to the risk of pregnancy – remember to take condoms with you just in case. Condoms should be kept in a cool dry place or they may crack and perish

Emergency contraception is most effective if taken within 24 hours after unprotected sex. The International Planned Parent Federation (www.ippf.org) can advise about the availability of contraception in different countries. Tampons are almost impossible to find in Iran, but sanitary towels are available in cities.

Travelling during pregnancy is usually possible but there are important things to consider. Have a medical check-up before embarking on your trip. The most risky times for travel are during the first 12 weeks of pregnancy, when miscarriage is most likely, and after 30 weeks, when complications such as high blood pressure and premature delivery can occur. Most airlines will not accept a traveller after 28 to 32 weeks of pregnancy, and long-haul flights in the later stages can be very uncomfortable. Antenatal facilities vary greatly between countries in the Middle East and you should think carefully before travelling to a country with poor medical facilities or where there are major cultural and language differences from home. Taking written records of the pregnancy including details of your blood group are likely to be helpful if you need medical attention while away. Ensure your insurance policy covers pregnancy delivery and postnatal care, but remember insurance policies are only as good as the facilities available.

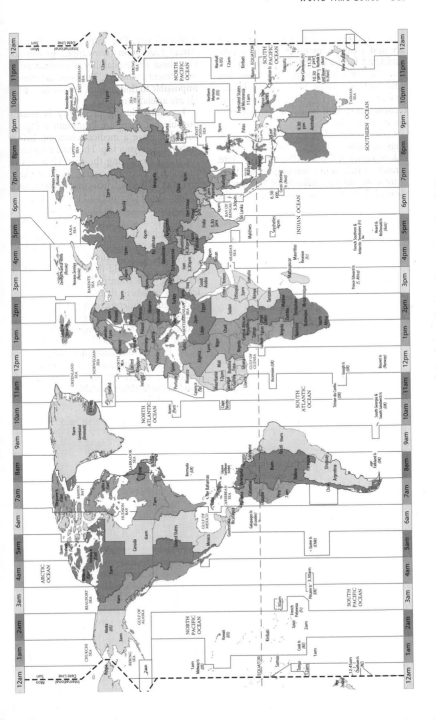

Language

CONTENTS

Farsi (or Persian as it's also known) is an Indo-Iranian language and a member of the Indo-European language family. It's written in Arabic script, which runs from right to left, but the language itself isn't related to Arabic at all. There are a number of different mutually-intelligible dialects spoken in Iran. The words and phrases in this language guide are based on the Tehrani dialect, and reflect mostly colloquial, everyday speech. Tehrani is considered to be the standard dialect, and the one spoken by most Farsi speakers. This is distinct from Classical Farsi, which is not an everyday language, but a literary form, normally used only in books or speeches.

For a more comprehensive guide to the language, pick up a copy of Lonely Planet's *Farsi (Persian) Phrasebook*.

TRANSLITERATION

Transliterating from non-Roman script into the Roman alphabet is always a tricky affair. Formal transliterations of Farsi are overly complicated in the way they represent vowels, and they do not accurately represent the spoken language. In this language guide the system used is designed to be as simple as possible for spoken communication, even at the expense of absolute accuracy.

PRONUNCIATION

Hyphens have been used between compound words that are pronounced as one word but written as two, and where a combination of consonants would otherwise be mispronounced.

In general, the last syllable of a multi-syllable word is stressed, unless the last vowel in the word is a short vowel.

Vowels

a	as in 'father'
e	as in 'bed'
i	as in 'marine'
o	as in 'mole'
u	as in 'rule'

Consonants

The letters **b**, **d**, **f**, **j**, **m**, **n**, **p**, **sh**, **t** and **z** are pronounced as in English.

ch	as in 'cheese'
g	as in 'goose'
gh	a guttural sound like a heavy French 'r' pronounced at the back of the mouth
h	as in 'hot'
kh	as the 'ch' in Scottish loch
l	always as in 'leg', never as in 'roll' (see note below)
r	trilled
s	as in 'sin'
y	as in 'yak'
zh	as the 'g' in 'mirage'
'	a very weak glottal stop, like the sound made between the words 'uh-oh' or the 'tt' in Cockney 'bottle'

Note: doubled consonants are always pronounced as two distinct sounds, as in 'hat'-'trick' not 'battle'; the sole exception is *Allah* (God), in which the l's are swallowed as in English 'doll'.

BE POLITE!

When addressing a stranger, especially one older than you, it's polite to include *agha* (sir) or *khanom* (madam) at the beginning of the first sentence, or after one of the standard greetings. *Agha ye* and *Khanom e*

HELP! I CAN'T SPEAK FARSI

English is understood by well-educated people in the major cities, by some employees of middle and top-end restaurants and hotels, and by just about everyone working at a travel agency or airline office. Away from tourist areas, however, very few people speak English and when they do, because they are not used to listening to native speakers, they may not be able to understand your replies, making for some very frustrating 'conversations'. Since Iran does more business with France and Germany than with the English-speaking countries, you may have better success with French or German.

If you're travelling independently and using budget accommodation and restaurants, it would certainly help to learn a few basic Farsi phrases. At the very least, learn the Arabic numerals so you can identify prices, bus and train numbers, and addresses.

Whenever possible get your hotel receptionist to write down the Farsi for wherever you're going so you can show it to people. And don't forget to pick up your hotel's bilingual business card in case you get lost!

Thankfully, just about every village, town and city, and most streets and squares within the towns and cities, have signs in English.

are the equivalents of Mr, and Mrs/Miss/Ms. *Agha* can be used before or after the first name as a title of respect, eg Mohammad Agha or, more likely, Agha Mohammad.

The pronoun *shoma* is the polite form of 'you' singular, and should be used when addressing people you don't know well – *to* is only generally used when talking to close friends and relatives of the same generation or older, and to children and animals.

ACCOMMODATION

Do you have any rooms available?
   otagh khali darin

I'd like a ... room.	*ye otagh e ... mikham*
single	*taki*
shared	*moshtarak*

How much is it for ...?	*baraye ... cheghadr mishe?*
one night	*ye shab*

a week	*ye hafte*
two people	*do nafar*

We want a room with a ...	*ma ye otagh ba ye ... mikhayim*
bathroom	*dastshuyi*
shower	*dush*
TV	*televiziyon*
window	*panjere*

CONVERSATION & ESSENTIALS

The all-purpose greeting in Iran is *salam aleykom*, which does duty for 'good morning', 'good afternoon' and 'good evening'. The same expression is used throughout the Muslim world, so if you learn only one phrase in Iran, this is it!

Welcome.	*khosh amadin*
Greetings.	*salam aleykom*
Hello.	*salam*
Good morning.	*sob bekheyr*
Good day. (noon)	*rux bekheyr*
Good evening.	*shab bekheyr*
Goodbye.	*khoda hafez*
How are you?	*haletun chetor e?*
Fine – and you?	*khubam – shoma chetoin?*
Yes.	*bale*
No.	*na*
Please.	*lotfan*
Thank you.	*motashakkeram*
Thank you very much.	*kheyli mamnum*
You're welcome.	*khahesh mikonam*
Excuse me/I'm sorry.	*bebakhshid*
I like ...	*man ... dust daram*
I don't like ...	*man ... dust nadaram*
What's your name?	*esmetun chi ye?*
My name is ...	*esmam ... e*
Where are you from?	*kojayi hastin?*
I'm from ...	*man ahl e ... am*
It is God's will.	*mashallah*

mother	*madar*
father	*pedar*
sister	*khahar*
brother	*bavadar*
daughter	*dokhtar*
son	*pesar*
aunt	*ameh* (maternal)/ *khaleh* (paternal)
uncle	*amu* (maternal)/ *dai* (paternal)
wife	*zan*
husband	*shohar*

LANGUAGE

DIRECTIONS

Where is the ...?	... koja st?
Can you show me (on the map)?	mishe (tu naghshe) be man neshun bedin?
Is it far from here?	un az inja dur e?
Go straight ahead.	mostaghim berin
To the left.	samt e chap
To the right.	samt e rast
here	inja
there	unja

SIGNS

Entrance	ورود
Exit	خروج
Open	باز
Closed	بسته
No Entry	ورود ممنوع
No Smoking	دخانیات ممنوع
Prohibited	ممنوع
Hot	گرم
Cold	سرد
Toilets	توالت
Men	مردانه
Women	زنانه

behind	posht
in front of	jeloye
far (from)	dur az
near (to)	nazdik be
opposite	moghabele

HEALTH

Where is the ...?	... koja st?
chemist	darukhune
dentist	dandun pezeshk
doctor	doktor
hospital	bimarestan
I'm sick.	mariz am

I have ...	... daram
anaemia	kam khuni
asthma	asm
diabetes	diyabet

I'm allergic to ...	be ... hassasiyat daram
antibiotics	antibiyutik
aspirin	asperin
bees	zanbur
peanuts	badum zanini
penicillin	penisilin

antiseptic	zedd e ufuni konande
aspirin	asperin

EMERGENCIES

Help!	komak!
Stop!	ist!
Go away!	gom sho!

I wish to contact my embassy/consulate.
  mikham ba sefarat/konsulgari khod am tamas begiram

Where is the toilet?
  tuvalet koja st?

Shame on you!
  khejalat bekesh! (said by a woman to a man bothering her)

Call ...!	... khabar konin!
a doctor	ye doktor
an ambulance	ye ambulans
the police	polis o

condom	kandom
contraceptive	zedd e hamelegi
diarrhoea	es-hal
medicine	daru
sunblock	kerem e zedd e aftab
tampon	tampon

LANGUAGE DIFFICULTIES

Do you speak English?
  shoma ingilisi baladin?

Does anyone here speak English?
  inja kesi ingilisi balad e?

I understand.
  mifahman

I don't understand.
  na mifahman

How do you say ... in Farsi?
  ... ro dar farsi chetori migin?

What does ... mean?
  ma'ni ye ... chi ye?

Please write it down.
  lotfan un o benevisin

NUMBERS

0	sefr	٠
1	yek	١
2	do	٢
3	se	٣
4	chahar	٤
5	panj	٥
6	shish	٦
7	haft	٧
8	hasht	٨
9	noh	٩
10	dah	١٠

11	*yazdah*	۱۱
12	*davazdah*	۱۲
13	*sizdah*	۱۳
14	*chahardah*	۱۴
15	*punzdah*	۱۵
16	*shanzdah*	۱۶
17	*hifdah*	۱۷
18	*hijdah*	۱۸
19	*nuzdah*	۱۹
20	*bist*	۲۰
21	*bist o yek*	۲۱
22	*bist o do*	۲۲
30	*si*	۳۰
40	*chehel*	۴۰
50	*panjah*	۵۰
60	*shast*	۶۰
70	*haftad*	۷۰
80	*hashtad*	۸۰
90	*navad*	۹۰
100	*sad*	۱۰۰
167	*sad o shast o haft*	۱۶۷
200	*divist*	۲۰۰
1000	*hezar*	۱۰۰۰

one million   *yek milyon*

PAPERWORK
name   *esm*
nationality   *melliyyat*
date/place of birth   *tarikh/mahalle tavallod*
sex/gender   *jensiyat*
passport   *gozarname*
visa   *viza*

QUESTION WORDS
Who?   *ki?*
What?   *che?*
When?   *key?*
Where?   *koja?*
Which?   *kodam?*
Why?   *chera?*
How?   *chetor?*

SHOPPING & SERVICES
Where is the ...?   *... koja st?*
  bank   *bank*
  church   *kelisa*
  city centre   *markaz e shahr*
  consulate   *konsulgari*
  embassy   *sefarat*
  hotel   *hotel*
  lodging house   *mosaferkhùneh*
  mosque   *masjed*
  market   *bazar*
  police   *polis*

post office   *edare ye post*
public telephone   *telefon e umumi*
public toilet   *tuvalet e umumi*
tourist office   *edare ye jahangardi*
town square   *meydun a shahr*

I'd like to buy ...   *mikham ... bekharan*
How much is it?   *che ghadr?*
I don't like it.   *az un khosh am nemiyad*
May I look at it?   *mishe negali esh konam?*
I'm just looking.   *faghat negah mikonam*
I think it's too expensive.   *fekr mikonam un kheyli gerun e*
I'll take it.   *un o mikharam*

Do you accept credit cards?
  karte e e'tebari ghabul mikonin?
Do you accept travellers cheques?
  shoma cheke mosaferati ghabul mikonin?

more   *ziyad*
less   *kam*
smaller   *kuchiktar*
bigger   *bozorgtar*

TIME & DATES
What time is it?   *sa'at chand e?*
today   *emruz*
tomorrow   *farda*
yesterday   *diruz*
tonight   *emshab*
morning, am   *sob*
afternoon, pm   *ba'd az zohr*
day   *ruz*
month   *mah*
year   *sal*

Monday   *dos hanbe*
Tuesday   *se shanbe*
Wednesday   *chahar shanbe*
Thursday   *panj shanbe*
Friday   *jom'e*
Saturday   *shanbe*
Sunday   *yekshanbe*

TRANSPORT
Public Transport
Where is the ...?   *... koja st?*
  airport   *furudgah*
  bus stop   *istgah e utubus*
  train station   *istgah e ghatar*

What time does the ... leave/arrive?   *... che sa'ati harekat mikone/mirese?*
  boat   *ghayegh*
  bus   *utubus*

ROAD SIGNS

Give Way	حق تقدم
Danger	خطر
No Parking	پارک ممنوع
Entry	ورود
No Overtaking	سبقت ممنوع
Slow Down	آهسته حرکت کنید
No Entry	ورود ممنوع
One Way	یکطرفه
Exit	خروج
Tollway	اتوبان

plane	havapeyma
train	ghatar

What time is the ... bus? utubus e ... key miyad?
first avval
last akhar
next ba'di

I'd like a ... . mikham
one-way ticket belit e ye sare
return ticket belit e do sare

1st class daraje yek
2nd class daraje do

Private Transport

I'd like to hire a ... mikham ... keraye konam
car mashin
4WD patrol
motorbike motorsiklet
bicycle docharkhe

Is this the road to ...?
in jadde be ... mire?

Where's a service station?
pomp e benzin e ba'di kojast?
Please fill it up.
lotfan bak o por konin
I'd like ... litres.
... litr benzin mikham
diesel gazoyil
leaded petrol ma'muli
unleaded (petrol) bedun e sorb

How long can we park here?
che ghadr mishe inja park kard?
(I/We) need a mechanic.
ye mekanik (mikhaham/mikhayim)
The car/motorbike has broken down at ...
mashin/mororsiklet dar ... kharab shode
I have a flat tyre.
ye charkh am panchar shode
I've run out of petrol.
benzin am tamum shode
I had an accident.
man tasadof kardam

TRAVEL WITH CHILDREN

Is there a/an ...? yek....hast?
I need a ... man yek....lazem daram
baby change room otaghe avaz kardane bachche
car baby seat sandaliye bachche
children's menu liste ghazaye bachche ha
disposable nappies/ pushak
diapers
formula (infant milk) shire khoshk
highchair sandaliye boland
potty lagane bachche
stroller kaleske

Are children allowed? bachche ha ejaze darand?

Glossary

Here, with definitions, are some unfamiliar words and abbreviations that you may encounter in this book. Generally the Farsi words in this book are transliterations of colloquial usage. See the Language chapter for other useful words and phrases.

agha – sir; gentleman
Allah – Muslim name for God
andaruni – private part of a traditional home, where only immediate family are welcome (see *biruni*)
aramgah – resting place; burial place; tomb
arg, ark – citadel
astan-e – sanctuary; threshold
ateshkadeh – a Zoroastrian fire temple where a flame was always kept burning
ayatollah – Shiite cleric of the highest rank, used as a title before the name; literally means a 'sign or miracle of God'
azad – free; liberated
azadi – freedom

badgir – windtower or ventilation shaft used to catch breezes and funnel them down into a building to cool it
bagh – garden
bandar – port; harbour
Bandari – indigenous inhabitant of the Persian Gulf coast and islands
bastan – ancient; ancient history; antiquity
bazar – bazaar; market place
bazari – shopkeeper in the bazaar
behesht – paradise
biruni – outer part of a traditional home, where guests are entertained
bolvar – boulevard
boq'eh – mausoleum
borj – tower
burqa – a mask with tiny slits for the eyes worn by some Bandari women
bozorg – big, large, great

caliphate – the dynasty of the successors of the Prophet Mohammed as rulers of the Islamic world
caravanserai – an inn or way-station for camel trains; usually consisting of rooms arranged around a courtyard
chador – literally 'tent'; a cloak, usually black, covering all parts of a woman's body except the hands, feet and face
chay – tea
chaykhuneh – teahouse ('chaykhaneh' in Kerman province)

dar baste – closed door, used in taxis to indicate you want a private hire

darvazeh – gate or gateway, especially a city gate
darya – sea
dasht – plain; plateau; desert, specifically one of sand or gravel

eivan – see *iwan*
emam – see *imam*
enqelab – revolution

farsh – carpet
Farsi – Persian language or people
Ferdosi – one of the great Persian poets, born about AD 940 in Tus, near Mashhad; wrote the first epic poem, the *Shahnamah*
fire temple – see *ateshkadeh*

gabbeh – rug
golestan – rose garden; name of poem by Sa'di
gonbad – dome, domed monument or tower tomb; also written 'gombad'

Hafez – one of the great Persian poets, born in Shiraz in about AD 1324
haj – pilgrimage to Mecca
halal – permitted by Islamic law; lawful to eat or drink
hammam – bath, public bathhouse; bathroom
Hazrat-e – title used before the name of Mohammed, any other apostle of Islam or a Christian saint
hejab – veil; the 'modest dress' required of Muslim women and girls
Hossein – the third of the 12 *imams* recognised by Shiites as successors of the Prophet Mohammed; he was martyred at the battle of Karbala, an event that is commemorated in rituals acted out during the mourning month of Moharram
Hosseinieh – see *takieh*

imam – emam in Farsi; religious leader, also title of one of the 12 descendants of Mohammed who, according to Shiite belief, succeeded him as religious and temporal leader of the Muslims
Imam Reza – the eighth Shiite *imam*, also known as the Hidden One or the Mahdi; he is said to have disappeared in AD 878, and his return will, it is believed, signal an end to tyranny and injustice
imamzadeh – descendant of an imam; shrine or mausoleum of an imamzadeh
in sh'Allah – if God wills it
istgah – station (especially railway station)
ITTIC – corporate arm of the *ITTO*; it runs hotels and the occasional restaurant, but does not have very much information

ITTO – Iranian Touring & Tourism Organisation; a government-run travel agency

iwan – eivan in Farsi; rectangular hall opening onto a courtyard

Jameh Mosque – Masjed-e Jameh in Farsi; meaning Friday Mosque, this is the mosque Muslims go to on their holy day, Friday

kabir – great

kalisa – church (sometimes cathedral)

kavir – salt desert

khalij – gulf; bay

khan – feudal lord, title of respect

kheyabun – street; avenue

khoda hafez – farewell greeting meaning 'God be with you' and used whenever you part ways with anyone

khuneh – house; home

Komiteh – local 'committee' of the Islamic Revolutionary Guards Corps, or religious police; now disbanded

kuche – lane; alley

Kufic – Ancient script found on many buildings dating from the about the 7th to 13th centuries

madraseh – school; also Muslim theological college

Majlis – Iranian Parliament

manar – minaret: tower of a mosque

markaz – centre; headquarters

markazi telefon – main telephone office

masjed – mosque: Muslim place of worship

Masjed-e Jameh – see *Jameh Mosque*

mehmun – guest

mehmunkhuneh – hotel

mehmunpazir – a simple hotel

mehmunsara – government-owned resthouse or hotel

mihrab – niche inside a mosque indicating the direction of Mecca, often ornately decorated with tiling and calligraphy; in Iran, specifically the hole cut in the ground before the niche

minbar – pulpit of a mosque

Moharram – first month of the Muslim lunar calendar, the Shiite month of mourning

mosaferkhuneh – lodging-house or hotel of the cheapest, simplest kind; 'mosafer' means traveller or passenger

muezzin – person at mosque who calls Muslims to prayer

mullah – Islamic cleric; title of respect

No Ruz – Iranian New Year's Day, celebrated on the vernal equinox (usually around 21 March)

Omar Khayyam – born in Neishabur in about 1047 and famous as a poet, mathematician, historian and astronomer; his best-known poem is the Rubaïyat

Parsi – Farsi for Persia or Iran

pasazh – passage; shopping arcade

Persia – old name for Iran

Persian – adjective and noun frequently used to describe the Iranian language, people and culture

pik-up – utility with a canvas cover

pol – bridge

qal'eh – fortress; fortified walled village

qalyan – water pipe, usually smoked in traditional teahouses

qanat – underground water channel

qar – cave

Quran – Muslim holy book

Ramazan – ninth month in the Muslim lunar calendar; the month of fasting

rial – currency of Iran; equal to one-tenth of a *toman*

rud, rudkhuneh – river; stream

ruz – day

Sa'di – one of the great Persian poets (AD 1207–91); his most famous works are the *Golestan* (Rose Garden) and Bustan (Garden of Trees)

sahn – court; courtyard

sardar – military governor

savari – private car; local word for a shared taxi, often refers to longer trips between cities

shah – king; the usual title of the Persian monarch

shahid – martyr; used as a title before the forename of a fighter killed during the Islamic Revolution or the Iran-Iraq War

shahr – town or city

Shahnamah – *Ferdosi's* famous epic poem

shared taxi – common form of public transport within cities; they usually run on set routes and generally don't leave until full

takht – throne

takieh – building used during the rituals to commemorate the death of Imam Hossein during Moharram; sometimes called a *Hosseinieh*

tappeh – hill; mound

terminal – terminal; bus station

timches – domed halls

toman – unit of currency equal to 10 *rials*

zarih – the gilded and latticed 'cage' that sits over a tomb, such as that of *Imam Reza*

ziggurat – pyramidal temple with a series of tiers on a square or rectangular plan

Zoroastrianism – ancient religion, the state creed before the Islamic conquest; today, Zoroastrians are found mainly in Yazd, Shiraz, Kerman, Tehran and Esfahan

zurkhaneh – house of strength

Behind the Scenes

THIS BOOK

This is the fourth edition of *Iran*. The first edition, written by David St Vincent, appeared in 1992. Paul Greenway updated the second edition; Pat Yale and Anthony Ham researched and wrote the third edition. This edition was researched and updated by Andrew Burke and Mark Elliott; Kamin Mohammadi researched and wrote the Culture chapter and updated the Arts chapter.

THANKS from the Authors

Andrew Burke Iran is the kind of place where a simple *'mersi'* can never really convey the thanks I owe to so many people. My deepest gratitude to the lovely Maryam Julazadeh in Tehran, whose friendship and prompt replies to countless emails were invaluable. Also in Tehran, Marty, Mohammad and Mohsen Shams and family fed, informed and lobbied for me in a visa crisis; Chris Taylor was the perfect host; and Mohammad at Hotel Naderi was all gentle persuasion when I was under arrest.

In Bam, special thanks to Hossein Vatany, Jalal Mehdizadeh, Mohammad Ali and especially Panjalizadeh Akbar and family for the very essence of Iranian hospitality in the face of near-total loss. In Yazd, thanks to Hadi Safaeian, Mohsen Hajisaeed, Ali and Hossein; and, in Mashhad, Hajj Ali Khatib and Towhid for expert and passionate guiding. Thanks to Wendy Gootjes and Saeed Iranzad in Bushehr; Massoud Nematollahi and staff in Shiraz; Maziar and Ariane in Garmeh; and fellow travellers Kate O'Rourke, Alex, Tobias Stein, Yves 'Zigoto', Coen, Karin-Marijke and Andrew Fisher for company and valuable feedback.

In Hong Kong, thanks to a great group of friends (you know who you are); and in Sydney my family provided their usual (and underappreciated) bedrock of love and support. At LP, thanks to the professional and patient Will, Julia, Sarah, Joanne, Elizabeth, Emma; to Tony Wheeler for test-driving the book; and to my dedicated co-authors Mark Elliott and Kamin Mohammadi. Finally, *kheyli mamnun* to the wonderful people of Iran – *khoda hafez*.

Mark Elliott Enormous thanks to a myriad hospitable and inspiring Iranians and some thoughtful fellow-travellers. Notable thanks to Parvis and Jounes Gholbazi in Zanjan, Nasser Khan, Mansur, Hadi, and Hossein in Tabriz, Nika 'Bek' in Ahar, Coen and Karin-Marijke in Sanandaj, Habib Rajabi and his six brothers in Bin Jafar, Esakh Siyabush in Shushtar, Abdel and Ahmed in Marivan, Arash in Dorud, Hamid in Ahvaz, Ali A at Takht-e Soleiman, Sohrab and crew for opening my blind eyes in Khorramabad and Sanandaj, Farkhad Taqadosi in Shush, Dariush at Choqa Zanbil, Shirmar Glamali on the mad Andimeshk train ride, Masud Daradi in Khorramabad, Hamid, Mujitaba and all the gang in Bisheh, Sam Golshan at Ganjnameh, Mohammad Siyarpush and Hadieyeh Ajodany in Qazvin, Louise Firouz and friends in GTS, Behman in Rasht, Mohammad, Mila, Manuchem and the two Mammuds in Rasht, Ali Fagani in Kordkuy, Abdul Rahman in Aliabad, Daz Gumbadi in Gorgan, Naib and Roalla in Amol, Davud in Chaldoran, Borzou in Piranshahr, Islam Suleymani in Maku, Maria O'Shea, Tobias Steino, Zahra Vesal, Sebastien Reichel, Wieland de Hoon, Paul Clammer, Mohammad Fathi,

THE LONELY PLANET STORY

The story begins with a classic travel adventure: Tony and Maureen Wheeler's 1972 journey across Europe and Asia to Australia. There was no useful information about the overland trail then, so Tony and Maureen published the first Lonely Planet guidebook to meet a growing need.

From a kitchen table, Lonely Planet has grown to become the largest independent travel publisher in the world, with offices in Melbourne (Australia), Oakland (USA), London (UK) and Paris (France).

Today Lonely Planet guidebooks cover the globe. There is an ever-growing list of books and information in a variety of media. Some things haven't changed. The main aim is still to make it possible for adventurous travellers to get out there – to explore and better understand the world.

At Lonely Planet we believe travellers can make a positive contribution to the countries they visit – if they respect their host communities and spend their money wisely.

Zangengeh Bar Sasan, Bruce Thompson, Michael Abbot, Nasrin Harris, Pamela Yuille, Ruth Staines, Linda Shen, Sadegh Aghajani, Mohsen Aghajani and many more whose names I never knew. Thanks, too, to the LP team, thoughtful fellow author Andrew and inspiringly encouraging commissioning editor Will. Most of all eternal thanks to my long-suffering parents and my 'wife' Dani Systermans who between them give me the love that makes everything worthwhile.

CREDITS

This book was commissioned and briefed in Lonely Planet's Melbourne office by Will Gourlay. Joanne Newell completed the manuscript assessment and Emma Koch oversaw things while Will was on holidays. The project manager was Andrew Weatherill. Editing was coordinated by Julia Taylor with invaluable assistance from Joanne Newell, Elizabeth Swan and Anne Mulvaney. Thanks also to Carly Hall and Carolyn Boicos. Cartography was coordinated by Sarah Sloane, with assistance from Jacqui Saunders, Louise Klep, Amanda Sierp, Kusnandar, Julie Sheridan and Chris Thomas. David Kemp designed the colour pages and Margaret Jung laid the book out. James Hardy designed the cover. Overseeing production were Danielle North and Kerryn Burgess (managing editors) and Shahara Ahmed (managing cartographer). Quentin Frayne compiled the Language chapter and he would like to thank Dr Yavar Dehghani.

THANKS from Lonely Planet

Many thanks to the travellers who used the last edition and wrote to us with helpful hints, useful advice and interesting anecdotes:

Diana Ader, Nick Adlam, Yiota Amanatidou, Eva Andersson, Johann Annuar, Jun Asakura, Marzieh Asgari-Targhi, Amir Asgary, Chingiz Askarov, Peter & Rosemary Balmford, Grace Barran, David Barrett, Daniel Bauer, Daniel Bayard, Klaus Becker, G Beerepoot, Marcel Bellorini, Jose Benavides, PM Berry, Alain Bertallo, Antonia Bertschinger, Ivana Bezecna, Einar Bjorge, John Blackburn, Lenore Blackwood, Jane Bobko, Jurgen Bohler, Kim Boreham, Andreas Bosshard, Achille Brambilla, Kathryn Briggs, Eric Bringuier, Ron Broadfoot, Gail Brooks, Alain Broutain, Martin Brunner, Hans J Buhrmester, Emma Bush, Luigi Cavaleri, Sam Chamberlain, Reza Zare Chian, Davide Chiapasco, Martin Civin, Chrissy & Malcolm Clark, Margaret & Michael Clark, Dorothy Cockrell, Sarah Cottam, Christer Daatland, Hamid Dafileh, Ashk P Dahlen, Oystein Bornes Dalijord, Shaun Daly, Angela Davies, Irene de Charriere, Bruno de Cordier, Eduardo de Francisco, Joost de Graaf, Jeroen de Haan, Dale Dewar, Joel Didomizio, Marijke Dijkgraaf, Oyuna Dougarova, Petr Drbohlav, Kristina & Magnus Duhring, Behzad Eghtesad, Peter Eller, RA Elliott, Stephan Ellis, Kari Eloranta, Richard Entwistle,

Wayne Erb, Mohsen Fakhari, Anna Fayeg, Una Freeston, Mechthild Fuchs, Bernadette Gabris, James Gaffney, Frederic Gangloff, Betty Gardiner, Denis Garnier, Jan Garvelink, Stefan Gerber, Gabriele Gierke, Marc Glaudemans, Ashley Goldstraw, Helmut Goller, Davis Goodman, Wendy Gootjes, Jacqueline Graf, Amparo Granada, Alain Grand, Phil Greg, Nancy Greig, Josef Grieshuber, Ulrich Grothus, Virginie Guignard, Marc Guitering, Gell Gunther, Stefan & Thomas Haefliger, Bart Haenen, Guy Hagan, James Halton, Evans Harrell, Paul Harris, David Havelin, Tim Hawley, Brendon Hayes, Jeremy Hillman, Gordon Hodgkinson, Geoff & Carol Hodgson, Abbas Hormati, Matt Howes, Herman Hulsinga, Bram Hulzebos, Clephane Hume, Mats Hyttmark, Theo Jager, Martin Jameson, Pete Jameson, Volkmar E Janicke, Rok Jarc, David Javaheri, Stephen Jennings, Peter Jensen, Tove Grønbæk Jensen, Visi Baek Jensen, Ola Joernmark, Morten Johansen, Carolyn Johnson, Roger Jones, Boris Josipovic, Encarna Juarez, Martijn Kaal, Lucia Kadijk, Martin Kalenberg, Simone Karlhuber, Andrew Karney, Wouter Karst, L Birt Kellam, Paul Key, Rafi Khankhajeh, Majid Khoshrou, Lucie Kinkorova, Andrew Knoedler, Cynthia Koens, Jolanda Koopmans, Elena Krashia, Walter Kunze, Nikolaj Ladegaard, Siyyid Farid Laghai, Ibrahim Leadley, Vassili Lebedev, Min-jeong Lee, William Lee, Mark Levitin, Laurent Licari, Alain Liger, Jos Limpens, Jordi Llorens Estape, Alex Loucaides, Guido Lovati, Janine Lucas, Zhiyu Lui, Pavel Luksha, Damian MacCormack, Hejo Mackenschins, Elizabeth Madigan Jost, Leif Madsen, Laurence Makowy, Delyan Manchev, Brian Mariotti, Marius Massimo, David Mast, Duncan McDuie, Alex Melbourne, Jean-Marc Mojon, Esther Monfulleda, Ronan Moore, Christian Mooser, Pedro Muroa,

SEND US YOUR FEEDBACK

We love to hear from travellers – your comments keep us on our toes and help make our books better. Our well-travelled team reads every word on what you loved or loathed about this book. Although we cannot reply individually to postal submissions, we always guarantee that your feedback goes straight to the appropriate authors, in time for the next edition. Each person who sends us information is thanked in the next edition – and the most useful submissions are rewarded with a free book.

To send us your updates – and find out about LP events, newsletters and travel news – visit our award-winning website: **www.lonelyplanet.com**.

Note: We may edit, reproduce and incorporate your comments in Lonely Planet products such as guidebooks, websites and digital products, so let us know if you don't want your comments reproduced or your name acknowledged. For a copy of our privacy policy visit www.lonelyplanet.com/privacy.

Bartosz Musialowicz, Emma Nahvi, Sana Namazie, Joanna Nathan, Jose Antonio, Elena, Eloy & Alberto Navarro, Sina Nielsen, Willem Nijkerk, Elizabeth North, Luka Novak, Sarah Ohring, Lars Olberg, Margarette Oniye, Max Oppen, Anthony Paine, Myriam & Jofre Palau, Michèle Pascal, Carlo & Emanuela Paschetto, Tanya, Jason & Snortie Paterson, John Patterson, Marketa Peckova, Susanne Petschan, Dr Hellmuth Pickel, Anna Piller, David Plested, Oksana Podolyak, Harm Poelman, Oliver Pogatsnik, Jacques Poitras, Robert Potocrik, David Prache, Anne Price, Oliver Progatsnik, Leila Qizilbash, Gunter Quaisser, Loretta Rafter, Andrew Ratcliffe, Rob Reijnders, Rob & Len Reijnders, Elisabeth Remund, Thilo Reusch, Nina Reznick, Marcus Rhinelander, Mary Roberts, Frederic Rolet, Skip Roothans, Hans Peter Ros, Hans Rossel, Reza Saberi, Ali Sabetian, Ali Sadeghi, Tajalli Saghaee, Maja Sajovic, Toni Salvado-i-Nayach, Betty Sam, I Samran, Robert Sare, Kath Sargent, George Schaller, Rudolf Schilling, Ute Schneemann, Annekatrin Scholze, Ralf Schwate, Jennifer Scott, Mario Secen, Roger Secker Walker, Gavin Sexton, Francis & Nicole Seys, Marty Shams, Dahlia Shamsuddin, Adrian Shariati, David Shariatmadari, John Sharp, Ann Shrigley, Philippe Sibelly, St John Simpson, Annarosa Sinopoli, Kelly Sobczak, Denise Solis, Gavin Staton, Brano Stefanik, Jay Stephens, Jonathan Stock, Gwen Strickland, Artur & Agnieszka Styrna, Marek Aziz Szymanowicz, Massimo Taddei, Joshua Taylor Barnes, Thibaud Taudin Chabot, Maike Tausch, Andrea Terbijhe, Drew Terenzini, Carina Thees, Bruce Thompson, Diana Thorburn, Vazgin Timas, Sato Tomoko, Arnaud Toussaint, Charlotte Ulfsparre, Tanya & Urs Unternahrer, Mike Vafai, Wim van Ranst, Agnes van Veen, Erik Vanem, Arjan Veersma, Martina Vercikova, Haman Veyseh, E Villemin, Tommaso Vistosi, Barli (Christoph) von Toggenburg, Arno Waal, Judith Waegell, Steve Walker, Scott Wallace, Domenic Wasescha, Pierre Watrinet, Stella Wegman, Francisco Welber, John Whittaker, Bronwen Williams, W Williams, Edina Winternitz, Martyna Wolinska, Adrian Wright, Daniela Wyttenbach, Cheryl Young.

ACKNOWLEDGMENTS

Many thanks to the following for the use of their content:

Globe on back cover © Mountain High Maps 1993 Digital Wisdom, Inc.

Index

INDEX

000 Map pages
000 Location of colour photographs

INDEX

INDEX

MAP LEGEND

ROUTES

Tollway	One-Way Street
Freeway	Unsealed Road
Primary Road	Street Mall/Steps
Secondary Road	Tunnel
Tertiary Road	Walking Tour
Lane	Walking Tour Detour
Under Construction	Walking Trail
Track	Walking Path

TRANSPORT

Ferry	Bus Route
Metro	Rail

HYDROGRAPHY

River, Creek	Water

BOUNDARIES

International	Ancient Wall

AREA FEATURES

Airport	Land
Area of Interest	Park
Beach, Desert	Sports
Building	Urban
Campus	

POPULATION

☼ CAPITAL (NATIONAL)	◉ CAPITAL (STATE)
● Large City	● Medium City
○ Small City	○ Town, Village

SYMBOLS

Sights/Activities
- Beach
- Castle, Fortress
- Christian
- Islamic
- Monument
- Museum, Gallery
- Ruin
- Skiing

Eating
- Eating

Drinking
- Café

Entertainment
- Entertainment

Shopping
- Shopping

Sleeping
- Sleeping

Transport
- Airport, Airfield
- Border Crossing
- Bus Station
- Cycling, Bicycle Path
- Savaris/Shared Taxis

Other
- Parking Area

Information
- Bank, ATM
- Embassy/Consulate
- Hospital, Medical
- Information
- Internet Facilities
- Petrol Station
- Police Station
- Post Office, GPO
- Telephone
- Toilets

Geographic
- Lookout
- ▲ Mountain, Volcano
- National Park

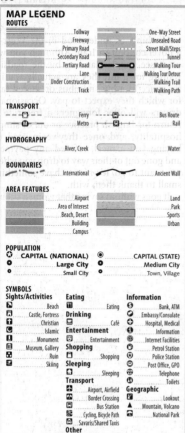

LONELY PLANET OFFICES

Australia
Head Office
Locked Bag 1, Footscray, Victoria 3011
☎ 03 8379 8000, fax 03 8379 8111
talk2us@lonelyplanet.com.au

USA
150 Linden St, Oakland, CA 94607
☎ 510 893 8555, toll free 800 275 8555
fax 510 893 8572, info@lonelyplanet.com

UK
72–82 Rosebery Ave,
Clerkenwell, London EC1R 4RW
☎ 020 7841 9000, fax 020 7841 9001
go@lonelyplanet.co.uk

Published by Lonely Planet Publications Pty Ltd
ABN 36 005 607 983

© Lonely Planet 2004

© photographers as indicated 2004

Cover photographs by Lonely Planet Images: Henna-decorated hand of Afghani girl, Mark Daffey (front); Reflections inside the 17th century Imam Mosque of Esfahan, Chris Mellor (back). Many of the images in this guide are available for licensing from Lonely Planet Images: www.lonelyplanetimages.com.

All rights reserved. No part of this publication may be copied, stored in a retrieval system, or transmitted in any form by any means, electronic, mechanical, recording or otherwise, except brief extracts for the purpose of review, and no part of this publication may be sold or hired, without the written permission of the publisher.

Printed through Colorcraft Ltd, Hong Kong.
Printed in China

Lonely Planet and the Lonely Planet logo are trademarks of Lonely Planet and are registered in the US Patent and Trademark Office and in other countries.

Lonely Planet does not allow its name or logo to be appropriated by commercial establishments, such as retailers, restaurants or hotels. Please let us know of any misuses: www.lonelyplanet.com/ip.

Although the authors and Lonely Planet have taken all reasonable care in preparing this book, we make no warranty about the accuracy or completeness of its content and, to the maximum extent permitted, disclaim all liability arising from its use.